DATE DUE

Dictionary of Latin American Racial and Ethnic Terminology

Dictionary of Latin American Racial and Ethnic Terminology

Part I. Spanish American Terms

Part II. Brazilian Portuguese Terms

Thomas M. Stephens

University of Florida Press
Gainesville

Library of Congress Cataloging-in-Publication Data

Stephens, Thomas M.
    Dictionary of Latin American racial and ethnic terminology /
Thomas M. Stephens.

    p.   cm. —
    Bibliography : p.
    Includes index.
    Contents: pt. 1. Spanish American terms—pt. 2. Brazilian
Portuguese terms.
    ISBN 0-8130-0965-0 (alk. paper)
    1. Ethnology—Latin America—Dictionaries—Spanish. 2. Eth-
nology—Latin America–Dictionaries—Portuguese. I. Title.
GN564.L29S84   1990
305.8′003—dc20   89–33416
                                                       CIP

The University of Florida Press is a member of University Presses of Florida, the scholarly publishing agency of the State University System of
Florida. Books are selected for publication by the faculty editorial
committees of Florida's nine university presses: Florida A&M University
Press (Tallahassee), Florida Atlantic University Press (Boca Raton), Florida International University Press (Miami), Florida State University
Press (Tallahassee), University of Central Florida Press (Orlando), University of Florida Press (Gainesville), University of North Florida Press
(Jacksonville), University of South Florida Press (Tampa), University of
West Florida Press (Pensacola).
    Orders for books published by all member presses should be addressed
to University Presses of Florida, 15 NW 15th Street, Gainesville, FL
32603.

Contents

Preface and Acknowledgments

Branco é quem tem dinheiro.
— Brazilian proverb

El que no tiene dinga tiene mandinga.
— Spanish American proverb

The entries found in the *Dictionary of Latin American Racial and Ethnic Terminology* represent the fruition of almost a decade of researching, assembling, sorting, and revising the verbal intricacies of human race and ethnicity. In the process of preparing them, I have had to re-examine my own views concerning race and ethnicity and have thus come to an understanding of the roots of prejudice, my own as well as the prejudices of others.

When I started the research for this dictionary, I realized there could be pitfalls. First, the very fact of studying race and ethnicity offers the possibility that the researcher will be pegged a racist. On the contrary, I believe that *not* studying race and ethnicity sanctions ignorance and intolerance. Study alone will not eliminate prejudices but, together with understanding, it will at least make us aware that they exist. Second, I often discovered that I needed that so-hard-to-find, and therefore seldom-found, native informant capable of clarifying certain words or definitions. Finally, I realized that, because of the dynamic nature of race and ethnicity, no time allotted will ever produce a truly complete set of Latin American racial and ethnic terms and their definitions.

The type of work attempted here must by nature rely on material that others have collected. The compiling of dictionaries, although rewarding in its outcome, requires much time, great patience, and a relatively clear understanding that the words collected are meant to give others some insight into another aspect of human thinking. It is therefore impossible to organize a word list without the input of many other persons along the way; the long roster of contributors to this study shows that it is no exception.

The personal informants, designated by the abbreviation "p.c." (for "personal communication"), were invaluable to me; they were (with their country of origin or expertise in parentheses): Dr.

Lawrence B. Kiddle (United States, Latin America), Dr. Paola Bentivoglio (Italy, Venezuela), Hersilia Alvarez (Chile), Imants Kuga (Argentina), Dr. Gustavo Pérez-Firmat (Cuba, Florida), María Lamigueiro (Cuba), Pedro Gómez (Cuba), Ana León (Venezuela), Dr. Rei Berroa (Dominican Republic), Amarfi Herrera (Dominican Republic), Dr. Stanley McCray (United States, Dominican Republic), Diana Argersinger (Mexico, Texas), Elna de la Bandera (Uruguay), Dr. Gabriela Mora (Chile), Lori Diehl (New Mexico), Nívea Pereira Parsons (Ceará state, Brazil), an Amazon River tour guide (Manaus, Amazonas state, Brazil), and a Manaus hotel bellboy (Brazil). Furthermore, I am grateful to Dr. John M. Lipski, Dr. William W. Megenney, and Dr. Francisco Gomes de Matos, reviewers for the University of Florida Press, who made invaluable contributions to this work regarding both Spanish America and Brazil.

Acknowledgments must be made to Professors Steven N. Dworkin, Raleigh Morgan, Jr., Ernst Pulgram, David Wolfe, and Thomas Toon of the University of Michigan, who read an earlier version of part of this research. I give special thanks to Professor Lawrence B. Kiddle, formerly of the University of Michigan, who suggested the idea to me, and to the Research Council of Rutgers University, which graciously supported portions of this project.

I also wish to acknowledge the many colleagues and friends who gave me encouragement and/or professional advice during this research: Carl Kirschner, Margo Persin, Frank Dauster, Mary Lee Bretz, Phyllis Zatlin, Janet DeCesaris, John Earl Joseph, Stanley and Christy McCray, Paul Roberge, Marion Elias, Kathy Barnes, Lynn and Jean Harrill, Robert Sabatine, John Burger, George and Doris McClellan, Johnny Tucker, and William and Barbara Wadsworth.

Special thanks and love go to my family, Talmadge and Telewene Whittle Stephens, J. Lewis Stephens, and Cathy Stephens Grubbs; they now truly have a 'book.'

Finally I must express utmost gratitude to my friend James A. McClellan, who saw me through all of this. For his kindness and words of wisdom I will forever be indebted.

Abbreviations and Symbols

Abbreviation	Label	Abbreviation	Label
abbr.	abbreviated, abbreviation	CO	Colorado
		colloq.	colloquial
AC	Acre	comp(s).	compiler(s)
acc.	according to	contemp.	contemptuous
adj.	adjective	coord(s).	coordinator(s)
affect.	affectionate	CR	Costa Rica
AHD	*American Heritage Dictionary*	CT	Connecticut
		Cu	Cuba
AL	Alagoas	c.w.	central-west, central-western
AM	Amazonas		
Amer.	American	DC	District of Columbia
An	Antilles	deriv(s).	derivative(s)
anal.	analogy	derog.	derogatory
ant(s).	antonym(s)	desc.	descriptive
anthro.	anthropological	df(s).	definition(s)
AP	Amapá	DF	Distrito Federal
Ar	Argentina	DH	*Diccionario Histórico de la Lengua Española*
att.	attested		
aug.	augmentative		
AZ	Arizona	dim.	diminutive
BA	Bahia	dir(s).	director(s)
Bo	Bolivia	DR	Dominican Republic
Br	Brazil	DRAE	*Diccionario de la Real Academia Española*
Br-PR	Paraná		
Brz.	Brazilian	ea.	east, eastern
CA	California	Ec	Ecuador
ce.	central	ed.	edited, edition
CE	Ceará	e.g.	for example, as an example
CeA	Central America		
cent.	century	Engl.	English
cf.	compare	equiv(s).	equivalent(s)
Ch	Chile	ES	Espírito Santo
cl, cl.	colonial	esp.	especially
Co	Colombia	euph.	euphemistic

ix

exc.	except	obs.	obsolete
excl.	exclusive	OED	*Oxford English*
ext.	extension		*Dictionary*
f.	feminine	opp.	opposed, opposition
facet.	facetious	p(p).	page(s)
fig.	figurative	Pa	Panama
FL	Florida	PA	Pará
Fr.	French	partic.	participle
ftn.	footnote	PB	Paraíba
GO	Goiás	p.c.	personal
Gu	Guatemala		communication
Ho	Honduras	Pe	Peru
humor.	humorous	PE	Pernambuco
i.e.	that is	pejor.	pejorative
IL	Illinois	Pg	Paraguay
injur.	injurious	phr(s).	phrase(s)
insult.	insulting	PI	Piaui
interj.	interjection	pl.	plural
iron.	ironic	poss.	possessive
joc.	jocular	PR	Puerto Rico
LA	Louisiana	pref.	prefix
lg.	language	pron.	pronoun
m.	masculine	Ptg.	Portuguese
MA	Maranhão	ref.	reference
MG	Minas Gerais	region.	regionalism
MI	Michigan	rel.	related
Michaelis	*New Michaelis*	repr.	reprinted
	Dictionary	respect.	respectful
MS	Mato Grosso do Sul	RJ	Rio de Janeiro
MT	Mato Grosso	RN	Rio Grande do Norte
Mx	Mexico	RO	Rondônia
n.	noun	RP	River Plate region
NC	North Carolina	RR	Roraima
n.d.	no date	RS	Rio Grande do Sul
n.e.	northeast,	Sa	El Salvador
	northeastern	SA	Spanish America
Ni	Nicaragua	sarc.	sarcastic
NJ	New Jersey	SC	Santa Catarina
NM	New Mexico	scorn.	scornful
no., No.	north, northern	s.e.	southeast,
NoA	North America		southeastern
NV	Nevada	SE	Sergipe
n.w.	northwest,	sim.	similar
	northwestern	sing.	singular
NY	New York	so.	south, southern

SoA	South America	trans.	translated, translation
So. Amer.	Southern (North)	TX	Texas
	American	Ur	Uruguay
Sp.	Spanish	US	United States
SP	São Paulo	var(s).	variant(s)
std.	standard	Ve	Venezuela
suf.	suffix	vol(s).	volume(s)
s.w.	southwest,	vulg.	vulgar
	southwestern	we.	west, western
syn(s).	synonym(s)	WI	Wisconsin

Symbol	*Label*	*Symbol*	*Label*
<	comes from, derives from, is derived from	+	plus, in addition to
		‖	in an entry, to separate areas or
>	becomes, goes to, gives		times of use
		*	unattested form

Introduction

Overview

Modern Latin American societies manifest a racial and ethnic composition resulting from a mixture of human contacts that have not occurred anywhere else on earth. The records that have been kept since the arrival of the first Europeans in the New World document the racial types in epistolaries, dictionaries, parochial files, and colonial censuses (Borah and Cook 1961:70) and mirror the patterns of birth, baptism, marriage, and death for persons of all races. These documents are therefore a rich source of racial and ethnic terminology, since chroniclers, scribes, and historians meticulously noted the racial and ethnic composition of the new Americans, certainly those of non-European and mixed race.

The Americas have traditionally been the meeting place, forced and otherwise, of the world's racial and ethnic communities. As is common in such mass-migration areas, encounters of different social or racial groups often cause ill feelings; this is especially true in the Americas, where many differing peoples have constituted the underclasses and few the privileged classes. Historically in Latin America, the many racial and ethnic admixtures have produced myriad human phenotypes acknowledged in complex racial and ethnic classification systems. Cultural amalgamation in the Americas has created its own havoc in the social values of peoples, values that cannot be totally attributed to ancient European traditions. Tuttle (1976) has discussed the hybridization of European and Amerindian ethnic groups and the resulting linguistic mixtures and has found, not surprisingly, that many factors combined to precipitate the struggles between races, classes, and ethnic groups in America.

The present dictionary of racial and ethnic terms is warranted as a record of one form of human response to other humans, namely, the labels and other monickers used in the Americas. It is designed as a reference for speakers of English interested in topics of race and ethnicity in Spanish America and Brazil. This work, containing well over a thousand entries, incorporates historical, literary, political, sociological, anthropological, and some linguistic information as well as current colloquialisms.

These two dictionaries in one are composed of Spanish and Portuguese terms and expressions referring to physical type, skin color, ethnically marked national, regional, or geographic origin, social class, religion, and combinations thereof, many of which are charged with judgmental or prejudicial significance relating to the period and place of use. This work connects each term to time, place, and social significance whenever possible. The strong influences of the social and cultural customs of the people at a given time provide insights into the opinions, prejudices, and other impressionistic views that peoples share about each other. It is the nature of human beings to make choices and indicate preferences, and it can therefore be said that every person is prejudiced to some degree. This is not to say, however, that human beings cannot control emotional responses to others, only that too often they do not.

Latin America, Spanish America, and Brazil

The term "Latin America" is often misused or unexplained. In this book, "Latin America(n)" refers only to Spanish America and Brazil and does not include French-speaking America in the broader sense of the term. Racial terms from French-speaking and English-speaking America are used only when they may offer a comparison with those from Spanish and Portuguese.

"Spanish America," often confused with the term "Latin America," herein encompasses all the traditional, Spanish-speaking countries of America as well as part of the United States. Although some may believe that "Hispanic America" is a more precise way of expressing the idea of "Spanish America," others would counter that, in its broadest sense, "Hispanic" could just as easily include "Luso-Brazilian." Thus, in order to avoid further controversy, I have chosen "Spanish America," imprecise though it may be, for this work.

In some cases, both for Spanish America and Brazil, certain authors have given only general areas of use for extremely valuable and revealing entries. Examples of these broad geographic designations are the River Plate, the Antilles, Central America, the southwestern United States, and northeastern Brazil. I have not attempted to decipher completely the intentions of the authors and have tended not to interpret what geographical boundaries a specific area may embrace. Generally, however, for Spanish America, the Antilles are the Spanish-speaking islands of the Caribbean, namely, Cuba, the Dominican Republic, and Puerto Rico. The southwestern United States could represent any or all of the states of California, Arizona, New Mexico, Colorado, and Texas. River Plate is usually that area of Argentina and Uruguay near the mouth of the rivers that empty into the Atlantic between Buenos Aires and Montevideo. In Brazil, the North encompasses the states and territories of Acre, Amapá, Amazonas, Pará, Rondônia, and Roraima; the Northeast includes the states of Alagoas, Bahia, Ceará, Maranhão, Paraíba, Pernambuco, Piaui, Rio Grande do Norte, and Sergipe; the Central-West comprises the states of Goiás, Mato Grosso, Mato Grosso do Sul, Tocantins, and Brazil's capital, Brasília, Distrito Federal; the Southeast is constituted by the states of Espírito Santo, Minas Gerais, Rio de Janeiro, and São Paulo; and the South is made up of the states of Paraná, Rio Grande do Sul, and Santa Catarina.

Race and Ethnic Group

Today it is often the case, correctly or incorrectly, that *race* and *ethnic group* are interchangeable terms, quasi-synonyms. In the present work, however, the manner in which one human group classifies or identifies other individuals or human groups considered different from themselves broadly defines the term *race*. Depending on the field of inquiry (e.g., physical anthropology, zoology, politics, literature, social structures, etc.), *race* can beget quite divers though interrelated meanings. The term *race* has taken on disagreeable connotations (as per Pulgram 1958:75) to such an extent that many scholars have substituted for it the phrase *ethnic group*. In essence, *ethnic group* designates any group of humans that shares social or cultural traits (Whitten 1965:89; Moreno Navarro 1973:33, 35). These traits may include language variety, religion, national or regional origin, and at times phenotype.

If all of the above-mentioned characteristics did not originally mark ethnic type, they have lately acquired significance as ethnic identifiers. Consider terms denoting geographic, regional, or na-

3

tional origin. They often can be utilized to imply something about the identity or place of origin of the person so indicated. For example, in American English, the stereotypical Southerner speaks with a drawl, is slow of manner and slower in comprehension, propagates racist ideas, and does not like "Yankees." Even though the term "Southerner" indicates regional origin, many people attach a negative connotation to its usage or often infer one from its context and/or the tone of voice of the speaker. A similar denotative/connotative problem also exists for the American Spanish terms *puertorriqueñeo* 'Puerto Rican,' the derogatory and often self-deprecating variant of *puertorriqueño,* and *brasilero* 'Brazilian,' in lieu of standard *brasileño.* These examples show that the distinction between an ethnic and a national/regional/geographic significance of a term is often not clear.

The phrase *ethnic group* has unfortunately acquired many odious implications and pejorative connotations; it often serves only as a thinly disguised euphemism for *race,* as briefly noted above. For example, Kany (1960b:34) related racial nicknames to euphemism and slang in Spanish America. That is to say, he considered pejoration a part of humor, which arose as a "result of the natural rivalries among competitive social classes and among neighbors," thus classifying ethnic terms "in their relationship to races, to neighboring regions within a country" (1960b:34). Therefore, in the present work, I shall use *race* and *racial* in the broadest of senses to refer to the physical, social, and cultural characteristics of a human group and shall reserve *ethnic* and *ethnic group* to refer to traits of geography, national origin, religion, language, and other cultural references of a narrower nature. Indeed, the uses of *race* and *ethnic group* will often overlap, thus demonstrating that social factors often mitigate physical traits in Latin American classification systems.

Racial nomenclature in Latin America differs greatly both in nature and type from that found in Anglo America, specifically the United States. Two distinctions help separate Latin American and Anglo American racial classification systems. First, the North American system of racial classification is based on an oft-misunderstood dichotomy between nonwhite and white, in the sense of true racial prejudice. In fact, most prejudices amongst North Americans depend on stereotype by skin color or other physical characteristics, although in the twentieth century ethnic or cultural groups such as Hispanics, American Indians, and Jews have been racialized in the Anglo-dominant environment. Second, Latin American systems of racial and ethnic classification rely on a

4

complex of social factors and other class-related criteria to modify the impact of racial or ethnic categories (Harris 1964b:24; Solaún and Kronus 1973:162-3). That is to say, in Latin America but not in the United States, social indicators can alter ethnic or racial categories.

One can understand, in view of the unequivocal linguistic reality of the terms in these dictionaries, that Latin Americans themselves are acutely aware of race and ethnicity based on a multitude of factors, especially the so-called racial elements of skin color, hair type, and nose shape. Even though other factors must not be forgotten, policy makers, sociologists, historians, anthropologists, and others interested in Latin American racial and ethnic issues should appreciate the important, in many cases primordial, role that oft-ignored racial or physical characteristics play in Latin American racial and ethnic naming.

In summary, it should be remembered that racial and ethnic nicknames arise most often from obvious physiognomic or cultural traits and create or reinforce social classes. That is to say, these terms are imbued with the function of maintaining order in the social structure through the linguistic manifestations, often in the form of biases, of the Latin Americans who use them. Fromkin and Rodman (1988:287) have aptly observed that institutionalized social attitudes regularly surface in language usage, thus causing language to have positive or negative connotations. They have elucidated the pivotal nature of language in society by observing (1988:287): "When everyone in society is truly created equal and treated as such, there will be little concern for the asymmetries that exist in language." Latin American racial and ethnic terminology effectively demonstrates the judgmental function language performs in society.

Methodology, Collection of Data, and Commentary on Sources Consulted

In order to establish the bases for and development of racial and ethnic terminology in the Spanish and Portuguese of the Americas, I have studied anthropological texts such as Harris (1964a) and Mörner (1967), which clarified historical data and social consequences of racial epithets. The works of Woodbridge (1948), Aguirre Beltrán (1972), and Alvarez Nazario (1974) have shown that modern usage depends on previous manifestations of racial identifications and that terms previously not marked for race or

5

ethnicity assumed new characteristics in America.

The works mentioned above offer generally well-developed theses which have contributed greatly to the understanding of racial terminology in Latin America. The studies of Woodbridge (1948), Pérez de Barradas (1948), and Levine (1980) approach the scope of the present volumes. Those of Alvarez Nazario (1974), Aguirre Beltrán (1972), and Harris and Kottak (1963) have helped define the races and ethnic groups of Spanish American and Brazilian societies. Alvarez Nazario's findings on the African accretions of language, culture, and peoples to Puerto Rican life may be applied to the rest of Latin America as well. Aquirre Beltrán, who has investigated the influences that indigenous populations had on Mexico, believes that the native peoples there had input equal to that of the Europeans in founding the Mexican culture, a logical but novel concept for anthropological studies of Spanish American societies. Similarly, Harris and Kottak have studied race names and racial awareness in the multi-ethnic Northeast of Brazil, where they have found a plethora of phenotypes and a multifaceted naming system.

Harris (1970) and others have determined that the relative position of persons at the lower end of the social scale is often improved if there is semantic confusion in the terminological system. Racial and ethnic terms in many parts of Latin America, therefore, do not always distinguish types but rather muddle the classification in order to retain or increase ambiguity in the system. Borah and Cook (1961:67) have noted that social factors often outweigh racial ones in the naming process and facilitate the blurring of the racial or ethnic classification. Proof of this theory can be seen in the Spanish term *turco* 'Turk', which has come to mean 'person from the Middle East' in many parts of Spanish America.

Previous works have dealt almost solely with one region or country of Latin America at one specific time. Generally these works revolved around one type of investigation, either historical, anthropological, social, ethnological, or linguistic (e.g., Chance and Taylor 1977, Solaún and Kronus 1973, Woodbridge 1948, or Wagley 1949). The present work offers a relatively exhaustive view of race and ethnicity in Latin America, by using resources available in the United States from a wide variety of disciplines, and giving definitions from all periods of Latin American history from the earliest European settlement to the present day.

Introduction

Organization of a Definition

The racial and ethnic terms in these dictionaries are arranged using English-language, word-by-word alphabetization, including Spanish and Portuguese graphemes such as ç, ch, ll, rr, and ~. Words spelled the same except for accent marks are alphabetized in this order: unaccented word, word accented with ´, word accented with ^. Each entry is composed of the parts explained in (a) through (d) below:

(a) The term, in boldface, given in the masculine unless otherwise noted in the explanation; feminine and plural forms follow regular rules for Spanish and Portuguese unless otherwise noted in the explanation.

(b) A literal or "dictionary" definition in English, enclosed in single quotes immediately after the entry and given only if the term has a standard meaning in some variety of Spanish or Portuguese.

(c) The racial or ethnic definition(s), numbered sequentially from 1 if more than one definition exists; related or subsidiary definitions representing slight variations in meaning marked sequentially from a; definition consists of meaning, country and/or region of use, source of the information, historical period of use.

(d) A commentary, enclosed in square brackets immediately following the definition(s); may contain (1) information of an etymological or explanatory nature, (2) part of speech or type of phrase in which the entry usually appears, (3) derivative(s), (4) variant(s), (5) synonym(s), (6) antonym(s) and/or (7) cross-reference(s) to other entries of similar usage or meaning in either Spanish or Portuguese.

A typical entry will have the following layout (the information given in these entries is *pure invention for illustration only*):

gris 'gray'
person with white skin color; white person. *Mx* (Smith 1982:21) cl.
[M., f. Derog. Sim. in meaning to Black Amer. Engl. *honky.* Acc. Jones (1987:33), excl. to cl. Mx. Syn., deriv. *grisito.* Ants. *blanco, indio, negro.* Cf. **blanco, grisito, indio, negro,** Ptg. **cinzento.**]

or

cinzento 'gray'
1. person with white skin color; white person. *Br-n.e.* (Johnson 1976:234) cl–20.

7

2. black person. *Br-n.e.* (Smith 1982:22) 17–18 ‖ *Br-PR* (Cabral 1913:220) early20.
3a. person of mixed race. *Br-PR* (Olivares 1952:231) mid19–20.
3b. person of mixed race, usually of black and white parentage. *Br* (Gomes 1964:220) early20prior.
3c. person of mixed race, usually of white and Indian; mestizo. *Br-so.* (Graciano 1975:65) 20.
   [Df. 2 euph., iron. Df. 3 euph. Syn. df. 3b *mulato.* Acc. Gamba (1981:45), also found in c.w. Br. Deriv. *cinzentinho.* Cf. **mestiço, mulato,** Sp. **gris.**]

By way of explanation, for the Spanish term *gris,* the definition tells us that it is used in colonial Mexico, is unchangeable for masculine or feminine, is derogatory in its usage, has synonyms, and can be cross-referenced to both the synonyms and a Portuguese term. For the Portuguese term *cinzento,* the definition relates its various uses to time (e.g., "early20prior" in reference to a period up to and including the early twentieth century) and place (e.g., *Br-PR,* the abbreviation for the state of Paraná in southern Brazil), describes some of its uses as euphemistic or ironic, and gives us derivatives and cross-references. Definition 2 is offered by two authors (divided by a pair of vertical bars, ‖) for different areas and times.

The reader should remember several points and be aware of certain *caveats* while using these dictionaries:

(1) Some entries are subdivided in order to give more precise definitions or to present more accurately the intent of the source cited.

(2) A few abbreviations are personal invention; most, including those referring to states of the United States and of Brazil, nonetheless reflect accepted standard.

(3) In many entries referring to the colonial period, the authors cited (anthropologists, historians, sociologists, and so on) have calculated the percentage of each race that a person of mixed ancestry might have, a practice perceived by some as by nature an odious, racist tactic. These calculations, however, were most often an academic exercise meant to explain racial mixtures of the colonial period and to help decipher what colonial "ethnographers" were describing rather than to harm specific persons or groups. I have therefore included the percentages along with the definitions for the sake of completeness.

(4) The "colonial" period itself is not easily defined. Most authors do not explain their exact intent when discussing events

from colonial times and thus the term may mean different things to different people. Generally the period lasts from the discovery of the New World to the nineteenth century.

(5) In ascertaining the entries for this work, I have taken great pains to note for each one the intent, connotation, judgmental significance, or impact, including pejoration, derogation, slur, euphemism, or affection, whenever so indicated by the sources. I have, however, occasionally hazarded to note a term's intent when the author has not given direct indication, but have done so only when other factors point in a specific direction. For further information concerning these matters, the reader is urged to consult the sources listed with each definition.

(6) Each entry and the dictionaries themselves are by nature incomplete, since I have not been able to consult every possible source. Therefore, many terms, especially the rich set of categories referring to national, regional, or geographic origin or to American Indian groups will not be entirely represented herein. The dictionaries should nonetheless serve as a good starting point for those difficult-to-encounter definitions of some of the lexical items.

Part I.

Spanish American Terms

A

abajeño 'lowland; lowlander'
1. person from the coast or lowlands. *Mx PR* (Malaret 1931:3) mid20 ‖ *Co* (Alario di Filippo 1964:1); *Bo Co PR Mx* (Tobón Betancourt 1953:25); *PR SA* (Morínigo 1966:17) 20.
2. person from a seaport. *PR SA-so.* (Morínigo 1966:17) 20.
3. person from northern, generally coastal, departments of Co. *Co* (Morínigo 1966:17) 20.
4. southern Californian living somewhere between Santa Barbara and San Diego. *US-CA* (Blanco 1971:163) cl.
[Acc. DRAE (2), < *abajo* 'below' + adj. suf. *-eño.* Cf. **abajino, arribeño, bajero, nortino.**]

abajero — See *bajero*

abajino
person from northern or central Ch, acc. southern Chileans; northerner. *Ch* (Rodríguez 1875:6) 19; (Malaret 1931:3) mid20.
[Cf. **abajeño, arribano, nortino.**]

abejón colorado 'red drone'
mulatto with kinky, reddish hair. *DR* (Patín Maceo 1940:7) mid20.
[< *abeja* 'bee' + aug. suf. *-ón.* Cf. **color, mulato, pelo malo, quemado, rosado.**]

aborigen 'aborigine, native'
Native American; American Indian. *SA* (Gillin 1949:162) cl.
[Acc. Gillin, *aborígena* [*sic*] < *aborigen* + suf. *-ena* by anal. to *indígena.* Cf. **amerindio, indígena, indio,** Ptg. **amerígena.**]

aborígena — See *aborigen*

abrasilerado 'Brazilianized'
person who imitates Brazilians or adopts their customs. *Ur* (Mieres et al. 1966:15) 20.
[< *a-* + *brasilero* 'Brazilian' + adj. suf. *-ado,* probably pejor. Cf. **achapinado, achilenado, brasilero,** Ptg. **castelhano.**]

acanelado 'cinnamon-like'
person with reddish-brown skin color. *Co-Corozal, -Villanueva, -Carmen, -Mompós, -San Onofre, -San Juan, -La Cruz* (Flórez 1969:120) 20 ‖ *Co-Cartagena* (Solaún et al. 1987:19) late20.
[< *a-* + *canela* 'cinnamon' + suf. *-ado;* probably euph. Acc. Flórez, *acanelao* [*sic*]. Cf. **canelo.**]

acanelao — See *acanelado*

achapinado
person who has acquired the characteristics of a Guatemalan.

Ni (Castellón 1939:18) mid20.
[Acc. Castellón, < *achapinarse* 'to acquire the characteristics of a Guatemalan.' Probably pejor. Cf. **achilenado, agauchado, chapín.**]
achilenado 'Chileanized'
person who has acquired the manners and customs of a Chilean. *Bo* (Fernández and Fernández 1967:14) 20.
[< *a*- + *chileno* 'Chilean' + -*ado*. Generally pejor., esp. prevalent after the Chaco War of 1832–35 between Ch, Bo, and Pe, acc. Fernández and Fernández. Cf. **abrasilerado.**]
achinado
1. offspring of a mulatto and a black. *Cu* (Boyd-Bowman 1984:2171) 19.
2. person with the skin color and features of a *chino,* or offspring of an Indian and a *zambo. Ar* (Garzón 1910:6); *Ar-Buenos Aires, -so.* (Saubidet 1943:3) 19–early20.
3. person of mixed white and Indian race whose skin color and features are Indian-like. *Ar* (Segovia 1911:106) early20 ‖ *Ch Pe* (Malaret 1942:58) mid20 ‖ *Ur* (Cowles 1952:7; Mieres et al. 1966:15); *RP* (Guarnieri 1967:22) 20.
4. person of low social standing whose physical traits reflect an Indian heritage. *Ar Pg Ur* (Morínigo 1966:28) 20.
5. illicit lover of a *china,* or Indian woman. *Ch Pe* (Malaret 1942:58) mid20.
[< *a*- + *chino* + -*ado;* df. 1 vulg. Acc. Boyd-Bowman, syn. df. 1 *atezado.* Acc. Lipski (1988:p.c.), *ojos achinados* 'slanted eyes.' Cf. **aindiado, atezado, chino.**]
achocolatado 'chocolate-colored'
person with brown or chocolate-colored skin. *Mx SA* (Diggs 1953:407) early cl–18 ‖ *Co-Bata* (Flórez 1969:120) 20.
[< *a*- + *chocolate* 'chocolate' + -*ado;* generally desc., found in many Mexican laws in ref. to nonwhites. Cf. **negro achocolatado.**]
acholado '*cholo*-like'
1a. person with the physical features of a *cholo,* or mestizo. *CR* (Villegas 1952:2); *CR* (Cowles 1952:8); *Ch SA* (Yrarrázaval 1945:63) 20.
1b. person with the physical features of either a *cholo* or an Indian. *CR* (Gagini 1918:47) early20.
2. offspring of a European white and an Indian; mestizo. *Ch* (Yrarrázaval 1945:63) 20.
3. person who has taken on the attitudes or customs of a *cholo. Ar Bo Ch Pe* (Morínigo 1966:29) 20.
[< *a*- + *cholo* + -*ado.* Acc. Cowles, var. *acholao* in CeA, SoA no. of

14

RP. Cf. **achapinado, achinado, acriollado, cholo.**]
acholao — See *acholado*
acriollado 'creole-like'
1. foreigner who acquires the local customs and manners. *SA* (Morínigo 1966:26); *Pe* (Paz Soldán 1938:60); *SA Ur* (Cowles 1952:5) 20prior.
2. Basque, generally male, newly arrived among the gauchos, who acquired gaucho manners and customs faster than others as a result of his skills as a horseman. *Ar* (Laxalt 1980:499) late19–early20.
[Acc. Malaret (1947:15), < *acriollarse* 'to acclimate, become accustomed to.' Cf. **agauchado, criollo,** Ptg. **crioulo.**]
africano 'African'
1. black person. *Mx* (Aguirre Beltrán 1972:157) cl.
2. slave. *Mx* (Aguirre Beltrán 1972:157) cl.
[Acc. DRAE (33), syn. *afro.* Cf. **esclavo, negro, prieto,** Ptg. **africano.**]
afro — See *africano*
afroamericano 'Afro-American'
descendant of African blacks who were brought to America as slaves and remained in the New World after the abolition of slavery. *SA* (Vergara Martín 1922:229; Santamaría 1942:1.51) 20prior.
[Equiv. to No. Amer. Engl. *Afro-American,* which came into broad use in the 1960s. Cf. **africano, afroantillano, afrocolonial, afrocubano, afromestizo, americano, negro, prieto,** Ptg. **afronegro.**]
afroantillano 'Afro-Antillean'
any West Indian. *Pa* (Lipski 1988:p.c.) late20.
[Acc. Lipski, official designation used widely in print. Cf. **afroamericano, afrocolonial, afrocubano, afromestizo.**]
afrocolonial 'Afro-colonial'
any descendant of black African slaves. *Pa* (Lipski 1988:p.c.) late20.
[Acc. Lipski, official designation used widely in print. Cf. **afroamericano, afroantillano, afrocubano, afromestizo.**]
afrocubano 'Afro-Cuban'
American-born black slave who often served as a domestic in the master's city dwelling. *Cu* (Nuñez 1980:14) late cl.
[Acc. Nuñez, syn. *criollo.* Cf. **afroamericano, afroantillano, afrocolonial, afromestizo, criollo,** Ptg. **afro-brasileiro.**]
afromestizo 'Afro-mestizo'
1. offspring of a black and a person of any other race. *Mx*

15

(Aguirre Beltrán 1972:222) 20.

2a. person of mixed race in whom Negroid features predominate. *SA* (Urbanski 1978:155) 20.

2b. person of mixed race who has some physical features of a black but who is identified with whites. *SA* (Nuñez 1980:15) 20.

[Acc. Urbanski, term coined by the Chilean scholar Rolando Mellafe, in opp. to **euromestizo**. Cf. **africano, afroamericano, afroantillano, afrocolonial, afrocubano, americano, euromestizo, mestizo, negro, prieto,** Ptg. **afro-brasileiro, afro-negro.**]

afuerano — See *afuereño*

afuereño 'outsider'

foreigner, not native to the region or country. *Co* (Alario di Filippo 1964:6); *Co Ec Gu* (Malaret 1947:192) 20.

[< *afuera* 'outside' + adj. suf. *-eño*. Vars. *afuerino* in Ch, *ajuereño* in almost all other areas. Acc. Megenney (1988:p.c.), vars. *afuerano, ajuerano* in Ar and Ur. Cf. **abajeño.**]

afuerino — See *afuereño*

agabachado — See *gabacho*

agabacho — See *gabacho*

agauchado 'gaucho-like'

person who attempts to imitate the manners and customs of a gaucho. *Ar* (Garzón 1910:10; Segovia 1911:150; Saubidet 1943:6) early20 ‖ *Ar Ch Pg Ur* (Morínigo 1966:34) 20.

[< *agaucharse* 'to take on the customs of a gaucho,' ultimately < *gaucho*. Acc. Saubidet, var. *agauchao* in Buenos Aires. Cf. **achapinado, achinado, acriollado, afuereño, gaucho.** Ptg. **agauchado.**]

agauchao — See *agauchado*

agregado 'newly added, recently arrived'

1. squatter, or any poor person living on the land that belongs to another. *Ar* (Garzón 1910:10); *Ar Co* (DRAE 37) 20.

2. landowner. *Co* (Cowles 1952:12) mid20.

3. Indian or mestizo from the Peruvian highlands who works for the rich haciendas as a type of sharecropper and lives on a small piece of land there. *Ar Co Pe PR Ve* (Cowles 1952:12) mid20.

4. Indian who is taken into another Indian community and who holds relatively high social status. *SA-Andes* (Levine 1980:4) 20.

[< *agregar* 'to join, add to.' Widely used in SA. Syn. df. 1 *allegado* Syn. df. 4 *originario*. Acc. Guarnieri (1968:17), var. *agregao* in RP. Cf. **achocolatado, agregado al país, afuereño, originario,** Ptg. **agregado.**]

agregado a la hacienda — See *indio agregado*

16

agregado al país 'newly arrived in the country'
foreigner; gringo. *RP* (Guarnieri 1967:25 and 1979:14) 20.
[Cf. **afuereño, agauchado, agregado.**]
agregao — See *agregado*
agrifado '*grifo*-like'
person whose skin color is sim. to that of a *grifo*, or black person; colored person. *PR* (Malaret 1937:80) mid20.
[< *a-* + *grifo* + *-ado*. Cf. **grifo, persona de color.**]
agringado 'gringo-like'
1a. person who has the manners and customs of a gringo. *Bo*
(Fernández and Fernández 1967:16); *SA* (Morínigo 1966:35) 20.
1b. any non-North American who imitates the manners or has
been influenced by the customs of US. *Mx-Sonora* (Sobarzo 1966:6);
Ch Gu Ho Mx (Cowles 1952:12) 20.
2. person sim. in features to a *gringo*, or blond from NoA or
Europe. *Ch Gu Ho Mx* (Cowles 1952:12) 20.
[< *a-* + *gringo* + *-ado*. Cf. **agauchado, gringo, pocho.**]
aguador — See *aguatero*
aguatero 'water carrier, water seller'
person, usually a black slave or child, who sells water in urban
areas. *RP* (Guarnieri 1979:15) cl.
[< *agua* 'water' + suf. *-tero*. Var. *aguador.*]
ahí te estás 'there you are'
1. offspring of an Indian and a *coyote;* 43.15% white, 51.35% Indian, 5.5% black. *Mx* (Pérez de Barradas 1948:191) cl.
2. offspring of a *coyote* and a mestizo. *Mx* (Santamaría
1942:1.64; León 1924:21; Woodbridge 1948:356) cl ‖ *SA* (Vergara
Martín 1922:229) n.d.
3. offspring of a *coyote mestizo* and a mulatto. *Mx* (Monteforte
Toledo 1959:171; Woodbridge 1948:356; León 1924:47–48) cl;
(Mörner 1967:58) 18.
4. offspring of a *no te entiendo* and an Indian; 15.62% white,
59.38% Indian, 25% black, or 12.5% white, 70.3% Indian, 17.2%
black. *Mx* (Pérez de Barradas 1948:191; Woodbridge 1948:356) cl.
5. person of racial mixture whose physical traits do not correspond to those of whites, blacks, or Indians. *Mx* (Moreno Navarro
1973:143) 18.
[M., f. Acc. Diggs (1953:407), invented by scholars and clerics to
refer to a racial cross known in cl. SA. Df. 5 sim. to *tente en el aire*.
Vars. *ahí-te-estás, allí te estás.* Cf. **coyote, mestizo, no te
entiendo, tente en el aire.**]
ahí-te-estás — See *ahí te estás*

aibino
Indian of the Pima nation. *Mx-Sonora* (Sobarzo 1966:8) 20.
[Acc. Sobarzo, syn. *nebome bajo,* probably of Amerindian origin. Var. *aivino.* See also Santamaría (1942:1.66). Cf. **yanacona, yucateco.**]
aindiado 'Indian-like'
1. person with Indian-like features, esp. with respect to hair color and other physical features. *Co-no.* (Sundheim 1922:19; Revollo 1942:9) 20.
2. person with Indian-like features, esp. with respect to skin color, which ranges from reddish to copper-colored. *Ar* (Grenón 1930:242) late18 ‖ *Ar* (Segovia 1911:106; Garzón 1910:14; Saubidet 1943:8; Cowles 1952:19); *Ur* (Cowles 1952:19); *Cu RP* (Granada 1957:1.63); *RP* (Guarnieri 1979:16); *Co* (Alario di Filippo 1964:9); *SA* (Morínigo 1966:39) 20.
[< *a-* + *indio* 'Indian' + -*ado.* Df. 2 sim. to *achinado.* Cf. **achinado, amulatado.**]
aivino — See *aibino*
ajuerano — See *afuereño*
ajuereño — See *afuereño*
aladinado '*ladino*-like'
Indian who has acquired the manners and customs of either a mestizo or a white; acculturated Indian. *Gu* (Batres Jáuregui 1892:81–82) late19; (Cowles 1952:21) 20.
[< *a-* + *ladino* + -*ado.* Cf. **ladino.**]
alazán — See *alazano*
alazano 'sorrel-colored'
person with brownish or light brown skin color. *Co-Cimitarra* (Flórez 1969:120) 20.
[Acc. DRAE (49), var. *alazán.* Cf. **ruano.**]
albarasado — See *albarazado*
albarazado 'leprous, whitish; poorly matched'
1. person with whitish skin color, acc. parish records. *Mx* (Roncal 1944:533) cl.
2a. offspring of a *cambujo* and a mulatto. *Mx* (Vergara Martín 1922:229; Woodbridge 1948:356; Santamaría 1942:1.74; Monteforte Toledo 1959:171; Mörner 1967:58) cl.
2b. offspring of a *cambujo* and a mulatto; 30.86% white, 43.75% Indian, 25.39% black. *Mx* (Pérez de Barradas 1948:191) cl.
3. offspring of a *cambujo* and a white. *Mx* (Vergara Martín 1922:229; Woodbridge 1948:356) cl.
4. offspring of a *cambujo* and an Indian. *Mx* (Vergara Martín 1922:229; Woodbridge 1948:356) cl.

5. offspring of a *chino* and a *genízaro*. *Mx* (Vergara Martín 1922:229; Malaret 1931:22; Woodbridge 1948:356) cl.

6. offspring of a *lobo* and an Indian. *Mx* (Woodbridge 1948:355, 356; Pérez de Barradas 1948:191) cl.

7. offspring of a *zambaigo* and an Indian. *Mx* (Woodbridge 1948:356) cl.

8a. offspring of a *gíbaro* and an Indian. *Mx* (León 1924:9; Woodbridge 1948:356) cl.

8b. offspring of a *gíbaro* and an Indian; 24.22% white, 56.25% Indian, 19.53% black. *Mx* (Pérez de Barradas 1948:191) cl.

9a. offspring of a *gíbaro* and a mulatto. *Mx* (Monteforte Toledo 1959:171; Woodbridge 1948:356) cl; (McAlister 1963:354) 19.

9b. offspring of a *gíbaro* and a mulatto; 58.6% white, 6.25% Indian, 35.15% black. *Mx* (Pérez de Barradas 1948:191) cl.

10a. offspring of a *coyote* and a *morisco*. *Mx* (Woodbridge 1948:356; León 1924:39–40) cl.

10b. offspring of a *coyote* and a *morisco;* 62.5% white, 18.75% Indian, 18.75% black. *Mx* (Pérez de Barradas 1948:185) cl.

11a. offspring of a *tente en el aire* and a mulatto. *Mx* (Vergara Martín 1922:229; Woodbridge 1948:356; León 1924:20–21) cl.

11b. offspring of a *tente en el aire* and a mulatto; 25% white, 40.62% Indian, 34.38% black. *Mx* (Pérez de Barradas 1948:191; León 1924:20–21, plate 2) cl.

12a. offspring of a *chino* and an Indian. *Mx* (O'Crouley 1972:19) 18.

12b. offspring of a *chino* and an Indian; dihybrid, fourth-generation offspring of 3 parts black and 5 parts Indian. *Mx* (Moreno Navarro 1973: 129–31; Solano 1975:85) 18.

13. trihybrid, sixth-generation offspring of 11 parts black, 8 parts white, and 13 parts Indian. *Mx* (Moreno Navarro 1973:129–31; Solano 1975:84) 18.

14. dihybrid, seventh-generation offspring of 15 parts black and 49 parts Indian, i.e., offspring of a *genízaro* and another racial type. *Mx* (Moreno Navarro 1973:129–31; Solano 1975:85) 18. [Acc. Corominas (1954–57:1.83), < *abarazado* 'sick with leprosy.' Acc. Diggs (1953:407, mocking, joc.; term invented by clerics and others to describe new racial types. Excl. to cl. Mx, never widespread. Vars. *albarasado, albarrazado, alvarazado.* Cf. **albino, alcanzado, tente en el aire.**]

albarrazado — See *albarazado*

alvarazado — See *albarazado*

albino 'albino, white'

1a. person with white skin, acc. parish records. *Mx* (Roncal

1944:533) cl.

1b. person with either white or light skin. *Co-Fomeque, -Turbaco, -San Onofre* (Flórez 1969:120) 20.

1c. person with white skin whose parents are blacks. *Mx* (Woodbridge 1948:356) cl ‖ *DR* (Malaret 1942:82) mid20.

2a. offspring of a *morisco* and a white person, the latter of which is most often either Spaniard or European. *DR Mx* (Woodbridge 1948:356; León 1924:21; Monteforte Toledo 1959:171; Pérez de Barradas 1948:189) cl ‖ *Mx* (Vergara Martín 1922:229; Malaret 1931:22; O'Crouley 1972:19; Mörner 1967:58) 18.

2b. offspring of a *morisco* and a white; 87.5% white, 12.5% black. *Mx* (Pérez de Barradas 1948:185, 189; León 1924:20–21, plate 3) cl.

3. *castizo,* or offspring of a white Spaniard and a mestizo. *Mx* (O'Crouley 1972:19) 18.

4a. offspring of a *zambo* and a white; dihybrid, fourth-generation offspring of 7 parts white and 1 part black. *Mx* (Moreno Navarro 1973:129–31; Solano 1975:85) 18.

4b. person of mixed race, of 7 parts white and 1 part black, with very light skin covered with small chestnut-colored spots. *Mx* (Moreno Navarro 1973:140) 18.

4c. person with 7 white grandparents and 1 black one. *Mx* (Solano 1975:83) 17.

[Acc. Cassidy and DeCamp (1966:129), considered a white man's term, < Ptg. *albino* 'white-type,' formerly with sim. meaning in Engl.-speaking An. Syn. df. 4b *quinterón de mulato* in SoA. Cf. **aibino, albarazado, alcanzado, agauchado, blanco, castizo, mestizo, morisco mulato, negro, quinterón de mulato, zambo,** Ptg. **aça, albino.**]

alcanzado 'hard-up, broke; achieved, reached'
Indian merchant who works in the outskirts of a town. *Pe* (Cowles 1952:23) mid20.
[Used in ref. to the Indian who has arrived at a new station in life, that of owner of a small business.]

alcatraz 'gannet, pelican'
offspring of a black and an Indian. *DR* (Exquemelin 1684:25) cl; (Domínguez 1973:109) late18.
[Sim. to *zambo.* Acc. Exquemelin (1684:25), nickname used in ref. to the dark color of the *zambo* in allusion to the color of the gannet. Cf. **cayubro, mono, zambo, zorro.**]

aldeado 'villager'
Indian reduced to living on a reservation or other closed community. *SA* (Vergara Martín 1922:229) n.d., probably cl.

[< *aldea* 'village.' Cf. **poblano, pueblano, pueblero.**]

aldeano — See *campirano*

alemán 'German'
person having ruddy, "German-like" skin color. *Ve* (Flórez 1969:123, ftn.) 20.
[Cf. **ruso,** Ptg. **alemão.**]

alemán de mierda 'shitty German'
German settler. *Ch* (Roback 1944:133; Levine 1980:5) 20.
[Pejor., slur. Acc. Lipski (1988:p.c.), epithet *de mierda* used often with racial, regional, or ethnic terms. Cf. **alemán,** Ptg. **alemão batata.**]

aliento vivo 'live breath'
black African slave. *SA* (Ramos 1944:173) cl.
[Used perhaps in ref. to the slave's cramped journey from Africa in a tiny boat; if still alive upon arrival in the New World, the slave could be sold at market. Cf. **pieza de Indias, pieza de registro,** Ptg. **peça da costa, peça de Guiné.**]

allegado — See *agregado*

allí te estás — See *ahí te estás*

alobado — See *indio alobado, lobo*

altureño 'highlander'
person from the interior or highlands. *PR* (Malaret 1937:84) mid20.
[< *altura* 'height' + suf. *-eño.* Cf. **serrano.**]

alunado 'lunatic; tainted'
person whose skin color indicates racial mixture. *Co-Capitanejo* (Flórez 1969:120) 20.
[Acc. Flórez, *alunao* [sic]. Cf. **abrasilerado, quemado.**]

alunao — See *alunado*

alvarazado — See *albarazado*

alzado 'rebel, runaway'
1. slave who rises up against or flees from captors. *Cu* (Pichardo 1953:34) 19.
2a. rebel, fugitive. *Ar* (Cowles 1952:28) mid20.
2b. rebel who flees to the mountains. *CR* (Cowles 1952:28) early–mid20.
[Used also in ref. to animals. Acc. Cowles, sim. to *cimarrón;* var. *alzao.* Acc. Boyd-Bowman (1971:52), used in late 16-cent. Pe in phr. *negro alzado.* Cf. **cimarrón,** Ptg. **mocambeiro, quilombola.**]

alzao — See *alzado*

ama 'housewife; housemaid, nursemaid'
black nursemaid. *SA* (Levine 1980:5) 20.

[F. Cf. Ptg. **ama, babá.**]

amarillento 'yellowish'

person with yellowish skin color. *Co-Onzaga* (Flórez 1969:120) 20.

[< *amarillo* 'yellow' + suf. *-ento.* Cf. **amarillito, amarillo, amarilloso,** Ptg. **amarelo.**]

amarillito 'little yellow one'

mulato pardo, or offspring of a black and an Indian. *Mx-Chiapas* (Alvarez Nazario 1974:351) cl.

[< *amarillo* + dim. suf. *-ito.* Cf. **amarillento, amarillo, amarilloso,** Ptg. **amarelo.**]

amarillo 'yellow'

1. Asian, i.e., Japanese, Chinese, Korean, etc. *Cu* (Vandiver 1949:143) 20.

2. person with yellow skin color. *Co-Facatativá, -Sabana de Torres* (Flórez 1969:120); *Co-Cartagena* (Solaún and Kronus 1973:166) 20.

[Df. 1 found in 1943 Cuban census, acc. Vandiver. No ref. to use as a racial term in cl. times. Derivs. *amarillento, amarillito, amarilloso.* Cf. **amarillento, amarillo, amarilloso, azul,** Ptg. **amarelo.**]

amarilloso 'yellowish'

person with yellowish skin color. *Co-Utica* (Flórez 1969:120) 20.

[< *amarillo* + suf. *-oso.* Cf. **amarillento, amarillito, amarillo,** Ptg. **amarelo.**]

ambujo

offspring of a mulatto and a black. *SA* (Nuñez 1980:25) n.d.

[Perhaps var. of *cambujo.* Cf. **cambujo.**]

amembrillado 'quince-like'

black person whose somewhat yellowish skin color is lighter than that of the *retinto. Mx* (Aguirre Beltrán 1945:214) 17.

[< *a-* + *membrillo* 'quince' + *-ado.* Syn. *negro amulatado.* Cf. **membrillo, retinto.**]

amembrillado cafre de pasa

black person with yellowish skin and kinky hair texture. *Mx* (Aguirre Beltrán 1945:214) 17.

[Syn. *amembrillado merino,* acc. Aguirre Beltrán. Cf. **amembrillado, membrillo.**]

amembrillado merino — See *amembrillado cafre de pasa*

americano 'American'

1a. American; citizen of or native to US. *Ar* (Segovia 1911:24) early20 ‖ *Co-coast* (Revollo 1942:12) mid20 ‖ *Pa* (Aguilera Patiño 1951:411); *SA* (Morínigo 1966:49) 20.

1b. American, or any US citizen, incl. non-Hispanics among

22

andícola

them, acc. Canary Islanders. *US-LA-St. Bernard Parish* (Mac-Curdy 1950:50) mid20.

2a. person who speaks English only, acc. those of Spanish heritage. *US-s.w.* (Morínigo 1966:49) 20.

2b. Anglo, or non-Spanish-speaking white person, acc. older Indo-Hispanic Americans. *US-NM, -CO-so.* (Cobos 1983:9) 20.

3. peninsular Spaniard who spent time in America only to return to Spain. *SA* (Vergara Martín 1922:229–30) cl.

[< *América.* Derog. syn. df. 1a *yanqui.* Ants. df. 1b *criollo, isleño.* Syn. df. 2b *anglo.* Syn. df. 3 *indiano.* Other syns. *américo, angloamericano, estadounidense, norteamericano, saxoamericano.* Cf. **anglo, perulero, yanqui.**]

américo — See *americano*

americucho

1. American; person from US mainland; statesider. *PR* (Gallo 1980:5) 20.

2. non-American who tries to act or speak like an American. *PR* (Gallo 1980:5) 20.

[Acc. Gallo, slang. Probably somewhat derog. Cf. **americano, continental, gringo.**]

amerindio 'Amerindian'

Indian of the Americas; Amerindian; American Indian. *SA* (Alonso 1958:1.316) 20.

[Term used by Anthropological Society of America in ref. to Native Americans or American Indians. Var. *amerindo.* Cf. **aborígena,** Ptg. **amerígena, amerindio.**]

amerindo — See *amerindio*

amestizado 'mestizo-like'

person who looks like a mestizo. *SA* (DRAE 78) 20.

[< pref. *a-* + *mestizo* 'mestizo' + suf. *-ado.* Also used in Spain. Cf. **mestizo.**]

amonado 'monkey-like'

person with very light chestnut hair color. *Co* (Alario di Filippo 1964:14); *Co-Cartagena* (Solaún and Kronus 1973:166) 20.

[< *a-* + *mono* 'monkey, blond' + suf. *-ado;* probably also indicates light skin color. Cf. **mono.**]

amulatado 'mulatto-like'

person who looks like a mulatto. *SA* (DRAE 82) 20.

[< *a-* + *mulato* 'mulatto' + suf. *-ado.* Also used in Spain. Cf. **amestizado, negro amulatado,** Ptg. **amulatado.**]

anacona — See *yanacona*

andícola 'Andean'

person from the Andes Mountains. *SA* (Malaret 1947:194)

mid20.

[Acc. Alonso (1958:1.349), Americanism < *andi-* 'Andes' + Latin *colere* 'to cultivate, to inhabit.' Cf. **andino, andínico.**]

andínico 'Andean'

person from the Andes Mountains. *SA* (Malaret 1947:194) mid20.

[Cf. **andícola, andino.**]

andino 'Andean'

person native to the Andes Mountains. *SA* (Morínigo 1966:53; Alonso 1958:1.349) 20.

[Cf. **andícola, andínico.**]

anémico 'anemic'

person with light-colored skin. *Co-Timaná* (Flórez 1969:120) 20.

[Cf. **albino, blanco, cara pálida.**]

anglo 'Anglo'

1a. white, English-speaking person not native to the area. *US-NM, -CO* (Cobos 1983:10) 20.

1b. white, English-speaking American, acc. Hispanics. *US* (Fox 1988:235) 20–late20.

2. English-speaking American, acc. Hispanics. *US* (Gann and Duignan 1986:xiii) 20.

[Acc. Cobos, df. 1a used in ref. to an outsider coming into s.w. US. Df. 1b also used in Amer. Engl.; opp. to *hispano* or *latino*. Derog. syn. df. 2 *anglosajón*. Cf. **americano, bolillo, californio, gabacho, hispano, latino, nuevo mexicano, tejano.**]

angloamericano — See *americano*

anglosajón — See *anglo*

angola 'Angola'

1. black person from Angola, Africa. *Cu* (Pichardo 1953:39) 19 ‖ *Cu-Havana Mx-Puebla* (Boyd-Bowman 1971:62) 16 ‖ *Ar* (Garzón 1910:26; Segovia 1911:107, 153, 581) early20.

2. person with dark or black skin color. *Ar* (Garzón 1910:26) early20.

[Acc. Boyd-Bowman (1971:62), cited as *de nación Angola*. Acc. Garzón, syn. *bozal*. In Cu *venir* or *ser de Angola* 'to be stupid,' acc. Pichardo and Alonso (1958:1.362). Other syns. *negro angolo, angola fino*. 17-cent. var. *angolo*, acc. Boyd-Bowman (1983:188). Cf. **bozal, de nación Angola, negro angolo.**]

angola fino — See *angola*

angolo — See *angola*

antioqueño 'person from Antioquia'
white person or mestizo from the department of Antioquia, Co. *Co-Unguía, -Chocó* (Wade 1985:239) 20.
[< *Antioquia* + suf. *-eño*. Cf. **apaisado.**]

apaisado *'paisa*-like'
person who has become more like an *antioqueño*, i.e., more successful as a farmer. *Co-Unguía, -Chocó* (Wade 1985:241) 20.
[< *a-* + *paisa* 'antioqueño' (< *paisano*) + suf. *-ado*. Cf. **antioqueño, paisa.**]

apalencado *'palenque*-dweller'
1. runaway slave who gathered into a group of 7 or more such slaves in the wilds where there were *palenques* 'runaway slave outposts.' *PR* (Alvarez Nazario 1974:342) cl.
2. any foreigner who has adopted Cuban customs and has become familiar with Cuban people and ways; Cubanized foreigner. *Cu* (Vergara Martín 1922:230) n.d.
[< *a-* + *palenque* + adj. suf. *-ado*. Cf. **acriollado, agauchado, palenquero,** Ptg. **quilombola.**]

apampado
person who has the characteristics of a Pampa Indian. *Ar* (Morínigo 1966:57) 20.
[< *a-* + *pampa* + *-ado*. Cf. **abrasilerado, achapinado, achilenado, aladinado, amestizado, amulatado, apalencado.**]

aperlado 'pearly'
person with light-creamy, or pearly, skin color. *Co-San Vicente* (Flórez 1969:120) 20.
[< *a-* + *perla* 'pearl' + *-ado*. Acc. Flórez, *aperlao* [*sic*]. Acc. DRAE (102), var. of *perlado*. Cf. **anénico, quemado, rosado.**]

aperlao — See *aperlado*

apiñonado 'toasted pine nut-colored'
person with brown hair; brunet. *Mx* (Kany 1960b:48) 20.
[Acc. Kany, < *piñón* 'pine nut.' Cf. **moreno, morocho.**]

aplatanado 'nativized'
foreigner who can pass for a native of the country by having adopted the language and customs of the people; nativized foreigner. *Cu PR* (Morínigo 1966:60); *Cu* (Espina Pérez 1972:10) 20 ‖
Cu (Vergara Martín 1922:230) n.d.
[< *a-* + *plátano* 'plantain, or banana native to America' + adj. suf. *-ado*. Used esp. in ref. to the foreigner from Europe, acc. Santamaría (1942:1.116). Cf. **acriollado, agauchado, apalencado, criollo.**]

aprietado — See *prieto*

araba — See *árabe*
áraba — See *árabe*
arabe — See *árabe*
árabe 'Arab, Arabic'
1. person whose skin color is sim. to that of an Arab. *Co-Cartagena* (Solaún and Kronus 1973:166) 20.
2. Arab, Lebanese, or Syrian. *Co-Cartagena* (Solaún and Kronus 1973:166) ‖ *US-NM, -CO* (Cobos 1983:11) 20.
[M., f. Acc. Cobos, also f. form *áraba*. Acc. Cobos, *araba, arabe* [*sic*]. Cf. **turco**, Ptg. **árabe, turco.**]
arará
black person, native to the Arara region of Africa, known for distinctive facial features generally characterized by scarring and decorative stripes. *Cu* (Pichardo 1953:46) 19 ‖ *SA* (Vergara Martín 1922:230) n.d.
[M., f. Acc. Alonso (1958:1.452), also 'type of wild tree native to Cu.' Cf. **angola.**]
arrabalero — See *orillero*
arrendero — See *indio agregado*
arribano
southerner. *Ch* (Malaret 1931:3) mid20.
[Cf. **abajeño, arribeño, sureño.**]
arribeño 'inlander, highlander'
1a. inhabitant of the interior of the country. *Ar-Buenos Aires* (Bayo 1910:21) early20.
1b. native of the northern provinces of Ar and Bo. *Ar-Buenos Aires* (Garzón 1910:34) early20.
2. native or inhabitant of the interior or highland states, acc. coastal dwellers. *Mx* (Cowles 1952:50) mid20.
3. native of highland areas. *Ar SA* (Cowles 1952:50) mid20.
4. inhabitant or native of the southern highlands. *Co* (Tobón Betancourt 1953:38) 20.
5. highlander, esp. a person who lives along the Rio Grande north of La Bajada in Santa Fe County. *US-NM* (Cobos 1983:12) 20.
6. northern Californian. *US-CA* (Blanco 1971:163, 169) 20prior.
[< *arriba* 'up, above' + suf. *-eño.* Cf. **abajeño, arribero, nortino.**]
arribero 'southerner'
native of the south; southerner. *Ch* (Bayo 1931:29) mid20.
[< *arriba.* Ant. *abajeño.* Acc. Bayo, no. Ch known as *abajo* and so. Ch as *arriba;* ant. *abajeño.* Cf. **abajeño, arribano, arribeño.**]

artesano 'artisan'

black person, considered a second-class citizen of the artisan class. *PR* (Alvarez Nazario 1974:347) 20prior; (Zenón Cruz 1975: 1.249) 20.

[Generally social classification; blacks were often craftsmen and artisans of various types, such as blacksmiths and potters, during and after the cl. period. Syns. *clase artesana, clase de artesanos.*]

asiano — See *asiático*

asiático 'Asiatic, Asian'

1. Oriental, or Asiatic, person; Asian. *Ch* (Kany 1960b:38) 20.

2. person with the skin color of an Asian. *Co-Cartagena* (Solaún and Kronus 1973:166) 20.

3. native of China who contracted to serve or work in Cu, often in a type of disguised slavery; indentured Chinese servant. *Cu* (Macías 1885:98) 19; (Pichardo 1953:52) 20.

[Acc. Kany, term used to avoid *chino,* which had several native and Sp. meanings. Acc. DRAE (131), obs. var. *asiano.* Cf. **amarillo, chale, chino, chino manila.**]

atezado 'blackened'

1. black slave. *Mx-Puebla* (Boyd-Bowman 1969:137) cl ‖ *Mx* (Aguirre Beltrán 1945:213) 17.

2. offspring of a mulatto and a black. *Cu* (Boyd-Bowman 1984:2171) 19.

[< *a-* + *tez* 'coloring, complexion' + suf. *-ado.* Acc. Boyd-Bowman (1971:94), att. as *una esclava negra atezada ladina* in 16 cent. Syn. df. 1 *negro retinto;* syn. df. 2 *achinado.* Df. 2 vulg. Cf. **achinado, negro, negro atezado, negro retinto.**]

atravesado 'crossed, mongrel, crossbred'

1. mestizo. *Pe* (Cowles 1952:57) mid20.

2. mulatto or mestizo. *SA* (Alonso 1958:1.565) 20.

[Acc. Alonso, used also in ref. to 'hybrid animal' or 'person with a perverse attitude or intention.' Cf. **mestizo, mulato,** Ptg. **misturado.**]

auca

Araucanian Indian, generally considered rebellious. *Ch* (Armengol Valenzuela 1914:10.185; Malaret 1947:197) 20prior.

[M., f. Acc. Armengol Valenzuela, < Quechua and Aimara *auca* 'unruly, warlike, runaway, rebellious.' Syns. *indio auca, indio de guerra.*]

azul 'blue'

black person with very dark skin. *Pe-Piura* (Kany 1960b:35) 20.

[Facet.; derog. Reminiscent of the So. Amer. Engl. expression *blue-gummed Negro,* a very dark black person, whose gums, when show-

27

ing through a smile, allegedly had a bluish hue. Cf. **amarillo, blanco, negro, negro azul.**]

B

babeco — See *bebeco*

bachaco

1. person with physical characteristics of black race but with light-colored eyes, hair, or skin. *Ve-Caracas* (Bentivoglio 1977:295) 20.

2. person with Negroid features and white skin. *Ve-Caracas, -Malabo* (Bentivoglio 1984:p.c.) 20.

[Acc. Bentivoglio, < Amerindian word meaning 'ant of dark-reddish color,' possibly excl. to Ve as a racial term. Cf. **candelo, güero, mono, rubio.**]

bachicha 'Italian, wop'

1. Italian. *Ar* (Cara-Walker 1987:46) late19–early20 ‖ *Ar-Buenos Aires* (Chamberlain 1981:419); *Bo* (Fernández and Fernández 1967:25); *Ec* (Morínigo 1966:81); *Pe* (Paz Soldán 1938:223; Morínigo 1966:81) 20 ‖ *Pe* (Malaret 1942:160) early20prior.

2. non-Spaniard foreigner, esp. Italian. *Ar* (Garzón 1910:44) 20.

3a. uncultured or uneducated Italian, often a poor neighborhood grocer. *Ar Pe Ec* (Kany 1960b:37) 20.

3b. uneducated Italian, most often Genoese. *Ar Ch Pg Pe Ur* (Morínigo 1966:81) prior20.

3c. Italian, esp. Genoese. *Ar RP* (Segovia 1911:108) early20.

[M., f. Df. 1 pejor. Acc. Alonso (1958:1.610–11), Kany, Morínigo, and Segovia, < Genoese name *Baciccia,* hypocoristic form of the common Italian surname Battista. Lunfardo term found in Buenos Aires. Regional vars. *bachiche* in Pe and Ec, *bachichi* in Bo. Cf. **carcamán, gallego, godo, gringo, tano.**]

bachiche — See *bachicha*

bachichi — See *bachicha*

backra

white man. *SA* (Levine 1980:10) n.d.

[Acc. Levine, < Ibo *mbakara* 'white man.' Att. in Gullah and Engl. as *buckra* and Virgin Islands Engl. as *bukra* 'white man, planter.']

bagazo 'residue; useless person'

person of little esteem or low social standing. *Co* (Malaret 1937: 94–95; Revollo 1942:24; Alario di Filippo 1964:25); *CR Cu PR* (Malaret 1937:94–95; Revollo 1942:24); *SA* (Malaret 1937:94–95); *An*

Co SA-ce. (Alonso 1958:1.613) 20.
[Att. in phr. *al bagazo poco caso.*]
baisano — See *paisano*
bajeño 'lowland, lowlander'
person who lives near valleys or mountains; person who lives on the coast of the province of Los Santos. *Pa* (Aguilera Patiño 1951:416) mid20.
[Cf. **abajeño, bajero.**]
bajero 'lower; lowland, lowlander'
1. lowlander. *Co* (Tobón Betancourt 1953:41; Revollo 1942:24; Alario di Filippo 1964:26) 20.
2. person from the lower Magdalena River area of Co. *Co* (Alario di Filippo 1964:26; Revollo 1942:24) 20.
[Syn. df. 1 *abajeño.* Excl. to Co. Cf. **abajeño, abajero, bajero.**]
bajo de color 'low in color'
black person. *DR* (Kany 1960b:35) 20.
[Acc. Kany, semi-humor. or semi-euph., used not only in ref. to skin color but also to the low social status of the black. Cf. **gente de color, persona de color.**]
bamba
black person. *DR* (Vergara Martín 1922:230; Kany 1960b:35) 20.
[M., f. Acc. Kany, semi-humor. or semi-derog., excl. to DR. Rel. to African word *bembo* 'thick-lipped.' In Br 'dance done by blacks,' acc. Santamaría (1942:1.182). Acc. Alonso (1958:1.629), < onomatopoeic form *bamb* 'presumptuous and stupid person.' Cf. **bembón, bembo, negro bembón.**]
bandido — See *gauderio*
bantú — See *negro de gelofe*
baqueano — See *baquiano*
baquiano 'expert, practiced; guide'
1. person practical in things of the land or of the rural areas; guide; scout. *SA* (Alcedo 1786–89:5.16) late18prior ‖ *Pe* (Paz Soldán 1938:93) 19 ‖ *SA* (Malaret 1947:28; Bayo 1910:27–28); *CR* (Gagini 1918:69) 20.
2. colonizer who could resist the fatigue of work in America. *SoA* (Vergara Martín 1922:230) cl.
[Acc. Malkiel (1976:583), < Arawak (Cu or Haiti) form meaning 'guide.' Acc. Armengol Valenzuela (1914:10.190–91), < truncation of Sp. *vavaquia* 'boldness.' Acc. Boyd-Bowman (1971:111), 'old soldier' in 16-cent. Pe. Acc. Corominas (1973:84), Americanism documented from 1555. Vars. *baqueano, vaquiano, huaquiano, guaquiano.* Cf. **chapetón, gachupín, gaucho, ladino,** Ptg. **baqueano.**]

bárbaro 'wild, barbaric'
tribal or uncivilized Indian. *Bo-ea.* (Levine 1980:12) 20.
[Acc. Levine, pejor. Cf. **indio.**]

barbimono
man with a red or blond beard. *Co* (Alario di Filippo 1964:29)
20.
[< *barba* 'beard' + *mono* 'blond.' Syns. *barbirrubio, barbirrojo.* Cf.
mono.]

barbirrojo — See *barbimono*

barbirrubio — See *barbimono*

barbudo 'bearded'
Cuban who was a member of Fidel Castro's army that helped
overthrow Batista's government in the late 1950s. *Cu US-FL-so.*
(Rieff 1987:153) 20.
[Often derog., esp. amongst Cuban-Americans in FL. Cf. **batis-
tiano, brigadista, gusano.**]

barcino
1. offspring of an *albarazado* and a white. *Mx* (Woodbridge
1948:356; Santamaría 1942:1.189) cl ‖ *SA* (Vergara Martín
1922:230) n.d.
2a. offspring of an *albarazado* and an Indian. *SA* (Vergara
Martín 1922:230) n.d.
2b. offspring of an *albarazado* and an Indian; 12.5% white,
70.3% Indian, 17.2% black. *Mx* (Woodbridge 1948:356; Pérez de
Barradas 1948:191; León 1924:20–21, plate 4) cl.
3. offspring of a *gíbaro* and a *lobo.* *Mx* (Woodbridge 1948:356) cl
‖ *SA* (Vergara Martín 1922:230) n.d.
4a. offspring of an *albarazado* and a mulatto. *SA* (Vergara
Martín 1922:230) n.d.
4b. offspring of an *albarazado* and a mulatto; 40.43% white,
21.87% Indian, 37.7% black. *Mx* (Pérez de Barradas 1948:192;
Woodbridge 1948:356; Monteforte Toledo 1959:171) cl; (Mörner
1967:58) 18.
5. offspring of an *albarazado* and a mestizo. *Mx* (Woodbridge
1948:355, 356; Pérez de Barradas 1948:192) cl.
6. person whose hair color is a mixture of white, brown, and
often reddish. *Co-we.* (Velásquez 1962:115) prior20.
7. trihybrid, seventh-generation offspring of 11 parts black, 45
parts Indian, and 8 parts white. *Mx* (Moreno Navarro
1973:129–30; Solano 1975:84) 18.
[Acc. Moreno Navarro (1973:142), "animal with a brown or reddish-
white coat or hair, like some pigs, dogs, or cows." Vars. *barnocino,
baroina, barzino, barzina, barquina, borcino.* Cf. **albarazado,**

30

gíbaro, lobo, mestizo, mulato.]

barnocino — See *barcino*

baroina — See *barcino*

barquina — See *barcino*

barranquero 'riverbank dweller'
person who lives along the banks of a river. *SA-RP* (Morínigo 1966:87) 20.
[< *barranca* 'riverbank' + suf. *-ero*. Acc. Morínigo, also ref. to animals. Cf. **serrano, blanco de la barranca.**]

barriotero
person of low social class, of no financial means, or without social distinction. *Cu* (Malaret 1942:177) mid20.
[< *barrio* 'community, slum' + suf. *-(t)ero*. Cf. **aguatero.**]

barzina — See *barcino*

barzino — See *barcino*

bastante claro 'light enough'
person who is generally light-skinned. *Co* (Solaún and Kronus 1973:166) 20.
[Cf. **claro.**]

batistiano
Cuban who supported Fulgencio Batista's military dictatorship. *Cu US-FL-so.* (Rieff 1987:154–59) 20.
[< *Batista* + suf. *-iano*. Often derog. in Cu. Cf. **barbudo, brigadista, gusano.**]

batuco
Opata Indian of the Tegui family formerly residing in the village of Batuco. *Mx-Sonora* (Sobarzo 1966:38) 20.
[Cf. **indio.**]

baturro 'uncouth; Aragonese peasant'
Spaniard. *Bo* (Fernández and Fernández 1967:27) 20.
[Acc. DRAE (173), < *bato* 'stupid or rustic type' + suf. *-urro*. Probably pejor. Cf. **chapetón, gachupín, gallego**, Ptg. **galego.**]

bayano 'Bahian'
mulatto of sallow skin color, common to Br. *RP Ur* (Guarnieri 1967:43) 20.
[< Brz. Ptg. *baiano* 'native of Bahia,' acc. Guarnieri. Cf. Ptg. **baiano.**]

bayetero 'flannel maker'
Indian flannel-cloth weaver. *Pe* (Cowles 1952:79) mid20.
[< *bayeta* 'baize, a type of flannel used for blankets' + suf. *-ero.*]

bayunco 'silly, uncouth; rustic'
1. fat, rustic person. *Ho* (Membreño 1897:19–20); *Gu* (Batres

Jáuregui 1892:132) late19.

2. inhabitant of the *valle,* or outback; country hick. *CR* (Gagini 1918:71) early20.

3. Salvadoran, Nicaraguan, Honduran, or other Central American not from Gu. *Gu* (Kany 1960b:40) 20.

[Excl. to CeA. Acc. Lipski (1988:p.c.), now 'stupid,' esp. in Sa. Acc. Gagini, < *valle* 'valley.' Acc. Membreño, possibly < *bayuca* 'tavern' or < dim. of *valle*. Vars. *vallunco, valluno*.]

bebeco

1. albino. *Co* (Bayo 1931:34) mid20 ‖ *Co* (Acuña 1951:23; Cowles 1952:79; Tobón Betancourt 1953:44; Alario di Filippo 1964:32; Flórez 1969:120); *Cu* (Tobón Betancourt 1953:44) 20.

2. non-Spaniard foreigner. *Co* (Bayo 1931:34; Santamaría 1942:1.198) mid20.

[Var. *babeco*. Cf. **chele, gringo, jorongo, yanqui,** Ptg. **babeco**.]

befo — See *bembo*

belfo — See *bembo*

belfudo 'horse-lipped, thick-lipped'

black person with very dark skin. *Mx* (Aguirre Beltrán 1945:213) 17.

[< *belfo* 'large lower lip' + suf. *-udo*. Acc. Aguirre Beltrán, syn. *retinto*. Cf. **bembo, retinto**.]

bemba — See *bembo*

bembe — See *bembo*

bembo 'thick-lipped'

1a. person with thick lips, usually characteristic of a black. *Cono.* (Sundheim 1922:80–81) early20 ‖ *Ve* (Bayo 1931:40; Santamaría 1942:1.205) early–mid20 ‖ *Cu* (Espina Pérez 1972:18); *An Co Cu Pe Ve* (Cowles 1952:81); *An Co Mx-Tabasco Pe Ve* (Morínigo 1966:92) 20.

1b. tall person with a large mouth and thick lips. *Ho* (Membreño 1897:20) late19.

2a. person of African origin; black person. *Cu* (Pichardo 1953:90) 19; (Santamaría 1942:1.205) mid20.

2b. black African or African recently arrived in the New World. *An Co Cu Pe Ve* (Cowles 1952:81) prior20.

2c. Afro-Cuban with predominantly black physical features. *Cu* (Nuñez 1980:67) 20.

3. insignificant person. *Cu* (Espina Pérez 1972:18) 20.

[Df. 1a *bembo, bezudo,* or *bembón*. Df. 1b *bimba*. Acc. Morínigo, df. 1 vulg. Acc. Cowles (1952:81), *bembo, bemba, bembe, bembón* < African language; syns. df. 2b *negro bozal, negro africano*. Acc. Megenney (1983:3), *bemba* < LiNgala lg. of Zaire *mbembo* 'very large

lower lip'; pejor. Acc. Zenón Cruz (1975:1.247), *bembe* 'thick lip,' pejor. in PR; derivs. *bembón, bemboso, bembú, bembeteo.* Syns. *bezo, bezudo, befo, belfo, belfudo, bembudo, bimba.* Cf. **afrocubano, belfudo, getudo, jetón, negro bembón, trompudo.**]
bembón — See *bembo, negro bembón*
bembú — See *bembo*
bembudo — See *bembo*
berberisco 'Berber'
Berber, generally white, slave from North Africa. *Mx* (Aguirre Beltrán 1972:104) cl ‖ *Pe* (Boyd-Bowman 1971:120) mid–late16. [Syn. *beréber.* Cf. **árabe, turco.**]
beréber — See *berberisco*
bermejo 'red, reddish'
1. Spaniard. *SA* (Diggs 1953:405) cl.
2a. white person or Spaniard characterized by ruddy or reddish skin color. *Mx* (Aguirre Beltrán 1945:213) 17.
2b. white person. *Mx* (Aguirre Beltrán 1972:166) cl.
[Acc. Corominas (1954–57:1.445), first att. in the Cid with meaning 'blond, reddish.' Cf. **blanco, rubio.**]
betún 'bitumen; shoe polish'
black man. *RP* (Guarnieri 1967:44) 20.
[Cf. **negro, retinto.**]
bezo — See *bembo*
bezudo — See *bembo*
biche
1. weak, thin person with bad skin color. *Ar* (Morínigo 1966:93) 20.
2. person with blond hair; blond. *Mx-Oaxaca* (Morínigo 1966:93) 20.
[Acc. Santamaría (1942:1.209) and Blanco (1971:173), < Zapotec *bichi* 'blond, yellow.' Acc. Alonso (1958:1.696), < Quechua *huischi* 'lamb.' Cf. **bicho, chele, mono, rubio.**]
bicho 'weak animal; ridiculous person'
white person with blue eyes. *Mx* (Levine 1980:14) mid20.
[Acc. Levine, 1930s slang.]
bien — See *persona bien*
bimba — See *bembo*
blanco 'white'
1. white person. *SA* (Esteva Fabregat 1964:280); *PR* (Tumin and Feldman 1969:199); *Cu* (Pichardo 1953:98) cl–20.
2. Spaniard. *Mx* (Aguirre Beltrán 1972:166) cl; (Chance 1979:154) 19.

3a. person who has white skin color but is not necessarily all white by descent; anyone who is not Indian or black. *Mx* (Fuente 1947:65) 19–20 ‖ *SA* (Harris 1964a:115) 20.

3b. person with white skin color. *Co* (Solaún and Kronus 1973:166); *Co Ve* (Flórez 1969:123) 20.

4. offspring of a white and a *tercerón*. *PR* (Alvarez Nazario 1974:357) late18.

5. offspring of a white and a *cuarterón*. *DR* (Alvarez Nazario 1974:357) 18.

6. person who is 1/8 Indian or 1/16 black; offspring of a white Spaniard and a *castizo* or of a white and a *quinterón*. *SA* (Rosenblat 1954:2.137) cl.

7a. person with visible white characteristics enjoying the highest social standing. *Co-Zarzal, -highland valley* (Sayres 1956:223) 20.

7b. rich person who owns land and cattle, who has good social standing, and who may or may not have white skin. *Co-Atlantic coast* (Alario di Filippo 1964:36) 20.

7c. mestizo, mulatto, or white of the middle or upper class who has some degree of good social standing. *Ec-n.w. coast* (Whitten 1965:91) 20.

7d. highlander of the middle or upper class who is given some respect. *Ec-n.w. coast* (Whitten 1965:92) 20.

7e. person of some wealth, not necessarily having white skin, known for self-importance and tyranny, acc. those of the lower social strata. *Pe SA* (Kany 1960b:38) 20.

7f. light-skinned mulatto of the upper social strata. *SA* (Levine 1980:17).

7g. person of mixed race who is treated socially as white, esp. in the lower classes. *Co-Cartagena* (Solaún et al. 1987:19) 20.

7h. person of the highest social classes. *Pa-interior* (Aguilera Patiño 1951:419) 20.

7i. person in social or economic favor who has good manners, can grow a moustache, or shows any other feature characteristic of a white. *Co-Zarzal, -highland valley* (Sayres 1956:224) 20.

8. any white or nonwhite person considered important, wealthy, or dictatorial, acc. the lower classes. *Co Pa Pe* (Kany 1960b:38) 20.

9. Bribri, Cabezar, or Tiribi Indian of Costa Rica, acc. Spaniards. *CR* (Vergara Martín 1922:230) n.d.

[Acc. Rosenblat (1954:2.138), affect. as in phr. *mi blanco*, sim. to *negrito* or *cholito*. Syns. *español, európido, gente de razón.* All parts of df. 7 refer to social standing; often derog. Df. 8 derog., iron. Cf. **indio, mestizo, mulato, negro,** Ptg. **branco.**]

blanco aindiado 'Indian-like white'
white person showing some Indian features. *Co-Cartagena* (Solaún et al. 1987:19) late20.
[Cf. **aindiado, blanco moreno, indio alobado.**]

blanco claro 'light white'
white person with light or pale white skin color. *Co-Cartagena* (Solaún et al. 1987:19) late20.
[Probably indicates lack of racial mixing. Cf. **trigueño claro.**]

blanco con negro 'white with black'
white person with black features. *Co-Cartagena* (Solaún and Kronus 1973:166) 20.
[Cf. **blanco, negro, blanco con poco negro.**]

blanco con poco negro 'white with a little black'
white person with some black features. *Co-Cartagena* (Solaún and Kronus 1973:166, 168) 20.
[Cf. **blanco, blanco con negro, blanco con tinta, negro.**]

blanco con tinta 'white with ink added'
white person with black features. *Co-Cartagena* (Solaún and Kronus 1973:166) 20.
[Cf. **blanco, blanco con negro, blanco con tinta negroide, retinto, tinta.**]

blanco con tinta negroide 'white with black ink added'
white person with dark skin color, generally indicating black ancestry. *Co-Cartagena* (Solaún and Kronus 1973:166) 20.
[Cf. **blanco, blanco con tinta, blanco moreno, tinta.**]

blanco criollo — See *blanco del país*

blanco de color moreno subido 'white with very dark skin'
mestizo; white whose skin color is dark brown. *Bo* (Kany 1960b:35) 20.
[Acc. Kany, humor. or pejor. Cf. **blanco, blanco moreno, moreno.**]

blanco de la barranca 'white from the gutter'
nonwhite person who pretends to be white. *DR* (Patín Maceo 1940:24) mid20.
[Acc. Patín Maceo, sarc. Cf. **barranquero, blanco.**]

blanco de la tierra — See *criollo*

blanco de tierra
native of PR. *PR* (Vergara Martín 1922: 230) early20.
[Acc. Vergara Martín, syn. *jíbaro.* Cf. **blanco del país, criollo, jíbaro.**

blanco del país 'white from the country'
descendant of whites and Africans. *PR* (Alvarez Nazario 1974:356) cl–19.
[Obs. Near syn. *blanco criollo* 'white native to the country.' Cf. **blanco.**]

blanco moreno 'brown-skinned or brunet white'
white person with dark or brown skin color. *Co-Cartagena* (Solaún and Kronus 1973:166) 20.
[Cf. **blanco, blanco de color moreno subido, moreno.**]

blanco no del todo 'not all white'
person who is not completely white. *Co-Cartagena* (Solaún et al. 1987:19) late20.
[Euph., acc. Solaún et al. Cf. **blanco con negro, blanco moreno, no blanco del todo.**]

blanco quemado 'burnt white'
white person with burned or suntan-like skin. *Co-Cartagena* (Solaún et al. 1987:19) late20.
[Possibly euph.; could indicate some racial mixture. Cf. **blanco moreno, blanco rosado.**]

blanco rosado 'white with rosy skin'
white person with rosy or reddish skin color. *Co-Cartagena* (Solaún and Kronus 1973:166) 20.
[Cf. **blanco, blanco moreno, blanco trigueño, rosado,** Ptg. **rosado.**]

blanco trigueño 'white with wheat-colored skin'
white person with light brown skin color. *Co-Cartagena* (Solaún and Kronus 1973:166) 20.
[Cf. **blanco, blanco quemado, blanco rosado.**]

blanco y ñato 'white and flat-nosed'
white person who has a wide nose like a black. *Co* (Levine 1980:18); *Co-Cartagena* (Solaún and Kronus 1973:166) 20.
[Probably indicates some racial mixture. Cf. **pelo malo.**]

blanconazo
1. mestizo who is almost white. *Cu* (Espina Pérez 1972:19) 20.
2. light-skinned mulatto. *Cu* (Kany 1960b:35; Alonso 1958: 1.716) 20.
3. person who is not totally white as a result of some black ancestry. *Cu* (Malaret 1942:190) mid20.
[Excl. to Cu. Df. 1 syn. *ochavón.* Acc. Kany, df. 2 semi-humor. Cf. **blanco, ochavón.**]

blanconazo mulatico
Dominican who is part black or somewhat mulatto, acc. Cubans. *US-NY* (Domínguez 1973:150) 20.

[Somewhat derog. Cf. **blanconazo, mulato.**]

blancote 'sickly white; coward'

tall, fat, white person. *DR* (Patín Maceo 1940:24) mid20.
[Acc. Alonso (1958:1.716), *blanco* + pejor. aug. suf. *-ote*. Cf. **blanco.**]

blancuso — See *blancuzco*

blancuzco 'whitish'

white person. *Ar* (Garzón 1910:58) early20.
[Derog. Acc. Corominas (1954–57:1.470), first att. mid-19 cent.
Derog. Var. *blancuso* 'white person' used by blacks, acc. Santamaría (1942:1.214). Other vars. *blancuso, blancuzo, blanquecino, blanquizco*. Cf. **blanco, blancote.**]

blancuzo — See *blancuzco*

blanquecino — See *blancuzco*

blanquito

1. white person. *PR* (Zenón Cruz 1975:1.258) 20.

2. upper-class or rich person, referring vaguely to white skin color. *PR* (Gallo 1980:11) 20.

3. dark-skinned person, not fully white, who is trying to pass for white, acc. Cubans, Dominicans, and Puerto Ricans. *Cu DR PR US-NY* (Domínguez 1973:189) 20.

4. black person with straight or wavy, but not kinky, hair texture. *An* (Domínguez 1986:275) 20.
[< *blanco* + dim. suf. *-ito*. Acc. Zenón Cruz, df. 1 injur. or insult., referring to one's class. Acc. Gallo, df. 2 neutral, slang ref. to one's wealth. Acc. Domínguez (1986), df. 4 affect.; syn. *indio*, who has only straight hair. Cf. **blanco no del todo.**]

blanquizco — See *blancuzco*

blondo 'blond'

1. person with blond hair. *Gu* (Batres Jáuregui 1892:134) late19 ‖ *Gu* (Santamaría 1942:1.214) 20.

2. person with curly or kinky hair. *Ch* (Batres Jáuregui 1892:134) late19 ‖ *SA* (Santamaría 1942:1.214); *Co-coast* (Revollo 1942:32) mid20.
[Acc. Revollo, incorrect nickname for *crespo* or *rizado* 'curly or kinky hair.' Cf. **albino, chele, güero, mono, rubio.**]

boca abajo — See *bocabajo*

boca bajo — See *bocabajo*

bocabajo 'down in the mouth'

black person. *PR* (Alvarez Nazario 1974:343, 380) 20.
[Pejor.; fig. *Bocabajo*, or *boca bajo*, 'instrument of punishment used to make slaves behave,' making their 'mouths hang down,' acc. Cowles (1952:87), Espina Pérez (1972:20), and Sobarzo (1966:44).

Acc. Sobarzo, deriv. *bocabajeado* 'depressed person' in Sonora, Mx. Vars. *boca abajo, boca bajo.*]

boga — See *bogo*

bogo

1. Indian employed as a canoe man. *Co* (Levine 1980:77) cl.

2. offspring of a black and an Indian, who can be found in the jungles of the Magdalena River and has savage customs; person of color from the department of Boga, Co. *Co* (Vergara Martín 1922:230) n.d., probably early20.

[Acc. Vergara Martín, syn. *zambo.* Acc. Levine, invariably *boga.* Cf. **carguero, libre de color.**]

bolaño 'rock pellet; stone'

California Indian from the coast near San Rafael. *US-CA* (Blanco 1971:175) cl.

[Cf. **bolillo.**]

boliche 'small ball'

Bolivian. *SA* (Kany 1960b:39) 20.

[Acc. Kany, derog., play on name *Bolivia;* also 'ball used in the game *pigeon-holes.*']

bolillo 'white bread roll'

Anglo-Saxon; white North American; white person; non-Indo-Hispanic white person. *US-TX* (Kany 1960b:38); *US-CO, -NM* (Cobos 1983:19) 20.

[Acc. Alonso (1958:1.735) and Kany, < Mexican Sp. *bolillo* 'chunk of white bread.' Acc. Cobos, 'type of white breakfast roll.' Often derog. or facet. Cf. **americano, anglo, gabacho, gabardino, gringo.**]

borcino — See *barcino*

boricano — See *boricua*

boricua

Puerto Rican. *PR* (Cowles 1952:96; Gallo 1980:13) 20.

[M., f. Acc. Cowles, < Arawak *Boriquén* 'PR.' Vars. *boricano, borincano, boriqueño, boriquense, borinqueño, borinqueño, boriquense.* Cf. **portorriqueño, puertorriqueño.**]

borincano — See *boricua*

borinqueño — See *boricua*

boriqueño — See *boricua*

boriquense — See *boricua*

box

native of the Yucatán Peninsula. *Mx* (Kany 1960b:42) 20.

[Acc. Kany, < Mayan *box* 'black.' Deriv. *boxito.*]

boxito — See *box*

bozal 'new, untamed, stupid; muzzle'

1a. black slave brought directly from Africa to America. *PR* (Zenón Cruz 1975:1.250) cl.

1b. black slave recently arrived from Africa, esp. one who does not speak Spanish or Portuguese, who is not Christian, who is untrained in Western ways, and/or who is unskilled labor. *SA* (Alvarez Nazario 1974:333; Bayo 1910:36 and 1931:47; Rout 1976: xiv); *Cu* (Cowles 1952:99; Pichardo 1953:110); *Co-we.* (Velásquez 1962:114); *PR* (Alleyne 1963:98) cl ‖ *SA* (Alcedo 1786–89:5.19) late18.

2a. person, esp. black, who speaks Spanish poorly. *An SA* (Santamaría 1942:1.231) mid20.

2b. black, Indian, or foreigner who speaks bad Spanish. *Ar* (Segovia 1911:110) early20.

2c. person, esp. Indian, who speaks Spanish badly. *SA* (Zenón Cruz 1975:1.250) 20.

[Acc. Cobarruvias (1611:223), Wilson (1939:172), Aguirre Beltrán (1972:158), and Alvarez Nazario, df. 1 att. in Golden Age Spain. Acc. Corominas (1954–57:1.507), used by Nebrija in 1492. Acc. Zenón Cruz, Sp. > Ptg. *boçal* > Papiamentu *busá* 'stupid, simple.' Cf. **bozal torpe, bozalón, criollo, ladino, negro bozal.**]

bozal potreador 'fearsome *bozal*'

strong black slave recently arrived from Africa who was used to break colts. *RP* (Guarnieri 1979:36) cl.

[Cf. **bozal.**]

bozal torpe 'stupid *bozal*'

black slave who was put to labor easily, who spoke Spanish imperfectly or not at all, and who was thus deemed ignorant in the eyes of the slave masters. *Mx SA* (Aguirre Beltrán 1972:160); *Cu PR* (Alvarez Nazario 1974:334) cl.

[Cf. **bozal, bozal potreador, bozalón, ladino.**]

bozalón

1. slave who spoke Spanish imperfectly. *SA* (Aguirre Beltrán 1972:160); *Co-we.* (Velásquez 1962:114); *PR* (Alvarez Nazario 1974:334) cl.

2a. Indian who speaks Spanish badly. *Ec* (Alonso 1958:1.762) 20.

2b. Indian or mountain-dwelling peasant who speaks Spanish poorly, often mixing it with Quechua. *Ec* (Zenón Cruz 1975:1.250) 20.

[< *bozal* + aug. suf. *-ón.* Syn. *bozal torpe.* Cf. **bozal, bozal potreador, bozal torpe, ladino.**]

bracero 'day laborer'
1. Mexican day laborer or farm worker; Mexican migrant worker. *US-CO, -NM* (Cobos 1983:20); *Mx US* (Bailey and Nasatir 1973:766) 20.
2. legal Mexican migrant worker contracted as an agricultural laborer. *US-s.w.* (Gann and Duignan 1986:46) mid20.
[< *brazo* 'arm.' Acc. Bailey and Nasatir, like Engl. *field hand.* Cf. **chicano, mojado, pocho.**]

brasileño — See *brasilero*

brasilero 'Brazilian'
Brazilian. *Ar* (Segovia 1911:164) early20 ‖ *SA* (Bayo 1931:47) mid20.
[< Ptg. *brasileiro* 'Brazilian' in contrast to std. Sp. *brasileño.* Possibly derog. Cf. **gallego.**]

brícamo
black person native to the Carabali region of Africa. *Cu* (Pichardo 1953:111) mid19.
[Acc. Pichardo, these people use wooden harmonicas and drums in their festivals. Acc. Santamaría (1942:1.233), also used in 20 cent. Cf. **angola, briche.**]

briche
black person native to the Carabali region of Africa. *Cu* (Pichardo 1953:111) mid19.
[Acc. Pichardo, these people are distinguished by their prominent and decoratively scarred forehead. Acc. Dunbar-Nelson (1916:361), LA Fr. *briqué* 'scrubbed' used in 19 cent. by nonwhites to distinguish skin color. Cuban Sp. term probably < Fr. Cf. **angola, brícamo.**]

brigadista 'brigade member'
Cuban rebel-fighter who went to the Bay of Pigs in 1961 with Brigade 2506 in the vain attempt to liberate Cu from Fidel Castro. *US-FL-so.* (Rieff 1987:160–61) 20.
[M. < *brigada* 'brigade, squad' + suf. *-ista.* Acc. Rieff, Brigade 2506 consisted of a CIA force of 1400 Cuban exiles, several hundred of whom were captured in the ill-fated Bay of Pigs invasion. Cf. **barbudo, batistiano, gusano.**]

brucú
black slave recently arrived from Guinea in Africa. *Cu* (Vergara Martín 1922:231) cl.
[Cf. **angola, bozal, brícamo, briche, guineo.**]

buchi
1. farmer, or rustic person; person who acts like a farmer. *Pa* (Aguilera Patiño 1951:421) mid20; (Kany 1960b:41) 20.

2. barbarian; barbaric or savage man. *Pa* (Levine 1980:22) 20.
[Acc. Aguilera Patiño and Levine, < Engl. *bush(man)*. Acc. Vergara
Martín (1922:231), *boschnegers, bosh,* or *bush* were "runaway black
slaves, usually from the Auca, Saramacca, Maesinga, or Beca tribes,
who lived in the interior jungles of Surinam." Var. *buchí.* Cf. **buchi
gringo.**]
buchi gringo
North American with no education; person whose actions indicate a lack of education or training. *Pa* (Aguilera Patiño 1951:421)
mid20.
[Cf. **buchi, gringo.**]
buchí — See *buchi*
bugre 'savage'
savage or wild Indian. *SA-so.* (Bayo 1910:38) early20.
[Acc. Bayo (1910:38 and 1931:49), maps of Bo, Pe, and Pg often
noted *"Aquí empiezan los bugres,"* as ancient texts noted *"Hic sunt
leones"*; < Brz. Ptg. *bugre.* Syns. in Bo and Pe *chuncho,'gíbaro.* Cf.
indio, Ptg. **abugrado, bugre.**]
bundo
native of Angola, Africa; Angolan black. *Ur* (Tenório
d'Albuquerque 1954:31); *RP* (Pereda Valdés 1937:72) mid20.
[Acc. Machado (1952–59:1.417), < Kimbundu *mbundu* 'black.' Acc.
Schneider (1985:230), Brz. *bundo* 'incorrect way of speaking' < Kimbundu *ambundo* 'group of people.' Cf. **angola, brícamo, briche,
negro angola.**]

C

caballero 'gentleman'
Spanish gentleman or horseman. *SA* (Bailey and Nasatir
1973:766) cl.
[M. only. Cf. **español, cachupín.**]
cabecita — See *cabeza negra*
cabecita negra — See *cabeza negra*
cabeza cuadrada 'square head'
German. *SA* (Roback 1944:133) mid20.
[Acc. Roback, slur. Cf. **alemán de mierda, carcamán, mojado,
nación, paisano.**]
cabeza negra 'black head'
1. poor, rural Argentine dispossessed from the land. *RP*
(Guarnieri 1967:53) 20.
2. *morocho* from the interior of the country. *Ar* (Guarnieri
1967:53) 20.

3. black person. *Ar* (Kuga 1982:p.c.) 20.
[Used in ref. to both Amerindian and black phenotypes. Dim. deriv.
cabecita. Syn. *cabecita negra.* Syn. df. 3 *pardo.* Cf. **morocho,
negro, pardo.**]
cabinda
black person from the Cabinda region of Africa. *Ur* (Tenório
d'Albuquerque 1954:31; Pereda Valdés 1937:72) mid20.
[M., f. < *Cabinda* 'small territory, presently part of Angola, located
on the s.w. coast of Africa.']
caboclo
settler new to the country; colonizer. *Co* (Malaret 1931:85); *Ur*
(Malaret 1942:222) mid20 ‖ *Co* (Cowles 1952:109; Tobón Betancourt 1953:53; Alario di Filippo 1964:45) 20.
[Probably < Ptg. *caboclo.* Cf. Ptg. **caboclo.**]
cachaco 'dandy'
1. Spaniard, esp. one with revolutionary ideas. *PR* (Malaret
1937:114); *SA* (Cowles 1952:113–14) mid20.
2. person from the interior of the country, acc. coastal dwellers.
Co (Kany 1960b:41; Alario di Filippo 1964:46; Revollo 1942:42) 20.
3. person of high class or society. *Co* (Alario di Filippo 1964:46)
20.
4. soldier from the department of Antioquia, Co. *Pa* (Cowles
1952:113–14) mid20.
[Acc. Kany, df. 2 derog. Df. 3 generally derog., probably used by
person from the lower classes. Df. 4 probably derog. Extremely
derog. syn. *cachuzo.* See also Santamaría (1942:1.255–58). Cf. **persona bien.**]
cachimbazo — See *cachimbo*
cachimbito — See *cachimbo*
cachimbo 'pipe'
1a. black person. *Cu* (Pichardo 1953:128–29) 19.
1b. black slave. *Cu* (Macías 1885:220) 19.
2. person of little economic means. *Cu* (Santamaría 1942:1.260)
20.
3. person with a very prominent lower jaw. *Ec* (Malaret
1942:232) mid20.
[Acc. Pereda Valdés (1937:72–73), < Kimbundu *kisima* 'pipe.' Acc.
Pichardo, df. 1a scorn.; 'pipe used by blacks outside of the city.' Acc.
Macías, df. 1b injur.; 'pipe used in the fields by slaves as they
worked'; aug. deriv. *cachimbazo;* affect. dim. deriv. *cachimbito.* Cf.
negro.]
cachupín
1. European or Spaniard. *Mx* (Alcedo 1786–89:5.22) late18 ‖

CeA Ve (Malaret 1947:35) mid20.

2a. Spaniard, acc. Indians. *Co Mx* (Tascón 1961:90) cl.

2b. low-class Spaniard. *SA* (Malaret 1942:234) mid20 ‖ *US-CO, -NM* (Cobos 1983:23); *CeA Mx* (Kany 1960b:37) 20.

2c. Spaniard. *US-CO, -NM* (Cobos 1983:23) 20.

2d. Spanish settlers unknowledgeable of American ways. *CeA Mx* (Kany 1960b:37) cl.

2e. Spanish settler, esp. one unknowledgeable of American ways and interested mostly in economic improvement. *SA* (Morínigo 1966:113) cl.

[Df. 2e derog. Acc. Tascón, < Nahuatl (Aztec) *cacchopín* 'shod viper.' Acc. Kany, < *cachopo* 'hollow tree trunk.' Acc. Cobos, Malaret, and Morínigo, var. *gachupín* in Mx. Cf. **chapetón, gachupín.**]

cachuzo

1. person of low class from the interior of the country. *Co-Cartagena* (Revollo 1942:42) mid20.

2. person from the interior of the country, acc. coastal dwellers. *Co* (Kany 1960b:41) 20.

[Extremely derog., acc. Kany. Cf. **cachaco, centrano, reinoso.**]

cacique 'chief'

Indian chief or tribal leader. *SA* (Bailey and Nasatir 1973:766); *RP SoA* (Guarnieri 1979:39) cl.

[Acc. Bailey and Nasatir, chief often retained as local village authority under the Spaniards; today often 'political boss.']

cafingo

pure black person. *Co-coast* (Alario di Filippo 1964:49) 20.

[Probably of African origin. Cf. **negro retinto.**]

cafre 'cruel; infidel'

1. black slave, usually Islamic, from the east African coast. *Mx* (Aguirre Beltrán 1972:144) cl.

2. bad-mannered, rude, eccentric, unpopular or otherwise unpleasant person. *PR* (Gallo 1980:18) 20.

[Acc. Alvarez Nazario (1974:44), Tenório d'Albuquerque (1954:32), and DRAE (223), < Arabic *kafir* 'infidel.' Acc. Chaudenson (1974:78, 81), Indian Ocean Fr. creole pejor. form *kaf* 'black African with very dark skin.' Acc. Aguirre Beltrán, usually first slaves brought to New World. Df. 2 slang, acc. Gallo. Syns. *negro cafre, negro cafre de pasa, esclavo de la India de Portugal.* Cf. **cafre de pasa, esclavo, esclavo de la India de Portugal, negro cafre.**]

cafre de pasa 'infidel with tight curly hair'

black person whose hair is short and tightly curled. *SA* (Diggs 1953:406) cl.

[*Pasa* 'raisin,' also 'short crisp rolls of hair, characteristic of blacks.'

Cf. **cafre, negro amembrillado, negro amembrillado de los cafres de pasa, negro pasudo, pelo pasa.**]

caído 'fallen; pale'

person with pale skin. *Co-Tona* (Flórez 1969:121) 20.

[Usually in phr. *caído de color.* Cf. **anémico, saltatrás, tornatrás,** Ptg. **caído.**]

calentano

person from a warm area; warm-weather lover. *Co* (Tobón Betancourt 1953:56) mid20.

[< *caliente* 'warm.']

califa

California boy; any Californian. *US-AZ* (Barker 1950:33) mid20.

[Mostly m. Abbr. from state name *California.* Acc. Barker, Pachuco slang.]

californio 'Californian'

1. person of Spanish or Hispanic descent from CA. *US-CA, -s.w.* (Marden and Meyer 1978:242) 19.

2. Spanish-speaking Californian, acc. himself or herself. *US-CA* (Gann and Duignan 1986:xiii) 19.

[< *California.* Cf. **califa, chicano, hispano, latino, nuevo mexicano, tejano.**]

calmapulo — See *calpamulato*

calpalmulato —See *calpamulato*

calpamuato — See *calpamulato*

calpamulato

1. offspring of a mulatto and an Indian; 25% white, 50% Indian, 25% black. *Mx* (Pérez de Barradas 1948:184–85; Woodbridge 1948:356) cl.

2a. offspring of a mulatto and a *zambo. Mx* (Herrera and Cícero 1895:90) cl.

2b. offspring of a mulatto and a *zambo,* the latter of which was of black and Indian mixture; 25% white, 25% Indian, 50% black. *Mx* (Pérez de Barradas 1948:356) cl.

3a. offspring of a *sambaigo* and a *lobo. SA* (Vergara Martín 1922:231–32) cl.

3b. offspring of a *sambaigo* and a *lobo;* 30.76% white, 38.28% Indian, 30.96% black. *Mx* (Woodbridge 1948:356; Pérez de Barradas 1948:192) cl; (McAlister 1963:354) 19.

4a. offspring of a mulatto and a mestizo. *SA* (Vergara Martín 1922:231–32) cl.

4b. offspring of a mulatto and a mestizo; 25% white, 50% Indian, 25% black. *Mx* (Woodbridge 1948:356; Pérez de Barradas 1948:192) cl.

5a. offspring of a *barcino* and an Indian. *SA* (Vergara Martín 1922:231–32) cl.

5b. offspring of a *barcino* and an Indian; 6.25% white, 85.15% Indian, 8.6% black. *Mx* (Woodbridge 1948:356; Pérez de Barradas 1948:192; León 1924:20–21, plate 6) cl.

6. offspring of a *sambaigo* and a mulatto. *Mx* (Woodbridge 1948:356) cl.

7. offspring of a *sambaigo* and an Indian. *Mx* (Monteforte Toledo 1959: 171) cl.

8a. offspring of an *albarazado* and a black. *Mx* (Vergara Martín 1922:232; Malaret 1931:97; Woodbridge 1948:356; Santamaría 1942:1.276; Alonso 1958:1.865) cl.

8b. dihybrid, eighth-generation offspring of 79 parts black and 49 parts Indian, i.e., offspring of an *albarazado* and a black. *Mx* (Solano 1975:85; Moreno Navarro 1973:129–31) 18.

9. person of mixed race whose physical features tend toward those of a black. *Mx* (Moreno Navarro 1973:143) cl.

[Probably excl. to cl. Mx invented by parish priests interested in such classifications. Vars. *campa mulato, campa-mulato, calpanmulato, calmapulo, calpamuato, calpamulo, campomulato, calpan mulato, calpan-mulato, campamulato, calpulmulato, calpalmulato.* Cf. **albarazado, barcino, cambujo, mestizo, moreno, mulato, sambaigo.**]

calpamulo — See *calpamulato*

calpan mulato —See *calpamulato*

calpan-mulato —See *calpamulato*

calpanmulato — See *calpamulato*

calpulmulato — See *calpamulato*

calungo 'hairless'
coastal dweller. *Co* (Kany 1960b:41) 20.
[Cf. **cachaco, cachuzo.**]

camagüeyano 'Camagueyan'
person from the city or province of Camagüey, Cu. *Cu* (Espina Pérez 1972:29) 20.
[< *Camagüey.* Cf. **antioqueño, habanero.**]

camba
1a. Indian. *Bo* (Vergara Martín 1922:232) n.d.

1b. Indian, acc. whites of the town of Santa Cruz. *Bo-Santa Cruz* (Bayo 1910:45 and 1931:59) early–mid20.

1c. Chiriguano Indian. *Bo-ea.* (Bayo 1910:45 and 1931:59) early–mid20.

2. Bolivian from the high plateau. *Bo-Santa Cruz* (Bayo 1931:59) mid20.

3. semi-savage Indian from northern and eastern Bo. *Bo* (Alonso 1958:1.874) 20.

[M., f. Df. 1b pejor., acc. Bayo. Acc. Santamaría (1942:1.281), < Tupi-Guarani *cambá* 'black person.' Acc. Bayo, syns. df. 1c *tambeta, tembeta;* these Indians of the Chiriguano tribes bartered door to door when spring arrived.]

cambujo 'dark, swarthy'

1. person with dark skin. *Mx* (Roncal 1944:533) cl; (Herrera and Cícero 1895:90) late19.

2. offspring of a black and a white; *mulato pardo. Mx-Oaxaca* (Woodbridge 1948:356; Aguirre Beltrán 1972:169) cl; (Aguirre Beltrán 1945:216) 17.

3a. offspring of a black and an Indian. *Mx RP* (Woodbridge 1948:356) cl ‖ *Mx* (Alcedo 1786–89:5.104) late18.

3b. offspring of a black and an Indian; 50% black, 50% Indian. *Mx* (Pérez de Barradas 1948:190) cl.

3c. dihybrid, second-generation offspring of black and Indian; *lobo. Mx* (Moreno Navarro 1973:129–31; Solano 1975:85) 18.

3d. dihybrid, fifth-generation of 18 parts black and 6 parts Indian. *Mx* (Moreno Navarro 1973:129–31; Solano 1975:85) 18.

4. offspring of a *zambaigo* and a mulatto. *Mx* (Woodbridge 1948:357) cl ‖ *SA* (Vergara Martín 1922:232) n.d.

5. offspring of a *zambaigo* and a *chino. Mx* (Woodbridge 1948:357) cl.

6a. offspring of a *zambaigo* and an Indian. *SA* (Vergara Martín 1922:232) n.d.

6b. offspring of a *zambaigo* and an Indian; 11.7% white, 87.5% Indian, 0.8% black. *Mx* (Pérez de Barradas 1948:192; Monteforte Toledo 1959:171) cl; (Mörner 1967:58) 18.

7a. offspring of an *albarazado* and a black. *SA* (Vergara Martín 1922:232) n.d.

7b. offspring of an *albarazado* and a black; 29.3% white, 3.13% Indian, 67.57% black. *Mx* (Pérez de Barradas 1948:192; Woodbridge 1948:356; Monteforte Toledo 1959:171) cl; (McAlister 1963:354) 19.

8. offspring of an *albarazado* and an Indian; 24.22% white, 56.25% Indian, 19.53% black. *Mx* (Pérez de Barradas 1948:192) cl.

9a. offspring of a *chino* and an Indian. *SA* (Vergara Martín 1922:232) n.d.

9b. offspring of a *chino* and an Indian; 62.5% Indian, 37.5% black. *Mx* (León 1924:20–21, plate 5; Woodbridge 1948:356; Pérez de Barradas 1948:191) cl.

10a. offspring of a *lobo* and an Indian. *Mx* (Santamaría 1942:1.281; Woodbridge 1948:356) cl ‖ *SA* (Vergara Martín 1922:232) n.d.

10b. offspring of a *lobo* and an Indian; 75% Indian, 25% black. *Gu Mx* (Pérez de Barradas 1948:185, 191) cl.

11. offspring of a *cambujo* and an Indian. *SA* (Vergara Martín 1922:232) n.d.

12. person with very dark skin, considered stupid or ignorant. *SA* (Santamaría 1942:1.281; Woodbridge 1948:356; Diggs 1953: 407) cl ‖ *Mx CeA* (Malaret 1947:204; Morínigo 1966:118); *Mx* (Crépeau 1973:30) 20.
[Acc. Roncal, df. 1 acc. parish records; acc. Herrera and Cícero, df. 1 insult. Df. 12 derog., has come to mean 'stupid, ignorant.' Acc. Corominas (1954–57:1.614–15), 'mestizo with very dark skin color, bird with black or dark meat.' Acc. Moreno Navarro, 'horse or mare of reddish black coat, duck with dark red feet.' Acc. Diggs, 'color of a horse, bird with dark meat and feathers' in Mx. Syns. *zambaigo, zambayo, zambo, zambo de indio, lobo, mulato pardo.* Cf. **albarazado, chino, mulato pardo, zambaigo, zambo.**]

camilucho 'laborer'
1. Indian day laborer on a large farm. *Ar* (Malaret 1942:252) mid20 ‖ *Ar Mx* (Morínigo 1966:119) prior20 ‖ *SA* (Alonso 1958:1.879) 20.

2a. gaucho. *Ar* (Malaret 1942:252; Alonso 1958:1.879; Corominas 1954–57:1.616–17) 20.

2b. gaucho day laborer on a large farm. *Ar Mx* (Morínigo 1966:119) prior20.

2c. uncouth gaucho. *RP* (Kany 1960b:40) 20.
[Acc. Corominas, att. SA 1840; probably < Amerindian language. Cf. **gaucho, indio, jornalero.**]

campa mulato — See *calpamulato*

campa-mulato — See *calpamulato*

campamulato — See *calpamulato*

campechano
rustic type; hick. *CR* (Villegas 1952:24) mid20.
[Slang, acc. Villegas. Cf. **campero, camperuso, campesino.**]

campero 'rustic'
person dexterous in the ways of country life; rural type; hick; woodsman; cattle farmer. *Ch RP Ur* (Cowles 1952:134); *RP* (Malaret 1947:204); *Ar Co-Ocana* (Revollo 1942:48) mid20 ‖ *Ar Ur*

(Morínigo 1966:119–20); *Mx-Sonora* (Sobarzo 1966:58) 20.

[Syn. *campesino*. Cf. **campechano, camperuso, campesino,** Ptg. **campeiro.**]

camperuso 'hick'

peasant; rustic type. *Ve* (Kany 1960b:41) 20.

[Var. *campiruso*, acc. Kany. Cf. **campero, campirano, campiruso, campesino.**]

campesino 'peasant; farmer; poor peasant; country hick'

1. white Dominican peasant. *DR* (Hoetink 1973:16) 20.

2. peasant, usually Indian. *SA* (Levine 1980:26) 20.

3. Indian. *Bo* (Levine 1980:26) mid20.

[Cf. **campechano, campero, camperuso, concho, criollo, jíbaro, paisano,** Ptg. **campeiro.**]

campirano 'hick'

peasant; rustic type. *CR* (Salesiano 1938:48) mid20; (Kany 1960b:42) 20 ‖ *Mx* (Malaret 1947:204) mid20 ‖ *Mx-Sonora* (Sobarzo 1966:58); *Bo Mx* (Morínigo 1966:120) 20.

[Syn. *concho*, acc. Kany. Acc. Salesiano, 1930s syns. in CR *aldeano, campiruso, campista, campuso, paleto, rústico.* Acc. Morínigo, syn. in Bo *patán.* Cf. **camperano, campero, campesino, campiruso, campusano, campusio, chapetas, concho, pato.**]

campiruso 'hick'

peasant; rustic type. *CeA CR* (Cowles 1952:134) mid20 ‖ *CR* (Kany 1960b:42) 20.

[Syn. *concho*, acc. Kany. Acc. Cowles, syn. in CR *rústico;* syns. in CeA *campesino, charro, grosero, rústico.* Cf. **camperano, campero, campesino, campirano, campusano, campusio, concho.**]

campista 'rustic type; hick'

1. peasant. *CeA* (Bayo 1931:59) mid20.

2a. country person, esp. one who cares for cattle. *Ho Mx-Tabasco* (Morínigo 1966:120) 20.

2b. woodsman; person who lives in the country; country bumpkin. *CeA* (Bayo 1931:59) mid20 ‖ *Mx PR* (Morínigo 1966:120) 20.

[M., f. Syn. *campirano.* Cf. **campero, campesino, campirano, campiruso, campisto,** Ptg. **caipira, campeiro.**]

campisto 'rustic type; hick'

1. peasant; rural dweller. *PR Ve* (Malaret 1937:119); *Ni* (Castellón 1939:36) mid20 ‖ *CR* (Morínigo 1966:120) 20.

2. savannah dweller. *Ni* (Castellón 1939:36) mid20.

[Probably < *campista.* Syns. *campesino, sabanero.* Cf. **campesino, campirano, campiruso, campista,** Ptg. **caipira, campeiro.**]

campomulato — See *calpamulato*

campuno 'peasant'
peasant; country bumpkin. *DR* (Cowles 1952:134) mid20.
[Syn. *campesino.* Cf. **campesino, campirano, campista, campisto.**]

campusano 'hick'
rustic type; peasant; person who lives in the country. *Pa* (Aguilera Patiño 1951:424); *Ar Pa Ur* (Cowles 1952:134) mid20 ‖ *RP* (Kany 1960b:40) 20.
[Syn. *campesino.* Cf. **camperano, campesino, campirano, campiruso, campusio.**]

campusio 'hick'
rustic person; peasant. *Ur* (Kany 1960b:40) 20.
[Cf. **camperano, campesino, campirano, campiruso, campusano.**]

campuso 'hick'
uncouth peasant. *CR* (Kany 1960b:42) 20.
[Syn. *concho.* Cf. **camperano, campesino, campirano, campiruso, campusano, campusio, concho.**]

canaca 'Chinese'
Chinese person; Oriental; Asian. *Ch* (Kany 1960b:38; DRAE 240); *Ch Ec Pe* (Morínigo 1966:120) 20.
[M., f. Acc. DRAE, derog.; < Pacific Ocean lg.; in Ch also 'owner of a bordello.' Cf. **asiático, oriental.**]

canalla — See *gente de orilla*

canario — See *isleño, raza inferior*

canche 'blond'
person with blond hair. *Gu* (Batres Jáuregui 1892:161) late19; (Santamaría 1942:1.289) mid20 ‖ *CeA* (Malaret 1942:258) mid20; (Alonso 1958:1.892) 20.
[Acc. Corominas (1954–57:1.627), < Quechua *kancha* 'area standing out on the skin.' Cf. **candelo, canelo, chele, rubio.**]

candelo 'reddish-blond'
person with reddish or blond hair and perhaps light skin color. *Co-Santo Domingo, -Yolombó, -Jardín, -Cimitarra* (Flórez 1969:121) 20.
[Acc. Santamaría (1942:1.291), 'light-colored medicinal plant, *Rondeletia pubescens,* found in Co.' Cf. **canelo.**]

canela — See *canelo*

canelo 'cinnamon-colored'
1. person with cinnamon-colored or reddish-brown skin. *Co-Barbacoas, -Piedecuesta* (Flórez 1969:121) 20.

2. person with blond hair. *CR* (Villegas 1952:25; Cowles 1952:138) mid20.

3a. mulatto woman with light skin and good facial features. *Cu* (Pichardo 1953:147–48) late19.

3b. mulatto girl. *Cu PR* (Kany 1960b:45) 20.

[Sim. to *acanelado*. Df. 3 f. form *canela*. Cf. **acanelado, candelo, mulato,** Ptg. **caneludo.**]

cangrejo 'crab'

person with reddish hair or skin color. *Ch* (Flórez 1969:123) 20.

[Acc. Alonso (1958:1.898), 'reddish color; person with reddish hair,' in Burgos, Spain. Cf. **candelo, canelo, chele, rubio.**]

canisa

offspring of a mestizo, or any person of mixed race, and an Indian. *Mx* (Roback 1944:133) 19–20.

[M., f. Acc. Roback, slur.]

cano 'gray-haired'

person with gray hair or light skin color. *Co-Ricaurte* (Flórez 1969:121) 20.

[Acc. Cobarruvias (1611:287), 'person with gray hair or anything that is graying or whitening.' Cf. **candelo, canelo, chele, rubio.**]

capirro

1. person with red hair. *Cu* (Santamaría 1942:1.304) 20.

2. mulatto. *Cu* (Santamaría 1942:1.304; Alonso 1958:1.919) 20.

3. nonwhite person who wants to pass for white. *Cu* (Santamaría 1942:1.304; Alonso 1958:1.919) 20.

4. person of mixed race or caste. *Cu* (Alonso 1958:1.919) 20.

[Df. 3 joc., acc. Santamaría and Alonso. Excl. to Cu. Cf. **barbimono, candelo, canelo, chele, mulato, rubio.**]

capochín — See *cachupín, gachupín*

cara pálida 'pale face'

white person, acc. Indians. *SA* (Vergara Martín 1922:232) n.d.

[Sim. to No. Amer. Engl. *paleface* 'white man,' used by Indians. Syn. *rostro pálido.*]

carabalí

black slave native to the Carabali region of Africa. *Cu* (Vergara Martín 1922) prior20.

[M., f. Cf. **angola, brícamo, briche, carabela.**]

carabela 'caravel'

black African slave, acc. other slaves on the same slaver's ship. *Cu* (Levine 1980:28) prior20.

[M., f. Rel. to Engl. *caravelle* 'type of sailing ship.' Sim. to cl. Brz. Ptg. *malungo.* Cf. Ptg. **malungo.**]

carapachayo

person who lives on an island in the Paraná River delta. *SA* (Bayo 1910:49 and 1931:65) early–mid20.

[Var. *carapacho,* acc. Morínigo (1966:126). Cf. **isleño.**]

carapacho — See *carapachayo*

caratejo

person whose skin has the appearance of *carate,* or mange. *Co-Yarumal, -Heliconia* (Flórez 1969:121) 20.

[Acc. Santamaría (1942:1.315), < std. *cartoso* 'one who suffers from the itch of *carate,* type of skin disease perhaps transported from Africa and common to SoA and CeA.']

carayano

white person, acc. Indians of eastern Bo. *Bo* (Bayo 1910:49 and 1931:65) early–mid20.

[Acc. Bayo, < Quechua *kcara* or *kcala* 'bald.' Acc. Santamaría (1942:1.315), perhaps < Guarani *caraya* or *carayá* 'large monkey native to Br and RP.' Cf. **canelo, cano, cara pálida, caratejo.**]

carcamán 'tub-like boat; low-class foreign immigrant'

1a. foreigner, generally poorly educated and of humble economic conditions, but who has pretensions to a higher social position. *Cu* (Pichardo 1953:161) late19 ‖ *Cu* (Espina Pérez 1972:36); *Cu Ur* (Cowles 1952:151); *Ar Cu Pe Ur* (Morínigo 1966:127) 20.

1b. rude or ill-manned foreigner. *Cu* (Macías 1885:279) 19.

2a. Italian, generally a new immigrant. *Ar-Buenos Aires* (Chamberlain 1981:420) 20.

2b. Italian, esp. Genoese. *Ar* (Santamaría 1942:1.316) mid20; (Segovia 1911:170) early20.

[Df. 1a derog. Df. 2a excl. to Lunfardo speech of Buenos Aires. Acc. Morínigo and Pichardo, < *carcamal.* Acc. Corominas (1954–57:1.677 and 1973:131–32), *carcamal* < *cárcamo* 'old ship with sails.' Perhaps these types of ships brought immigrants to the New World. Acc. Cobos (1983:28), also 'game of chance in which dice are used to guess the lucky number in a raffle' in 20-cent. Mx. Cf. **cafre, carabela, gachupín,** Ptg. **carcamano.**]

cargamento de ébano 'load of ebony'

black slave in transit from Africa, acc. slavers. *SA* (Alvarez Nazario 1974:356) cl.

[Sim. to *pieza de ébano.* Cf. **bozal, carabela, pieza de Indias, pieza de ébano.**]

carguero 'cargo carrier'

Indian carrier. *Co* (Levine 1980:77) cl.

[Acc. Levine, *cargero* [*sic*]. Cf. **boga, libre de color.**]

caribe 'cannibal'

1. black person from the north coast of Ho. *Ho* (Bayo 1931:65) 20.

2. fierce, cannibalistic Indian. *SA* (Oviedo 1945:14.200) cl.

[Acc. Gili y Gaya (1960:1.487), att. early 17 cent. as 'flesh-eating Amerindian.']

caribeño 'Caribbean'

native of the Caribbean. *Ur* (Mieres et al. 1966:40) 20.

[Cf. **caribe.**]

carija — See *carijo*

carijo

1. Indian from between Cananea and the River Patos, in the state of SC, southern Br. *SA* (Santamaría 1942: 1.323) 20.

2. Indian of pre-Columbian SoA. *SA* (Santamaría 1942: 1.323) 20prior.

3. Indian from the Amazon River area. *SA* (Santamaría 1942:1.323) 20.

4. Carib Indian who lives in the upper Yapurá with the Uitotes and the Macuches in Br. *SA* (Santamaría 1942:1.323) 20.

[Acc. Machado (1952–59:1.510), < *carajó* < Tupi *caray-yó* 'descendant of the *carahybas.*' Vars. *carijó, carija, carijona.* Cf. **yanacona, yaro,** Ptg. **carijó.**]

carijó — See *carijo*

carijona — See *carijo*

carmelito 'Carmelite'

person with light brown hair or skin. *Co-Facatativá* (Flórez 1969:121) 20.

[Acc. Corominas (1954–57:1.690), first att. in Spain about 1600. Acc. Santamaría (1942:1.324), Alonso (1958:1.952), and Kany (1960b:46), < light brown or chestnut color of the habit worn by the Carmelite order of nuns. Cf. **castaño, moreno.**]

carolo — See *negro carolo*

carraco 'hick'

rustic type; peasant. *CR* (Villegas 1952:26) mid20.

[Cf. **campesino, campista, campirano, campuno.**]

cartago

inhabitant from the province of Cartago or any other interior area. *CR* (Cowles 1952:158; Kany 1960b:41) 20.

[Acc. Cowles, used on Atlantic coast. Acc. Kany, derog. syn. *cartucho.* Cf. **nicaregalado.**]

cartucho — See *cartago*

casco 'cask; helmet'
offspring of two mulattoes. *SA* (Johnston 1910:55) early20prior.
[Acc. Reuter (1918:13), also found in Engl. Cf. **mulato.**]
casi limpio 'almost clean'
offspring of a Spaniard and a *gente blanca. SA* (Vergara Martín 1922:232) n.d.
[Probably cl. Cf. **gente blanca, cuasi limpio de origen.**]
casta 'breed'
  1a. person of mixed racial background, generally of low social class. *SA* (Romero 1944:375; Gibson 1966:116; Diggs 1953:404; Rout 1976:xiv); *Mx* (Velasco Valdés 1957:26); *SA* (Velásquez 1962:115) cl ‖ *SA* (Mörner 1967:39); *Mx-Oaxaca* (Chance and Taylor 1977:461) 18 ‖ *SA* (Thompson addition to Alcedo 1786 −89:5.28) late18−early19.
  1b. person of mixed blood, free or slave. *SA* (Levine 1980:30) prior20.
  2. any non-Indian. *Pe* (Sánchez-Albornoz 1974:111) 19.
  3. person of low class. *Co-s.w.* (Velásquez 1962:115) prior20.
  4. Moorish slave of Islamic religion. *Mx* (Aguirre Beltrán 1972:105) cl.
[Acc. Castro (1973:31), att. in Spain as df. 1 in 15–17 cent. Acc. León (1924:16), derog. ref. to mixed race, acc. those of non-mixed race, and positive ref. to themselves by those of mixed race in Mx. Cf. **casta de mezcla.**]
casta de mezcla 'mixed breed'
offspring of parents of different racial backgrounds or different racial mixtures. *SA* (Sánchez-Albornoz 1974:129; Rosenblat 1954: 1.71) cl.
[Syn. in 18-cent. Mx *casta infectada,* acc. Boyd-Bowman (1982:523). Cf. **casta, gente decente, mezcla.**]
casta de Mozambique
black, east African slave from Mozambique who was generally shipped to the New World across the Pacific. *SA* (Levine 1980:31) prior20.
[Cf. **casta, casta de ríos de Guinea, mozambique,** Ptg. **moçambique.**]
casta de ríos de Guinea
black slave native to the Guinea region of west Africa. *SA* (Levine 1980:31) prior20.
[Acc. Levine, person could be from the African *gelofe, biafra,* or *mandingo* tribes. Cf. **casta.**]
casta de San Tomé
black African slave from São Tomé, an island off the west Afri-

can coast. *SA* (Levine 1980:31) late16.

[Cf. **casta, casta de Mozambique, casta de ríos de Guinea.**]

casta infectada — See *casta de mezcla*

castaño 'chestnut-colored'

person with light brown hair or skin color. *Co-Villacaro* (Flórez 1969:121) 20.

[Acc. Corominas (1954–57:1.724 and 1973:138), att. as adj. in 10- or 11-cent. Spain in ref. to the chestnut color of a horse or mule. See also Cobarruvias (1611:317). Cf. Ptg. **acastanhado.**]

castao

Puerto Rican native. *PR* (Gallo 1980:186) 20.

[Probably < *castado*. Acc. Gallo, slang. Syn. *criollo*. Cf. **criollo, puertorriqueño.**]

castellano 'Castilian'

1. white descendant of Spanish colonizers. *Ch* (Cowles 1952:160) mid20.

2. white person. *CR* (Villegas 1952:27; Cowles 1952:160) mid20.

[Syn. df. 1, *gente blanca*. Other syns. *blanco, español, gachupín, europeo, peninsular,* acc. León (1924:16). Cf. **blanco, español, europeo, gente blanca, gachupín, peninsular.**]

castizo 'pure; pureblood'

1. mestizo; offspring of a white and an Indian. *Co-no.* (Sundheim 1922:145) early20.

2a. offspring of a white and a mestizo; 75% white, 25% Indian. *Mx* (Woodbridge 1948:355, 357; Pérez de Barradas 1948:184, 188; Monteforte Toledo 1959:171; Santamaría 1942: 1.334; Roncal 1944:533; León 1924:20–21, plate 7) cl; (Mörner 1967:58; O'Crouley 1972:19) 18; (McAlister 1963:354) 19 ‖ *Mx PR* (Morínigo 1966:131) 20 ‖ *SA* (Alba 1969:34) 20prior.

2b. offspring of a mestizo and a white, i.e., 3 parts white and 1 part Indian. *Mx* (Moreno Navarro 1973:139) 18.

2c. dihybrid, third-generation offspring of a white and a mestizo. *Mx* (Moreno Navarro 1973:129–31; Solano 1975:85) 18.

2d. person who has 3 white grandparents and 1 Indian one. *Mx* (Solano 1975:83) 17.

3. offspring of a white and a *mestizo blanco*. *Mx* (Aguirre Beltrán 1972:171) cl.

[Acc. Castro (1973:31), 'blue-blood, or someone of noble heritage without racial mixture' in 17-cent. Spain. Acc. Aguirre Beltrán (1945:218), often confused with white persons in 17-cent. Mx. Acc. Chance and Taylor (1977:460), also att. in 18-cent. Oaxaca, Mx. First att. in 16 cent., < *casta* + dim. suf. *-izo,* acc. Corominas (1954–57:1.723 and 1973:138) and Alonso (1958:1.984). Syn. df. 2a *albino*, acc. O'Crouley. Syn. df. 2b *cuarterón de mestizo* in SoA. Syn. df. 3 *mestizo castizo* in cl. Mx, acc. Aguirre Beltrán. Cf. **albino, casta, castizo cuatralbo, cuarterón, mestizo, mestizo castizo, mestizo blanco.**]

castizo cuatralbo
offspring of a mestizo and a white; 75% white, 25% Indian. *Mx* (León 1924:20–21, 22; Woodbridge 1948:357; Pérez de Barradas 1948:188) cl.
[Acc. Roncal (1944:533), phr. used in parish baptismal records and other documents in cl. Mx. Vars. *castizo cuatraluo, castizo cuatrialbo.* Cf. **casta, castizo, mestizo.**]

castizo cuatraluo — See *castizo cualtralbo*
castizo cuatrialbo — See *castizo cuatralbo*
castizo mestizo
offspring of a mestizo and a white Spaniard. *Mx* (Aguirre Beltrán 1945:217–18) 17.
[Acc. Aguirre Beltrán, syn. *castizo.* Cf. **castizo, mestizo.**]

casto
person who is of mixed racial background; half-breed. *US-CO, -NM* (Cobos 1983:30) 20.
[Acc. Cobos, < *casta.* Cf. **casta.**]

catedrático 'chaired professor'
1. black person, usually male, whose affected phrases and fancy words show that he is living beyond his linguistic means. *Cu* (Pichardo 1953:175) 19; (Cowles 1952:161) mid20.
2. person who was born on a street close to the city's cathedral. *Ec-Guayaquil* (Santamaría 1942:1.336) 20.
[Sim. to, but not syn. with, the racially charged term *professor* used by some So. Amer. whites in ref. to a respected or semi-respected black teacher who, in their opinion, does not deserve the appellation *Mr.* Cf. **negro catedrático.**]

catinga 'body odor'
black person. *RP* (Guarnieri 1979:50) 20.
[M., f. Acc. DRAE (279), < Guarani. Acc. Guarnieri and Granada (1957:1.155), < *catinga* 'gland of some animals which makes their meat smell bad.' Acc. Ayrosa (1937:145–46), < Tupi-Guarani *catim* 'body odor, bad odor.' Cf. **catingudo.**]

catingudo 'stinky from body odor'
1. black person who smells bad. *RP* (Guarnieri 1979:50) 20.
2. person who has the stink of a black person. *Ar* (Segovia 1911:173) early20.
[Cf. **catinga.**]

catire 'blond'

1a. person with blond hair. *Co* (Acuña 1951:33; Morínigo 1966:132; Cowles 1952:162; Bayo 1931:68; Tobón Betancourt 1953: 66); *Ve* (Morínigo 1966:132; Alonso 1958:1.944; Cowles 1952:162); *Ec* (Cowles 1952:162; Bayo 1931:68); *Pe* (Malaret 1942:297–98; Cowles 1952:162); *Ec Pe* (Alonso 1958:1.994) 20.

1b. person with blond hair and perhaps light skin color. *Co Ve* (Flórez 1969:121, 123) 20.

1c. person with reddish-blond hair. *SA* (Alonso 1958:1.994) 20.

2. person who has white skin, black eyes, and brown hair. *Ve* (Alonso 1958:1.994) 20.

3. person with red hair; redhead. *Pe-Lima* (Malaret 1942: 297–98; Alonso 1958:1.994) 20.

4. black person. *Co* (Tobón Betancourt 1953:66); *Co Ec-coast* (Kany 1960b:46–47) 20.

[Acc. Tobón Betancourt, df. 4 iron. Acc. Santamaría (1942:1.336) and Morínigo (1966:132), probably < Cumanagota (Amerindian) *catire* 'blond.' Syns. dfs. 1, 2, 3 *güero, chele, rubio*. Vars. *catiri, catiro, catirro*. Cf. **candelo, canelo, chele, güero, rubio, tela-moco**.]

catiri — See *catire*

catiro — See *catire*

catirro — See *catire*

catracho

Honduran. *CeA* (Castellón 1939:39; Cowles 1952:162; Alonso 1958:1.996; Kany 1960b:40) 20.

[Cf. **nica, nigüento, tico**.]

catrín 'dandy'

white person. *Mx* (Chance 1979:154) 20.

[Acc. Santamaría (1942:1.337) and Alonso (1958:1.996), 'elegant, polished to excess,' by ext. 'lazy vagrant who is well-dressed.' Cf. **gente de razón, gente decente**.]

cayubro 'reddish-blond'

1. person with reddish blond or dark yellow hair. *Co* (Tobón Betancourt 1953:66; Alario di Filippo 1964:67; Morínigo 1966: 132–33) 20.

2. person with reddish-blond hair and probably light skin color. *Co-Yolombó* (Flórez 1969:121) 20.

[< *cayubra* 'red-colored ant which gives a painful bite,' acc. Tobón Betancourt, Alario di Filippo, Morínigo, Santamaría (1942:1.340), and Alonso (1958:1.1004). Excl. to Co as racial term. Probably < Amerindian lg. Cf. **catire, chele, güero, rubio**.]

cenizo 'ashen'
person with ashen or grayish skin color. *Co-Yolombó* (Flórez 1969:121) 20.
[Acc. Corominas (1954–57:1.762), first att. in Spain early–mid-17 cent.]

centrano
person from the interior highland, non-coastal departments of Co. *Co-coast* (Revollo 1942:42) mid20.
[Cf. **cachaco, cachuzo, reinoso.**]

cerdudo 'hog farmer'
1. person with long, thick, straight hair. *RP* (Guarnieri 1967: 67) 20.
2. man who has thick, dense hair on his chest. *SA* (Alonso 1958:1.1037) 20.
[Acc. Corominas (1973:146), 'pig' att. 1682; *cerda* 'hard, thick hairs of certain animals, esp. horses and pigs,' att. 1495.]

chabacano 'vulgar'
person with no education; uncultured person. *Ar* (Garzón 1910:140) early20.
[Att. in Spain 1525, acc. Corominas (1954–57:2.1). See also Alonso (1958:1.1319).]

chacho
1. servant. *Mx* (Morínigo 1966:169) 20.
2. twin brother. *CeA* (Santamaría 1942:1.453) 20.
[Affect.; apheresis of *muchacho*, acc. Alonso (1958:1.1321) and Corominas (1954–57.3:468). Cf. **muchacho.**]

chacra — See *chagra*

chacracama
Indian in charge of planting crops. *Ec* (Cowles 1952:229) mid20.
[Generally m. Acc. Santamaría (1942:1.451–52) and Corominas (1973:188), < Quechua *chagra* or *chajra* 'cornfield' + *cama* 'Indian (worker).' Cf. **chagra.**]

chafalote 'common; knife'
1. uncultured, ill-mannered person. *Ar Ur* (Cowles 1952:231) mid20.
2. Indian of the indigenous tribes of Sonora, Mx, who disappeared soon after the arrival of the Spaniards. *SA* (Santamaría 1942:1.454) cl.
[Acc. Corominas (1954–57:2.48), 'knife used to peel potatoes' in Chiloé, < *chifla* 'wide knife with a curved cutting edge, used for removing skins from animals.' Cf. **chabacano.**]

cháfiro

Guatemalan. *CeA* (Salazar García 1910:85) early20.

[Syn. *chapín.* Cf. **chapín.**]

chagra

farmer; peasant; person not from the city. *Ec* (Vergara Martín 1922:234) n.d.; (Armengol Valenzuela 1915:16.283–84) early20; (Carvalho-Neto 1964:157; Morínigo 1966:170) 20 ‖ *Co* (Morínigo 1966:170) 20.

[Generally m. < Old Quechua *chakra* 'cornfield,' acc. Corominas (1954–57:2.4), Santamaría (1942:1.454) and Morínigo (1966:170). Var. *chacra.* Cf. **chacracama, gaucho, guajiro, guaso, jarocho, sabanero.**]

chajal

1. Indian man who served a priest. *Gu* (Batres Jáuregui 1892:197–98) late19 ‖ *Ec* (Alonso 1958:1.1323; Santamaría 1942:1.456) cl–18.

2. Indian woman who did domestic work. *Gu* (Batres Jáuregui 1892:197–98) late19 ‖ *Ec* (Alonso 1958:1.1323; Santamaría 1942:1.456) cl–18.

3. servant. *Ec* (DRAE 403) 20.

[M., f. Probably < Amerindian lg. Cf. **chabacano, chacracama.**]

chal — See *chale*

chale

Chinese person; person born in China. *Mx-no.* (Cumberland 1960:203); *Mx* (León 1924:69) early20 ‖ *Mx Ni* (Malaret 1931:174) mid20 ‖ *Ni* (Kany 1960b:38); *Mx Ni* (Santamaría 1942:1.457); *Mx* (Velasco Valdés 1957:34; Kany 1960b:38) 20.

[Df. 2 derog., syns. *chino, asiático.* Roughly equiv. to derog. Engl. term *chink.* Acc. Malaret, *chal* in Ni, *chale* in Mx. Possibly < Engl. name *Charles* or affect. *Charlie,* so often used by the Chinese in ref. to the white man. Var. *chal.* Cf. **asiático, canisa, chino.**]

chamiso

1a. offspring of an Indian and a *coyote,* the latter of which is a mulatto and a *barcino;* 22.6% white, 55.5% Indian, 21.9% black. *Mx* (León 1924:20–21, plate 15; Monteforte Toledo 1959:171; Woodbridge 1948:357; Pérez de Barradas 1948:192) cl.

1b. offspring of an Indian and a *coyote,* the latter of which is an Indian and a mestizo; 12.5% white, 87.5% Indian. *Mx* (Pérez de Barradas 1948:188) cl.

2. offspring of an Indian and a mulatto; 25% white, 50% Indian, 25% black. *Mx* (Pérez de Barradas 1948:193) cl.

3. offspring of a *saltatrás* and an Indian; 43.75% white, 50% Indian, 6.25% black. *Mx* (Pérez de Barradas 1948:192) cl.

4a. offspring of a mestizo and a *castizo;* 63.5% white, 36.5% Indian. *Mx* (Woodbridge 1948:357; Pérez de Barradas 1948:188) cl.

4b. dihybrid, fourth-generation offspring of 5 parts white and 3 parts Indian, i.e., offspring of a mestizo and a *castizo. Mx* (Moreno Navarro 1973:129–31; Solano 1975:85) 18.

5. offspring of a *coyote* and a mestizo. *Mx* (Mörner 1967:58) 18.

6. offspring of a *coyote* and a *lobo. SA* (Vergara Martín 1922:234) n.d.

[Skin color term used in cl. Mx parish records, acc. Roncal (1944:533). Acc. León (1924:22), 'wild medicinal herb.' Acc. Moreno Navarro (1973:142), 'tree or wood scorched or half-burned,' ext. to ref. to skin color of mestizos. Var. *chamizo.* Almost excl. to cl. Mx. Cf. **barcino, castizo, indio, mestizo, moreno, mulato, saltatrás.**]

chamizo — See *chamiso*

chanate

1. mulatto. *US-NM, -TX* (Cobos 1983) 20.

2. black person. *US-AZ* (Barker 1950:33) mid20.

[Acc. Cobos, < Nahuatl *zanatl* 'kind of blackbird.' Acc. Barker, also 'coffee' in Pachuco slang. Acc. Kany (1960b:35), var. of *zanate* or *sanate* 'type of blackbird.' Cf. **mulato.**]

chancla — See *chancle*

chancle

rich person of high social class who dresses well; person who dresses well. *Gu* (Cowles 1952:238) mid20.

[Acc. Cowles, < apocope of *chancletudo;* f. form *chancla;* often derog. Cf. **chancletudo.**]

chancletero — See *chancletudo*

chancletudo 'common, low-class'

shod city dwellers; by ext., rich person of the upper class who dressed well, acc. the country folk, who went shoeless. *Ho* (Membreño 1897:48) late19 ‖ *CR Gu* (Cowles 1952:238–39) mid20.

[Derog. < *chancleta* + adj. suf. *-udo.* Acc. Cowles and Cobarruvias (1611:432), *chancleta* 'type of heel-less shoe.' Acc. Corominas (1973:190), *chanclo* 'wooden sandal' att. 1693. Var. *chancletero.* Cf. **chabacano.**]

chango

1. Bolivian born or living on the northern Chilean coast, an area taken from Bo. *Bo Ch* (Cowles 1952:240; Morínigo 1966:175; Bayo 1910:72) 20.

2. Indian from the Antofagasta area of the northern Pacific coast of Ch, formerly Bo. *Bo Ch* (Bayo 1931:92) mid20.

3a. fisherman from the northern coast. *Ch* (Cowles 1952:240) mid20.

3b. Indian fisherman from the northern coast. *Ch* (Armengol Valenzuela 1914:16.296) early20prior.

4. person with very bad manners. *Mx PR* (Alonso 1958:1.1330) 20.

5. vain person; joker. *PR* (Zenón Cruz 1975:1.248) 20.

6. person from the lower Rio Grande villages of NM, acc. northern New Mexicans. *US-NM* (Cobos 1983:43) 20.

7. any boy or child. *Mx* (Alonso 1958:1.1330) 20.

8. child houseservant. *Ar Ur* (Morínigo 1966:175) 20.

[Df. 2 by ext. of 1; derog. Acc. Santamaría (1942:1.465), 'small monkey found in Mx.' Df. 3a derog. Df. 4 reminiscent of monkey's manners, acc. Alonso (1958:1.1330). Acc. Armengol Valenzuela, < Quechua *chancu* 'dwarf, rascal.' Acc. Megenney (1983:5), Manganja lg. of Mozambique *tsanga* 'lemur macaco monkey.' Acc. Zenón Cruz, *changa* 'insect,' *chango* 'type of bird.' Acc. Cobos, 'monkey; clownish, stupid'; df. 6 thus derog. or insult. Cf. **chabacano, chango prieto, changó, macaco.**]

chango prieto

black person. *PR* (Nuñez 1980:122) n.d.

[Probably 20 cent. Cf. **chango, changó.**]

changó

black person living on the Pacific coast. *Ec* (Nuñez 1980:121) 20prior.

[< Bantu, acc. Nuñez. Cf. **chango, chango prieto.**]

chapa

Indian spy. *Co* (Morínigo 1966:176); *SoA* (Alonso 1958:1.1331) 20.

[Generally m. Acc. Morínigo, < Quechua *chapa* 'Indian spy'; now 'policeman' in Co and Ec.]

chapaco

peasant from the department of Tarija, Bo. *Bo* (Fernández and Fernández 1967:51) 20.

[Cf. **campesino.**]

chapaneco

1. short, fat person with brown hair or skin color. *CR* (Villegas 1952:42) mid20.

2. person from the state of Chiapas, in southern Mx. *Mx* (Santamaría 1942:1.467) 20.

[Var. df. 2 *chiapaneco.*]

chapapote 'asphalt'

black person with dark brown skin. *Cu Ve* (Espina Pérez

1972:59); *Cu* (Lamigueiro 1982:p.c.) 20.

[Joc. Used in phrs. such as *negro como un chapapote, blanco como un coco,* acc. Lamigueiro. Syn. *negrito prieto.* Acc. Santamaría (1942:1.467–68), < Aztec *chapapotl,* from *tzauctli* 'gum, sticky material' + *popochitli* 'perfume.' Acc. Espina Pérez, < Caribbean lg.; original use almost excl. to Co, Cu, and Ve. Var. *chapopote.* Cf. **negrito prieto.**]

chapeado 'veneered; rosy'

1. person whose skin color is rosy and clear, usually indicative of a white person. *Co-Quetame* (Flórez 1969:121) 20.

2. person with reddish or suntanned skin color. *Mx-Oaxaca* (Garza Cuarón 1987:64) late20.

[Acc. Flórez, *chapiao* [*sic*]. Syn. df. 2 *colorado.* Acc. Alonso (1958:1.1332), 'of good color' in SA. Cf. **chapudo, colorado.**]

chapeta 'hick; board, plank; rouge; good sense'

uncouth peasant; hick. *CR* (Kany 1960b:42) 20.

[M., f. < *chapa* 'plate, sheet.' Syn. *concho.* Cf. **campirano, campiruso, campuso, chayote, concho, pato.**]

chapetón 'awkward; tenderfoot'

1. Creole Spaniard, i.e, white born in the New World. *SA* (Pérez de Barradas 1948:174) cl; (Gibson 1966:130) 17–18 ‖ *Ho* (Membreño 1897:48) late19.

2a. white European or Spaniard. *Pe* (Rosenblat 1954:1.71) cl.

2b. white European, generally a Spaniard, newly arrived in America. *SA* (Morínigo 1966:177) cl; (Alcedo 1786–89:5.30) late18 ‖ *SoA* (Woodbridge 1948:353) cl, generally 17; (Vergara Martín 1922:234) n.d. ‖ *Bo Ch CR Ec Ho Pe* (Malaret 1931:179) mid20.

2c. white Spaniard newly arrived from Spain. *SA* (Batres Jáuregui 1892:204) cl–late19 ‖ *SoA* (Bailey and Nasatir 1973:767) cl ‖ *Pe* (Vergara Martín 1922:234) n.d.

2d. peninsular Spaniard. *Bo Ch Ec Pe CeA Ve* (Malaret 1947:61) mid20.

2e. Spaniard. *Bo* (Fernández and Fernández 1967:51) 19 ‖ *Pe* (Paz Soldán 1938:163) cl–19 ‖ *SA* (Bayo 1910:72 and 1931:92) cl–20 ‖ *Co* (Acuña 1951:43) 20.

2f. male Spaniard known for his long *chape,* or pigtail, apparently the symbol of his authority in the New World. *Ch* (Rodríguez 1875:148–49) 19prior.

2g. white Spaniard born in Spain. *RP* (Fontanella de Weinberg 1982:44) 16–17.

3. foreigner, or any newly arrived person, unfamiliar with the land and the customs of the people. *Ar* (Segovia 1911:116) early20 ‖ *CR* (Salesiano 1938:57); *Ar CR Ch Ec Ur* (Cowles 1952:243);

CeA SoA (Kany 1960b:36); *RP* (Guarnieri 1967:83) 20.
[Df. 1 derog. Df. 2b derog., acc. Malaret. Dfs. 2e, 2g pejor. Acc. Corominas (1954–57:2.22–23) and Kany (1960b:35), < *chapín* 'cork-soled clog.' Acc. Corominas (1973:191) and Kany (1960b:36), 'sandals'; by ext. 'inexpert, unfamiliar with the territory, newcomer.' Acc. Alonso (1958:1.1333), 'stupid,' 'person who walks with difficulty.' Acc. Santamaría (1942:1.469), first used in SA in ref. to recently arrived soldiers. Acc. Boyd-Bowman (1971:254), att. in 16-cent. Co as *indio chapetón.* Cf. **chapín, criollo, español, gachupín, gaucho, indio chapetón.**]

chapiao — See *chapeado*

chapín 'crooked leg; cork-soled clog'
   1. Guatemalan. *Sa* (Vergara Martín 1922:234) n.d. ‖ *Ho* (Membreño 1897:49) 19 ‖ *CeA* (Salazar García 1910:85) early20 ‖ *CR Ho Sa* (Malaret 1931:179–80) mid20 ‖ *CeA* (Gagini 1918:109; Arriola 1941:57–59; Kany 1960b:40; Cowles 1952:243; Morínigo 1966:177); *CR* (Villegas 1952:43); *CR Sa* (Bayo 1931:93); *Ho* (Castellón 1939: 48); *Mx CeA* (Santamaría 1942:1.469) 20.
   2. Nicaraguan. *Ni* (Gagini 1918:109) early20; (Castellón 1939:48) mid20.
   [Acc. Kany (1960b:40), 'crooked-footed, waddling.' Also 'cork-bottomed shoes for women,' acc. Cobarruvias (1611:432), Corominas (1954–57:2.23 and 1973:191) and Santamaría (1942:1.469). Syn. *cháfiro.* Syn. df. 2 *nigüento.* Cf. **cháfiro, chapetón, criollo, gachupín, nigüento.**]

chapopote — See *chapapote*

chapudo
   1. person with good, rosy skin color. *Pe SA* (Cowles 1952:244) mid20.
   2. person who has either rouged or naturally rosy cheeks. *Ec* (Alonso 1958:1.1334) 20.
   [Probably indicates white person. < *chapa* 'rouge' + adj. suf. *-udo.* Cf. **chapeado.**]

charro
   1. Mexican peasant who is characterized by a special outfit typical of the relative social position of the person and who is dexterous in things of the farm. *Mx* (Malaret 1947:62; Morínigo 1966:179) 20.
   2. peasant; rustic type. *CeA* (Cowles 1952:134) mid20.
   [Acc. Santamaría (1942:1.474) and Morínigo, used in Spain as 'villager from Salamanca, Spain,' a person who is also characterized by the wearing of a special outfit to indicate relative social position or place of origin. Syns. *campesino, campiruso, grosero,* acc. Cowles. Cf. **campiruso, gaucho.**]

charrúa 'Uruguayan'
native of Ur; Uruguayan. *RP* (Guarnieri 1967:84–85) 20.
[M., f. Acc. Guarnieri, < *charrua* 'name of Indian tribe found in Ur
until 1850s.' Acc. Fontanella de Weinberg (1982:46), found in 17
cent. text as 'indios charruas amigos.' Cf. **oriental.**]

chasco
person whose hair is coarse and straight, often in elongated
waves or braids. *Ar Bo* (Garzón 1910:149; Malaret 1947:63;
Morínigo 1966:180) 20.
[Also applied to animals. Acc. Morínigo, < Quechua *chasca* 'shock of
tangled hair.' Var. *chascudo,* acc. Bayo (1910:73). Cf. **pelo pasa.**]

chascudo — See *chasco*

chaso — See *chazo*

chato 'flat-nosed'
1. person with a flattened nose. *Gu SA* (Batres Jáuregui
1892:207) late19.
2. short person with dark brown, dark red, or Indian-like skin
color. *RP Ur* (Guarnieri 1968:59) 20.
[Acc. Batres Jáuregui (1892:207), affect. in late 19-cent. Gu. Var.
ñato. Cf. **ñato, romo.**]

chayón
1. albino. *Ec* (Morínigo 1966:181) 20.
2. person who cannot see well in light as a result of having very
blond eyelashes and very blue eyes. *Ec* (Alonso 1958:1.1340) 20.
[Probably < Quechua. Cf. **albino.**]

chayote 'hick'
uncouth peasant. *CR* (Kany 1960b:42) 20.
[Syn. *concho.* Cf. **campirano, campiruso, campuso, chapetas,
concho, pato.**]

chazo 'remnant, piece'
1. non-indigenous or non-Indian peasant. *Ec* (Malaret 1947:
214) mid20; (Alonso 1958:1.1341) 20.
2. hick; peasant; rustic type; native of the province of Loja, Ec.
Ec (Cowles 1952:247) mid20.
[Acc. Cowles, syn. df. 2 *guajiro; chaso* [*sic*]. Cf. **chacracama,
guajiro.**]

che
1. Bolivian. *Ch* (Kany 1960b:39) 20.
2. Argentine. *CR* (Villegas 1952:44); *Ch* (Kany 1960b:39) 20.
3. any person; guy. *Ar Bo Ur* (Cowles 1952:250) mid20.
[Acc. Cowles, used in many parts of SA as 'hi'; perhaps < Guarani
chi 'hello,' or Guarani or Arawak interj. for gaining someone's at-
tention. Acc. Kany, ext. in ref. to Argentines by all their neighbors

as a result of overuse of the interj. in Ar. Acc. Santamaría (1942:1.477), possibly < Andalusian Sp. in the sense of the interj. *ce*. Var. *chey*.]

chele

1. person with blond hair and generally with blue eyes. *Ho* (Membreño 1897:49); *Gu Sa* (Batres Jáuregui 1892:161, 209) late19 ‖ *Ni* (Castellón 1939:49) mid20 ‖ *CR* (Gagini 1918:110) early20 ‖ *CR* (Salesiano 1938:58) mid20 ‖ *Sa* (Kany 1960b:38); *CeA* (Morínigo 1966:182; Cowles 1952:251); *CR* (Villegas 1952:44) 20.

2. foreigner, esp. North American Anglo. *CeA* (Cowles 1952:251); *Ec* (Morínigo 1966:182); *Sa* (Kany 1960b:38) 20; (Vergara Martín 1922:234) n.d.

[Df. 2 by ext. of df. 1. Acc. Gagini, < Maya *chele* 'blue; blue-eyed person.' Var. in Mx *chelo*. Cf. **chapetón, chapín, gachupín, güero.**]

chelo — See *chele*

chey — See *che*

chiapaneco — See *chapaneco*

chicano

1. Mexican. *US-AZ* (Barker 1950:33) mid20.

2a. Mexican-American; anyone of Mexican background. *US-s.w.* (Galván and Teschner 1985:35) 20.

2b. Mexican-American without an Anglo self-image; un-Americanized Mexican-American. *US* (Marden and Meyer 1978:255–56) 20.

2c. militant Mexican-American, esp. a student, during the second half of the 20 cent., acc. himself or herself. *US* (Gann and Duignan 1986:xii, xiii) 20.

[Acc. Barker, df. 1 Pachuco slang. Acc. Gann and Duignan, df. 2c often derog. amongst older Mexican-American population. Acc. Marden and Meyer, < *(me)jicano*. Cf. **californio, hispano, latino, nuevo mexicano, tejano.**]

chicas patas — See *chicaspatas*

chicaspatas 'smallfoot'

Mexican. *US-AZ* (Barker 1950:33) mid20 ‖ *US-TX* (Kany 1960b:40) 20.

[Acc. Barker, Pachuco slang. Acc. Kany, var. *chicas patas*. Cf. **chicano.**]

chilango

1. person from the interior. *Mx-Veracruz* (Kany 1960b:42) 20.

2. person from the capital; Mexico City native. *Mx* (Lipski 1988:p.c.) late20.

[Probably pejor. Acc. Kany, *shilango* [*sic*]; < Mayan *xilaan* 'unkempt, disheveled.' Cf. **chicano, jarocho, pocho, tapatío.**]

chillo
person with very dark black skin color. *Pe* (Morínigo 1966:188) 20.
[Perhaps < Amerindian lg. Sim. to *chilo* 'very dark black person' in Bo. Cf. **chilo.**]

chilo
person with very dark black skin color. *Bo* (Fernández and Fernández 1967:53) 20.
[Cf. **chillo.**]

chimayó
Indian or *genízaro* no longer part of a tribe. *US-NM* (Cobos 1983:46) 20.
[Acc. Cobos, < Tewa *tsimajó* 'obsidian flake,' also NM placename and Indian-type blanket. Cf. **genízaro.**]

china — See *chino*

china poblana
1. Mexican woman, usually from the pueblo, characterized by a type of bright clothing. *Mx* (Morínigo 1966:191; Aguirre Beltrán 1972:179) 20.
2. Mexican woman, usually an Indian or mestizo. *SA* (Corominas 1954–57:2.53; Santamaría 1942:1.500) 20.
3. servant, usually a mestizo woman. *Mx RP* (Alonso 1958:1.1351) 20.
[Acc. Corominas (1954–57:2.53 and 1973:195), *china* < Quechua *china* 'female of animals, female servant,' whence the deriv. *chino* 'mestizo.' *Poblana* 'native of Puebla, Mx.' Use of Quechua word in Mx, where it was never spoken, unexplained. Cf. **charro, chazo, chino.**]

chinacate — See *chinaco*

chinaco
1. warrior who fought against the French invasion of Mx in 19 cent. *Mx* (Aguirre Beltrán 1972:179) 19–20.
2. person of the low social standing. *Mx* (Santamaría 1942:1.501) 20.
[Usually m. pl. Syn. df. 2 *chinacate*. Cf. **china poblana, chino.**]

chinero
man of good social standing who prefers *chinas,* i.e., Indian or mestizo women, as sexual partners. *Ar* (Segovia 1911:190) early20.
[< *chino* + adj. suf. *-ero*. Cf. **mulatero, negrero,** Ptg. **chineiro.**]

chingo 'small; flat-nosed'
person with a flat, sometimes mutilated, nose. *Ve* (Malaret

1947:70; Alario di Filippo 1964:98; Santamaría 1942:1.509) 20.
[Cf. **chato, ñato, romo.**]
chinito 'small *chino*'
young mestizo or Amerindian. *Ar* (Segovia 1911:117) early20.
[< *chino* + dim. suf. *-ito.* Affect. in phr. *mi chinito* in 19 cent. Ch,
acc. Rodríguez (1875:164), and in early 20-cent. Ar, acc. Segovia
(1911:191). Cf. **chino, negrito, negro.**]
chino 'Chinese; Indian'
   1. person with yellowish or brown skin color. *Pe* (Romero
1944:375) cl ‖ *Co-Cartagena* (Solaún and Kronus 1973:166) 20.
   2a. Indian. *SA* (Malaret 1942:422) cl ‖ *Ar* (Bayo 1910:78)
early20 ‖ *Ar Ch Ve* (Malaret 1931:193–94) prior20 ‖ *Ch*
(Yrarrázaval 1945:52) mid20 ‖ *Ar* (Garzón 1910:155–56; Segovia
1911:117, 583) early20; (Vergara Martín 1922:234) n.d.
   2b. Goajiro Indian. *Co* (Malaret 1942:422) mid20.
   2c. Goajiro Indian, who happens to look Chinese. *Ve* (Vergara
Martín 1922:234) n.d.
   3. offspring of an Indian and a *lobo,* used in baptismal records
and other official documents. *Mx* (Roncal 1944:533) cl.
   4. offspring of a mulatto and an Indian; 25% white, 50% Indian,
25% black. *Pe* (Pérez de Barradas 1948:186; Woodbridge 1948:357)
cl; (Mörner 1967:59) 18; (Vergara Martín 1922:234) n.d.
   5. offspring of a *zambo* and an Indian. *Mx* (Woodbridge
1948:357) cl ‖ *SA* (Yrarrázaval 1945:72) mid20 ‖ *SA* (Garzón
1910:155–56) early20.
   6. offspring of a *saltatrás* and an Indian. *Mx* (Woodbridge
1948:357) cl ‖ *Pe* (Vergara Martín 1922:234) n.d.
   7a. offspring of a black and an Indian. *Ar* (Woodbridge
1948:357); *Mx* (Love 1971:81; Aguirre Beltrán 1972:179); *Mx Pe*
(Humboldt 1941:2.140–41) cl ‖ *Ar* (Garzón 1910:155–56) early20
‖ *Pe* (Millones Santagadea 1973:66) late18–early19; (Malaret
1942:442) mid20; (Morínigo 1966:191) 20.
   7b. *zambo,* or offspring of a black and an Indian. *SA* (Vergara
Martín 1922:234) n.d.
   8. offspring of a white and a black; mulatto. *Mx* (Love 1971:81;
Aguirre Beltrán 1972:169, 179; Woodbridge 1948:357) cl ‖ *Ar*
(Garzón 1910:155–56) early20; (Vergara Martín 1922:234) n.d.
   9a. offspring of a white and an Indian; mestizo. *Ar Pg Ur*
(Woodbridge 1948:357) cl ‖ *Ar* (Segovia 1911:117) early20 ‖ *Ur*
(Mieres et al. 1966:52) 20 ‖ *Ar-so.* (Vergara Martín 1922:234) n.d.
   9b. offspring of a white European and an Indian, with regular
features and very white skin. *SA* (Alcedo 1786–89:5.31) late18.
   10a. offspring of a black and a mulatto. *Cu* (Woodbridge

1948:357) cl; (Pichardo 1953:249; Martinez-Alier 1974:94) 19; (Malaret 1931:193–94) mid20; (Dihigo 1966:102; Espina Pérez 1972:61; Morínigo 1966:191) 20; (Vergara Martín 1922:234) n.d.

10b. offspring of a mulatto and a black, who had skin the color of Malays and who were mistaken for Chinese. *Cu* (Macías 1885:436) 19.

11a. offspring of a black and a *lobo;* 25% Indian, 75% black. *Mx* (Woodbridge 1948:357); *Mx Pe* (Pérez de Barradas 1948:191; León 1924:20–21, plate 16) cl.

11b. offspring of a black and a *lobo* or *cambujo;* dihybrid, third-generation offspring of 3 parts black and 1 part Indian. *Mx* (Moreno Navarro 1973:129–31; Solano 1975:85) 18.

11c. *zambo prieto,* or offspring of a black and a *lobo. SA* (Vergara Martín 1922:234) n.d.

12a. offspring of a white and a *morisco. SA* (Alba 1969:34) n.d.

12b. offspring of a white and a *morisco;* 87.5% white, 12.5% black. *Mx* (Pérez de Barradas 1948:190; Woodbridge 1948:357; Monteforte Toledo 1959:171) cl; (McAlister 1963:354) 19 ‖ *SA* (Alba 1969:34) n.d.

12c. *quinterón,* or offspring of a *morisco* and a white Spaniard. *Mx* (Vergara Martín 1922:234) n.d., probably cl.

13a. Asian; Oriental person. *Mx* (Aguirre Beltrán 1972:52; Love 1971:81) cl ‖ *Cu* (Pichardo 1953:249) 19 ‖ *SA* (DRAE 411) 20.

13b. native of China; Chinese. *Cu* (Macías 1885:436) 19.

13c. slave from the Orient. *Mx* (Aguirre Beltrán 1972:52) cl ‖ *Cu* (Pichardo 1953:249) 19.

13d. slave brought from the Philippines, of Mongoloid race. *Mx* (Aguirre Beltrán 1972:144; Love 1971:81) cl.

13e. African slave taken from Mozambique and brought to the New World across the Pacific. *Mx* (Levine 1980:34) prior20.

14a. Indian, usually a woman, who worked for a soldier as a servant. *Ch* (Cowles 1952:261) 20 ‖ *CeA SA* (Bayo 1931:101) mid20.

14b. Indian woman. *RP* (Guarnieri 1979:68) 20.

14c. woman with Indian-like, dark skin and straight, black hair. *RP* (Guarnieri 1979:68) 20.

14d. young female Indian who served in a convent. *Ec* (Carvalho-Neto 1964:173) late18.

14e. Indian woman who served as a servant or domestic. *SA* (Vergara Martín 1922:234) n.d.

14f. Pampa Indian woman, generally characterized by her *trigueño,* or light brown, skin color. *Ur* (Mieres et al. 1966:52) 20 ‖ *Ch Co Ec Pe Ur Ve* (Cowles 1952:261) mid20.

14g. wife of a gaucho or of an Indian. *RP* (Guarnieri 1967:87 and 1979:68); *Ar* (Laxalt 1980:486) 20.

14h. pretty mestizo woman who is perceived to be a lively dresser and to lead a good life. *Mx* (Moreno Navarro 1973:142) 20.

14i. prostitute, in the sense of 'woman of a soldier.' *Mx* (Aguirre Beltrán 1972:179) cl.

14j. any woman. *Mx SA* (Vergara Martín 1922:234) n.d.

14k. countrywoman, no matter what her race. *Ur* (Mieres et al. 1966:52) 20.

15. person who has dark skin and other physical features, thus resembling an Amerindian. *Ar Ch Pg Ur Ve* (Morínigo 1966: 190–91); *RP* (Guarnieri 1979:69); *Co-Zarzal* (Sayres 1956: 223) 20.

16. uncivilized Indian. *Co* (Morínigo 1966:191) 20.

17. civilized or cultured Indian. *CeA SA* (Bayo 1931:101) mid20.

18. child, esp. an Indian child. *Co* (Tascón 1961:145) 20.

19. servant. *Ar* (Morínigo 1966:191) 20 ‖ *Ch* (Cowles 1952: 261) mid20.

20. low-class or nonwhite person, including Indian, mestizo, mulatto, or *zambo;* plebeian. *SA,* esp. *Ch* (Rodríguez 1875:162–64) 19prior.

21. Filipino; person born in the Philippines. *Mx-DF* (Love 1971:81) mid17–mid18.

[Df. 2 possibly derog. in Ar, acc. Bayo (1910:78) or in Ar, Ch and Ve, acc. Malaret (1931:193–94). Syn. df. 2 *chino cholo,* used to distinguish Indian from the Asian *chino.* Acc. Malaret (1931:193–94), in Bilbao, Spain, 'black, mulatto.' Df. 5 of little use in Ch, acc. Yrarrázaval. Df. 13e confused with those Asian slaves brought across the Pacific, acc. Levine. F. form *china* used esp. for df. 14. Df. 15 indicates lowest of 12 social positions in Zarzal, Co, acc. Sayres. Acc. Sayres (227), very insult.; extremely derog. in family banter; used in ref. to 'Indian' or 'pig'; in early 1950s also meant 'enemy' in Co, only SoA country to send troops to Korea. Df. 14j syns. in Spain *chula, manola,* acc. Vergara Martín. Acc. Corominas (1954–57:2.53 and 1973:195) and Moreno Navarro (1973:142), 'maid' in the Andes probably < Quechua *china* 'female animal.' Acc. Santamaría (1942:1.510) and Garzón (1910:155–56), possibly < Aztec *chinoa* 'toasted,' alluding to the skin color. Acc. Malaret (1947:71), Morínigo (1966:191), and Santamaría (1942:1.510), may also refer to the crisp, curly hair of the *chino* in 20-cent. Mx. Acc. Alario di Filippo (1964:99) and Morínigo, may also refer to the stiff hair of the Indian in 20-cent. Co. Acc. Moreno Navarro, now folkloric type of Mexican, esp. in Puebla. Also affect. as in *mi chino, mi china,* acc. Pichardo (1953:249) in 19-cent. Cu and acc. Revollo (1942:94) in mid-20 cent. Co. *Chinerío* or *chinaje* 'group of *chinos*,' sim. to *negrerío* 'group of blacks,' acc. Morínigo (1966:189–90). Syn. *aindiado*. Syn. *mulato pardo* in 17-cent. Puebla, Mx, acc. Aguirre Beltrán (1945:216 and 1972:169). Other deriv. *achinado*. Cf. **aindiado, asiático, castizo, chapín, china poblana, chino cambujo, indio, lobo, moreno, mulato, negro, oriental, pardo, zambo, zobo.**]

chino blancoide
offspring of a white and Chinese. *Pe* (Gutiérrez Saco 1965: 262) 20.
[Acc. Gutiérrez Saco, anthro.; used in opp. to *chino indioide* and *chino negroide*. Syn. *injerto*. Cf. **blanco, chino, chino negroide, chino indioide.**]

chino cambujo
1. offspring of an Indian and a *lobo*. *Mx* (O'Crouley 1972:19) 18.
2. offspring of a chino and a *cambujo*. *Mx* (León 1924:23) cl.
[Cf. **cambujo, chino, lobo.**]

chino cholo
offspring of a black and an Indian. *Pe* (Romero 1944:375; Woodbridge 1948:357) cl.
[Term used to avoid confusion with *chino* 'Chinese.' Syn. *chino*. Var. *chino-cholo*. Cf. **chino, cholo.**]

chino-cholo — See *chino cholo*

chino claro
light-skinned person of mixed race. *Pe* (Romero 1944:375) cl.
[Cf. **chino, claro.**]

chino-claro — See *chino claro*

chino de Manila — See *chino manila*

chino grifo
offspring of a mulatto and an Indian. *Mx* (O'Crouley 1972:19) 18.
[Acc. O'Crouley, '*chino* with kinky hair,' in ref. to the black traits of this tri-racial mixture. Cf. **chino, chino cambujo, grifo.**]

chino indioide
offspring of an Indian and a Chinese; *injerto*. *Pe* (Gutiérrez Saco 1965:262) 20.
[Acc. Gutiérrez Saco, *chino indiode* [*sic*]; anthro.; used in opp. to *chino blancoide* and *chino negroide,* all commonly called *injerto*. Acc. Kiddle (1984:p.c.), *indioide* < *indio* + *-oide* by anal. to *negroide* or *blancoide*. Cf. **chino, chino blancoide, chino negroide, indio, injerto.**]

chino manila
1. Asiatic slave. *Cu* (Pichardo 1953:52) 19.

2. Asian colonist contracted to work under poor working conditions. *Cu* (Macías 1885:436, 820) 19.

[Acc. Pichardo and Macías, used to distinguish 'Asian' from 'off-spring of a black and a mulatto.' Acc. Macías, generally Chinese and not necessarily Filipino. Syns. df. 1 *asiático, chino.* Ant. *chino cholo.* Vars. *chino de Manila, chino manilo, chino-manila, chinomanila.* Cf. **asiático, chino, chino cholo.**]

chino manilo — See *chino manila*

chino-manila — See *chino manila*

chino negroide

offspring of a black and a Chinese; *injerto. Pe* (Gutiérrez Saco 1965:262) 20.

[Acc. Gutiérrez Saco, anthro.; used in opp. to *chino blancoide* and *chino indioide.* Cf. **chino, chino blancoide, chino indioide, injerto, negro, negroide.**]

chino prieto

person of mixed race whose skin color is black or very dark. *Pe* (Romero 1944:375 and 1965:233) cl.

[Var. *chino-prieto.* Cf. **chino, chino claro, prieto.**]

chino-prieto — See *chino prieto*

chino puro 'pure Chinese'

person who is considered to be pure Chinese or Asian. *Co-Cartagena* (Solaún and Kronus 1973:166) 20.

[Cf. **chino, negro puro.**]

chino rechino

person who is considered to have extremely Chinese or Asian features. *Pe* (Romero 1965:166) cl.

[*Rechino < chino* by anal. to the pair *tinto -retinto.* Cf. **chino, negro retinto, retinto.**]

chino y blanco

person of mixed European and Asian parentage. *Co-Cartagena* (Solaún and Kronus 1973:166) 20.

[Cf. **blanco, chino, chino cambujo, chino puro.**]

chinomanila — See *chino manila*

chinonga

native, generally Indian, maid of poor appearance. *Ar* (Morínigo 1966:191) 20.

[F. Acc. Morínigo, < *china* 'servant, usually Indian' + pejor. suf. *-onga.* Cf. **china poblana, chino.**]

chiquito 'very small'

civilized Bolivian Indian of very small stature. *Bo RP* (Bayo 1910:79 and 1931:102) 18–20.

[Cf. **camba, indio.**]

chivo 'goat'

person from the highlands of western Gu. *Gu* (Kany 1960b:42) 20.

[Acc. Kany, highlander is generally a goatherd or shepherd. Cf. **guájiro, serrano.**]

choco 'curly-haired; dark red'

1. person with very brown or dark skin color. *Co* (Morínigo 1966:197) 20.

2. pure-blooded Indian. *Mx-Tabasco* (Morínigo 1966:197) 20.

3. person with kinky hair, esp. one with a flat nose. *Ch Ec* (Santamaría 1942:1.527) 20.

[Acc. Corominas (1954–57:1.74), 'small cuttlefish.' In Bo, 'dark red color.' In Ec, 'chocolate color.' In Ch and Ec, 'reddish curly hair style.']

chocoano 'person from the Chocó, Co'

black person. *Co* (Solaún and Kronus 1973:43); *Co-Unguía, -Chocó* (Wade 1985:239, 242) 20.

[Acc. Solaún and Kronus, region. Sim. to *choco,* but probably < *Chocaá* 'name of an Indian tribe on the Chocó River in the we. ranges of the Andes and on the Pacific coast of Co,' acc. Santamaría (1942:1.527), + suf. *-ano.* Ext. to 'black person' unexplained. Acc. Wade, syn. *verdadero negro;* often a farmer or laborer. Cf. **choco.**]

cholito — See *cholo*

cholo 'half-breed'

1a. offspring of an Indian and a mestizo; 25% white, 75% Indian. *Mx* (León 1924:20–21, plate 17; Pérez de Barradas 1948:188); *Pe* (Pérez de Barradas 1948:186) cl ‖ *Pe* (Mörner 1967:59) 18 ‖ *SA* (Vergara Martín 1922:235) n.d.

1b. dihybrid, third-generation offspring of 3 parts Indian and 1 part white. *Mx* (Moreno Navarro 1973:129–31; Solano 1975:85) 18.

2a. mestizo; offspring of a white and an Indian. *Pe* (Paz Soldán 1938:170–72; Sánchez-Albornoz 1974:137); *Ar Bo Ch Ec Pe* (Santamaría 1942:1.531; Woodbridge 1948:357) cl ‖ *Bo* (Levine 1980:34–35) pre19; (Bailey and Nasatir 1973:767) 20 ‖ *Pe-Lima* (Boyd-Bowman 1984:874) 19 ‖ *Ar* (Segovia 1911:117); *Ch* (Armengol Valenzuela 1916:17.301) early20 ‖ *SA* (Malaret 1942:437–38); *SA exc. Ch* (Malaret 1947:74) mid20 ‖ *Bo* (Fernández and Fernández 1967:55; Bailey and Nasatir 1973:767); *Pe* (Kany 1960b:35; Simmons 1955:108); *Pa* (Nack 1980:38); *SA* (Bayo 1910:80 and 1931:104); *SoA-Andes* (Ferguson 1963:120; Alba 1969:34; Urbanski 1978:154) 20 ‖ *Ar-no.* (Vergara Martín 1922:235) n.d.

2b. offspring of an Indian and a white Spaniard, the latter being offspring of a pure white and a *castizo;* 48.25% white, 51.75% Indian. *Pe* (Pérez de Barradas 1948:188) cl.

2c. mestizo who is trying to improve social standing. *Pe* (Bourricaud 1975:350–51) 20.

2d. mestizo who has improved social standing through education. *SA* (Konetzke 1961:197) 20.

2e. mestizo whose Indian physical traits are dominant. *Pe* (Woodbridge 1948:357) cl.

2f. mestizo who lives in the highlands. *Pe* (Gillin 1949:162) cl.

2g. mestizo of low social standing. *Ch Pe* (Rodríguez 1875:170) 19 ‖ *Ec-n.w.* (Whitten 1965:92) 20.

2h. person who occupies a social position between the mestizo and Indian worlds, usually offspring of white and Indian. *Pe* (Fried 1961:25; Mörner 1967:68–69) 20.

2i. dark-skinned soldier or any dark-skinned person, generally offspring of a white and an Indian. *Co-Santanderes* (Kany 1960b:34) 20.

3. dark-skinned person from the coast, or *costeño,* who generally has straight hair and lacks any specific color designation, but who is often a mixture of black and Indian. *Ec-n.w.-Esmeraldas* (Whitten 1965:91) 20.

4a. Peruvian. *Pe* (Malaret 1942:437–38) mid20 ‖ *Ch* (Bayo 1931:104); *Co* (Alario di Filippo 1964:102); *Ch Co Ec* (Kany 1960b:39) 20.

4b. Peruvian or Bolivian of the lower classes. *Ch* (Armengol Valenzuela 1916:17.301) early20.

5a. *serrano,* or person from the highlands, who wants to pass for *criollo. Pe-Lima* (Bourricaud 1975:384) 20.

5b. migrant worker or person moving from the highlands. *Pe-Lima* (Wallace 1984:64) 20.

5c. *criollo* who is of part Indian ancestry. *Pe* (Vergara Martín 1922:235) n.d.

6. any dark-skinned person, varying from Indian to mestizo, who wears typical Indian clothing and carries other items indicating adoption of Indian culture. *CR* (Woodbridge 1948:357; Santamaría 1942:1.531) cl ‖ *Ar Bo Ch CR Ec Pe* (Cowles 1952:277–78); *Ec* (Carvalho-Neto 1964:175–76) 20 ‖ *CR* (Salesiano 1938:61; Gagini 1918:117) early20 ‖ *CR* (Malaret 1942:437–38) mid20.

7a. civilized Indian. *Pa* (Morínigo 1966:198; Aguilera Patiño 1951:439); *Pe* (Pitt-Rivers 1968:272); *SA exc. Ch* (Yrarrázaval 1945:72); *Pa Pe* (Cowles 1952:277–78) 20.

7b. Indian, generally young, who has been reared among Europeans, is knowledgeable of their customs, and speaks Spanish. *SA* (Alcedo 1786–89:5.32) late18.

7c. semi-civilized Indian. *Pa* (Malaret 1942:437–38) mid20 ‖ *Pe* (Vergara Martín 1922:235) n.d.

7d. pure-blooded Indian. *Pe* (León 1924:23) early20 ‖ *Ch-so. CR* (Malaret 1942:437–38) mid20.

7e. Indian who has the cunning of a gypsy and who speaks both Spanish and the native lg. *Bo* (Levine 1980:34–35) 20.

8. low-class or inferior person, usually from the interior of Mx. *US-CA* (Blanco 1971:195) cl.

9. person who is a mixture of black, Indian, and white, or of black and Indian. *Co-Zarzal* (Sayres 1956:223) 20.

10. servant. *Mx* (Armengol Valenzuela 1916:17.301) early20.

[Syn. df. 1b *coyote*. Dfs. 2c, 2i pejor. Df. 6 derog. Acc. Sayres, df. 9 combines all bad stereotypical qualities of a black (ugliness) and a mulatto (unreliability); occupies the 6th highest social class. Skin color term used in parish records and other official documents in cl. Mx, acc. Roncal (1944:533) and in cl. Pe, acc. Romero (1944:375). Acc. Fernández and Fernández and Corominas (1954–57:2.92–93), < *chulo* 'gaudy,flashy.' Acc. Armengol Valenzuela and Paz Soldán, < Aymara *chulu* 'mestizo.' Acc. Cowles, < *Cholula* 'distict in Mx,' or < Aymara *chhulu* 'mestizo,' or < *cholo* 'mulatto' in the Windward Islands. Acc. Aguilera Patiño, < *chole* 'pre-Colombian, Central American Indian tribe.' Acc. Armengol Valenzuela, df. 10 < Nahautl or Mexican *xolo*. Affect. when used for friends and close relatives, sim. to *cholito*, in Ec-n.w., acc. Whitten, in CR, acc. Salesiano and Gagini, and in Pe, acc. Pitt-Rivers. Derivs. *acholado, cholito*. Cf. **blanco, castizo, chino, chulo, costeño, coyote, español blanco, mestizo, mulato, negro, serrano**.]

cholo chino
offspring of a black and a Chinese or Asian. *Pe* (Woodbridge 1948:357; Santamaría 1942:1.531) cl.

[Var. *cholo-chino*. Cf. **asiático, chino, chino cholo, chino manila, cholo, oriental**.]

cholo-chino — See *cholo chino*

chombo
1. black person from the English-speaking An. *Pa* (Malaret 1942:438) mid20; (Malaret 1947:75; Aguilera Patiño 1951:439; Rout 1976:xiv; Alonso 1958:1.1366; Kany 1960b:35) 20.

2. black person. *Pa* (Cowles 1952:278) 20.

3. offspring of a black and an Indian. *Pa* (Malaret 1942:438) mid20; (Alonso 1958:1.1366) 20.

[Excl. to Pa. Acc. Rout, insult. Var. *chumbo*. Acc. Kany, 'buzzard.'

Cf. **afroantillano, chumagra, chumeca, mestizo, negro, prieto.**]

chonta 'blockhead'

mestizo. *Pe* (Kany 1960b:35) 20.

[M., f. Acc. Kany, humor. or pejor. Acc. Santamaría (1942:1.533), < Quechua *chunta* 'palm, palm tree, wood of dark color.' Var. *chontano.* Cf. **chonta-campas, chontal.**]

chonta-campas

Indian from the department of Loreto, Pe. *Pe* (Santamaría 1942:1.533) 20.

[Usually m. pl. Cf. **chonta, chontal, loretano.**]

chontal 'wild; rustic, crude'

1a. uncivilized or unruly Indian of southern Mx, Gu, and Ni. *CeA Mx* (Morínigo 1966:199) cl ‖ *Gu* (Batres Jáuregui 1892:227) late19.

1b. uncultured or illiterate Indian. *SoA* (Vergara Martín 1922:235) n.d.

2. fugitive or otherwise unruly Indian, considered uncultured and uneducated. *CeA* (Morínigo 1966:199) 20.

3. Indian slave who does not speak Spanish and is not familiar with Hispanic customs. *Cu* (Macías 1885:755) 19.

4. Lenca Indian, acc. Niquira Indians. *Ni-ea.* (Vergara Martín 1922:235) n.d.

[Acc. Morínigo, < Nahuatl *chontali* 'wild.' Cf. **chonta, ladino.**]

chontano — See *chonta*

chorizo 'pork sausage'

1. black person or mulatto. *Cu* (Kany 1960b:35; Alonso 1958: 1.1368) 20.

2. black person, acc. whites. *Cu* (Vergara Martín 1922:235) n.d.

[Df. 1 facet., acc. Kany; derog., acc. Alonso. Df. 2 derog., acc. Vergara Martín. Cf. **negro azabache, nigüento.**]

chorote 'drinking chocolate'

1. friendly Indian living on the Pg-Ar-Bo border. *Ar* (Morínigo 1966:200) 20.

2. Indian. *Mx-Tabasco* (Santamaría 1942:1.538) 20.

[Cf. **achocolatado, indio.**]

chota

young female Indian who is almost a woman; young Indian woman entering puberty. *Bo* (Morínigo 1966:200; Santamaría 1942:1.539) 20.

[F. Acc. Cobarruvias (1611:438), Morínigo (1966:201), and Alonso (1958:1.1369), < *choto* 'person or animal which is still a suckling.']

chucho
Indian from the province of Chumbivilcas. *Pe* (Cowles 1952:283) mid20.
[Possibly reduplicative form of the initial syllable of the name of the province. Cf. **chonta-campas.**]

chuco — See *pachuco*

chulo 'amusing, charming'
1. mulatto. *Co* (Kany 1960b:35–36) 20.
2. person with black skin color. *Co* (Santamaría 1942:1.545) 20.
[Df. 1 facet. Df. 2 derog. Acc. Corominas (1973:199), *chulo* 'boy' first att. in Spain 1666 as 'low class person.' Acc. Kany, 'turkey buzzard, type of black insect.' Rel. to *cholo*. Cf. **choco, cholo, mulato, negro.**]

chumagra
1. black person. *CR* (Salesiano 1938:62) early20.
2. white person or mestizo, acc. the *garífunas* of Ho. Ho (Lipski 1988:p.c.) late20.
[M., f. Possibly rel. to *chumeca*. Cf. **chulo, chumeca, congo, negro, prieto.**]

chumbo — See *chombo*

chumeca
1. black person from Jamaica. *CR* (Gagini 1918:119) early20; (Malaret 1931:205) mid20; (Kany 1960b:36; Santamaría 1942:1.546; Morínigo 1966:203; Alonso 1958:1.1374) 20.
2. black person. *CR* (Gagini 1918:119) early20; (Salesiano 1938:62; Cowles 1952:286; Villegas 1952:52) 20.
[M., f. Df. 1 facet. Df. 2 slang. Excl. to CR. Acc. Morínigo, Malaret, Gagini, Villegas, and Cowles, < Sp. imitation of Jamaicans' pronunciation for the name of the island *Jamaica*. Acc. Villegas, *chumeco* [*sic*]. Var. *yumeca*. Cf. **chumagra, congo, negro.**]

chumeco — See *chumeca*

chuncano
uncouth peasant. *Ar-San Luis* (Kany 1960b:40) 20.
[Cf. **camilucho, campusano, concho, pajuerano.**]

chuncho 'savage; rustic'
1. savage or uncivilized Indian from eastern Pe. *Pe* (Paz Soldán 1938:173) 19; (Bayo 1910:82 and 1931:106; Cowles 1952:9; Morínigo 1966:203) 20.
2. Bolivian, acc. coastal Peruvians. *Pe* (Santamaría 1942:1.547) 20.
[Acc. Cowles, < Quechua *ch'unchu* 'savage man.' Acc. Bayo (1910:82) and Alonso (1958:1.1375), < Aymara *chuncho* 'savage.' Cf. **chonta, cholo, chucho.**]

churrapaco 'stubby; short; thick-lipped'
1. mestizo. *Pe* (Kany 1960b:35) 20.
2a. somewhat civilized Indian. *Pe* (Alonso 1958:1.1378) 20.
2b. Indian. *Pe* (Kany 1960b:35) 20prior.
[Df. 1 pejor., humor. Syn. df. 2a, *chuto, cholo.* Acc. Kany, originally, 'thick-lipped.' Cf. **bembón, cholo, chuto, indio, mestizo, negro bembón.**]

chuto 'thick-lipped'
Indian or mestizo. *Pe* (Cowles 1952:292; Kany 1960b:35; Morínigo 1966:207) 20.
[Derog., humor. Acc. Cowles, < Quechua *chchutu* 'thick-lipped'; possibly derog. for *cholo.* Acc. Alonso (1958:1.1380), in Bo and Ve, 'flat and small,' in Bo 'timid and poor.' Cf. **chato, cholo, churrupaco, indio, mestizo.**]

cimarrón 'runaway'
1. savage, semi-savage, or crude person. *SA* (Cowles 1952:171–72; Malaret 1947:44); *PR* (Malaret 1937:129); *RP* (Guarnieri 1968:47) 20.
2. person, esp. a boy, who is short and timid; uncouth person. *Mx-Sonora* (Sobarzo 1966:67) 20.
3. runaway slave, generally black, Indian, or of mixed race, who fled the plantation and often hid out in the outback, forests, swamps, or hills. *Pe* (Grenón 1930:271) early17 ‖ *SA* (Alcedo 1786–89:5.33) late18; (Bailey and Nasatir 1973:767) cl ‖ *CR* (Gagini 1918:92); *SA* (Alvarez Nazario 1974:341; Morínigo 1966: 136); *Pe* (Paz Soldán 1938:128–30); *PR* (Alvarez Nazario 1974:380); *Pa* (Aguilera Patiño 1951:428); *Cu* (Cowles 1952:171–72) cl–19 ‖ *Cu* (Macías 1885:327–28) 19 ‖ *SA* (Vergara Martín 1922:232) pre20.
4. black person. *Pe* (Vergara Martín 1922:232) pre20.
[Acc. Morínigo, att. 1535 as 'fugitive.' Acc. Alvarez Nazario, < *cima* 'top' + suf. *-arrón,* of Antillean origin. Acc. Macías, var. *simarrón.* Acc. Boyd-Bowman (1971:189), vars. *simarrón, zimarrón.* Cf. **injerto, negro, negro cimarrón,** Ptg. **fugido.**]

cincha — See *tener cincha*

claro 'light'
1. person with light skin color. *Co-Turbaco* (Flórez 1969:121) 20 ‖ *Co-Cartagena* (Solaún et al. 1987:19) late20.
2. light-skinned person, used by the working class in order not to imply racial connotations. *Co-Cartagena* (Solaún and Kronus 1973:166, 180) 20.
[Acc. Boggs et al. (1946:116–17), att. as 'blond' in ref. to color of eyelashes in 17-cent. Spain. Cf. **mulato claro, negro claro,** Ptg. **claro.**]

clase artesana — See *artesano*

clase de artesanos — See *artesano*

clavero 'key keeper; gatekeeper'

servant, usually neophyte Indian, who is employed to work in the service of a mission. *US-CA* (Blanco 1971:185) cl.

[< *clave* 'key' + suf. *-ero.*]

coartado

slave who acquired freedom through negotiations with and payment to the master. *SA* (Alvarez Nazario 1974:345); *Cu* (Pichardo 1953:188) cl.

[< *coartar* 'to limit.' Cf. **liberto, libre.**]

cobrizo 'copper-colored'

1. mestizo. *Ni* (Vandiver 1949:144) early20.

2. person with reddish-brown or copperish skin color. *Co-Capitanejo* (Flórez 1969:121) 20 ‖ *Co-Cartagena* (Solaún et al. 1987:19) late20.

3. Indian. *SA Ve* (Mörner 1961:285) 20.

[Acc. Vandiver, df. 1 used in 1920 Ni census. Acc. Solaún et al., df. 2 not a racial term. Acc. Mörner, df. 3 anthro., desc. < *cobre* 'copper' + adj. suf. *-izo.*]

cocho 'cooked'

mulato pardo, or offspring of a black and an Indian. *Mx-Michoacán* (Aguirre Beltrán 1945:216) 17; (Woodbridge 1948:357; Aguirre Beltrán 1972:169) cl ‖ *Mx* (Levine 1980:36) cl.

[Acc. Levine, 'dirty.' Cf. **membrillo cocho.**]

cocoliche

1a. Italian immigrant, usually speaking the pidginized lg. common to the RP Italian population. *RP* (Kany 1960b:37; Cammarota 1963:23; Guarnieri 1967:70) 20.

1b. Italian trying to pass for native or for a gaucho, characterized by mixed lg. and crude manners. *Ar* (Cara-Walker 1987:43) late19–early20.

2. foreigner, usually Italian, who speaks bad Spanish. *Ur* (Malaret 1942:318) mid20.

[< *cocoliche* 'creoloid lg. with both Sp. and Italian elements used by new Italian immigrants to Ar and Ur.' Acc. Santamaría (1942:1.367), var. *cocolinche.* Acc. Cara-Walker, generally pejor., mainly literary character or caricature.]

cocolinche — See *cocoliche*

cocolo

1. black person from the Windward Islands brought to DR to work the sugar plantations. *DR* (Patín Maceo 1940:39) mid20.

2. black person from the English-speaking An. *DR PR* (Alvarez Nazario 1974:67); *DR* (Domínguez 1973:106) 19 ‖ *PR* (Zenón Cruz 1975:1.248) pre20; (Malaret 1937:131 and 1942:318) mid20; (Gallo 1980:24) 20 ‖ *An* (Alonso 1958:1.1106) 20.

3. black person. *An PR* (Domínguez 1986:275) 20.

4. Afro-American, or black North American, acc. young Hispanics. *US-NY* (Domínguez 1973:187) 20.

[Acc. Zenón Cruz, df. 2 now pejor., close to pure African in type, like the *angolo* or *congo*. Acc. Gallo, df. 2 slang. Acc. Domínguez (1986), df. 3 pejor. Acc. Domínguez (1973), df. 4 used by young Puerto Ricans, Dominicans, and Cubans in Washington Heights, New York City. Cf. **angolo, congo, moreno de Barlovento, negro cocolo.**]

cocoroco 'brazen; vain'

1. chief of an African community, acc. white people. *PR* (Zenón Cruz 1975:1.248) pre20.

2. person with economic or political power. *PR* (Zenón Cruz 1975:1.248) 20.

[Acc. Zenón Cruz, df. 1 in ref. to black chief's frequent request for a drink of the same name. Cf. **cocolo.**]

colla 'greedy'

1. Aymara Indian. *SA* (Bayo 1931:74) mid20.

2. Bolivian Indian. *Ar Bo Pe* (Morínigo 1966:145) 20 ‖ *Bo* (Vergara Martín 1922:233) n.d.

3. mestizo who is part Indian. *Ar* (Alonso 1958:1.1134) 20.

4. Bolivian. *Ar* (Bayo 1910:59–60; Segovia 1911:178) early20.

5. inhabitant of the Andean mesetas. *Bo* (Alonso 1958:1.1134; DRAE 325) 20.

[M., f. Df. 3 region., syn. *indio mestizo,* acc. Alonso. In Pe 'stingy, miserly,' acc. Alonso. Acc. Bayo (1931:74), 'inhabitant of the *collao,* or high plateau.' Used among the Incas as a syn. for *infante* 'prince.' Acc. Morínigo, < Quechua *kolla* 'highlander.' Acc. Segovia, var. *coya.* Cf. **camba, coya, cullaca, negro cocolo.**]

colono 'colonist; settler; tenant farmer'

1a. tenant farmer. *Gu* (Morínigo 1966:144); *SA-Andes* (Levine 1980:37) 20.

1b. highland farmer of the Andes, who uses the land in return for labor. *SA-Andes* (Bailey and Nasatir 1973:767) 20.

1c. independent farmer, usually white, who owns land and grows sugar cane. *An* (Levine 1980:37) 20.

2. Indian servant. *SA-Andes* (Levine 1980:37) 20.

[Cf. **pegujalero, sayañero.**]

colono africano 'African colonist'
black African slave brought illegally to America from west Africa after the abolition of direct slave trading. *Pe* (Nuñez 1980:134) mid19.
[Cf. **africano, colono.**]

color achocolatado 'chocolate-colored'
person who is not clearly a Spaniard or European, i.e., not totally white. *Mx* (McAlister 1963:368) cl
[*Achocolatado* < *a-* + *chocolate* + adj. suf. *-ado.* Generally in phr. *de color achocolatado.* Cf. **negro achocolatado,** Ptg. **chocolate.**]

color amarillito 'yellowish'
person with yellowish, i.e., nonwhite, skin color. *SA* (Diggs 1953:406) cl.
[Acc. Diggs, class distinction. Cf. **amarillo.**]

color champurrado 'mixed color'
person of mixed race with dark or chocolate skin color. *SA* (Diggs 1953:406) cl.
[Acc. Diggs, class distinction; *champurrado* < *cha(m)purrar* 'to mix liquors; to mix chocolate with *atole* and not water.' Cf. **color achocolatado, color amarillito, color inferior.**]

color cocho 'cooked color'
person with bronzed or dark brown skin color. *SA* (Diggs 1953:406) cl.
[Acc. Diggs, skin color classification. Acc. Aguirre Beltrán (1945:216), att. 17-cent. Mx. Cf. **cocho, color amarillito, color champurrado, membrillo cocho.**]

color de coche nuevo 'color of a new car'
1. person with very black skin color. *Pa* (Aguilera Patiño 1951:430) mid20.
2. mulatto. *Pa* (Kany 1960b:35) 20.
[Df. 1 facet., in ref. to shiny black color of early automobiles. Excl. to Pa. Cf. **color achocolatado, color de membrillo.**]

color de membrillo 'color of quince'
person with quince-colored, or light brown, skin. *SA* (Diggs 1953:406) cl.
[Acc. Diggs, skin color distinction. Cf. **color achocolatado, color de membrillo cocho, negro amembrillado.**]

color de membrillo cocho 'color of cooked quince'
slave whose skin color was dark brown like that of cooked quince. *Mx-Puebla* (Boyd-Bowman 1969:137) cl.
[Var. *color de membrillo cocido* in 15-cent. Spain, acc. Domínguez Ortiz (1952:371). Cf. **color achocolatado, color de membrillo, negro amembrillado.**]

color de membrillo cocido — See *color de membrillo cocho*

color de rapadura 'color of wood shavings'
person with light brown skin color. *SA* (Diggs 1953:406) cl.
[Cf. **color achocolatado.**]

color honesto 'honest color'
1. mulatto. *Pe* (Kany 1960b:35) 20.
2. person not considered white. *Pe* (Paz Soldán 1938:289) 19–20.
[Df. 1 euph., facet. Df. 2 euph. used to avoid ref. to skin color. Cf. **color achocolatado, de color, medio pelo.**]

color inferior 'inferior color'
person with some black ancestry. *Mx* (Roncal 1944:533) cl.
[Acc. Roncal, found in parish records; indicates low standing of anyone with black ancestry. Syns. *color quebrado, moreno, pardo.* Cf. **color achocolatado, color quebrado, moreno, pardo.**]

color le ofende 'his/her color holds him/her back'
person whose black ancestry prohibits movement to a higher social status. *Pa* (Nuñez 1980:135) 20.
[M., f. Cf. **tente en el aire.**]

color loro 'dark-colored'
person with dark skin color. *SA* (Diggs 1953:406) cl.
[Acc. Aguirre Beltrán (1945:216), att. 17-cent. Mx. Cf. **color achocolatado, loro.**]

color pardo 'brown-colored'
person with brown skin color. *SA* (Diggs 1953:406) cl.
[Cf. **color loro, pardo.**]

color quebrado 'broken color'
1. nonwhite person of low social class. *SA* (Diggs 1953:406) cl.
2. person with some black ancestry, acc. parish records. *Mx* (Roncal 1944:533) cl.
[Acc. Aguirre Beltrán (1945:216), att. 17-cent. Mx. Syns. *color inferior, pardo, moreno.* Cf. **color inferior, moreno, pardo.**]

color sepia — See *sepia*

color zambaigo — See *zambaigo*

colorado 'red, reddish'
1a. person with reddish skin color. *Co-Heliconia, -Remedios, -Yarumal* (Flórez 1969:121) 20.
1b. person with reddish or suntanned skin color. *Mx-Oaxaca* (Garza Cuarón 1987:64) late20.
2. person with red hair; redhead. *US-CO, -NM* (Cobos 1983:33) 20.
[Syn. df. 1b *chapeado.* Std. syn. df. 2 *pelirrojo.* Cf. **abejón**

colorado, chapeado, pelicandelo.]
colorete 'rouge'
person with reddish skin color. *Co-Sonsón* (Flórez 1969:121) 20.
[Cf. **chapeado, color achocolatado, colorín.**]
colorín 'reddish-blond'
person with blond or reddish hair and/or beard. *SA* (Bayo 1931:74); *Ch* (Malaret 1947:46; Cowles 1952:185; Morínigo 1966:144) 20.
[Acc. Gili y Gaya (1960:1.587), att. in Spain 1616 as 'red.' Cf. **color achocolatado, colorado, colorete.**]
comadre — See *compadre*
comadrita — See *compadrito*
comecamote 'root-eater'
Indian of a tribe by the same name. *US-NM* (Kany 1960b:35) 20.
[Cf. **comecrudos, comechingón, comepescados.**]
comechingón
1. Indian descendant of the tribe by the same name which once lived in the highlands south of Córdoba near San Luis. *Ar* (Cowles 1952:187) mid20.
2. Indian who once lived in caves. *Ar* (Alonso 1958:1.1138) 20.
3. Indian of a tribe by the same name. *Ar* (Kany 1960b:35) 20.
[Generally m. pl. Cf. **yaro.**]
comecrudos
Indian of a tribe by the same name. *US-NM* (Kany 1960b:35) 20.
[Generally m. pl. Cf. **comecamote, comechingón, comepescados.**]
comepescados 'fish-eater'
Indian of a tribe by the same name. *Mx* (Kany 1960b:35) 20.
[Generally m. pl. Cf. **comecamote, comechingón, comecrudos.**]
compadre 'godfather/father relationship; pal'
white worker, acc. Indian co-workers. *SA* (Ferguson 1963:119–20) 20.
[F. form *comadre.* Acc. Ferguson, also iron., in ref. to man and woman. Acc. Kany (1960b:38), var. in 20-cent. Ch *compale,* < Chinese pronunciation of *compadre.* Cf. **compadrito.**]
compadrito
1. black vendor in the marketplace. *Cu-Tierradentro* (Macías 1885:873) 19.
2. vain or conceited person of low class. *SA* (Malaret 1947:46) mid20.

[F. form *comadrita,* acc. Macías. < *compadre* + dim. suf. *-ito.* Acc. Malaret, syn. df. 2 *chulo.* Cf. **compadre.**]

compadrón

vain or conceited person of low class. *Ar Ur* (Malaret 1947:47) mid20.

[Cf. **compadrito.**]

compale — See *compadre*

concertado 'methodical'

servant. *CR* (Cowles 1952:189) mid20.

[Acc. Cobarruvias (1611:345–46), < *concertar* 'to be well arranged'; *hombre concertado* 'one who lives an orderly life.']

conche

1. Anglo-Saxon, generally an English-speaking North American. *Gu* (Kany 1960b:38) 20.

2. foreigner of Saxon race; white foreigner. *Gu* (Vergara Martín 1922:233) n.d.

[Excl. to Gu. Cf. **candelo, chele, concho, rubio, güero.**]

concho 'brown-colored; color of beer sediment'

Costa Rican peasant or rustic. *CR* (Salesiano 1938:52) mid20; (Kany 1960b:42) 20 ‖ *CR Ni* (Cowles 1952:190) mid20; (Alonso 1958:1.1164) 20.

[Acc. Kany, < nickname *Concho* < *Concepción,* name commonly used among peasants. Syns. *campirano, campiruso, campuso, chapetas, chayote, pato.*]

coñete 'mean, cruel'

stingy Spaniard. *Ch* (Alvarez 1980:p.c.) 20.

[< *coño* 'vagina' + suf. *-ete.* Acc. Alonso (1958:1.1213), att. as 'cheap, stingy' in both Ch and Pe. Cf. **coño.**]

congo 'black person'

1a. black person. *CR* (Salesiano 1938:53); *An SoA* (Kany 1960b:35); *Cu SA* (Santamaría 1942:1.388) 20.

1b. person with distinctive African features. *PR* (Zenón Cruz 1975:1.248) 20.

2. black African slave native to the Congo, who is known and desired for loyalty but not for hard work. *Cu* (Pichardo 1953:202) 19.

3. black African from the Congo, now Zaire. *SA* (Alcedo 1786–89:5.36) late18; (Alonso 1958:1.1176) 20.

[Df. 1 semi-euph., humor. Acc. Boyd-Bowman (1971:213), def, 2 in 16-cent. Cu. Acc. Alcedo, skin color jet black and shiny. Acc. Lipski (1985:24–25), abbr. for *negro congo* 'folkloric figure of Caribbean coast of Pa.' Acc. Megenney (1983:5, 10), today 'black person; any person from Africa'; synechdoche used in ref. to the geographical origin of many black slaves; sim. to No. Amer. Engl. use of *Guinea man* 'African' during slave trade period. Cf. **africano, angola, cocolo, guineo, negro, negro angolo, negro congo.**]

coño 'vagina'
Spaniard. *Ch* (Kany 1960b:36) 20.
[Acc. Kany, used in ref. to Spaniards known for their frequent use of this often-vulg. epithet. Acc. Armengol Valenzuela (1914:12.291), < *coñue* < *coñihue* 'place where Chilean colonization took place in the department of Villa Rica.' Syn. *godo.* Cf. **chapetón, coñete, español, gachupín, godo.**]

continental 'continental'
American; mainlander. *PR* (Gallo 1980:27) 20.
[Acc. Gallo, slang. Cf. **americucho.**]

contra 'contra'
anti-Sandinista and generally anti-communist Nicaraguan rebel-fighter. *SA US-FL-so.* (Rieff 1987:201–3) late20.
[M., f. Acc. Rieff, such troops have had bases in other countries, esp Ho, and CR. Also used in Amer. Engl. Used in opp. to *sandinista.* Cf. **gusano.**]

conuquero '*conuco* farmer'
slave who farmed for his own benefit or subsistence a *conuco* or small plot of the master's sugar plantation. *Cu* (Nuñez 1980:142) cl.
[< *conuco* 'small plot of land' + suf. *-ero.* Cf. **negro de conuco.**]

correcto 'correct'
white person, generally of high social class. *Mx* (Chance 1979:154) 20.
[Syn. *gente de razón.* Acc. Cobarruvias (1611:363) and Alonso (1958:1.1235), 'free of defects.' Cf. **gente de razón.**]

costanero — See *costeño*

costañero — See *costeño*

costarricense — See *tico*

costeño 'coastal; coastal dweller'
1a. person from the coastal areas. *Co* (Alario di Filippo 1964:380; Revollo 1942:79); *Pe* (Cowles 1952:201); *CR* (Salesiano 1938:54) 20.
1b. person from the coast, regardless of skin color or type, acc. the highland mestizo and the northern Ecuadorian from Esmeraldas. *Ec-n.w.* (Whitten 1965:90–91) 20.
2. person from the coast who probably has dark skin. *Ve* (Flórez 1969:123) 20.
3. person of mixed race from the Atlantic coastal region. *Co-Unguía, -Chocó* (Wade 1985:239) 20.

4. black person. *Co* (Solaún and Kronus 1973:43) 20.

5. Colombian of mixed Spanish, African, and Indian race, usually with dark complexion, from the coastal areas, acc. Colombians
in Chicago. *US-IL* (Gann and Duignan 1986:122) 20.

6. person, esp. one from the coastal areas, whose skin color is
either black, copperish-brown, or mulatto-like. *Mx-Oaxaca* (Garza
Cuarón 1987:64.

[< *costa* 'coast' + adj. suf. *-eño*. Df. 4 region. Df. 5 also used in Co.
Df. 6 covers *negro, moreno,* or *mulato.* Vars. *costanero, costañero,
costero, costino.* Cf. **cachuzo, colla, comechingón, moreno,
moreno, negro, serrano.**]

costero — See *costeño*

costino — See *costeño*

coya

Bolivian Indian. *Ar* (Segovia 1911:114) early20prior.

[M., f. Acc. Segovia, < Quechua *kkoya* 'queen, woman of the Inca.'
Var. *colla.* Cf. **colla.**]

coyota — See *coyote*

coyote 'coyote'

1a. *mestizo pardo* or *mestizo blanco* with yellowish-gray skin
color. *Mx* (Woodbridge 1948:357) cl.

1b. offspring of a white and an Indian; *mestizo blanco. Mx*
(Sobarzo 1966:84; Aguirre Beltrán 1972:171) cl; (Aguirre Beltrán
1945:217–18) 17.

1c. person of mixed race; *mestizo pardo. Mx* (Aguirre Beltrán
1972:171) cl; (Aguirre Beltrán 1945:217–18) 17.

2a. offspring of a mestizo and an Indian; 25% white, 75% Indian. *Mx* (León 1924:20–21, plate 9); Woodbridge 1948:355, 357;
Pérez de Barradas 1948:188) cl ‖ (O'Crouley 1972:19; Moreno Navarro 1973:142) 18.

2b. offspring of a mestizo and an Indian. *Mx* (Vergara Martín
1922:233) n.d.

2c. dihybrid, third-generation offspring of a mestizo and an Indian, i.e., 3 parts Indian and 1 part white. *Mx* (Moreno Navarro
1973:129–31; Solano 1975:85) 18.

3. offspring of an Indian and a mulatto. *Mx* (Roncal 1944:533)
cl.

4. offspring of an Indian and a black. *SA* (Gibson 1966:116) cl.

5a. offspring of a mulatto and a *barcino,* the latter of which is a
mulatto and an *albarazado. Mx* (Mörner 1967:58; Woodbridge
1948:357; Pérez de Barradas 1948:192; Monteforte Toledo
1959:171) cl.

5b. offspring of a mulatto and a *barcino*. *Mx* (Vergara Martín 1922:233) n.d.

6. offspring of a mestizo and a quadroon; 50% white, 37.5% Indian, 12.5% black. *Mx* (Pérez de Barradas 1948:185, 192; Woodbridge 1948:357) cl.

7. trihybrid, seventh-generation offspring of 29 parts black, 7 parts Indian, and 28 parts white. *Mx* (Moreno Navarro 1973:129–31; Solano 1975:84) 18.

8. white person, acc. Spanish-speaking Indians. *Mx* (Kany 1960b:38) 20.

9. mestizo. *Mx* (Love 1971:81) cl ‖ *US-NM* (Kany 1960b:38) 20.

10. *zambo*. *Pe* (Levine 1980:41) n.d.

11. Mexican Indian. *Mx* (Vergara Martín 1922:233) n.d.

12. offspring of European parentage; *criollo*. *Mx* (Santamaría 1942:1.411) mid20 ‖ *US-CO, -NM* (Cobos 1983:37) 20.

13a. offspring of an Anglo-American and an Indo-Hispanic. *US-CO, -NM* (Cobos 1983:37) 20 ‖ *US-NM* (Diehl 1986:p.c.) late20.

13b. offspring of an Anglo-Hispanic marriage. *US-NM* (Marden and Meyer 1978:258) 20.

14. person who works as a usurer or money exchanger. *Mx* (Alonso 1958:1.1257) 20.

15. youngest child of a family. *US-CO, -NM* (Cobos 1983:37) 20. [F. form *coyote* or *coyota*. Acc. Santamaría, Morínigo (1966:156), Alonso, Corominas (1973:177), and León, < Nahuatl *coyotl* 'coyote (animal).' Acc. Marden and Meyer, 'unpredictable' (like the coyote) in ref. to which parent the child will come to resemble. Acc. Alcedo (1786–89:5.38), ref. to things or products from cl. Mx. Df. 9 pejor. Df. 10 contemp. Df. 13a personal self-description, acc. Diehl. Acc. Roncal, used in baptismal records of cl. Mx. Present usage almost excl. to Mx and s.w. US. Cf. **albarazado, chino, cholo, mestizo, mestizo blanco, mestizo pardo, mulato.**]

coyote mestizo

1a. offspring of a *chamiso* and a mestizo; 36.3% white, 52.7% Indian, 11% black. *Mx* (León 1924:20–21, plate 10; Woodbridge 1948:357; Monteforte Toledo 1959:171) cl ‖ (Mörner 1967:58) 18.

1b. offspring of a *chamiso* and a mestizo. *Mx* (Vergara Martín 1922:233) n.d.

2. offspring of a mulatto and a *chamiso,* the latter of which is an Indian and a *coyote;* 36.3% white, 52.7% Indian, 11% black. *Mx* (Pérez de Barradas 1948:192) cl.

3. offspring of an Indian and a *coyote,* the latter of which is an Indian and a mestizo; 12.5% white, 87.5% Indian. *Mx* (Pérez de Barradas 1948:188) cl.

[Cf. **chamiso, coyote, mestizo, mulato.**]

coyotero — See *tonto*

crema 'cream'

person of the upper classes or social strata. *Co* (Alario di Filippo 1964:83) 20.

[F. Sim. to Fr. *crème de la crème,* also borrowed into Engl. Cf.
gente de razón, gente decente.]

criada 'servant'

dark-skinned, generally Indian, woman who served a Spaniard
as a slave and/or concubine. *Pe* (Harth-Terré 1965:133) cl.

[Cf. **moza.**]

criollazo — See *criollo*

criollito — See *criollo*

criollo 'creole; native'

1a. white or white Spaniard born in America; pure white person. *Mx* (Herrera and Cícero 1895:87; Aguirre Beltrán 1972:174;
Rosenblat 1954:2.18); *Pe* (Simmons 1955:108); *SA* (Johnson
1971:73; Rosenblat 1954:1.71; Malaret 1947:51; Morínigo
1966:158; Bayo 1931:80; Cowles 1952:206; Diggs 1953:407); *SA*
(Esteva Fabregat 1964:281; Barón Castro 1946:793; Bailey and
Nasatir 1973:768) cl ‖ *Mx* (Gibson 1966:130) 17–18 ‖ *SA* (Rout
1976:xiv) cl–19 ‖ *RP* (Fontanella de Weinberg 1982:45) 16–17 ‖
Cu (Pichardo 1953:216–17) 19 ‖ *Ar* (Segovia 1911:114) early20 ‖
Pe (Bourricaud 1975:353) cl–20.

1b. offspring of European parents, principally born in America
or other colonies. *SA* (Vergara Martín 1922:233) n.d.

2a. black or mulatto born in America. *SA* (Diggs 1953:407); *Mx*
(Boyd-Bowman 1969:143); *Co Mx Pa Pe Ve* (Velásquez 1962:114) cl
‖ *Cu* (Pichardo 1953:216–27) 19.

2b. black born in America, acc. blacks. *SA* (Vergara Martín
1922:233) n.d.

2c. Malaysian or mulatto born in America. *Pe-Lima* (Vergara
Martín 1922:233) n.d.

2d. offspring of persons who are mostly black; *zambo. Pe-Lima*
(Wallace 1984:64–65) 20.

2e. black person native to the country or area. *Ar* (Cara-Walker
1987:50) late19–early20.

3a. person born in America. *SA* (Morínigo 1966:158; Malaret
1947:211); *PR* (Malaret 1937:139) cl ‖ *SA* (Gibson 1966:130) cl–18
‖ *Ar* (Segovia 1911:114) early20 ‖ *Co-coast* (Revollo 1942:80)
mid20.

3b. white or black born in the New World. *SA* (Zenón Cruz

1975:1.251) 16.

3c. person born in America of foreign parents. *RP* (Granada 1957:1.172) mid20.

4. offspring of Spanish parents, or offspring of parents of slightly mixed race. *Ur-interior* (Vergara Martín 1922:233) n.d.

5. offspring of foreigners, or non-Americans, born in the RP region. *RP* (Granada 1957:1.172) 20.

6a. person native to the country where residing. *SA* (Boyd-Bowman 1984:799) 19; (Cowles 1952:206) 20.

6b. person native to Lima. *Pe-Lima* (Wallace 1984:64–65) 20.

6c. person native to PR, esp. one from the city of Caguas. *PR* (Gallo 1980:29) 20.

6d. white person from the highlands of PR; *jíbaro*. *PR* (Zenón Cruz 1975:1.249) 20.

6e. person native to the country and knowledgeable of the native customs; gaucho. *RP SoA* (Guarnieri 1979:60) 20.

7. member of elite society, even a mestizo, born in the New World. *SA* (Levine 1980:42) prior20.

8. white person who is descended from early Spanish colonizers or *conquistadores*. *Cu* (Gann and Duignan 1986:97) mid20.

9. Hispanic from St. Bernard Parish, LA. *US-LA-St. Bernard Parish* (MacCurdy 1950:50) mid20

[Syn. df. 1a *español americano*. Controversy surrounds to whom term first refers. Acc. Mellafe (1975:116), ref. to people of completely European appearance born in the Amer. colonies. Acc. Boyd-Bowman (1983:714), 'native to the land' in the early 17 cent. Acc. Bailey and Nasatir, never used in ref. to racial mixture in cl. times. Acc. Corominas (1954–57:1.943–54 and 1973:178), Sp.< Ptg. *crioulo* < *cria* + dim. suf. *-oulo* or *-elo*. Acc. Solaún and Kronus (1973:166), used as skin color term in Cartagena, Co. Acc. Segovia, df. 3a incorrect. Acc. Boyd-Bowman, df. 6a possibly derog. Acc. Gallo, in ref. to df. 6c, also 'member of the Caguas basefall team,' i.e., the Caguas Criollos. Acc. MacCurdy, ants. df. 9 *americano, isleño*. Acc. Bourricaud (1975:384), used as skin color term in the shanty towns of Lima. Acc. Tascón (1961:130), 'coward' in Cauca, Co. See also Corominas and Pascual (1980, vol. 2). For an explanation of this term in other languages, see Chaudenson (1974), OED (1971), AHD (1976), Imbs (1978), Zaccaria (1927), Stephens (1983), and Goodman (1964). Syns. *jíbaro, hijo de la tierra, blanco de la tierra, zambo*. Derivs. *acriollado, criollazo, criollito*. Cf. **americano, bozal, chino, coyote, criollo mestizo, criollo moreno, criollo rellollo, gachupín, gallego, gaucho, godo, hijo de la tierra, isleño, jíbaro, mestizo, mulato, polaco, zambo,** Ptg. **crioulo.**]

criollo de Curazao 'Curaçao creole'
free mulatto born on the island of Curaçao who settled in the
Spanish-speaking An and who had characteristic speech patterns,
costume, songs, and dances. *An* (Nuñez 1980:149) early19.
[Acc. Nuñez, syn. *mulato holandés.* Cf. **criollo, mulato holandés,
negro criollo.**]
criollo mestizo
1. person born in America of mixed parentage. *SA* (Gibson
1966:80–81, plate 16) cl.
2. offspring of a white and a mestizo. *Pe* (Santamaría
1942:1.413) 20.
[Cf. **blanco, criollo, mestizo.**]
criollo moreno
black person born in America, esp. one whose parents are
bozales. SA (Rout 1976:xv) cl; (Levine 1980:42) prior20.
[Cf. **bozal, criollo, moreno.**]
criollo rellollo
offspring of parents who were born in the country. *Cu* (Macías
1885:387) 19.
[Acc. Macías, used in the playful phrase *soy criollo, rellollo y
tatararellollo,* sim. in sense to the Amer. Engl. phrase "my
ancestors came over on the Mayflower." Cf. **criollo, coyote,
rellollo.**]
cristal 'crystal'
white North American or Anglo-Saxon. *US-TX* (Kany 1960b:38)
20.
[Acc. Kany, syn. *cristalino.* Cf. **bolillo, gabacho, yanqui.**]
cristalino — See *cristal*
cristiano 'Christian; human being'
1. civilized person; non-Indian. *SA* (Bayo 1910:65 and
1931:80–81); *Ur* (Cowles 1952:206); *Ar Pg* (Morínigo 1966:158) 20.
2. rational person. *Mx* (Aguirre Beltrán 1972:155) cl.
[Acc. Castro (1973:30), 'person who took sides against the Moors' in
medieval Spain. Acc. Alonso (1958:1.1272), *cristiano viejo* 'person
not of Moorish or Jewish ancestry.' Acc. Boyd-Bowman (1971:239),
'Spaniard' throughout cl. SA. Cf. Ptg. **cristão.**]
cruzado 'mixed, crossed'
offspring of a white and an Indian. *Co-Zarzal* (Sayres 1956:223,
225) 20.
[Acc. Sayres, 4th highest social class in Zarzal, Co; sim. to mestizo,
indicates racial and cultural mixing or acculturation toward white
society and customs. < *cruzar* 'to mix.' Cf. **aladinado, criollo,
ladino, mestizo, mulato, zambo,** Ptg. **cruza, misturado.**]

cuarterón 'quadroon'

1. quadroon, acc. parish records and other documents. *Mx* (Roncal 1944:533); *Pe* (Romero 1944:375) cl.

2a. offspring of a white and a *tercerón;* 87.5% white, 12.5% black. *Co Mx* (León 1924:20–21, plate 11; Woodbridge 1948:357) cl.

2b. offspring of a white and a *tercerón. SoA* (Grenón 1930:281) mid18 ‖ *DR* (Domínguez 1973:108) late18.

3a. offspring of a white and a mulatto; 75% white, 25% black. *Cu* (Woodbridge 1948:357) cl ‖ *Cu* (Pichardo 1953:220) 19 ‖ *PR* (Alvarez Nazario 1974:354, 380; Malaret 1937:140); *An Cu SoA* (Cowles 1952:210); *An SoA* (Morínigo 1966:160) 20.

3b. offspring of a white and a mulatto. *SA* (Vergara Martín 1922:233) n.d. ‖ *SoA* (Grenón 1930:281) mid18 ‖ *PR* (Zenón Cruz 1975:1.251) cl–20 ‖ *Cu* (Macías 1885:392) 19prior ‖ *An SoA* (Malaret 1931:160) mid20 ‖ *RP SoA* (Guarnieri 1979:61) 20.

4a. offspring of a white and a mestizo; 75% white, 25% Indian. *SA* (Santamaría 1942:1.419; Woodbridge 1948:357) cl ‖ *Mx* (Sundheim 1922:145) early20 ‖ *An SA* (Morínigo 1966:160) 20.

4b. offspring of a white and a mestizo. *SA* (Vergara Martín 1922:233) n.d. ‖ *Cu* (Macías 1885:392) 19prior ‖ *An SoA* (Malaret 1931:160) mid20 ‖ *SA* exc. *Pe* (Malaret 1942:353) mid20.

5. offspring of a mulatto and a mestizo; 50% white, 25% Indian, 25% black. *Mx* (Pérez de Barradas 1948:185, 192; Woodbridge 1948:357; Mörner 1967:110) cl.

6. mulatto with good, i.e., not kinky, hair. *Cu* (Macías 1885:392) 19prior.

[Acc. Tuttle (1976:611), Sp. *cuarterón* > Engl. *quadroon* and provided model for *octoroon.* Syn. *pardo* in 18-cent. Potosí, Mx, acc. Boyd-Bowman (1982:821). Syn. *cuatratuo.* Vars. *cuartón, quarterón.* Cf. **cuarterón cuatralbo, mestizo, mulato, ochavón.**]

cuarterón cuatralbo

offspring of a white and a mulatto; 75% white, 25% black. *Mx* (Pérez de Barradas 1948:189) cl.

[Acc. Corominas (1954–57:1.958), *cuatralbo* 'animal which has four white paws or feet' in 18 cent. Var. *cuarterón cuatraluo.* Cf. **cuarterón, cuatralbo, tercerón, ochavón.**]

cuarterón cuatraluo — See ***cuarterón cuatralbo***

cuarterón de chino

1. quadroon of mixed parentage, acc. parish records. *Mx* (Roncal 1944:533) cl.

2a. offspring of a white and a *chino,* the latter of which is a black and a lobo; 50% white, 12.5% Indian, 37.5% black. *Mx* (Pérez de Barradas 1948:192) cl.

2b. offspring of a white and a *chino;* 56.25% white, 6.25% Indian, 37.5% black. *Mx* (Woodbridge 1948:357; León 1924:20–21, plate 12; Santamaría 1942:1.419) cl.

2c. offspring of a white and a *chino,* the latter of which is the offspring of a *saltatrás* and an Indian; 62.5% white, 25% Indian, 12.5% black. *Pe* (Pérez de Barradas 1948:186, 192) cl ‖ (Mörner 1967:59) 18.

2d. offspring of a white and a *chino. SA* (Vergara Martín 1922:233) n.d.

[Cf. **chino, cuarterón de mestizo, cuarterón de mulato.**]

cuarterón de mestizo

1. quadroon of mixed parentage, acc. parish records. *Mx* (Roncal 1944:533) cl.

2. offspring of a white and a *castizo,* the latter of which is of a mestizo and a white; 87.5% white, 12.5% Indian. *Mx* (Pérez de Barradas 1948:188) cl.

3a. offspring of a white and a mestizo; 75% white, 25% Indian. *Mx* (Woodbridge 1948:357; León 1924:20–21, plate 13); *Pe* (Pérez de Barradas 1948:185, 186, 188) cl ‖ *SA* (Santamaría 1942:1.419) cl ‖ *SA* (Mörner 1967:58) 18.

3b. offspring of a white and a mestizo. *SA* (Vergara Martín 1922:233) n.d.

[Syns. *español, castizo, cuatralbo.* Cf. **cuarterón de chino, cuarterón de mulato, cuarterón de saltatrás, mestizo.**]

cuarterón de mulato

1. quadroon of mixed parentage, acc. parish records. *Mx* (Roncal 1944:533) cl.

2. offspring of a *cambujo* and a *chino. Mx* (Woodbridge 1948:357) cl.

3a. offspring of a white and a mulatto; 75% white, 25% black. *Mx* (León 1924:20–21, plate 14; Woodbridge 1948:357; Santamaría 1942:1.419); *Pe* (Pérez de Barradas 1948:186, 189) cl ‖ *Pe* (Mörner 1967:58) 18.

3b. offspring of a white and a mulatto. *SA* (Vergara Martín 1922:233) n.d.

[Cf. **cuarterón de chino, cuarterón de mestizo, cuarterón de saltatrás, mulato.**]

cuarterón de saltatrás

1. quadroon of mixed parentage, acc. parish records. *Mx* (Roncal 1944:533) cl.

2. offspring of a *tercerón* and a black. *Mx* (Woodbridge 1948:357; Santamaría 1942:1.419) cl ‖ *SA* (Vergara Martín 1922:233) n.d.

[Acc. Vergara Martín, var. *cuarterón salta atrás.* Cf. **cuarterón de chino, cuarterón de mestizo, cuarterón de mulato, saltatrás, tercerón.**]

cuarterón salta atrás — See *cuarterón de saltatrás*

cuarterón y grifo

person of mixed race who has some black ancestry. *An* (Nuñez 1980:151) prior20.

[Cf. **cuarterón, grifo.**]

cuartón — See *cuarterón*

cuasi limpio de origen 'almost clean by origin'

offspring of a white and a *gente blanca,* the latter of which is a white and a *requinterón de mulato;* 98.44% white, 1.56% black. *Pe* (Pérez de Barradas 1948:190) cl.

[Cf. **gente blanca, limpio de origen, quasi limpio en su origen, requinterón de mulato.**]

cuatralbo 'having four white feet'

offspring of a white Spaniard and a mestizo; 75% white, 25% Indian. *SA* (Pérez de Barradas 1948:189) cl.

[Acc. Santamaría (1942:1.421) and Vergara Martín (1922:233), syn. *cuarterón de mestizo.* Cf. **cuarterón de chino, cuarterón de mestizo, cuatratuo.**]

cuatratuo

offspring of a mestizo and a white person or Spaniard; quadroon born in America. *SA* (Alonso 1958:1.1288) cl.

[Acc. Vergara Martín (1922:233), syn. *cuarterón.* Var. *cuatratúo.* Cf. **cuarterón, cuarterón cuatralbo.**]

cuatratúo — See *cuatratuo*

cubiche

Cuban. *An* (Kany 1960b:40; Morínigo 1966:161); *CR* (Villegas 1952:35); *Mx* (Velasco Valdés 1957:31) 20.

[Humor. Cf. **jíbaro.**]

cucarrón

person whose skin color indicates racial mixture. *Co-Rionegro* (Flórez 1969:121) 20.

[Acc. Santamaría (1942:1.424), 'type of orchid or animal.']

cuentayo

Indian in charge of the hacienda's livestock. *Ec* (Cowles 1952:215) mid20.

[Cf. **cuico, indio.**]

cuico 'thin; foreigner'

1. dwarfish, emaciated Indian; dwarf Indian. *SA* (Bayo 1910:66) and 1931:83) early20 ‖ *Bo* (Malaret 1942:363) mid20; (Alonso 1958:1.1301) 20.

2. Indian or mestizo. *Ar* (Garzón 1910:136); *Ch Pe RP* (Kany 1960b:39) 20.

3. Bolivian, esp. during the war of 1879. *Ch* (Bayo 1910:66); *Ch Pe* (Cowles 1952:217); *SA* (Simmons 1955:109) 19–20 ‖ *Ch* (Rodríguez 1875:134) 19; (Armengol Valenzuela 1915:13.131) early20 ‖ (Vergara Martín 1922:234) n.d. ‖ *Pe* (Malaret 1942:363) mid20 ‖ *Ch Pe RP* (Kany 1960b:39) 20.

4a. Mexican of the lower classes. *Cu* (Pichardo 1953:225) 19.

4b. Mexican. *Cu* (Rodríguez 1875:134) 19; (Kany 1960b:40) 20.

4c. Mexican peasant who immigrated to Cu. *Cu* (Vergara Martín 1922:234) prior20

5. offspring of an Indian and a white; *indio mestizo*. *Bo Pe* (Vergara Martín 1922:234) n.d.; (Santamaría 1942:1.432) 20 ‖ *Bo* (Malaret 1942:363) mid20.

6. offspring of a Quechua Indian and a white European. *Ur* (Alonso 1958:1.1301) 20.

7a. Bolivian Indian. *Ch Pe* (Alonso 1958:1.1301) 20; (Malaret 1942:363) mid20.

7b. Quechua Indian. *Ur* (Alonso 1958:1.1301) 20.

7c. Colla (or Coya) Indian of Ur. *RP SoA* (Guarnieri 1979:62) prior20.

8. person native to other regions. *Ar Ch* (Malaret 1931:165) mid20.

9. any nonwhite, esp. Indian, rival, acc. whites. *RP SoA* (Guarnieri 1979:62) prior20.

[Df. 4a joc. Df. 4c injur. Acc. Cowles, 'rural policeman or rural police force' in 20 cent. Mx. Acc. Armengol Valenzuela, < Quechua *kuyca* or Aymara *ccoica* 'earthworm,' sim. to Araucanian *cùyco* 'transparent, diaphanous.' Cf. **colla, indio, mestizo.**]

cullaca

Aymara Indian woman. *Bo* (Cowles 1952:220) mid20.

[F. Cf. **camba, colla, coya.**]

curiche 'black; black person'

dark-skinned black person. *Ch* (Armengol Valenzuela 1915:13.148) early20; (Cowles 1952:223; Alonso 1958:1.1313) mid20.

[Acc. Cowles, < Mapuche *curi* 'black' + *che* 'people.' Acc. Santamaría (1942:1.443), < Arawak *curi* 'black' + human suf. *-che.* Acc. Armengol Valenzuela, < Araucanian *curi-* or *curu-* 'black' + *che* 'man.' Cf.

negro.]
curro 'smart; free-spirited'
1. free or freed slave of the former Havana suburb called Barrio del Manglar. *Cu* (Cowles 1952:224) cl–19.
2. Andalusian Spaniard; person born in Andalusia, Spain. *Mx Cu* (Santamaría 1942:1.444) mid20 ‖ *Cu* (Vergara Martín 1922:234) n.d.
[Df. 1 ext. of df. 2 because Cuban blacks seemed to pronounce Sp. like *curros,* or Andalusians. Cf. **curro del Manglar.**]

curro del Manglar
black person born in the area of Havana, Cu, identified by certain actions and turns of phrase. *Cu* (Macías 1885:815) 19.
[Syns. *negro curro, negro del Manglar. Manglar* 'former community of Havana.' Cf. **curro.**]

curunco
blond; blond-haired person. *Gu Sa* (Morínigo 1966:166) 20.
[Acc. Kany (1960b:48), < *curunco* 'type of red ant.' Cf. **chele, güero, rubio.**]

cusco
black person or mulatto. *Co-Betania* (Flórez 1969:121); *Ec* (Kany 1960b:35) 20.
[Acc. Santamaría (1942:1.445), perhaps < *sijú cuco* 'type of bird' in Co. Acc. Kany, < Quechua *cuscu* 'black corn.' Cf. **curiche, negro.**]

cuyano 'native of Cuyo'
Argentine. *Ch* (Yrarrázaval 1945:154); *Ar Ch* (Cowles 1952:227) mid20.
[< *Cuyo,* ext. from original meaning; former province now formed from provinces of Mendoza, San Juan, and San Luis, acc. Kany (1960b:39).]

cuyuco
black bodyguard. *Pe* (Morínigo 1966:167) 20.
[Perhaps of Amerindian origins.]

D

de clase — See *ser de clase*
de color 'of color; colored'
1. person who does not have white skin color; nonwhite; colored person; person of color. *Pe* (Paz Soldán 1938:289) early–mid20 ‖ *DR* (Domínguez 1973:109) late18.
2. black person. *SA* (Malaret 1931:143) mid20 ‖ *PR* (Zenón Cruz 1975:1.250–51) cl–20.

3. mulatto. *SA* (Malaret 1931:143) mid20.
[Euph. Usually in phrs. *ser de color, gente de color, persona de color.* Cf. **color honesto, color achocolatado, de color medio, de medio pelo, gente de color, mulato, persona de color, ser de clase,** Ptg. **gente de cor, pessoa de cor.**]

de color medio 'of medium color'
person who is not white. *DR* (Hoetink 1973:23–24) late18.
[Usually in phrs. *ser de color medio* or *persona de color medio.* Cf. **color honesto, de color,** Ptg. **médio.**]

de la clase 'of the class'
black person. *SA* (Kany 1960b:35) 20.
[Euph. Possibly < *(persona) de la clase (negra)* or *(persona) de la clase (baja).* Usually in phr. *ser de la clase.* Cf. **de color, de medio pelo.**]

de medio pelo 'of medium hair'
1. person who is not of the upper classes; dark-skinned person; person with little or no education. *Mx* (Santamaría 1942:2.439–40) mid20.
2. person of color; person of mixed race; nonwhite person. *PR* (Santamaría 1942:2.439–40) mid20.
3. person with some black ancestry. *Pe* (Kany 1960b:36) 20.
[Acc. Kany, def. 3 facet. Ref. to hair reminiscent of the texture or color of a black person's hair. Cf. **de color, medio pelo, pelo malo,** Ptg. **ser ruim de cabelo.**]

de nación — See *nación, natural*
de nación Angola — See *angola*
de nariz chata — See *chato, ñato*
de orozuz — See *muñeco de orozuz*
de sangre azul 'blue-blooded'
person of the upper class, of a Christian background, or of the nobility; white Spaniard; descendant of whites. *SA* (Castillo 1974:146) cl–20.
[Often in phr. *persona de sangre azul, ser de sangre azul,* or *hombre de sangre azul.* Cf. **castizo, de color, de medio pelo, gente de razón, gente decente,** Ptg. **cristão.**]

de tierra — See *natural*
decente 'decent; of good quality'
1. person of the bourgeoisie or high society. *Pe* (Kany 1960b:39) 20.
2. person of white race, generally of the upper classes. *Pe* (Kany 1960b:39) 20.

[Acc. Kany, def. 2 ext. of def. 1.; excludes any Indian, *cholo,* or *zambo.* Cf. **gente de razón, gente decente.**]

del color 'of color; colored'

1. white person, acc. some lower-class people. *Co-Cartagena* (Solaún and Kronus 1973:166, 167) 20.

2. nonwhite person, acc. educated or upper-class people. *Co-Cartagena* (Solaún and Kronus 1973:166, 167) 20.

[Derog. Cf. **de color, de medio pelo.**]

del color pero castaño 'colored but with chestnut hair'

person with chestnut hair and/or brown skin. *Co-Cartagena* (Solaún and Kronus 1973:166) 20.

[Cf. **de color, de medio pelo, del color,** Ptg. **acastanhado.**]

del país 'of the country'

native of PR; native to the country. *PR* (Gallo 1980:81) 20.

[Acc. Gallo, slang. Possibly pejor. Often in phr. *ser del país.* Cf. **criollo, del patio.**]

del patio 'from the patio'

resident of the area; native to PR. *PR* (Gallo 1980:81) 20.

[Acc. Gallo, slang. Possibly pejor. Often in phr. *ser del patio.* Cf. **criollo, del país.**]

desaguado 'drained'

person with light or pallid skin color. *Co-Potosí* (Flórez 1969:121) 20.

[Acc. Boyd-Bowman (1971:292), past partic. of *desaguar* 'to drain,' used in Co from 1547.]

diablito 'little devil'

ridiculously dressed black person who does pirouettes in the streets during certain holidays. *Cu* (Morínigo 1966:221) 20.

[< *diablo* 'devil' + dim. suf. *-ito.* Cf. **negro.**]

dinga y mandinga

white person who may also have black and/or Indian ancestry. *PR* (Zenón Cruz 1975:1.255) 20.

[M., f. Acc. Zenón Cruz, insult given in response to a white who has insulted a black, thus accusing the white of also having nonwhite ancestors. Sim. to Amer. Engl. phr. *darkie* or *nigger in the woodpile.* Cf. **mandinga.**]

doña 'lady'

Indian woman. *Ec* (Cowles 1952:306) mid20.

[Form of direct address. Acc. Boyd-Bowman (1971:326), 'doña Juana, (india)' att. in mid-16 cent. Mx. Cf. **cullaca, indio,** Ptg. **sinhá.**]

E

ébano humano 'human ebony'
    black slave; shipment of black slaves. *Ar* (Segovia 1911:55) prior20.
    [Cf. **aliento vivo, ébano vivo, esclavo, negro.**]
ébano vivo 'live ebony'
    black African slave, ạcc. slavers. *SA* (Alvarez Nazario 1974:336; DRAE 500) cl.
    [Cf. **aliento vivo, cargamento de ébano, ébano humano, pieza de ébano, pieza de indias, pieza de registro.**]
elemento 'element'
    1. person of little depth or importance. *Ch DR Pe PR* (Malaret 1947:80; Morínigo 1966:228) 20.
    2. people in general. *Cu* (Cowles 1952:310) mid20.
    [M. Acc. Cowles, also *elemento feminino* 'women.' Cf. **catedrático, diablito,** Ptg. **negrada.**]
emancipado 'emancipated, freed'
    black African slave, freed by British and released in Cu, only to be re-enslaved there. *Cu* (Rout 1976:xv) 19; (Levine 1980:48) cl.
    [Acc. Corominas (1973:226), first att. 1604. Cf. **horro, liberto, libre.**]
embocaba
    white Spaniard, acc. Caribe Indians. *SA* (Vergara Martín 1922:235) n.d., probably early cl.
    [Generally m. Acc. Vergara Martín, ref. to Spaniards because they had hairy calves like a parrot's feet.]
empingorotado 'stuck-up, snobbish'
    person of high social class or category. *Co-Bogotá* (Acuña 1951:64) mid20.
    [Cf. **decente, ser de clase.**]
endizuelo 'little Indian'
    small Indian; Indian child. *Ec* (Cowles 1952:318) mid20.
    [Acc. Cowles, generally derog.; syns. *indizuelo, indiecillo.* Cf. **indizuelo.**]
enrazado 'half-breed'
    mestizo. *Co* (Alario di Filippo 1964:128; Morínigo 1966:244) 20.
    [Acc. Alonso (1958:2.1734), used in Andalusia, Spain, as 'animal of known or pure race'; < *enrazar* 'to mix; to get mixed up.' Cf. **mestizo, mezcla,** Ptg. **misturado.**]
equipación 'baggage'
    black slave being transported to America, acc. slavers. *PR* (Alvarez Nazario 1974:380) cl.

[F. Cf. **aliento vivo, ébano vivo, pieza de ébano, pieza de registro.**]

esclava mulata de color de pera cocha 'mulatto slave woman whose skin color was that of cooked pears'
> mulatto slave woman. *SA* (Torre Revollo 1927:270) early16.
> [Acc. Torre Revollo, cited in a Real Cédula; desc. Cf. **esclavo.**]

esclavo 'slave'
> Sinca Indian of southeastern Gu. *Gu-s.e.* (Vergara Martín 1922:235; Santamaría 1942:1.617) prior20.
> [Acc. Boyd-Bowman (1971:367), first att. as 'slave' in Mx 1516. Acc. Espina Pérez (1972:75), used in ref. to blacks, Indians, and North Africans in SA and Br. Cf. **africano, ébano vivo, esclavo berberisco, esclavo blanco, negro, pieza de registro.**]

esclavo berberisco 'Berber slave'
> non-Christian slave. *DR* (Hoetink 1973:58) early16.
> [Originally used in ref. to Berbers, the nomadic, Caucasoid tribes of North Africa absorbed by the Arabs on their march we. toward Iberia. Syn. *esclavo de casta de moros.* Cf. **berberisco, esclavo blanco.**]

esclavo blanco 'white slave'
> 1. white Arabic or Berber slave from North Africa, generally a Moslem. *Mx* (Aguirre Beltrán 1972:156) cl.
> 2. Moroccan, Moorish, Berber, or Jewish slave taken in Zafi as a result of battles against Islam. *Mx SA* (Aguirre Beltrán 1972:104) cl.
> [Syn. def. 1 *morisco.* Acc. Pike (1967:344), used for 'Moorish or morisco slave' in 16 cent. Spain, esp. those captured as prisoners of war in campaigns by the Christians in North Africa. Those that came from southern Spain, mostly Granada, were the so-called *moriscos,* persons of Moorish descent left in Spain after 1492, who had not converted to Christianity from Islam. Free *moriscos* did live in Seville in the early 16 cent. Cf. **blanco, esclavo berberisco, esclavo de buena guerra.**]

esclavo coartado
> black slave who could by law purchase his/her freedom for a pre-set price. *Cu SA* (Nuñez 1980:180) cl.
> [Cf. **coartado, esclavo, esclavo entero, esclavo jornalero.**]

esclavo de buena guerra 'slave taken during a war'
> Indian slave taken during an insurrection or war. *Mx-Jalisco* (Boyd-Bowman 1969:136) mid16.
> [Excl. to Mx. Cf. **esclavo, esclavo berberisco, esclavo de casta de moros.**]

esclavo de casta de moros 'Moorish slave'
> non-Christian slave. *DR* (Hoetink 1973:58) early16.

[Syn. *esclavo berberisco.* Cf. **esclavo berberisco, esclavo de buena guerra.**]

esclavo de la India de Portugal 'slave from the Indian Ocean area'

slave introduced into Mx from the Indian Ocean area, generally Mozambique, Java, and the Spice Islands. *Mx* (Aguirre Beltrán 1972:143) cl.

[Early Ptg. sailors and traders, the first known Europeans in the East Indies, were thought to have brought these slaves to the New World. Cf. **esclavo berberisco, esclavo de levante.**]

esclavo de levante 'slave from the Middle East'

slave taken from Asia Minor or the Middle East. *Mx* (Aguirre Beltrán 1972:106) cl.

[Also used in Spain. Cf. **esclavo berberisco, esclavo de casta de moros, esclavo judío.**]

esclavo entero 'complete slave'

black slave who could not change masters without his/her own master's consent. *SA* (Nuñez 1980:180–81) cl.

[Acc. Nuñez, opp. to *esclavo coartado.* Cf. **esclavo, esclavo coartado.**]

esclavo jornalero 'day-laborer slave'

black slave who worked for wages in the town or another plantation as per the master's desires. *SA* (Nuñez 1980:181) cl.

[Cf. **esclavo, esclavo coartado, jornalero.**]

esclavo judío 'Jewish slave'

non-Christian, esp. Jewish, slave. *DR* (Hoetink 1973:58) early16.

[Syn. *esclavo berberisco,* i.e., considered the same as a slave of Islamic religion. Cf. **esclavo berberisco, esclavo de casta de moros, esclavo de la India de Portugal, esclavo de levante, judío.**]

esclavo ladino

person who has been a slave for more than 1 year. *Cu* (Macías 1885:755) 19.

[Cf. **esclavo, ladino.**]

escolorido 'discolored'

person whose skin color is pallid, white, or washed out. *Co-Quetame, -San Faustino* (Flórez 1969:121) 20.

[Probably phonetic mutation of term *descolorido* 'discolored, washed out, pallid, white.' Cf. **cara pálida.**]

espalda mojada 'wet back'

illegal Mexican immigrant. *US-s.w.* (Galván and Teschner 1985:52) 20.

[M., f. Very derog., perhaps < Amer. Engl. *wetback*. Cf. **chicano.**]

españo-americano
Spaniard or person of Spanish descent living in US. *US-CA* (Blanco 1971:201–2) cl.

[Cf. **español.**]

español 'Spanish, Spaniard'
1a. white person. *Mx* (Love 1971:81) cl.

1b. white person, but not necessarily someone who was of pure white race. *Mx* (Love 1971:82) cl.

1c. white person, acc. baptismal records and censuses. *Mx* (Roncal 1944:533) cl ‖ *Ar* (Bayo 1910:91 and 1931:114) early–mid20.

1d. any person, even a mestizo, considered white. *Mx* (Chance 1979:164) early19.

1e. white person, usually used to denote a person who is the skin color of a white Spaniard. *Mx* (Crépeau 1973:27); *CR* (Cowles 1952:160); *Ve* (Flórez 1969:123) 20.

1f. white person, generally of Spanish descent, born in America; creole. *Mx-Oaxaca* (Chance and Taylor 1977:460) 18 ‖ *Pg* (Hollanda 1956:74–75) cl ‖ *SA* (Vergara Martín 1922: 236) n.d.

1g. white person born in Spain or America. *RP* (Fontanella de Weinberg 1982:44) 16–17.

1h. offspring of pure white Spaniards. *Ec-Quito* (Vergara Martín 1922:236) n.d.

2a. offspring of a white and a *castizo;* 87.5% white, 12.5% Indian. *Mx* (León 1924:20–21, plate 18; Pérez de Barradas 1948:188) cl; (O'Crouley 1972:19; Moreno Navarro 1973:139–40) 18.

2b. dihybrid, fourth-generation offspring of 7 parts white and 1 part Indian; offspring of a white and a *castizo*. *Mx* (Moreno Navarro 1973:129–31; Solano 1975:85) 18.

2c. offspring of a white and a *castizo*. *Mx* (Woodbridge 1948:357; Monteforte Toledo 1959:171; Pérez de Barradas 1948: 188) cl.

3. offspring of a white and a *quinterón de mestizo;* 93.75% white, 6.25% Indian. *Mx* (Woodbridge 1948:357; Pérez de Barradas 1948:186) cl.

4. dihybrid, fifth-generation offspring of 15 parts white and 1 part Indian; offspring of a white and an *español*. *Mx* (Moreno Navarro 1973:129–31; Solano 1975:85); *SoA* (Moreno Navarro 1973:139–40) 18.

5. dihybrid, sixth-generation offspring of 31 parts white and 1 part black; offspring of a white and a *tornatrás*. *Mx* (Moreno Navarro 1973:129–31; Solano 1975:85) 18.

6. offspring of a *quinterón de mulato* and a *requinterón de mulato*. *Mx* (Woodbridge 1948:357) cl.

7. Venezuelan or foreigner, usually white, acc. Guarano Indians of the Paraguaná Peninsula. *Ve* (Vergara Martín 1922:236) n.d.

[Acc. Boyd-Bowman (1971:373), att. as 'white person' in early 16 cent. Mx. Acc. Moreno Navarro (1973:139–40), syn. *puchuel* in 17 cent. Mx. Other syns. *blanco, requinterón de mestizo, castellano, puro español.* Var. *españolo.* Cf. **blanco, castellano, chapetón, español americano, gachupín, requinterón de mestizo.**]

español americano 'American Spaniard'

white person of European parents born in America. *SA* (Rosenblat 1954:1.38, 71); *Mx* (Aguirre Beltrán 1972:174) cl.

[Acc. Rosenblat, self-ref.; syns. *criollo, americano;* these people gave up their identification with Spain to take up the fight for independence from Sp. cl. rule. Ant. *español europeo.* Cf. **españoamericano, español criollo, español europeo.**]

español criollo 'creole Spaniard'

white European born in America, who occupied the second rung of the social ladder after the *español europeo. SA* (Pérez de Barradas 1948:174) cl–late19.

[Cf. **criollo, español americano, español europeo.**]

español europeo 'European Spaniard'

1. white Spaniard born in Spain, i.e., a person who possessed all the rights of a person born in Spain but living in America. *Mx* (Aguirre Beltrán 1972:174) cl ‖ *Mx-Oaxaca* (Chance and Taylor 1977:460) 18.

2. white or Spaniard. *SA* (Rosenblat 1954:1.71) cl.

[Df. 1 derog. Cf. **español americano.**]

españolo

1. peninsular Spaniard, acc. parish records. *Mx* (Roncal 1944:533) cl.

2. offspring of a white and a *castizo;* 87.5% white, 12.5% Indian. *Mx* (León 1924:20–21, plate 18) cl.

[Syn. df. 2 *español.* Cf. **castellano, español.**]

estadounidense — See *americano*

estibador 'stevadore'

black man who worked in the sugar cane warehouses on the wharves of western Cu. *Cu* (Pichardo 1953:291) 19.

[Acc. Pichardo, *estivador* [sic]. M. Excl. to black slaves.]

estivador — See *estibador*

euromestizo

1. native-born person who is the offspring of a European white

and either an Indian or a black African. *Mx* (Aguirre Beltrán 1972:222) cl.

2. native-born American whose phenotype was predominantly white even after racial mixture. *Mx* (Aguirre Beltrán 1972:246) cl.

3. offspring of a white European and either a creole or a white mestizo. *SA* (Urbanski 1978:155) n.d.

[Anthro.; 20 cent. term used to characterize cl. person. Acc. Urbanski, term invented by Chilean scholar Rolando Mellafe. Ant. *afromestizo.* Cf. **español americano, español europeo, mestizo.**]

europeo 'European'

white person, usually of European descent. *PR US* (Gann and Duignan 1986:80) 20.

[Acc. Gann and Duignan, color classification in PR. Cf. **gente de color, moreno, trigueño.**]

európido

white person. *SA* (Esteva Fabregat 1964:280) 20.

[Acc. Esteva Fabregat, anthro.; common to SA and Br. Syn. *blanco.* Cf. **blanco.**]

F

fardo 'bundle; bundle of rags'

black slave, acc. slavers. *PR SA* (Alvarez Nazario 1974:336, 380) cl.

[Acc. Cobarruvias (1611:585), att. as 'bag or sack in which something is poured that turns black, such as wool bound from Spain to Italy.' Cf. **aliento vivo, ébano vivo, equipación, pieza de ébano, pieza de registro.**]

farruco

Asturian or Galician Spaniard. *Cu* (Vergara Martín 1922:236; DRAE 610) n.d.

[Acc. Vergara Martín, deriv. *farruquiño* 'young *farruco.*' Cf. **español, gallego.**]

farruquiño — See *farruco*

fatuto

1. person without racial mixture; pure-blood. *Co* (Acuña 1951:75); *Co-coast* (Revollo 1942:120) mid20.

2. foreigner who does not speak Spanish. *Co-coast* (Revollo 1942:120) mid20.

[Syn. *fotuto* 'pure,' in ref. to a foreigner who does not know how to speak Spanish, acc. Revollo and Santamaría (1942:1.637). Acc. Alonso (1958:2.1973) and Revollo, *indio fatuto* 'Indian with no racial mixture.' Cf. **bozal, fotuto, indio fatuto, ladino.**]

101

fiscal

1. Spanish king's solicitor-general, attorney general, or censurer in the New World. *SA* (Alcedo 1786–89:5.44) late18.

2. Bolivian or Peruvian Indian who took a turn in the domestic service of the priest. *SA* (Bayo 1910:95) early20; (Bayo 1931:118) mid20.

[Acc. Santamaría (1942:1.640–41), service for the priest brought much respect to the Indian. Acc. Boyd-Bowman (1971:406), att. as 'Indian in domestic service' in Ch 1587. Cf. **colla, coya.**]

flechado 'arrow-like'

person, esp. Indian, with straight, thick hair. *Co* (Alario di Filippo 1964:142) 20.

[Cf. **indio, pelo bueno, pelo malo.**]

fluminense

native of Rio de Janeiro, Br. *Ar* (Segovia 1911:63) early20 ‖ *SA* (Morínigo 1966:267) mid20prior.

[< Brz. Ptg. cognate *fluminense*. Acc. Morínigo, obs. Cf. **brasilero.**]

forano — See *fuerano*

fotuto

1. native person without racial mixture. *Co-coast* (Revollo 1942:120) mid20.

2. person with very rustic or backward customs. *Ve-Andes* (Cowles 1952:344) mid20.

[Syn. df. 1 *fatuto*. Acc. Corominas (1954–57:2.560 and 1973:279), first att. mid 16 cent.; probably Americanism from either Pe or An. Cf. **fatuto, indio fatuto.**]

francés de agua dulce 'freshwater Frenchman'

person native to the country, but who wants to pass for a foreigner. *CR* (Salesiano 1938:82) early20.

[Syn. *hechizo*. Cf. **hechizo.**]

franchute

native of France. *Bo* (Fernández and Fernández 1967:71) 20.

[Derog. Cf. **francés de agua dulce,** Ptg. **francês.**]

fuerano 'outsider'

1. peasant; rustic type. *Ni* (Cowles 1952:347) mid20 ‖ *RP* (Kany 1960b:41) 20.

2. foreigner. *Ho* (Membreño 1897:81) late19 ‖ *Ni* (Castellón 1939:64) mid20.

[< *fuera* 'outside' + suf. *-ano*. Acc. Kany, var. *juerano*. Acc. Cowles, ref. to anyone outside capital of Ni; derog. Acc. Membreño and Castellón, df. 2 < *forano*. Cf. **pajuerano.**]

fuereño 'outsider'

1. foreigner. *Mx* (Malaret 1947:220) mid20.

2. person not from the capital; provincial type; peasant. *Mx* (Rubio 1919:116–17) early20; (Velasco Valdés 1957:57; Morínigo 1966:271) 20.

[< *fuera* 'outside' + suf. *-eño.* Acc. Velasco Valdés, syns. *payo, pueblerino.* Cf. **fuerano, fuerero, pajuerano, payo.**]

fuerero 'outsider'

foreigner; outsider. *CR* (Villegas 1952:65) mid20.

[< *fuera* 'outside' + suf. *-ero.* Acc. Villegas, popular slang. Cf. **fuerano, fuereño, pajuerano.**]

fuerino 'outsider'

foreigner; outsider. *Ch* (Malaret 1947:220) mid20.

[< *fuera* + suf. *-ino.* Cf. **fuerano, fuereño, fuerero.**]

fugido 'fugitive'

fugitive slave. *SA* (Pescatello 1975:247) prior20.

[Sim. in Brz. Ptg.]

fula — See *fulo*

fulenco

person who is almost blond. *Pa* (Malaret 1944:23) mid20.

[Derog. < *fulo.* Cf. **fulo.**]

fulito — See *fulo*

fulo 'blond'

1. person with blond hair; blond. *Pa* (Malaret 1944:23; Aguilera Patiño 1951:451; Cowles 1952:347; Alonso 1958:2.2072–73) mid20.

2. black person or mulatto whose skin color tends toward light pallid yellow. *SA* (Santamaría 1942:1.656) mid20.

[Df. 1 probably < Latin *fulvus* 'tawny, yellowish, blond.' Acc. Megenney (1978:159), df. 2 first att. in ref. to the Fulanese people, who had lighter skin than the average African as a result of their mixture with the non-Negroid Moslems. Var. *fula.* Deriv. *fulito.* Cf. **candelo, canelo, negro angolo, negro de Guinea, rubio.**]

G

gaba — See *gabacho*

gabacho 'Pyrenean'

1. Frenchman residing in Mx. *Mx* (Velasco Valdés 1957:58) 20.

2. North American Anglo; American. *US-AZ* (Barker 1950:33) mid20 ‖ *US-TX* (Kany 1960b:39) 20.

3. foreigner; Anglo-American; gringo. *US-CO, -NM* (Cobos 1983:76) 20.

[Acc. Spaulding (1943:217), < Fr. *gave* 'torrential stream; person

from the French Pyrenees,' ext. to 'native of France.' Acc. Corominas (1954–57:2.603–4), < Occitan *gavach* 'crude mountainman.'
Acc. Cobos, < Fr. *gavache* 'southern Frenchman.' Syns. df. 2 *gaba,
gabardino.* Acc. Miller (1987:166), derivs. *agabachado* 'Americanized,' *agabacho.* Vars. *gaba, gavacho.* Cf. **gringo.**]

gabardino — See *gabacho*

gachupata

Spaniard born in Spain. *CeA Mx* (Cowles 1952:350) mid20.
[M., f. Acc. Cowles, derog.; probably < Aztec *cactil* 'shoe' + Sp. *pata*
'paw'; even more pejor. than *gachupín.* Cf. **gachupín.**]

gachupín 'Spaniard'

1a. Spaniard of generally crude manners born in Europe. *Mx*
(Aguirre Beltrán 1972:158–59); *SA* (Woodbridge 1948:353; Rosenblat 1954:1.71) cl ‖ *SA* (Gibson 1966:130) cl–18 ‖ *Mx* (McAlister
1963:363) cl–20 ‖ *Cu SA* (Pichardo 1953:368) 19 ‖ *SA* (Bayo
1910:97) 20 ‖ *Mx* (Rubio 1919:121) early20; (Velasco Valdés
1957:58) 20 ‖ *CeA Mx* (Malaret 1947:87) mid20 ‖ *CeA Mx* (Kany
1960b:37; Morínigo 1966:274) 20.

1b. Spaniard; recently arrived Spaniard; Spaniard established
in the New World. *Mx* (Macías 1885:561–62) late19; (Bailey and
Nasatir 1973:770) 19prior ‖ *CeA Mx* (Cowles 1952:350) mid20.

1c. Spaniard, no matter of what social standing. *Mx* (Malaret
1944:26) mid20.

1d. Spaniard living in SoA. *SoA* (Vergara Martín 1922:236) n.d.

2. person born in Europe who acquired high social position in
America. *SA* (Pérez de Barradas 1948:174) late19.

3. person who speaks with a twang. *US-CO, -NM* (Cobos
1983:74) 20.

[Df. 1a slanderous; df. 1b injur.; df. 2 derog.; df. 3 usually
adverbial, as in *Elena habla muy gachupín,* acc. Cobos. Acc. Bailey
and Nasatir, *gachupín* 'one who wears spurs.' Acc. Pichardo,
Morínigo, and Kany, < Ptg. *cachopo* 'child,' applied to early Sp.
settlers because of their ignorance of American ways and things.
Acc. Velasco Valdés, ant. *español* 'Spaniard of good character.' Acc.
Macías, syns. *patón* or *gorrión* in Cu, *godo* in Buenos Aires, and
chapetón in Pe. Vars. *cachopín, cachupín, cachupo, gachupo.* Cf.
cachupín, chapetón, gachupata, gorrión, patón.]

gachupincito

Spaniard. *Mx* (Vergara Martín 1922:236) early20.
[< *gachupín* + dim. affect. suf. *-cito.* Acc. Vergara Martín,
gachupinsito [*sic*]. Cf. **gachupín, gallego.**]

gachupo — See *gachupín*

gaita 'bagpipe'

Spaniard. *Ar* (Kany 1960b:37) 20.

[M., f. Acc. Kany, ext. from 'bagpipe, Galician musical instrument' > 'Galician' > 'any Spaniard,' since many of the poorer immigrants to America came from Galicia. Cf. **gallego.**]

galfarro 'lazy'

offspring of a black and a mulatto; 25% white, 75% black. *Mx* (Pérez de Barradas 1948:190; Woodbridge 1948:357) cl.

[Acc. Cobarruvias (1611:621), att. as 'young, roguish, semi-ruffian, or vagrant type.' Acc. León (1924:23), < *gafar* 'unpleasant, idle vagrant.' Cf. **mulato, negro.**]

gallego 'Galician'

1. peninsular Spaniard, no matter from what region; European-born Spaniard. *SoA* (Macías 1885:566) 19prior ‖ *Ar* (Segovia 1911:122) early20 ‖ *Ar Bo PR* (Malaret 1931:259) mid20 ‖ *SA* (Santamaría 1942:2.12) mid20 ‖ *SA* (Bayo 1910:97 and 1931:121; Kany 1960b:37) 20 ‖ *Ar* (Garzón 1910:221); *RP Ur* (Guarnieri 1957:94 and 1968:76) 20 ‖ *SoA* (Vergara Martín 1922:236) n.d.

2. uneducated or uncultured peninsular Spaniard; simpleton. *CR* (Villegas 1952:66); *SoA* (Morínigo 1966:275) 20.

3. recent white Spanish immigrant, esp. from northwestern Spain. *Cu* (Gann and Duignan 1986:97) 20.

[Df. 1 pejor. Acc. Vergara Martín, 'cheap person' in Spain. Acc. Santamaría, now 'servant' in Cu. Acc. Boyd-Bowman (1971:422), att. in Cuba 1570. Cf. **chapetón, criollo, gachupín, godo, polaco.**]

gallina 'hen; chicken'

Peruvian. *Ec* (Kany 1960b:39) 20.

[Derog. Sim. to Amer. Engl. *chicken* 'coward.' Cf. **gallinazo.**]

gallinazo 'turkey buzzard; black buzzard'

mulatto. *Ec Pe* (Kany 1960b:36) 20.

[Facet. Acc. Kany, deriv. *gallinacera* 'group of blacks.' Cf. **gallina, mulato,** Ptg. **urubu.**]

gañán 'young, strong laborer'

Indian volunteer who worked on the hacienda for the land-owner at a fixed contractual wage. *SA* (Mörner 1967:93) cl.

[Acc. Boyd-Bowman (1971:424), att. with racial meaning in mid-16 cent. Mx.]

gandul 'vagabond'

1a. Indian. *RP* (Fontanella de Weinberg 1982:46) 17.

1b. Indian who sits around in public places. *SA* (Levine 1980:56) 20.

2. vagrant, vagabond, or lazy person. *SA* (Levine 1980:56) 20.

[Acc. Fontanella de Weinberg, df. 1a pejor., cited as in *gandules agresores* 'aggressive or belligerent Indians.' Cf. **indio, pieza.**]

gangá

black person native to the African Gangá area, which comprises the Longobá, Maní, Quisí, etc. *Cu* (Pichardo 1953:322) 19.

[M., f. Acc. Alonso (1958:2.2104), < African origins, 'name given to priests of blacks in Angola, the Congo, and other countries of we. Africa.' Cf. **angolo.**]

gato 'cat'

person with blue, green, or hazel eyes. *CR* (Salesiano 1938:78; Cowles 1952:357; Villegas 1952:68) mid20.

[F. form *gata*. Cf. **zarco.**]

gauchita — See *gaucho*

gauchito — See *gaucho*

gaucho 'cowboy; gaucho'

1a. Argentine peasant or cowboy, usually living on the pampas. *Ar* (Saubidet 1943:178–81) 19; (Garzón 1910:225–27) early20 ‖ *SA* (Cowles 1952:358) mid20 ‖ *SA* (Bayo 1931:123; Malaret 1947:89); *Ar Ur* (Laxalt 1980:493); *SA* (Morínigo 1966:279) 20.

1b. horseman of the pampas; cowboy. *Ar SoA Ur* (Bailey and Nasatir 1973:770) n.d.

2. Argentine. *SA* (Simmons 1955:109) 20.

3. mestizo; offspring of a white Spaniard and an Indian. *Ar* (Echaiz 1955:23; Vergara Martín 1922:236); *Ar Pg Ur* (Laxalt 1980:482) prior20.

4. rustic type; man of the fields, dexterous with horses. *Ar* (Segovia 1911:431) early20.

5. peasant of Buenos Aires or Montevideo. *RP* (Vergara Martín 1922:236) n.d.

6. vagrant. *RP* (Vergara Martín 1922:236) n.d.

[Origin uncertain. Acc. Cowles, < Arawak *cauchu* 'vagrant.' Acc. Corominas (1954–57:2.706), < Quechua *wahca* 'poor'; first att. 1782. Syns. *baqueano, hombre de campo*. Derivs. *agauchado, gauchito; gauchesco, gauchita* 'pretty, well-dressed peasant woman,' acc. Morínigo. Cf. **baqueano, gauderio,** Ptg. **gaúcho.**]

gaucho criollo

Italian immigrant who has become like a gaucho and can pass for a native. *Ar* (Cara-Walker 1987:50) late19–early20.

[Cf. **cocoliche, criollo, gaucho, tano.**]

gauderio

1. gaucho. *RP* (Morínigo 1966:283) 18 ‖ *SA* (Bayo 1931:123); *Ar* (Garzón 1910:227; Segovia 1911:431) prior20.

2. Uruguayan gaucho, acc. Spaniards. *Ur* (Vergara Martín

1922:236) prior20.
[Acc. Corominas (1954–57:2.706), att. late 18 or early 19 cent. Acc. Segovia and Morínigo, obs. Acc. Vergara Martín, syn. df. 2 *bandido*. Cf. **gaucho**, Ptg. **gaudério**.]

gavacho — See *gabacho*

gavalín
American. *US-AZ* (Barker 1950:33) mid20.
[Acc. Barker, Pachuco slang. Cf. **gabacho, gabardino**.]

gelofe — See *negro de gelofe*

genízaro
1. person of mixed race and nonwhite skin color, acc. parish records and other documents *Mx* (Roncal 1944:533) cl.

2a. offspring of a *barcino* and a *zambaigo;* 17.975% white, 72.65% Indian, 9.375% black. *Mx* (Woodbridge 1948:357; León 1924:20–21, plate 19) cl.

2b. offspring of a *barcino,* which is an Indian and an *albarazado,* and a *sambayo,* which is an Indian and a *lobo;* 6.25% white, 75.78% Indian, 17.97% black. *Mx* (Pérez de Barradas 1948:193) cl.

2c. offspring of a *barcino* and a *zambaigo. SA* (Vergara Martín 1922:236) n.d.

3. offspring of a *chino* and a *cambujo. SA* (Santamaría 1942:2.26) cl; (Vergara Martín 1922:236) n.d.

4. dihybrid, sixth-generation offspring of 7 parts black and 25 parts Indian. *Mx* (Moreno Navarro 1973:129–31; Solano 1975:85) 18.

5. offspring of non-European parents of mixed race. *US-CO, -NM* (Cobos 1983:76) 20.

6. non-Pueblo Indian captive rescued by the Spanish settlers from nomadic tribes. *US-CO, -NM* (Cobos 1983:76) prior20.
[Acc. Cobarruvias (1611:636), att. as 'offspring of Christian and Turkish parents.' Acc. Alonso (1958:2.2131), used in ref. to a Turkish soldier in Spain up to 20 cent.; first att. 1599. Sim. to Engl. *janissary* 'Turkish soldier.' Var. *jenízaro*. Cf. **albarazado, barcino, lobo, zambaigo**.]

gente 'people'
1. person of distinction or merit, usually of the upper classes. *Ho* (Membreño 1897:84); *CR* (Salesiano 1938:79); *Co* (Tobón Betancourt 1953:131) cl–20 ‖ *Ar* (Segovia 1911:123) early20 ‖ *Ch* (Rodríguez 1875:269) 19.

2. Indian. *Co* (Cowles 1952:359) mid20.
[Syns. *gente bien, gente de sociedad, gente de bien, gente decente.* Acc. Rodríguez, *jente* [sic]. Cf. **gente bien, gente blanca**.]

gente bien 'high-classed people'
1. white person, generally of the upper class. *Co-coast* (Revollo 1942:30) mid20.
2. person of good class, decent and educated. *Ar-Buenos Aires* (Segovia 1911:220) early20.
[Acc. Santamaría (1942:2.26), used throughout SA. Syns. *gente de calidad, persona de pro, persona distinguida, persona decente.* Var. *gente de bien.* Cf. **gente, gente blanca, gente decente, persona bien.**]

gente blanca 'white people'
1. skin color expression used in ref. to both whites and persons of mixed race, acc. parish records and other official documents. *Mx* (Roncal 1944:533) cl.
2. person of pure white race; person with absolutely no racial mixture. *Co Ec Pa Pe Ve* (Konetzke 1946:234) cl.
3a. offspring of a white Spaniard and a *requinterón de mulato,* the latter of which is a white and a *quinterón de mulato;* 96.87% white, 3.13% black. *Mx* (León 1924:23, 20–21, plate 20) cl.
3b. offspring of a white Spaniard and a *requinterón de mulato,* the latter of which is a white and a *quinterón de mulato;* 96.88% white, 3.12% black. *Mx* (Pérez de Barradas 1948:186, 190; Santamaría 1942: 2.26) cl.
3c. offspring of a white and a *requinterón de mulato.* SA (Vergara Martín 1922:236) n.d.
4. dihybrid, seventh-generation offspring of 63 parts white and 1 part black; offspring of a white and an *español. Mx* (Moreno Navarro 1973:129–31; Solano 1975:85) 18.
[Cf. **blanco, gente, gente bien, gente decente.**]

gente de bien — See **gente bien**

gente de casta limpia 'person of a clean caste'
white person with no known racial mixture; pure white person. *SA* (Nuñez 1980:208) early16.
[Cf. **casta, de color, gente, gente bien, gente de color, gente decente, gente de castas.**]

gente de castas 'person from the castes'
person of lower class, usually a nonwhite slave. *Ve* (Vallenilla Lanz 1921:111) late18.
[Cf. **casta.**]

gente de categoría — See *gente decente*

gente de clase 'people of class'
Afro-Argentine, or black Argentinian, acc. himself or herself. *Ar-Buenos Aires* (Andrews 1979:39) 20prior.

[Class distinction with racial connotations. Syn. *gente de color*. Cf. **gente, gente de color.**]

gente de color 'people of color, colored people'

1a. colored person; nonwhite. *SA* (Alvarez Nazario 1974:349) cl–20.

1b. free person of color. *SA* (Diggs 1953:407) late cl.

2a. black person. *SA* (Mörner 1961:281) late18 ‖ *SA* (Kany 1960b:35); *Pa* (Aguilera Patiño 1951:453); *PR* (Alvarez Nazario 1974:347, 380) 20.

2b. Afro-Argentine, or black Argentinian, acc. himself or herself. *Ar-Buenos Aires* (Andrews 1979:39) 20prior.

3a. black person or mulatto. *Cu* (Reuter 1918:60) 20.

3b. black person or mulatto, but not a Chinese. *SA* (Vergara Martín 1922:236) n.d.

3c. black person or any person with dark skin color. *PR US* (Gann and Duignan 1986:80) 20.

4. any nonwhite, especially black person or mulatto. *Co-no.* (Sundheim 1922:161) 20.

5. free person of the lower classes. *SA* (Diggs 1953:407) cl.

6. non-Indian, acc. Chiricano Indians. *Pa* (Aguilera Patiño 1951:453) mid20.

[Dfs. 2, 3a, and 5 euph. Acc. Gann and Duignan, df. 3c color classification in PR. Acc. Chaudenson (1974:79), sim. to Engl. *colored people* or *people of color,* Fr. *gens de couleur,* Mauritian Creole *dimun kulèr.* Syns. *hombre de color, pardo, persona de color.* Cf. **europeo, gente de clase, hombre de color, moreno, persona de color, trigueño,** Ptg. **gente de cor.**]

gente de mala raza — See *mala raza*

gente de medio pelo 'lower-middle-class people'

1. person who tries to pass as rich and well-appointed. *Ar* (Segovia 1911:220) early20.

2. person of the middle class, who has more in common with the lower classes than with the upper. *Co* (Alario di Filippo 1964:212) 20.

[Df. 1 used in opp. to *gente de pelo* 'one who is rich.' Cf. **de medio pelo, gente, gente de pelo, medio pelo.**]

gente de orilla 'riverbank people'

person of the lower classes. *DR* (Patín Maceo 1940:86) mid20.

[Syns. *canalla, gente menuda, gente ruin, plebe, populacho.* Cf. **gente de segunda,** Ptg. **caboclo.**]

gente de pelo 'rich people'

person who is rich and well-appointed. *Ar* (Segovia 1911:220) early20.

[Acc. DRAE (662), syn. *gente de pelusa*. Cf. **gente, gente de medio pelo, gente de razón.**]

gente de pelusa — See *gente de pelo*

gente de primera 'first-class people'
person of the upper classes. *DR* (Domínguez 1973:115) 20.
[Acc. Domínguez, social and racial distinction, implying person is white. Ant. *gente de segunda.* Cf. **gente de pelo, gente de razón, gente de segunda.**]

gente de pro
person of distinction, class, social rank, or some merit. *Ar* (Segovia 1911:65) early20.
[Cf. **gente, gente bien, gente de primera, gente de razón, gente decente.**]

gente de razón 'people of reason'
1. Spanish-speaking Catholic. *Mx* (Cowles 1952:359) mid20.
2. Christian, i.e., a white Spaniard or blueblood. *Mx SA* (Aguirre Beltrán 1972:158) cl.
3. Mexican of Spanish descent, acc. Mexicans of Spanish descent. *Mx* (Chance 1979:154) 20.
4a. any non-Indian. *Mx* (Rosenblat 1954:1.33) cl ‖ *US-CA* (Blanco 1971:73) 16.
4b. non-Indian who followed Spanish rather than Indian customs or way of life. *US-CO, -NM* (Cobos 1983:76) prior20.
5a. person who had the ability to reason, i.e., white person and not slaves or Indians. *SA* (Bailey and Nasatir 1973:770) cl.
5b. educated person. *US-CO, -NM* (Cobos 1983:76) 20.
[Acc. Aguirre Beltrán, also att. in Spain. Acc. Rosenblat, *vestirse de razón* 'to adopt the dress of whites.' Acc. Chance, phr. used to indicate that the person is not an Indian. Syns. *catrín, cristiano, español, gente decente, vecino, correcto, mexicano.* Cf. **gente, gente decente.**]

gente de segunda 'second-class people'
1. person not of the upper social or racial classes. *DR* (Domínguez 1973:115) 20.
2. person who is not white, most often a black person involved in manual labor and not a profession. *PR* (Zenón Cruz 1975:1.250) 20.
[Acc. Domínguez, ant. *gente de primera* in both social and racial contexts. Acc. DRAE (662), considered bandits. Cf. **gente, gente de medio pelo, gente de primera, gente de razón.**]

gente de servicio 'people of service'
1. servant, usually Canary Islander, known for being a servant. *Ve* (Vallenilla Lanz 1921:110) late18.

2. black person or person of mixed race. *Ve* (Vallenilla Lanz 1921:110) late18.
[Acc. Vallenilla Lanz, df. 2 ext. from df. 1. Ants. *gente decente, gente de razón.*]

gente de sociedad — See *gente*

gente de tomuza 'people with stiff hair'
black person or mulatto. *Ve* (Kany 1960b:36) 20.
[Acc. Kany, facet.; *tomuza* 'stiff, tangled hair,' var. of std. Sp. *tomiza* 'esparto rope.' Cf. **gente.**]

gente decente 'decent people'
1. Spanish colonizer of America. *SA* (Rodríguez Molas 1961: 101) cl.
2. person of a good background and education. *Ar* (Segovia 1911:220) early20.
3. white person. *Mx* (Levine 1980:57) 19.
[Syns. *gente de categoría, gente de razón, persona decente.* Cf. **decente, gente de categoría, gente de pelo, gente de primera, gente de razón, pelado.**]

gente fina 'fine people'
person of the elite social classes. *US-Co, -NM* (Cobos 1983:76) 20.
[Cf. **gente de categoría, gente de pelo, gente de primera, gente decente, pelado.**]

gente inilustrada 'unenlightened people'
Indian. *SA* (Gillin 1949:162) cl.
[Cf. **gente, gente de segunda, gente de servicio, indio.**]

gente menuda — See *gente de orilla*

gente principal 'principal people'
person known for noble background but more for meritorious service. *Ar* (Segovia 1911:65) early20.
[Cf. **gente de categoría, gente de pelo, gente decente.**]

gente que no es blanca 'nonwhite people'
black person. *PR* (Alvarez Nazario 1974:347) cl–20.
[Acc. Zenón Cruz (1975:1.254), euph. for *negro* or *prieto* in PR. Cf. **blanco, gente de color.**]

gente ruin — See *gente de orilla*

gentil 'gentile; pagan'
non-Christian Indian. *SA* (Gillin 1949:162) cl ‖ *RP* (Fontanella de Weinberg 1982:46) 17.
[Acc. Fontanella de Weinberg, used by Catholic bishops to identify Indians. Cf. **gente.**]

getudo 'big-mouthed; big-lipped'
person with thick lips and a flattened nose. *Co-no.* (Sundheim 1922:81) early20.
[< *jeta* 'thick lips' + pejor. adj. suf. *-udo.* Var. of *jetudo.* Cf. **chato, ñato, negro getudo, romo.**]
gíbaro 'wild'
   1. offspring of a *lobo* and a mulatto. *Mx* (Woodbridge 1948: 358) cl.
   2. offspring of an *albarazado* and a *calpamulo. Mx PR* (Woodbridge 1948:358) cl.
   3. offspring of an *albarazado* and a *grifo. Mx* (Woodbridge 1948:358) cl.
   4. offspring of a *zambo* and a *grifo. Mx* (Woodbridge 1948:358) cl.
   5. offspring of a *chino* and a mulatto. *Mx* (Woodbridge 1948:358) cl.
   6a. offspring of a *lobo* and a *chino. Mx* (McAlister 1963:354) 19.
   6b. offspring of a *chino,* which is a black and a *lobo,* and a *lobo,* which is an Indian and a *cambujo;* 37.5% Indian, 62.5% black. *Mx* (Pérez de Barradas 1948:191) cl.
   6c. offspring of a *lobo,* which is a mulatto and a *saltatrás,* and a *chino,* which is a black and a *lobo;* 67.19% white, 12.5% Indian, 20.31% black. *Mx* (León 1924:20–21, plate 21; Pérez de Barradas 1948:193; Woodbridge 1948:358) cl.
   7a. offspring of a *calpamulato* and an Indian. *Mx* (Woodbridge 1948:358) cl.
   7b. offspring of a *calpamulato* and an Indian; 12.5% white, 75% Indian, 12.5% black. *Mx* (Pérez de Barradas 1948:193) cl.
   8. offspring of a *zobo,* which is part Indian and part black, and a mulatto woman. *SA* (Levine 1980:57) 20.
   [Acc. Roncal (1944:533), also skin color term used in parish records and other official documents of cl. Mx. Acc. Diggs (1953:407), insult.; scholarly term used in classifying skin color in cl. SA. Var. *gívaro.* Cf. **jíbaro, lobo, zobo.**]
gívaro — See *gíbaro, jíbaro*
goagiro — See *guajiro*
goahiro — See *guajiro*
goajiro — See *guajiro*
gocho 'pig'
   person from the Andes who is a lazy speaker. *Ve* (Ana León 1980:p.c.) 20.
   [Acc. Lipski (1988:p.c.), also commonly used in Co. Cf. **andino, serrano.**]

godito — See *godo*
godo 'Goth'
    1. peninsular Spaniard. *Ar Ch Ve* (Cowles 1952:360) cl ‖ *Ar Ch* (Malaret 1947:92; Morínigo 1966:284); *Ch Pg RP* (Kany 1960b:37); *Ch* (Bayo 1910:123; Alario di Filippo 1964:153–54) 20.
    2. Spaniard, esp. one who supported the Spanish regime during independence or who kept ties with Spain. *Ar Ch Ur* (Vergara Martín 1922:236) n.d. ‖ *Ar Ch Ve* (Cowles 1952:360) 19prior ‖ *Ar-Buenos Aires SoA* (Macías 1885:583); *RP SoA* (Guarnieri 1979:96) 19 ‖ *Ar* (Segovia 1911:221) early20.
    [Derog. Acc. Bailey and Nasatir (1973:770), sarc. ref. to 'blond or ancient Gothic Spaniards,' ext. to 'any Spaniard in America during the wars for independence.' Acc. Segovia, little used by early 20 cent. Acc. Cowles, df. 2 derog. in Ar and Ch. Acc. Megenney (1988:p.c.), 'member of the Conservative Party' in Co. Syns. *gachupín, español,* acc. Alonso (1958:2.2152). Other syn. *coño.* Deriv. *godito.* Cf. **chapetón, gachupín, gallego, guacamayo.**]

gorrión — See *gachupín, patón*
granadillo
    person with yellowish red skin color. *Co-Jardín* (Flórez 1969:121) 20.
    [Acc. Alonso (1958:2.2168), 'tree with hard, compact wood, of fine grain and a yellowish red color.' Cf. **granadino.**]

granadino 'of Granada; Granadan'
    Colombian. *SA* (Bayo 1931:124) early20.
    [Ext. from former name of Colombia, part of the cl. Nuevo Reino de Granada, a Sp. viceroyalty.]

grasiento 'greasy'
    offspring of whites, Indians, and blacks of the lower classes and of apathetic demeanor. *US-CA* (Blanco 1971:207–8) 19.
    [Acc. Blanco, these people worked with animal skins and the grease from them, whence the name. Form sim. to Amer. Engl. *greaser.*]

grébano 'Italian'
    1. any foreigner of whatever class. *Ar* (Garzón 1910:230) early20.
    2. Italian. *Ar* (Kany 1960b:37) 20.
    [Df. 1 derog. Var. *grévano.* Acc. Kany, originally 'peasant from the Piedmont, region in northern Italy.' Excl. to Ar, with its many Italian immigrants. Cf. **bachicha, cocoliche, tano,** Ptg. **bachicha.**]

greciano
    Greek; person from Greece. *CR* (Salesiano 1938:79) mid20.
    [Std. Sp. *griego.*]

grévano — See *grébano*

grifado — See *grifo*

grifo 'kinky-haired; griffin'

1a. person whose skin color was not white, acc. parish records and other documents. *Mx* (Roncal 1944:533); *PR* (Alvarez Nazario 1974:380) cl.

1b. person of color. *Cu PR* (Malaret 1931:268 and 1937:181) mid20.

2a. black person. *Cu PR* (Malaret 1937:181); *An* (Woodbridge 1948:358; Morínigo 1966:286) 20.

2b. black person, or any person with kinky hair. *An* (Alvarez Nazario 1974:355; Kany 1960b:35, 191) 20.

3a. offspring of an Indian and a *lobo,* which is an Indian and a black; 25% white, 50% Indian, 25% black. *Mx* (Pérez de Barradas 1948:193) cl.

3b. offspring of an Indian and a *lobo;* 30% white, 20.7% Indian, 49.3% black. *Mx* (León 1924:20–21, plate 22; Woodbridge 1948:358) cl.

4a. mulatto; offspring of a black and a white; any person with kinky hair. *Mx* (Woodbridge 1948:358) cl–20; (Moreno Navarro 1973:142) 18; (Aguirre Beltrán 1972:177) 20 ‖ *PR* (Alvarez Nazario 1974:355); *An Cu* (Dihigo 1966:141) 20.

4b. light-skinned person with kinky hair. *PR* (Zenón Cruz 1975:1.252) 20.

5a. offspring of a mulatto and a black. *PR* (Zenón Cruz 1975:1.252) cl ‖ *DR PR* (Alvarez Nazario 1974:354) 18–19.

5b. offspring of mulattoes or blacks, esp. one with black skin. *DR* (Domínguez 1973:109) late18.

6. offspring of a black person and an Indian. *DR* (Domínguez 1973:109) late18.

7. offspring of 2 quadroons, of 2 mulattoes, or of 2 mestizos. *SA* (León 1924:23) cl.

8. person under the influence of marijuana. *Co* (Tobón Betancourt 1953:132; Morínigo 1966:286) 20.

[Syn. df. 3a *tente en el aire.* Df. 2b semi-euph. Df. 6 pejor. Acc. Cobarruvias (1611:658), *grifo* 'griffin of Greek mythology with the body and claws of a lion, tail of a snake, wings of a vulture, and head of an eagle,' i.e., an animal of mixed types; ext. to humans of mixed race. Acc. Boyd-Bowman (1982:1462), 'mulatto-black mixture' in Santo Domingo 1762. Acc. Moreno Navarro, used infrequently in 18 cent. Mx; 'type of mulatto' in Fr. An. Acc. Vergara Martín (1922:236, 245), syn. *tente en el aire.* Sim. to Louisiana Fr. *griffe* and Haitian Creole *griffone.* Derivs. *agrifado, grifado.* Cf. **grifado,**

indio, negro parejero, tente en el aire.]
grifo parejero
nonwhite who pretends to the higher social position of the white, acc. whites. *PR* (Zenón Cruz 1975:1.257) 20.
[Acc. Zenón Cruz, term used to indicate the place of the nonwhite in the social structure. Syn. *negro parao.* Cf. **grifo, negro parejero.**]
gringo 'foreigner'
    1a. foreigner, esp. an Englishman or North American, often blond and definitely English-speaking. *Ho* (Membreño 1897); *Gu* (Batres Jáuregui 1892:303) late19 ‖ *Mx* (Velasco Valdés 1957:61) 19–20 ‖ *Pa* (Sundheim 1922:335) early20 ‖ *Pa* (Aguilera Patiño 1951:453); *Co* (Alario di Filippo 1964:6); *An CeA Mx* (Kany 1960b: 39); *Ec* (Carvalho-Neto 1964:227); *Co Gu Ve* (Alonso 1958: 2.2178) 20 ‖ *Ch Gu Pa Pe US-NM* (Morínigo 1966:362–63) 20 ‖ *SA* (Vergara Martín 1922:236–37) n.d.
    1b. North American immigrant, generally English-speaking. *Ni* (Castellón 1939:67) 20.
    1c. American. *PR* (Gallo 1980:51); *Pa* (Aguilera Patiño 1951: 453) 20.
    1d. English-speaking white person; American; Yankee. *US-CO, -NM* (Cobos 1983:77) 20.
    1e. American, or any North American English speaker, acc. Cubans and Cuban-Americans. *Cu US* (Gann and Duignan 1986:95) 20.
    1f. Anglo, or any English speaker, acc. Hispanics. *US* (Abalos 1986:176) 20.
    2a. foreigner, esp. one who does not speak Spanish. *Ar* (Garzón 1910:230) early20 ‖ *Co Mx RP* (Tobón Betancourt 1953:133) mid20 ‖ *Ec-n.w.* (Whitten 1965:91); *Co* (Alario di Filippo 1964: 156); *Pe* (Kiddle 1984:p.c.) 20.
    2b. foreigner who does not speak Spanish or speaks it badly; foreigner whose native lg. is not Spanish. *Ar* (Vergara Martín 1922:236–37) n.d.
    2c. foreigner who is not from the Iberian Peninsula. *Ar* (Bayo 1910:101 and 1931:124) early–mid20 ‖ *RP* (Granada 1957:2.33; Guarnieri 1968:79 and 1979:97) 20.
    2d. foreigner, esp. an Italian. *Ar* (Cara-Walker 1987:40) late19–early20; (Segovia 1911:123) early20 ‖ *Ar Ur* (Cowles 1952: 362–63) mid20 ‖ *RP* (Kany 1960b:38; Guarnieri 1968:79 and 1979:97); *Ar* (Gobello and Payet 1959:44) 20.
    2e. foreigner of non-Latin heritage. *Mx* (Vergara Martín 1922:236–37) n.d.
    2f. foreigner who speaks with an accent in Spanish, esp. an

Irishman. *Ar* (Segovia 1911:123) early20.

2g. European foreigner, neither Spaniard nor Italian, esp. an Anglo-Saxon. *Ar* (Segovia 1911:123) early20.

2h. white foreigner. *US-CO, -NM* (Cobos 1983:77) 20.

3. person with blond hair and light complexion, acc. family and friends. *Pe* (Kiddle 1984:p.c.) 20.

4. Englishman or Englishwoman. *Pe* (Paz Soldán 1938:223) mid20.

[Df. 1c slang. Df. 3 affect. Acc. Kiddle, ext. to mean 'dumbbell.' Acc. Corominas (1954–57:2.783–85 and 1973:304) and corroborated by Kiddle, < *griego* 'incomprehensible jargon or language,' probably altered to **grigo* and then to *gringo;* first att. mid-18 cent. Acc. Alario di Filippo, deriv. *engringarse* 'to imitate the customs of a *gringo,* or foreigner.' Less derog. syn. df. 1 often *norteamericano.* Cf. **americano, americucho, anglo, bolillo, chele, continental, criollo, joroncho, paisano, saxo-americano, yanqui.**]

gringo acriollado 'nativized foreigner'
nativized Italian. *Ar* (Cara-Walker 1987:56) late19–early20.
[Cf. **gaucho criollo, gringo bachiche.**]

gringo bachiche
foreigner who speaks Italian; Italian. *Pe* (Kiddle 1984:p.c.) 20.
[Cf. **bachicha, gringo, gringo acriollado, gringo pichicuma.**]

gringo pichicuma
foreigner who speaks English. *Pe* (Kiddle 1984:p.c.) 20.
[Acc. Kiddle, *pichicuma* < Engl. *beachcomber,* implying one who comes from NoA or Great Britain. Cf. **gringo, gringo bachiche.**]

gringo salado 'salty gringo'
American of dull demeanor. *US-CO, -NM* (Cobos 1983:77) 20.
[Acc. Cobos, insult. Also probably iron. Cf. **gringo.**]

grisoso 'grayish, ashen'
person with ashen skin color. *Co-Tona* (Flórez 1969:121) 20.
[< adj. *gris* 'gray' + adj. suf. *-oso.*]

grosero — See *campiruso, charro*

guacamayo 'type of parrot; type of fish; absurdly dressed'
1. Spaniard, esp. during the war for independence from Spain. *Cu* (Kany 1960b:37; Santamaría 1942:2.35) late19–early20.

2. person who wears clothes of many colors. *PR* (Morínigo 1966:287) 20.

3. old person who is ridiculous in appearance and dress. *Ar Ur* (Morínigo 1966:287) 20.

[Acc. Santamaría (1942:2.35), < Arawak *huacamaya* 'type of bird.' Acc. Kany, *guacamaya* 'type of red and yellow-colored fish,' applied to Spaniards during the war of independence as a result of the color

of the Sp. flag. Cf. **catedrático, gallego, godo, gringo.**]
guache 'hick'
man from a small town; country man. *Co* (Alario di Filippo
1964:158) 20
[Cf. **campesino, gaucho, gente, guachile.**]
guachile
Mexican. *US-AZ* (Barker 1950:33) mid20.
[Cf. **chicano, guachinango, mexicano.**]
guachinango 'astute'
1a. resident of the Valle de México or the Mexican highlands,
acc. person from the Veracruz coastal area. *Mx* (Malaret 1944:49;
Velasco Valdés 1957:61; Morínigo 1966:288) 20.
1b. person from the Mexican interior. *Mx-Veracruz* (Vergara
Martín 1922:237) n.d.
2. Mexican. *Cu* (Macías 1885:603–4) 19; (Vergara Martín
1922:237) early20; (Kany 1960b:40) 20.
3. person who is astute or sturdy of body. *Cu Mx* (Vergara
Martín 1922:237) n.d.
[Acc. Vergara Martín, df. 2 joc. Acc. Kany, 'type of common fish.'
Acc. Santamaría (1942:2.40), perhaps < Aztec.]
guacho — See *gaucho*
guáfiro 'silly; foolish; dumb'
Guatemalan or other Central American born outside Guatemala City. *Gu* (Kany 1960b:42) 20.
[Syns. *guájiro, guanaco.* Cf. **guájiro, guanaco.**]
guagiro — See *guajiro*
guahiro — See *guajiro*
guairo — See *guajiro*
guajero — See *guajiro*
guajiro 'peasant; hick'
1a. white peasant from Cu. *Cu* (Malaret 1931:273; Cowles
1952:370) mid20; (Hoetink 1973:16; Espina Pérez 1972:90; Malaret 1947:95; Morínigo 1966:290) 20; (Vergara Martín 1922:237)
n.d. ‖ *An* (Malaret 1947:95) mid20.
1b. peasant. *DR* (Morínigo 1966:290); *Cu* (Macías 1885:616–19;
Pichardo 1953:343–44) 19; (Cowles 1952:370; Dihigo 1966:
150–51) 20 ‖ *Cu DR* (Kany 1960b:42) 20.
2a. Cuban not from Havana. *Cu* (Espina Pérez 1972:90) 20.
2b. Cuban worker on a sugar plantation. *Cu* (Bailey and
Nasatir 1973:771) 20.
3. chief, head. *An* (Oviedo 1945.14:209) cl ‖ (Pichardo 1953:
343–44) cl–19.

4. Central American not born in Guatemala City. *Gu* (Alonso 1958:2.2186) 20.

[Acc. Alonso (1958:2.2186) and Cowles, < Yucatec *guajiro* 'man, gentleman.' Acc. Boyd-Bowman (1971:438), att. as 'man' in Co 1537. Acc. Alba (1969:34), like *jíbaro*, often 'black person' or 'mulatto' in some SA countries. Vars. *goagiro, goahiro, goajiro, guagiro, guahiro, guaxiro, guairo, guajero, gualiro,* Syns. *aldeano, campesino.* Cf. **guajiro cepillado, guanaco, jíbaro.**]

guajiro cepillado 'combed peasant'
peasant with little formal education. *Cu* (Espina Pérez 1972:90) 20.

[Cf. **guajiro.**]

guájiro 'dumb; foolish'
Guatemalan or other Central American born outside Guatemala City. *Gu* (Kany 1960b:42) 20.

[Syns. *guáfiro, guanaco.* Cf. **guáfiro, guanaco.**]

gualiro — See *guajiro*

guanaco 'simple'
1. native of Sa. *Ar CeA* (Cowles 1952:372–73) mid20.
2. native of Sa or Ni. *Gu* (Kany 1960b:40) 20.
3. native of Sa, Ni, or Ho. *Gu* (Castellón 1939:68; Arriola 1941:78) mid20.
4a. Central American born outside Guatemala City. *Gu* (Batres Jáuregui 1892:308–9) late19; (Kany 1960b:42) 20 ‖ *Ho* (Membreño 1897:86) late19.
4b. Central American other than Guatemalan. *Gu* (Malaret 1931:275) mid20.
4c. Central American other than Guatemalan, esp. Salvadoran. *Gu* (Vergara Martín 1922:237) n.d.
4d. Salvadoran. *CeA* (Lipski 1988:p.c.) late20.

[Acc. Kany, probably < Aztec *cuanaca* 'hen,' modern 'coward, fool.' In this sense, sim. to Amer. Engl. *chicken* 'coward.' Acc. Cowles, Morínigo (1966:291), Santamaría (1942:2.53), and Corominas (1954–57:2.810 and 1973:307), < Quechua *wanáku* or *huanacu* 'type of pack animal.' Acc. Salesiano (1938:80), deriv. *Guanacia* 'republics of Honduras and El Salvador, countries of the *guanacos*,' as for *Tiquicia* 'republic of Costa Rica, country of the *ticos*.' Var. *huanaco.* Syns. df. 4a *guáfiro, guájiro.* Cf. **gallina, guáfiro, guajiro, guájiro, nica, nigüento, tico.**]

guanche
native of the Canary Islands. *Cu* (Rout 1976:17) 19.

[Acc. Rout (1976:334), used in ref. to the native populations of the Canaries. Cf. **isleño.**]

guanco
1. mountainman. *Mx-Guerrero* (Malaret 1944:56) mid20.
2. quintessential rural person, or rustic type, who wears an expression considered stupid. *Ho* (Membreño 1897:86) late19.
[Cf. **guachinango.**]

guarachudo 'shod; sandal-wearing'
Indian who wears the rough *guarache*. *Mx-Sonora* (Sobarzo 1966:155) 20.
[Derog. < Mexican Sp. *guarache* 'sandal' + adj. suf. *-udo.*]

guarín
Otomi Indian who does not speak Spanish. *Mx* (Morínigo 1966:295) 20.
[Cf. **gringo, ladino.**]

guaso 'coarse; peasant'
1a. rustic type; peasant. *Ch* (Rodríguez 1875:241–42) 19 ‖ *Ar Ch* (Bayo 1910:106) early20 ‖ *Ar Ch Cu SA* (Cowles 1952:381) mid20 ‖ *Ar Cu Ec Ur* (Morínigo 1966:296) 20.
1b. peasant from the plains; plainsman. *SoA* (Vergara Martín 1922:237) n.d.
1c. person from the rural areas, esp. a horseman. *Ch* (Rodríguez 1875:241–42) 19.
1d. highland peasant. *Ar Ch Cu SoA* (Cowles 1952:381) mid20.
2. Chilean peasant, laborer, or cowboy. *Ch* (Garzón 1910:235–36) early20 ‖ *Ar Ch* (Bayo 1931:136) mid20 ‖ *Ch* (Morínigo 1966:296) 20.
3a. mestizo; offspring of a white Spaniard and an Indian. *Ar Bo Ch* (Santamaría 1942:2.67) mid20.
3b. mestizo; offspring of Spanish colonizers and Indians, usually peasants or laborers. *Ch* (Vergara Martín 1922:237) n.d.
[Acc. Granada (1957:2.42–43), Garzón, Alonso (1958:2.2198), and Cowles, < Quechua *huasu* 'rustic.' Acc. Rodríguez, sim. to Mexican *jarocho;* < Quechua *huasa* 'back and haunches of a beast.' Vars. *guazo, huaso.* Cf. **gíbaro, huaso, jíbaro.**]

guata
person from or inhabitant of the interior of Co, esp. Antioquia. *Co* (Kany 1960b:41) 20.
[Var. of *guate.* Cf. **guate, huaso, motoso.**]

guata de manteca 'belly of butter'
Guatemalan. *Ch* (Kany 1960b:40) 20.
[M., f. Acc. Kany, vars. *guat'e manteca* and *guata mala* 'bad belly.' Used to burlesque Guatemalans. Cf. **guacamayo, guajiro, guanaco.**]

guataco

Indian. *Co* (Alario di Filippo 1964:162; Morínigo 1966:296) 20.
[Derog. Acc. Alonso (1958:2.2198) and Revollo (1942:132), < *Guataco* 'name of an Indian tribe in Co.]

guate 'belly; inhabitant of the interior'

1a. Colombian, esp. inhabitant of the interior highlands. *Co Ve* (Cowles 1952:381–82) mid20 ‖ *Ve* (Kany 1960b:39) 20.

1b. person from the interior of the country. *Pa* (Malaret 1944:67) mid20.

2a. any Colombian or inhabitant of the Andean highlands, acc. *llaneros,* or plainsmen. *Ve* (Cowles 1952:381–82) mid20.

2b. inhabitant of the highlands. *Ve* (Malaret 1944:67) mid20; (Kany 1960b:41) 20.

[Df. 2a derog. Acc. Alonso (1958:2.2198), < Aztec *ohuatl* 'tender corn stalk.' Vars. *guata, huate.* Cf. **guata.**]

guatuso 'blond'

1. Indian with red hair. *Ni* (Castellón 1939:69) mid20 ‖ *CR* (Santamaría 1942:2.69) mid20.

2. person with blond hair; blond. *CeA* (Alonso 1958:2.2199) 20.
[Var. *guatuzo.* Cf. **chele.**]

guatuzo — See *guatuso*

guaxiro — See *guajiro*

guazo — See *guaso*

güerinche

person with blondish hair and a light complexion. *US-CO, -NM* (Cobos 1983:79) 20.
[Var. *güeruncho.* Cf. **güero, huero.**]

güero 'blond'

1. person with blond hair. *Mx* (Fuente 1947:66); *Gu Mx* (Malaret 1947:98) mid20 ‖ *Gu Mx* (Morínigo 1966:299) 20.

2a. person with a light complexion, usually with blond hair. *US-CO, -NM* (Cobos 1983:79) 20.

2b. person with light skin or hair color. *Mx-Oaxaca* (Garza Cuarón 1987:53, 64) late20.

3. North American Anglo. *US-TX* (Kany 1960b:39) 20.
[Acc. Kany (1960b:47), 'blond' < 'pallid, pale' < 'rotten egg.' Vars. *güiro, huero.* Cf. **claro, huero.**]

güero enchilado 'reddish-blond'

person with reddish-blond hair; redhead. *Mx* (Kany 1960b:48) 20.
[Acc. Kany, *enchilado* < *chile* 'red pepper.' Cf. **candelo, catire, cayubro, colorín, mono.**]

güeruncho — See *güerinche*

guineo 'Guinean'

black person native to Guinea, in Africa. *PR* (Zenón Cruz 1975:1.248) 20 ‖ *SA* (Alonso 1958:2.2206) cl–20.

[Acc. Brown (1967:471), att. as early as 14 cent. in Europe and North Africa, perhaps borrowed from the Berbers; used in ref. to person who was unintelligent. Sim. to Amer. Engl. *Guinea Negro* 'black slave newly arrived from Africa' during the slaving period, acc. Dunlap and Weslager (1947:85). Var. *guinea, guineu.* Cf. **canario, esclavo, negro, negro de Guinea, pieza de registro.**]

güiro — See *güero*

gusano 'worm'

Cuban or Cuban-American who fought against the government of Fidel Castro; expatriated Cuban; anti-Castro Cuban; Cuban-American. *Cu US-FL-so.* (Rieff 1987:41) 20.

[Very derog. ref. to anyone in opp. to late 1950s Cuban revolution led by Fidel Castro.]

H

habado — See *jabado*

habanero 'native of Havana'

Spaniard who returns to Spain after becoming rich in America. *Cu* (Espina Pérez 1972:97) 20.

[Used in ref. to 'white person from Spain'; < *Habana* 'Havana, capital of Cu.' Cf. **perulero.**]

harnizo

1a. offspring of a white and a *coyote;* 84.4% white, 12.5% Indian, 3.1% black. *Mx* (León 1924:23; Santamaría 1942:2.90; Woodbridge 1948:358) cl.

1b. offspring of a white and a *coyote;* 37.5% white, 62.5% Indian. *Mx* (Pérez de Barradas 1948:188) cl.

1c. offspring of a white and a *coyote.* *SA* (Vergara Martín 1922:237) n.d.

2. person of mixed race, acc. parish records. *Mx* (Roncal 1944:533) cl.

[Cf. **coyote.**]

hay te estás 'there you are'

1. offspring of a *no te entiendo* and an Indian; 15.62% white, 59.38% Indian, 25% black. *Mx* (León 1924:20–21, plate 1; Woodbridge 1948:358) cl.

2. person of mixed race, acc. parish records. *Mx* (Roncal 1944:533) cl.
[Acc. Roncal, used by priests to describe the new racial mixes found in America. Phonological var. of *allí te estás, ahí te estás.* Excl. to cl. Mx. Cf. **ahí te estás, no te entiendo, tente en el aire.**]

hechizo 'artificial; homemade'
native to the country; creole. *CR* (Salesiano 1938:82) mid20.
[Syns. *criollo, francés de agua dulce.* Cf. **criollo, francés de agua dulce.**]

hijo de estas provincias — See *hijo de la tierra*

hijo de la tierra 'son of the land'
offspring of white Spaniards born in America. *RP* (Fontanella de Weinberg 1982:45) 16–17.
[Syns. *criollo, hijo de estas provincias* 'son of these provinces,' *mancebo de la tierra, natural de la tierra.* Cf. **criollo, hijo del país, mancebo de la tierra, natural de la tierra.**]

hijo del país 'son of the country'
1. native-born offspring of peninsular Spaniards who had emigrated to Mx. *Mx* (Vergara Martín 1922:237) n.d.
2. creole; native to the country. *Pg* (Vergara Martín 1922:237) n.d.
[Syn. df. 2 *criollo.* Cf. **criollo, hijo de la tierra.**]

hijo del sol 'son of the sun'
white Spaniard, acc. Peruvian Indians. *Pe* (Vergara Martín 1922:237) early cl.
[Acc. Vergara Martín, used by Indians in ref. to the Spaniards' whiteness, their bright armor, and their supposed management of sunlight.]

hipato — See *jipato*

hispánico — See *hispano*

hispano 'Hispanic; Spanish; Spaniard'
1. person native to southwestern US of either Spanish or mixed Indian and Spanish descent. *US-CO, -NM* (Cobos 1983:83) 20.
2. Hispanic-American; Hispanic. *US* (Fox 1988:235) 20–late20.
3a. Spanish speaker, usually acc. non-Spanish speakers. *US* (Gann and Duignan 1986:25) 20.
3b. Spanish speaker descended from the Spanish or Spanish-Mexican lineage of the 16 cent. explorations of the American Southwest, esp. during the time of the annexation of former Mexican territories to US. *US-CO, -NM, -s.w.* (Marden and Meyer 1978:256–57) 19.
[Acc. Fox, df. 2 often self-description sim. to *latino,* the latter of

which may indicate a different social class. Also in Amer. Engl. as racial or ethnic category *Hispanic*. In the Engl. of some Hispanics, *Spanish* used as desc. of oneself. Syn. at times *hispánico*. Cf. **americano, anglo, californio, hispanoamericano, latino, nuevo mexicano, tejano.**]

hispanoamericano 'Spanish American'
person native to SA. *Ar* (Segovia 1911:124) early20.
[Cf. **españo-americano, hispano.**]

hombre de baja estofa 'man of low class'
male servant who has no education and is of little economic means. *Ar* (Segovia 1911:68) early20.
[M. Cf. **gente inilustrada.**]

hombre de color — See *gente de color*

hombre de la otra banda 'man from the other zone'
peninsular Spaniard, or any European, who settled in America and who was considered a bit sickly. *SA* (Levine 1980:63) n.d.
[Acc. Levine, considered sickly in contrast to the more healthy, native-born Americans. Cf. **hijo de la tierra, natural de la tierra.**]

hombre de razón 'rational man'
white person. *Mx* (Sánchez-Albornoz 1974:78) cl.
[Cf. **gente de razón, persona de razón.**]

hombre de sangre azul — See *de sangre azul*

hombre decente 'decent man'
man of good social standing. *Ar* (Segovia 1911:190) early20.
[Cf. **chinero, decente, gente decente, hombre de razón.**]

hombre del pueblo 'man of the people'
man of the working class, of low social standing and humble lineage. *Ar* (Segovia 1911:68) early20.
[Cf. **hombre de baja estofa.**]

horro — See *negro horro*

hosco — See *josco*

huanaco — See *guanaco*

huaquiano — See *baquiano*

huasipunguero
1. Indian who is the occupant of a *huasipungo*. *Ec* (Carvalho-Neto 1964:243) 20.
2. black person or Indian who works as a daily laborer on a hacienda. *Ec* (Klumpp 1970:248; Alonso 1958:2.2319) 20.
[Acc. Carvalho-Neto, *huasipungu* or *huasipungo* 'piece of land given by the landowner as partial payment for services.' Acc. Klumpp, prior to the 1960s farm land reforms in Ec, most black farmers were

huasipungueros, who worked the landlord's land for a small plot of land and a minimal daily wage. Cf. **huaso.**]

huaso 'peasant'

1. mestizo. *Ch* (Echaiz 1955:29) late cl.

2a. cowhand, cowboy, or peasant. *Ch* (Malaret 1947:101; Cowles 1952:406; Morínigo 1966:313; Bailey and Nasatir 1973: 771; Laxalt 1980:493) 20.

2b. countryman; Chilean peasant. *Ch* (Alonso 1958:2.2320) 20.

2c. poorly dressed peasant, who is considered loquacious, picturesque, and happy. *Ch* (Armengol Valenzuela 1914:20.288) early20prior.

2d. poor, rural peasant. *Ch* (Mora 1988:p.c.) 20.

[Acc. Armengol Valenzuela, < Latin *gavisus* 'happy, joyful.' Acc. Echaiz, sim. to *roto.* Acc. Cowles, < Quechua *huaso* 'rustic.' Acc. Echaiz, sim. to *roto,* another type of mestizo in Ch; *huaso* lives rural lifestyle, has the possibility of becoming rich, and is generally descendant of Andalusians. Acc. Mora, opp. to *roto* 'urban bum, ragamuffin,' but sim. to *jíbaro* 'rural peasant' in PR. Var. *guaso.* Cf. **gaucho, guaso, jíbaro, huasipunguero, roto,** Ptg. **caipira.**]

huate — See *guate*

hueñi

servant; any person with dark or swarthy skin color. *Ch* (Kany 1960b:34) 20.

[Acc. Kany, < Indian tribal name. Cf. **ama, chontal, colla.**]

huero

person with blond hair; blond. *Gu Mx US-NM* (Cowles 1952:408) mid20 ‖ *Gu Mx* (Alonso 1958:2.2321) 20.

[Acc. Corominas (1954–57:2.969), att. in Spain 1400. Var. of *güero.* Cf. **barbimono, chele, guanaco, güero, jíbaro, rubio.**]

huesero

inhabitant of the suburbs of a large city. *Cu* (Morínigo 1966:315) mid20prior.

[Acc. Morínigo, generally in ref. to poor person, slum dweller; < *hueso* 'bone' + suf. *-ero,* in ref. to women in slums of Havana who bought and sold bones and other parts of the cattle killed in the slaughterhouses.]

húngaro 'Hungarian'

gypsy. *Mx* (León 1937:36–37) mid20.

[Acc. León, used in ref. to supposed origin of gypsies in Hungary. Cf. Ptg. **cigano.**]

I

indezuelo — See *indiecito*

indiaco

1. person who has the cultural traits of an Indian. *Ar* (Garzón 1910:251) early20.

2. person of low social standing. *Bo* (Fernández and Fernández 1967:82) 20.

[< *indio* + suf. -*aco*. Df. 2 scorn., reflecting social implications of being a native American. Syn. *aindiado*. Cf. **indiecito, indio.**]

indiado

Indian. *US-CA-so*. (Blanco 1971:210) cl.

[Cf. **indiaco, indio.**]

indiano

1a. Spaniard who goes to America only to return to Spain. *SA* (Vergara Martín 1922:229–30) cl.

1b. Spaniard who returns to Spain after having acquired wealth in America. *SA* (Vergara Martín 1922:238; Roback 1944:134; Mosél 1945:23) cl.

1c. peninsular Spaniard who resided in America for a long time. *SA* (Urbanski 1978:171) cl.

2. Asian Indian; native to the East Indies. *SA* (DRAE 740) 20.

[Acc. Vergara Martín, syns. *americano, américo.* Acc. Roback, df. 1b slur; in Spain, *indiano de hilo,* literally 'thread Indian,' 'miser, skinflint.' Cf. **godo, indiaco, indio, perulero.**]

indiecito

Indian. *Co-Bogotá* (Acuña 1951:93); *Bo* (Fernández and Fernández 1967:82) 20.

[Euph. < *indio* + dim. suf. -*cito.* Syn. *indezuelo.* Cf. **indizuelo, indiaco, indígena, indio.**]

indígena 'indigenous; native to the country'

1. Indian. *Ho* (Membreño 1897:95) late19 ‖ *Ar* (Segovia 1911:125) early20 ‖ *SA* (Santamaría 1942:2.120) mid20 ‖ *RP* (Granada 1957:2.56); *SA* (Kany 1960b:34) 20.

2. person with predominantly Indian physical traits. *Co* (Sayres 1956:223, 227) 20.

3. any uneducated or crude person. *SA* (Santamaría 1942:2.120) 20.

[Df. 1 euph. Acc. Sayres, df. 2 in ref. to 10th highest social ranking, just above *natural;* less euph. than *indio.* Cf. **aborígena, indiaco, indio, natural.**]

indio 'Indian'

1a. Indian; native of the Americas; Amerindian. *Mx* (Love

1971:81) cl ‖ *RP* (Fontanella de Weinberg 1982:46) 16–17 ‖ *Cu* (Pichardo 1953:390) late19 ‖ *SA* (Bayo 1910:114) early20 ‖ *Ec* (Whitten 1965:91); *SA* (Esteva Fabregat 1964:280; Morínigo 1966:322) 20; (Vergara Martín 1922:238) n.d.

1b. Indian, native of America, acc. baptismal and other records. *Mx* (Roncal 1944:533; Aguirre Beltrán 1972:155) cl.

1c. Indian, often implying a dim-witted, surly type. *Mx* (Fuente 1947:66; Rosenblat 1954:1.33; Velasco Valdés 1957:67; Sobarzo 1966:171; Crépeau 1973:30; Malaret 1947:102); *Pe* (Malaret 1947:102; Bourricaud 1975:384) 20.

1d. Indian; person with bronze skin color, indicating Indian ancestry. *Mx* (Aguirre Beltrán 1945:213) 17.

2a. person whose skin color is like that of an Indian. *Co-Pacho* (Flórez 1969:121); *Co-Cartagena* (Solaún and Kronus 1973:166); *Ve* (Flórez 1969:123) 20.

2b. person of dark Indian-like skin color, with black, straight hair and body traits of an Indian. *RP* (Guarnieri 1967:127, 1968:84, and 1979:105) 20.

2c. person with the copper-colored skin of an Indian. *SA* (Pérez de Barradas 1948:174) late19–early20.

2d. person with copper-colored skin, indicating descent from Indians. *Ar* (Segovia 1911:126) early20.

2e. peasant or any person with the skin color and physical appearance of an Indian. *Cu-Tierradentro* (Macías 1885:704) late19.

2f. person with predominantly Indian physical features. *Co-Zarzal* (Sayres 1956:223, 227) 20.

3. offspring of an Indian and a *coyote*. *Mx* (O'Crouley 1972:19) 18.

4. courageous gaucho; person who is arrogant. *RP SoA* (Guarnieri 1979:105) 20.

5a. black person whose hair is wavy or straight, not kinky. *DR PR* (Domínguez 1986:275) 20.

5b. dark-skinned person with straight hair. *PR* (Zenón Cruz 1975:1.252) 20.

5c. mulatto with straight hair and brown skin color. *DR* (Domínguez 1973:110) late18.

6. Asian Indian; native to the East Indies. *SA* (DRAE 741) 20.

[Df. 1c derog. Acc. Sayres, df. 2f used in ref. to 9th highest social ranking; very euph. in ref. to Indian. Acc. Domínguez, df. 5a opp. to *trigueño* 'black person with kinky hair.' Acc. Domínguez (1973:184), represents intermediate class between black and white in DR and among Dominicans in NY. Derivs. *aindiado, indiecito, indizuelo*.

Also used in Spain. Cf. **aborígena, grifo, indígena,** Ptg. **índio.**]

indio agregado
Indian who received a wage for working on the hacienda. *Pe-s.e.*
(Mörner 1967:96) cl.
[Syn. *arrendero,* literally 'added pieces or parts of the farm.' Often
in phr. *agregado a la hacienda.* Cf. **agregado, agregado al país,
indio.**]

indio alobado *'lobo*-like Indian'
offspring of a *mulato alobado* and an Indian, esp. one lacking
many black features. *Mx* (Woodbridge 1948:358; Aguirre Beltrán
1945:217 and 1972:170) cl–17.
[Acc. Mellafe (1975:89), phr. often shortened to *alobado,* person had
very Indian-like characteristics and could pass for pure Indian. Syn.
lobo. Cf. **indio, lobo, mulato alobado.**]

indio amigo — See *indio de paz*

indio arcaico — See *indio de montaña*

indio auca — See *auca*

indio bárbaro
1. war-like, or otherwise unfriendly Indian, most often a Chichi-
meco. *Mx* (Aguirre Beltrán 1972:155) cl.
2. uncivilized Indian. *Mx SA* (Vergara Martín 1922:238) n.d.
[Sim. to *salvaje.* Syns. *indio infiel, indio gentil, indio rayado.* Cf.
indio, indio de paz, salvaje, Ptg. **índio bárbaro.**]

indio blanco 'white Indian'
Indian with near-white skin of the Guainar tribe from the Up-
per Orinoco river area. *SoA-no.* (Santamaría 1942:2.120) mid20;
(Vergara Martín 1922:238) n.d.
[Cf. **blanco, indio.**]

indio bravo 'wild Indian'
1. Indian runaway or rebel who commits excesses in the
countryside. *Cu* (Macías 1885:704) 19.
2. Indian who lives in a wild, primitive, and independent state.
Ve (Vergara Martín 1922:238) n.d.
3. desert Indian from the state of Sonora. *Mx* (Vergara Martín
1922:238) n.d.
[Cf. **indio,** Ptg. **índio bravo.**]

indio caballero — See *indio jinete*

indio castellano 'Castilianized Indian'
Indian who could speak Spanish or who had acquired some
Hispanic customs. *RP* (Bayo 1931:68) cl–early 20.
[Syn. *ladino.* Cf. **castellano, indio, ladino.**]

indio catequizado 'baptized Indian'
Indian who has been christianized but who retains tribal lg. and customs. *Ve* (Vergara Martín 1922:238) n.d.
[Syn. *indio redimido.*]

indio claro 'light Indian'
light-skinned mulatto. *DR* (Berroa 1987:p.c.) 20.
[Euph. for dark-skinned person, used on official forms as a racial category, like *indio oscuro.* Cf. **indio, indio oscuro.**]

indio coyote
Indian native to NM. *US-NM* (Cobos 1983:37) 20
[Cf. **coyote, indio.**]

indio de carga — See *yanacona*

indio de Filipinas
1. Oriental, Filipino, or Indonesian slave transported to the New World through Manila. *Mx* (Aguirre Beltrán 1972:149) cl.
2. freed slave, either Oriental, Filipino, or even mulatto, who founded a community at the small port of Coyuca. *Mx* (Aguirre Beltrán 1972:50) early17.
[Acc. Aguirre Beltrán, these slaves were not all from the Philippines themselves but were from various parts of the Orient, since many were mulattoes. Cf. **asiático, chino manila.**]

indio de Garabito
Indian of the Chorotega tribe from the province of Garabito, CR. *CR* (Vergara Martín 1922:238) n.d.
[Cf. **auca, indio.**]

indio de guerra — See *auca*

indio de montaña 'mountain Indian'
Indian from the mountainous areas at the time of the arrival of the Spaniards. *Mx* (Vergara Martín 1922:238) cl.
[Cf. **indio.**]

indio de paz
peaceful Indian who aided the white conquerors. *SA* (Rosenblat 1954:1.66) cl.
[Syn. *indio amigo.* Cf. **indio bárbaro.**]

indio de pelea 'fighting Indian'
any healthy or robust male, from 16 to 50 years of age. *Ar-Buenos Aires* (Boyd-Bowman 1984:1728) 19.
[Perhaps indicates male of fighting age for armed forces.]

indio del Perú 'Indian from Peru'
Indian of the Callahagua tribe of Pe who emigrated to Ar in order to trade in medicinal herbs. *Ar* (Vergara Martín 1922:238) n.d.

indio fatuto
pure-blooded Indian; Indian with no racial mixture. *Co* (Revollo 1942:120; Alonso 1958:2.1973) 20.
[Syns. *fatuto, fotuto.* Cf. **fatuto, fotuto, indio.**]

indio gaucho
Indian not subjugated or enslaved, acc. other Indians. *Ar-Buenos Aires* (Boyd-Bowman 1984:1728) 19.
[Cf. **gaucho, indio.**]

indio gentil — See *indio bárbaro*

indio gringo 'fair-skinned or blond Indian'
Indian. *Pe-no. Andes* (Pitt-Rivers 1967:549 and 1968:271) 20.
[Acc. Pitt-Rivers, used in ref. to social classification for an Indian and not to phenotype. Cf. **gringo, indio.**]

indio infiel — See *indio bárbaro*

indio infiel de montaña
unfriendly highland Indian of pure ancestry. *Pe* (Pérez de Barradas 1948:185) cl.
[Acc. Pérez de Barradas, 100% Indian. Cf. **indio bárbaro, indio de montaña, indio infiel, infiel.**]

indio jinete 'horseman Indian'
Indian of the Guaicuru tribe of ce. SoA, known for excellent horsemanship. *SoA* (Vergara Martín 1922:238) n.d.
[Syn. *indio caballero.* Cf. **caballero, gaucho, indio.**]

indio ladino
Christianized Indian who willingly adopted Spanish customs and lg., or one who was enslaved forcibly. *Mx* (Aguirre Beltrán 1972:155; Love 1971:81) cl–18.
[Syn. *indio reducido.* Cf. **indio, ladino.**]

indio manso 'tame Indian'
1. Newly enslaved Indian. *Mx* (Aguirre Beltrán 1972:155) cl.
2. Indian who converted to Catholicism and adopted Spanish lg. and customs. *Ve* (Vergara Martín 1922:238) n.d.
[Syns. *indio reducido, indio neófito, indio sometido.* Cf. **indio bárbaro, indio catequizado, indio ladino, indio de paz,** Ptg. **índio manso.**]

indio mestizo — See *colla*

indio mitayo
Indian used in forced labor. *Pe* (Mörner 1967:96) cl.
[Acc. Mörner, < *mita* 'forced labor.' Cf. **indio ladino, indio manso.**]

indio naborí
Indian who was subjected to various forms of servitude even

though considered free. *Ni* (Levine 1980:67); *SA* (DRAE 908) cl.
[Acc. Levine, *indio naborio* [*sic*]. Cf. **indio.**]

indio naborio — See *indio naborí*

indio neófito 'neophyte Indian'
Indian enslaved by the Spanish conquerors. *Mx* (Aguirre
Beltrán 1972:155) cl.
[Syns. *indio manso, indio reducido;* often placed in *reducciones,* or
reservations, away from the rest of humanity, sim. to treatment af-
forded No. Amer. Indians in 18–19 cent. These *neófitos* included
indios ladinos, who spoke Sp., and *indios torpes,* who did not. Cf.
**indio bárbaro, indio ladino, indio manso, indio reducido,
indio torpe.**]

indio originario
Indian who possessed no land and lived with the landlord. *Pg*
(Hollanda 1956:73) cl.
[Syn. *indio yanacona.* Cf. **indio, yanacona.**]

indio oscuro 'dark Indian'
very dark-skinned black person. *DR* (McCray 1980:p.c.) 20.
[Euph. for *negro* used in the census and official documents. Sim. to
So. Amer. Engl. *Florida Indian,* joc. euph. for 'black person,' supposedly anyone darkened by the hot sun of Florida. Cf. **indio, indio
claro, oscuro.**]

indio picota 'peak Indian'
Indian *cacique,* or chief. *Pe-s.e.* (Mörner 1967:96) cl.
[Cf. **cacique, indio mitayo.**]

indio pongo
Indian who serves as a domestic. *Pe* (Levine 1980:67) cl ‖ *Bo
Pe* (DRAE 1048) 20.
[Cf. **indio, pongo.**]

indio rayado 'striped Indian'
war-like Indian of the northern plains of cl. Mx, now part of US.
Mx (Aguirre Beltrán 1972:156) cl.
[Acc. Aguirre Beltrán, this Indian marked (or striped) the face with
ritualistic tribal scars and paints. Acc. Boyd-Bowman (1983:1288),
att. in 17 cent. Cf. **indio bárbaro.**]

indio redimido — See *indio catequizado*

indio reducido — See *indio manso, indio neófito*

indio salvaje — See *salvaje*

indio serrano 'highland Indian'
highland Indian of pure ancestry. *Pe* (Pérez de Barradas
1948:185–86) cl.
[Syn. *tributario civilizado* 'civilized taxpayer.' Cf. **indio, indio
infiel de montaña, serrano.**]

indio sometido — See *indio manso*
indio torpe 'stupid Indian'
   Indian who did not speak Spanish. *Mx* (Aguirre Beltrán 1972:155) cl.
   [Derog. Ants. *indio ladino, indio castellano.* Cf. **indio castellano, indio ladino.**]
indio y negro 'Indian and black'
   person with both black and Indian physical traits. *Co-Cartagena* (Solaún and Kronus 1973:166) 20.
   [Cf. **indio, negro.**]
indio yanacona — See *indio originario*
indiobruto
   Indian worker who is brutish in nature. *Bo Pe* (Levine 1980:66) 20.
   [Acc. Levine, pejor. Cf. **indio.**]
indiote 'big Indian'
   Indian. *Mx* (Rosenblat 1954:1.33; Fuente 1947:66) 20.
   [Derog. < *indio* + aug. pejor. suf. *-ote.* Cf. **indizuelo, mulecote.**]
indita 'little female Indian'
   Indian maiden. *US-CO, -NM* (Cobos 1983:87) 20.
   [Acc. Cobos, used in allusion to the virgin Guadalupe, the dark-skinned patron saint of Mx. Cf. **indio, indito.**]
indito 'little Indian'
   1. Indian, acc. *ladinos,* or 'hispanized mestizos.' *Mx-Chiapas* (van den Berghe 1967:54) 20.
   2. little Indian; any primitive or backward child. *SA* (Abalos 1986:43) 20.
   3. peasant, acc. persons of the middle class. *SA* (Abalos 1986:43) 20.
   [Acc. van den Berghe, indicates simplemindedness, irresponsibility, and childishness on the part of the Indian. Generally derog. Cf. **huaso, indio, indita, jíbaro, roto.**]
indizuelo 'small Indian'
   Indian. *Gu* (Batres Jáuregui 1892:336) late19 ‖ *Sa* (Cowles 1952:416) mid20.
   [< *indio* + dim. suf. *-zuelo.* Var. *endizuelo.* Cf. **indiecito, indiote.**]
indoeuropeo 'Indo-European'
   offspring of a mestizo and a European white. *Mx* (León 1937:37) mid20prior.
   [Acc. León, originally 'Aryans from India who spread throughout Europe.' Cf. **euromestizo, indiolatino, indomestizo.**]

indolatino
mestizo; offspring of an Indian and a white. *Mx* (León 1936-supplement:4) mid20prior.
[Acc. León, used until 1934 in Mexican constitution and other laws. Acc. León (1937:37), formed by anal. to *indoeuropeo.* Cf. **euromestizo, indoeuropeo, indomestizo, ladino, latino.**]
indomestizo
person with predominantly Indian physical features, generally offspring of an Indian and person of another race. *Mx* (Aguirre Beltrán 1972:222) cl.
[Sim. to *indolatino.* Cf. **indolatino, indoeuropeo, euromestizo, mestizo.**]
infiel 'unfaithful; infidel'
1. uncivilized Indian from eastern Ec. *Ec* (Bayo 1910:114) early20.
2. any Indian considered uncivilized. *RP SoA* (Guarnieri 1979:105) 20prior.
[Cf. **indio bárbaro.**]
inglés 'English; Englishman'
black, English-speaking immigrant from An. *Ve* (Levine 1980:67) early20; (Ferguson 1963:122) 20.
[Cf. **chumeca, negro.**]
injerto 'graft, grafting'
1a. offspring of a Japanese and any Peruvian, apparently either white or *cholo. Pe-Lima* (Mörner 1967:132) cl–20.
1b. offspring of an Oriental and an Indian. *Pe* (Santamaría 1942:2.122) mid20.
2. mestizo with some Chinese ancestry. *Pe* (Millones Santagadea 1973:62) 20.
3. person whose skin color indicates mixed race. *Co-Pacho* (Flórez 1969:121) 20.
[Acc. Millones Santagadea, colloq. Cf. **asiático, cholo, oriental.**]
inquilino 'resident'
person who lives in a remote area of the country. *Ch* (Rodríguez 1875:264–65) 19.
[Acc. Rodríguez, sim. to *naborio* of Mx or *yanacona* of Pe. Cf. **indio naborí, yanacona.**]
irlandés porteño 'port Irishman'
Argentine of Irish origin, esp. a farmer or shepherd. *Ar* (Ferguson 1963:122) 20.
[*Porteño* generally indicates 'from Buenos Aires.']
isleño 'islander'
1a. person from the Canary Islands. *Cu* (Macías 1885:708) 19;

(Vergara Martín 1922:238) n.d. ‖ *Cu PR* (Malaret 1937:194; Revollo 1942:138) mid20 ‖ *US-LA* (Lipski 1987:320) 20prior.

1b. native of or descendant of natives of the Canary Islands. *US-LA-St. Bernard Parish* (MacCurdy 1950:68) mid20.

2. person from San Andrés or Providencia islands. *Co* (Revollo 1942:138) mid20.

3. person from Margarita Island. *Ve* (Revollo 1942:138) mid20.

4a. inhabitant of St. Bernard Parish, LA. *US-LA-St. Bernard Parish* (MacCurdy 1950:68) mid20.

4b. Hispanic native of St. Bernard Parish, LA. *US-LA-St. Bernard Parish* (MacCurdy 1950:50) mid20.

4c. person, usually Spanish-speaking, from Delacroix Island, LA, or its environs. *US-LA* (Lipski 1987:320) 20prior.

[Acc. Revollo, 'Canary Islander' in Spain. Dfs. 1b, 4 current today. Acc. MacCurdy, syn. df. 4b *criollo;* ant. *americano.* Cf. **canario.**]

J

jabado 'off-white color with dark spots'

1. person of mixed race who has hair and skin color of a white person and kinky hair texture or other physical features of a black person. *Cu PR* (Alvarez Nazario 1974:356); *Cu* (Gómez 1980:p.c.) 20.

2. mestizo or mulatto who wants or tries to pass for white. *Cu* (Morínigo 1966:328) 20.

3. mestizo. *Cu* (Espina Pérez 1972:104) 20.

4. mulatto; offspring of a black and a white, whose skin color is yellowish and whose hair color is light. *Cu* (Barnet 1971:202) 19–20.

5. offspring of a white and a mulatto who has white skin color and blond, kinky hair. *An* (Nuñez 1980:244) 20.

6. person who vacillates between 2 opinions; fence-straddler. *Cu* (Alonso 1958:2.2434; Morínigo 1966:328) 20.

[Df. 2 and 3 pejor. Var. of *habado.* Acc. Alvarez Nazario and Morínigo, original ref. to 'rooster or chicken with two-toned feathers, often off-white with black or dark brown.' Acc. Pichardo (1953:394–95) and Alonso (1958:2.2434), < Antillean Indian word *jaba* for which they offer no definition. Acc. Santamaría (1942:2.132), originally from Murcia or Andalusia used in ref. to 'bird or chicken of varigated coloration.' Var. *jabao.* Cf. **mestizo, mulato.**]

jabanés
person native to Havana, Cu. *SA* (Vergara Martín 1922:238) prior20.
[Var. of std. Sp. *habanero* 'native of Havana.']
jabao —See *jabado*
jacoibo
Jewish person; Jew. *Ch* (Kany 1960b:37) 20.
[Pejor. Cf. **judío, ruso,** Ptg. **judeu.**]
jalof — See *negro de gelofe*
jamaicano — See *jamaiquino*
jamaiquino 'Jamaican'
black person who speaks English. ·*Cu* (Ferguson 1963:122) 20.
[< *Jamaica* 'Jamaica' + suf. *-ino.* Syn. *jamaicano.* Cf. **chumeca, inglés.**]
jarochito — See *jarocho*
jarocho
1. person whose skin color indicated mixed race, acc. parish records and other documents. *Mx* (Roncal 1944:533); *SA* (Mörner 1967:59) cl.
2a. offspring of a black and an Indian; 50% Indian, 50% black. *Mx* (León 1924:20–21, plate 24; Woodbridge 1948:358; Pérez de Barradas 1948:190) cl.
2b. *mulato pardo,* or offspring of a black and an Indian. *Mx-Veracruz* (Woodbridge 1948:358; Aguirre Beltrán 1945:216 and 1972:169) cl–17.
2c. person whose physical traits indicate a mixture of black and Indian blood. *Mx-Veracruz* (Moreno Navarro 1973:142–43) 18.
3. black person; person of African descent. *Cu* (Macías 1885:724) late19 ‖ *Mx* (Vergara Martín 1922:239) n.d.
4. mulatto. *Mx* (Vergara Martín 1922:239) n.d.
5a. native of the state of Veracruz, esp. from coastal areas. *Cu* (Macías 1885:724) late19 ‖ *Mx* (Malaret 1931:303) mid20; (Fuente 1947:65; Velasco Valdés 1957:70; Morínigo 1966:333; DRAE 767) 20.
5b. rural peasant from the Veracruz coastal area. *Mx* (Herrera and Cícero 1895:72) late19prior.
6a. coastal peasant. *Mx* (Kany 1960b:42) 20.
6b. peasant. *Mx* (Vergara Martín 1922:239) n.d.
6c. cattle herdsman. *Mx* (Herrera and Cícero 1895:72) late19prior.
[Acc. Velasco Valdés, Fuente, and Morínigo, df. 5a ext. from former meaning 'offspring of a black and an Indian.' Acc. Aguirre Beltrán (1972:179), < Moslem Sp. *jaro* 'wild pig' + suf. *-cho;* once derog. Acc.

Moreno Navarro, < Arabic *jaro* 'wild pig.' Acc. Alvar (1987:144), < Arabic *xarût* 'bad woman.' Deriv. *jarochito.* Syn. *mulato pardo.* Cf. **chilango, jenízaro, mulato pardo, tapatío.**]

jáyaro 'poorly mannered'
rustic type; hick. *Ec* (Cowles 1952:426) mid20; (Morínigo 1966:334) 20.
[Syns. *patán, rústico.* Cf. **campesino.**]

jenízaro 'mixed'
1. offspring of a mulatto and an Indian. *Mx* (Morínigo 1966:335) cl.
2. offspring of a *cambujo* and a *chino.* *Mx* (Santamaría 1942:2.144) mid20prior.
3. offspring of parents from different countries. *Mx* (Alonso 1958:2.2450) 20.
4. person of mixed race. *US-CO, -NM* (Cobos 1983:90) 20.
5. Indian captured by other Indians, rescued by Spaniards, and then used by them as a domestic or soldier; descendant of these Indians. *US-CO, -NM* (Cobos 1983:90) prior20.
6. person who is dark-skinned. *US-CO, -NM* (Cobos 1983:90) 20prior.
[Acc. DRAE 768), df. 3 std. Var. *genízaro.* Cf. **genízaro.**]

jente — See *gente*

jetón 'thick-lipped; big-lipped'
person, esp. black, with a large flat nose and large lips. *RP SoA* (Guarnieri 1979:108); *Bo* (Fernández and Fernández 1967:84) 20.
[< *jeta* 'large lip' + suf. *-ón.* Syns. *jetudo, negro jetón.* Cf. **bembón, bembudo, getudo.**]

jetudo — See *getudo, jetón*

jíbaro 'peasant'
1. offspring of a *lobo* and a mulatto; 48.44% white, 12.5% Indian, 39.06% black. *Mx* (Pérez de Barradas 1948:193) cl.
2. offspring of a *lobo* and a *chino.* *Mx* (Vergara Martín 1922:239; Monteforte Toledo 1959:171) cl.
3. offspring of a *calpamulato* and an Indian; 12.5% white, 75% Indian, 12.5% black. *Mx* (Pérez de Barradas 1948:185) cl.
4. offspring of a *calpamulo* and an *albarazado.* *Mx* (Vergara Martín 1922:239; Malaret 1931:304) cl.
5. offspring of a *zambo* and a *grifo.* *Mx* (Vergara Martín 1922:239) cl.
6. Indian. *Ec* (Bayo 1931:144); *Ec Pe* (Morínigo 1966: 336) 20.
7. person who is the product of the mixing of blacks, whites, and Indians. *PR* (Coll y Toste 1924:127) early20.

8a. white Puerto Rican peasant. *PR* (Malaret 1931:304 and 1937: 196–97; Cowles 1952:429; Kany 1960b:42; Morínigo 1966: 336; Hoetink 1973:16; Hernández Aquino 1969:222–23; Cortina Gómez 1978:72) 20.

8b. rural Puerto Rican or person from the interior mountain region. *PR* (Gallo 1980:58) 20.

8c. peasant; rustic type, generally rural. *Ho* (Membreño 1897:99); *Cu* (Pichardo 1953:408); *Cu-Santiago PR* (Macías 1885:732–33) late19 ‖ *SA* (Yrarrázaval 1945:76); *An Cu Mx-Tabasco* (Cowles 1952:429); *Ho* (Morínigo 1966:336); *DR* (Kany 1960b:42); *PR* (Mora 1988:p.c.) 20 ‖ *SA* (Vergara Martín 1922:239) n.d.

9. person native to PR; Puerto Rican. *PR* (Malaret 1937: 196–97; Cowles 1952:429; Kany 1960b:42; Morínigo 1966:336; Hoetink 1973:16; Hernández Aquino 1969:222–23; Vergara Martín 1922:230) 20.

[Acc. Cortina Gómez, possibly < Taino lg. of Arawak Indians. Acc. Kany, < *Jíbaro* 'savage Indian tribe of cl. An.' Acc. Gallo, df. 8b slang; sim. to Amer. Engl. *hillbilly* or Cuban *guajiro*. Df. 9 ext. from 8a. Acc. Mörner (1967:59) and Woodbridge, used in cl. SA documents and official records. Acc. Alba (1969:34), sim. to *guajiro;* also used in ref. to 'black or mulatto peasant' in some countries. Acc. Vergara Martín, syn. df. 9 *blanco de tierra.* Other syn. *criollo.* Vars. *gíbaro, gívaro; jívaro, xíbaro.* Cf. **blanco de tierra, campesino, criollo, gíbaro, guajiro, huaso, roto,** Ptg. **caboclo, caipira.**]

jicaque

person who is rude or uncouth, esp. a peasant. *Gu Ho* (Kany 1960b:34) 20.

[Cf. **jíbaro.**]

jincho 'bloated'

white person with very pale skin and a bloated body. *PR* (Malaret 1937:198; Alonso 1958:2.2454) 20.

[Var. of std. Sp. *hinchado* 'bloated.' Cf. **jíbaro.**]

jipato 'pale'

white person who is very pale or anemic. *An CeA Ch Co Ec Mx Ve* (Morínigo 1966:338) 20.

[Acc. Macías (1885:737), var. *hipato;* < std. Sp. *hepático* 'yellowish color of hepatitis victim.' Cf. **anémico, jincho.**]

jornalero 'day laborer'

black dayworker or journeyman. *PR* (Alvarez Nazario 1974: 380) 20.

[Cf. **indio mitayo, indio picota.**]

jorongo 'poncho'
1. gringo; North American. *SA* (Bayo 1931:145) mid20.
2. foreigner. *SA* (Bayo 1931:145) mid20 ‖ *Ve* (Cowles 1952:
440; Morínigo 1966:341, 345) 20.
[Generally 'type of poncho worn by Mexican peasants.' Vars.
jorungo, jurungo, yurungo. Cf. **gringo.**]

jorungo — See *jorongo*

josco 'dark brown'
person with dark, usually black or dark brown, skin color. *PR*
(Morínigo 1966:341) 20.
[Acc. DRAE (721), color rel. to Indians and mulattoes. Acc. Cowles
(1952:435) 'pearl-colored, or off-white' in Gu. Acc. Santamaría
(1942:2.157) and Alonso (1958:2.2459), originally ref. to cattle hair.
Var. *hosco*.]

juaquinero
Indian from the area of the San Joaquín river. *US-CA* (Blanco
1971:212) 19.
[Cf. **califa.**]

judío 'Jew; Jewish'
1. foreigner or irreligious person. *Cu* (Pichardo 1953:417;
Macías 1885:746) late19.
2. any white person, acc. Dominicans in New York City. *US-NY*
(Gann and Duignan 1986:116) late20.
[Acc. Pichardo, scorn. Acc. Macías, derog. Acc. Gann and Duignan,
in many New York City neighborhoods in which Dominicans found
themselves, Jews were the predominant white group. Cf. **jacoibo,
ruso,** Ptg. **judeu.**]

juerano — See *fuerano*

jurungo — See *jorongo*

juyungo 'black person'
1. black person, acc. Cayapa Indians. *Ec-Esmeraldas* (Cowles
1952:440) mid20 ‖ *Co-so. Ec* (Kany 1960b:35) 20.
2. black person or mulatto with very dark skin. *Ec* (Morínigo
1966:345) 20.
[Acc. Cowles, < Cayapa Indian lg. *juyungo* 'monkey, devil, bad.']

L

labión 'large lip; large-lipped'
person with large lips. *Mx-Oaxaca* (Garza Cuarón 1987:63)
late20.
[Syns. *labiudo, trompudo*. Cf. **bembón, bembudo, trompudo.**]

labiudo — See *labión, trompudo*
laborio — See *naborio*
laborío — See *naborio*
ladino 'cunning; astute'

1. black slave first brought to Spain who learned to speak Spanish and assimilated some of the culture before being sold in America. *SA* (Alvarez Nazario 1974:332; Mörner 1967:16); *Cu* (Pichardo 1953:423); *PR* (Alleyne 1963:96); *Co-we.* (Velásquez 1962:114); *PR SA* (Zenón Cruz 1975:1.252) cl.

2a. offspring of black African slaves born in America; any hispanized black person. *SA* (Rout 1976:xv) cl.

2b. civilized and acculturated black African. *Cu* (Malaret 1931:311) mid20prior.

3a. Indian who has learned to speak Spanish. *Gu* (Batres Jáuregui 1892:356–57) late19 ‖ *Co Ec* (Malaret 1944:112–13); *Ar Pe* (Malaret 1931:311) mid20 ‖ *RP* (Granada 1957:2.66) 20 ‖ *Ar CeA Co Ec Pe* (Morínigo 1966:349) 20 ‖ *US-CO, -NM* (Cobos 1983:95) cl–20.

3b. modernized, Spanish-speaking Indian. *Gu* (Bailey and Nasatir 1973:772) 20.

3c. any person who speaks Spanish and adopts the *ladino* way of life, i.e., mostly Spanish customs. *Gu* (Pinkerton 1986:696) 20.

4a. mestizo; offspring of a white and an Indian. *CeA Mx-Tabasco SoA* (Woodbridge 1948:358) cl ‖ *CeA* (Salazar García 1910:167) early20 ‖ *Mx* (Cámara Barbachano 1964:61) early18 ‖ *CeA* (Mörner 1967:106; Morínigo 1966:349); *Ni Sa* (Vergara Martín 1922:239); *Gu* (Malaret 1931:311) mid20; (Alba 1969:34) 20 ‖ *US-CO, -NM* (Cobos 1983:95) cl–20.

4b. hispanized or acculturated mestizo. *Mx-Chiapas* (van den Berghe 1967:54) 20.

4c. white person or mestizo, acc. Indians. *Mx* (Woodbridge 1948:358) cl ‖ *CeA Mx* (Cowles 1952:446); *Mx* (Morínigo 1966:349) 20.

4d. non-Indian. *Gu* (Vandiver 1949:143) late19–early20 ‖ *CeA Mx* (Harris 1964a:116); *Gu Mx-Chiapas* (Fuente 1947:65) 20.

[Black, Sp.-speaking (*ladino*) slaves brought a higher price than the *bozales* 'slaves newly arrived from Africa' and often worked in domestic service rather than in the fields, acc. Alvarez Nazario, Mörner, and Pichardo. Acc. Salazar García, df. 4a barbarism or provincialism; syns. *mestizo, cholo, mestezuelo.* Often used in phr. *indio ladino* or *negro ladino.* Acc. Cobarruvias (1611:747), '*morisco* or foreigner who learned Sp.' in Spain. Acc. Malaret (1944:112–13), in Spain ref. to 'Moor who spoke Latin or Spanish.' Acc. Segovia

(1911:127), came to refer to 'person who is intelligent or astute' in early 20 cent. Ar. Acc. Boyd-Bowman (1971:515), att. as *negro ladino* in Cu 1520. Acc. Alvarez Nazario, syns. *negro de Castilla, negro de Portugal.* Acc. Boyd-Bowman (1982:1746), att. as 'fluent, literate' in 18 cent. Mx. See also Alonso (1958:2.2490) and Santamaría (1942:2.168). Cf. **bozal, cholo, esclavo ladino, indio ladino, latino, mestizo, negro ladino.**]

lanudo 'wooly; shaggy, unkempt; rustic'

1. rustic island native who came to the port of Cartagena, Co, to do business. *SA* (Alcedo 1786–89:5.54) late18.

2. person from Bogotá, Co, and any cold regions surrounding it. *Co* (Kany 1960b:41) 20.

3. rustic type; peasant. *Ec Ve* (Morínigo 1966:352) 20.

[Df. 1 probably indicates black creoles. Syn. df. 2 *rolo.* Syn. df. 3 *patán, rústico.* Cf. **isleño.**]

latino 'Latin, Latino'

1. white person. *Mx* (León 1936:supplement.4) mid20prior.

2. Hispanic-American; Latin. *US* (Fox 1988:235) 20–late20.

[Acc. León, df. 1 opp. to *indio* in Mexican constitution and other laws up to 1934. Acc. Fox, df. 2 sim. in use to *hispano* 'Hispanic,' esp. when politically expedient; can have class or status connotations. Often used in opp. to *anglo* 'Anglo, English-speaking (white) American' as catch-all term for 'Spanish-speaker in US.' Also used in Amer. Engl. as *Latin* or *Latino.* Cf. **anglo, californio, hispano, indolatino, indio, ladino, nuevo mexicano, tejano.**]

lavado 'washed'

mulatto whose skin color is lighter and other physical features more Caucasian than those of most other mulattoes. *Ec PR* (Alvarez Nazario 1974:356) 20.

[Acc. Alvarez Nazario, considered more delicate, i.e., more acceptable than darker skin and fewer Caucasoid features. Acc. Malaret (1931:315), Santamaría (1942:2.175), and Alonso (1958:2.2524), first att. in ref. to cattle with reddish and white hair or hide. Var. *lavao.* Cf. **mulato.**]

lavao — See *lavado*

leído 'read'

1. any person of culture or high society, acc. peasants or lower-class people. *Ch* (Cowles 1952:453) mid20.

2. literate person, usually Indian, acc. Indians. *Pe* (Cowles 1952:453) mid20.

[Df. 2 usually in phr. *leído y escribido* 'read and written.' Cf. **gente de razón, indio.**]

leonado 'tawny; dark blond color'

person with dark skin, esp. black person or mulatto. *SA*

(Domínguez Ortiz 1952:371) cl; (Boyd-Bowman 1971:524) 16.
[Acc. Domínguez Ortiz, att. in 15-cent. Spain with ref. to the skin color of blacks, mulattoes, or dark-skinned Berbers. Acc. Boyd-Bowman, att. as racial term in mid-16 cent. SA.]

lépero 'leprous; ordinary'
1. offspring of a white Spaniard and an Indian. *Mx* (Vergara Martín 1922:239) n.d.

2a. low-class city dweller. *Mx* (Vergara Martín 1922:239) n.d.

2b. underemployed man of the lower classes, usually of part Indian ancestry, who lurked in the outskirts of Mexico City and begged or stole to support his family. *Mx* (Levine 1980:77) cl–19.

2c. person of low social class. *Mx* (Cowles 1952:454–55) mid20 ‖ *CeA Mx* (Malaret 1947:226; Morínigo 1966:359) 20.

3. low-class Mexican. *Ec* (Kany 1960b:40) 20.
[Cf. **ladino, mestizo.**]

libanés — See *turco*

liberto 'freed, free'
1. freed slave. *PR* (Alvarez Nazario 1974:346) 20prior.

2. offspring of slaves who was freed by 'free-womb' laws of 19 cent. *Ar Pe Pg Ur* (Rout 1976:xv) 19.

3. offspring of a black and a mulatto. *DR* (Domínguez 1973:109) late18.
[Syn. *negro libre.* Cf. **manumiso, manumitido.**]

liberto de la República del Paraguay 'Paraguayan freedman'
any person born of a slave mother who was declared free on 1 January 1843 by the government of Carlos A. López. *Pg* (Vergara Martín 1922:239) 19–early20.
[Cf. **liberto.**]

liborio
Cuban. *Cu SA* (Vergara Martín 1922:239) n.d.
[Acc. Vergara Martín, sim. to *Juan Español* 'Spaniard.']

libre 'free'
white person. *Ve* (Mörner 1961:285) late18.
[Cf. **liberto.**]

libre de color 'free person of color'
free black person who suffered the same racial and social restrictions as black slaves. *SA* (Levine 1980:77) prior20.
[Cf. **liberto, libre.**]

limpio 'clean, neat'
1. person whose skin color indicated slightly mixed race, acc. parish records. *Mx* (Roncal 1944:533) cl.

2. offspring of a white and *gente blanca;* 99% white, 1% black.

Mx (Woodbridge 1948:358; León 1924:20–21, plate 25) cl.
[Acc. Cobarruvias (1611:767), att. as 'Christian Spaniard with no Moorish or Jewish blood.' Acc. Boyd-Bowman (1971:531), att. in phr. *'persona ... de limpia generación'* in late 16 cent. Mx. Cf. **cuasi limpio de origen, limpio de origen, quasi limpio en su origen.**]
limpio de origen 'clean by origin'
offspring of a *cuasi limpio de origen* and a white; 99.22% white, 0.78% black. *Mx* (Pérez de Barradas 1948:190) cl.
[Cf. **cuasi limpio de origen, limpio, quasi limpio en su origen.**]
litoraleño 'coastal'
person native to a coastal province. *Ar* (Segovia 1911:236–37) early20.
[Cf. **costeño.**]
llanero 'plainsman'
1a. plainsman; cowhand; inhabitant of the *llanos* of Co and Ve. *Cu* (Pichardo 1953:435) late19 ‖ *SA* (Bayo 1910:128 and 1931:153); *Ve* (Malaret 1947:108; Cowles 1952:465); *Co* (Alario di Filippo 1964:192); *Co Ve* (Morínigo 1966:370; Laxalt 1980:493) 20.
1b. plainsman of San Martín and Casanare, Co. *Co SA* (Vergara Martín 1922:239) early20.
2a. mestizo of the plains of Ve who leads the nomadic life of a shepherd. *Ve* (Echaiz 1955:22) 20.
2b. mestizo who was a shepherd and led a nomadic life in some South American countries. *SA* (Vergara Martín 1922:239) n.d.
[< *llano* 'plain' + adj. suf. *-ero*. Sim. in meaning to *roto, gaucho, huaso.* Cf. **gaucho, guate, huaso, mestizo, palmarote, roto.**]
llavera — See *madre abadesa*
lobo 'wolf; shrewd'
1. person whose skin color indicates racial mixture of black and Indian, acc. the *Periquillo Sarniento. Mx* (Chance 1979:164) early19.
2a. offspring of a black and an Indian. *Mx* (León 1924:20–21, plate 26; Roncal 1944:533; Woodbridge 1948:358; Pérez de Barradas 1948:188; Mörner 1967:74; Rubio 1919:143) cl; (O'Crouley 1972:19); (Moreno Navarro 1973:141) 18; (Malaret 1931:321) prior20; (Vergara Martín 1922:239) n.d. ‖ *Mx US-NM* (Cowles 1952:460) 20.
2b. offspring of a black and an Indian; 50% black, 50% Indian. *Mx* (Pérez de Barradas 1948:190) cl.
2c. *cambujo;* dihybrid, second-generation offspring of a black and an Indian. *Mx* (Moreno Navarro 1973:129–31; Solano 1975:85) 18.

3a. offspring of a *saltatrás* and a mulatto; 46.88% white, 25% Indian, 28.12% black. *Mx* (Pérez de Barradas 1948:193) cl.

3b. offspring of a *saltatrás* and a mulatto. *Mx* (Rubio 1919:143; Woodbridge 1948:358; Monteforte Toledo 1959:171) cl; (McAlister 1963:354) 19 ‖ *SA* (Alba 1969:34) cl; (Vergara Martín 1922:239) n.d.

3c. offspring of a *chino,* which is the offspring of an Indian and a mulatto, and a mulatto; 46.88% white, 25% Indian, 28.12% black. *Mx* (Pérez de Barradas 1948:193; Woodbridge 1948:358) cl.

4a. offspring of an Indian and a *tornatrás;* 46.88% white, 50% Indian, 3.12% black. *Mx* (Pérez de Barradas 1948:193) cl.

4b. offspring of an Indian and a *tornatrás. Mx* (Rubio 1919:143; Woodbridge 1948:358; Monteforte Toledo 1959:171; Mörner 1967: 58) cl ‖ *SA* (Vergara Martín 1922:239) n.d.

5. offspring of a *chino cambujo* and an Indian. *Mx* (Rubio 1919:143; Woodbridge 1948:355, 358) cl.

6. offspring of an Indian and a *cambujo,* which is offspring of an Indian and a black; 75% Indian, 25% black. *Mx* (Pérez de Barradas 1948:190) cl.

7. offspring of an Indian and a mulatto; *sambayo. Mx* (O'Crouley 1972:19) 18.

8a. *mulato lobo. Mx* (Aguirre Beltrán 1972:170) cl; (Love 1971:81) 17–18.

8b. *mulato lobo, mulato alobado,* or *indio alobado. Mx* (Aguirre Beltrán 1945:216–17 and 1972:170) 16–17.

9. trihybrid, sixth-generation offspring of 15 parts white, 9 parts black, and 8 parts Indian. *Mx* (Solano 1975:84) 18.

[Acc. DRAE (811), syn. df. 2 *zambo.* Acc. Moreno Navarro (1973:141), ref. to dusky color of wolf's coat, sim. to skin color of a person so described; sim to *zambo* of earlier times. Acc. Malaret (1931:321), ethnographic term no longer used. Acc. Aguirre Beltrán (1945:216–17), syns. in 17 cent. Mx *mulato lobo, mulato alobado, indio alobado.* Cf. **indio alobado, mestizo, mulato alobado, mulato lobo, zambaigo, zambo.**]

lobo tornatrás

offspring of a *lobo* and an Indian. *Mx* (Woodbridge 1948:358; Santamaría 1942:2.189) cl ‖ *SA* (Vergara Martín 1922:239) n.d.

[Cf. **lobo, tornatrás.**]

locho 'reddish'

person with reddish hair. *Co* (Alario di Filippo 1964:189; Morínigo 1966:365); *Co-Araticam, -Sardinata, -Simacota, -Suaita* (Flórez 1969:122) 20.

[Acc. Alario di Filippo and Morínigo, < Quechua *locho* 'deer.' Acc.

Malaret (1931:321), < *loche* 'type of crow with lustrous reddish feather covering, < Quechua *lluchu* 'deer.' Cf. **chele, güero, lobo, longo, loro, rubio.**]

longo 'Indian youth'
Indian, esp. young one. *Ec* (Malaret 1931:322 and 1947:226; Cowles 1952:462; Santamaría 1942:2.191; Alonso 1958:2.2602) 20.
[Acc. Cowles, < Quechua *longo* 'Indian youth.' Cf. **indiecito, indizuelo.**]

loretano 'someone or something from Loreto'
mestizo, or offspring of a white and an Indian, who is native to the department of Loreto, Pe. *Pe* (Cowles 1952:462) mid20.
[Cf. **chino, cholo, mestizo.**]

loro 'dark brown'
1. Indian of An. *SA* (Alvarez Nazario 1974:350–51) late15–early16; (Oviedo 1945:14.212) cl.
2. dark-skinned person verging on black; *moreno. SA* (Barón Castro 1946:790) cl ‖ *PR* (Alvarez Nazario 1974:380) cl.
3. dark-skinned person. *Gu* (Batres Jáuregui 1892:365) late19.
4. person with an aquiline nose. *Bo* (Fernández and Fernández 1967:89) 20.
5. offspring of a white and a black. *SA* (Nuñez 1980:277) cl.
[Acc. Alvarez Nazario (1974:350), < Latin *laurus* 'laurel,' originally alluded to the dark color of the plant. Acc. Zenón Cruz (1975:1.252), oldest Sp. word for 'mulatto'; also 'any animal with dark skin.' Df. 2 also att. in 15-cent. Spain, acc. Seminario (1975:25) and Barón Castro (1946:790). Syns. *mulato pardo, amarillito, membrillo* in cl. Chiapas, Mx, acc. Woodbridge (1948:358), Aguirre Beltrán (1945:216 and 1972:196), and Alvarez Nazario (1974:351). Syn. df. 3 *indio amulatado*. Acc. Simonet (1888:316–17), att. as 'brown color leaning toward black, and yellow or blond, applied to wheat.' Acc. Verlinden (1955:280, 366), att. as 'mulatto' and 'blond' as early as 13 cent. Acc. Boyd-Bowman (1983:1428), used in ref. to a black slave in phr. *de color loro* in 17 cent. Gu. Should not be confused with homonym *loro* 'parrot.' Cf. **amarillito, membrillo, moreno, mulato, mulato pardo,** Ptg. **louro.**]

lucumi — See *lucumí*
lucumí
1. black person from Nigeria and other sub-Saharan regions of Africa, esp. from the Gulf of Guinea. *Cu* (Barnet 1971:203) 19–20.
2. black slave of the Yoruba tribes of west Africa. *Co Cu Mx* (Levine 1980:79); *Cu* (Nuñez 1980:280) cl.
[Probably of African origins. Var. *lucumi*. Cf. **guineo, nagó.**]

lunarejo 'spotty-faced'
person whose skin color indicates mixed race, acc. parish rec-

ords and other documents. *SA* (Mörner 1967:59); *Mx* (Roncal 1944:533; Pérez de Barradas 1948:193; León 1924:20–21, plate 27) cl.

[Acc. Corominas (1973:367), < *lunar* 'mole.' Acc. Malaret (1931:323), 'any person or animal with moles on the skin.' Cf. **lobo, loro, moreno, mulato.**]

lunero

Mexican mestizo or Indian paid wages for 1 day of work per week. *Mx* (Levine 1980:79) 20.

[Acc. Levine, < *lunes* 'Monday,' day the worker was paid. Cf. **jornalero.**]

lunfa — See *lunfardo*

lunfardo 'lg. of the underworld; thieves' jargon'

delinquent, usually Italian. *Ar-Buenos Aires RP* (Guarnieri 1979:115) late19.

[Shortened form *lunfa.* Acc. Megenney (1988:p.c.), majority of ethnic jargon from Buenos Aires area based on Italian. Cf. **bachicha, cocoliche,** Ptg. **bachicha.**]

M

ma Fulana — See *taita*

macaco 'deformed; monkey'

1. Chinese. *Ec Mx* (Malaret 1931:326); *Pa* (Aguilera Patiño 1951:465) mid20 ‖ *Ec Mx Pa Pe* (Cowles 1952:468; Kany 1960b:38) 20.

2. Brazilian. *Ar* (Segovia 1911:238) early20; (Garzón 1910:290; Bayo 1910:129 and 1931:154) 20 ‖ *Bo* (Fernández and Fernández 1967:90) 20.

3. person who is ugly or deformed. *Ch Cu* (Dihigo 1966:173) 20.

[Acc. Malaret, df. 1 derog. Acc. Segovia, df. 2 vulg. nickname. < Ptg. < Angolese or Congolese lg., used in ref to 'type of monkey known for its mimicking abilities,' acc. Alonso (1958:2.2631) and Dihigo (1966:173). Acc. Kany and Aguilera Patiño, < *Macao* 'Indo-Chinese island' because many Chinese came to America from there. Cf. **asiático, brasilero, chino,** Ptg. **macaco.**]

machango — See *mono moreno*

macho 'male; strong'

1a. foreigner. *CR* (Gagini 1918:173; Cowles 1952:473) early–mid20.

1b. foreigner, usually a blond or redhead of English or North

American origin. *CR* (Salesiano 1938:91; Cowles 1952:473; Villegas 1952:86; Kany 1960b:39) 20.

2. person with a ruddy face and blond hair, usually Anglo-Saxon. *CR* (Malaret 1931:329) mid20; (Kany 1960b:209) 20prior.

[Acc. Kany, used in ref. to foreigners since they appeared physically larger and more powerful than the natives of the country. Acc. Corominas (1954–57:3.178–79), < Ptg. *muacho* 'mule.' Acc. Boyd-Bowman (1982:1844), first att. as racial category in 18-cent. no. SoA. Cf. **chele, gringo.**]

machucón 'bruise'
black person. *US-AZ* (Barker 1950:34; Kany 1960b:36) mid20.
[Acc. Barker, Pachuco slang.]

machulla
1. offspring of a white European and an Indian. *Ch* (Morínigo 1966:378; Santamaría 1942:2.211) 20.
2. Indian of the Mapuche tribes of southern SA. *Ch* (Santamaría 1942:2.211) 20.
[M., f. Probably < indigenous Chilean lg. Cf. **mestizo.**]

macjta — See *majta*

maco 'rogue'
slave or prisoner of war reduced to slavery, acc. Caribe Indians. *SA* (Vergara Martín 1922:239) cl.
[Cf. **cargamento de ébano.**]

macuá
1. black person, usually a slave, from the Macua region of Africa. *Cu* (Pichardo 1953:440) 19.
2. Indian. *Mx-interior* (Santamaría 1942:2.206) 20.
[M., f. Acc. Escalante (1964:177), 'small bird dried and pulverized to be used in acts of love magic' on the Atlantic coast of Co. Acc. Santamaría, vars. *macurino, maje, majigua, macucué, macuche.* Df. 2 rel. to *macuache.* Cf. **macuache.**]

macuache
1. Indian not educated or instructed in any manner. *Mx* (Vergara Martín 1922:239; Alonso 1958:2.2638) prior20.
2. worthless or contemptible Indian. *Mx* (Alonso 1958:2.2638) 20.
[Acc. Alonso (1958:2.2638), < Nahuatl *macchualtic* 'poor' < *macehua* 'despicable being;' var. *macuachi.* Cf. **macuá.**]

macuachi — See *macuache*

macuche — See *macuá*

macucué — See *macuá*

macuito

black person. *Pe* (Morínigo 1966:377) prior20; (Santamaría 1942:2.207; Alonso 1958:2.2638) 20 ‖ *Pe-Lima SoA* (Malaret 1944:141) mid20.

[< *macuá* + dim. suf. *-ito.* Acc. Malaret, joc. nickname sim. to *mohino.* Cf. **mohino, muzucuco.**]

macurino — See *macuá*

madera de ébano 'ebony wood'

black African slave, acc. slave traders. *PR SA* (Alvarez Nazario 1974:356, 380) cl.

[Euph. ref. to dark or ebony skin color. Cf. **cargamento de ébano, ébano, ébano vivo.**]

madre abadesa

Indian woman, usually unwed or widowed, who kept order and held the keys to the mission's monastery. *US-CA* (Blanco 1971:216) cl.

[F. only. Acc. Blanco, syn. *llavera.*]

maestro — See *taita*

maicero 'corn eater'

person from Antioquia, Co. *Co* (Kany 1960b:41) 20.

[Acc. Kany, much corn is grown and eaten in this area. Cf. **mazamorrero, negro, patojo, sabanero.**]

maje — See *macuá*

majigua — See *macuá*

majta

cholo, or mestizo. *Pe* (Cowles 1952:477) mid20.

[M., f. Acc. Cowles, < Amerindian lg., most probably < Quechua, esp. in light of its phonetic shape and vars. *macjta, mak'ta, maqt'a.* Cf. **cholo, mestizo.**]

mala

Hispanic suffering from the feelings of middle age; middle-aged Hispanic. *US-FL-so.* (Pérez-Firmat 1988:p.c.) late20.

[M., f. Acronym < Engl. phr. *middle-aged, Latin, and anguished,* acc. Pérez-Firmat. Cf. **yuca.**]

mala casta — See *mala raza*

mala raza 'bad race'

1. slave. *Mx* (Aguirre Beltrán 1972:267) cl.

2. any Moor, Jew, black, or Indian, acc. Spanish colonizers. *SA* (Rodríguez Molas 1961:101) cl.

[Slaver's or slave trader's shorthand. Acc. Rodríguez Mola, used to emphasize one's *limpieza de sangre,* or pure-bloodness or lack thereof. Usually in phrs. *persona de mala raza* or *gente de mala raza.* Acc. Mellafe (1964:87), syn. *mala casta.* Cf. **casta, raza.**]

mallate — See *mayate*

mambí

1. runaway slave or fugitive from justice. *PR* (Zenón Cruz 1975:1.248–49) prior20.

2. rebel who fought against the cl. Spanish government. *PR* (Zenón Cruz 1975:1.248–49); *Cu* (DRAE 833) 19.

[Generally m. Acc. Zenón Cruz, < Antillean lg. root meaning 'bad, not good,' now means 'ferocious or cruel animal.' Acc. DRAE, *mambís* [sic].]

mambís — See *mambí*

mameluco 'overall; mestizo'

1a. offspring of a white Portuguese and an Indian from southern Br who raided missions or land in RP for slaves and cattle. *Ar* (Segovia 1911:586) early20 ‖ *Ar Pg Ur* (Morínigo 1966:385); *SA* (Bayo 1910:133 and 1931:158) prior20.

1b. offspring of a Portuguese and an Indian; Brazilian mestizo. *RP* (Guarnieri 1979:121) 20prior.

2a. person from or native to São Paulo, Br; *paulista. Ar* (Segovia 1911:239) early20 ‖ *SA* (Alonso 1958:2.2675; Santamaría 1942:2.224) 20.

2b. cruel person native to the state of São Paulo, Br. *Ar* (Segovia 1911:239) early20.

3. prostitute. *Ch* (Malaret 1931:335) mid20.

[Acc. Malaret, df. 2b sim. in cruelty to the *mameluco* of Egypt. Perhaps < Arabic *mamluk* 'one who is enslaved,' participle of *malaka* 'to own or govern,' acc. Souza (1961:189), Corominas (1954–57:3.213–14 and 1973:376), Alonso (1958:2.2675), and Machado (1952–59:2.1406). Acc. Corominas (1954–57:3.213–14) and Alonso (1958:2.2675), first att. 1585. Alternatively, acc. Souza (1961:198) and Santamaría (1942:2.224), possibly < Tupi-Guarani *mamaruca* < *mamã* 'to mix' + *ruca* or *yruuca* 'to throw.' Sim. to Haitian Fr. Creole *mamelouque* or LA Fr. *meamelouc.* Cf. Ptg. **mameluco paulista.**]

mamplora

rustic type; sodomite; hermaphrodite. *Ho* (Membreño 1897:111) late19.

[M., f. Now 'homosexual' in CeA. Cf. **campesino,** Ptg. **caipira.**]

managuaco

peasant with a very rustic appearance; hick. *Cu* (Morínigo 1966:387; Espina Pérez 1972:121) 20.

[Joc. Cf. **campesino, mamplora.**]

mancebo de la tierra 'boy native to the country'
offspring of white Spaniards born in SA. *RP* (Fontanella de Weinberg 1982:45) 16–17.
[Acc. Fontanella de Weinberg, *mançevo de la tierra* [*sic*]; syns. *hijo de la tierra, natural de la tierra, mancebo nacido en la tierra.* Cf. **criollo, español.**]

mancebo nacido en la tierra — See *mancebo de la tierra*

mançevo de la tierra — See *mancebo de la tierra*

mancha del plátano — See *platanero*

mandinga 'effeminate; devil; black person'
1. black slave brought to America from the area of Africa to the north of the equator and between the Senegal and Niger rivers. *Cu* (Pichardo 1953:457) 19 ‖ *PR* (Malaret 1937:211); *Co-coast* (Revollo 1942:163); *Co* (Alario di Filippo 1964:200); *Cu PR* (Cowles 1952:484–85) mid20.
2. person who is not pure white, esp. one who has some black ancestry. *Pe* (Santamaría 1942:2.228) 20.
3. black person. *RP* (Guarnieri 1979:121) 20.
[M., f. < *Mandinga* 'African tribe from no. Guinea or we. Sudan.' Possible var. *mandingo*. Acc. Megenney (1983:7), phr. *mandinga tsivī* 'evil or the evil-doer; the devil,' < Kimbundu. Acc. Boyd-Bowman (1971:555), first att. in phr. '(negro) Pedro, mandinga' in Puebla, Mx, 1555. Acc. Gallo (1980:67), often found in the phr. *el que no tiene dinga tiene Mandinga* 'one who has no Indian (Inca) blood has black blood.' Cf. **chino manila, esclavo, negro africano, negro de gelofe.**]

mandingo — See *mandinga, negro de gelofe*

mango 'mango (fruit); handle'
offspring of a black and a *sambo*. *SA* (Reuter 1918:13) n.d.
[Cf. **negro, sambo.**]

manigüero
1. rural peasant type; inland peasant; hick. *Cu* (Espina Pérez 1972:122) 20.
2. rebel who takes to the countryside or jungle. *An* (Morínigo 1966:391) 20.
3. inhabitant of the *manigua,* or swampy wetlands. *An* (Morínigo 1966:391) 20.
[< *manigua* 'countryside, jungle, scrubland' + suf. *-ero.* Acc. Espina Pérez, df. 1 derog.; syns. *campesino, montuno.* Also 'athlete, player, sportsman.' Cf. **campesino, montuno.**]

mantuano 'Mantuan; native of Mantua, Italy'
1a. person of good social or economic standing, or one who is taken for such, usually white. *Ve* (Morínigo 1966:393) 20.

1b. white creole, or white born in America. *Co* (Vergara Martín 1922:240) prior20.

2. person of distinction, since only those of good standing wore a *manto,* or cape. *Ve* (Bayo 1931:160) 20.

3. person pertaining to the upper, noble, or aristocratic classes. *Ve* (Cowles 1952:490) mid20prior.

4. offspring of an Indian and a noble Spaniard. *Ve* (Santamaría 1942:2.236; Alonso 1958:2.2704) prior20.

[Acc. Alonso (1958:2.2704) and Cowles, < *Mantua* 'town in Italy.' Cf. **gente de pro, gente de razón.**]

manumido 'freed'

child of black slaves who was considered free if born after 1821. *Co SoA-no.* (Nuñez 1980:299) cl.

[Var. of *manumiso* or *manumitido.* Cf. **liberto, manumiso, manumitido.**]

manumiso 'freed'

freed slave, usually black. *Co Ec Ve* (Rout 1976:xv; Levine 1980:82) prior20.

[Cf. **liberto, manumido, manumitido, negro horro, negro libre.**]

manumitido 'freed'

freed slave, usually black. *PR* (Alvarez Nazario 1974:346) cl.

[First att. 1726, acc. Alonso (1958:2.2705). Cf. **liberto, manumido, manumiso, negro horro, negro libre.**]

manuto 'rustic'

rustic type; hick. *Pa* (Aguilera Patiño 1951:469) mid20.

[Cf. **campesino.**]

manzanero 'apple picker; apple grower'

Patagonian Indian. *SA* (Vergara Martín 1922:240) cl.

[< *manzana* 'apple.' Acc. Vergara Martín, Spaniards found these Indians drunk on alcoholic cider.]

marabú 'marabou'

offspring of a *grifo* and a black. *PR* (Alvarez Nazario 1974:354) cl.

[Acc. Alonso (1958:2.2711), < Arabic *marabut* 'ascetic; saint; African stork, considered a holy animal since it eats various pesky insects.' Acc. Pescatello (1975:248), 'Muslim hermit.' Sim. to Haitian Fr. Creole *marabout* 'white and blackish-green bird,' 'offspring of a black and a quadroon,' acc. Alvarez Nazario (1974:354). Acc. Reuter (1918:12), *marabon* 'offspring of a mulatto and a *griffe*' in LA Fr. Cf. **cuarterón, grifo.**]

maracucho

1. person with dark skin color. *Ve* (Flórez 1969:123) 20.

2. person from Maracaibo. *Ve* (Alonso 1958:2.2711) 20.
[Df. 2 nickname ext. of df. 1, since many Maracaibans have dark skin color. < *Maracaibo* 'Venezuelan seaport,' which has a large black population.]

marielito
Cuban emigré, often black, illiterate, homosexual, and/or criminal, who arrived in southern FL on the Mariel boat lifts in 1980. *US-FL-so.* (Rieff 1987:29–31, 46) late20.
[< *el Mariel* 'port town ea. of Havana from which these people departed Cu' + suf. *-ito.* Acc. Rieff, often very derog. ref. to any Cuban immigrant, considered an undesirable, who came to US on the boatlifts. Also used in Amer. Engl. Cf. **gusano.**]

marimbero 'marimba player'
1. offspring of a Chontal Indian and a white, esp. one who plays the marimba. *Mx-s.w.* (Herrera and Cícero 1895:72) 19prior.
2. person who deals cocaine or marijuana. *Co-coast* (Megenney 1988:p.c.) late20.
[< *marimba* 'resonant musical instrument' + suf. *-ero.* Cf. **mestizo.**]

marimbo — See *güero*

marismeño 'lowlander; marsh dweller'
Pima Indian who lived on the banks of the Colorado River. *Mx-Sonora* (Sobarzo 1966:201) 20prior.
[< *marisma* 'low, marshy land frequently inundated' + adj. suf. *-eño.* Perhaps obs.]

marrón 'chestnut-colored, brown'
1. runaway slave. *PR* (Alvarez Nazario 1974:342) cl.
2. brown-skinned person who has curly hair. *Co* (Revollo 1942:169) mid20.
[Acc. Santamaría (1942:2.251), used in ref. to a woman's curls. Most probably < apheresis of *cimarrón* 'runaway slave.' Alternatively, acc. Alvarez Nazario (1974:342) and Alonso (1958:2.2728), < Fr. *marron* 'chestnut brown.' Engl. *maroon* < Sp. Cf. **cimarrón.**]

marrueco 'Moroccan'
person from the Virgin Islands. *PR* (Cowles 1952:498) mid20.
[Cf. **isleño.**]

más o menos blanco 'more or less white'
person whose skin color indicates racial mixture. *Co-Cartagena* (Solaún and Kronus 1973:166, 168) 20.
[Cf. **blanco.**]

mateo 'Matthew'
Mexican immigrant. *US-CO, -NM* (Cobos 1983:108) late19–20.
[Acc. Cobos, euph. for the derog. *mato* (< *surumato*). Cf. **surumato.**]

mato — See *mateo, surumato*

matucho 'agile; astute; devil'
peninsular Spaniard. *SA* (Bayo 1910:139) early20 ‖ *Ch* (Kany 1960b:37; Santamaría 1942:2.260) mid20prior.
[Acc. Corominas (1954–57:3.292), < *matar* 'to kill.' Acc. Kany, obs. Cf. **chapetón, gachupín, gallego, godo.**]

maturrango 'clumsy; poor horseman'
la. Spaniard. *Ar Ur* (Cowles 1952:505) mid20.
1b. Spaniard, formerly considered clumsy or not aware of customs in the New World. *Ch* (Kany 1960b:37) 20prior.
1c. Spaniard during the wars of independence. *RP* (Guarnieri 1979:126) 19.
2. person recently arrived in the country. *Ar* (Santamaría 1942:2.260); *SA* (Alonso 1958:2.2747) 20.
[Acc. Santamaría (1942:2.260), < *matungo* 'old; old horse; poor horsemanship.' Acc. Guarnieri, 'inexpert, esp. at horsemanship.' Acc. Kany, obs. Cf. **criollo, gachupín, godo, matucho.**]

mayate 'black bug; black beetle'
black person. *US-AZ* (Barker 1950:34) mid20 ‖ *US-NM* (Kany 1960b:36) 20.
[Acc. Barker, Pachuco slang. Acc. Kany, Pachuco slang; < Nahuatl (Aztec) *mayatl* 'type of black beetle.' Var. *mallate.* Cf. **de medio pelo, gente de tomuza, mallate, matucho, maturrango.**]

mazamorrero 'corn mush eater'
person native to Lima, Pe. *Pe* (Kany 1960b:41) 20.
[Acc. Kany, < *mazamorra* 'corn mush.' Acc. Megenney (1988:p.c.), 'person who gets into trouble' in coastal Co. Cf. **maicero, motoso.**]

mazombo
black person from Africa; black African. *An* (Alvarez Nazario 1974:356) cl.
[Probably indicates 'slave.' Acc. Alvarez Nazario (1974:356), < *Mozambique* 's.e. African country from which many black slaves were taken.' Vars. *mosombo, mozombo, mozambo.* Cf. **criollo,** Ptg. **mazombo.**]

meco 'silly, stupid; left-handed person'
1. black Jamaican. *Pa* (Aguilera Patiño 1951:470) mid20.
2. wild, uncivilized, uncultured, or savage Indian. *US-CA* (Blanco 1971:219) cl ‖ *Mx-Zacatecas, -Querétaro, -Durango* (Malaret 1944:183) mid20 ‖ *Mx* (Santamaría 1942:2.266; Cowles 1952:508; Alonso 1958:2.2758) 20; (Vergara Martín 1922:240) n.d.
3. Indian. *Mx* (Santamaría 1942:2.266; Cowles 1952:508; Alonso 1958:2.2758); *US-CO, -NM* (Cobos 1983:109) 20.
[Df. 1 probably < apheresis of Engl. *Jamaican.* Df. 2 < *Chichimecan*

'Indian tribe of Mx,' acc. Santamaría (1942:2.266) and Kany (1960b:34). Acc. Cobos, < Mexican Sp. *chichimeca* 'Indian tribe from the Valley of Mexico at the time of Aztec colonization, sim. to Apaches in demeanor.' Df. 3 generally pejor. Cf. **chumagra, chumeco.**]

medio color 'half color'

mulatto. *US-LA-St. Bernard Parish* (MacCurdy 1950:72) mid20.

[Cf. **de color medio,** Ptg. **médio.**]

medio pelo — See *mediopelo*

mediopelo

1. mulatto. *Mx* (Alario di Filippo 1964:212; Santamaría 1942:2.268) 20.

2. person, esp. a woman, of low social class who uses dress and actions to feign a higher one. *Bo* (Fernández and Fernández 1967:96) 20.

3. person who does not belong to the higher classes. *Co Mx* (Alario di Filippo 1964:259) 20.

4. person with nonwhite skin color. *Pe* (Paz Soldán 1938:389) late19–early20.

[Df. 4 euph. Acc. Alonso (1958:2.2765), 'person with little hair' in Aragon and Navarra regions of Spain. Usually found in phr. *de mediopelo* or *gente de mediopelo.* Var. *medio pelo.* Cf. **color de mediopelo, color honesto, gente de mediopelo.**]

mejicano 'Mexican'

1. person from NM of mixed Indian and Hispanic descent. *US-CO, -NM* (Cobos 1983:109) 20.

2. Mexican. *US-CO, -NM* (Cobos 1983:109) 20.

[Cf. **chicano, gente de razón, mexicano, pachuco.**]

membrillo 'quince'

mulato pardo, or offspring of a black and an Indian. *Mx-Chiapas* (Alvarez Nazario 1974:351) cl.

[Acc. Boyd-Bowman (1971:578), att. in Puebla, Mx, 1554 as *de color de membrillo cocho.* Usually in phr. *color (de) membrillo.*]

mengala — See *mengalo*

mengalo

1. person, usually a woman, from the middle class. *Sa* (Cowles 1952:511) mid20.

2a. country girl, or *ladina. Gu* (Cowles 1952:511) mid20.

2b. young woman from the country, usually very poor. *CeA* (Cowles 1952:511); *Ho* (Santamaría 1942:2.272) mid20.

3. Indian girl. *Gu* (Alonso 1958:2.2786) 20.

[F. form dfs. 2, 3 *mengala;* m. counterpart *el lana,* acc. Cowles. Acc.

Cobarruvias (1611:799), *mengala* 'very delicate cloth or veil brought from the province of Mengala, India.']

mequimisto

person with dark skin color, implying a mixture of white and Indian, acc. parish records and other documents. *Mx* (Roncal 1944:533; León 1924:20–21, plate 28; Pérez de Barradas 1948:193); *SA* (Mörner 1967:59) cl.

[Vars. *mequimixt, mequimixto.*]

mequimixt — See *mequimisto*

mequimixto — See *mequimisto*

merino 'wool'

negro amembrillado, or black person with dark skin and generally curly or kinky hair. *SA* (Diggs 1953:406) cl.

[Cf. **negro amembrillado.**]

mestenco —See *mostrenco*

mesteño —See *mostrenco*

mestezuelo

mestizo; *ladino. CeA* (Salazar García 1910:167) early20.

[Cf. **ladino, mestizo.**]

mestindio

1a. person with dark skin color, implying mixed race, acc. parish records and other documents. *Mx* (Roncal 1944:533) cl.

1b. offspring in any combination of white and Indian, acc. parish priests. *Mx-Oaxaca* (Chance and Taylor 1977:461) 18.

2a. offspring of an Indian and a mestizo; 25% white, 75% Indian. *Mx* (León 1924:58; 20–21, plate 29; Woodbridge 1948:358; Pérez de Barradas 1948:189) cl.

2b. offspring of a *mestizo blanco* and and Indian; 25% white, 75% Indian. *Mx* (Woodbridge 1948:358; Aguirre Beltrán 1972:172) cl.

2c. offspring of a white mestizo and an Indian, identified with the Indian population. *Mx* (Aguirre Beltrán 1945:218) 17

[< *mesti-* 'mixed' + *indio* 'Indian.' Cf. **mequimisto, mestizo.**]

mestizo 'half-breed; mestizo'

1. person whose skin color indicates racial mixture. *Co* (Flórez 1969:122; Solaún and Kronus 1973:166) 20.

2a. offspring of a white and an Indian; 50% white, 50% Indian. *Pe* (Pérez de Barradas 1948:184, 185, 186, 188) cl.

2b. offspring of a white and an Indian. *DR* (Exquemelin 1684, chap. 3); *SA* (Gibson 1966:116; Mörner 1967:34; Rosenblat 1954: 1.71; León 1924:24–25; Woodbridge 1948:358); *Mx* (McAlister 1963:354; Woodbridge 1948:355; Monteforte Toledo 1959:171; Love

1971:81; Roncal 1944:533; Aguirre Beltrán 1972:170; León 1924:20–21, plate 30) cl ‖ *Mx* (Aguirre Beltrán 1945:217) 17 ‖ *Mx* (Mörner 1967:58; O'Crouley 1972:19); *Pe* (Mörner 1967:58); *SA* (Barón Castro 1946:798–99) 18 ‖ *DR* (Domínguez 1973:108–9) late18 ‖ *Mx* (McAlister 1963:354); *SA* (Pérez de Barradas 1948:174) 19 ‖ *SA* (Bayo 1910:142) early20 ‖ *Mx* (Cowles 1952:513) mid20 ‖ *SA* (Esteva Fabregat 1964:281); *Co-Zarzal* (Sayres 1956:223); *SA* (Bailey and Nasatir 1973:773) 20 ‖ *An Co-Cartagena* (Solaún et al. 1987:18) late20.

2c. offspring of a white European and an Indian, of lighter color than the Indian more resembling the European, and known for thievery, sensuality, and drunk behavior. *SA* (Alcedo 1786–89:5.64) late18.

2d. dihybrid, second-generation offspring of a white and an Indian. *Mx* (Moreno Navarro 1973:129–31; Solano 1975:85) 18.

3a. any person of mixed race, but usually of white and Indian. *RP* (Woodbridge 1948:358); *SA* (Gibson 1966:116); *Mx* (McAlister 1963:354) cl; (Moreno Navarro 1973:139) 18 ‖ *Pa* (Vandiver 1949:140) mid20 ‖ *SA* (Vergara Martín 1922:240) 20prior ‖ *SA* (Morínigo 1966:412); *Ec-n.w.* (Whitten 1965:92); *Pe* (Bourricaud 1975:350) 20.

3b. any person of mixed race, with no black ancestors. *Co-Zarzal* (Sayres 1956:224–25) 20.

4a. offspring of a white and a quadroon. *PR* (Alvarez Nazario 1974:354) cl–late18.

4b. offspring of a quadroon. *DR* (Domínguez 1973:108–9) late18.

5. offspring of 2 mestizos; 50% white, 50% Indian. *Pe* (Pérez de Barradas 1948:185) cl.

6. any person who has some Indian ancestry. *Pe SA* (Romero 1944:375) cl.

7a. person who is illegitimate. *Mx-Oaxaca* (Chance and Taylor 1977:463) cl–late18.

7b. mestizo who is by implication illegitimate. *Mx* (Solano 1975:77) 17.

8. offspring of a white and a black; mulatto. *Cu* (Woodbridge 1948:358) cl.

9. offspring of a white and black, Chinese and black, or Chinese and mulatto parents. *Cu* (Vandiver 1949:143) mid20.

10. any non-Indian of low social standing. *Ec* (Klumpp 1970:262) 20.

11. *cholo,* or offspring of a white and an Indian. *SA* (Santamaría 1942:2.275) 20.

[Acc. Sayres, df. 2b 3rd highest social rank in Zarzal, Co. Df. 7 pejor. Df. 10 social term. Acc. Vergara Martín, also 'bosomy, large-breasted.' First att. in Spain about 1600, acc. Alonso (1958:2.2807) and Corominas (1954–57:3.316). Acc. Boyd-Bowman (1971:585), first att. in Mx 1564 and in Pe 1570. Acc. Olaechea Labayen (1985:124–5), used in SA from 1533 as 'offspring of Spaniard and Indian.' Acc. Salazar García, syns. *ladino, cholo, mestezuelo.* Cf. **chino, cholo, ladino, mestezuelo, mestindio, mulato, zambo,** Ptg. **mameluco, mestiço, misturado.**]

mestizo amulatado 'mulatto-like mestizo'
offspring of a *mestizo blanco* and a *mulatto pardo. Mx* (Aguirre Beltrán 1972:171) cl; (Aguirre Beltrán 1945:218) 17 ‖ *Ar-Santiago de Estero* (Grenón 1929:17) 18.
[*Amulatado* < *a-* + *mulato* + *-ado*. Syns. *coyote, mestizo pardo.* Cf. **coyote, mestizo blanco, mestizo pardo, mulato pardo.**]

mestizo blanco 'white mestizo'
offspring of a white and an Indian; *coyote. Mx* (Aguirre Beltrán 1972:171; Woodbridge 1948:358) cl.
[Cf. **blanco, coyote, mestizo amulatado.**]

mestizo castizo
offspring of a white and a *mestizo blanco; castizo. Mx* (Aguirre Beltrán 1972:171; Woodbridge 1948:358) cl.
[Acc. Aguirre Beltrán, light-skinned person, often confused with a pure Spaniard. Cf. **castizo, mestizo, mestizo blanco.**]

mestizo claro 'light mestizo'
person of mixed race with light skin color. *Co-Cartagena* (Solaún and Kronus 1973:166) 20.
[Cf. **claro, mestizo,** Ptg. **mestiço claro.**]

mestizo indoespañol — See *cholo*

mestizo mezclado 'mixed mestizo'
person whose skin color indicates mixed race, probably at least part Indian. *Co-Cartagena* (Solaún and Kronus 1973:166) 20.
[Acc. Solaún and Kronus (1973:166), *mestizo mesclado* [*sic*]. Cf. **mezcla.**]

mestizo moreno 'brown mestizo'
person of mixed race with brown skin color. *Co-Cartagena* (Solaún and Kronus 1973:166) 20.
[Cf. **mestizo pardo, moreno.**]

mestizo pardo 'dark brown mestizo'
1. person of mixed race with dark brown skin color. *SA* (Diggs 1953:406) cl.
2a. offspring of a *mestizo blanco* and a *mulatto pardo. Mx* (Aguirre Beltrán 1972:171; Woodbridge 1948:358) cl.

2b. offspring of a mestizo and a dark mulatto. *Mx* (Aguirre Beltrán 1945:218) 17.

[Acc. Aguirre Beltrán, syns. *mestizo amulatado, coyote.* Cf. **coyote, mestizo amulatado, mestizo blanco, mulato pardo.**]

mestizo prieto 'black mestizo'

1. person of mixed race with black skin color. *SA* (Diggs 1953:406) cl.

2. offspring of a *mestizo blanco* and a black, usually with obvious black features. *Mx* (Aguirre Beltrán 1972:171; Woodbridge 1948:358) cl.

3. offspring of a mestizo and a black, usually with obvious black features. *Mx* (Aguirre Beltrán 1945:218) 17.

[Syn. *mulato amestizado.* Cf. **mulato amestizado, prieto.**]

mestizo real 'royal or real mestizo'

offspring of a Spaniard and an Indian. *Pe* (Alonso 1958:2.2807) probably cl.

[Cf. **mestizo.**]

mestizo sambaigo

person of mixed race, probably of Indian, black, and white. *Ar* (Grenón 1930:357) early19.

[Cf. **mestizo, mestizo amulatado, sambaigo.**]

mestizón

1. person whose skin color indicates mixed race. *Co-Cartagena* (Solaún and Kronus 1973:166, 168) 20.

2. offspring of a mestizo and a *criollo. Ar* (Santamaría 1942:2.275) 20.

[Df. 1 often f.; sexual overtones. < *mestizo* + pejor. aug. suf. *-ón.* Cf. **criollo, mestizo.**]

mestrenco — See *mostrenco*

mestreño — See *mostrenco*

mexicano 'Mexican'

1. Mexican. *US-CO, -NM* (Cobos 1983:111) 20.

2. New Mexican of Mexican background. *US-CO, -NM* (Cobos 1983:111) 20.

[Syn. and var. *mejicano.* Cf. **gente de razón, mejicano.**]

mezcla 'mixture'

person whose skin color indicates mixed race. *Co-Cartagena* (Solaún and Kronus 1973:166) 20.

[Cf. **mestizo mezclado,** Ptg. **cruza.**]

mezcla clara 'light mixture'

person of mixed race with light skin color. *Co-Cartagena* (Solaún and Kronus 1973:166) 20.

[Cf. **claro, mestizo mezclado.**]

minuán

Indian who lived on the northern bank of the Paraná River near the mouth of the Salado, during the time of the discovery of America. *Ar* (Garzón 1910:312; Alonso (1958:2.2841) cl.

[Var. *minuano.*]

minuano — See *minuán*

miste

1. mestizo or mulatto from the coastal areas. *Pe* (Kany 1960b:36) 20.

2. white person or mestizo, acc. Indians. *Pe* (Cowles 1952:520) mid20.

3. white person, acc. Indians. *Bo Pe* (Cowles 1952:520) mid20.

[Df. 1 facet. Perhaps < *mixtura* 'mixture.' Var. *misti,* acc. Cowles. Cf. **mestizo.**]

míster

1. person who is probably an outsider or foreigner. *Co-Villapinzón* (Flórez 1969:122) 20.

2. older male or male teacher. *PR* (Gallo 1980:71) 20.

[M. < Engl. *mister.* Df. 2 Puerto Rican slang. Acc. Alonso (1958:2.2852), 'gentleman,' respect. in Engl.; Sp. equiv. *señor.* Cf. **musiú, yanqui.**]

misti — See *miste*

mitayo

Indian given work through a lottery system or used in public jobs. *SA* (Vergara Martín 1922:240) n.d.

[< *mita* 'tribute paid by Indians,' prior 20-cent. Cf. **indio.**]

mohino 'gloomy; sullen; offspring of a horse and a donkey; black'

1. person whose skin color implies racial mixture. *Ve* (Flórez 1969:123) 20.

2. black person. *Pe* (Cowles 1952:523) mid20.

3. black person with very dark skin. *Co* (Alario di Filippo 1964:218); *Mx* (Santamaría 1942:2.290) 20.

[Var. *mojino.* Syns. *macuito, muzucuco.* Cf. **macuito.**]

mojado 'wet'

1. peninsular Spaniard. *PR* (Malaret 1937:221) prior20.

2. Mexican migrant worker who crossed the US-Mx border illegally; wetback. *Mx US* (Gann and Duignan 1986:129) 20.

[Acc. Alonso (1958:2.2865), df. 1 also used in ref. to person who was sympathetic to cl. Sp. sovereignty in PR. Df. 2 often derog. Cf. **bracero, pocho.**]

mojino — See *mohino*

moleca — See *muleque*

moleque — See *muleque*

molleto

black person or anyone with very dark skin, generally not muscular. *PR* (Gallo 1980:72) 20.

[Acc. Gallo, slang. Cf. **morado, moreno, negro.**]

mono 'monkey; blond; cute'

1. person with light hair color and perhaps light skin color. *Co* (Flórez 1969:122, 123) 20.

2a. person with blond or very light brown hair color. *Co-Bogotá* (Acuña 1951:113) mid20.

2b. person with golden blond hair. *Co* (Santamaría 1942:2.295; Alonso 1958:2.2878) 20.

2c. person with red hair but never a blond. *Co-coast* (Revollo 1942:178); *Co* (Malaret 1931:362) mid20.

3. Chinese. *Pe* (Malaret 1944:201) mid20; (Kany 1960b:38) 20.

4. coastal dweller, acc. highlanders. *Ec* (Carvalho-Neto 1964: 298) 20.

5. person generally considered white, esp. young person with white features. *Co-Zarzal* (Sayres 1956:223) 20.

6. Ecuadorian. *SA* (Simmons 1955:109); *Pe* (Kany 1960b:39) 20.

7. any handsome, pretty, or nice person. *SA* (Santamaría 1942:2.295) 20.

[Df. 4 derog.; syn. *costeño*. Df. 5 familiar; 2nd highest social rank in Zarzal, Co, acc. Sayres. Possibly < *mono* 'monkey with light body hair in the Andean highlands.' Cf. **chele, pelicandelo, rubio,** Ptg. **louro.**]

mono blanco 'white monkey'

person with light hair color. *Co-Cartagena* (Solaún and Kronus 1973:166) 20.

[Acc. Santamaría (1942:2.295), 'little So. Amer. monkey with light hair.' Cf. **mono.**]

mono colorado 'red monkey'

person with red or reddish hair color. *Co-coast* (Revollo 1942:178) mid20.

[Acc. Santamaría (1942:2.295), 'type of So. Amer. monkey.' Cf. **colorado, mono, mono blanco, mono moreno.**]

mono de orozuz — See *muñeco de orozuz*

mono moreno 'brown monkey'

person with brown hair color. *Co-Cartagena* (Solaún and Kronus 1973:166) 20.

[Acc. Santamaría (1942:2.295), 'type of So. Amer. monkey.' Syn. *machango*. Cf. **mono, mono blanco, mono colorado, moreno.**]

monstruos-rompecielos — See *rompecielos*

montañero 'peasant; mountain dweller'

peasant, esp. one who lives in or near the mountains; person from Antioquia or Caldas. *Co* (Alario di Filippo 1964:221) 20.

[Cf. **campesino, montañés.**]

montañés 'mountain dweller'

1. mountain dweller; mountaineer. *SA* (Alonso 1958:2.2885) 20.

2. mestizo. *Pe Pg* (Rosenblat 1954:2.88, 116) 16.

[< *montaña* 'mountain' + suf. *-és.* Cf. **cholo, costeño, guajiro, jíbaro, ladino, mestizo, montañero, serrano.**]

montubio

1. mestizo whose ancestry includes white, black, and Indian. *Ec-no.* (Rosenblat 1954:2.82) mid20.

2. coastal-dwelling, Spanish-speaking Indian. *Ec-n.w., -so.* (Whitten 1965:91) 20.

3. peasant or dirt farmer, usually from the coastal areas. *Ec Pe* (Cowles 1952:526; Santamaría 1942:2.297; Alonso 1958:2.2887) mid20 ‖ *Ec* (Carvalho-Neto 1964:298–99; Malaret 1947:122; Bayo 1931:170) 20.

4. uncivilized, dangerous, and ill-kept person. *Ec-n.w.* (Whitten 1965:91) 20.

5. light-skinned person of the lower classes from the provinces of Manabi or Guayas. *Ec-n.w.* (Whitten 1965:91) 20.

6. light-skinned coastal dweller, esp. from the provinces of Manabi or Guayas, who has no outstanding black features. *Ec-n.w.* (Whitten 1965:92) 20.

7. black runaway slave who often took an Indian wife. *SA* (Urbanski 1978:217) cl.

[Acc. Alonso (1958:2.2887), excl. to coastal areas of Ec, Pe, and Co. Sim. to *chagra, charro, jíbaro, guajiro, concho, guaso, guacho* of other areas. Var. *montuvio.* Cf. **cholo, costeño, serrano.**]

montuno 'rustic; wild'

1. peasant; *guajiro. Cu-ea.* (Vergara Martín 1922:240) n.d. ‖ *Cu* (Pichardo 1953:487); *Cu-Vueltarriba* (Macías 1885:866) 19 ‖ *Co-coast Cu* (Revollo 1942:179); *An Ch Co Pa Ve* (Malaret 1937:222 and 1947:122; Cowles 1952:526); *Pa* (Aguilera Patiño 1951:473) mid20 ‖ *Ch Co Cu PR Ve* (Alario di Filippo 1964:221); *Cu Ve* (Dihigo 1966:182; Espina Pérez 1972:131) 20.

2. stupid or uncivilized person. *Cu-we.* (Vergara Martín 1922:240) n.d.

[Syns. *campesino, guajiro, montañés.* Cf. **cholo, guajiro, montubio, roto.**]

montuvio — See *montubio*

morado 'purple'
person whose skin color is very dark. *Ar* (Cowles 1952:527) mid20 ‖ *Co-Baraya* (Flórez 1969:122) 20.
[Var. *morao*. Cf. **morejón.**]

morao — See *morado*

morcilla 'blood sausage; black pudding'
black person. *US* (de la Bandera 1989:p.c.) 20–late20.
[M., f. Acc. de la Bandera, euph. formulated by blue-collar Uru-guayans in US; derog. syn. *teléfono;* syn. in Ur *negrito*. Cf. **negrito, negro, negro como una paila, muñeco de orozuz, teléfono.**]

morejón
black person considered ugly or ordinary. *DR* (Patín Maceo 1940:118; Alonso 1958:2.2893) 20.
[Probably derog. F. form *morejona*. < *mora* 'mulberry' + *-ej-* + aug. pejor. suf. *-ón.* Cf. **morado, negro, pardejón.**]

morejona — See *morejón*

morena caliente 'hot brunette'
sexually attractive woman whose darkish skin color and dark hair indicate racial mixture. *Co-Cartagena* (Solaún and Kronus 1973:166) 20.
[Usually f. Cf. **moreno, moreno alisado, moreno bastante, moreno criollo,** Ptg. **mulata quente.**]

morenito 'little brown or brunet one'
black person. *Ur* (Cowles 1952:527) mid20.
[Euph. < *moreno* + dim. suf. *-ito.* Cf. **moreno.**]

morenito acrespado 'little brown, kinky-haired one'
person of mixed race with kinky hair. *Co-Cartagena* (Solaún and Kronus 1973:166, 168) 20.
[Acc. Solaún and Kronus, considered paternalistic or affect. *Acrespado* < *a-* + *crespo* 'kinky, curly' + adj. suf. *-ado.* Cf. **morado, morenito, moreno.**]

moreno 'brown; brunet'
1. person whose skin color ranges from white or light brown to very black, acc. parish records, literary works, and other documents. *Mx* (Chance 1979:164) early19; (Chance and Taylor 1977:164) 19 ‖ *Ve Co* (Flórez 1969:122, 123); *SA* (Pitt-Rivers 1967:548) 20.
2a. black person. *Mx* (Aguirre Beltrán 1972:173; Love 1971:81); *SA* (Mörner 1967:44; Alvarez Nazario 1974:348) cl ‖ *PR* (Alvarez Nazario 1974:380) cl–20 ‖ *Cu* (Martinez-Alier 1974:17) 18–19 ‖ *Mx* (O'Crouley 1972:19) 18 ‖ *Ar* (Andrews 1979:21) 19 ‖ *Cu*

(Vergara Martín 1922:240) early20 ‖ *Pe* (Paz Soldán 1938:289); *Gu* (Cowles 1952:527) mid20 ‖ *Cu* (Dihigo 1966:183; Santamaría 1942:2.299); *PR* (Zenón Cruz 1975:1.254); *RP* (Guarnieri 1967:149); *SA* (Kany 1960b:35; Nuñez 1980:323) 20.

2b. black person or mulatto. *SA* (Rosenblat 1954:2.157); *Mx* (Love 1971:81) cl ‖ *Cu* (Dihigo 1966:183) 20.

2c. Afro-American, or black person native to US, acc. adult Cubans, Dominicans, and Puerto Ricans of Washington Heights, New York City. *US-NY* (Domínguez 1973:186) 20.

2d. black American. *PR US* (Gann and Duignan 1986:80) 20.

3a. any person of color with light skin. *An SA* (Sánchez-Albornoz 1974:130) cl.

3b. person with copperish-brown skin color. *Mx-Oaxaca* (Garza Cuarón 1987:64) late20.

4a. any free person, usually dark-skinned, of the lower class. *SA* (Diggs 1953:407) late cl.

4b. any free black. *PR* (Alvarez Nazario 1974:346–47); *PR SA* (Zenón Cruz 1975:1.252) cl.

4c. free person of color with dark skin, acc. mid-19 cent. censuses. *PR* (Domínguez 1973:123) mid19.

5. mestizo. *Mx* (Mörner 1967:82) late18–early19.

6a. any person with some black ancestry, acc. parish records. *Mx* (Roncal 1944:533) cl.

6b. adult person of mixed race. *Co-Cartagena* (Solaún et al. 1987:18–19) late20.

6c. person of mixed race with predominantly black features. *Co-Zarzal* (Sayres 1956:223) 20.

7. black person, *zambo,* or mulatto, acc. himself or herself. *Ec-n.w.-coast* (Whitten 1965:90) 20.

8a. black person, considered brunet. *SA* (Kany 1960b:35) 20.

8b. dark-skinned person of African descent, considered brunet. *Cu* (Rout 1976:xv) cl–20.

8c. white person, person of mixed race, or black person, considered brunet. *Co-Cartagena* (Solaún and Kronus 1973:164, 166, 183) 20.

8d. white person with brunet hair. *Co-Cartagena* (Solaún et al. 1987:18–19) late20.

[Dfs. 2a, 2b, 3a, 4 euph. Acc. Gann and Duignan, df. 2d color classification in PR, opp. to *gente de color* 'black or dark-skinned Puerto Rican'; used esp. by Puerto Ricans in US. Df. 6c 7th highest social rank in Zarzal, Co, acc. Sayres. Df. 8c highly ambiguous. Acc. Solaún et al., indicates both blackness and whiteness and thus terminological mixing. Acc. Boyd-Bowman (1971:602), att. as a skin color in Mx 1532. Deriv. *morenito.* Cf. **color inferior, colorado, costeño, europeo, gente de color, güero, mestizo, morenito, morenito acrespado, mulato, negro, pardo, prieto, quebrado, trigueño, zambo,** Ptg. **moreno.**]

moreno alisado

black person, usually a woman, who greases her hair in order to eliminate the kinkiness. *Co-Cartagena* (Solaún and Kronus 1973:134) 20.

[Usually in f. form *morena alisada. Alisado* 'smoothed' < *a-* + *liso* 'smooth' + adj. suf. *-ado.* Acc. Solaún and Kronus, equiv. to old So. Amer. Engl. phr. *mammy's leg.* Cf. **moreno, mulato.**]

moreno avanzado 'advanced brown or brunet'

person whose skin color is probably very dark. *Co-Cartagena* (Solaún and Kronus 1973:166) 20.

[Cf. **moreno, moreno alisado.**]

moreno bastante 'brunet enough'

person whose skin color indicates racial mixture. *Co-Cartagena* (Solaún and Kronus 1973:166) 20.

[Cf. **morena caliente, moreno, moreno avanzado.**]

moreno caliente — See *morena caliente*

moreno claro 'light brunet'

person whose social class requires a lighter racial category than is otherwise indicated by dark skin color. *Co-Cartagena* (Solaún et al. 1987:19) late20.

[Acc. Solaún et al., ambiguous term, perhaps euph. Cf. **morena caliente, moreno, moreno criollo,** Ptg. **moreno claro.**]

moreno criollo 'creole brunet'

black person born in PR. *PR* (Alvarez Nazario 1974:248) late18.
[Acc. Boyd-Bowman (1983:1587), att. in SA early 17 cent.; ant. *moreno de Barlovento.* Cf. **chumeca, criollo, moreno, moreno de Barlovento.**]

moreno de Barlovento 'black from the Windward Islands'

1. black slave not born in PR. *PR* (Alvarez Nazario 1974:348) 18.
2. black person from Barlovento, Ve. *Ve* (Megenney 1988:p.c.) late20.

[*Barlovento* 'island off the we. African coast through which many black slaves passed on their way to America.' Acc. Lipski (1988:p.c.), 'Cape Verde Island or Windward Islands of the Caribbean.' Cf. **libre, libre de color, moreno, moreno criollo.**]

moreno libre 'free black person'

black person or mulatto not subject to slavery; free black or mulatto. *SA* (Barón Castro 1946:797) cl.

[Cf. **moreno.**]

moreno o mestizo
person whose skin color implies some unclassifiable racial mixture. *Co-Cartagena* (Solaún and Kronus 1973:166) 20.
[Sim. to *más o menos blanco*. Cf. **más o menos blanco, moreno, mulato, moreno mulato.**]

moreno oscuro 'dark brown or brunet'
person with dark skin color. *Co-Cartagena* (Solaún and Kronus 1973:166) 20.
[Cf. **moreno, moreno subido, moreno tostado, oscuro.**]

moreno subido 'dark brunet'
person with dark skin color. *Co-Cartagena* (Solaún and Kronus 1973:166) 20.
[Cf. **moreno, moreno oscuro, moreno tostado.**]

moreno tostado 'toasted brunet'
person with dark skin color. *Co-Cartagena* (Solaún and Kronus 1973:166) 20.
[Cf. **moreno, moreno oscuro, moreno subido, moreno trigueño.**]

moreno trigueño 'wheat-colored brunet'
person with light brown skin color. *Co-Cartagena* (Solaún and Kronus 1973:166) 20.
[Cf. **moreno, moreno oscuro, moreno subido, moreno tostado, trigueño.**]

morisco 'Moorish'
1. person with the dark skin color reminiscent of a Moor, acc. parish records and provincial documents. *Mx-Oaxaca* (Chance and Taylor 1977:460) 18.
2a. offspring of a white and a mulatto; 75% white, 25% black. *Mx* (León 1924:25, 20–21, plate 31; Woodbridge 1948:355, 358; Pérez de Barradas 1948:184, 189) cl.
2b. offspring of a white and a mulatto. *Mx* (Aguirre Beltrán 1972:162; Roncal 1944:533; Love 1971:81; Monteforte Toledo 1959:171) cl; (Mörner 1967:58; O'Crouley 1972:19) 18; (McAlister 1963:354) 19; ‖ *SA* (Kany 1960b:35) 20.
2c. offspring of a mulatto and a white European. *Mx* (Vergara Martín 1922:240; Santamaría 1942:2.299; Alonso 1958:2.2896) cl; (Aguirre Beltrán 1945:214) 17; (Malaret 1931:364) prior20.
2d. offspring of a mulatto and a white Spaniard. *SA* (Vergara Martín 1922:240) cl.
2e. offspring of 3 white grandparents and 1 black one. *Mx* (Solano 1975:83) 17; (Moreno Navarro 1973:140) 18.
2f. dihybrid, third-generation offspring of a mulatto and a white. *Mx* (Moreno Navarro 1973:129–31; Solano 1975:85) 18.

3. offspring of a black and a white Spaniard. *Mx* (Aguirre Beltrán 1972:162) cl.

4. white slave from No. Africa, often of Arabic or Berber descent. *Mx* (Aguirre Beltrán 1972:156) cl.

[< *moro* 'Moor' + adj. suf. *-isco* '-ish.' Df. 2c could pass for white, usually with reddish or white skin color, acc. Aguirre Beltrán. Acc. Moreno Navarro, df. 2e skin color lighter than mulatto's; syn. in SoA *cuarterón de mulato.* Df. 3 often replaced by syn. *mulato,* acc. Aguirre Beltrán. Syn. df. 4 *esclavo blanco.* Acc. Castro (1948:57), 'Moor living under Christian rule' in medieval Spain. Acc. Cobarruvias (1611:815), 'Moorish converts to Christianity.' Acc. Aguirre Beltrán (1972:167), syn. *mulato morisco* in cl. Mx. Cf. **esclavo blanco, mulato, mulato morisco.**]

morlaco 'silly'

1. *cholo* from Cuenca who wears bright blouses and dresses. *Ec* (Carvalho-Neto 1964:301) 20.

2. person from Azuay, also known as Morlaquía. *Ec* (Alonso 1958:2.2896) 20.

[Df. 2 derog. Acc. Corominas (1954–57:3.443), 'one who feigns stupidity or ignorance;' < Italian *morlacco* 'rustic type; inhabitant of Morlaquía, a Slavic region in the mountains of Dalmatia.' Cf. **cholo.**]

moro 'Moor; Moorish'

dark-skinned slave, sometimes of Islamic religion. *Mx* (Aguirre Beltrán 1972:104–5) cl.

[Syns. *casta, esclavo moro.* Acc. Hole (1958:46), 'Andalusian,' used in 20-cent. Spain in ref. to the swarthy complexion of those Spaniards. Acc. Cobb (1972:36), 'dark-skinned or black person' in 20-cent. Spain. Acc. Corominas (1973:404), 'North African' from 1091; 'dark color' from about 1200. Cf. **casta, esclavo, esclavo moro, morisco.**]

morocho 'dark'

1a. person with dark skin color. *Co-Cachira* (Flórez 1969:12) 20.

1b. person with dark skin; black person. *RP* (Guarnieri 1968:101 and 1979:130) 20.

1c. black person, acc. peasants. *RP* (Guarnieri 1967:149) 20.

2a. person with brown skin. *Ar* (Bayo 1910:148) early20 ‖ *SoA* (Malaret 1947:123); *Ar SoA Ur* (Cowles 1952:529) mid20 ‖ *Pe RP* (Granada 1957:2.109) 20.

2b. person with brownish or bronzish skin color. *Ar* (Segovia 1911:131) early20.

3. white person, esp. one who is young and beautiful, with brown or brunet hair. *Ar* (Garzón 1910:219) early20.

[Df. 1b euph. Acc. Guarnieri (1979:130), syn. *moreno*. < Quechua *muruchu* or *muruch'u* 'hard, strong, brown, dark, chestnut-colored,' acc. Alonso (1958:2.2897), Santamaría (1942:2.300), Corominas (1954–57:3.444 and 1973:404), Guarnieri (1979:130), and Cowles. Vars. *morucho, murusho, muruxo*. Cf. **moreno, trigueño**, Ptg. **morocho**.]

morochón
> attractive, dark-skinned person. *RP* (Guarnieri 1979:130) 20.
> [< *morocho* + suf. *-ón*. Cf. **morocho**.]

morucho — See *morocho*

mosombo — See *mazombo*

mosquito de la costa — See *mosquito-zambo*

mosquito-zambo
> 1. inhabitant of the interior of the country. *SA*, probably *CeA* (Vergara Martín 1922:241) probably cl.
> 2. offspring of an Indian and a black; *zambo. SA*, probably *CeA* (Vergara Martín 1922:241) probably cl.
> [Acc. Vergara Martín, df. 1 < name *Mosquitia* 'interior of the country' so called by the Engl. sailors; term used to distinguish these persons from *mosquitos de la costa*. Cf. **zambo, zambo mosquito**.]

mostrenco 'homeless'
> very poor, wretched Indian. *Pe* (Cowles 1952:530) mid20.
> [Extremely insult. Acc. Cobarruvias (1611:816), 'any lost head of cattle with no obvious owner.' Acc. Santamaría (1942:2.303), 'spiny bush,' 'any domestic animal with no value' in SA. Vars. *mesteño, mestreño, mestrenco*.]

motocho
> person with brown skin color; *moreno. Ar Ch Pe Ur* (Flórez 1969:123) 20.
> [Sim. to *motoso* or *motudo*. Cf. **moreno, motoso, motudo**.]

motoso 'hairy'
> 1a. person with curly or kinky hair. *Ar Co* (Alario di Filippo 1964:224; Santamaría 1942:2.308); *Ar Co Ec* (Kany 1960b:55) 20.
> 1b. any person with the crisp, curly ringlets characteristic of a black person. *Ar* (Segovia 1911:131) early20.
> 2. Indian who speaks bad Spanish. *Pe* (Santamaría 1942:2.308) 20.
> 3. highlander; peasant; Motero Indian. *Pe* (Alonso 1958:2.2907; Kany 1960b:41) 20.
> [Acc. Kany, df. 1 < *mota* 'tight lock of kinky hair' + adj. suf. *-oso*. Acc. Kany, df. 3 < *mote* 'type of boiled corn,' considered the main food of the highland peasant. Acc. Bayo (1931:171) and Patín Maceo

(1940:119), *mota* 'kinky or bad hair of the black.' Cf. **motocho, motudo.**]

motudo 'hairy'
person, usually black, who has thick, tightly curled locks of hair called *motas* or *pasas*. *RP* (Guarnieri 1967:150); *Ar Ch* (Santamaría 1942:2.309); *Ch* (Alonso 1958:2.2908) 20.
[Acc. Kany (1960b:55), < *mota* + pejor. suf. *-udo*. Excl. to extreme so. SA. Cf. **motocho, motoso, pelo pasa.**]

moza 'girl servant'
white slave or concubine. *Pe* (Harth-Terré 1965:133) cl.
[F. only. Euph. Cf. **chacracama, criada, mozo, mucama.**]

mozambique 'Mozambique'
black person from Mozambique. *RP* (Pereda Valdés 1937:77) mid20 ‖ *PR* (Zenón Cruz 1975:1.249) 20.
[Acc. Zenón Cruz, 'type of black bird.' Cf. **angola, mazombo,** Ptg. **moçambique.**]

mozambo — See *mazombo*

mozo 'boy'
humble day laborer from rural areas. *Gu* (Cowles 1952:531) mid20.
[Cf. **moza.**]

mozombo — See *mazombo*

mucama 'maid servant'
1. female house servant. *Ar Pe* (Santamaría 1942:2.310) 20.
2. young, female African black who served as maidservant to the lady of the house. *Ar* (Segovia 1911:131) 19prior.
[F. only. Acc. Corominas (1973:406), Sp. term < Brz. Ptg. Acc. Megenney (1983:8), 'black or mulatto slave girl'; < Fulani *mukama* 'one of the emir's chief slaves who was the almsgiver'; or perhaps < Kikongo *mu'kami* 'pupil; child; orphan;' used as a personal name in Gullah, Engl.-based creole lg. of coastal areas of s.e. US. Cf. **ama, chacracama, criada, moza, mucamo,** Ptg. **babá, mucama.**]

mucamo
1. houseboy. *Ar* (Segovia 1911:131) early20.
2. servant of color. *Ar Ch* (Malaret 1931:367) prior20.
[M. only. Acc. Segovia, < *mucama*. Cf. **mucama.**]

muchacho 'boy'
black person. *Cu* (Pichardo 1953:490; Macías 1885:873) 19 ‖ *SA* (Kany 1960b:35) 20.
[F. form *muchacha*. Euph. in direct address for *negro*. Syn. *moreno*. Sim. in use to Amer. Engl. *boy,* derog. form of direct address, esp. in so. US. Cf. **moreno.**]

muchinga
black person. *RP* (Guarnieri 1967:151 and 1968:101) 20.
[M., f. Acc. Guarnieri, possibly < African lg. Cf. **negro.**]
muco
Nicaraguan. *CeA* (Lipski 1988:p.c.) late20.
[Acc. Lipski, originally 'cow without horns.' Cf. **nica.**]
mujico
black person with very dark skin. *Co-Tarra* (Flórez 1969:122) 20.
[Cf. **moreno tostado, negro.**]
mulañero
man who prefers mulatto women as sexual partners. *Cu* (Espina Pérez 1972:135) 20.
[< *mulata* 'mulatto woman' + suf. *-ñero* by anal. to *puta* 'whore,' *putañero* 'pimp, whoremonger.' Cf. **mulatero.**]
mulatero 'mule driver; mule owner'
1. non-mulatto who affiliates with mulattoes. *Ar* (Garzón 1910:323) early20.
2a. man who prefers mulatto women as sexual partners. *Cu* (Pichardo 1953:491; Macías 1885:875) 19.
2b. white man who prefers mulatto women as sexual partners. *Cu* (Santamaría 1942:2.314; Alonso 1958:2.2919) 20.
[< *mulata* + adj. suf. *-ero.* Syn. *mulañero.* Cf. **mulañero,** Ptg. **mulateiro.**]
mulatico 'little mulatto'
1a. mulatto. *Cu* (Pichardo 1953:491) 19.
1b. small mulatto. *Cu* (Macías 1885:875) 19.
2. *chino,* or person of mixed race. *Mx* (Boyd-Bowman 1984:2171) 19.
3. brown-skinned person. *Cu* (Macías 1885:875) 19.
[Df. 1a euph. Df. 3 affect. < *mulato* + affect. dim. suf. *-ico.* Var. *mulatillo* in 17 cent. Var. *mulito.* Cf. **chino, mulato.**]
mulatillo — See *mulatico, mulato*
mulato 'mulatto'
1a. person whose skin color implies racial mixture, generally between blacks and whites. *Pe* (Romero 1944:375); *Mx* (Aguirre Beltrán 1972:178) cl ‖ *Mx-Oaxaca* (Chance and Taylor 1977:460) 18 ‖ *Mx* (Chance 1979:164) 19 ‖ *Co-Cartagena* (Solaún and Kronus 1973:166); *SA* (Bailey and Nasatir 1973:773) 20.
1b. person who has some black ancestry. *Cu* (Macías 1885:875) 19.
2a. offspring of a black and a white; 50% white, 50% black. *An*

mulato   PART I

(Alvarez Nazario 1974:351); *Mx* (Woodbridge 1948:355); *Mx Pe SoA-no.* (Velásquez 1962:114); *Ar Mx* (Woodbridge 1948:359); *SA* (Aguirre Beltrán 1972:159); *SA* (Gibson 1966:116); *DR* (Exquemelin 1684, chap. 3); *Mx* (Roncal 1944:533; Pérez de Barradas 1948:184, 186, 188, 189; León 1924:20–21, plate 32); *Pe SA* (Barón Castro 1946, plate X); *An PR SA* (Alvarez Nazario 1974:351); *Mx* (Love 1971:81; Monteforte Toledo 1959:171) cl ‖ *Pe* (Rogers 1712:203) 17–18 ‖ *Mx Pe* (Mörner 1967:58) 18 ‖ *Mx* (O'Crouley 1972:19) cl–18 ‖ *Mx* (Moreno Navarro 1973:140) 18 ‖ *SA* (Alcedo 1786–89:5.68); *DR* (Domínguez 1973:108) late18 ‖ *Cu* (Pichardo 1953:491; Macías 1885:875); *Mx* (McAlister 1963:354) 19 ‖ *SA* (Pérez de Barradas 1948:174) late19 ‖ *Cu* (Rout 1976:xv) cl–20 ‖ *Mx* (Cowles 1952:533) mid20 ‖ *Co-Zarzal* (Sayres 1956:223); *RP* (Guarnieri 1979:132); *Ec-n.w.* (Whitten 1965:92); *SA* (Alonso 1958:2.2919; Esteva Fabregat 1964:281) 20 ‖ *SA* (Vergara Martín 1922:241) n.d.

2b. dihybrid, second-generation offspring of a black and a white. *Mx* (Moreno Navarro 1973:129–31; Solano 1975:85) 18.

2c. person who is descended from a mixture of blacks and whites. *An Co-Cartagena* (Solaún et al. 1987:18) late20.

3. offspring of a white and a *zambo*. *Pe* (Santamaría 1942: 2.314; Woodbridge 1948:358) cl.

4. offspring of a white and a mulatto. *Cu* (Woodbridge 1948:358) cl; (Pichardo 1953:491) 19; (Vergara Martín 1922:241) n.d.

5. enslaved mestizo. *PR* (Alvarez Nazario 1974:347) cl.

6. offspring of a black and an Indian; *zambaigo*. *Mx* (Aguirre Beltrán 1972:162) 16.

7. *morisco, pardo,* or mulatto, acc. official administrative sources. *Mx-Oaxaca* (Chance and Taylor 1977:460) 18.

8. offspring of 2 mulattoes; 50% black, 50% white. *Pe* (Pérez de Barradas 1948:186; Barón Castro 1946, plate X); *DR* (Woodbridge 1948:358) cl; (Santamaría 1942:2.314) mid20; (Vergara Martín 1922:241) n.d. ‖ *Cu* (Macías 1885:875) 19.

9. person of mixed race, including Indian, black and white. *Mx* (Aguirre Beltrán 1945:214) 17 ‖ *Co-Zarzal* (Sayres 1956:223) 20.

10. very light-skinned person from the coast. *Ec-n.w.* (Whitten 1965:91) 20.

11. taxpayer of the lower classes; dangerous person. *Mx-Oaxaca* (Chance and Taylor 1977:463) 18.

12. any beautiful woman. *Cu* (Macías 1885:875) 19.

[Syn. df. 2a *pardo*, acc. Domínguez. Syn. df. 6 *zambaigo*. Acc. Sayres, dfs. 2a and 9 are 5th highest social rank in Zarzal, Co; more

168

admired than *negro* and considered mentally quick but lacking re-
sponsibility. Acc. Pichardo, affect. in 19-cent. Havana, Cu. Acc.
Zenón Cruz, implies slavery or poor social status. Acc. Cobarruvias
(1611:819), sim. to a mule, *mulato* is a hybrid animal. Acc. Corominas (1954–57:3.475), first applied to 'offspring of a European and
Moor' in 16-cent. Spain, then to 'offspring of a black and an Indian'
in SA 16 cent. Acc. Boyd-Bowman (1971:609), first att. as a racial
term in Pa 1550. Var. *mulat*. Dim. *mulatillo* in late 18-cent. Ar,
acc. Grenón (1929:229). Engl. *mulatto*, Fr. *mulâtre* < Sp. Cf. **mestizo, moreno, morisco, pardo, prieto, zambaigo, zambo,** Ptg.
mulato.]

mulato alobado
offspring of a *mulato lobo* and an Indian, whose features tend
toward those of the Indian. *Mx* (Aguirre Beltrán 1972:170) cl;
(Aguirre Beltrán 1945:217) 17.
[*Alobado* < *a-* + *lobo* 'wolf' + adj. suf. *-ado*. Cf. **mestizo amulatado,
mulato amestizado, mulato anegrado.**]

mulato amarillo 'yellow mulatto'
mulatto with yellowish skin color. *An* (Nuñez 1980:328) 20.
[Cf. **amarillo, mulato, mulato amestizado, mulato membrillo,
mulato pardo.**]

mulato amestizado 'mestizo-like mulatto'
offspring of a *mestizo blanco* and a black; *mestizo prieto*. *Mx*
(Aguirre Beltrán 1972:171) cl; (Aguirre Beltrán 1945:218) 17.
[*Amestizado* < *a-* + *mestizo* + *-ado*. Cf. **mestizo, mestizo alobado,
mestizo anegrado, mestizo prieto.**]

mulato anegrado 'blackened mulatto'
1. mulatto with the dark skin or other features of a black person. *SA* (Diggs 1953:406) cl.
2. mulatto with many black traits, including big lips, kinky
hair, etc.; *mulato prieto. Mx* (Aguirre Beltrán 1945:216) 17.
[*Anegrado* < *a-* + *negro* + suf. *-ado*. Syn. df. 2 *mulato prieto*. Cf.
mestizo prieto, mulato amestizado, mulato prieto.]

mulato blanco 'white mulatto'
1. offspring of a white and a black; *mulato claro; mulato. Mx*
(Aguirre Beltrán 1972:167; Alvarez Nazario 1974:351; Love
1971:81; Woodbridge 1948:359) cl.
2. white or light mulatto. *SA* (Diggs 1953:406) cl ‖ *Mx-Oaxaca*
(Chance and Taylor 1977:461) 18.
3. person with one black parent but whose white features predominate, acc. baptismal records. *CR* (Levine 1980:90) 18.
[Acc. Alvarez Nazario, first att. in 16 and 17-cent. Mx, then spread
to SoA. Syn. *mulato claro*. Cf. **mestizo blanco.**]

mulato chino
mulatto with Oriental features or skin color. *Cu* (Levine 1980:90) 20.
[Cf. **chino, mulato, mulato blanco, mulato amestizado.**]
mulato claro 'light mulatto'
1. person of mixed race with light skin color. *Pe* (Romero 1944:375) cl ‖ *Co-Cartagena* (Solaún and Kronus 1973:166) 20.
2. *mulato blanco,* or offspring of a black and a white. *Mx* (Aguirre Beltrán 1972:167) cl.
3. light mulatto. *SA* (Diggs 1953:406) cl.
[Syn. *mulato blanco.* Cf. **claro, mulato, mulato blanco,** Ptg. **mulato claro.**]
mulato criollo 'creole mulatto'
mulatto native to the region. *SA-no.* (Boyd-Bowman 1983) 17.
[Cf. **criollo, mulato.**]
mulato cuarterón 'quadroon mulatto'
1. quadroon. *An* (Alvarez Nazario 1974:354) 18–19.
2. offspring of a white Spaniard and a mulatto. *DR* (Boyd-Bowman 1982) 18.
[Syn. *cuarterón.* Cf. **cuarterón, mulato, mulato criollo.**]
mulato holandés 'Dutch mulatto'
mulatto born in the Dutch-speaking An. *SA* (Nuñez 1980:329) cl.
[Syn. *criollo de Curazao,* acc. Nuñez. Cf. **criollo de Curazao, mulato.**]
mulato lavado 'washed mulatto'
mulatto whose skin color is lighter than that of most mulattoes. *Co-Cartagena* (Solaún and Kronus 1973:166, 168) 20.
[*Lavado* < *lavar* 'to wash.']
mulato lobo
1. offspring of a *mulato pardo* and an Indian. *Mx* (Alvarez Nazario 1974:351; Woodbridge 1948:359; Aguirre Beltrán 1972:170) cl; (Aguirre Beltrán 1945:216) 17.
2. offspring of a *pardo* and an Indian. *Mx* (Love 1971:81); *SA* (Mellafe 1964:89) cl.
[Syn. *lobo.* Cf. **mulato alobado, mulato pardo.**]
mulato loro
dark-skinned mulatto. *An* (Nuñez 1980:329) 20.
[Cf. **loro, mulato, mulato pardo.**]
mulato membrillo 'quince-colored mulatto'
mulatto with yellowish skin color. *An* (Nuñez 1980:329) 20.
[Cf. **mulato, mulato amarillo, mulato loro, negro amembrillado.**]

mulato morisco 'Moorish mulatto'

1. offspring of a *mulato blanco* and a white. *Mx* (Aguirre Beltrán 1972:167; Alvarez Nazario 1974:351; Woodbridge 1948:359) cl.

2. dark mulatto. *SA* (Diggs 1953:406); *Pe* (Romero 1965:233) cl.
[Acc. Aguirre Beltrán (1945:214), syn. *morisco* in 17-cent. Mx. Acc. Mellafe (1964:88), generally 'blond with light-colored eyes.' Cf. **morisco, mulato blanco**.]

mulato negro 'black mulatto'

mulatto whose skin color tends toward black. *Co-Cartagena* (Solaún and Kronus 1973:166) 20.
[Cf. **mulato morisco, mulato oscuro, negro**.]

mulato obscuro — See *mulato oscuro*

mulato oscuro 'dark mulatto'

1. mulatto with dark skin color, acc. parish records and other documents. *Mx* (Roncal 1944:533); *Pe* (Romero 1944:375 and 1965:233) cl.

2. offspring of a mulatto and an Indian; 25% white, 25% black, 50% Indian. *Mx* (León 1924:25, 20–21, plate 33; Woodbridge 1948:359; Pérez de Barradas 1948:193) cl.
[Var. *mulato obscuro*. Cf. **mulato morisco**.]

mulato pardo 'dark-brown mulatto'

offspring of a black and an Indian. *Mx* (Aguirre Beltrán 1972:169; Woodbridge 1948:359; Alvarez Nazario 1974:351) cl.
[Acc. Aguirre Beltrán (1945:216 and 1972:169), term modified acc. person's skin color, e.g., *color pardo, color de rapadura, color champurrado, color amarillito, color de membrillo, color quebrado, color cocho, color zambaigo, color loro*. Cf. **mulato negro, mulato oscuro, pardo, mulato prieto, zambaigo**.]

mulato prieto 'black mulatto'

1. mulatto with black skin color. *SA* (Diggs 1953:406) 20.

2. offspring of a *mulato pardo* and a black, whose skin color approaches black. *Mx* (Aguirre Beltrán 1972:168; Woodbridge 1948:359; Alvarez Nazario 1974:351) cl; (Aguirre Beltrán 1945:215) 17.

3. offspring of a black and a *pardo*. *Mx* (Love 1971:81) cl.

4. dark mulatto, acc. parish priests. *Mx-Oaxaca* (Chance and Taylor 1977:461) 18.

5. person with dark skin, esp. offspring of blacks and Indians. *Mx* (Aguirre Beltrán 1945:215) 17.
[Acc. Mellafe (1964:89), could pass for black in cl. SA. Acc. Woodbridge, syn. *mulato anegrado*. Cf. **mulato, mulato anegrado, mulato oscuro, pardo, prieto**, Ptg. **mulato preto**.]

mulato primerizo

first-generation mulatto; offspring of a pure white and a pure black. *DR* (Hoetink 1973:25) late18.

[Cf. **mulato, mulato blanco, mulato prieto.**]

mulato tornatrás

offspring of a mestizo and a mulatto. *Mx* (Woodbridge 1948:359; Santamaría 1942:2.314) cl ‖ *SA* (Vergara Martín 1922:241) n.d.

[Indicates that person has fewer white traits than either of the parents. Cf. **mulato, mulato oscuro, mulato primerizo, tornatrás.**]

mulatona 'large mulatto woman'

mulatto woman who is sexually attractive or desirable. *Co-Cartagena* (Solaún and Kronus 1973:166, 168) 20.

[F. < *mulato* + aug. suf. *-ona*. Cf. **mulato, mulatico.**]

muleca — See *muleque*

muleco — See *muleque*

mulecón

1. black slave, acc. slavers in the market. *PR* (Alvarez Nazario 1974:336, 337, 380) cl.

2a. young, African-born black between childhood and puberty. *Cu* (Pichardo 1953:491; Macías 1885:875) 19.

2b. African-born black over ten years of age. *Cu* (Vergara Martín 1922:241) n.d.

2c. black slave between seven and twelve years of age. *Cu* (Rout 1976:xv) 19.

2d. black, generally a slave, between twelve and eighteen years of age. *Co-we.* (Velásquez 1962:114) cl.

2e. black, generally a slave, between fourteen and eighteen years of age. *PR* (Alvarez Nazario 1974:337) cl.

[Acc. Alonso (1958:2.2919), < *muleque* + aug. suf. *-ón*. Indicates that person identified is younger than the *muleque*. Cf. **muleque, negro bozal.**]

muleque

1. black slave, acc. slavers. *PR* (Alvarez Nazario 1974:336, 337, 380) cl.

2a. young black, usually a slave. *Cu* (Pichardo 1953:491) 19 ‖ *RP* (Granada 1957:2.113) cl–19 ‖ *Ur* (Mieres et al. 1966:94; Tenório d'Albuquerque 1954:34); *Cu RP* (Espina Pérez 1972:135) 20.

2b. black slave between twelve and sixteen years of age. *Cu* (Rout 1976:xv) 19.

2c. black slave between six and fourteen years of age, acc. slavers. *PR* (Alvarez Nazario 1974:337) cl.

2d. young or small black slave between seven and ten years of age. *Cu* (Malaret 1931:368; Dihigo 1966:183–84; Espina Pérez 1972:135; Segovia 1911:246; DRAE 903); *Co-we*. (Velásquez 1962:114) cl–prior20.

2e. young black recently arrived from Africa between seven and ten years of age. *Cu* (Macías 1885:875) 19; (Vergara Martín 1922:241) n.d.

3a. young or small black slave or servant; child of color. *Ar Cu Ur* (Alonso 1958:2.2919) 20 ‖ *Ar* (Segovia 1911:131) prior20.

3b. small black child. *Ar* (Segovia 1911:131) early20 ‖ *Ar Cu* (Malaret 1931:368); *Ur* (Malaret 1944:213) mid20 ‖ *RP* (Guarnieri 1979:132) 20.

[F. form *muleca*. Acc. Macías, df. 2e derog. Acc. Alvarez Nazario (1974:338), possibly < Caribbean lg. (Arawak or Taino), perhaps *moulékê, muleki,* or *mureko* 'little boy; boy.' Acc. Segovia (1911:246), < Congo lg. Syn. *negrito* 'little black boy,' acc. Pereda Valdés (1937:77). Vars. *moleque, moleca, muleco*. Cf. **moza, mucama, muchacho, mulecón, negrito,** Ptg. **moleque.**]

mulequillo
1. black child from birth to six years of age. *PR* (Alvarez Nazario 1974:337) cl.

2. black slave, acc. slavers. *PR* (Alvarez Nazario 1974:380) cl.

[< *muleque* + dim. suf. *-illo*. Cf. **mulecón, muleque, mulequín, mulequito.**]

mulequín
black child from birth to six years of age. *PR* (Alvarez Nazario 1974:337–38) cl.

[Acc. Alvarez Nazario, < *muleque* + dim. suf. *-ín*. Cf. **mulecón, muleque, mulequillo, mulequito.**]

mulequito
muleque, or small black child. *PR* (Alvarez Nazario 1974:337) cl.

[< *muleque* + dim. suf. *-ito,* acc. Alvarez Nazario. Cf. **mulecón, muleque, mulequillo, mulequín.**]

mulito — See *mulatico*

muñeca de orozuz — See *muñeco de orozuz*

muñeco de orozuz 'licorice doll; black doll'
black person. *Mx US-TX* (Argersinger 1989:p.c.) 20–late20.

[F. form *muñeca de orozuz*. Acc. Argersinger, euph.; derog. syn. *mono de orozuz*. Cf. **gabacho, morcilla, negro, negro como una paila, teléfono.**]

murusho — See *morocho*

muruxo — See *morocho*

musiú
any foreigner. *Ve* (Megenney 1988:p.c.) late20.
[Acc. Megenney, < Fr. *monsieur* 'sir, gentleman.' Cf. **afuereño, míster.**]

musolino
immigrant from south Italy; bandit. *RP* (Guarnieri 1967:152 and 1979:132) 20.
[Acc. Gobello and Payet (1959:54), < Lunfardo *musolino* < *(José) Musolino* 'famous bandit who escaped from jail in 1899 and was condemned to a life sentence in 1901'; now 'city street sweeper.' Cf. **cocoliche.**]

muy blanquito 'very white'
white person whose skin color is very pale, acc. Dominicans, Puerto Ricans, and Cubans of New York City. *US-NY* (Domínguez 1973:189) 20.
[< *blanco* 'white' + dim. suf. *-ito.* Cf. **blanco.**]

muzucuco — See *macuito, mojino*

N

ña — See *taita*

naborí
Indian slave serving a nobleman or plantation owner. *Cu* (Macías 1885:880) 19; (Vergara Martín 1922:241) early cl.
[Acc. Macías, var. of *laboría* < *labor* 'work.' Cf. **naboria, naborio.**]

naboria
free Indian used in domestic service. *SA* (Vergara Martín 1922:241) n.d.
[Acc. Vergara Martín, syn. *naborí.* Cf. **naborí, naborio.**]

naborio
Indian who was exempt from formal slave labor but was subject to forced, low-wage, mine labor. *Mx* (Levine 1980:92) 18.
[Syns. *laborio, laborío.* Cf. **indio naborí, naborí, naboria.**]

nación 'nation'
1a. foreigner. *Bo* (Alonso 1958:3.2935) 18–20 ‖ *SA* (Bayo 1931:173); *Ar Bo Ur* (Cowles 1952:536–37) 20 ‖ *RP* (Guarnieri 1967:152); *Ur* (Mieres et al. 1966:95) 20.

1b. foreigner who does not speak Spanish. *Ar* (Morínigo 1966:419) 20.

1c. foreigner, esp. an Italian immigrant. *RP* (Kany 1960b:38) 20.

2. any Italian. *Ar* (Gobello and Payet 1959:54) 20.
[M., f. Acc. Santamaría (1942:2.321), 'group of Indians who speak basically the same lg., whether they live in the same villages or not.' Common in phr. *de nación* or m. form *el nación*. Cf. **bachiche, cocoliche, gringo, musolino,** Ptg. **de nação.**]

naco 'stupid'
  1. Indian who has innate inferior qualities. *Mx* (Rosenblat 1954:1.33; Fuente 1947:66) 20.
  2. Indian, usually considered ignorant. *Mx-Guerrero* (Morínigo 1966:419) 20.
  3. semi-civilized Indian. *Mx* (Velasco Valdés 1957:87) 20.
  4. Indian who wears white pants. *Mx-Tlaxcala* (Santamaría 1942:2.321).
  5. Indian. *Mx* (Malaret 1944:218) mid20.
  [Df. 1 derog. Df. 5 nickname. Acc. Velasco Valdés (1957:87), < *Naco* 'town in the state of Sonora, n.w. Mx.' Alternately, acc. Santamaría (1942:2.321), < Otomi *naco* 'brother-in-law.' Excl. to Mx.]

nagó
  black slave of Yoruba origin. *SA* exc. *Co Cu Mx* (Levine 1980:79) cl.
  [Acc. Levine, *nago* [*sic*]. Cf. **africano, mozambique, negro,** Ptg. **nagô.**]

ñajal
  white person, esp. white master, acc. Indians. *US-CA* (Blanco 1971:223) cl.
  [Acc. Blanco, syn. *gente de razón;* dim. form *ñajalito.* Cf. **blanco, gente de razón.**]

ñajalito — See *ñajal*

ñamiñami
  black person recently arrived from the Guinea region of west Africa. *SA* (Vergara Martín 1922:241) prior20.
  [M., f. Cf. **africano, guineo, nagó, negro de Guinea.**]

ñapango
  1a. mestizo. *Bo* (Kany 1960b:35) 20.
  1b. mestizo or mulatto. *Co* (Malaret 1947:127; Alonso 1958:3.3003) 20.
  2. town boy. *Co* (Alonso 1958:3.3003) 20.
  [Df. 2 m. only. Acc. Santamaría (1942:2.340), Alonso, and Kany, < Quechua *llapanku* or *llapangu* 'barefoot, without shoes.' Used by ext. in ref. to mulattoes and mestizos who must have gone barefoot. Excl. to Co. Cf. **mestizo, mulato.**]

nápiro
  black person. *CR* (Villegas 1952:97) mid20.

[Cf. **chumeca, negro.**]
nápoles
person from Naples, Italy; Neapolitan. *Ar* (Cowles 1952:539) mid20.
[Syns. *napolitano, tano.* Cf. **bachicha, cocoliche, gringo, tano.**]
napolés — See *tano*
napoletano — See *tano*
napolitano — See *nápoles, tano*
narigón 'large nose'
person with a large nose, acc. the upper classes. *Mx-Oaxaca* (Garza Cuarón 1987:62) late20.
[< *nariz* 'nose' + aug. suf. *-gón.* Cf. **chato, narizón, ñato.**]
narizón 'big nose'
person with a big nose, acc. the lower classes. *Mx-Oaxaca* (Garza Cuarón 1987:62) late20.
[< *nariz* 'nose' + aug. suf. *-ón.* Cf. **chato, narigón, ñato.**]
narra
Chinese person; Oriental. *Cu US-NY* (Gómez 1980:p.c.) 20.
[M., f. Derog. Used among Cubans of New York City. Cf. **asiático, chale, oriental.**]
nativo — See *natural*
ñato 'flat-nosed'
person with a flat, large, and/or wide nose, generally character-istic of blacks. *Ar Ch Pe* (Rodríguez 1875:329–30) 19 ‖ *Ho* (Membreño 1897:124) late19 ‖ *SA* (Corominas 1944:15; Malaret 1931:376 and 1947:127); *Ar Ch CR Ur* (Cowles 1952:551); *Co-coast* (Revollo 1942:186); *PR* (Malaret 1937:229) mid20 ‖ *Co* (Tobón Betancourt 1952:183; Alario di Filippo 1964:232); *SA* (Espina Pérez 1972:140) 20.
[Acc. Rodríguez, familiar, affect. Acc. Malaret (1937:229), *ñatu* in Asturias, Spain. Acc. Tobón Betancourt, Corominas, and Alario di Filippo, < Quechua *ñatu* 'flat-nosed.' Syns. *chato, romo, de nariz chata.* Cf. **chato, romo.**]
natural 'natural; native'
1a. Indian, acc. non-Indians. *Mx* (Love 1971:82–83) cl ‖ *Pe* (Paz Soldán 1938:289) 19 ‖ *SA* (Kany 1960b:34) 20.
1b. Indian, acc. Indians. *CeA Mx* (Cowles 1952:446) mid20.
1c. Indian. *RP* (Fontanella de Weinberg 1982:46) 16–17.
2. non-Indian. *CeA Mx Sa* (Cowles 1952:446) mid20.
3. *cholo,* or mestizo. *Pe* (Santamaría 1942:2.326) mid20.
4. person with predominantly Indian features. *Co-Zarzal* (Sayres 1956:223) 20.

[Df. 1a euph. Df. 1c neutral, generic. Acc. Sayres, df. 4 is 11th (or next to lowest) social rank in Zarzal, Co; evokes disapproval and linked to illegitimacy. Acc. Cobarruvias (1611:824), 'bastard; naive.' Acc. Alonso (1958:3.2944–45), syn. *nativo* 'belonging to a place or region.' Acc. Aguirre Beltrán (1972:161), other syns. in Mx *de nación, de tierra*. Cf. **cholo, indio, mestizo.**]

natural de la tierra 'native of the land'
offspring of white Spaniards born in the New World. *RP* (Fontanella de Weinberg 1982:45) 16–17.
[Cf. **bozal, chapetón, criollo, gachupín, gente de razón, mancebo de la tierra, natural.**]

negrada — See *negro*

negrazo
black person with a very large body. *Cu* (Macías 1885:886; Pichardo 1953:499) 19.
[< *negro* + aug. suf. *-azo*. Cf. **negrito, negro,** Ptg. **pretão.**]

negrecito 'little black one'
black person; person with what is considered blackened skin. *Co-no.* (Sundheim 1922:459) early20.
[< *negro* + dim. suf. *-cito*. Cf. **negrito, negro.**]

negrería — See *negro*

negrerío — See *negro*

negrero 'slaver; slave trader; slave driver'
1. white man who prefers black women as sexual partners. *Cu* (Pichardo 1953:499; Santamaría 1942:2.328) 19.

2a. person who deals in the black slave trade; slaver. *Cu* (Alonso 1958:3.2956) cl–19.

2b. white man who deals in black slaves. *Cu* (Macías 1885:886) 19.

3. person who exploits workers, esp. foreign, at the lowest salaries. *SA* (Morínigo 1966:421) 20.

4. white person who seeks out the intimate company of blacks. *Co* (Tascón 1961:279) 20.
[Dfs. 1, 2 m. only. Acc. Corominas (1973:413), first att. 1836; Fr. *négrier* 'slave trader' first att. 1752. < *negro* + adj. suf. *-ero,* sim. to *mulatero.* Cf. **chinero, mulañero, mulatero, negro,** Ptg. **negreiro.**]

negrete
1. intimate friend. *PR* (Morínigo 1966:421) 20.
2. boy. *PR* (Santamaría 1942:2.328) mid20.
[Generally m. Affect. direct address. Acc. Corominas (1973:413), < *negro* + dim. suf. *-ete.* Cf. **negrecito, negrito, negro.**]

negrillo 'small black'

pygmy. *SA* (Alonso 1958:3.2956) 20.

[< *negro* + dim. suf. *-illo*. Acc. Steiner (1985:95), att. late 16-cent. Spain as 'small blackamoor, negro.' Acc. Boyd-Bowman (1971:621), att. in Puebla 1554, and (1983:1625), in 18-cent. Mexico City. Cf. **negrecito, negrito, negro,** Ptg. **negrilho.**]

negrín

person with black skin color. *Ve* (Flórez 1969:123) 20.

[Affect., usually in phr. *mi negrín.* < *negro* + dim. or affect. suf. *-ín.* Cf. **negrecito, negrito, negro,** Ptg. **negrinho.**]

negrito 'small black person'

1a. black person. *PR* (Alvarez Nazario 1974:349) cl–20.

1b. black person; little black person. *Cu* (Pichardo 1953:499) 19.

2. any person or child regardless of skin color. *Co-Antioquia* (Bayo 1931:174); *CR* (Villegas 1952:97) mid20 ‖ *Co-Cartagena* (Solaún and Kronus 1973:166, 168) 20.

[Df. 1 euph. Df. 3 affect. or endearing. Acc. Boggs et al. (1946:356), < *negro* + modern dim. suf. *-ito;* Old Sp. *negriello.* Acc. Zenón Cruz (1975:1.253), tone of voice implies either affect. or pejor.; often used by black nursemaids to children of the master in cl. PR. Often in phrs. *mi negrito, mi negrita.* Cf. **negrecito, negrete, negro.**]

negrito prieto 'small very black person'

black person with accentuated black features. *PR-Loíza Aldea* (Alvarez Nazario 1974:347) 20.

[Very pejor. Cf. **negrito, negro, prieto.**]

negro 'black'

1. person with black skin color. *Co* (Flórez 1969:122); *Co-Cartagena* (Solaún and Kronus 1973:166); *Mx* (Roncal 1944:533) 20.

2a. pure black person. *Mx* (Love 1971:81) cl ‖ *Cu* (Pichardo 1953:499) 19 ‖ *PR* (Tumin and Feldman 1969:199) 20.

2b. black person. *Mx* (Crépeau 1973:30); *PR* (Alvarez Nazario 1974:346) 20 ‖ *An Co-Cartagena* (Solaún et al. 1987:18) late20.

2c. black slave. *Mx* (Aguirre Beltrán 1972:157) cl.

2d. offspring of two blacks recently arrived from Guinea, Africa. *Pe SA* (Barón Castro 1946, plate XI) cl.

2e. black person, acc. other blacks. *Ec-n.w.* (Whitten 1965:91) 20.

2f. black Jamaican who came to work in the Canal Zone and who retained the English lg. and Protestant religion. *Pa* (Pitt-Rivers 1968:270) 20.

2g. person, generally black, of low social standing. *Mx Pe SA-*

_no._ (Velásquez 1962:114) cl.

2h. person with predominantly black features. _Co-Zarzal_ (Sayres 1956:223).

3a. person from the coast with dark skin color, acc. highlanders. _Ec-n.w._ (Whitten 1965:92) 20.

3b. person with very dark brown skin color. _Co_ (Flórez 1969:123) 20.

3c. person whose features are black, i.e., dark skin, kinky hair, thick lips, and a flat nose. _SA_ (Esteva Fabregat 1964:280–81) 20.

3d. dark-skinned person who tries to speak and act like whites or those of higher classes; _negro catedrático. Cu PR_ (Morínigo 1966:422) 20.

4. black, _zambo,_ or mulatto, acc. non-blacks. _Ec-n.w._ (Whitten 1965:91) 20.

5. Cauca Valley native. _Co_ (Kany 1960b:41) 20.

6. city slum-dweller. _Co-Barranquilla_ (Pitt-Rivers 1967:548 and 1968:270) 20.

7. any person or child regardless of color. _Ec-n.w._ (Whitten 1965:91); _CR, Ur_ (Cowles 1952:541); _CR_ (Salesiano 1938:96); _Bo_ (Fernández and Fernández 1967:101); _Co_ (Alario di Filippo 1964:229; Tobón Betancourt 1953:179); _SA_ (Morínigo 1966:422; Gillin 1961:77) 20.

8. Brazilian. _Bo_ (Fernández and Fernández 1967:101) 20.

9. offspring of a black man and a _china. Pe_ (Millones Santagadea 1973:66) late18–early19.

10. slave. _PR_ (Zenón Cruz 1975:1.252–53) cl.

11. person of color. _PR_ (Malaret 1931:372) mid20.

12. Californian, acc. other Californians. _US-CA_ (Blanco 1971:222) cl.

[Often pejor. or derog. with the weight of No. Amer. Engl. _nigger,_ acc. Aguirre Beltrán and Crépeau. Df. 2b very insult.; syns. in Mx _africano, esclavo._ Df. 2g 8th highest social rank in Zarzal, Co, acc. Sayres. Df. 4 insult. Syn. df. 5 _patojo_ 'lame; street urchin,' in 20-cent. Co, acc. Kany. Df. 7 term of affect. or endearment, usually in phrs. _mi negra, mi negro._ Df. 9 different from _zambo-chino_ 'offspring of a black woman and a _chino,_' acc. Millones Santagadea. Df. 11 derog. Df. 12 affect. Acc. Whitten (1965:91), can be insult. or affect., depending on context, in San Lorenzo, Ec. Acc. Segovia (1911:132), like _negrito_ term of affect. in Ar. Term of affect. amongst family and/or friends in 19-cent. SoA, acc. Rodríguez (1875:327), in mid-20 cent. An, Co, and Ch, acc. Malaret (1931:372), in 20-cent. RP, acc. Guarnieri (1979:133), and in 20-cent. PR slang, acc. Gallo (1980:74). Acc. Zenón Cruz, implied slavery and social badness in cl. times. Derivs. _negrada, negrería, negrerío_ 'group of blacks or black slaves' in 19-cent. Cu, acc. Pichardo (1953:499); 'group of blacks' in 20-cent. Ar, Co, Cu, Ec, Gu, Pe, PR, and Ur, acc. Morínigo (1966:421). Cf. **africano, blanco, bozal, esclavo, indio, moreno, negro catedrático, prieto,** Ptg. **negro, preto.**]

negro achocolatado 'chocolate-skinned black person'
person whose skin color is chocolate-brown. *PR* (Alvarez Nazario 1974:355) 19.
[Acc. Alvarez Nazario, *negra achocolatada* [*sic*]. Cf. **mulato anegrado, negro, color achocolatado.**]

negro africano 'African black'
person whose black skin color implies low social standing. *SA* (Pérez de Barradas 1948:174) late19.
[Acc. Pérez de Barradas, African-born blacks held in low esteem, including among blacks born in America (called *criollos* or *negros criollos*). Cf. **bozal, criollo, negro.**]

negro alforrado
freed black slave who often had to live with the stigma of having been a slave. *Mx* (Aguirre Beltrán 1972:280–81) cl.
[*Alforrado* < *forro* 'free.' Cf. **negro forro, negro horro.**]

negro alzado — See *alzado*

negro amembrillado 'quince-colored black'
black person whose yellowish skin color was less dark than that of the *negros atezados. Mx* (Aguirre Beltrán 1972:166) cl.
[Acc. Diggs (1953:406), divided into two groups, *negro amembrillado de los cafres de pasa* and *negro amembrillado de los merinos,* in cl. SA. Syn. *negro amulatado.* Cf. **membrillo, mulato membrillo, negro amembrillado de los cafres de pasa, negro amembrillado de los merinos.**]

negro amembrillado cafre de pasa — See *negro amembrillado de los cafres de pasa*

negro amembrillado de los cafres de pasa
black person, often with light skin and with hair in short, tight curls like raisins. *Mx* (Aguirre Beltrán 1972:167); *SA* (Diggs 1953:406) cl; (Aguirre Beltrán 1945:214) 17.
[Acc. Aguirre Beltrán (1945:214), var. *negro amembrillado cafre de pasa.* Cf. **cafre, negro amembrillado, negro amembrillado de los merinos, negro amulatado, pelo pasa.**]

negro amembrillado de los merinos
black person, often with light skin, whose hair is rolled into long spires like the long, wooly curls of a sheep. *Mx* (Aguirre Beltrán 1972:167); *SA* (Diggs 1953:406) cl; (Aguirre Beltrán 1945:214) 17.
[*Merino* 'type of sheep known for its high-quality wool.' Var. *negro*

negro boni

amembrillado merino, acc. Aguirre Beltrán (1945:214). Cf. **merino, negro amembrillado, negro amembrillado de los cafres de pasa, negro amulatado.**]

negro amembrillado merino — See *negro amembrillado de los merinos*

negro amulatado 'mulatto-like black'
person whose skin color, generally lighter than that of a pure black, implies racial mixture. *Mx* (Aguirre Beltrán 1972:166); *SA* (Diggs 1953:406) cl ‖ *Mx* (Aguirre Beltrán 1945:214) 17.
[Acc. Aguirre Beltrán (1945:214), syns. *amembrillado, negro amembrillado.* Cf. **amembrillado, mulato amestizado, negro, negro amembrillado.**]

negro angolo 'Angola black'
black person, supposedly from Angola, in southwestern Africa. *PR* (Alvarez Nazario 1974:380) cl.
[Derog. *Angolo < Angola* 'country in s.w. Africa at the so. end of the Congo, which was the homeland of many black slaves who were forcibly exported to America.' Cf. **angola, criollo, mandinga,** Ptg. **negro angola.**]

negro atezado 'blackened black'
black person, usually a slave from Africa, with very dark skin color. *SA* (Diggs 1953:406; Rout 1976:24); *Mx* (Aguirre Beltrán 1972:166) cl.
[Acc. Aguirre Beltrán (1945:213), syns. in 17-cent. Mx *atezado, negro retinto.* Cf. **atezado, negro, negro retinto.**]

negro azabache 'jet-black person'
black person with very dark skin color. *Co-coast* (Revollo 1942:183) mid20.
[*Azabache* 'jet, a shiny black mineral.' Var. *negro de azabache.* Cf. **negro atezado, negro retinto.**]

negro azul 'blue-toned black'
1. black person whose skin color appears bluish. *Co-Cartagena* (Solaún and Kronus 1973:166) 20.
2. near-pure black person. *Co* (Levine 1980:95) 20.
[Possibly sim. to So. Amer. Engl. *blue-gummed Negro,* both joc. and derog. Cf. **azul, negro atezado, negro amulatado.**]

negro bembón 'thick-lipped black'
black person with large thick lips. *Cu* (Pereda Valdés 1970:164) 20prior; (Nicolás Guillén) 20.
[Taken from Guillén's poem 'Negro bembón.' Cf. **bembo.**]

negro boni
black person who lives in the remotest parts of Guyana, in northeastern SoA. *SA* (Vergara Martín 1922:241; Santamaría

1942:2.328) 20.

[*Boni* perhaps < from African lg. Cf. **chumeca, negro bosh.**]

negro bosh

black rebel who fled to the interior of Dutch Guyana, now Surinam. *SA* (Vergara Martín 1922:241; Santamaría 1942:2.328) prior20.

[Used in ref. to Bush Negroes of Surinam. Cf. **buchi, negro boni.**]

negro bozal

black slave brought directly to America from Africa. *PR* (Alvarez Nazario 1974:365) cl ‖ *Cu* (Macías 1885:191) 19.

[Ant. *negro ladino* 'black slave taken to America via the Iberian Peninsula.' Acc. Macías, syn. *negro de nación.* Cf. **bozal, criollo, ladino, negro de nación, negro ladino.**]

negro bozal de Guinea

black slave, considered pure black, from Guinea on the west African coast. *Pe* (Pérez de Barradas 1948:186) cl.

[Cf. **bozal, mandinga, negro angolo, negro bozal, negro cabo verde.**]

negro cabo verde 'Cape Verdean black'

black slave from Cape Verde Island off the west African coast. *Mx* (Aguirre Beltrán 1972:114–15) cl.

[Syns. *negro caboverdiano, guineo.* African slaves often passed through Cape Verde on their journey to America. Cf. **guineo, moreno cabo verde, moreno de Barlovento,** Ptg. **cabo verde.**]

negro caboverdiano — See *negro cabo verde*

negro cafre de pasa 'kinky-haired black'

black slave from the east African coast. *Mx* (Alvarez Nazario 1974:358; Aguirre Beltrán 1972:144) cl.

[Cf. **cafre, esclavo de la India de Portugal, negro amembrillado de los cafres de pasa.**]

negro carolo

1. black person known for cute and daring acts or gestures. *PR* (Alvarez Nazario 1974:350) cl.

2. black person known for being insolent to or contemptuous of others. *SA* (Nuñez 1980:344) 20prior.

[Acc. Alvarez Nazario, often abbr. to *carolo* < *cara* 'face' + suf. *-olo.* Acc. Nuñez, used esp. in areas with large concentrations of blacks. Var. **carolo.** Cf. **criollo de Curazao, negro catedrático, negro criollo.**]

negro catedrático

1. black person who feigns education; black person who misuses lg. and shows other signs of not being educated. *An* (Malaret 1937:227) mid20.

2. black person who speaks and acts with intelligence and polish, in allusion to a certain theatrical type of black developed in 19-cent. Cuban literature. *Cu PR* (Alvarez Nazario 1974:361) 19–20.
[Df. 2 joc. Cf. **catedrático, negro carolo.**]

negro cimarrón 'runaway black'
black runaway slave. *SA* (Rosenblat 1954:2.69; Mörner 1967: 76) cl.
[Cf. **cimarrón, negro, negro bosh.**]

negro claro 'light-skinned black'
black person with light skin color. *Co-Cartagena* (Solaún and Kronus 1973:166) 20.
[Cf. **claro.**]

negro cocolo
black person. *PR* (Alvarez Nazario 1974:349, 380) cl ‖ *DR* (Megenney 1988:p.c.) late20.
[Pejor. Cf. **cocolo.**]

negro como una paila 'black as a pot; black as a frying pan'
black person, esp. one with very dark skin color. *DR* (Herrera 1989:p.c.) late20.
[M., f. Acc. Herrera, common among peasants; syn. *negro como una pailita*. Cf. **cocolo, indio oscuro, muñeco de orozuz, negro como un tizón.**]

negro como una pailita — See *negro como una paila*

negro como un tizón 'black as a smudge'
pure black African; person who by all appearances is pure black. *PR* (Alvarez Nazario 1974:349) 20.
[Pejor. Sim. to *negrito prieto.* Cf. **negrito prieto, negro azabache.**]

negro congo 'Congo black'
1. black African, generally a slave. *PR* (Alvarez Nazario 1974:349) cl.
2. black person who seems very dark-skinned. *PR* (Alvarez Nazario 1974:349) cl.
3. black person, known for creolized or stylized speech patterns, who performs during the carnival season. *Pa-Caribbean coast* (Lipski 1985:24–25) 20.
[Dfs. 1, 2 pejor. *Congo* 'region on we. African coast,' from which many black slaves came. Acc. Lipski, df. 3 folkloric performer. Cf. **negro africano, negro angolo, negro cabo verde,** Ptg. **negro angola.**]

negro coyote
person whose skin color indicates racial mixture. *Ve* (Vallenilla Lanz 1921:111) late19.

[*Coyote* usually 'offspring of Indian and white,' esp. in Mx. Cf. **coyote, negro.**]

negro criollo 'creole black'

black person, generally a slave, born in the New World. *PR* (Alvarez Nazario 1974:380); *SA* (Diggs 1953:417) cl ‖ *Mx* (Aguirre Beltrán 1972:161) 18–19.

[Ants. *negro de nación, negro de tierra* 'foreign-born black.' Sim. to Fr. *nègre créole,* Engl. *creole negro.* Cf. **bozal, criollo, criollo de Curazao, ladino, negro, negro bozal, negro carolo, negro de nación,** Ptg. **negro crioulo.**]

negro curro — See *curro*

negro de alquiler 'black for rent'

black slave hired out by the master for the master's profit. *SA* (Pescatello 1975:248) prior20.

[Acc. Pescatello, *negro de aluguel* [*sic*]. Cf. **negro de gaño,** Ptg. **preto de aluguel.**]

negro de azabache — See *negro azabache*

negro de casa 'house black'

black domestic slave. *PR* (Alvarez Nazario 1974:380) cl.

[Syn. *negro doméstico.* Cf. **moza, mucama, muchacho, negro doméstico.**]

negro de Castilla — See *ladino, negro ladino*

negro de conuco

black person who has been given a small plantation. *PR* (Alvarez Nazario 1974:380) cl.

[Acc. Alvarez Nazario, *conuco* 'small plantation.' Cf. **conuquero, negro de tala.**]

negro de gaño

black slave who did hired work and gave the master a fixed part of the earnings. *SA* (Pescatello 1975:248) prior20.

[Acc. Pescatello, *negro de ganho* [*sic*]. Cf. **negro de alquiler,** Ptg. **negro de ganho, preto de aluguel, preto de ganho.**]

negro de gelofe

black slave from sub-Saharan Africa. *SA* (Rout 1976:16; Levine 1980:96) 15–16.

[Acc. Levine, syn. *mandingo* 16-cent. Acc. Rout, these slaves came from between Sierra Leone and the Senegal River area; syns. *mandingo, bantú.* Vars. *gelofe, jalof, negro de jalof.*]

negro de Guinea 'Guinea black'

black slave from the Guinea river area of west Africa. *Mx* (Aguirre Beltrán 1972:115) cl.

[Cf. **guineo, negro angolo, negro bozal de Guinea,** Ptg. **negro de Guiné.**]

negro de humo — See *negro humo*

negro de jalof — See *negro de gelofe*

negro de la India de Portugal
black slave from the Indian Ocean region of east Africa or the islands off Africa. *Mx* (Aguirre Beltrán 1972:144) cl.
[Used in ref. to blacks brought to America by Ptg. ships which cruised to all parts of the Indian Ocean and Africa. Cf. **negro africano, negro angolo, negro cabo verde, negro congo, negro de Guinea.**]

negro de nación 'native black'
1. black slave born in Africa. *PR* (Alvarez Nazario 1974:334, 380) cl ‖ *Cu* (Pichardo 1953:110) 19.
2. black African. *Cu* (Macías 1885:881) 19.
[Acc. Macías, df. 2 ant. *criollo*. Cf. **nación, negro bozal, negro criollo, negro ladino.**]

negro de pañuelo 'black person with a handkerchief'
black person who is culturally and physically very African. *PR* (Alvarez Nazario 1974:350, 380) cl.
[Pejor., usually f. Syn. *negro de pañuelo de Madrás*. Sim. to LA Fr. *tignon de Madras*. Cf. **negro catedrático.**]

negro de pañuelo de Madrás — See *negro de pañuelo*

negro de Portugal — See *ladino, negro ladino*

negro de tala
black person who owns a small farm or plantation. *PR* (Alvarez Nazario 1974:380) cl.
[Pejor. Sim. to *negro de conuco*. *Tala* 'small vegetable garden' in PR. Cf. **negro de conuco.**]

negro de tierra — See *natural, negro criollo*

negro del Manglar — See *curro del Manglar*

negro del país 'native black'
black person born in America. *Pe* (Barón Castro 1946:plate X) cl.
[*Del país* 'native to the same country.' Syn. *negro criollo*. Ants. *negro africano, negro criollo, negro de nación*. Cf. **negro, negro africano, negro criollo, negro de nación.**]

negro doméstico 'domestic black'
black domestic slave. *PR* (Alvarez Nazario 1974:380) cl.
[Syn. *negro de casa*. Cf. **criada, moza, mucama, negro de casa.**]

negro esclavo 'black slave'
black person who is not respected or who is a member of another group. *Pe* (Millones Santagadea 1973:19) 20.
[Acc. Millones Santagadea, colloq.; used in ref. to football team

members; ant. *zambo.* Cf. **esclavo, negro, zambo.**]

negro fileno 'delicate black'
black person with a straight or aquiline nose. *Co-Cartagena* (Solaún et al. 1987:19) late20.
[Cf. **chato, ñato, negro, romo.**]

negro forro — See **negro horro**

negro horro 'free black'
free or freed black slave; *negro alforrado. Mx-Puebla* (Boyd-Bowman 1969:149); *Mx SA* (Aguirre Beltrán 1972:280–81); *PR* (Alvarez Nazario 1974:346) cl.
[Syns. *negro alforrado, negro forro, negro libre.* Acc. Domínguez Ortiz (1952:386), many slave owners in Andalusia sent slaves out to sell wares on the street, either to earn a living on their own or to make money for their owner. If the slaves did earn their keep, then the master expected a percentage of the earnings, a practice which made it possible for some slaves to buy their freedom (to become *horros* or *libertos*) through saving their money (thus the Sp. verb *ahorrar* 'to save') and that of their families; customary throughout Br and SA. Cf. **horro, liberto, negro alforrado, negro de alquiler, negro de gaño,** Ptg. **negro forro.**]

negro humo 'smoke black'
black person with smoke-black skin color. *Co-coast* (Revollo 1942:183) mid20.
[Vars. *negro de humo, negro-humo.* Cf. **negro azabache.**]

negro-humo — See **negro humo**

negro jetón 'thick-lipped black'
black person who has very thick lips, or who has a pendulous lower lip. *Bo* (Fernández and Fernández 1967:84) 20.
[Acc. Fernández and Fernández, *jetón* 'thick or hanging lower lip,' characteristic of some blacks; < *jeta* 'thick lips' + aug. suf. *-ón.* Cf. **jetón, labión, negro bembón.**]

negro ladino 'astute black one'
1. black slave totally or partially assimilated to Iberian lgs. and culture before arriving in America. *SA* (Aguirre Beltrán 1972:157) cl ‖ *PR* (Alvarez Nazario 1974:17, 365) 15–early cl.
2. Berber, Jewish, or Moorish slave. *PR SA* (Coll y Toste 1924:141) cl.
[Acc. Barón Castro (1946:788), said of black slave who had stayed a minimum of 2 years in the Iberian Peninsula before being sent to America. Df. 1 also in 15-cent. Spain. Formed by anal. to *moro ladino.* Cf. **ladino, negro bozal.**]

negro libre 'free black'
freed black slave. *PR* (Alvarez Nazario 1974:346) cl.

[Syns. *coartado, liberto, manumiso, manumitido, negro horro.* Cf. **liberto, negro alforrado, negro horro.**]

negro lindo 'pretty black one'
boyfriend or girlfriend; lover; fianceé; spouse. *Mx* (Velasco Valdés 1957:88) 20.
[M., f. No necessary ref. to skin color.]

negro o mulato 'black or mulatto'
person with dark or black skin color. *Co-Cartagena* (Solaún and Kronus 1973:166) 20.
[Cf. **más o menos blanco, moreno o mestizo.**]

negro parao
nonwhite who pretends to the social position of the white, acc. whites. *PR* (Zenón Cruz 1975:1.257) 20.
[Syn. *grifo parejero.* Cf. **grifo parejero, negro parejero.**]

negro parejero 'bold black one'
person of color who pretends to be on a par with persons of higher social status. *PR* (Alvarez Nazario 1974:361) cl.
[Pejor. *Parejero* 'bold, brazen; social climbing.' Syn. *grifo parejero.* Cf. **grifo parejero.**]

negro pasudo 'kinky-haired black'
black person with tight kinky hair. *Co* (Tobón Betancourt 1953:193) mid20.
[*Pasudo < pasa* 'raisin' + adj. suf. *-udo.* Cf. **pelo pasa, pasa, pasudo.**]

negro por el pelo 'black by the hair'
person who is identified as black by kinky hair texture. *Co-Cartagena* (Solaún et al. 1987:19) late20.
[Cf. **negro pasudo, pelo malo, pelo pasa.**]

negro prieto 'very black person'
person of pure black race. *PR* (Alvarez Nazario 1974:349) cl.
[Intensifier. Cf. **negro, negro puro, prieto,** Ptg. **negro preto.**]

negro puro 'pure black'
person whose skin color indicates pure black race. *Co-Cartagena* (Solaún and Kronus 1973:166) 20.
[Cf. **africano, negro prieto.**]

negro retinto 'redyed black person'
1. very dark-skinned black person, once a slave. *SA* (Diggs 1953:406) cl ‖ *PR SA* (Alvarez Nazario 1974:349, 380) cl–20.
2. black person with very dark skin color. *Mx* (Aguirre Beltrán 1945:213) 17.
[Pejor. Syns. *atezado, negro atezado.* Cf. **atezado, negro, negro atezado, retinto.**]

negro sucio 'dirty black person'
white person. *PR* (Zenón Cruz 1975:1.258) 20.
[Insult.; iron. Cf. Ptg. **negro ruim, negro sujo.**]

negro timba
very dark-skinned black person. *Pa* (Aguilera Patiño 1951:474) mid20.
[Acc. Aguilera Patiño, *timba* 'hand in a card game; low-life gambling house; water bucket.' Probably < African lg. Cf. **negro.**]

negroide 'Negroid'
1. person whose skin color is black. *Co-Cartagena* (Solaún and Kronus 1973:166) 20.
2. person who has the facial or other features resembling those of a black. *SA* (Morínigo 1966:422) 20.
[< *negro.* Cf. **negro, negrolo.**]

negrolo
1a. person of color, acc. other persons of color. *PR* (Alvarez Nazario 1974:350) cl.
1b. black person, acc. other blacks. *PR* (Gallo 1980:74) 20.
2. any person with the features of a black person. *PR* (Alvarez Nazario 1974:350) cl.
[Acc. Gallo, df. 1b affect. in direct address. Acc. Alvarez Nazario, df. 2 affect., joc.; < *negro* + suf. *-olo;* like *carolo,* formed by anal. to *angolo* and *cocolo.* Cf. **blanco indioide, negro, negro carolo, negroide.**]

negruzco — See *prietuzco*

nengre — See *nengro*

nengro
black person. *Bo* (Fernández and Fernández 1967:101) 20.
[< *negro* through progressive assimilation. Acc. Lipski (1988:p.c.), used in *bozal* Sp. since Golden-Age Spain; used throughout SA; var. *nengre.* Cf. **negro.**]

neorriqueño 'Nuyorican'
1. Puerto Rican from or living in New York City or environs. *PR* (Gallo 1980:74) 20 ‖ *PR US* (Lipski 1988:p.c.) late20.
2. Americanized Puerto Rican born or living in New York City. *PR* (Abalos 1986:43) 20.
[Acc. Gallo, slang. Acc. Lipski, var. *nuyorican* common in US and PR. Acc. Abalos, often derog. Cf. **mojado, pocho, puertorriqueño.**]

ñero
person from Margarita Island, Ve. *Ve* (León 1980:p.c) 20.
[Known for speaking like Andalusians. Cf. **isleño.**]

nica
Nicaraguan. *CR* (Malaret 1944:222; Villegas 1952:97; Cowles 1952:542; Salesiano 1938:96) mid20 ‖ *CeA* (Kany 1960b:40; Cowles 1952:542; Alonso 1958:3.2973) 20.
[M., f. Pejor. abbr. of *nicaragüense.* Acc. Malaret, festive nickname. Syn. *nicaragua* 'name of the CeA country.' Cf. **muco, nigüento.**]

nicaragua — See *nica*

nicaragüense — See *nica*

nicaregalado
native of the province of Guanacaste, CR. *CR* (Lipski 1988:p.c.) late20.
[Cf. **nica, tico.**]

niche
black person. *Cu* (Levine 1980:96) 20.
[Slur. Acc. Levine, sim. to No. Amer. Engl. *nigger.* Acc. Lipski (1988:p.c.), also common in Ho and perhaps elsewhere. Cf. **negro.**]

nigüento 'flea-riddled'
Guatemalan. *Ni* (Castellón 1939:48) mid20.
[Probably derog. Acc. Alonso (1958:3.2976), 'something which has *niguas,* or sand fleas, which are found throughout An, CeA, Co, and Ec.' Syn. *chapín.* Cf. **chapín, nica.**]

niño 'young; young child'
1a. white master, acc. slaves or servants. *Cu* (Dihigo 1966:185; Espina Pérez 1972:138; Alonso 1958:3.2977) cl–19 ‖ *Pe* (Paz Soldán 1938:289) 19 ‖ *Ar CeA DR Mx Pe PR Pg* (Morínigo 1966:423) 20.
1b. master, or any white person, acc. blacks and mulattoes. *Cu* (Malaret 1931:373) cl.
2a. any white person, generally a child. *Cu* (Dihigo 1966:185; Espina Pérez 1972:138; Alonso 1958:3.2977) cl–19 ‖ *Pe* (Paz Soldán 1938:289) 19 ‖ *Ar CeA DR Mx Pe PR Pg* (Morínigo 1966:423) 20.
2b. child of the master or patron. *Ar* (Segovia 1911:132) early20.
2c. child, relative, or friend of the master, no matter what age, acc. persons of color. *Cu SoA* (Macías 1885:890) 19prior.
[Generally respect. Df. 2 by ext. from df. 1. Acc. Paz Soldán, used in opp. to *muchacho* 'black child.' Cf. **muchacho, niño de color.**]

niño de color 'child of color'
small black child. *PR* (Zenón Cruz 1975:1.250–51) 20.
[Acc. Zenón Cruz, syn. *negrito.* Cf. **negrito, negro.**]

nipón

Japanese. *Ar* (Segovia 1911:85) early20.

[F. *nipona*. Acc. Segovia, < Japanese *nippon* 'rising sun.' Cf. **asiático, oriental,** Ptg. **japonês.**]

nipona — See *nipón*

ño — See *taita*

no blanco del todo 'not all white'

person who is not completely white. *Co-Cartagena* (Solaún and Kronus 1973:166, 168) 20.

[Cf. **blanco no del todo, moreno o mestizo, negro o mulato.**]

no te entiendo 'I do not understand you'

1a. person whose skin color suggests unknown or mixed race, acc. parish records. *Mx* (Roncal 1944:533) cl.

1b. racially mixed person who has no physical traits from the parents or who shows recessive traits from ancestors. *Mx* (Moreno Navarro 1973:143) 18.

2a. offspring of a *tente en el aire* and a mulatto. *Mx* (León 1924:9, 25; Woodbridge 1948:359; Monteforte Toledo 1959:171) cl; (McAlister 1963:354) 19 ‖ *SA* (Vergara Martín 1922:241) n.d.

2b. offspring of a mulatto and a *tente en el aire,* the latter of which is offspring of a *calpamulato* and a *zambo;* 31.25% white, 18.75% Indian, 50% black. *Mx* (Santamaría 1942:2.335; Pérez de Barradas 1948:193) cl.

2c. offspring of a mulatto and a *tente en el aire,* the latter of which is offspring of an Indian and a *cambujo;* 25% white, 40.6% Indian, 34.4% black (León 1924:20–21; Pérez de Barradas 1948:193) cl.

2d. offspring of a mulatto and a *tente en el aire,* the latter of which is offspring of a *cambujo* and a *calpamulato;* 40% white, 10.35% Indian, 49.65% black. *Mx* (Pérez de Barradas 1948:193; León 1924:20–21, plate 34) cl.

[M., f. Acc. Mellafe (1964:90), humor. Excl. to cl. Mx. Var. *no-te-entiendo.* Cf. **calpamulato, cambujo, indio, mulato, no blanco del todo, tentenelaire.**]

no-te-entiendo — See *no te entiendo*

nopo

European Spaniard. *Pe* (Alcedo 1786–89:5.70) late18.

[Cf. **ñopo.**]

ñopo

1. Spaniard. *Pa* (Cowles 1952:552; Alonso 1958:3.3005; Kany 1960b:48) 20.

2. person who is white or has blond hair. *Pa* (Alonso 1958:3.3005; Kany 1960b:48) 20.

3. person who is flat-nosed. *Co* (Malaret 1931:377) mid20; (Santamaría 1942:2.343; Alonso 1958:3.3005) 20.

[Possibly < phonetic distortion of *español*. Syn. df. 3 *chato*. Cf. **chato, español, ñato, romo.**]

norteamericano — See *americano, anglosajón, gabacho, gringo, yanqui*

nortino 'northern; northerner'
inhabitant of the north of the country; northerner. *Ch Pe* (Malaret 1947:126) mid20; (Morínigo 1966:424) 20.

[Cf. **arribeño, sureño.**]

nuestros primos — See *primo*

nuevo mexicano 'New Mexican'
1. person of Spanish descent from NM. *US-NM, -s.w.* (Marden and Meyer 1978:242) 19.

2. Spanish-speaking person descended from the earliest colonizers from Spain, acc. himself or herself. *US-NM* (Gann and Duignan 1986:xii) 20prior.

[Acc. Gann and Duignan, syn. *hispano*. Cf. **californio, hispano, latino, tejano.**]

nuevo-mexicano — See *nuevo méxico*

nuevo méxico
New Mexican. *US-CA* (Blanco 1971:223) cl.

[Acc. Blanco, syn. *nuevo-mexicano*. < *Nuevo México*.]

nuyorican — See *neorriqueño*

O

ochavina — See *octavón*

ochavón 'octoroon'
1a. offspring of a white and a quadroon. *Cu* (Pichardo 1953:507) 19; (Malaret 1931:378) mid20; (Dihigo 1966:187; Espina Pérez 1972:141; Santamaría 1942:2.349; Alonso 1958:3.3021) 20.

1b. offspring of a white and a *cuarterón de negro*. *Cu* (Vergara Martín 1922:242) n.d.

2. offspring of two quadroons. *Cu* (Pichardo 1953:507) 19.

3. offspring of a white and a *cuatralbo;* 87.5% white, 12.5% Indian. *Mx* (León 1924:20–21, plate 35) cl.

[Vars. *octavón, octarón*. Cf. **cuarterón, octavón,** Ptg. **oitavão.**]

ochavón blanco 'white octoroon'
octoroon with white or light skin color. *Pe* (León 1924:26) cl.
[Cf. **blanco, negro blanco, octavón indio, octavón negro.**]

octarón — See *ochavón, octavón*

octavón 'octoroon'
1. octoroon, acc. parish records. *Mx* (Roncal 1944:533) cl.
2a. offspring of a white and a *cuarterón de mulato,* the latter of which is offspring of a white and a mulatto; 87.5% white, 12.5% black. *Mx* (León 1924:25; Pérez de Barradas 1948:189) cl.
2b. offspring of a white and a quadroon; 87.5% white, 12.5% black. *Mx* (León 1924:25; Woodbridge 1948:359; Pérez de Barradas 1948:189) cl.
3. offspring of a white and a *cuatralbo;* 87.5% white, 12.5% Indian. *Mx* (León 1924:20–21, plate 35) cl.
[Acc. Alvarez Nazario (1974:354), syn. *quinterón de mulato.* F. var. *ochavina,* acc. León (1924:25). Engl. *octoroon* < Sp. Cf. **ochavón, quinterón de mulato.**]

octavón indio 'Indian octoroon'
offspring of a white and a person of Indian admixture; 12.5% Indian, 87.5% white. *Mx* (Woodbridge 1948:359) cl.
[Acc. Woodbridge, clarifies *octavón.* Cf. **octavón, octavón negro, ochavón blanco.**]

octavón negro 'black octoroon'
offspring of a black and a white; 87.5% white, 12.5% black. *Mx* (Woodbridge 1948:359) cl.
[Acc. Woodbridge, clarifies *octavón.* Cf. **octavón, octavón indio.**]

orejano 'ownerless; peasant'
1. countryman, dirt farmer, or peasant. *Cu* (Pichardo 1953:510) 19 ‖ *Pa* (Aguilera Patiño 1951:476; Alonso 1958:3.3059; Morínigo 1966:437); *DR* (Morínigo 1966:437) 20.
2. Indian who had elongated ears like those of a donkey. *Pa* (Aguilera Patiño 1951:476) 19.
[Df. 1 used in ref. to any non-city dweller. Acc. Aguilera Patiño, df. 2 helped to perpetuate myth that Indians, usually rural dwellers, were dumber than whites, usually urban dwellers; < *oreja* 'ear.' Var. *orejeado.* Cf. **campesino, orejón,** Ptg. **caipira.**]

orejeado — See *orejano*

orejón 'rough; crude'
1a. noble Indian who had his earlobe enlarged and elongated by the use of adornments which indicated his distinction. *Pe* (Bayo 1931:179–80; Morínigo 1966:438) cl.

1b. Indian who was a nobleman, acc. Spaniards. *SA* (Vergara Martín 1922:242) n.d.

1c. Indian known for great shouts, acc. Spaniards. *Ch* (Rodríguez 1875:148–49) 19prior.

2. person with big ears. *Ho* (Membreño 1897:126) late19.

3. plainsman. *Co* (Kany 1960b:41) 20.

[Generally m. Acc. Boyd-Bowman (1971:649), < *oreja* 'ear' + aug. suf. *-ón*. Acc. Kany, df. 3 < *orejonas* 'large spurs used by plainsmen.' Cf. **orejano.**]

oriental 'oriental; eastern'

1. Uruguayan. *Ar* (Cara-Walker 1987:59) late19–early20; (Garzón 1910:342; Bayo 1910:158 and 1931:180; Segovia 1911:251) early–mid20 ‖ *Ur* (Mieres et al. 1966:98) 20.

2. person from the province of Oriente, Cu. *Cu* (Espina Pérez 1972:143) 20.

3. person from the Orient; Asian; Oriental. *SA* (Alonso 1958:3.3063) 20.

[Acc. Segovia (1911:608), f. *orientala* < by anal. to *esquimala* or *provenzala*. Df. 1 < *(República) Oriental (del Uruguay)*. Cf. **asiático,** Ptg. **oriental.**]

orientala — See *oriental*

originario 'original; aboriginal'

Indian who owns ancestral lands. *SA* (Bayo 1931:180) early–mid20.

[Cf. **aborígena, agregado.**]

orillero

1. slum dweller, peasant, or other person of low class, generally without education. *CR* (Salesiano 1938:99) mid20; (Morínigo 1966:438) 20.

2. slum dweller. *Ar CeA Cu Pg Ur Ve* (Morínigo 1966:438); *Ar CeA Cu Ur Ve* (Espina Pérez 1972:143) 20.

[< *orilla* 'bank, rim, side' + suf. *-ero*. Syn. df. 2 *arrabalero*.]

overo 'peach-colored'

person, usually black, mulatto, or dark-skinned white, who has white spots on the body, esp. on the hands and face. *Cu* (Pichardo 1953:510; Vergara Martín 1922:242) 19.

[Acc. Santamaría (1942:2.363) and Boyd-Bowman (1971:654), 'color of horses or cattle, white with spots.' Acc. Pichardo, also in ref. to some *blancos trigueños*. Acc. DRAE (954), 'peach-colored, esp. in ref. to horses.' Acc. Corominas (1973:429), att. in Spain 1495 as 'spotted.' Cf. **blanco trigueño, jabado.**]

P

pachuco
man from El Paso, TX. *US-AZ* (Barber 1950:34) mid20.
[Acc. Barber, slang. < *Pachuco* 'border lingo of Mexicans or Mexi-can-Americans.' Acc. Lipski (1988:p.c.), current in CA and TX; var. *chuco.* Cf. **chicano, mexicano, pasiente.**]
paio — See *payo*
paisa
1. Colombian. *Ec* (Kany 1960b:39) 20.
2. Chinese person. *Pe* (Kany 1960b:38) 20.
3. native of the department of Antioquia, Co. *Co* (Tobón Betan-court 1953:188; Cowles 1952:565; Alario di Filippo 1964:240) mid20.
4. rough, Andean soldier. *Ve* (Cowles 1952:565) mid20.
[M., f. Df. 4 pejor. Acc. Cowles and Kany, < apocopation of *paisano* 'peasant.' Acc. Tobón Betancourt, used in ref. to person from Antio-quia since *antioqueños* overuse the term. Syn. and deriv. *paisita.* Cf. **chale, chino, oriental, paisano.**]
paisano 'peasant; native to the same country'
1. Chinese. *Ch Pe* (Kany 1960b:38) 20.
2. Spaniard. *Mx* (Kany 1960b:37; Morínigo 1966:444) 20.
3a. peasant or farmer. *Ar* (Morínigo 1966:444); *RP* (Guarnieri 1967:157) 20.
3b. peasant; person from the countryside; person practical in country things. *Ar* (Segovia 1911:443) early20.
4a. Arabic speaker. *Ar* (Morínigo 1966:444) 20.
4b. any foreigner, esp. one from the Middle East. *DR* (Morínigo 1966:444) 20.
5. Italian, acc. other Italians. *RP* (Guarnieri 1967:157); *Ar* (Morínigo 1966:444) 20.
6a. person from the highlands, often Indian. *Ec* (Cowles 1952:565); *Ec Pe* (Morínigo 1966:444; Kany 1960b:35) 20.
6b. Indian. *Ar* (Cowles 1952:565) mid20.
7. fellow Hispanic or Latino, acc. U.S. Hispanics. *US* (Abalos 1986:171) 20.
[Df. 2 derog. Df. 4a vulgar. Df. 4b syn. *turco.* Df. 6a humor. or derog.; syn. *serrano,* esp. if Indian. Sim. to Italian *paesano* 'peas-ant' and Fr. *paysan.* Var. *paisa.* Deriv. *paisanaje* 'group of peas-ants.' Cf. **chino, gringo, indio, paisano criollo, serrano, turco.**]
paisano criollo
native to the area; local guy. *Ar* (Cara-Walker 1987:60) late19–early20.

[Cf. **criollo, paisano.**]

paisita — See *paisa*

pajón 'coarse straw; lank; straight'
uncouth person, often with hair which is straight, stiff, and bristly. *Mx-Zacatecas* (Morínigo 1966:446) 20.
[< *paja* 'straw' + suf. *-ón*. Cf. **pelo malo.**]

pajuerano 'provincial'
1. provincial or rural type. *Ar-Buenos Aires* (Cammorota 1963:47); *Ar* (Kany 1960b:40) 20.
2. rural type or peasant who comes to an urban area. *Ar Bo Ur* (Malaret 1947:131; Morínigo 1966:446) mid20.
[Acc. Cammorota, Kany, and Morínigo, < *p'ajuera* < *para afuera* 'from the outskirts' + suf. *-ano*. Acc. Morínigo, now obs. Cf. **campesino, campirano, paisano,** Ptg. **caboclo, caipira.**]

palanqueta 'small lever; sugary confection'
Chinese. *Cu* (Kany 1960b:38) 20.
[M., f. Acc. Kany, perhaps < color of *palanqueta* 'confection made of ground corn and honey,' or < Chinese vendors of this confection, called *chinopote* in Tabasco, Mx. Cf. **asiático, chale, chino, oriental, paisa.**]

palenquero
1. black person or almost totally black person who lives in remote areas and retains African customs. *Co-Cartagena* (Solaún and Kronus 1973:150, 160) 20.
2. inhabitant of Palenque de San Basilio, a village located south of Cartagena, Co. *Co* (Megenney 1988:p.c.) late20.
[Acc. Alvarez Nazario (1974:380), < *palenque* 'maroon colony;' now 'fence; palisade.' Acc. Corominas (1954–57:3.626), specialized in SA in ref. to 'black or Indian runaway slave hideout.' Cf. **cimarrón, marrón, negro, pardo,** Ptg. **mocambeiro, quilombola.**]

palestino — See *turco*

paleto — See *campirano*

pálido 'pallid'
person with very light or pallid skin color. *Co-Yolombo* (Flórez 1969:122) 20.
[Cf. **anémico,** Ptg. **pálido, verde.**]

palilla
peasant. *CR* (Villegas 1952:102) mid20.
[M., f. Acc. Villegas, slang. Possibly < *palillo* 'stick; toothpick.' Cf. **campesino, campirano, paisano, pajón, pajuerano,** Ptg. **caboclo, caipira.**]

palmarote
rustic or uncivilized plainsman. *Ve* (Kany 1960b:41) 20.

[Acc. Kany, syn. *sabanero.*]

palomo 'dove, pigeon'

person whose skin color indicates mixed race. *Co-Guaca* (Flórez 1969:122) 20.

[Acc. Santamaría (1942:2.390), used in ref. to color of horses or cattle.]

pampeado

native of the Pampa. *Ar* (Segovia 1911:253) early20.

[< *pampa* 'grassy plains of SoA.' Cf. **gaucho, pampeano, pampeño, pampino, sabanero.**]

pampeano

person native to the Pampa; person living in the Pampa. *SoA* (Malaret 1947:234) mid20 ‖ *Ar Ur* (Morínigo 1966:451) 20.

[< *pampa.* Cf. **gaucho, pampeado, pampeño, pampino.**]

pampeño

person from or native to the Pampa. *Co Pe* (Cowles 1952:573) mid20.

[< *pampa.* Syn. *pampero.* Cf. **gaucho, llanero, pampeado, pampeano, pampino.**]

pampero — See *pampeño*

pampino

1. inhabitant of the interior of the Chilean provinces that produce nitrate. *Ch Pe* (Malaret 1947:132); *Ch* (Cowles 1952:573) mid20.

2. inhabitant of the northern pampa lands. *Ch* (Morínigo 1966:451) 20.

[< *pampa.* Cf. **pampeado, pampeano, pampeño.**]

panamericano 'Pan American'

inhabitant of the American continents. *Ar* (Segovia 1911:253) early20.

[Cf. **americano.**]

pancutra — See *pantruca*

pando 'sagging; person of great heaviness'

mestizo. *Co-Corozal* (Flórez 1969:122) 20.

[Acc. Santamaría (1942:2.396), also 'person or animal with an arched back or curved spine,' 'one with a distended belly.' Cf. **mestizo, mulato, pardo.**]

pantruca

person with pallid skin. *Ch* (Flórez 1969:123) 20.

[M., f. Acc. Santamaría (1942:2.399), var. *pancutra;* perhaps < Quechua *p'ancu* 'pale.' Cf. **anémico, trigueño.**]

panza verde 'green belly'
native to or resident of the city of León de las Aldamas, Guanajuato. *Mx* (Velasco Valdés 1957:96) 20.
[M., f. Acc. Velasco Valdés, used in ref. to these people because of the large quantities of lettuce the women generally carried in front of them supported by their hands.]

papolitano
Italian. *Ar* (Cara-Walker 1987:44) late19–early20.
[Acc. Cara-Walker, cocoliche slang < *papo* 'chat aimlessly, blabber' + *tano* 'Italian.' Possibly var. of *napolitano* 'Neapolitan.' Cf. **cocoliche, nápoles, tano.**]

paquete 'packet'
black slave, acc. slavers. *SA* (Alvarez Nazario 1974:356) cl.
[Cf. **cargamento de ébano, carabela, pieza de ébano, muleque,** Ptg. **malungo.**]

parameño
highlander; uplander. *Ve* (Morínigo 1966:458) 20.
[< *páramo* 'plateau, mountainous highland.' Cf. **paramero, paramuno, serrano.**]

paramero
highlander; uplander. *Co Ve* (Moríngino 1966:458) 20.
[< *páramo* 'plateau, upland.' Syn. in Co *paramuno,* acc. Tobón Betancourt (1953:192). Cf. **parameño, paramuno, serrano.**]

paramuno
highlander; uplander. *Co* (Malaret 1947:234) mid20; (Tobón Betancourt 1953:192; Morínigo 1966:458) 20.
[< *páramo* 'plateau, highland.' Syn. in Co *paramero.* Cf. **parameño, paramero, serrano.**]

pardejón 'brownish'
1. person with traits of a *pardo* or mulatto. *Ar* (Segovia 1911:134) early20; (Morínigo 1966:459) 20; *RP* (Granada 1957:2.138) 20.
2. offspring of a black and a white. *RP* (Guarnieri 1979:143) 20.
[Df. 1 obs.; derog. Acc. Guarnieri, df. 2 identifies person of lighter skin than a *pardo.* < *pardo* + *-ej-* + augmentative *-ón.* Cf. **morejón, pardo,** Ptg. **pardavasco.**]

pardito 'little brown person'
mulatto. *An SoA* (Santamaría 1942:2.411) 20.
[Euph. < *pardo* + dim. suf. *-ito.* Cf. **negrito, pardejón.**]

pardo 'brown'
1. person whose skin color generally indicates mixed race, usually including black. *PR* (Alvarez Nazario 1974:24); *Mx* (Roncal 1944:533) cl ‖ *Mx-Oaxaca* (Chance and Taylor 1977:460) 18 ‖

SA (Kany 1960b:35) 20.

2a. offspring of a white and a black; mulatto. *An Ar* (Woodbridge 1948:359); *SA* (Mörner 1967:44); *Mx* (Aguirre Beltrán 1972:173) cl ‖ *Mx* (O'Crouley 1972:21) 18 ‖ *Cu* (Martinez-Alier 1974:11–12, 17); *DR-Santo Domingo* (Domínguez 1973:108) late18 ‖ *Cu* (Pichardo 1953:526; Macías 1885:935–36) 19 ‖ *Ar* (Saubidet 1943:276) early–mid20 ‖ *Ar* (Garzón 1910:355) early20 ‖ *PR* (Malaret 1931:394 and 1937:236); *SA* exc. *Pe* (Malaret 1944: 263) mid20 ‖ *An Ar* (Morínigo 1966:459; Santamaría 1942:2.411); *Cu PR* (Dihigo 1966:192; Espina Pérez 1972:148) 20 ‖ *Cu PR* (Vergara Martín 1922:242) n.d.

2b. offspring of a black and a white, with dark skin and kinky hair. *RP* (Guarnieri 1979:143) 20.

3. any nonwhite. *Mx* (Roncal 1944:533); *Pe SA* (Romero 1944:375); *SA* (Romero 1944:385); *An Ar* (Sánchez-Albornoz 1974:130) cl ‖ *SA-we. coast* (Rout 1976:xv; Rosenblat 1954:2.157; Kany 1960b:35) cl–20 ‖ *Mx* (O'Crouley 1972:21) 18 ‖ *Pe* (Cowles 1952:580); *SA* (Granada 1957:2.138) prior20 ‖ *SA Ur Ve* (Cowles 1952:580) mid20 ‖ *RP* (Guarnieri 1967:159–60); *An Ar* (Morínigo 1966:459) 20.

4a. offspring of free blacks. *RP* (Granada 1957:2.138) prior20.

4b. black person. *Pg* (Pescatello 1975:249) 20prior ‖ *SA* (Kany 1960b:35) 20.

5a. free mestizo. *PR* (Alvarez Nazario 1974:347) cl.

5b. free mulatto or mestizo. *PR SA* (Zenón Cruz 1975:1.252) cl.

5c. free mulatto. *Cu* (Macías 1885:935–36) 19.

5d. free person of mixed race. *PR* (Domínguez 1973:80) late18.

5e. free person of color with light skin. *PR* (Domínguez 1973:123) mid19.

5f. person of dark skin color who is the offspring of at least one black parent. *Pe SA* (Roncal 1944:375) cl ‖ *RP* (Guarnieri 1967:159–60) 20.

6. person of humble social standing. *Mx-Tabasco* (Morínigo 1966:459; Santamaría 1942:2.411) 20.

7a. offspring of a white and an Indian; mestizo. *Cu PR* (Woodbridge 1948:359) cl.

7b. offspring of a white Spaniard and an Indian. *Ve* (Vergara Martín 1922:242) n.d.

8. offspring of a white and a mulatto. *Cu* (Woodbridge 1948:359) cl–20.

9. offspring of a black and an Indian; *zambo*. *Mx* (Love 1971:81) cl ‖ *RP* (Granada 1957:2.138) 20.

10. person of low social standing or of native origin. *Ar* (Garzón

1910:355) early20.

11a. mulatto or other person of color, acc. military services. *Mx* (Aguirre Beltrán 1972:173); *SA* (Mörner 1967:44; Rout 1976:xv) cl.

11b. any person of color, mulatto, or black. *Ar* (Segovia 1911:134) early20 ‖ *SA* (Malaret 1931:394) mid20.

11c. person whose dark skin color is between *morocho* and *negro*. *RP* (Guarnieri 1957:139) 20.

11d. offspring of a Spaniard or European and an Indian or black; any person of color. *Cu PR SA* (Santamaría 1942:2.411) 20.

11e. person of mixed race, usually white and black. *Ar* (Andrews 1979:21) 19.

[Df. 2a ranges from pejor. to respect. Df. 2b syn. *mulato*. Df. 3 euph. Df. 4 syn. *moreno*. Df. 5 syn. *mestizo libre*. Df. 6 used in opp. to *gente decente*. Df. 11a euph. used to allow the military to conscribe this person into the service, otherwise prohibited to blacks and mulattoes. Df. 12 includes *negro del país*. Also used in 15- and 16-cent. Spain. Other syn. *zambo* 'offspring of a black and an Indian,' acc. Mellafe (1964:89). Cf. **color inferior, indio, mestizo, moreno, morocho, mulato, negro, zambo.**]

pardo loro

person with brown or light brown skin color. *CR* (Levine 1980:102) 18.

[Cf. **loro, pardo.**]

pariente 'family relative'

1. person from the same country, or fellow countryman, acc. *negros ladinos*. *Cu* (Pichardo 1953:526) 19.

2. black person or creole from the coastal areas. *PR* (Zenón Cruz 1975:1.257–58) 16–18.

[Df. 1 syn. *paisano*. Df. 2 greatly insult.; often in phr. *tener parientes en la costa*. Cf. **ladino, paisano.**]

pasa 'raisin; tightly rolled kinky hair'

person with short, kinky, or matted hair, reminiscent of a black person or a mulatto. *PR SA* (Alvarez Nazario 1974:357–58) cl ‖ *Cu DR PR* (Cowles 1952:581) mid20.

[Usually in phr. *tener pasa*. Acc. Alvarez Nazario, also used in Canary Islands. Usually in phr. *pelo de pasa* or *pelo pasa*. Cf. **negro pelo pasa, pasita.**]

pasiente

native or resident of El Paso, TX. *US-AZ* (Barker 1950:34) mid20.

[Acc. Barker, Pachuco slang. Cf. **chicano, mexicano, pachuco.**]

pasita 'little raisin; tight curls'

1. person whose hair is kinky, like that of a black person. *Co*

(Alario di Filippo 1964:252) 20.

2. Indian of an ancient Tamaulipan tribe. *Mx* (Santamaría 1942:2.418) 20.

[Usually in phr. *tener pelo pasita. Pasita* < *pasa* 'raisin' + dim suf. *-ito.* Cf. **pasa, negro pelo pasa.**]

pasmarote — See *payo*

pasudo 'kinky-haired'

person whose hair is short, kinky, tight-rolled, or matted hair, like that of a black person. *Co* (Tobón Betancourt 1953:193); *Co Cu PR Ve* (Malaret 1931:397) mid20 ‖ *Co* (Tascón 1961:295); *Mx* (Morínigo 1966:463); *PR* (Alvarez Nazario 1974:358); *Co Mx Ve* (Alario di Filippo 1964:253); *Co Ve* (Alonso 1958:3.3171); *SA* (Santamaría 1942:2.421–22) 20.

[< *pasa* + adj. suf. *-udo.* Var. *pasúo.* Cf. **negro pasudo, pasuriento, pasita.**]

pasúo — See *pasudo*

pasuriento 'kinky-haired'

person, generally black, whose hair is kinky or tightly matted in *pasas. PR* (Alvarez Nazario 1974:358) 20.

[< *pasa* + adj. suf. *-uriento.* Cf. **pasita, pasudo, pasurín, pasuso.**]

pasurín 'kinky-haired'

black person whose hair is kinky or tightly matted in *pasas. PR* (Alvarez Nazario 1974:358; Alleyne 1963:97) 20 ‖ *PR SA* (Alvarez Nazario 1974:358) cl–20.

[Acc. Alvarez Nazario, also used in Canary Islands. < *pasa* + *-ur-* + dim. suf. *-ín.* Cf. **pasa, pasita, pasudo, pasuso.**]

pasuso 'kinky-haired'

black person whose hair is kinky or tightly matted in *pasas. CR* (Morínigo 1966:463); *Ve* (Alvarez Nazario 1974:358); *CR* (Alario di Filippo 1964:253) 20.

[< *pasa* + suf. *-uso.* Cf. **pasa, pasita, pasudo, pasuriento.**]

patán — See *campesino, campirano, jáyaro*

patapila — See *pila*

patillo — See *pato*

pato 'duck'

farmer; rustic or rural type. *CR* (Salesiano 1938:102; Villegas 1952:106; Cowles 1952:587–88) mid20; (Kany 1960b:42) 20.

[Acc. Villegas, slang. Dim. syn. *patillo.* Excl. to CR. Syns. *concho, campirano,* acc. Kany. Cf. **campesino, campirano, concho, paisano, polo.**]

patojo

person from the Cauca Valley, Co. *Co* (Kany 1960b:41) 20.

[Syn. *negro.*]

patón 'clumsy-footed'

1a. peninsular Spaniard. *Cu PR* (Malaret 1931:399) mid20 ‖
Cu PR (Kany 1960b:37; Santamaría 1942:2.427); *Cu* (Morínigo
1966:466) 20.

1b. Spaniard, acc. person of the lower classes. *SA* (Vergara
Martín 1922:242) n.d.

2. person native to the Canary Islands. *Ve* (Malaret 1931:399)
mid20; (Kany 1960b:37; Santamaría 1942:2.427) 20; (Vergara
Martín 1922:242) n.d.

[Df. 1 insult., derog. Df. 2 indicates cowardice. < *pata* 'paw, foot' +
aug. suf. *-ón,* literally 'someone with big feet.' Cf. **chapetón,
gachupín, gorrión, isleño, ñopo.**]

patricio 'patrician'

Brazilian. *Ur* (Cowles 1952:587–88) mid20.

[Acc. Cowles, used in ref. to Brazilians because they employ the
term so much in the sense of *paisano* 'compatriot.' Cf. **brasilero,
gaucho, negro,** Ptg. **castelhano.**]

payé — See *payo*

payo 'albino; peasant'

1. albino. *SA* (Bayo 1910:172 and 1931:189) early–mid20 ‖ *Ar
Bo* (Cowles 1952:590) mid20 ‖ *Ar* (Garzón 1910:365); *Ar-interior*
(Segovia 1911:257) early20; (Morínigo 1966:468) 20 ‖ *RP* (Santa-
maría 1942:2.431) 20.

2. person with very light blond or white hair. *Ar* (Garzón
1910:365); *Ar-interior* (Segovia 1911:257) early20 ‖ *Ar* (Cowles
1952:565); *Ar Bo* (Cowles 1952:590); *RP* (Santamaría 1942:2.431)
mid20.

3a. crude or untravelled peasant. *Ar* (Garzón 1910:364) early20
‖ *RP* (Kany 1960b:40) 20 ‖ *Mx* (Malaret 1947:135) mid20;
(Velasco Valdés 1957:97) 20.

3b. peasant, visiting a city for the first time, who is surprised by
everything around. *Mx* (Morínigo 1966:468) 20.

3c. ordinary, shy, or unsociable peasant. *Ar* (Saubidet
1943:284) early–mid20.

[Acc. Corominas (1954–57:3.701), att. in 16-cent. Sp. slang. Acc.
Garzón, 'Catalan or Balearic Island peasant' in Spain. Syns. df. 3a
fuereño, pueblerino. Syns. df. 3a *payuco, payuca, payucano,
payuscano.* Syn. df. 3b *pasmarote.* Vars. for df. 3 *paio, payé,
payesa.* Cf. **albino, campesino, chele, guaso, güero, paisano,
palmarote, rubio.**]

payuca — See *payo*

payucano — See *payo*

payuco — See *payo*

payuscano — See *payo*

pegujalero

1. Indian servant or slave. *Bo* (Levine 1980:37) 20.

2. sharecropper; farmer who works land of another. *Bo* (Levine 1980:37) 20.

[Acc. DRAE (997), < *pegujal* 'hacienda, tract of land.' Cf. **colono, sayañero.**]

pehuenche

1. Mapuche Indian from the pinelands. *Ch* (Cowles 1952:593) mid20.

2. inhabitant, often Indian, of the Andean highlands. *Ch* (Cowles 1952:593) mid20; (DRAE 997) 20.

[Df. 2 derog. Acc. Cowles, < Mapuche *pehuén* 'Araucanian pine' + *che* 'people.' Cf. **serrano.**]

pelado 'hairless; coarse, rude'

1. person with brown skin. *Mx* (Levine 1980:104) 19.

2. Indian. *Mx* (Vergara Martín 1922: 243) n.d.

3. person of low class or social standing; riff-raff. *Mx* (Levine 1980:104) 19; (Malaret 1947:136) mid20; (Vergara Martín 1922:243) n.d.

4. peasant; small farmer. *Mx* (Vergara Martín 1922:243) n.d.

[Cf. **campesino, pardo, payo, pelo malo.**]

pelicandelo

person with red hair; redhead. *Co* (Alario di Filippo 1964:259) 20.

[< *pelo* 'hair' + *candelo* 'reddish-blond' by anal. to *pelirrojo* 'redhead' and *pelirrubio* 'blond.' Std. syn. *pelirrojo*. Cf. **colorado, chelo, güero, puca.**]

peliduro

person whose hair is kinky or matted like that of a black person. *Pa* (Aguilera Patiño 1951:482) mid20.

[< *pelo* 'hair' + *duro* 'hard' by anal. to *pelirrojo*, as in *pelicandelo*. Cf. **motoso, motudo, pelo pasa.**]

pelirrojo — See *colorado, pelicandelo*

pelo apretado 'tight hair'

black person whose hair is kinky or in tight curls. *PR* (Alvarez Nazario 1974:358) 20.

[Often in phr. *tener pelo apretado*. Cf. **pelo pasa.**]

pelo bueno 'good hair'

person who has wavy hair. *Cu DR PR US-New York City*

(Domínguez 1973:190); *PR* (Alvarez Nazario 1974:358) 20.
[Used in opp. to *pelo malo.* Usually in phr. *tener pelo bueno.* Cf.
pelo apretado, pelo malo, pelo muerto, pelo vivo.]

pelo de pasa — See *pasa*

pelo malo 'bad hair'
any person, often white, who has kinky hair. *PR* (Alvarez Nazario 1974:355) 20.
[Acc. Alvarez Nazario and Domínguez (1973:190), *pelo bueno* used
in ref. to 'straight hair of the white person.' Usually in phr. *tener
pelo malo;* indicates undesirable 'kinky hair' in almost all of SA,
acc. Alba (1969:34). Syn. *grifo.* Cf. **grifo, motudo, negro por el
pelo, pelo pasa,** Ptg. **ser ruim de cabelo.**]

pelo moreno 'brown or brunet hair'
person whose dark hair color may indicate racial mixing. *Co-
Cartagena* (Solaún and Kronus 1973:166) 20.
[Usually in phr. *por el pelo moreno* 'by the brunet hair.' Cf. **negro
por el pelo, pelo apretado, pelo malo, pasa.**]

pelo muerto 'dead hair'
person who has straight hair. *Cu DR PR US-New York City*
(Domínguez 1973:190) 20.
[Usually in phr. *tener pelo muerto.* Used in opp. to *pelo bueno, pelo
malo,* or *pelo vivo.* Cf. **pasa, pelo bueno, pelo malo, pelo vivo.**]

pelo pasa — See *pasa*

pelo pasa largo 'long raisin hair'
person whose hair is in long, tight curls. *PR* (Alvarez Nazario
1974:358) late19.
[Acc. Alvarez Nazario, found in the Registro Central de Esclavos of
1872. Usually in phr. *tener pelo pasa largo.* Cf. **pasa.**]

pelo pasita — See *pasita*

pelo vivo 'live hair'
person with curly hair. *Cu DR PR US-New York City*
(Domínguez 1973:190) 20.
[Usually in phr. *tener pelo vivo.* Cf. **pelo bueno, pelo malo, pelo
muerto.**]

peninsular
1a. peninsular Spaniard. *SA* (Pérez de Barradas 1948:174) cl;
(Rout 1976:xiv) cl–20; (Vergara Martín 1922:243) n.d. ‖ *Ar*
(Segovia 1911:258) early20.
1b. person born in the Iberian Peninsula rather than America.
SA (Bailey and Nasatir 1973:775) n.d.
2. person from the Yucatán peninsula. *Mx* (Santamaría
1942:2.443) 20.
[Syns. df. 1a *gachupín, chapetón, español europeo.* Cf. **chapetón,**

gachupín, español europeo, Ptg. peninsular.]
peón 'peon; peasant; laborer'
  1. descendant of Indians who served the master as a servant and followed him north across the Rio Grande. *Mx US-TX* (Gonzalez de Mireles 1939:498) cl.
  2. poor Mexican immigrant who comes to the United States in search of a job. *US* (Gonzalez de Mireles 1939:498) mid20.
  [Cf. **bracero, peón de raya, pocho.**]
peón de raya
  farm worker, usually Indian or mestizo, of low social status who was paid poor wages and some food for nine months of work per year. *Mx* (Levine 1980:105) prior20.
  [Cf. **pegujalero.**]
perlado — See *aperlado*
pernambucano 'Pernambucan'
  person from or native to PE, Br. *Ur* (Mieres et al. 1966:105) 20.
  [Cf. **brasilero, paulista,** Ptg. **castelhano.**]
persona bien 'good person'
  person of high social standing. *Co-coast* (Revollo 1942:208) mid20.
  [Syn. *bien.* Acc. Boyd-Bowman (1971:693), att. as *persona (de) bien* in Puebla, Mx. Cf. **bien, gente bien.**]
persona de bien — See *persona bien*
persona de color 'person of color'
  1. person of color; colored person. *Co-Cartagena* (Solaún and Kronus 1973:148) 20.
  2. mulatto. *PR* (Alvarez Nazario 1974:352) cl–20.
  [Df. 2 euph. Cf. **de color, gente de color.**]
persona de la clase — See *de la clase*
persona de limpia generación — See *limpio*
persona de mala raza — See *mala raza*
persona de razón — See *gente de razón*
persona de sangre azul — See *de sangre azul*
persona decente — See *gente decente, plebe*
persona que no es blanca 'person who is not white'
  black person. *PR* (Zenón Cruz 1975:1.254) 20.
  [Euph. Acc. Zenón Cruz, *personas que no son blancas* [*sic*]. Cf. **gente que no es blanca.**]
perulero 'type of earthen jar; Peruvian'
  1a. Peruvian, acc. Spaniards. *Pe* (Paz Soldán 1938:163) 19prior.
  1b. Peruvian, esp. one who is wealthy by tradition. *SA* (Kany

1960b:39) 20.

2a. rich Spaniard-Peruvian. *Pe SA* (Bayo 1910:177 and 1931: 192) early–mid20.

2b. Spaniard who has gotten rich in America, esp. in Pe. *SA* (Cobarruvias 1611:867; Santamaría 1942.1:452; Alonso 1958: 3.3245) cl; (Vergara Martín 1922:243) n.d.

3. person from SA; *americano*. *SA* (Vergara Martín 1922:243) n.d.

[Often pejor. Also used in Spain. < *Peru* + adj. suf. *-(l)ero*. Cf. **americano, español, gachupín, godo.**]

petiyanqui — See *pitiyanqui*

pichín

1. Italian, esp. a grocer. *Pe* (Morínigo 1966:488) 20.

2. Peruvian-born child of an Italian. *Pe* (Alonso 1958:3.3265) 20.

[Acc. Morínigo and Alonso, < Italian *piccino* 'small lad; little.' Cf. **piquinini.**]

pichón

native-born person of foreign-born parents. *Cu* (Vergara Martín 1922:243) 20prior.

[Acc. Vergara Martín, usually in phrs. such as *pichón de española* or *pichón de asturiano* in which one or both of the parents' nationalities are mentioned. Cf. **criollo.**]

pieza 'piece (of cloth); something owned; coin'

1a. black slave, acc. slavers. *PR SA* (Alvarez Nazario 1974:380); *Cu* (Levine 1980:107); *SA* (Morínigo 1966:490) cl.

1b. black slave. *Cu* (Santamaría 1942:2.470) prior20 ‖ *DR* (Boyd-Bowman 1971:702) early16.

1c. Indian or black slave at the disposal of the landowner, acc. slave traders. *SA* (Morínigo 1966:490) cl.

2. person captured or imprisoned by Indian foes. *Mx-Sonora* (Sobarzo 1966:246) 20.

3. Indian woman or child. *RP* (Fontanella de Weinberg 1982:46) 16–17.

4. concubine or loved-one. *Cu* (Morínigo 1966:490) 20.

[M., f. Df. 1b euph. Syns. df. 1a, *pieza de ébano, pieza de Indias*. Cf. **indio, pieza de Indias, pieza de registro**, Ptg. **peça de Índias.**]

pieza de ébano — See *pieza*

pieza de esclavos

1. black slave on the slave ship. *Mx SA* (Aguirre Beltrán 1972:40) cl.

2. any slave. *Mx-Puebla* (Boyd-Bowman 1969:138) cl.

[On a bill of sale, a 'head of slaves,' like a head of cattle, acc. Boyd-

Bowman. Cf. **pieza, pieza de Indias,** Ptg. **peça de escravo.**]

pieza de Indias 'piece of the Indies'

1a. black slave in the slave market. *SA* (Alvarez Nazario 1974:336, 380) cl.

1b. slave, acc. slavers. *Cu* (Levine 1980:107) cl.

2a. black African slave of great value in the marketplace, esp. one in the prime of life. *SA* (Bailey and Nasatir 1973:775; Sánchez-Albornoz 1974:74) cl.

2b. black African, usually a slave, between eighteen and thirty years of age, having no obvious physical defects and standing no less than five feet tall. *SA* (Rout 1976:xii) cl.

2c. black slave between eighteen and thirty-five years of age. *Co-we.* (Velásquez 1962:114) cl.

[Acc. Mörner (1967:17), used as common slave analyzing device, i.e., 1 male slave in good condition = 1 *pieza;* 2 in poor condition = 1 *pieza,* etc. Cf. **pieza, pieza de esclavo, pieza de registro,** Ptg. **peça de Índias.**]

pieza de registro 'piece of the register'

black slave registered on the slave ship. *Mx SA* (Aguirre Beltrán 1972:40) cl.

[Cf. **pieza de Indias.**]

pieza de roza 'piece for planting'

black slave used to grow the master's food; black fieldhand. *SA* (Nuñez 1980:383) prior20.

[Cf. **pieza, pieza de Indias, pieza de registro.**]

pijotero 'tedious; wretched'

Italian immigrant. *Ar* (Levine 1980:107) 20prior.

[Acc. Levine, syn. *gringo.* Cf. **cocoliche, gringo, nápoles, pichín.**]

pila 'hairless dog; bare, nude'

Paraguayan soldier during the Chaco War. *Bo* (Kany 1960b: 39) mid19.

[M. Syn. *patapila* 'barefoot'; used in ref. to ragged state of these soldiers.]

pililo 'dirty or ragged person'

person of the lowest possible social class, even lower than the *roto. Ch* (Rodríguez 1875:374) 19.

[Acc. Rodríguez, sim. to Mexican *lépero.* Cf. **roto.**]

pillán

Spaniard, acc. Indians. *Ch* (Kany 1960b:37) cl.

[Acc. Kany, 'devil of thunder and lightening,' in ref. to the firearms of the Spaniards.]

pinacate 'black beetle'
1. woman of color; black girl or woman. *US-AZ* (Barker 1950:34) mid20.
2. black person. *Pe* (Kany 1960b:36) 20.
[Derog. Df. 1 f. only. Acc. Barker, 'colored girl;' Pachuco slang. Acc. Kany, 'type of black beetle,' < Aztec *pinacatl.* Cf. **chulo, mayate.**]

pinolero
Nicaraguan. *CR* (Bayo 1931:198); *CeA* (Cowles 1952:617) mid20 ‖ *Ho* (Morínigo 1966:496); *CeA* (Kany 1960b:40) 20.
[Acc. Cowles, < *pinol* 'type of cold drink.' Acc. Kany, 'national drink of Nicaragua, made of ground corn, sugar, and ice.' Cf. **nica, pipe.**]

pinta 'spot; paint, painted'
black person. *DR* (Malaret 1944:304) mid20; (Kany 1960b:36; Morínigo 1966:496) 20.
[Facet. Usually in phr. *ser de la pinta* < abbr. of *ser de la raza pinta* 'to be of the painted or colored race.' Acc. Santamaría (1942:2.479), also 'color of animals, generally cattle and chickens.' Cf. **negro, persona de color, pinto,** Ptg. **ter pinta.**]

pinto 'painted'
Nicaraguan Indian, usually having white spots on brown skin, and generally deriving from a mixture of various Indian tribes. *Ni* (Vergara Martín 1922:243) n.d.
[Acc. Cowles (1952:158) 'animal with black and white hair or coat.' Cf. **indio, rayado.**]

piojo 'louse'
Mexican. *US-AZ* (Barker 1950:34) mid20.
[Acc. Barker, Pachuco slang. Cf. **chicano, mexicano, pasiente.**]

piolo
1. mestizo who prefers white women as sexual partners. *Cu* (Espina Pérez 1972:158) 20.
2. white man who prefers mestizo women as sexual partners. *Cu* (Espina Pérez 1972:158) 20.
[Cf. **mulañero, mulatero, negrero.**]

pipe
Nicaraguan. *CR* (Kany 1960b:40) 20.
[Acc. Kany, < *pipil* 'name of a local Indian tribe.' Cf. **nica, pinolero, pipil.**]

pipil 'Mexican'
1. Mexican. *CeA* (Kany 1960b:40; Morínigo 1966:498) 20.
2. Toltec Indian of Sa who spoke very bad Nahuatl. *Sa* (Vergara Martín 1922:243) n.d.

3. Salvadoran. *CeA* (Lipski 1988:p.c.) late20.

[Joc. Acc. Santamaría (1942:2.484), 'boy, people of the Pipila tribe, rel. to the Aztecs, who supposedly spoke the lg. of the Aztecs like children.' Cf. **pipe.**]

piquichón

black person or *chino* who is overcome in a fit of pique. *Pe* (Vergara Martín 1922:243) n.d.

[Cf. **chino.**]

piquinini 'pickaninny'

1a. black or mulatto child. *Cu Pe* (Alvarez Nazario 1974:339) cl ‖ *Pe* (Morínigo 1966:499) 20.

1b. small child. *Pe* (Paz Soldán 1938:323) 19 ‖ *An Ni* (Morínigo 1966:499) 20.

2a. small person or child, esp. black. *Cu* (Morínigo 1966:499) 20.

2b. small person. *Ar-interior Ch Co* (Morínigo 1966:499–500) 20.

3. black person, generally a slave, recently arrived from Africa. *Cu* (Macías 1885:976) 19prior; (Santamaría 1942:2.487) prior20.

[M., f. Acc. Paz Soldán, < Sp. *pequeño niño* 'small child.' Acc. Morínigo, < Ptg. *pequenino.* Var. df. 2b *piquinino.* Perhaps < deformation of Sp. or Ptg. word used by black slaves and their master speaking a form of creolized language. Acc. Paz Soldán, in so. US *pickaninny* used by whites in ref. to 'black or mulatto child' and by blacks in ref. to 'any white child.' Cf. **muleque, negrito.**]

piquinino — See *piquinini*

pisco 'turkey'

person whose skin color indicates mixed race. *Co-Jardín* (Flórez 1969:122) 20.

[Acc. Alonso (1958:3.3297), < Quechua *pisco* 'bird.']

pitiyanqui

person belonging to the statehood party, acc. socialists and other political opponents. *PR* (Gallo 1980:87) 20.

[Acc. Gallo, pejor. slang; indicates that person would rather cast aside native culture to become American. Acc. Lipski (1988:p.c.), var. *petiyanqui.* Cf. **yanqui.**]

platanero 'banana grower'

Puerto Rican. *PR* (Kany 1960b:42) 20.

[Acc. Kany, sim. to phr. *tener la mancha del plátano* 'to have the stain of the banana,' i.e, 'to be typically a native of PR.' Acc. Lipski (1988:p.c.), *mancha del plátano* 'appearance of being Puerto Rican.' Cf. **neorriqueño, puertorriqueño.**]

playero 'beachcomber'

1. person who lives on or near the coast. *PR* (Malaret 1937:247) mid20 ‖ *Cu Mx PR* (Morínigo 1966:508) 20.

2. person of the lower classes; riff-raff. *PR* (Malaret 1937:247) mid20.

3. person of little economic means who makes a living by selling scraps found on the beach for a few cents. *Ch* (Morínigo 1966:508) 20.

[< *playa* 'beach' + suf. -*ero.* Cf. Ptg. **caiçara.**]

plebe 'common people'

person who is Indian or black, or any person of mixed race such as mestizo, mulatto, *cholo,* or *zambo;* nonwhite; person of color. *Ar* (Bayo 1910:91, 183) early20.

[F. Ants. *español, gente decente, persona decente.* Acc. Megenney (1988:p.c.), 'children' in NM. Cf. **español, gente decente, gente de orilla.**]

poblano 'town, village; villager'

1. person who lives in a town or village. *SoA* (Malaret 1947:238) mid20 ‖ *Bo* (Fernández and Fernández 1967:114); *SoA* exc. *Ar Bo Ch Pg Ur* (Morínigo 1966:510) 20 ‖ *Pe* (Paz Soldán 1938:327) n.d.

2. person native to or living in Puebla, Mx. *Mx* (Morínigo 1966:510) 20.

[Acc. Paz Soldán, *pueblero* in gaucho speech. < *pueblo* 'town, village.' Cf. **pueblano, pueblero.**]

pochi — See *pocho*

pochito — See *pocho*

pocho 'faded, discolored; malnourished, pale'

1. Mexican living in southwestern US; Mexican-American. *Mx* (Morínigo 1966:510); *Mx-Sonora* (Sobarzo 1966:258); *US-CO, -NM* (Cobos 1983:136) 20.

2a. Americanized Mexican born or living in the United States. *Mx* (Abalos 1986:43) 20.

2b. any Mexican-American who abandons native Mexican culture and Spanish lg. in becoming Americanized. *US-CA, -s.w.* (Rodriguez 1982:29) 20.

[Acc. Morínigo, used in ref. to the bastardized Tex-Mex lingo common to persons along US-Mx border. Acc. Abalos, df. 2a often derog. Acc. Cobos, < Mexican Sp. *pocho* < Yaqui *pochio* 'dull.' Acc. Rodriguez, affect. or joc. dim. df. 2b *mi pochito* 'my little *pocho*' or 'my sweetie.' Var. *pochi,* acc. Sobarzo. Syn. *agringado.* Cf. **bracero, chicano, gabacho, mexicano, mojado, nuyorican, piojo.**]

polaca 'Polish woman'

prostitute. *Ar* (Roback 1944:136) mid20.

[F. only. Acc. Roback, slur; *polacca*[*sic*]; < *polaco* 'Polish,' since white slaves were once drawn from Poland. Cf. **polaco.**]

polaco 'Polish, Pole'
1. Jewish person; Jew. *Co* (Ferguson 1963:122) 20 ‖ *Cu* (Lipski 1988:p.c.) late20.
2. white Eastern European, esp. Jewish. *Cu* (Gann and Duignan 1986:97) mid20.
[Cf. **jacoibo, judío, polonés, ruso,** Ptg. **judeu, polaco.**]

polo
rustic type; hick. *CR* (Villegas 1952:113) mid20.
[Acc. Villegas, slang. Cf. **campesino, paisano, pato.**]

polonés 'Polish, Pole'
Christian person of Polish descent. *Co* (Ferguson 1963:122) 20.
[Cf. **polaco.**]

pongo 'Indian servant'
1. Indian resident or tenant farmer of a hacienda who serves a week in the master's city home and who is often rented out for other jobs by the master. *Bo Pe* (Bayo 1931:202) 20.
2a. Indian servant. *Bo Ec Pe* (Malaret 1947:239) mid20.
2b. Indian servant, usually of the hacienda, who is generally not paid for whatever manner of odious job performed. *Bo Ec Pe* (Cowles 1952:633) mid20.
2c. Indian servant who works on a large farm in exchange for the right to sharecrop a small plot of land. *Bo Ch Ec Pe* (Morínigo 1966:514) 20.
2d. Indian who does domestic service. *SoA* (Malaret 1944:322) mid20.
3. servant. *SoA-no.* (Boyd-Bowman 1982:2338) 18.
[Acc. Morínigo and Alonso, < Quechua *puncu* or *punco* 'door.' Acc. Malaret and Cowles, < Aymara *puncai* 'guardian.' Cf. **chacracama, criada, indio pongo, moza, mucama.**]

populacho — See *gente de orilla*
por el pelo moreno — See *pelo moreno*
poroto 'type of bean'
Chilean. *Ch* (Kany 1960b:41) 20.
[Acc. Kany, *porotos* 'beans' figure greatly in the Chilean diet. Cf. **guaso, roto.**]

porteño 'port dweller'
1. native of Buenos Aires city or province. *Ar* (Segovia 1911:265) early20; (Malaret 1947:146) mid20 ‖ *Ar Ur* (Cowles 1952:637) mid20 ‖ *SA* (Ferguson 1963:122) 20.
2. native of Valparaiso, Ch. *Ch* (Cowles 1952:637) mid20.
[< *puerto* 'port' + suf. *-eño.* Deriv. used in Ur *aporteñarse* 'to take on traits of a *porteño*,' acc. Mieres et al. (1966:22). Cf. **irlandés porteño,** Ptg. **carioca.**]

portorricense
Puerto Rican. *PR* (Malaret 1937:248; Alonso 1958:3.3360) 20.
[Derog. var. *puertorriqueñeo.* Acc. Lipski (1988:p.c.), var. *portorro,*
probably derog. Std. Sp. *puertorriqueño.* Cf. **cubiche, nica,
nigüento, puertorriqueño.**]

portorriqueño — See *puertorriqueño*

portorro — See *portorricense*

portuga
Brazilian or Portuguese person, esp. during the wars of inde-
pendence. *Ur* (Mieres et al. 1966:110) 19.
[M., f. Acc. Mieres et al., derog.; < abbr. of *portugalés* 'Portuguese.'
Cf. **brasilero.**]

postizo 'false'
offspring of a *castizo* and a white. *Mx* (León 1924:25; Woodbridge 1948:359; Santamaría 1942:2.520) cl ‖ *SA* (Vergara
Martín 1922:243) n.d.
[Cf. **castizo, mestizo.**]

potón 'rustic'
rustic type; hick. *Ch* (Morínigo 1966:517) 20.
[Acc. Morínigo, < Mapuche *poto* 'rearend, behind'; syn. *patán.* Cf.
campesino, campirano, paisano, polo.]

prieto 'blackish, black'
1a. black person; person with black skin color. *PR* (Alvarez Nazario 1974:380) cl ‖ *Mx* (Chance 1979:164) early19 ‖ *Cu Sa*
(Cowles 1952:641) mid20 ‖ *Co-Yolombó* (Flórez 1969:122) 20.

1b. black person. *PR* (Alvarez Nazario 1974:346) cl–20; (Zenón
Cruz 1975:1.254; Gallo 1980:90) 20 ‖ *SA* (Kany 1960b:35) 20.

1c. Hispanic of African descent; Afro-Hispanic. *Cu DR PR US-
New York City* (Domínguez 1973:187) 20.

2. person whose hair is *moreno* or *trigueño,* i.e., a shade of
brown. *Co Mx* (Alario di Filippo 1964:284); *Mx* (Santamaría
1942:2.524) 20.

3. woman with dark skin and/or brunet hair. *Mx* (Morínigo
1966:520) 20.

4. person of color. *Mx-Puebla* (Boyd-Bowman 1971:742) mid16.
[Df. 1b. euph., acc. Kany; derog., uncultured, acc. Alvarez Nazario;
slang, acc. Gallo; social euph. esp. applied to a woman, acc. Zenón
Cruz. Df. 1c syn. *trigueño.* Df. 3 term of affect. or flirtation. Acc.
Malkiel (1953:18–35) and Corominas (1973:58), < *apretar* 'to
tighten, to stretch.' Acc. Cowles (1952:43), var. *aprietado* in 20-cent.
Sa. Acc. Corominas, att. in Spain 1272 as 'tight, thick'; dialectal
with meaning 'black.' Deriv. *aprietado.* Cf. **moreno, mulato,
negro, pardo, trigueño,** Ptg. **negro, preto.**]

prieto como un chorizo 'black as a sausage'
person with very dark skin like that of a sausage. *Cu* (Espina Pérez 1972:162) 20.
[Cf. **chorizo, negro como un tizón, prieto.**]

prietuzco 'blackish, darkish'
1. any nonwhite person. *PR* (Domínguez 1973:94) late19.
2. person with blackish skin. *An CeA Mx* (Morínigo 1966:520) 20.
[Syn. df. 2 *negruzco.* Cf. **prieto.**]

primo 'cousin'
North American. *Mx* (Kany 1960b:39) 20.
[Often in phr. *nuestros primos* 'our cousins (to the north).' Acc. Kany, 'dupe or simpleton.']

puca 'red'
person with red hair; redhead. *Ec* (Kany 1960b:48) 20.
[M., f. Cf. **pelicandelo.**]

puchuel
1. person whose skin color indicates racial mixing, acc. parish records. *Mx* (Roncal 1944:533) cl.
2. offspring of a *castizo* and a white. *Mx* (Woodbridge 1948:359) cl.
3. offspring of a *postizo* and a white. *Mx* (Woodbridge 1948:359) cl ‖ *SA* (Vergara Martín 1922:243) n.d.
4. offspring of a mestizo and a white. *Mx* (Woodbridge 1948:359; Santamaría 1942:2.528) cl.
5. offspring of an *ochavón* and a white, whose skin color is usually completely white. *Ve* (Woodbridge 1948:359) cl.
6. offspring of a white and a *cuarterón de mestizo,* the latter of which is offspring of a white and a *castizo;* 93.75% white, 6.25% Indian. *Mx* (León 1924:20–21; Pérez de Barradas 1948:189) cl.
7. offspring of an *octavón indio* and a white; 93.75% white, 6.25% Indian. *Mx* (León 1924:20–21, plate 36; Woodbridge 1948:359) cl.
8. offspring of a Spaniard and a quadroon. *DR-Santo Domingo* (Boyd-Bowman 1982:2449) 18.
[Also m. and f. var. *puchuela.* Probably < Amerindian lg. Almost excl. to Mx. Usually in ref. to white and Indian ancestry. Syns. *semiblanco, quinterón de mestizo.* Cf. **puchuela de blanco, puchuela de negro.**]

puchuela — See *puchuel*

puchuela de blanco
offspring of a white and an *ochavón blanco,* whose skin color is almost totally white. *Pe* (León 1924:25–26) cl.
   [Cf. **puchuel, puchuela de negro.**]
puchuela de negro
   1. person whose skin color indicates some black ancestry, acc. parish records. *Mx* (Roncal 1944:533) cl.
   2. offspring of a white and a *quinterón de mulato,* the latter which is offspring of a white and a *cuarterón de mulato;* 93.75% white, 6.25% black. *Mx* (León 1924:20–21, plate 37; Pérez de Barradas 1948:190) cl.
   3. offspring of an *octavón negro* and a white; 93.75% white, 6.25% black. *Mx* (León 1924:25; Woodbridge 1948:359) cl.
   [Excl. to cl. Mx. Usually in ref. to black and white racial mixture. Cf. **puchuel, puchuela de blanco.**]
pueblano 'villager'
   person who lives in the city or town. *DR-Santo Domingo Gu Ni Pa Pe-Ica* (Cowles 1952:644) mid20.
   [Acc. Cowles, corruption of *poblano.* Cf. **campesino, guajiro, poblano, puebleño, pueblero.**]
puebleño 'villager'
   1. rustic type. *Mx-Sonora* (Sobarzo 1966:264) 20.
   2. person native to a small town; simple or crude person. *Co* (Alario di Filippo 1964:287) 20.
   [Cf. **campesino, guajiro, jíbaro, poblano, pueblano, pueblero.**]
pueblerino — See *payo*
pueblero 'villager'
   1a. inhabitant of a town. *Ar Bo Ur Ve* (Malaret 1947:148) mid20.
   1b. inhabitant of a small town, acc. persons in the neighboring larger cities. *Mx* (Morínigo 1966:524) 20.
   2a. inhabitant or native of a city or town, usually unknowledgeable about things of the country. *Ar Bo Ur Ve* (Cowles 1952:645) mid20.
   2b. inhabitant of a city or town. *Pe* (Bayo 1931:204) mid20 ‖ *SoA* (Morínigo 1966:524); *Ve* (Kany 1960b:41) 20.
   3. inhabitant of an important town or city, acc. rural peasants. *Ar* (Saubidet 1943:312) 19.
   [Acc. Morínigo, df. 1b derog.; df. 2b ant. *paisano.* Cf. **campesino, guajiro, poblano, pueblano, puebleño.**]
puertorriqueñeo — See *puertorriqueño*

puertorriqueño 'Puerto Rican'
Puerto Rican. *PR* (Malaret 1937:250) mid20.
[Derog. var. *puertorriqueñeo*. Abbr. as *ricano, riqueño*. Cf. **porto-rricense.**]

puro 'pure'
Indian; full-blooded Indian. *Bo* (Fernández and Fernández 1967:117) 20.
[Syn. *indígena*. Cf. **indígena, negro puro, puro español.**]

puro español 'pure Spaniard'
person whose skin color indicates no racial mixture; white person. *Co-Cartagena* (Solaún and Kronus 1973:166) 20.
[Cf. **español, negro puro, puro.**]

Q

quasi limpio en su origen 'almost clean in origin'
offspring of a white and a *gente blanca;* 98.44% white, 1.56% black. *Pe* (Pérez de Barradas 1948:186) cl.
[*Quasi* obs. Cf. **cuasi limpio de origen, limpio de origen.**]

quebrado 'broken'
person with brunet hair color. *Ec-highlands* (Kany 1960b:49) 20.
[Cf. **moreno, trigueño.**]

quemado 'burnt; toasted'
person with dark or black skin color. *Co-San Juan* (Flórez 1969:122) 20.
[Acc. Flórez, *quemao* [sic]. Acc. Santamaría (1942:2.543), 'of dark tone, ranging from red to black.' Acc. DRAE (1090), Sp. slang 'black person.' Cf. **retinto, tostado.**]

quemao — See *quemado*

quinterón 'quintroon'
1. person whose skin color indicates racial mixture, acc. official documents. *Pe* (Romero 1944:375) cl.

2a. offspring of a white and a quadroon. *Mx* (Woodbridge 1948:359); *Pe* (Santamaría 1942:2.553); *SA* exc. *PR* (Alvarez Nazario 1974:380); *Pe* (Alonso 1958:3.3479) cl ‖ *Co-Cartagena* (Alvarez Nazario 1974:357) mid18 ‖ *SA* exc. *Pe* (Malaret 1944:343) 20 ‖ *SA* (Vergara Martín 1922:243) n.d.

2b. offspring of a white and a quadroon, which is a white and a *tercerón*. *SoA* (Grenón 1930:281) mid18.

3. offspring of a white and a *tercerón negro;* 87.5% white, 12.5% black. *Mx* (León 1924:20–21, plate 38; Woodbridge 1948:359) cl.

4. offspring of a white and a *cuarterón de mestizo*. *Pe* (Mörner 1967:58) 18.

5. offspring of a white and a *cuarterón de mulato*. *Pe* (Mörner 1967:58) 18.

6. offspring of a mestizo and a quadroon. *Cu* (Vergara Martín 1922:243) n.d.

[Acc. Vergara Martín, syn. *coyote*. Sim. to the former So. Amer. Engl. *octoroon* and *quintroon,* acc. Aguirre Beltrán (1972:178). Acc. Tuttle (1976:611), *cuarterón* and *quinterón* provided the anal. on which *ochavón* is based. Acc. Boyd-Bowman (1982:2497), *quinterón* known for reddish skin color; att. in Lima 1770. Cf. **cuarterón, moreno, mulato, ochavón, octavón, pardo.**]

quinterón de mestizo 'mestizo quintroon'

1. person whose skin color indicates white and Indian mixture, acc. parish records. *Mx* (Roncal 1944:533) cl.

2a. offspring of a white and a *cuarterón de mestizo,* the latter of which is a white and a mestizo; 87.5% white, 12.5% Indian. *Mx* (Woodbridge 1948:359; León 1924:20–21, plate 39); *Pe* (Pérez de Barradas 1948:185, 186, 189) cl.

2b. offspring of a white and a *cuarterón de mestizo,* the latter of which is a white and a *castizo;* 93.75% white, 6.25% Indian. *Mx* (Pérez de Barradas 1948:189) cl.

3. offspring of a white and a *castizo*. *Mx* (Woodbridge 1948:359) cl ‖ *SA* (Vergara Martín 1922:243) n.d.

[Acc. Vergara Martín, syns. *puchuel, postizo, octavón.* Cf. **octavón, quinterón, quinterón de mulato.**]

quinterón de mulato 'mulatto quintroon'

1a. offspring of a white and a quadroon. *Pe* (Alvarez Nazario 1974:354) cl.

1b. offspring of a white and a *cuarterón de mulato,* the latter of which is a white and a mulatto; 87.5% white, 12.5% black. *Mx* (Woodbridge 1948:359; Pérez de Barradas 1948:189; León 1924:20–21, plate 40); *Pe* (Pérez de Barradas 1948:186) cl.

2. offspring of a white and a *morisco*. *Mx* (Woodbridge 1948:359) cl ‖ *SA* (Vergara Martín 1922:243) n.d.

[Acc. Alvarez Nazario, syn. df. 1a in PR *cuarterón de mestizo,* sim. to No. Amer. Engl. *octoroon*. Cf. **cuarterón de mestizo, octavón, quinterón de mestizo.**]

quinterón de negro 'black quintroon'

person whose skin color indicates some black ancestry, acc. parish records. *Mx* (Roncal 1944:533) cl.

[Sim. to *quinterón de mulato,* acc. Roncal. Cf. **negro, quinterón de mulato.**]

quinterón de saltatrás
1. person whose skin color indicates mixed race, acc. parish records. *Mx* (Roncal 1944:533) cl.
2. offspring of a quadroon and a black. *Mx* (Woodbridge 1948:359) cl ‖ *SA* (Vergara Martín 1922:243) n.d.
[Var. *quinterón saltatrás* or *quinterón salta atrás.* Cf. **quinterón, quinterón de mestizo, quinterón de mulato, saltatrás.**]
quinterón salta atrás — See *quinterón de saltatrás*
quinterón saltatrás — See *quinterón de saltatrás*

R

racional 'rational; thinking being'
non-Indian who speaks Spanish. *Co Ve* (Rosenblat 1954:1.33) cl.
[Cf. **indio, ladino.**]
ragra-pocho
mestizo of the low classes; starving mestizo. *Pe* (Cowles 1952:666) mid20.
[Cf. **mestizo.**]
raído 'frayed, threadbare; shabby'
rustically or poorly dressed peasant or farmer. *Pg* (Morínigo 1966:541) 20.
[Cf. **campirano, campesino, paisano, pueblero,** Ptg. **caipira.**]
raja 'split, crack, line'
person with some black ancestry. *PR* (Zenón Cruz 1975:1.255; Gallo 1980:92) 20.
[Acc. Gallo, slang. Acc. Zenón Cruz, whiteness is broken by a line of black ancestry (*raja oscura*). Usually in phr. *tener raja.* Cf. **negro, prieto, tener raja, trigueño.**]
ralea 'breed, ilk'
1. black person. *SA* (Levine 1980:116) 20.
2. person of low-class lineage. *Co-we.* (Velásquez 1962:115) prior20.
[Usually derog., injur. Cf. **negro, raja.**]
ranchador — See *rancheador*
rancheador
person who pursued escaped runaway slaves. *SA* (Alvarez Nazario 1974:342) cl.
[< *ranchear* 'to loot; to build a camp.' Syns. *ranchador, recogedor.* Cf. **cimarrón.**]

ranchero
1. person who lives in a hut or shack. *Mx* (Cowles 1952:668) mid20.
2. mestizo who is a small landowner or farmer on the hacienda. *Mx* (Levine 1980:116) 20prior.
3. peasant, farmhand, or small farmer who lives in the quarters provided. *An Mx* (Morínigo 1966:543) 20.
[< *rancho* 'small farm, ranch, hut, crew's quarters' + suf. *-ero.* Cf. **mestizo, negro de conuco, negro de tala.**]

ranquel
savage Indian of the central Pampa region. *Ar* (Vergara Martín 1922:243) n.d.
[Cf. **indio.**]

rastreador 'tracker'
gaucho capable in tracking humans or animals. *Ar Ch* (Cowles 1952:670–71) mid20.
[< *rastrear* 'to track.' Var. in Ch *rastriao* and in Ar *rastriador.* Cf. **gaucho.**]

rastriador — See *rastreador*

rastriao — See *rastreador*

rayado 'striped'
1. person whose skin color possibly indicates some Indian ancestry. *Mx* (León 1924:20–21, plate 43; Pérez de Barradas 1948:193); *SA* (Mörner 1967:59) cl.
2. Jumano Indian, acc. early Spanish explorers. *US-CO, -NM* (Cobos 1983:145) cl.
[< *raya* 'stripe' + suf. *-ado,* perhaps in ref. to decorative stripes on natives' faces. Cf. **auca, indio, indio rayado, raja.**]

raza 'race'
mestizo, acc. Mexican-Americans. *US-CO, -NM* (Cobos 1983:145) 20.
[Cf. **mestizo, raza inferior.**]

raza inferior 'inferior race'
colonist from the Canary Islands. *Ve* (Vallenilla Lanz 1921:109) early20.
[F. Syn. *canario.* Acc. Cobarruvias (1611:896–97), 'type of branded horses; person of bad lineage as a result of racial mixing, esp. with Jewish or Moorish.' Cf. **isleño, raza.**]

rebeco 'chamois'
1. Anglo-Saxon; white person. *Co* (Kany 1960b:39) prior20.
2. white foreigner, esp. one of Anglo-Saxon origins. *Co* (Vergara Martín 1922:243) n.d.
[Acc. Corominas (1954–57:3.1029–30), < metathesis of *becerro*

'yearling calf; calfskin.' Cf. **chele, gringo, rubio.**]

recogedor — See *rancheador*

regular 'regular'

person whose skin color indicates that he or she is not totally white. *Co-Cartagena* (Solaún and Kronus 1973:166, 168) 20.

[Acc. Solaún and Kronus (1973:166), att. as *regular, moreno claro, mezcla* in ref. to 1 person. Cf. **mezcla, moreno claro,** Ptg. **regular.**]

reinoso 'inlander'

1. person from the interior of the country. *Co* (Morínigo 1966:554; Cowles 1952:678; Alario di Filippo 1964:303) 20.

2. Colombian. *Ve* (Santamaría 1942:3.25; Alario di Filippo 1964:303; Morínigo 1966:554) 20prior ‖ *Ve-we.* (Cowles 1952:678) mid20prior.

[Df. 2 obs. < *reino* 'kingdom.' Used to ref. to the cl. New Kingdom or Viceroy of Granada, centered in Bogotá, Co. Cf. Ptg. **reinol.**]

rellollo

black child of *negros criollos,* or blacks native to the country. *Cu* (Alvarez Nazario 1974:335) cl; (Santamaría 1942:3.27; Alonso 1958:3.3573) cl–20.

[Playful, joc. < pref. *re-* + reduplication of the last syllable of *criollo* 'double Creole.' Var. *reyoyo,* acc. Vergara Martín (1922:244). Cf. **criollo.**]

requinterón

1. person whose skin color indicates racial mixture. *SA* exc. *PR* (Alvarez Nazario 1974:380) cl.

2a. offspring of a white and a *quinterón. Mx* (Woodbridge 1948:359) cl ‖ *SA* exc. *Pe* (Malaret 1944:367) mid20 ‖ *SA* (Vergara Martín 1922:243–44) n.d.

2b. offspring of a white and a *quinterón de mulato. Pe* (Mörner 1967:58) 18

[< *requintar* 'to tighten; to insult,' acc. Cowles (1952.682). Acc. Zenón Cruz (1975:1.254), *requintar* 'to inherit recessive Negroid genes not present in the phenotype of the parents.' Cf. **cuarterón, quinterón.**]

requinterón de mestizo

1. offspring of a white and a *quinterón de mestizo. Mx* (León 1924:37–38; Woodbridge 1948:359) cl ‖ *Pe* (Mörner 1967:58) 18.

2. offspring of a white and either a *quinterón de mestizo* or a *puchuel;* 96.88% white, 3.12% Indian. *Mx* (León 1924:25; Pérez de Barradas 1948:189) cl.

3. offspring of a *quinterón de mestizo* and a *requinterón de mestizo;* 93.75% white, 6.25% Indian. *Mx* (León 1924:20–21, plate 41;

Woodbridge 1948:359) cl.

4. offspring of a white and a *quinterón de mestizo,* the latter of which is a white and a *castizo;* 93.75% white, 6.25% Indian. *Pe* (Pérez de Barradas 1948:189) cl.

[Syn. dfs. 1, 3 *español.* Cf. **castizo, español, quinterón, quinterón de mestizo, requinterón de mulato.**]

requinterón de mulato

1. person whose skin color indicates some black ancestry, acc. parish records. *Mx* (Roncal 1944:533) cl.

2. offspring of a white and a mestizo. *Pe* (Alvarez Nazario 1974:354) cl.

3. offspring of a white and a *quinterón de mulato;* 93.75% white, 6.25% black. *Pe* (León 1924:25; Pérez de Barradas 1948:189) cl.

4. offspring of a *requinterón de mulato* and a *quinterón de mulato;* 93.75% white, 6.25% black. *Mx* (León 1924:20–21, plate 42, 26; Woodbridge 1948:359); *Pe* (Pérez de Barradas 1948:186) cl.

[Syn. df. 2 *tercerón* in PR. Syn. df. 4 *español* in Pe. Cf. **español, requinterón de mestizo, tercerón.**]

retinto 'very dark; redyed'

1. very dark-skinned black person. *Cu* (Alvarez Nazario 1974:349) cl ‖ *Co Ec PR* (Alvarez Nazario 1974:349) 20 ‖ *Pe* (Rout 1976:xv) cl ‖ *Co Cu Ec PR* (Zenón Cruz 1975:1.255) cl–20.

2. nonblack with very dark skin color. *SA* (Santamaría 1942:3.34) mid20.

[< *re-* + *tinto* 'dyed.' Df. 1 pejor.; syn. *negro retinto.* Cf. **negro retinto, quemado, tinto, tostado,** Ptg. **retinto.**]

retorno 'return'

offspring of a mulatto and a black. *SA* (Vergara Martín 1922:243) n.d.

[Cf. **saltatrás, tornatrás, zambo.**]

revenido 'sweaty'

black person. *Co* (Tobón Betancourt 1953:223) mid20.

[< *revenir* 'to discharge moisture.' Cf. **negro, retinto.**]

reyoyo — See *rellollo*

riano 'river dweller'

inhabitant of the banks of the Magdalena or Cauca rivers. *Co-coast* (Revollo 1942:235; Alario di Filippo 1964:308) 20.

[< *río* 'river.' Syns. *ribeño, riberano, ribereño* elsewhere. Cf. Ptg. **caboclo.**]

ribeño — See *riano*

riberano — See *riano*

ribereño — See *riano*

ricano — See *puertorriqueño*

riograndense
1. native of the state of RS, Br. *Ar* (Garzón 1910:436) early20.
2. Brazilian. *Ar* (Garzón 1910:436) early20.
[Cf. **brasilero, riograndés,** Ptg. **rio-grandense-do-sul.**]

riograndés
native of the state of RS, Br. *Ar* (Segovia 1911:279) early20.
[Cf. **brasilero, portuga, riograndense,** Ptg. **gaúcho, guasca.**]

riojano 'Riojan'
native to the province of Rioja, Ar. *Ar* (Segovia 1911:278) early20.
[Cf. **riograndés.**]

rioplatense
native to the Río de la Plata region or the surrounding countries. *Ar* (Segovia 1911:279) early20 ‖ *Ar Ur* (Cowles 1952: 686) mid20.
[Cf. **oriental, riojano, riograndés.**]

riqueño — See *puertorriqueño*

rocoto 'large, round hot pepper; garlic'
Indian. *Ec* (Morínigo 1966:567) 20.
[Derog. Acc. Alonso (1958:3.3642) and Santamaría (1942:3.40), < Quechua *rucutu* 'type of hot chili pepper.' Acc. Kany (1960b:35), < Quechua for 'garlic.']

rolo
person from Bogotá or the cold regions surrounding it. *Co* (Kany 1960b:41) 20.
[Acc. Kany, syn. *lanudo.* Cf. **lanudo.**]

romito — See *romo*

romo 'snub-nosed'
person, esp. black African, with a short, flat nose. *Mx-no.* (León 1936:67) mid20.
[Acc. Boyd-Bowman (1971:821), att. as 'flat-nosed' in Pe 1570. Syn. and dim. deriv. *romito.* Cf. **chato, narigón, narizón, ñato.**]

rompecielos 'cloud-breaker'
white European explorers, acc. Indians. *An* (Maldonado de Guevara 1924:17) early cl.
[Generally pl. Used in ref. 'white conquerors,' who seemed to come from the sky, acc. Maldonado de Guevara. Var. *monstruos-rompecielos.*]

rorro 'baby'

blue-eyed blond. *Mx* (Kany 1960b:48) 20.

[Cf. **chele, pelicandelo, puca, rubio.**]

rosado 'pink'

person with rosy skin color. *Co* (Flórez 1969:122) 20.

[Acc. Flórez, *rosao* [*sic*]. Acc. Morínigo (1966:570), also 'color of horse hair between chestnut and white.' Cf. **overo, quemado,** Ptg. **rosado.**]

rosao — See *rosado*

rostro pálido — See *cara pálida*

roto 'broken; fop; half-breed'

1. Indian who dresses like a European. *Mx* (Rubio 1919:196–97) early20.

2a. mestizo who identified with whites. *Ch* (Echaiz 1955:18) 20.

2b. mestizo offspring of a white Spaniard and an Indian. *Ec* (Alonso 1958:3.3659) 20.

3a. low-class person of mixed race and dark skin. *Ch* (Mörner 1967:141) late19; (Hoetink 1973:125) 20.

3b. peasant of the lower class. *Ch Pe* (Cowles 1952:690) mid20.

3c. person of the lower class. *Ch* (Rodríguez 1875:427) 19; (Segovia 1911:141) early20.

3d. urban bum, usually astute in the ways of the city. *Ch* (Mora 1988:p.c.) 20

4a. Chilean. *Ar* (Segovia 1911:280) early20 ‖ *Ar Pe* (Malaret 1947:159) mid20; (Morínigo 1966:571; Kany 1960b:39) 20 ‖ *Bo* (Fernández and Fernández 1967:123); *SA* (Simmons 1955:109) 20.

4b. Chilean peasant or dirt farmer par excellence. *Ch* (Malaret 1947:159; Bayo 1931:220; Cowles 1952:690) mid20.

4c. type of Chilean gaucho. *Ch* (Vergara Martín 1922:244) n.d.

4d. Chilean miner or industrial worker. *Ch* (Bailey and Nasatir 1973:776) 20.

[Syns. df. 3c *cholo* in Pe, *lépero* in Mx. Acc. Mora, ant. df. 3d *huaso* 'poor rural peasant.' Df. 4a nickname; derog. Acc. Echaiz (1955:36), < *roto* 'nickname given to the explorer Pedro de Valdivia, who arrived in Pe poorly dressed and tired from his battles in Ch'; term used by ext. for his companions. Acc. Corominas (1954–57.4:59), 'poorly dressed person' ext. to Chileans in early 17 cent. Derivs. *rotería* 'group of *rotos*, lower-class people,' *rotaje, rotoso, rotuno.* Cf. **cholo, guaso, huaso, jíbaro, lépero, orillero,** Ptg. **caipira, roto.**]

rotoso

person of the lower classes. *Ar* (Segovia 1911:141) early20.

[< *roto.* Cf. **roto.**]

ruaco
albino. *Ve* (Morínigo 1966:571) 20.
[Cf. **albino,** Ptg. **preto-aça.**]

rubio 'fair-haired; blond'
1. person whose skin color generally indicates white race. *Co* (Flórez 1969:122; Solaún and Kronus 1973:166) 20.
2. person with blond hair. *Co-Cartagena* (Solaún et al. 1987:19) late20.
3. person of color. *PR* (Alvarez Nazario 1974:347) 20.
4a. black person. *Bo* (Fernández and Fernández 1967:123) 20.
4b. black or nonwhite person. *PR* (Zenón Cruz 1975:1.249) 20.
[Df. 2 iron.; used in attempt to avoid making a racial statement. Df. 3 joc. Df. 4a euph. Df. 4b joc. First att. as New World racial term in ref. to 'blond' in Mx 1532, acc. Boyd-Bowman (1971:824). Cf. **chele, güero, rucio, ruso.**]

rucio 'silver-gray; gray-haired'
1. person with blond hair. *Ch-so.* (Malaret 1947:243); *SoA* esp. *Ch-so.* (Malaret 1944:379) mid20.
2. person with gray hair. *Ch* (Kany 1960b:48) 20.
[Cf. **chele, güero, rubio, ruso.**]

rucutushca
old Indian. *Ec* (Cowles 1952:691) mid20.
[M., f. Probably < Quechua.]

runa
Indian, generally a man. *Ec* (Malaret 1944:380; Cowles 1952: 692) mid20.
[Generally m. Acc. Malaret, Cowles, Alonso (1958:3.3668), Santamaría (1942:3.48), and Kany (1960b:34), < Quechua *runa* 'man.' Cf. **indio, rucutushca.**]

runcho 'rustic; stupid; mean'
rustic type; hick. *Co* (Tobón Betancourt 1953:225) mid20.
[Syn. *rústico.* Cf. **campesino, huaso, jíbaro, roto.**]

rural 'rural'
country type; hick. *Ar* (Bayo 1910:202 and 1931:221) early–mid20.
[Acc. Bayo, gaucho expression. Syn. *campesino, rústico.* Cf. **campesino, guajiro, hauso, jíbaro, roto.**]

ruso 'Russian'
1. Jew; Jewish person. *Ar* (Gobello and Payet 1959:64; Ferguson 1963:123); *Ar-Buenos Aires* (Cammorota 1963:55) 20.
2. blond person with a reddish face. *RP* (Guarnieri 1967:186) 20.
[Df. 1 ext. from 'Russian,' since many Jews came from Russia. Acc.

Gobello and Payet, found in *lunfardo* speech. Df. 2 probably < Italian *russo* 'red.' Cf. **cara pálida, jacoibo, judío, pelicandelo, polaco, rubio,** Ptg. **russo.**]

rústico — See *campesino, campirano, campiruso, huaso, jáyaro, runcho, rural*

S

sabanero 'savannah-dweller'

1a. person who lives in the savannah or on the plains; plainsman. *SA* (Malaret 1947:161) mid20; (Morínigo 1966:574) 20.

1b. person who lives in the savannah or on the plains of Co; Colombian plainsman. *Co* (Bayo 1931:221) mid20.

2. countryman or peasant who herds cattle to the corral; herdsman. *Ni* (Castellón 1939:109) mid20.

3. native of the Savannahs of Bolívar. *Co-coast* (Revollo 1942:239) mid20.

[Acc. Revollo, Savannahs of Bolívar formerly called Savannahs of Corozal or of Tolu, including the towns of Corozal, Sincelejo, and Chinu in Co. Acc. Kany (1960b:41), syn. *orejón.* Cf. **llanero, orejón.**]

sacalagua

1a. person with white skin color whose hair or other physical features indicate black African ancestry. *Pe* (Morínigo 1966:575) 20.

1b. person, usually a mestizo with almost white skin, light-colored eyes, and blond or light-brown hair, whose freckles or kinky hair indicate black African ancestry. *Pe* (Malaret 1944:382) mid20.

1c. mestizo whose skin is almost white. *Pe* (Santamaría 1942:3.53) mid20.

1d. person with light skin color whose features and kinky hair indicate black ancestry. *Pe* (Kany 1960b:36) 20.

1e. coastal Peruvian with white skin, blond hair, and blue eyes but who has black ancestry. *Pe* (Paz Soldán 1938:349) mid20.

2. blond person with blue eyes. *Pe* (Bayo 1931:222) mid20.

3. type of mestizo. *Pe* (Vergara Martín 1922:244) n.d.

[M., f. Df. 1d. facet. Syn. df. 2 *catire* in Co. Acc. Paz Soldán (1938:349), < popular phr. *saca el agua del bautismo y se verá que no eres sino mezclado* 'throw out the baptismal water and we'll see you're (of) mixed (race).' Cf. **rubio, zambo.**]

sacatro

mestizo from Martinique. *SA* (Vergara Martín 1922:244) n.d.

[Acc. Vergara Martín, *saccatro* [*sic*]. Possibly < Fr. *sacatra* or

sacatre 'offspring of a black and a *grifo.*' Cf. **mestizo.**]
saco de carbón 'sack of coal'
   black person, acc. slavers. *SA* (Alvarez Nazario 1974:336) cl.
[Cf. **pieza de Indias, pieza de registro.**]
salta atrás, salta-atrás — See *saltatrás*
saltatrás 'jump back (from white)'
   1. person whose skin color indicates racial mixture, acc. parish
records. *Mx* (Roncal 1944:533); *Pe* (Romero 1944:375) cl ‖ *Co*
(Alario di Filippo 1964:317) 20.
   2a. offspring of a *chino* and an Indian. *Mx* (Monteforte Toledo
1959:171; Woodbridge 1948:359) cl; (McAlister 1963:354) 19 ‖ *SA*
(Vergara Martín 1922:244) n.d.
   2b. offspring of an Indian and a *chino,* which is a black and a
lobo; 43.75% white, 50% Indian, 6.25% black. *Mx* (Pérez de Barradas 1948:193) cl.
   2c. offspring of a Chinese and an Indian. *SA* (Alba 1969:34) n.d.
   3a. offspring of a quadroon and a mulatto; person whose parents are apparently white but whose recessive traits identify him
or her as having black ancestry. *Cu Mx Pe* (Woodbridge 1948:360)
cl.
   3b. offspring of a quadroon and a mulatto; person whose skin
color approaches that of a black. *SA* (Alcedo 1786–89:5.91) late18
‖ *Cu* (Macías 1885:1074) 19.
   4. offspring of a white Spaniard and a mulatto; 87.5% white,
12.5% black. *Mx* (Pérez de Barradas 1948:190) cl.
   5. offspring of a white Spaniard and a *morisco* or of a white and
an *albino. Mx* (O'Crouley 1972:19) 18.
   6a. offspring of a white and an *albino,* the latter of which is a
morisco and a white; 87.5% white, 12.5% black. *Mx* (Pérez de Barradas 1948:190) cl.
   6b. offspring of a white and an *albino;* 95.75% white, 4.25%
black. *Mx* (León 1924:20–21, plate 45; Woodbridge 1948:360) cl.
   7. offspring of an Indian and a mestizo. *Ve* (Woodbridge
1948:360) cl.
   8a. offspring of 2 whites who has the characteristics of a black
person. *Mx* (Woodbridge 1948:360) cl.
   8b. racially mixed person less similar to white than ancestors.
Mx (Moreno Navarro 1973:143) 18.
   8c. almost white person of some black African ancestry who
"regresses" by mixing with someone of black race. *Cu* (Pichardo
1953:605) 19.
   8d. person with black traits born to seemingly white parents.

SA (Diggs 1953:406) cl ‖ *Cu* (Santamaría 1942:3.60) 20.

8e. person of some black ancestry who mixes with a black person. *Cu* (Santamaría 1942:3.60) 20.

9. offspring of mestizos who has the characteristics of one of the original, i.e., nonwhite, races. *SA* (Alonso 1958:3.3695; DRAE 1174) 20.

10. offspring of a black and a white who identifies more with black than white. *Cu* (Macías 1885:1074) 19.

[M., f. Syn. df. 3b in cl. Mx *tornatrás.* E.g., *tornatrás* for df. 8b. < *saltar* 'to jump' + *atrás* 'back, backward.' Vars. *salta atrás, salta-atrás, salto atrás, salto-atrás, saltoatrás.* Acc. Boyd-Bowman (1982:1462), att. as 'offspring of a black and a *grifo*' in DR 1762. Syns. *tornatrás, seminegro.* Cf. **tornatrás,** Ptg. **salta-atrás.**]

saltatrás cuarterón

1. offspring of a black and a *cuarterón cuatralbo,* the latter of which is a black and a mulatto; 37.5% white, 62.5% black. *Mx* (León 1924:20–21, plate 46; Pérez de Barradas 1948:190) cl.

2. offspring of a black and a *tercerón;* 37.5% white, 62.5% black. *Mx* (León 1924:26; Pérez de Barradas 1948:190; Woodbridge 1948:360) cl.

[M., f. Cf. **cuarterón, saltatrás, saltatrás quinterón, tercerón.**]

saltatrás quinterón

1. offspring of a black and a *cuarterón de mulato,* the latter of which is the offspring of a white and a mulatto; 37.5% white, 62.5% black. *Mx* (León 1924:26; Pérez de Barradas 1948:360) cl.

2. offspring of a black and a quadroon; 43.75% white, 56.25% black. *Mx* (León 1924:20–21, plate 47; Woodbridge 1948:360) cl.

[M., f. Cf. **cuarterón de mulato, quinterón, saltatrás, saltatrás cuarterón.**]

salto atrás, salto-atrás — See *saltatrás*

saltoatrás — See *saltatrás*

salvaje 'wild, savage'

Indian. *SA* (Gillin 1949:162) cl.

[Acc. Gillin, cultural and social df. Syn. *indio salvaje* in Mx 1532, acc. Boyd-Bowman (1971:835). Cf. **indígena, indio, selvaje.**]

sambahigo — See *sambaigo*

sambaigo

1a. offspring of a *cambujo* and an Indian. *Mx* (Pérez de Barradas 1948:plate XV; Monteforte Toledo 1959:171) cl.

1b. offspring of an Indian and *cambujo,* the latter of which is a black and an *albarazado;* 14.65% white, 51.56% Indian, 33.79% black. *Mx* (Pérez de Barradas 1948:193) cl.

1c. offspring of a *cambujo* and an Indian; 23.45% white, 75%

Indian, 1.55% black. *Mx* (León 1924:26, 20–21, plate 44; Woodbridge 1948:360) cl.

1d. offspring of an Indian and a *cambujo,* the latter of which is an Indian and a *chino;* 81.25% Indian, 18.75% black. *Gu Mx* (León 1924:26; Pérez de Barradas 1948:191) cl.

1e. offspring of an Indian and a *cambujo;* 87.5% Indian, 12.5% black. *Mx* (Pérez de Barradas 1948:185) cl.

2a. offspring of a *lobo* and an Indian. *Mx* (Monteforte Toledo 1959:171) cl.

2b. offspring of an Indian and a *lobo,* the latter of which is a mulatto and either a *saltatrás* or a *tornatrás;* 23.45% white, 75% Indian, 1.55% black. *Mx* (Pérez de Barradas 1948:194) cl.

3. offspring of a *barcino* and an Indian. *Mx* (Woodbridge 1948:355) cl.

4. offspring of a black and an Indian. *Mx* (O'Crouley 1972:19) 18.

5. offspring of a *calpamulato* and a *zambo;* 12.5% white, 37.5% Indian, 50% black. *Mx* (Pérez de Barradas 1948:194) cl.

[Syn. df. 4 *lobo.* Vars. *sambahigo, sambaloo, sambaygo, sambayo, sambo higo, somboloro.* Cf. **zambaigo.**]

sambaloo — See *sambaigo*

sambaygo — See *sambaigo*

sambayo — See *sambaigo*

sambenito 'dishonor; inquisition cape'

person at least part black, mulatto, or another nonwhite race. *SA* (Vallenilla Lanz 1921:109) cl.

[Derog. Acc. Cobarruvias (1611:925), < *saco benedicto* 'sack cloth worn by the reconciled for penitence during the Inquisition.' Acc. Corominas (1954–57:4.143), 'scapular worn by Benedictine monks or those condemned to die in the Inquisition.' Cf. **mulato, sambo.**]

sambio

white person, acc. *cholos. Pe-Piura* (Kany 1960b:39) mid20.

[Derog. < *sambo.* Cf. **sambo.**]

sambo

1. person whose skin color indicates racial mixing. *Co-Cartagena* (Solaún and Kronus 1973:166) 20.

2. offspring of a black and an Indian. *Pe* (Rogers 1712:204) 17–18 ‖ *DR* (Alvarez Nazario 1974:355) late18.

3. offspring of a black and a mulatto. *Pe* (Alonso 1958:3.3700) 20.

[Sim. to *zambo.* Df. 2 sim. to No. Amer. and Jamaican Engl. *sambo;* obs. in NoA. Var. *sambio.* Cf. **zambaigo, zambo.**]

sambo de indio 'Indian sambo'
offspring of a black and an Indian; 50% black, 50% Indian. *Pe* (Pérez de Barradas 1948:186; Barón Castro 1946:plate XI) cl; (Mörner 1967:59) 18.
[Excl. to Pe. Cf. **sambo, sambo prieto.**]

sambo higo
offspring of a *sambo* and a mulatto. *Pe* (Alonso 1958:3.3700) 20.
[Var. of *sambaigo.* Cf. **sambaigo.**]

sambo-mosquito — See *zambo mosquito*

sambo prieto 'black *sambo*'
person whose skin color indicates part black ancestry. *SA* (Mörner 1967:59) cl–18.
[Cf. **prieto, sambo, sambo de indio, zambo.**]

sandinista — See *contra*

sangmelé
mestizo or person of mixed ancestry from Martinique. *SA* (Vergara Martín 1922:244) n.d.
[< Fr. *sang-mêlé* 'person of mixed blood.' Att. as 'offspring of a white and a quadroon' in 18-cent. Haiti and Fr. An, acc. Crépeau (1973:13) and Aguirre Beltrán (1972:178). Also att. in Fr.-speaking areas of so. US, acc. Reuter (1918:12). Cf. **mestizo, mulato.**]

sangraco 'blood sucker'
Indian medicine-doctor who practices bleeding as part of the treatment. *Pe* (Morínigo 1966:579) n.d.
[Probably < *sangre* 'blood.']

sanjuanero
native of San Juan, Cu. *Cu* (Dihigo 1966:253) 20.
[< *San Juan* + suf. *-ero.* Cf. **santiaguero.**]

santero
black leader of the *santería* cult. *Cu* (Nuñez 1980:420) 20prior.
[< *santo* 'saint' + suf. *-ero; santería* cults meld African religious traditions with Christian beliefs, sim. to Brz. *macumba, candomblé,* or *umbanda* cults in which the spiritual leader is called *pai-de-santo* or *mãe-de-santo.* Cf. **marabú,** Ptg. **malê.**]

santiaguero
native of the city of Santiago, Cu. *Cu* (Espina Pérez 1972:181) 20.
[< *Santiago* + suf. *-ero.* Cf. **sanjuanero.**]

saxoamericano — See *americano*

sayañero
person who is a sharecropper or tenant farmer; Indian servant, slave, or serf. *Bo-highlands* (Levine 1980:37) 20.

[Cf. **colono, negro de conuco, negro de tala, pegujalero, ranchero.**]

selvaje

Indian, acc. elite whites or mestizos. *SoA* (Levine 1980:124–25) 20.

[Probably pejor. Acc. Levine, condescending; connotes worship of pagan gods and lack of accepted manners or customs. < *selva* 'forest, jungle.' Acc. DRAE (1189), obs. var. of *salvaje*. Cf. **indio, salvaje.**]

semanero 'week laborer'

Indian offered by the pueblo to work for the priest, mission, or church. *US-CO, -NM* (Cobos 1983:154) 20prior.

[< *semana* 'week.' Cf. **indio, jornalero.**]

semiblanco — See *puchuel*

seminegro — See *saltatrás*

semita 'Semite'

1. mestizo. *Co Ch* (Bayo 1931:226) mid20.

2. Arab, Jew, or other Semitic or Turkish person. *SA* (Alonso 1958:3.3740) 20.

[M., f. Cf. **jacoibo, judío, ruso, turco.**]

señor de cuadrilla 'leader of the work-gang'

white owner of slaves who worked the mines. *Co* (Nuñez 1980:424) cl.

[Cf. Ptg. **senhor de engenho.**]

sepia 'cuttlefish which secretes a dark-brown inky fluid'

mulatto, acc. sports fans. *PR* (Alvarez Nazario 1974:352) 20.

[M., f. Euph. used in sports talk, acc. Alvarez Nazario. Often in phr. *color sepia*. Cf. **mulato.**]

septerón

person who is part black and part white; 12.5% white, 87.5% black. *SA* (Woodbridge 1948:360) mid20.

[Acc. Woodbridge, < *séptimo* 'seventh' for anthro. uses in 20 cent. by anal. to *cuarterón, quinterón,* and *tercerón*. Cf. **cuarterón, quinterón, tercerón.**]

ser de clase 'to be of the class'

person who may be of black race, acc. Afro-Argentines. *Ar-Buenos Aires* (Andrews 1979:39) 20.

[Acc. Andrews, used in question form to request the color or class of a person not present in the conversation, usually in phr. *es de clase*.]

ser de color — See *de color, persona de color*

ser de la clase — See *de la clase*

ser de la pinta — See *pinta*

ser de la raza pinta — See *pinta*
ser de sangre azul — See *de sangre azul*
ser más negro que el tizón — See *tizón*
serranito — See *serrano*
serrano 'highlander'
  1. mestizo. *Pe* (Rosenblat 1954:2.28) 18.
  2a. person from the mountain areas; highlander. *Pe* (Bourricaud 1975:382, 384); *Ec-n.w.* (Whitten 1965:91) 20.
  2b. anyone from the highlands, regardless of race. *Ec-n.w.* (Whitten 1965:91) 20.
  [Df. 2 pejor. Vars. in Ch *serruco, serrino,* acc. Cowles (1952:706); in Ni *sierreño,* acc. Castellón (1939:111). Acc. Boyd-Bowman (1971:857), att. in phr. *indio serrano* 'highland Indian' in Mx 1547. Dim. deriv. *serranito.* Cf. **costeño,** Ptg. **serrano.**]
serrino — See *serrano*
serruco — See *serrano*
servicial 'servant'
  servant; domestic. *SA* (Bayo 1910:206) early20 ‖ *Bo Co* (Morínigo 1966:585) 20.
  [M., f. Acc. Morínigo, syns. *sirviente, criado.* Acc. Bayo, syn. *mucamo* in Buenos Aires, *chino* in other areas of SA. Cf. **mucama, mucamo.**]
shilango — See *chilango*
siboney
  native of Cu; person born in Cu. *Cu* (Vergara Martín 1922:244) n.d.
  [Acc. Vergara Martín, name of aboriginal Cuban tribe. Cf. **criollo.**]
sierreño — See *serrano*
simarrón — See *cimarrón*
sirio — See *turco*
sololoi
  person whose skin color indicates racial mixture. *Co-Jardín* (Flórez 1969:122) 20.
  [Excl. to Co.]
somboloro — See *sambaigo*
sonoreño
  person from the state of Sonora, Mx. *US-CA* (Blanco 1971:230) cl.
  [< *Sonora* + suf. *-eño.* Var. *sonorense.* Cf. **chilango, jarocho, sonorense.**]
sonorense
  native of the state of Sonora. *Mx Mx-Sonora* (Sobarzo 1966:304) 20.

[< *Sonora* + suf. *-ense*. Cf. **sonoreño.**]
sungo 'black person with shiny skin'
1. black person. *Co* (Kany 1960b:44; Morínigo 1966:597, 692) 20.
2. person whose dark reddish sunburnt skin is sim. to that of the *sungo* or *chino* dogs. *Co* (Morínigo 1966:597) 20.
3. servant who is the offspring of a black person. *Co* (Santamaría 1942:3.326) 20.
[Acc. Santamaría (1942:3.105), < Quechua *sunku* or *sonku* 'type of dog,' colloq. 'heart; black person.' Var. *zungo*. Cf. **yanacona, yucateco.**]
super negro 'very dark black person'
person whose skin color is very dark black. *Co-Cartagena* (Solaún and Kronus 1973:166) 20.
[Cf. **negro, negro prieto.**]
sureño 'southerner; southern'
person who lives in the south of the country. *Ch* (Malaret 1931:471) mid20 ‖ *Ch DR* (Malaret 1947:245; Morínigo 1966:597) 20.
[< *sur* 'south' + suf. *-eño*. Cf. **arribeño, surero, suriano,** Ptg. **sulino, sulista.**]
surero 'southerner; southern'
native of the provinces to the south of Buenos Aires. *Ar* (Bayo 1931:232) mid20.
[< *sur* + suf. *-ero*. Ant. *arribeño*. Cf. **arribeño, sureño, suriano.**]
suriano 'southerner; southern'
native to the regions in the south of the country. *Mx* (Morínigo 1966:597) 20.
[< *sur* + suf. *-iano*. Cf. **sureño, surero.**]
surumato 'stunned; dazed; stupid'
low-classed farm worker from Mx, acc. Indo-Hispanics. *US-CO, -NM* (Cobos 1983:158) 19–20.
[Acc. Cobos, < *Surumato* 'toponym in the state of Jalisco, Mx.' Var. of std. Sp. *zurumato*.]

T

taco
Austrian; German colonist in St. Charles Parish, LA, along the Mississippi River. *US-LA-St. Bernard Parish* (MacCurdy 1950:83) mid20.

[Acc. MacCurdy, < Sp. *austriaco* 'Austrian,' in LA Fr. *tache.* Cf. **alemán,** Ptg. **alemão.**]

taita 'daddy'
any black male of age. *Cu-Tierradentro* (Macías 1885:873) 19.
[M. Generally respect. Syns. *maestro, ño;* f. syns. *ma Fulana, ña.* Cf. **tata.**]

talingo 'type of black bird'
black male. *Pa* (Cowles 1952:732) mid20.
[M. Ext. from name of bird to humans, acc. Cowles, Alonso (1958:3.3877), and Kany (1960b:36). Cf. **mayate, negro, pinacate.**]

tambeta — See *camba*

tameme 'Sherpa-like guide'
1. Indian who acts as a beast of burden to carry goods, usually for travellers, burro-style, or on the back. *SA US-FL* (Oviedo 1945:14.220; Rosenblat 1954:2.44); *Ch Mx Pe* (Morínigo 1966:606); *Mx Pe US-FL SoA* (Vergara Martín 1922:244) cl.
2. person who carries things; porter. *Ch Mx Pe Sa* (Cowles 1952:734) mid20.
[< Nahuatl *tlamama, tlameme, tlamema,* or *tlamame* 'one who carries cargo,' acc. Cowles, Morínigo, Alonso (1958:3.3882), Tuttle (1976:604), and Corominas (1954–57:4.361). Acc. Boyd-Bowman (1971:895), att. as 'porter' in Mexico City 1531. Var. *tamene,* acc. Vergara Martín (1922:244).]

tamene — See *tameme*

tano
1a. newly arrived Italian immigrant. *Ar* (Cara-Walker 1987:37, 44) 20prior.
1b. Neapolitan; any Italian. *Ar* (Segovia 1911:288) early20 ‖ *RP* (Kany 1960b:38) 20.
2. Indian from Tano, NM. *US-CO, -NM* (Cobos 1983:160) 20prior.
3. person from Galisteo, NM. *US-CO, -NM* (Cobos 1983:160) 20prior.
[Acc. Cara-Walker, df. 1 affect. or insult. Acc. Segovia, df. 1 < apheresis of *napolitano* 'Neapolitan.' Acc. Kany, syns. *nápoles, napoletano, napolitano.* Acc. Cobos, dfs. 2, 3 < Tewa *Tagno* 'placename, cl. Indian pueblo on the site of modern Galisteo, NM.' Cf. **tano agauchado.**]

tano agauchado
Italian who has become like a gaucho; acculturated Italian. *Ar* (Cara-Walker 1987:60) late19–early20.
[Cf. **agauchado, gaucho, tano.**]

tapatío
native or resident of Guadalajara, state of Jalisco, Mx. *Mx* (Malaret 1947:168; Morínigo 1966:609) 20.
[Acc. Morínigo, < *jarabe tapatío* 'popular dance native to Jalisco.' Cf. **chilango, jarocho.**]

tata 'dad, daddy, father'
landowner or visitor of high social rank. *Bo* (Levine 1980:132) 20.
[M. Acc. Levine, respect. Cf. **taita.**]

tecolote 'owl; grayish-brown, brown'
person whose skin color is brown or brownish. *CR* (Salesiano 1938:122) mid20.
[Vars. *tocolote, todolote.* < Nahuatl *tecolotl* 'owl,' acc. Malaret (1931:481) and Cobos (1983:162). Cf. **cholo, tecoloteño.**]

tecoloteño
native or resident of Tecolote, NM. *US-CO, -NM* (Cobos 1983:162) 20.
[< *Tecolote* 'placename in NM' < Nahuatl for 'owl,' acc. Cobos. Cf. **tecolote.**]

tecomate 'gourd; earthenware cup; pan'
native of Mx, acc. Spaniards in Mx. *Mx* (Vergara Martín 1922:245) n.d.
[Cf. **tecolote.**]

tehuano
native of Tehuantepec, Mx, and its surrounding areas. *Mx* (Morínigo 1966:615) 20.
[< apocopation of *Tehuantepec.* Cf. **sanjuanero, santiaguero.**]

tejano 'Texan'
1. white stranger, new to the area, from Tx or an eastern US state; gringo. *US-CO, -NM* (Cobos 1983:162) 20prior.
2. person of Spanish descent from TX. *MX US-s.w.* (Marden and Meyer 1978:242) 19.
3. Mexican-American from TX, acc. himself or herself. *US-TX* (Gann and Duignan 1986:xii) 20prior.
[Df. 1 derog. Syn. df. 3 *latino.* Var. *texano.* Cf. **bracero, californio, hispano, latino, nuevo mexicano, mojado, pocho.**]

teléfono 'telephone'
black person. *US* (de la Bandera 1989:p.c.) 20–late20.
[M., f. Acc. de la Bandera, often derog.; formulated by blue-collar Uruguayans in US in allusion to the black color of most telephones; syn. *morcilla;* syn. in Ur *negrito.* Cf. **morcilla, negrito, negro, muñeco de orozuz.**]

tembeta — See *camba*

tener cincha 'to have girth'
person who is part black or part Indian. *Co* (Kany 1960b:36) 20.
[Derog. verb phr. Cf. **tener raja.**]

tener la mancha del plátano — See *platanero*

tener pasa — See *pasa*

tener pasita — See *pasita*

tener pelo apretado — See *pelo apretado*

tener pelo bueno — See *pelo bueno*

tener pelo malo — See *pelo malo*

tener pelo muerto — See *pelo muerto*

tener pelo pasa largo — See *pelo pasa largo*

tener pelo vivo — See *pelo vivo*

tener raja 'to have a crack'
person who is part black. *PR* (Kany 1960b:36; Santamaría
1942:3.10) 20.
[Derog. verb phr. Acc. Santamaría, *raja* 'vulgar ref. to the vagina.'
Cf. **raja, ralea.**]

tente al aire — See *tente en el aire*

tente en el aire 'have yourself up in the air'
1a. person whose skin color or race is the same as that of the
parents, acc. parish records and other documents. *SA* (Diggs
1953:407); *Mx* (Roncal 1944:533); *Pe* (Romero 1944:375) cl.
1b. racially mixed person whose physical features did not ap-
proximate those of a white, Indian, or black. *Mx* (Moreno Navarro
1973:143) 18.
2a. offspring of 2 *mestizos de indio*. *Pe* (Woodbridge 1948:360)
cl.
2b. offspring of 2 mestizos. *Pe* (Woodbridge 1948:360) cl.
3a. offspring of an Indian and a *lobo;* 84.4% white, 12.5% Indian, 3.1% black. *Mx* (León 1924:20–21, plate 23; Woodbridge
1948:360; Santamaría 1942:3.155) cl.
3b. offspring of an Indian and a *lobo. SA* (Vergara Martín
1922:245) n.d.
4. offspring of a *calpamulato* and a *sambaigo. Mx* (León 1924:9;
Woodbridge 1948:360) cl.
5. offspring of a *zambo* and a *calpamulato. Mx* (Woodbridge
1948:360) cl.
6. offspring of a white or white Spaniard and a *requinterón. Mx*
(Woodbridge 1948:360; Santamaría 1942:3.155) cl ‖ *SA* (Vergara
Martín 1922:245) n.d.

7. offspring of 2 mulattoes. *Pe* (Woodbridge 1948:360) cl.

8. offspring of a quadroon and a mulatto. *Mx* (Woodbridge 1948:360) cl.

9. offspring of a *gíbaro* and an *albarazado*. *Mx* (Woodbridge 1948:360; Santamaría 1942:3.155) cl.

10a. offspring of a white and a *tornatrás*. *Mx* (Woodbridge 1948:355, 360) cl.

10b. offspring of a white and a *tornatrás,* the latter of which is a white and a mulatto; 96.88% white, 3.12% black. *Mx* (Pérez de Barradas 1948:190) cl.

11. offspring of a white and a *saltatrás;* person whose origins are not known. *Mx* (O'Crouley 1972:19) 18.

12. offspring of 2 quadroons. *Pe* (Woodbridge 1948:360) cl.

13. offspring of a *saltatrás* and an *albarazado*. *Mx* (Pérez de Barradas 1948:185; Woodbridge 1948:360) cl.

14a. offspring of a *calpamulato* and a *cambujo*. *Mx* (Woodbridge 1948:360; Monteforte Toledo 1959:171; Santamaría 1942:3.155) cl; (McAlister 1963:354) 19 ‖ *SA* (Vergara Martín 1922:245) n.d.

14b. offspring of a *cambujo* and a *calpamulato;* 30% white, 20.7% Indian, 49.3% black. *Mx* (Pérez de Barradas 1948:194) cl.

15a. offspring of an Indian and a *cambujo,* the latter of which is an Indian and a *chino;* 81.25% Indian, 18.75% black. *Mx* (León 1924:26, 20–21, plate 48; Pérez de Barradas 1948:191; Woodbridge 1948:360; Santamaría 1942:3.155) cl.

15b. offspring of an Indian and a *cambujo*. *SA* (Vergara Martín 1922:245) n.d.

16a. mulatto. *Ec* (Cowles 1952:751) mid20 ‖ *SA* (Kany 1960b:35) 20.

16b. mulatto whose skin color is closer to that of a white or a *mestizo amulatado*. *Mx* (Morínigo 1966:619) 20.

17. dihybrid, fifth-generation offspring of an Indian and an *albarazado;* 3 parts black and 13 parts Indian. *Mx* (Moreno Navarro 1973:129–31; Solano 1975:85) 18.

[M., f. Acc. Kany, df. 16a facet.; syns. *saltatrás, tornatrás.* Acc. Alvar (1987:194), person does not change race from the parents' generation to his or her own. Other syns. *grifo, mestizo amulatado.* Vars. *tentenelaire, tente al aire.* In parts of SoA, 'type of hummingbird,' acc. Santamaría. Acc. Mellafe (1964:90), humor. Vars. *tente-en-el-aire, tentenelaire, tente al aire, tenteenelaire.* Cf. **saltatrás, tornatrás.**]

tente-en-el-aire — See *tente en el aire*

tenteenelaire — See *tente en el aire*

tentenelaire — See *tente en el aire*

tercerón 'terceroon'
1. person whose skin color indicates mixed race, acc. official documents and parish records. *Pe* (Romero 1944:375) cl.
2a. offspring of a white and a mulatto. *Co Mx* (Woodbridge 1948:360; Santamaría 1942:3.161) cl ‖ *SoA* (Grenón 1930:281) mid18 ‖ *DR* (Domínguez 1973:108) late18 ‖ *PR* (Zenón Cruz 1975:1.255) cl–20.
2b. offspring of a white and a mulatto; 75% white, 25% black. *Mx* (León 1924:20–21, plate 49) cl.
2c. type of mulatto. *SA* (Alba 1969:34) n.d.
3. offspring of a white and a mestizo. *PR* (Alvarez Nazario 1974:354) late18.
[< *tercero* 'third' + aug. suf. *-ón* by anal. to *cuarterón* and *quinterón*. Acc. Cassidy (1961:162), in Jamaica *terceroon* or *mustee* 'next closest to black after quadroon;' little used. Acc. Boyd-Bowman (1982:2879), att. as 'offspring of a Spaniard and a mulatto' in Lima, Pe, 1770. Syn. *cuarterón cuatralbo*. Cf. **cuarterón cuatralbo, septerón.**, Ptg. **terceirão**.]

tercerón cuatralbo
offspring of a white and a mulatto; 75% white, 25% black. *Mx* (León 1924:26; Pérez de Barradas 1948:189) cl.
[Cf. **cuarterón cuatralbo, tercerón**.]

tercerón negro 'black terceroon'
person who is 33.3% black and 66.7% white. *SA* (Woodbridge 1948:359) cl.
[Acc. Rogers (1712:203), in 17- and 18-cent. Pe *terceroon de Negroes* = *terceroon de Indies*. Cf. **tercerón cuatralbo**.]

terrisureño
inhabitant of Baja California, Mx. *US-CA* (Blanco 1971:242) cl.
[< *tierra* 'land' + *sur* 'south' + suf. *-eño*. Cf. **sureño**.]

texano — See *tejano*

tía — See *tío*

tiburón 'shark'
Ceri or Seri Indian, esp. one living on Tiburón Island in the Gulf of California. *Mx-Sonora* (Sobarzo 1966:321) prior20 ‖ *Mx* (Vergara Martín 1922:245) n.d.
[Cf. **indio**.]

tico
Costa Rican; native of CR. *Ho* (Membreño 1897:171) late19 ‖ *CR* (Gagini 1918:231) late19–early20 ‖ *SA* (Bayo 1931:242); *CR*

(Salesiano 1938:123; Villegas 1952:135); *CeA* (Malaret 1931:485; Cowles 1952:756–57) mid20 ‖ *CeA* (Morínigo 1966:624; Kany 1960b:40) 20.

[Acc. Cowles, Kany, Morínigo, Gagini, Santamaría (1942:3.167), and Alonso (1958:3.3948), < overuse of dim. suf. *-(t)ico* by Costa Ricans, causing their neighbors to call them by this nickname. Acc. Salesiano (1938:80), deriv. *Tiquicia* 'land of the *ticos*,' like *Guanacia* 'land of the *guanacos*.' Std. syn. *costarricense*. Cf. **guanaco, nica, nicaregalado.**]

tierradentro 'inland'

Cuban from the central interior, not from the coast. *Cu* (Vergara Martín 1922:245) n.d.

[M., f. < *tierra* 'land' + *dentro* or *adentro* 'within.' Cf. **costeño, serrano, terrisureño.**]

tierrafría 'cold land'

inhabitant of the cold highlands or uplands. *Co* (Morínigo 1966:624) 20.

[M., f. Cf. **serrano, tierradentro.**]

tigua — See *tigüe*

tigüe

young black person; very dark-skinned young person. *Ho* (Morínigo 1966:625; Santamaría 1942:3.170) 20.

[F. form *tigua*. Cf. **timbo.**]

timanejo

1. native of the Neiva valley, Co. *Co* (Cowles 1952:759) mid20.

2. native of Timana. *SA* (Cowles 1952:759) mid20.

[< *Timana* + suf. *-ejo.*]

timbo

very black-skinned person; pure black. *Pa* (Aguilera Patiño 1951:501); *Co-coast* (Revollo 1942:261) mid20 ‖ *Co-Atlantic coast* (Escalante 1964:181) 20 ‖ *Co* (Alario di Filippo 1964:342; Alonso 1958:3.3955; Kany 1960b:36) 20.

[Cf. **negro timba, retinto.**]

tinto 'dyed, painted; dark red'

1. black person. *US-AZ* (Barker 1950:35) mid20 ‖ *US-CO, -NM* (Cobos 1983:165) 20.

2. dark-skinned person of color. *US-TX* (Kany 1960b:36) 20.

3. type of mulatto. *US-TX* (Kany 1960b:36) 20.

[Acc. Barker, df. 1 Pachuco slang. Df. 3 facet. Cf. **negro retinto, retinto.**]

tío 'uncle'

old African black; old black person. *Ar* (Segovia 1911:291) early20; (Santamaría 1942:3.176) mid20 ‖ *RP* (Granada

1957:2.221) 20.

[F. form *tía* 'aunt.' Sim. to So. Amer. Engl. *uncle* or *aunt,* respect., affect., or derog. to older blacks. Cf. **míster, muchacho, niño, sambo.**]

tizón 'spot; smudge; burnt piece of wood'
person with very dark skin color. *Cu* (Espina Pérez 1972:193) 20.

[Acc. Espina Pérez, joc., facet.; usually in phr. *ser más negro que el tizón.* Cf. **negro como un tizón, pinta.**]

tocolote — See *tecolote*

todolote — See *tecolote*

tojro
Peruvian. *Bo* (Fernández and Fernández 1967:133) 20.
[Acc. Fernández and Fernández, < Quechua *t'ojjro.*]

tomasino
native of the town of Santo Tomás in the province of Barranquilla, Co. *Co-coast* (Revollo 1942:263) mid20.
[< *Tomás.* Cf. **tomoco.**]

tomoco
Orejón Indian of the province of Santa María, Co. *Co* (Vergara Martín 1922:245) n.d.
[Acc. Vergara Martín, obs. Cf. **orejón, tiburón.**]

tonto 'foolish'
Apache Indian. *Mx-Sonora* (Sobarzo 1966:324) 20.
[Syn. *coyotero.*]

torna a español 'return to Spanish'
offspring of a white Spaniard and a *castizo;* 87.5% white, 12.5% Indian. *Gu Mx* (Pérez de Barradas 1948:184, 185, 188) cl
[M., f. Sim. to medieval Sp. *tornadizo* 'Moor who converted to Christianity,' acc. Castro (1948:53). Cf. **tornatrás.**]

torna atrás, torna-atrás — See *tornatrás*

tornatrás 'turn back (away from white)'
1. person whose skin color indicates racial mixture, generally away from white. *SA* (Diggs 1953:406); *Mx* (León 1924:26; Woodbridge 1948:360) cl.

2a. offspring of an *albino* and a white Spaniard. *Mx* (Woodbridge 1948:355, 360; Pérez de Barradas 1948:plate X; Monteforte Toledo 1959:171; Santamaría 1942:3.204) cl; (Mörner 1967:58) 18 ‖ *SA* (Vergara Martín 1922:245) n.d.

2b. offspring of a white or white Spaniard and an *albino,* the latter of which is a white and a *morisco;* 93.75% white, 6.25% black. *Gu Mx* (Pérez de Barradas 1948:184, 185, 189) cl.

2c. dihybrid, fifth-generation offspring of an *albino* and a white; 15 parts white, 1 part black. *Mx* (Moreno Navarro 1973:129–31, 140; Solano 1975:85) 18.

3a. offspring of an Indian and a *no te entiendo. Mx* (Woodbridge 1948:360; Monteforte Toledo 1959:171; Santamaría 1942:3.204) cl; (McAlister 1963:354) 19 ‖ *SA* (Vergara Martín 1922:245) n.d.

3b. offspring of an Indian and a *no te entiendo,* the latter of which is a mulatto and a *tente en el aire;* 20% white, 55.15% Indian, 24.85% black. *Mx* (Pérez de Barradas 1948:194) cl.

4. offspring of 2 mestizos who has traits of at least one of the original races. *SA* (Alonso 1958:3.3989) cl–20.

5. offspring of a mulatto and a quadroon. *Mx* (Alcedo 1786–89:5.91) late18

[M., f. Dfs. 1 and 5 syn. *saltatrás.* Acc. Vergara Martín, syns. *tente en el aire, grifo.* Acc. Moreno Navarro, syn. df. 2c *requinterón de mulato* in Mx and SoA prior to 18 cent. Acc. Woodbridge, implies return to features of a black in a racially mixed person. Acc. Santamaría, syn. *tente en el aire.* Vars. *torna atrás, torna-atrás.* Cf. **cuarterón, no te entiendo, saltatrás, tente en el aire.**]

tostado 'toasted, browned'
person whose skin is browned or darkened; person of color. *Co-Onzaga* (Flórez 1969:122) 20.
[Acc. Alonso (1958:3.3997), 'of very deep or dark color.' Var. *tostao.* Cf. **morado, quemado, retinto, rosado,** Ptg. **tostado.**]

tostao — See *tostado*

tramojo 'type of harness'
rustic type; mountaineer; highlander; hick. *Co* (Tobón Betancourt 1953:347) mid20.
[Cf. **campirano, campesino, serrano,** Ptg. **caipira.**]

tresalbo 'horse with three white extremities'
1. person whose skin color indicates racial mixture. *SA* (Mörner 1967:59) cl.

2. offspring of a mestizo and an Indian; 25% white, 75% Indian. *Mx Pe* (Woodbridge 1948:360); *Mx* (León 1924:26, 20–21, plate 50; Pérez de Barradas 1948:189) cl.
[Acc. Alonso (1958:3.4033), < *tres* 'three' + *albo* 'white.' Acc. Guarnieri (1979:185), used in 20-cent. RP as 'horse with three white extremities.' Var. *tresavo.* Cf. **cuatralbo, trigueño,** Ptg. **tresalbo.**]

tresavo — See *tresalbo*

tributario civilizado — See *indio serrano*

trigueño 'wheat-colored; light brown'
1a. person whose brown skin color indicates racial mixture. *Co-*

Cartagena (Solaún and Kronus 1973:164, 166) 20; (Solaún et al. 1987:19) late20; *Co Ve* (Flórez 1969:123) 20.

1b. person with light brown skin color who is often of mixed race. *PR US* (Gann and Duignan 1986:80) 20.

2a. type of mestizo, acc. 1920 census. *Ni* (Vandiver 1949:144) early–mid20.

2b. mestizo whose skin color is intermediate between 2 other stages. *Mx* (Fuente 1947:66) mid20.

3. person whose skin color is somewhat darkened or sim. to the color of wheat. *Cu* (Pichardo 1953:660–61) 19.

4a. mulatto. *PR* (Tumin and Feldman 1969:199) 20.

4b. light-skinned mulatto. *PR* (Zenón Cruz 1975:1.255) 20.

5. white person whose skin color is less light than that of the *mulato claro*. *PR* (Alvarez Nazario 1974:349) cl–20; (Zenón Cruz 1975:1.255) 20.

6a. black person. *Cu PR* (Alvarez Nazario 1974:347, 349, 380); *Cu PR* (Zenón Cruz 1975:1.254, 255) 20.

6b. black person with kinky hair. *DR PR* (Domínguez 1986:275) 20.

6c. Afro-Hispanic. *Cu DR PR US-New York City* (Domínguez 1973:187) 20.

[Acc. Gann and Duignan, df. 1b color classification in PR; used by Puerto Ricans in US. Df. 5 possibly iron., acc. Zenón Cruz. Df. 6a euph. for *negro* or *prieto;* acc. Zenón Cruz, social euph. for *pardo, prieto,* or *negro,* esp. in ref. to women. Df. 6c syn. *prieto.* < *trigo* 'wheat' + suf. *-eño.* Acc. Corominas (1954–57:4.575), syn. *moreno* in An and Andalusia. Acc. Boyd-Bowman (1971:942), att. as color in CR 1575. Cf. **europeo, gente de color, moreno, morisco, pardo,** Ptg. **trigueiro.**]

trigueño atezado 'darkened wheat-colored'
person with dark brown skin color. *Cu* (Macías 1885:1172–73) 19.

[Ant. *trigueño lavado,* acc. Macías. Cf. **atezado, trigueño, trigueño lavado.**]

trigueño claro 'light wheat-colored'
1. person whose skin color indicates racial mixture. *Co-Cartagena* (Solaún and Kronus 1973:166) 20.

2. person whose skin color is lighter than that of the *trigueño.* *Co-Cartagena* (Solaún et al. 1987:19) late20.

[Cf. **claro, trigueño oscuro.**]

trigueño de piel canela — See *trigueño piel canela*
trigueño lavado 'washed wheat-colored'
1. person whose skin color is a bit lighter than that of the

trigueño. Cu (Pichardo 1953:660–61) 19.

2. person with light brown skin color. *Cu* (Macías 1885: 1172–73) 19.

[Acc. Macías, df. 2 ant. *trigueño atezado.* Cf. **trigueño, trigueño atezado, trigueño claro.**]

trigueño oscuro 'dark wheat-colored'

person whose skin color is darker than that of the *trigueño. Co-Cartagena* (Solaún and Kronus 1973:166) 20.

[Cf. **trigueño, trigueño claro.**]

trigueño piel canela 'cinnamon wheat-colored skin'

mulatto. *PR* (Alvarez Nazario 1974:352) 20.

[Euph. Often in phr. *trigueño de piel canela.* Cf. **canela, trigueño.**]

trompudo 'thick-lipped'

1. black person with thick lips. *SA* (Morínigo 1966:645) 20.

2. person with big lips. *Mx-Oaxaca* (Garza Cuarón 1987:63) late20.

[Syn. df. 1 *jetudo.* Syns. df. 2 *labión, labiudo.* < *trompa* 'thick lip' + adj. suf. *-udo.* Cf. **bembón, bembudo, getudo, jetudo, labión.**]

trucho

1. mutilated slave. *Pa* (Levine 1980:137) prior20.

2. person missing a leg, ear, or other body part. *Pa* (Levine 1980:137) 20prior.

[Acc. Levine, used in ref. to animal or person. Cf. **tucho.**]

tucho

person who is very dark brown, ugly, and missing body parts. *Mx* (Morínigo 1966:648) 20.

['Type of monkey' native to Mx, acc. Santamaría (1942:3.226) and Morínigo. Acc. Santamaría, < Mayan *xtuch* 'monkey.' Cf. **mono, trucho.**]

tupamaro

1. Uruguayan gaucho, acc. Spaniards. *Ur* (Vergara Martín 1922:245) n.d.

2. native of Ur, acc. Spaniards. *Ur* (Cowles 1952:790–91) prior20.

[Acc. Cowles, iron. Acc. Cowles and Vergara Martín, < *Tupac-Amaru* 'name of a famous Indian insurgent leader.' Replaced older form *gauderio.* Cf. **gaucho, gauderio, oriental.**]

turco 'Turk; Middle-Easterner'

Arabic-speaking Middle-Eastern merchant, usually a small business man, who immigrated to America between 1890 and 1920. *SA* (Morínigo 1966:650–51); *DR* (Patín Maceo 1940:172); *Co* (Revollo 1942:271; Alario di Filippo 1964:355); *Ch Gu* (Cowles 1952:791) 20.

[Used in ref. to any Middle-Easterner, including *sirios, libaneses,* and *palestinos,* no matter what the racial or ethnic background of the person. Syns. *libanés, palestino, sirio.* Cf. **judío,** Ptg. **turco.**]

tútile
Italian. *CR* (Villegas 1952:141; Cowles 1952:793) mid20.
[Acc. Villegas, derog. Acc. Cowles, slang. Cf. **bachicha, tano.**]

tuve 'I had; I owned'
Cuban, acc. other Spanish-speaking Americans. *US* (Gann and Duignan 1986:110) 20.
[M., f. Acc. Gann and Duignan, joc. slang used in ref. to Cubans' supposed or real wealth before coming to US post-Castro. Cf. **brigadista.**]

V

vago 'vague; vagrant'
vagrant mestizo or mulatto. *SA* (Levine 1980:141–42) 16.
[Cf. **mestizo, mulato.**]

vallado 'valley dweller; type of fence'
rustic type, rural peasant, or hick who comes to the towns in shabby, country clothing. *PR* (Morínigo 1966:660) 20.
[Joc. < *valle* 'valley' + adj. suf. *-ado.* Cf. **jíbaro, vallero, vallino, valluno.**]

vallecaucano — See *patojo, negro, valluno*

valleclareño
native of the province of Las Villas, Cu. *Cu* (Espina Pérez 1972:203) 20.
[Cf. **vallado.**]

valleduparense — See *vallenato*

vallenato
native of Valledupar, Co, and its surrounding area. *Co-coast* (Revollo 1942:275) mid20 ‖ *Co* (Alario di Filippo 1964:360) 20.
[Acc. Revollo, also *valleduparense.*]

vallero
native to the valley. *Ar* (Segovia 1911:298) early20 ‖ *Mx Pe* (Morínigo 1966:660) 20.
[< *valle* 'valley' + suf. *-ero.* Acc. Morínigo, syns. *vallino* in Pe and *vallisto* in Ar and Mx. Cf. **vallado, valluno.**]

vallino — See *vallero*

vallisto — See *vallero*

valluco
rustic type; peasant; farmer. *Co* (Bayo 1931:255) mid20.

[Cf. **vallado, vallero, vallunco, valluno.**]

vallunco 'rustic; peasant'
rustic type; peasant; farmer. *CeA* (Bayo 1931:255) mid20; (Morínigo 1966:660) 20.
[Cf. **bayunco, vallado, vallero, valluco, valluno.**]

valluno
1. inhabitant of the valley. *Bo* (Fernández and Fernández 1967:138) 20.
2. native to or inhabitant of the Cauca Valley. *SA* (Cowles 1952:800) mid20 ‖ *Co* (Alario di Filippo 1964:360) 20.
[Acc. Cowles, syn. *timanejo* in Co. Acc. Alario di Filippo, syn. *vallecaucano* in Co. Acc. Kany (1960b:41), syns. *negro, patojo,* in Co. Cf. **vallado, vallero, valluco, vallunco.**]

vaqueano — See *baquiano*

vaquero 'cowboy'
1. mestizo of northern Mx or southwestern US. *Mx US-s.w.* (Echaiz 1955:21) 20.
2. gaucho; peasant; farmer. *Pg* (Laxalt 1980:493) 20.
[Cf. **gaucho, huaso, llanero, roto.**]

vaquiano — See *baquiano*

vecino 'neighbor'
1a. white person or Spaniard living in the cities. *SA* (Rosenblat 1954:2.135) cl.
1b. white person. *Mx* (Chance 1979:154) 20.
2. mestizo. *SA* (Rosenblat 1954:2.135) 16.
[Cf. **gente de razón, mestizo, vecino ladino.**]

vecino ladino 'mestizo neighbor'
1. mestizo. *CeA-no.* (Mörner 1967:99) late18.
2. mestizo living among Indians. *Mx* (Levine 1980:142) cl.
[Cf. **ladino, mestizo, vecino.**]

veguero 'plainsman; tobacco worker'
inhabitant of La Vega de Vuelta Abajo, Cu. *Cu* (Morínigo 1966:663) 20.
[< *vega* 'plain.']

verdadero jíbaro 'true peasant'
person of pure Spanish race with no racial mixture. *PR* (Coll y Toste 1924:127) early20.
[Cf. **jíbaro, verdadero negro.**]

verdadero negro 'true black person'
1. African black who generally arrived in Europe or America from the slave factories of Cabo Verde. *SA* (Aguirre Beltrán 1972:107, 113) 15–cl.

2. black person originally from the Chocó region of Co. *Co-Unguía, -Chocó* (Wade 1985:242) 20.

[Acc. Aguirre Beltrán, also used in Spain. Syn. df. 2 *chocoano*. Cf. **cabo verde, chocoano, negro cabo verde.**]

verraco 'boar, male pig'

1. person with blond hair and blue eyes. *Pe* (Morínigo 1966:666) 20.

2. person considered vulgar; low-life; trash. *Cu Mx* (Morínigo 1966:666; Santamaría 1942:3.258) 20.

[Acc. Megenney (1988:p.c.), 'person who does extraordinary things' in Co. Cf. **gringo, mono, rubio, tresalbo, zarco, zorro.**]

villano

rustic type; peasant. *Co* (Bayo 1931:255) mid20.

[Cf. **valluco.**]

villero

native of La Villa de San Benito Abad, Co. *Co* (Alario di Filippo 1964:365) 20.

[Cf. **valluco, vallunco.**]

vulgarejo 'vulgarism; vulgar thing'

person who is vulgar or crude. *Ec* (Morínigo 1966:673) 20.

[Cf. **campesino, jíbaro.**]

X

xíbaro — See *jíbaro*

xívaro

white rural peasant who tends to be crochety but likeable. *PR* (Hernández Aquino 1969:30; Levine 1980:147) 20prior.

[Acc. Levine, older version of *jíbaro*. Cf. **jíbaro.**]

Y

yanacón — See *yanacona*

yanacona 'Indian tenant farmer'

1a. Indian servant, acc. Spaniards. *SA* (Morínigo 1966:678; Santamaría 1942:3.285) cl.

1b. Indian who served Spaniards. *Pe* (Alcedo 1786–89:5.104) late18 ‖ *SA Pe* (Vergara Martín 1922:230) n.d.

2. Indian sharecropper or lessee of services on a farm. *Ar Bo Ch*

Pe (Malaret 1931:513 and 1947:252) mid20; Morínigo 1966:678) 20.

3. Indian born and reared in the master's house. *Pe* (Grenón 1929:227) early17.

4. laborer. *Bo* (Bailey and Nasatir 1973:778) 20.

[M., f. Acc. Morínigo, Oviedo (1945:14.226), Santamaría (1942: 3.285), Malaret (1931:513), and Alonso (1958:3.4215), < Quechua *yanacyani* 'to serve domestically' or *yanacuna* 'servitude.' Acc. Vergara Martín, syn. df. 1b *indio de carga, anacona.* Vars. *anacona, yanacón, yanacuna.*]

yanacuna — See *yanacona*

yankee — See *yanqui*

yanque — See *yanqui*

yanqui 'Yankee'

1. North American; gringo. *Cu* (Pichardo 1953:695) 19 ‖ *SA* (Morínigo 1966:678; Kany 1960b:39); *Ni* (Castellón 1939:125) 20.

2. North American English speaker, acc. Britons and others. *NoA SA* (Vergara Martín 1922:246) n.d.

[M., f. < Engl. *yankee* 'native of New England,' by ext. 'anyone from US,' acc. Alonso (1958:3.4215). Acc. Vergara Martín, possibly < Indians' pronunciation of *English* > *yanglese* > *yanque.* Vars. *yankee, yanque.* Cf. **gabacho, gringo, pitiyanqui.**]

yaro

Indian living on the eastern shore of the Uruguay River to the south of the Negro River. *Ur* (Mieres et al. 1966:133) 20.

[< *yaro* 'name of an Indian tribe'; var. *yaró,* acc. Alonso (1958: 3.4216).]

yaró — See *yaro*

yocalla

1. mestizo; street urchin. *Bo* (Morínigo 1966:681) 20.

2. child or servant of the house. *Bo* (Malaret 1944:508) mid20.

3. Indian peasant. *Bo* (Levine 1980:148) 20.

[Generally m. Acc. Malaret and Morínigo, < Aymara *llocalla* or *yocalla* 'child.' Acc. Santamaría (1942:3.299), < Quechua. Excl. to Bo. Cf. **tata, yanacona.**]

yuca

young adult Cuban-American of the middle or upper-middle class; Cuban-American yuppie. *US-FL-so.* (Rieff 1987:124; Pérez-Firmat 1988:p.c.) late20.

[M., f. Acc. Rieff, *yucca* [*sic*] < Engl acronym 'young, up-and-coming, Cuban-American.' Acc. Pérez-Firmat, Sp. acronym < Engl. phr. *young, upscale Cuban-American.* < by anal. to Engl. *yuppie* 'young, upscale professional'; perhaps bilingual play on Sp. *yuca* 'yucca plant,' ingredient in Latin meals. Cf. **mala.**]

yucateco

Mayan Indian. *Mx* (Morínigo 1966:682; Santamaría 1942:
3.301) 20.

[< *Yucatán* 'Mexican peninsula jutting into the Gulf of Mexico and
the Caribbean' + adj. suf. *-eco.* Cf. **yaro.**]

yudo

Jew; Jewish person. *Ar-Buenos Aires* (Cammorota 1963:62) 20.

[< Yiddish or German *Jude* 'Jew.' Cf. **jacoibo, judío, ruso.**]

yumbo

savage or uncivilized Indian from east of Quito or from the east
of the country. *Ec* (Morínigo 1966:682) 20; (Vergara Martín
1922:246) n.d.

[< *yumbo* 'name of an Indian tribe.' Cf. **yaro, yucateco.**]

yumeca

1. black Jamaican. *Co Pa* (Morínigo 1966:682) 20.

2. black from the English An; black from Curaçao. *Co-coast* (Revollo 1942:285) mid20.

[M., f. Acc. Morínigo, < Sp.-speakers' misinterpretation of Engl.
pronunciation of the word *Jamaica.* Cf. **chumeca.**]

yunga

1. person from the coast; coastal dweller. *Pe* (Malaret 1947:182)
mid20.

2. person from the hot valley lands. *Bo Ch Ec Pe* (Morínigo
1966:682) 20.

[M., f. Acc. Morínigo, < Quechua *yunca* 'hot land.' Cf. **costeño.**]

yunqueño

inhabitant of *yungas,* or hot valley lands, esp. an Indian from
the province of Muñecas. *Bo* (Bayo 1931:262) mid20.

[Cf. **yunga.**]

yuquero 'yucca grower'

crude peasant. *Co* (Kany 1960b:41) 20.

[< *yuca* 'yucca plant' + suf. *-ero.* Cf. **chagra, paisano, sabanero.**]

yurungo — See *jorongo*

Z

zambaigo

1. person whose skin color indicates racial mixture, acc. parish
records and other documents. *Mx* (Roncal 1944:533) cl.

2. offspring of a *chino* and an Indian. *Mx* (Malaret 1931:516;
Woodbridge 1948:361; Santamaría 1942:3.309) cl; (Morínigo

1966:685) 20; (Vergara Martín 1922:246) n.d.

3. offspring of a *barnocino* and an Indian; 12.5% white, 83.87% Indian, 3.63% black. *Mx* (Pérez de Barradas 1948:194; Woodbridge 1948:361) cl.

4. offspring of a *lobo* and an Indian. *Mx* (Woodbridge 1948:361) cl; (Mörner 1967:58) 18.

5a. offspring of a *cambujo* and an Indian. *Mx* (León 1924:9; Woodbridge 1948:361) cl; (McAlister 1963:354) 19.

5b. dihybrid, third-generation offspring of a *lobo* or *cambujo* and an Indian; 3 parts Indian, 1 part black. *Mx* (Moreno Navarro 1973:129–31; Solano 1975:85) 18.

6a. offspring of a black and an Indian. *SA* (Morínigo 1966:685; Aguirre Beltrán 1972:159; Rosenblat 1954:1.71); *Mx* (Pérez de Barradas 1948:190; Santamaría 1942:3.309); *CeA Mx* (Alvarez Nazario 1974:355) cl.

6b. offspring of a black and an Indian, of poor economic or social circumstances. *SA* (Vergara Martín 1922:246) n.d.

[Df. 6a. syn. *zambo*. Df. 6b syn. *mulato*. Acc. Aguirre Beltrán, Alvarez Nazario, and Romero (1965:233–34), < Mandinga *sambango* 'dark bay-colored horse.' Acc. Corominas (1954–57:4.818), perhaps < mispronunciation of *zambahigo* < *zambo hijo*. Vars. *zamboinga, zambinga, zambahigo, zambayo, sambaigo*. Syns. *cambujo, mestizo, zambo de indio, zambo, sambaigo*. Cf. **sambaigo, zambo de indio.**]

zambango
person whose kinky hair indicates some black ancestry. *PR* (Nuñez 1980:498) 20.
[Cf. **pelo malo.**]

zambayo
type of mestizo. *Ar* (Grenón 1929:229) late18.
[Syns. *cambujo, mestizo, sambayo*. Var. of *zambaigo*. Cf. **cambujo, mestizo, sambaigo, sambayo, zambo.**]

zambinga — See *zambaigo*

zambiricuco
mulatto or *sambo* who, while showing social upward mobility, retains vestiges of behavior characteristic of humble origins. *Pe* (Morínigo 1966:685) 20.
[Cf. **mulato, zambaigo.**]

zambito — See *zambo*

zambo 'knock-kneed; half-breed'
1. person whose skin color indicates racial mixture. *Pe* (Romero 1944:375); *PR* (Alvarez Nazario 1974:380) cl ‖ *Co-Barbacoas* (Flórez 1969:123) 20.

2a. offspring of a black and a mulatto; 25% white, 75% black. *Pe* (Pérez de Barradas 1948:186; Woodbridge 1948:361; Alvarez Nazario 1974:355) cl; (Mörner 1967:59) 18 ‖ *SA* (Rosenblat 1954:2.167) cl.

2b. offspring of a black and a mulatto who was despised for lack of civilities. *SA* (Alcedo 1786–89:5.104) late18.

2c. dihybrid, third-generation offspring of a black and a mulatto; 3 parts black, 1 part white. *Mx* (Moreno Navarro 1973:129–31; Solano 1975:85) 18.

2d. offspring of a black and a mulatto. *SA* (Vergara Martín 1922:246) n.d.

3. offspring of a black and a quadroon; 25% white, 75% black. *Pe* (Pérez de Barradas 1948:190) cl.

4. offspring of a black and a *chino. Pe* (Woodbridge 1948:361) cl.

5. offspring of a black and a white; mulatto. *Co Ch Pe* (Woodbridge 1948:361); *Pe* (Santamaría 1942:3.309) cl ‖ *SA* (Malaret 1947:183); *Ec* (Cowles 1952:828) mid20 ‖ *Bo Co Ch* (Malaret 1931:516) mid20; (Morínigo 1966:686) 20 ‖ *Co* (Kany 1960b:34–35) 20.

6a. offspring of a black and an Indian; 50% black, 50% Indian. *Mx* (León 1924:20–21, plate 51; McAlister 1963:354); *SA* (Gibson 1966:116; Rosenblat 1954:1.71; Diggs 1953:424; Mörner 1967:43); *SA* (Woodbridge 1948:361) cl; (Rout 1976:xv) cl–20; (Alvarez Nazario 1974:355; Pérez de Barradas 1948:190) prior20 ‖ *Ve* (Humboldt 1941:2.140–41) 18–19 ‖ *SA* (Pérez de Barradas 1948:174); *Ho* (Membreño 1897:194) late19 ‖ *Ar* (Segovia 1911:147); *SA* (Bayo 1910:247); *Ar* (Segovia 1911:147) early20 ‖ *Bo Co Ch Ur* (Cowles 1952:828); *SoA* (Malaret 1931:516); *SA* (Malaret 1947:183; Ramos 1941:537) mid20 ‖ *Bo-La Paz* (Alvarez Nazario 1974:355); *Co* (Kany 1960b:34–35; Tobón Betancourt 1953:263); *An* (Esteva Fabregat 1964:283); *SA CeA Mx* (Morínigo 1966:686; Santamaría 1942:3.309); *Pe* (Simmons 1955:108); *SoA RP* (Guarnieri 1979:197) 20 ‖ *An Co-Cartagena* (Solaún et al. 1987:18) late20 ‖ *SA* (Vergara Martín 1922:246; Bailey and Nasatir 1973:778) n.d.

6b. dark-skinned person whose ancestry includes black and Indian. *Mx* (Moreno Navarro 1973:141) 18.

7. offspring of a black and a mestizo. *Pe* (Simmons 1955:108) 20.

8. offspring of an Indian and a *cambujo,* the latter of which is an *albarazado* and an Indian; 6.05% white, 64.05% Indian, 29.9% black. *Mx* (Pérez de Barradas 1948:194) cl.

9. person with dark skin color. *Ur* (Cowles 1952:828) mid20 ‖ *Co* (Kany 1960b:34–35) 20.

10a. racially mixed person who is part black. *SA* (Woodbridge 1948:361) cl.

10b. racially mixed person who is mostly of black ancestry. *Pe-Lima* (Wallace 1984:65) 20.

10c. person of black race whose skin is cinnamon-colored. *DR Pe* (Malaret 1944:513) mid20.

11a. person who is tri-racial and tri-cultural, i.e., part Indian, part white, and part black. *Pe-coast* (Romero 1944:381) 20.

11b. person whose ancestry is considered bad because of racial mixtures with blacks and Indians. *Co-we.* (Velásquez 1962:115) prior20.

12. person of African origin. *An* (Alvarez Nazario 1974:356) late16.

13. any person who acts like a *zambo*. *Co* (Tobón Betancourt 1953:263) mid20.

14. person considered a bore. *Co* (Kany 1960b:34–35) 20; (Tobón Betancourt 1953:263) mid20.

[Df. 9 pejor. Df. 11b injur. Df. 13 derog. Df. 14 very derog. Acc. Alvarez Nazario, < Congolese lg. *nzambu* 'type of monkey' or < *Mozambique*. Acc. Rout (1976:xv), 'knock-kneed' in Spain. Syn. *mulato pardo* in 17-cent. Guerrero, Mx, acc. Aguirre Beltrán (1945:216 and 1972:169). Syn. *cambujo* in cl. Mx, acc. Woodbridge. Acc. Vergara Martín, syn. *cabra, grifo, retorno, zambaigo*. Acc. Pitt-Rivers (1968:272), affect. among friends in Pe, sim. to use of *negrito* or *cholito*. Italian borrowing att. as 'offspring of a black and American Indian,' acc. Zaccaria (1927:412). Derivs. *zambada, zambaje, zamberío* 'group of *zambos*.' Dim. deriv. *zambito*. Acc. Mellafe (1964:89), syn. *pardo*. Other syn. *mulato*. Vars. *sambo, zembo*. Cf. **cambujo, mulato, sambaigo, sambo, zambaigo,** Ptg. **zambo.**]

zambo chino

1. person whose skin color indicates racial mixing. *Pe* (Romero 1944:375) cl.

2. person whose ancestors include *chinos* and *negros*. *Pe* (Millones Santagadea 1973:66) late18–early19.

[Acc. Millones Santagadea, ant. df. 2 *negro*. Var. *zambo-chino*. Cf. **chino, negro, zambo.**]

zambo-chino — See *zambo chino*

zambo claro 'light *zambo*'

person whose dark skin color indicates racial mixture, acc. official documents and literary works. *Pe* (Romero 1944:375 and 1965:233) cl.

[Var. *zambo-claro*. Cf. **claro, zambo, zambo chino,** Ptg. **zambo claro.**]

zambo-claro — See *zambo claro*

zambo de indio 'Indian *zambo*'
offspring of a black and an Indian. *Pe* (Alvarez Nazario 1974:355); *Mx* (Alcedo 1786–89:5.104); (León 1924:27; Woodbridge 1948:361) cl.
[Syn. *cambujo* in Mx, acc. Alcedo, León, and Woodbridge. Acc. Vergara Martín, syns. *lobo* in Mx, *chino* in SA, *zambaigo.* Cf. **cambujo, indio, zambaigo, zambo.**]

zambo de mestizo 'mestizo *zambo*'
offspring of a black and an Indian who lived among the Indians, acc. religious and legal documents. *CR* (Levine 1980:148) cl.
[Cf. **mestizo, zambo, zambo de mulato.**]

zambo de mulato 'mulatto *zambo*'
1. offspring of a black and a *quinterón. SoA-no.* (Woodbridge 1948:361) cl.
2. offspring of a black and an Indian who lived among the blacks, acc. religious and legal records. *CR* (Levine 1980:148) cl.
[Cf. **mulato, zambo de indio, zambo de mestizo.**]

zambo de negro 'black *zambo*'
offspring of a black and a *quinterón. SoA-no.* (Woodbridge 1948:361) cl.
[Syns. *zambo de mulato, zambo de tercerón.* Cf. **negro, sambo, zambo de tercerón, zambo prieto.**]

zambo de tercerón 'terceroon *zambo*'
offspring of a black and a *quinterón. SoA-no.* (Woodbridge 1948:361) cl.
[Syns. *zambo de mulato, zambo de negro.* Cf. **tercerón, zambo, zambo de mestizo, zambo de mulato, zambo de negro.**]

zambo mosquito
1. offspring of a black worker from the English An and a native woman from the east coast of CeA. *Ho Ni* (Barón Castro 1946:798); *CeA Ni* (Rosenblat 1954:2.69) cl.
2. offspring of black fugitive slaves and *indios mosquitos. CeA* (Ferguson 1963:123) 20.
[< *mosquito* 'name of an Indian tribe; name of CeA coastline.' Vars. *sambo-mosquito, zambo-mosquito.* Cf. **mosquito-zambo, yaro, yucateco, zambo de indio.**]

zambo-mosquito — See *zambo mosquito*

zambo prieto 'dark *zambo*'
1. person whose dark skin color indicates racial mixture, acc. documents and records. *Pe* (Romero 1944:375) cl.
2. offspring of a *zambo* and a black; 75% black, 25% Indian. *Mx* (Pérez de Barradas 1948:190; León 1924:20–21, plate 52); *Mx Pe*

(León 1924:27; Woodbridge 1948:361) cl.

3. offspring of a black and a *lobo*. *Cu Mx* (Woodbridge 1948:361); *Mx* (Santamaría 1942:3.309) cl; (Vergara Martín 1922:246) n.d.

[Var. *zambo-prieto*. Cf. **prieto, zambo retorno,** Ptg. **zambo preto.**]

zambo-prieto — See *zambo prieto*

zamboide

offspring of an African black and a Germanic white, considered the 2 racial extremes. *SA* (Chávez González 1937:62) 20.

[Acc. Chávez González, racist anthro. term. Cf. **blancoide, indioide, negroide.**]

zamboinga — See *zambaigo*

zamuco

Chiquitano Indian who ran away from an old mission to the banks of the Paraguay River. *SA* (Bayo 1931:263) mid20.

[Cf. **indio.**]

zapoteco 'Zapotec'

1. inhabitant of the state of Oaxaca, Mx. *Mx* (Morínigo 1966:688) 20.

2. Zapotec Indian. *Mx* (Morínigo 1966:688) 20.

[Acc. Morínigo, Oaxaca is in region of the Zapotecs. Cf. **chilango, jarocho.**]

zarco 'light blue'

1. person with light skin color. *Co-San Agustín, -Yarumal* (Flórez 1969:123) 20.

2. person of white race. *Gu* (Malaret 1931:518) mid20; (Morínigo 1966:689) 20.

3a. person with light eyes. *Co-Bogotá* (Acuña 1951:177) mid20.

3b. person with eyes like an albino's. *Gu* (Cowles 1952:830) mid20.

3c. person, usually white, whose eyes are of a light blue color. *Gu* (Batres Jáuregui 1892: 559) late19.

3d. person having 2 differently colored eyes. *Bo* (Malaret 1931:518) mid20.

[Cf. **albino, claro, güero, rubio.**]

zembo — See *zambo*

zimarrón — See *cimarrón*

zíngaro

gypsy. *Ar* (Segovia 1911:303) early20.

[Acc. Segovia, < Italian *zingaro* 'gypsy.' Perhaps has Italian pronunciation. Cf. Ptg. **cigano.**]

zobo

racially mixed person of black African and Indian ancestry. *SA* (Levine 1980:149) cl.

[Acc. Levine, syns. *chino, zambo.* Cf. **zambo.**]

zonite 'of the Panama Canal Zone'

1. US citizen, usually white, who resides and works in the Panama Canal Zone. *Pa* (Rout 1976:xiv; Levine 1980:149) 20.

2. white born in the Panama Canal Zone who holds a job considered semi-inherited. *Pa* (Rout 1976:xiv) 20.

[< *zona* 'zone' + Engl. suf. *-ite.* Cf. **yanqui.**]

zorro 'fox; fox-colored'

person whose skin color indicates racial mixture. *Co-Rionegro* (Flórez 1969:123) 20.

[Acc. Santamaría (1942:3.323), 'Colombian game played with tokens in which the black tokens represent the fox and the whites the hens.' Thus, probably 'black person' in Co. Cf. **mono, tresalbo.**]

zungo

1. servant who is the offspring of blacks. *Co* (Malaret 1944:520) mid20.

2. black person. *Co* (Kany 1960b:36; Morínigo 1966:692) 20.

[Cf. **sungo.**]

zurumato — See *surumato*

Part II

Brazilian Portuguese Terms

A

abacaxi — See *galego*

abugrado
person who has features like those of a *bugre,* or Indian; Indian; descendant of Indians. *Br-RS* (Coruja et al. 1964:6) 20.
[Generally pejor. < pref. *a-* + *bugre* 'Indian' + suf. *-ado.* Cf. **bugre,** Sp. **aindiado.**]

aça 'albino'
1. offspring of a black and a white. *Br* (Woodbridge 1948:356) cl.
2. mulatto with light skin color. *Br* (Ramos 1941:537) mid20; (Buarque de Holanda 1975:14) 20.
3. albino. *Br* (Buarque de Holanda 1975:14) 20.
[M., f. Syn. df. 1 *mulato claro.* Probably < African lg. Acc. Buarque de Holanda, syn. df. 2 *mulato alvacento*; df. 3 used in ref. to person or animal; var. *aço.* Cf. **preto-aça.**]

acablocado — See *acaboclado*

acabocado — See *acaboclado*

acaboclado '*caboclo*-like'
1. person with bad manners sim. to a *caboclo*; rustic, brutish type. *Br-sertão* (Almeida Oliveira 1940:19) mid20.
2. person who has the features of an Indian. *Br-RS* (Coruja et al. 1964:6) 20.
[Syn. df. 2 *abugrado.* < *a-* + *caboclo* + *-ado.* Sim. to *pardavasco.* Acc. Buarque de Holanda (1975:15), other syns. *acaipirado, caipira, índio meio amulatado, pardavasco, rústico,* Vars. *acablocado, acabocado.* Cf. **abugrado, acaipirado, caboclo, caipira, pardavasco, rústico.**]

acabralhado '*cabra*-like'
1. offspring of a black and a mulatto. *Br* (Levine 1979:2) 20prior; (Levine 1980:2) 20.
2. mestizo, or person of mixed race sim. to a *cabra. Br* (Buarque de Holanda 1975:15) 20.
[< *a-* + *cabra* + *-(lh)ado.* Cf. **acaboclado, acaipirado, acrioulado, cabra.**]

acaipirado — See *caipira*

acastanhado 'chestnut-like'
person with chestnut-colored skin, acc. 1980 census. *Br* (Silva 1987:159) 20.
[< *a-* + *castanho* 'chestnut' + suf. *-ado.* Color classification, acc.

Silva. Cf. **agalegado, alvo, amorenado, gato negro, gazo, queimado de sol, moreno castanho, regular, vermelho.**]

aço — See *aça*

acrioulado 'creole-like'

person who adapts to new surroundings and takes on the local customs or traits of the natives of the area. *Br-RS* (Coruja et al. 1964:8) 20.

[Esp. in ref. to animals. Sim. to Sp. *acriollado.* < *acrioular-se* 'to acclimatize, adapt,' ultimately < *crioulo.* Cf. **crioulo,** Sp. **criollo.**]

acuém — See *xavante*

africano 'African'

1. black person. *Br-BA* (Sanjek 1971:1141) 20.

2a. person born in Africa. *Br-BA* (Pierson 1942:369) prior20.

2b. African-born slave. *Br* (Nuñez 1980:12) cl.

2c. Brazilian-born black who retained ancestral African beliefs and culture. *Br-BA* (Nuñez 1980:12–13) cl.

[Cf. **africano livre, afro-negro, escravo, negro, preto,** Sp. **africano.**]

africano livre 'free African'

1. African-born, unskilled black person brought to America to work in public jobs. *Br* (Nuñez 1980:13) mid19.

2. black slave freed after years of service to the master. *Br* (Silva 1987:263) prior20.

[Acc. Silva, census color classification. Cf. **africano, forro.**]

afro-asiático 'Afro-Asian'

person of mixed Asian and African parentage; person who is half Asian and half black. *Br* (Buarque de Holanda 1975:47) 20.

[< *afro* 'African' + *asiático* 'Asian.' Cf. **afro-brasileiro, afro-negro, asiático,** Sp. **afro, afroamericano, afrocubano, injerto.**]

afro-brasileiro 'Afro-Brazilian'

black Brazilian. *Br* (Buarque de Holanda 1975:47) 20.

[< *afro* 'African' + *brasileiro* 'Brz.' Cf. **afro-asiático, afro-negro, negro, preto,** Sp. **afroamericano, afrocubano.**]

afro-negro

black African. *Br* (Baldus and Willems 1939:20) early20.

[< *afro* 'African' + *negro* 'black.' Anthro. term used to separate African blacks from *negros* of Australia and the South Pacific, acc. Baldus and Willems. Cf. **africano, afro-asiático, afro-brasileiro,** Sp. **africano, afroamericano, afrocolonial, afrocubano, afro-mestizo.**]

agalegado '*galego*-like'

person whose skin color is reminiscent of that of a *galego,* acc. 1980 census. *Br* (Silva 1987:159) 20.

[< *a-* + *galego* 'Galician, person of Ptg. descent' + suf. *-ado.* Census color classification. Cf. **acastanhado, amorenado, galego, vermelho.**]

agauchado 'gaucho-like'

person who imitates the gaucho in customs, airs, or clothing. *Br-sertão* (Almeida Oliveira 1940:22); *Br-RS* (Coruja et al. 1964:11) 20.

[Acc. Morínigo (1966:34), < *agaucharse* 'to take on the customs of the gaucho, to become a cattleman, to imitate the gaucho.' Cf. **acrioulado, gaúcho,** Sp. **agauchado, gaucho.**]

agregado 'squatter'

1. squatter; any poor person living on land that belongs to another. *Br-RS* (Coruja et al. 1964:12) 20.

2. free or freed person of any color or race who lived under the protection of a family. *Br* (Mattoso 1986:250) prior20.

[< *agregar* 'to unite, collect.' Sim. to *agregado* in contiguous areas of SA. Cf. **acrioulado,** Sp. **agregado.**]

alamão

1. person of color, acc. country types. *Br-sertão* (Almeida Oliveira 1940:24) mid20.

2. person whose skin color is either black or white, acc. social context. *Br-BA-Salvador* (Sanjek 1971:1141) 20.

[Df. 1 pejor. Var. of *alemão* 'German, blond-haired, blue-eyed Aryan type.' Var. *lamão.* Cf. **alemão, branco,** Sp. **alemán.**]

albino 'albino'

1. offspring of a *morisco* and a white. *Br* (Woodbridge 1948:356; León 1924:21; Monteforte Toledo 1959:171; Pérez de Barradas 1948:189) cl.

2. mulatto; offspring of a black and a white. *Br* (Woodbridge 1948:356) cl; (Ramos 1941:537) mid20.

[Syn. *mulato.* Acc. Cassidy and DeCamp (1966:129), used by whites; Ptg. *albino* > Engl. 'white-type,' used formerly in Engl.-speaking An. Cf. **aça, branco, mulato,** Sp. **albino.**]

alemã — See *alemão*

alemão 'German'

1. German; person of German descent. *Br* (Buarque de Holanda 1975:65) 20prior.

2. any nonblack person. *Br-SP* (Paiva 1986:46) 20.

3. person whose skin color is generally white. *Br-BA-Salvador* (Sanjek 1971:1141) 20.

[Df. 2 att. in sentence "Você sabe, *alemão,* que só trabalho com coisa boa" from Paiva's novel *Blecaute.* Acc. Sanjek, f. form *alemã.* Cf. **alamão, alemão batata,** Sp. **alemán.**]

alemão batata 'potato German'

1. German settler. *Br* (Levine 1980:5) 20.

2. German. *Br* (Roback 1944:133) mid20.

[Df. 2 slur. Cf. **alemão,** Sp. **alemán de mierda.**]

alodê — See *boneco de alodê*

alvarento 'whitish; very light'

person with light skin color, acc. 1980 census. *Br* (Silva 1987:159) 20.

[Acc. Silva, census color classification. Cf. **alvo, alvo escuro, alvo rosado, vermelho.**]

alvinho 'white, whitish; little white one'

person whose skin color is light or white. *Br-BA-Salvador* (Sanjek 1971:1141); *Br* (Silva 1987:159) 20.

[< *alvo* 'white' + dim. suf. *-inho,* acc. Machado (1952:1.178). Acc. Silva, 1980 census color classification. Cf. **albino, alvo, branco, queimado de sol, vermelho.**]

alvo 'very white; very light-skinned'

1. person with thick lips, relatively straight hair, and a big nose. *Br* (Harris 1970:3); *Br-BA* (Sanjek 1971:1129) 20.

2. person with very white skin color, acc. 1980 census. *Br* (Silva 1987:159) 20.

[Df. 1 probably iron. Df. 2 color classification. Acc. Verlinden (1955:630), used in ref. to skin color of slaves bought and sold in Lisbon around 1460. Acc. Sanjek, one of 10 most used racial terms in Salvador. Euph., iron. Cf. **albino, alvinho, branco.**]

alvo cabelo ruim — See *alvo de cabelo ruim*

alvo de cabelo ruim 'white with bad hair'

person considered white but whose hair is kinky or curly like that of a black person. *Br-BA* (Sanjek 1971:1141) 20.

[Sim. to Sp. *pelo malo* 'bad hair.' Cf. **alvinho, alvo, negro de cabelo bom, negro de cabelo ruim, negro alvo,** Sp. **pelo malo.**]

alvo escuro 'dark white'

person whose skin color is darkish-white, acc. 1980 census. *Br* (Silva 1987:159) 20.

[Acc. Silva, census color classification. Cf. **alvo, queimado de sol, vermelho.**]

alvo rosado 'pinkish-white'

person with pinkish or pinkish-white skin color, acc. 1980 census. *Br* (Silva 1987:159) 20.

[Acc. Silva, census color classification. Cf. **alvarento, alvinho, alvo, alvo escuro, amarelo, vermelho.**]

ama 'nursemaid'

nursemaid, usually slave woman of color. *Br-BA* (Pierson

1942:369) prior20.

[F. Cf. **ama de criar, ama de leite, ama seca, babá, mucama,** Sp. **ama, baba.**]

ama de criar 'nursemaid'

nursemaid of color, often a former slave who was considered a member of the family and lived in the master's house. *Br* (Nuñez 1980:24) cl.

[F. Cf. **ama, ama de leite, ama seca.**]

ama de leite 'wet nurse'

black slave woman who served as wet nurse to the master's children. *Br* (Nuñez 1980:24) cl.

[F. Cf. **ama, ama de criar, ama seca.**]

ama seca 'dry nursemaid'

old black woman who cared for the master's children; black nanny. *Br* (Nuñez 1980:24) 20prior.

[F. Cf. **ama, ama de criar, ama de leite.**]

amarelado 'yellowed'

person with yellowed or yellowish skin color, acc. 1980 census. *Br* (Silva 1987:159) 20.

[< *amarelo* 'yellow' + suf. *-ado*. Acc. Silva, color classification. Cf. **agalegado, alvo, amorenado, avermelhado, queimado de sol, vermelho,** Sp. **amarillento.**]

amarelo 'yellow'

1. person with yellow or yellowish skin color. *Br* (Harris 1964a:58; Silva 1987:159); *Br-BA* (Sanjek 1971:1141) 20.

2. any Indian, *caboclo,* or sometimes Asian. *Br* (Azevedo 1953:125) cl.

3. any Oriental or Asian-Brazilian. *Br* (Levine 1980:5–6) 20.

4a. mulatto. *Br* (Nuñez 1980:24) n.d.

4b. mulatto with light skin color. *Br* (Levine 1980:5–6) 20.

[Acc. Silva, df. 1 1980 census color classification. Acc. Soares and Silva (1987:166), used in 1976 household census as a racial category. Sim. to Sp. *amarillo.* Cf. **alvo, amarelado, amarelo queimado, amareloso, amorenado, branco, negro, preto, queimado de sol, vermelho,** Sp. **amarillo.**]

amarelo de Goiana 'yellow-skinned person from Guiana'

person with very pallid skin color. *Br* (Cabral 1982:40) 20.

[Cf. **amarelo.**]

amarelo queimado 'burnt yellow'

person with reddish-yellow or dark yellow skin color, acc. 1980 census. *Br* (Silva 1987:159) 20.

[Acc. Silva, color classification. Cf. **alvo, alvo rosado, amarelo,**

amareloso, amorenado, avermelhado, queimado de sol, vermelho, Sp. **amarillo,**]

amareloso 'yellowish'

person with yellowish skin color, acc. 1980 census. *Br* (Silva 1987:159) 20.

[< *amarelo* 'yellow' + suf. *-oso.* Cf. **alvarento, alvo, amarelo, amarelo queimado, amorenado, avermelhado.**]

ambulante 'ambulatory'

outdoor-market, itinerant, or street vendor. *Br* (Gomes de Matos 1988:p.c.) late20.

[M., f. Syn. *feirante.*]

ameraba

native American, usually unassimilated; American Indian. *Br* (Souza 1961:11) 20.

[M., f. Acc. Souza, anthro. term proposed by Henrique Jorge Huxley as a more general category for 'American Indian' than *índio* or *indígena.* < *amer-* 'American' + Tupi *aba* 'man.' Syn. *ameríndio.* Acc. Rodrigues (1986:22), *abá* 'people, Indian' in Old Tupi. Cf. **amerígena, ameríndio, índio, indígena,** Sp. **aborígena.**]

amerígena

native American; Amerindian; American Indian. *Br* (Souza 1961:11) 20.

[M., f. Acc. Souza, anthro. term proposed by Saladino de Gusmão for 'Indian.' < *amer-* 'American' + *-ígena* by anal. to *indígena,* sim. to the formation of *ameraba.* Cf. **ameraba, ameríndio, indígena,** Sp. **aborígena.**]

ameríncola

native American; American Indian. *Br* (Souza 1961:11–12) 20.

[Anthro., acc. Souza. Cf. **ameraba, amerígena, ameríndio.**]

ameríndio 'Amerindian'

native American; American Indian. *Br* (Souza 1961:11–12; Cascudo 1962:38) 20.

[Anthro. term recommended by Charles Scott and John Wesley Powell, acc. Souza. Sim. to No. Amer. Engl. *Amerindian.* Acc. Baldus and Willems (1939:22), used to distinguish native American Indians (*índios*) from those of the Indian or Asian subcontinent (*indianos*). Var. *amerindo.* Cf. **ameraba, amerígena, ameríncola.**]

amerindo — See *ameríndio*

amisturado 'mixed'

person whose skin color indicates mixed racial background. *Br-BA* (Sanjek 1971:1141) 20.

[< *a-* + *mistura* 'mixture' + *-ado.* Cf. **mestiço, misturada, misturo.**]

amorenado 'browned; brownish'
person with brown or dark skin color, acc. 1980 census. *Br*
(Silva 1987:159) 20.
[< *a-* + *moreno* 'brown' + suf. *-ado*. Acc. Silva, color classification.
Var. *morenado,* acc. Buarque de Holanda (1975:945). Cf.
**acastanhado, agalegado, alvo, amarelado, avermelhado, bem
branco, morenado, moreno, vermelho.**]

amulatado 'mulatto-like'
person whose skin color and/or other physical features are like
those of a mulatto. *Br* (Moraes e Silva 1789:1.78) late18; (Buarque
de Holanda 1975:89) 20.
[< *a-* + *mulato* + suf. *-ado.* Cf. **amisturado, mulato,** Sp.
amulatado.]

angolense — See *angolo*

angolo
Angola-born black slave who worked on a sugar plantation. *Br*
(Nuñez 1980:29) prior20.
[Syn. *angolense.* Cf. Sp. **angola.**]

ao parecer branco 'seemingly white'
person whose white or light skin color may hide racial mixture.
Br (Russell-Wood 1982:25) cl.
[Cf. **branco,** Sp. **no blanco del todo.**]

árabe 'Arab, Arabic'
1. Arab; person of Arabic descent, esp. from North Africa. *Br*
(Buarque de Holanda 1975:123) 20.
2. Portuguese person. *Br-CE* (Parsons 1986:p.c.) 20.
[M.,f. Df. 2 probably derog. Syn. df. 2 *galego.* Cf. **galego, turco,**
Sp. **árabe, gallego, portuga.**]

araçuaba
1. offspring of a black and a white; mulatto. *Br-BA* (Woodbridge
1948:356) cl.
2. mulatto who has a lighter skin color than other mulattoes.
Br-BA (Ramos 1941:537) mid20.
3. person whose skin color indicates racial mixture. *Br* (Harris
1964a:58) 20.
[Syn. df. 1 *mulato claro.* Vars. *araçuabo, asaruabo, saruabo,* acc.
Sanjek (1971:1141). Cf. **mulato, mulato claro.**]

araçuabo — See *araçuaba*

ariboco
offspring of a black and an Indian. *Br* (Woodbridge 1948:356)
cl.
[Cf. **araçuaba, mulato.**]

arigó
   rustic, uncultured type; hick. *Br-SP* (Ayrosa 1937:80) mid20 ‖
Br-c.w., -RJ (Buarque de Holanda 1975:131) 20.
   [Syn. *caipira*. Cf. **caipira**.]
asaruabo — See *araçuaba*
avermelhado 'reddish; reddened'
   person with red, reddish, or sunburnt-type skin color, acc. 1980
census. *Br* (Silva 1987:159) 20.
   [< *a-* + *vermelho* 'red' + suf. *-ado*. Acc. Silva, color classification. Cf.
   **acastanhado, agalegado, alvo, amarelado, amorenado, bem
   branco, vermelho.**]
azul 'blue'
   person whose skin color is dark enough to appear blue or bluish,
acc. 1980 census. *Br* (Silva 1987:159) 20.
   [Acc. Silva, color classification. Cf. **acastanhado, agalegado, alvo,
   amarelado, amorenado, avermelhado, bem branco, vermelho,**
   Sp. **azul.**]
azul marinho 'navy blue'
   person whose skin color is dark enough to appear navy blue,
acc. 1980 census. *Br* (Silva 1987:159) 20.
   [Acc. Silva, color classification. Cf. **acastanhado, agalegado, alvo,
   amarelado, amorenado, avermelhado, azul, bem branco,
   vermelho.**]

B

babá
   1. black nursemaid. *Br* (Wagley 1971:21) cl; (Levine 1980:10)
20.
   2. leader, usually black, of an Afro-Brazilian religious cult. *Br*
(Buarque de Holanda 1975:1017) 20prior.
   [Df. 1 f.; syn. *ama*. Acc. Gomes de Matos (1988:p.c.), df. 1 may also
   be 'white nursemaid.' Df. 2 generally m.; syn. *pai-de-santo*. Possibly
   < Yoruba *baba* or *babá* 'father, ancestor' in Yoruba-based religious
   groups, acc. Schneider (1985:23). Df. 1 sim. to So. No. Amer. Engl.
   mammy. Cf. **ama, pai-de-santo,** Sp. **santero.**]
babalaô
   priest, generally black, of an Afro-Brazilian religious cult dedi-
cated to Ifá, god of guessing or riddles. *Br* (Buarque de Holanda
1975:171) 20prior.
   [Acc. Buarque de Holanda, < Yoruba *babaulá*. Cf. **babá, pai-de-
   santo.**]

babalorixá — See *pai-de-santo*

babaloxá — See *pai-de-santo*

babaquara
rustic, uncivilized type; hick. *Br-RJ* (Ayrosa 1937:80) mid20.
[M., f. Acc. Buarque de Holanda (1975:171), < Tupi *mbae'bé*
'nothing' + *kwa'á* 'to know;' now 'influential, important' in CE. Cf.
arigó, caipira.]

babeco
tall person with white skin color, blue eyes, and black hair. *Br-
PB* (Souza 1961:21) early–mid20; (Buarque de Holanda 1975:171)
20.
[Cf. **bebeco, gringo, yanqui,** Sp. **bebeco.**]

bachicha
foreigner. *Br-RJ* (Chamberlain 1981:419) 20.
[M., f. *Gíria* slang of Rio de Janeiro. Acc. Alonso (1958:1.610–11),
< common Genoese name *Baciccia,* hypocoristic for name Battista.
Also found in Lunfardo slang of Buenos Aires. Cf. Sp. **bachicha.**]

bagaceira 'trash heap; junk'
person of low class and poor manners; trash; low-class type. *Br-
so.* (Callage 1928) early20 ‖ *Br-RS* (Coruja et al. 1964:48) 20.
[F. Derog. Acc. Callage, used among gauchos. Cf. **bagaceiro,
bagagem, gentalha,** Sp. **bagazo.**]

bagaceiro 'trash'
person who lives among the lower classes. *Br-so.* (Callage
1928:22) early20.
[< *bagaceira.* Cf. **bagaceira, bagagem, gentalha.**]

bagagem 'baggage'
person of low class; trash; low-class type. *Br-so.* (Callage
1928:22) early20 ‖ *Br-RS* (Coruja et al. 1964:48) 20.
[F. Possibly euph. Syn. *bagaceira.* Acc. Machado (1952:1.299), < Fr.
bagage 'baggage.' Cf. **bagaceira, bagaceiro, gentalha.**]

bahiano — See *baiano*

baiana — See *baiano*

baiano 'Bahian'
1a. black person; person of color. *Br-so.* (Chamberlain and
Harmon 1983:38) 20.
1b. black woman from PE who is usually quite tall, beautiful,
graceful, and rhythmic of gait, and most probably of Sudanic
origins. *Br-BA* (Freyre 1964:275) 20.
2a. person from the north of the country. *Br* (Aguirre Beltrán
1972:178) cl ‖ *Br-RS* (Coruja et al. 1964:50) 20.
2b. person who does not know how to ride like a gaucho,

generally from BA or northeastern Br, acc. gauchos. *Br-so.* (Callage 1928:22) early20.

2c. northeasterner; person from northeastern Br. *Br-so.* (Chamberlain and Harmon 1983:38) 20.

2d. person from northeastern Br or anywhere outside the South. *Br-so.* (Silva 1987:171) late20.

3. rustic, uncivilized type; hick. *Br-PI* (Ayrosa 1937:81) mid20.

4. person with the skin color, probably dark, of a person from BA, acc. 1980 census. *Br* (Silva 1987:159) 20.

[Df. 1a colloq., pejor. Df. 2c. colloq. Df. 2d derog. Syn. df. 3 *caipira.* Acc. Silva, df. 4 color classification. < *bahia* or *baía* 'bay.' Joc. syn. *maleiro,* acc. Buarque de Holanda (1975:175). Std. syn. *baiense.* Var. *bahiano.* Cf. **acastanhado, agalegado, alvo, amarelado, avermelhado, bem branco, cearense, nordestino, pau-de-fumo, vermelho,** Sp. **bayano.**]

baiense — See *baiano*

banda-forra

offspring of a white and a black slave woman. *Br* (Diégues 1963:106) cl.

[M., f. Acc. Buarque de Holanda (1975:181), < *banda* 'side' + *forra* 'freed.' Cf. **mulato.**]

bandeirante

1a. soldier or explorer from SP, often a mestizo. *Br* (Rosenblat 1954:2.102) cl.

1b. mestizo. *Br* (Mörner 1967:72) cl.

2. person who participated in the *bandeiras,* often of Portuguese descent, adapted to Indian customs, and having Indian wives or concubines. *Br* (Levine 1979:24–25) late17–early18.

[Syn. df. 1b *mameluco.* Acc. Levine, < *bandeira* 'search or exploration for Indian slaves and gold.' Acc. Ramos (1944:27), these *bandeiras,* or expeditions, had flags carried at the front as a symbol of adventure; so. and c.w. Br opened for settlement by these explorer-adventurers. Cf. **mameluco.**]

banguela

person without teeth. *Br* (Cascudo 1962:92; Cabral 1982:94) 20.

[M., f. Acc. Cascudo, < *negros banguelos* 'African tribe known for sharpening incisors to triangular points.' Acc. Buarque de Holanda (1975:182), < *Banguela* 'African placename.' Acc. Cabral, many black Brz. slaves who had had teeth ceremonially extracted came from Banguela in we. Africa. Var. *banguelo.* Cf. **benguela.**]

banguelo — See *banguela*

banto — See *bantu*

bantu 'Bantu'
black person, not highly desired as a slave, from Angola, Congo, or Mozambique. *Br* (Levine 1980:11) 19prior.
[Acc. Cascudo (1962:93–94), *banto.* Cf. Sp. **angola, guineo.**]

baqueano
person practical in things of the land or of the rural areas; guide; scout. *Br* (Souza 1961:331); *Br-RS* (Coruja et al. 1964:477) 20.
[Vars. *baquiano, vaqueano, vaquiano.* Acc. Coruja et al., < Amer. Sp. *baquiano.* Cf. Sp. **baquiano.**]

baquiano — See *baqueano*

barbado 'bearded'
Guato Indian of MT, Br. *Br* (Vergara Martín 1922:230) n.d.
[Cf. **índio.**]

barriga verde — See *barriga-verde*

barriga-verde 'green belly'
native of the state of SC, Br. *Br* (Cascudo 1962:101); *Br-RS* (Coruja et al. 1964:57) 20.
[Acc. Cascudo, used in ref. to green vest or waistcoat worn in early 1800s by soldiers of Brigadier Silva Pais's battalion of riflemen. Syn. *catarinense.* Var. *barriga verde.* Cf. **baiano, gaúcho.**]

beato 'religious; devotee'
devotee of an Afro-Brazilian religious cult. *Br* (Gomes de Matos 1988:p.c.) 20.
[Cf. **babá, pai-de-santo.**]

beiço-de-pau — See *tapanhuna*

beiçoca — See *beiçudo*

beiçola — See *beiçudo*

beiçorra — See *beiçudo*

beiçudo 'big-lipped; devil'
person with big lips. *Br* (Buarque de Holanda 1975:195) 20.
[< *beiço* 'lip' + suf. *-udo.* Aug. syns. *beiçoca, beiçola, beiçorra.* Probably indicates 'black person.' Cf. Sp. **bembón, bembudo.**]

bem alvo 'very white'
person whose skin color is very light or white. *Br-BA-Salvador* (Sanjek 1971:1141) 20.
[Cf. **alvo, branco.**]

bem areado 'well-sandpapered; well-polished'
1a. person of mixed race with light skin color. *Br-BA* (Pierson 1942:139) mid20.
1b. person of mixed race identified with the white class. *Br-BA* (Nuñez 1980:67) 20.

2. mulatto with light skin color. *Br-BA* (Levine 1980:14) 20.

[Acc. Pierson, *bem areiada* [*sic*]. Acc. Nuñez, *bem areiado* [*sic*]. Acc. Levine, *bem ariada* [*sic*]. Cf. **bem alvo.**]

bem areiada, bem areiado — See *bem areado*

bem ariado — See *bem areado*

bem branco 'very white'

person with very white or light skin color, acc. 1980 census. *Br* (Silva 1987:159) 20.

[Acc. Silva, color classification. Cf. **acastanhado, agalegado, alvo, amarelado, avermelhado, bem claro, bem moreno, branco, vermelho.**]

bem claro 'very light'

person with very light or white skin color, acc. 1980 census. *Br* (Silva 1987:159) 20.

[Acc. Silva, color classification. Cf. **acastanhado, agalegado, alvo, amarelado, avermelhado, bem branco, bem moreno, claro, moreno, vermelho.**]

bem moreninho 'very little brown one or brunet'

person who has all the characteristics of a *moreno. Br-n.e.* (Hutchinson 1957:120) 20.

[Syn. *moreno fino.* Cf. **bem alvo, bem moreno, moreninho, moreno.**]

bem moreno 'very brown or brunet'

person with very brown or dark skin color, acc. 1980 census. *Br* (Silva 1987:159) 20.

[Acc. Silva, color classification. Cf. **acastanhado, agalegado, alvo, amarelado, avermelhado, bem branco, bem claro, bem moreninho, claro, moreno, vermelho.**]

bem pretinho 'very little black one'

person with very black skin color. *Br-n.e.* (Hutchinson 1957:120) 20.

[Cf. **bem preto, pretinho, preto.**]

bem preto 'very black'

person with very black skin. *Br-n.e.* (Hutchinson 1957:120) 20.

[Cf. **bem pretinho, preto.**]

bem sarará

person with all the qualities typical of a *sarará. Br-n.e.* (Hutchinson 1957:120) 20.

[Cf. **bem alvo, bem preto, sarará.**]

benguela

black African slave brought to America from Angola by the Portuguese. *Br* (Levine 1980:14) 19prior.

[Var. *benguelo.* Cf. **banguelo,** Sp. **angola.**]

benguelo — See *benguela*

benzedeiro — See *benzedor*

benzedor

person of an Afro-Brazilian cult who claims to cure illness with spells. *Br* (Buarque de Holanda 1975:199) 20.

[Syns. *benzedeiro, benzilhão.* Cf. **curador.**]

benzilhão — See *benzedor*

beribá — See *biriba*

beriva — See *biriba*

berivá — See *biriba*

besta de carga 'beast of burden'

black person. *Br* (Silva 1987:73) early20.

[Acc. Silva, pseudo-scientific term found in Euclides da Cunha. Syns. *filho das paisagens adustas, filho das paisagens bárbaras.* Cf. **filho das paisagens adustas, filho das paisagens bárbaras, negro, preto,** Sp. **yanacona.**]

bicudo — See *galego*

biriba

1a. person from rural SP or PR state who comes to the city to buy mules or horses; rustic type. *Br-RS* (Coruja et al. 1964:61) 20.

1b. inhabitant of the mountainous region of RS. *Br* (Buarque de Holanda 1975:208); *Br-RS* (Coruja et al. 1964:61) 20.

1c. rustic type; *caipira. Br* (Buarque de Holanda 1975:208) 20.

2. person from SP. *Br-RS* (Coruja et al. 1964:61); *Br* (Buarque de Holanda 1975:208) 20.

3. prostitute. *Br-PR, -so.* (Souto Maior 1980:14) 20–late20

[Acc. Buarque de Holanda, < Tupi *mbi'ribi* 'small, little, few.' Acc. Coruja et al., *beriva* [*sic*]. Vars. *beribá, beriva, berivá, biriva.* Cf. **caipira.**]

biriva — See *biriba*

boa gente 'good people'

white person; person of the upper classes. *Br* (Silva 1987:200) late20.

[Acc. Silva, syn. *gente fina.* Cf. **gente sinhá.**]

boaba — See *galego*

boava — See *galego*

boçal

black slave recently arrived from Africa, esp. one who did not speak Portuguese and was not Christian. *Br* (Moraes e Silva 1789:1.185) late18 ‖ *Br-sertão* (Almeida Oliveira 1940:47); *Br* (Souza 1961:42) cl.

[Syns. *escravo boçal, negro-novo, caramutanje,* acc. Buarque de Holanda (1975:212). Ant. *ladino.* Cf. **ladino,** Sp. **bozal.**]

boche
German, esp. one during the First and Second World Wars. *Br* (Buarque de Holanda 1975:65, 213) 20.
[Acc. Buarque de Holanda, < Fr. obs. slang *Boche* 'German;' derog. Perhaps obs., ultimately < *Bosch* 'German surname.' Cf. **alemão.**]

bode 'billy goat'
mulatto. *Br* (Nogueira 1959:177; Cascudo 1962:116; Levine 1979:33 and 1980:18) 20 ‖ *Br-sertão* (Almeida Oliveira 1940:47) mid20.
[Acc. Cascudo, syns. *mulato, mestiço, cabra, faiodermo.* Acc. Buarque de Holanda (1975:213), syn. *mulato crioulo.* Acc. Levine, slang. Acc. Souto Maior (1980:15), also 'menstruation' or 'man given to sexual conquests' in n.e. Br. Vars. *bode branco, bode preto.* Cf. **cabra, faiodermo, mestiço, mulato, mulato crioulo, preto.**]

bode branco — See *bode*

bode preto — See *bode*

bóia-fria 'cold lunch'
1. person from northeastern Br who travels south and eats food cold during the journey. *Br Br-so.* (Gomes de Matos 1988:p.c.) 20.
2. any northeasterner. *Br Br-so.* (Gomes de Matos 1988:p.c.) 20.
[M., f. Acc. Gomes de Matos, syn. *pau-de-arara.* Cf. **nordestino.**]

bom cidadão 'good citizen'
black person, esp. one who understands his or her place in the social structure. *Br* (Silva 1987:74) 20.
[M., f. Acc. Silva, sim. to *bom escravo* from slave period. Cf. **mau cidadão.**]

bom escravo — See *bom cidadão*

bom-cabelo 'good hair'
black person. *Br* (Chamberlain and Harmon 1983:74) 20.
[Slang. Cf. **branco cabelo bom,** Sp. **pelo bueno.**]

boneco de alodê
black person with very dark, shiny skin color. *Br-BA-Salvador* (Megenney 1978:46) 20.
[Ptg. *boneco* 'doll;' *alodê* < African lg., acc. Megenney. Cf. **preto retinto.**]

bororo
person of the Bororo or Boróro Indian tribe of central Br, esp. MT. *Br* (Buarque de Holanda 1975:220; Rodrigues 1986:49; Gomes de Matos 1988:p.c.) 20.

[Acc. Buarque de Holanda, syn. *otuque*. Var. *boróro*. Cf. **fulniô, tapanhuna.**]

boróro — See *bororo*

brancal 'whitish'
person with pale or whitish skin color and otherwise black physical features. *Br* (Nuñez 1980:86) 20.
[Cf. **branco.**]

brancão 'big white one'
1. mean or evil white man. *Br* (Nuñez 1980:86) n.d.
2. white man of poor social graces. *Br-PB* (Buarque de Holanda 1975:224) 20.
[M. Derog. Acc. Buarque de Holanda, df. 2 slang. Cf. **brancal, brancarão, branco.**]

brancarana — See *brancarano*

brancarano
light-skinned mulatto with many white features. *Br-Minas Velhas* (Souza 1961:198) cl ‖ *Br* (Chamberlain and Harmon 1983:79) 20.
[Acc. Souza, < *branco* 'white' + Tupi *rana* 'false.' Syn. *mulato claro*. Var. of *brancarão*. Acc. Chamberlain and Harmon, *brancarana* 'mulatto woman.' Cf. **branco, brancarão, mameluco.**]

brancarão
mulatto with very light, almost white, skin color. *Br* (Freyre 1964:405) cl.
[F. form *brancarona*. Acc. Mellafe (1975:115), Brz. equiv. of Sp. *mulato morisco* or *morisco* and Engl. *quadroon*. Syn. *mulato claro*. Cf. **branco, brancarano.**]

brancarona — See *brancarão*

brancarrão
mulatto who rose in social status as a result of light skin color. *Br* (Levine 1979:35) cl.
[F. form *brancarrona*. Cf. **brancarano, brancarão, branco.**]

brancarrona — See *brancarrão*

branco 'white'
1a. white person. *Br* (Hutchinson 1952:27–31 and 1957:117; Harris 1964a:58–59; Sanjek 1971:1129; Thompson 1965a:29) 20prior.
1b. person whose skin color is white, acc. 1976 household census. *Br* (Soares and Silva 1987:166) 20.
1c. white person of high social status, esp. in relation to the interlocutor. *Br-BA* (Pierson 1942:371) mid20.

1d. offspring of 2 whites; white person. *Br* (Diégues 1963:103) 20.

1e. white person, acc. blacks. *Br-n.e.* (Souza 1961:47) cl–20.

1f. person with white skin color, acc. 1980 census. *Br* (Silva 1987:159) 20.

2. person of any skin color who holds the high social status of a white. *Br* (Thompson 1965a:29; Wagley 1949:224) 20.

[Df. 1e submissive, affect., or respect., often in phr. *meu branco,* sim. to So. Amer. Engl. *boss* or *bossman,* but not sim. to Amer. Sp. *mi blanco* 'honey, my sweetie.' Acc. Silva, df. 1f color classification. Acc. Thompson, df. 2 can be *moreno* or any dark-skinned person as a result of social and financial importance, following the old adage "money whitens." Acc. Sanjek, 1 of ten most used racial terms in Salvador. Acc. Dirétoria Geral de Estátistica (1873–76) census figures of 1872, *branco,* along with *pardo, preto,* and *caboclo* could be free persons. Cf. **acastanhado, agalegado, alvo, amarelado, avermelhado, bem branco, brancarano, brancarão, brancarrão, vermelho,** Sp. **blanco.**]

branco africano 'African white'

person whose skin color is probably light and whose other physical features resemble those of a black, acc. survey. *Br* (Harris 1970:5) 20.

[Cf. **africano, branco.**]

branco amarelo 'yellow white person'

yellow-skinned white person, acc. survey. *Br* (Harris 1970:5) 20.

[Cf. **amarelo, branco, branco africano.**]

branco avermelhado 'reddish-white person'

person with reddish or reddish-white skin color, acc. 1980 census. *Br* (Silva 1987:159) 20.

[Acc. Silva, color classification. Cf. **acastanhado, agalegado, alvo, amarelado, avermelhado, bem branco, branco melado, branco moreno, branco pálido, branco queimado, branco sardento, branco sujo, vermelho.**]

branco cabelo bom 'white with good hair'

white or white-skinned person with straight hair. *Br-BA-Salvador* (Sanjek 1971:1140) 20.

[*Cabelo bom* 'good hair' and *cabelo ruim* 'bad hair' are factors in deciding Brz. races, sim. to Sp. Amer. *pelo bueno* or *pelo malo.* Var. *branco de cabelo bom.* Cf. **bom-cabelo, branco, branco de cabelo liso, branco de cabelo ruim,** Sp. **pelo bueno, pelo malo.**]

branco caboclado '*caboclo*-like white'

1a. white person who has traits of the mestizo. *Br* (Harris

1964a:58) 20.

1b. white person whose race is uncertain. *Br* (Levine 1980:21) 20

2. mulatto with light skin color. *Br* (Levine 1980:21) 20.
[Cf. **branco, caboclado, caboclo.**]

branco da Bahia 'Bahian white'

1a. mulatto. *Br-PA* (Souza 1961:47); *Br* (Levine 1980:21) 20.

1b. mulatto, esp. one from BA who can pass for white. *Br* (Chamberlain and Harmon 1983:80) 20.

2a. white person who has some small amount of black ancestry. *Br* (Degler 1971:99) 20.

2b. person whose skin color is almost white but who has black features. *Br* (Levine 1979:35) 20.

3. white person; person of mixed race with white skin. *Br* exc. *BA* (Pierson 1942:139) mid20.

[Generally euph. Acc. Levine, df. 1 mocking. Syn. df. 2a *branco da terra*. Acc. Levine, person defined in df. 2b could pass for white in US. Acc. Pierson, syn. df. 3 *branco por procuração*. Acc. van den Berghe (1967:71), var. *branco de Bahia*. Acc. Buarque de Holanda (1975:224), var. *branco-da-baía*; iron.; syn. *mulato*. Other var. *branco-da-bahia*. Cf. **branco, branco da terra.**]

branco-da-bahia — See *branco da Bahia*

branco-da-baía — See *branco da Bahia*

branco da terra 'white from the land'

1a. person whose features are those of a white but who has some blacks for ancestors. *Br-n.e.* (Hutchinson 1957:118) 20.

1b. white person with some black ancestry. *Br* (Kottak 1967:41; Hutchinson 1952:24, 27–31) 20.

2. *moreno* with yellowish skin color. *Br-n.e.* (Hutchinson 1957:118) 20.

[Acc. Alvarez Nazario (1974:357), sim. to Amer. Sp. *blanco del país*. Acc. Silva (1987:158), used also in BA. Acc. Degler (1971:103), person may pass completely for and receive same social treatment as white. Syn. *branco da Bahia*. Var. *branco de terra*. Cf. **branco, branco da Bahia,** Sp. **blanco, blanco del país.**]

branco de Bahia — See *branco da Bahia*

branco de cabelo bom — See *branco cabelo bom*

branco de cabelo liso 'white with straight hair'

white person with straight hair. *Br-BA-Salvador* (Sanjek 1971:1140) 20.

[Cf. **branco, branco de cabelo bom, branco de cabelo ruim.**]

branco de cabelo ruim 'white with bad hair'

white person whose hair texture indicates some black ancestry.

Br-BA-Salvador (Sanjek 1971:1140) 20.
   [Cf. **branco, branco de cabelo bom, branco de cabelo liso.**]

branco de terra — See *branco da terra*

branco em comissão — See *negro pó de arroz*

branco índio 'Indian white'
   person whose skin color looks sim. to that of an Indian, acc. survey. *Br* (Harris 1970:5) 20.
   [Cf. **branco, índio.**]

branco legítimo 'legitimate white'
   white person with no racial mixture. *Br-BA-Salvador* (Sanjek 1971:1140) 20.
   [Cf. **branco, branco limpo, negro legítimo.**]

branco limpo 'clean white'
   white person with no racial mixture. *Br-BA-Salvador* (Sanjek 1971:1140) 20.
   [Cf. **branco, branco legítimo.**]

branco louro 'blond white'
   person whose hair color indicates white race. *Br-BA-Salvador* (Sanjek 1971:1140) 20.
   [Cf. **branco, louro.**]

branco melado 'honey-colored white'
   person with honey-brown skin color, acc. 1980 census. *Br* (Silva 1987:159) 20.
   [Acc. Silva, color classification. Cf. **acastanhado, agalegado, alvo, amarelado, avermelhado, bem branco, branco avermelhado, branco moreno, branco pálido, melado, vermelho.**]

branco mestiço 'mestizo white'
   person whose skin color indicates racial mixture. *Br* (Harris 1970:5) 20.
   [Cf. **branco misturado, mestiço.**]

branco misturado 'mixed white'
   person whose skin color indicates racial mixture. *Br-SE* (Mott 1976:14) late18–early19.
   [Cf. **branco, branco caboclado, branco mestiço, misturado.**]

branco moreno 'brown or brunet white'
   1. light-skinned person of color. *Br* (Harris 1964b:21) 20.
   2. person with brown skin color, acc. 1980 census. *Br* (Silva 1987:159) 20.
   [Syn. df. 1 *pardo de matiz claro.* Acc. Silva, df. 2 color classification. Cf. **acastanhado, agalegado, alvo, amarelado, avermelhado, bem branco, branco, branco avermelhado,**

branco sujo, moreno, pardo de matiz claro.]
branco mulato 'mulatto white'
white person with features and skin color sim. to those of a
mulatto. *Br Br-BA-Arembepe* (Harris and Kottak 1963:203; Harris
1964a:58) 20.
[Cf. **branco, branco moreno, mulato.**]
branco nagô 'black African white'
white person whose skin color indicates racial mixture, acc.
survey. *Br* (Harris 1970:5) 20.
[Cf. **branco, nagô.**]
branco não legítimo 'not true white'
white person who is not all white. *Br-BA-Salvador* (Sanjek
1971:1140) 20.
[Cf. **branco, branco legítimo, branco limpo, branco sarará.**]
branco pálido 'pallid white'
person with pallid or very light skin color, acc. 1980 census. *Br*
(Silva 1987:159) 20.
[Acc. Silva, color classification. Cf. **acastanhado, agalegado, alvo,
amarelado, avermelhado, bem branco, branco, branco
avermelhado, branco melado, branco moreno, branco queimado, branco sardento, branco sujo, moreno.**]
branco por procuração 'white by proxy'
mulatto. *Br-BA* (Pierson 1942:139) mid20 ‖ *Br* (Levine
1980:21) 20.
[Acc. Levine, very mocking, used behind backs. Syn. *branco da
Bahia*. Cf. **branco da Bahia.**]
branco queimado 'burnt white'
person with reddish or browned-white skin color, acc. 1980
census. *Br* (Silva 1987:159) 20.
[Acc. Silva, color classification. Cf. **acastanhado, agalegado, alvo,
amarelado, avermelhado, bem branco, branco, branco
avermelhado, branco melado, branco moreno, branco pálido,
branco sardento, branco sujo, moreno.**]
branco rico 'rich white'
rich or well-off townsperson, usually white but sometimes
mulatto or black, acc. rural people. *Br* (Nuñez 1980:87) n.d.
[Cf. **branco, preto rico.**]
branco sarará '*sarará* white'
white person with the physical features of a *sarará*. *Br Br-BA-
Salvador* (Sanjek 1971:1140); *Br* (Harris 1964a:58 and 1970:5) 20.
[Acc. Harris (1970:5), *branco serará* [*sic*]. Cf. **branco, branco
moreno, branco mulato, sarará.**]

branco sardento 'freckled white'
person with freckled white skin color, acc. 1980 census. *Br*
(Silva 1987:159) 20.
[Acc. Silva, color classification. Cf. **acastanhado, agalegado, alvo,
amarelado, avermelhado, bem branco, branco, branco
avermelhado, branco melado, branco moreno, branco pálido,
branco queimado, branco sujo, moreno.**]

branco serará — See *branco sarará*

branco sujo 'dirty white'
person with dirty-white or brownish skin color, acc. 1980
census. *Br* (Silva 1987:159) 20.
[Acc. Silva, color classification. Cf. **acastanhado, agalegado, alvo,
amarelado, avermelhado, bem branco, branco, branco
avermelhado, branco melado, branco moreno, branco pálido,
branco queimado, branco sardento, moreno.**]

brancoso
very light-skinned or pallid person. *Br* (Buarque de Holanda
1975:224) 20.
[< *branco* 'white' + adj. suf. *-oso*. Cf. **branco.**]

brancozinho 'little white'
small white person; white person of mixed race. *Br-BA-
Salvador* (Sanjek 1971:1140) 20.
[< *branco* + dim. suf. *-zinho*. Cf. **brancarão, branco.**]

branqueado 'whitened'
person who is almost white; black person trying to pass for
white. *Br* (Nuñez 1980:88) 20prior.
[Cf. **brancal, branco.**]

branquiça — See *branquiço*

branquiço 'whitish'
person with dirty-white or whitish skin color, acc. 1980 census.
Br (Silva 1987:159) 20.
[Acc. Silva, color classification; *branquiça* [*sic*]. Cf. **acastanhado,
agalegado, alvo, amarelado, avermelhado, bem branco,
branco, branco avermelhado, branco melado, branco
moreno, branco pálido, branco queimado, branco sardento,
moreno.**]

branquinho 'little white one; whitish'
person with whitish skin color, acc. 1980 census. *Br* (Silva
1987:159) 20.
[< *branco* 'white' + dim. suf. *-inho*. Acc. Silva, color classification;
branquiça [*sic*]. Cf. **acastanhado, agalegado, alvo, amarelado,
avermelhado, bem branco, branco, branco avermelhado,**

branco melado, branco moreno, branco pálido, branco queimado, branco sardento, branquiço, moreno.]

brasilíndio 'Brazilian Indian'

Indian native to Br; Brazilian Indian. *Br* (Buarque de Holanda 1975:225–26) 20.

[Acc. Buarque, < *Brasil* + *índio,* recently coined but not widely accepted. Cf. **ameríndio.**]

bravi 'fierce ones'

1. black, *caboclo,* or *cabra* who fought in battles for whites. *Br* (Freyre 1964:405) cl.

2. black slave who defended the plantation against Indian attacks, protected the estate's autonomy, fought in battles against the Dutch, or attacked runaway slave camps. *Br* (Nuñez 1980:88) prior20.

[Generally m. pl. < *bravo* 'fierce.' Cf. **caboclo, cabra.**]

brum-brum

1. African or black who speaks Portuguese poorly or unintelligibly. *Br-RS* (Coruja et al. 1964:77) 20.

2. person who uses lg. poorly or with difficulty. *Br-RS* (Coruja et al. 1964:77) 20.

[Syn. *negro brum-brum.* Var. *brumbrum.* Cf. **boçal.**]

brumbrum — See *brum-brum*

bugra — See *bugre*

bugre 'bugger, sodomite; uncivilized'

1a. Indian. *Br* (Freyre 1964:406) cl; (Baldus and Willems 1939:35) early20.

1b. jungle-dwelling Indian, usually uncivilized. *Br-RS* (Coruja et al. 1964:79) 20.

1c. Botocudo Indian native to eastern Br, acc. Portuguese colonizers. *Br* (Vergara Martín 1922:231) cl.

2. uncivilized, jungle-dwelling person, esp. the fierce Amerindian or the *caboclo. Br* (Souza 1961:52) 20.

[M., f. Also f. form *bugra,* acc. Coruja et al. Df. 1a and 1b pejor., derog. Sim. to *chuncho* or *jívaro* of Bo and Pe. Acc. Alonso (1958: 1.793), < Fr. *bougre.* Acc. Bayo (1910:38 and 1931:49), old maps of Pe and Pg indicated warnings such as *"aquí empiezan los bugres"* 'here are the fierce Indians,' sim. to the ancient geographies' listing of *"hic sunt leones"* 'here begin the lions.' Cf. **bravi, índio.**]

bujamé

1. mulatto of light or clear skin color. *Br-CE* (Ramos 1941:537) mid20.

2. offspring of a black and a white; light mulatto. *Br-CE* (Woodbridge 1948:356) cl.

3. offspring of a black and a mulatto. *Br* (Buarque de Holanda 1975:233) 20.

[Syn. df. 2 *mulato claro*. Acc. Buarque, < African lg. Almost excl. to CE in n.e. Br.]

bundo 'incorrect manner of speaking; native of Angola'

black native of Angola. *Br* (Schneider 1985:230) 20.

[Acc. Schneider, < Kimbundu *ambundo* 'group of people.' Cf. Sp. **bundo.**]

burro-fugido 'fled donkey'

person of mixed race. *Br* (Silva 1987:158) mid20.

[Acc. Silva, color designation. Cf. **acastanhado, amarelado, avermelhado, bem moreno, mameluco, mestiço, moreno, branco, vermelho.**]

C

caatingueiro

person with Indian features. *Br-n.e.* (Hutchinson 1957:118) 20.

[Acc. Ayrosa (1937:67–70), < *caatinga* 'dry n. Brz. scrubland' (< *caá* 'leaf, tree, forest' + *tinga* 'white, whitish, powdery-dry white') + suf. *-eiro*. Syns. *caboclo, sertanejo*. Cf. **caboclo, sertanejo.**]

cabeça-chata 'dumb-head'

1. northeasterner, acc. southerners. *Br* (Cabral 1982:146) 19–20.

2. person from CE; by ext., any northerner. *Br* (Buarque de Holanda 1975:239–40) 20.

[M., f. Nickname. Syn. *nordestino*. Ant. *sulista*.]

cabeça-seca 'dry-head'

black slave. *Br-PE* (Buarque de Holanda 1975:240) prior20.

[M., f. Derog. nickname. Cf. **cabeça-chata.**]

cabelo corredio 'flowing hair'

person from Goa; any Asian with straight hair. *Br-MG* (Russell-Wood 1982:24–25) 18.

[Usually in phr. *ter o cabelo corredio*. Cf. **branco cabelo bom, cabelo de bom-bril.**]

cabelo de bom-bril 'Brillo-pad hair'

black person with kinky hair. *Br* (Chamberlain and Harmon 1983:90) 20.

[Usually in phr. *ter o cabelo de bom-bril*. Acc. Chamberlain and Harmon, slang, pejor.; *Bom-bril* 'popular type of steel wool pad.' Cf. **cabelo corredio.**]

cabelo-de-fogo 'fire-head'

person with red hair; redhead; carrot-top. *Br* (Chamberlain and Harmon 1983:91) 20.

[Acc. Chamberlain and Harmon, slang.]
cabo verde 'Cape Verdean'
1. offspring of an Indian and a black. *Br* (Woodbridge 1948:356)
cl ‖ *Br Br-BA* (Souza 1961:61; Ramos 1941:537); *Br-BA* (Diégues
1963:105) 20.
2. very dark-skinned person, though lighter than a *preto,* with
long straight black hair and fine facial features, including thin lips
and a narrow nose like those of a white. *Br-BA* (Pierson 1942:136)
mid20 ‖ *Br-n.e.* (Harris 1956:119; Hutchinson 1957:119; Kottak
1967:44); *Br* (Levine 1979:38) 20.
3. person whose skin color indicates African origins. *Br-BA*
(Sanjek 1971:1129); *Br* (Hutchinson 1952:27–31; Harris 1964a:58)
20.

[< *Cabo Verde* 'important island in the Atlantic off the we. African
coast, used as a port of departure for African slaves.' Acc. Sanjek
(1971:1129), 1 of 10 most used terms in Salvador. Vars. *caboverde,*
cabo-verde, caboverdiano. Syns. *caburé, cafuz.* Cf. **cabo verde**
claro, cabo verde escuro, cabo verde legítimo, caboré,
cafuso.]

cabo verde claro 'light Cape Verdean'
person whose skin color is usually very dark. *Br-BA-Salvador*
(Sanjek 1971:1141) 20.
[Euph. Cf. **cabo verde, cabo verde escuro, claro, moreno**
claro.]

cabo verde escuro 'dark Cape Verdean'
person whose skin color is very dark. *Br-BA-Salvador* (Sanjek
1971:1141) 20.
[Cf. **cabo verde, cabo verde claro, escuro.**]

cabo verde legítimo 'real Cape Verdean'
person whose skin color and other features fit all the traits of a
Cape Verdean. *Br-BA-Salvador* (Sanjek 1971:1141) 20.
[Cf. **cabo verde, cabo verde claro, cabo verde escuro, negro**
legítimo.]

cabo-verde — See *cabo verde*

cabocla — See *caboclo*

caboclado '*caboclo*-like'
person who has all the traits of a *caboclo. Br-n.e.* (Harris and
Kottak 1963:203); *Br-BA* (Sanjek 1971:1140) 20.
[< *caboclo* 'mestizo' + adj. suf. *-ado.* Cf. **caboclo, mestizo, mulato**
amestizado.]

caboclinho 'little *caboclo*'
small person or child whose traits are those of a *caboclo. Br-BA-*
Salvador (Sanjek 1971:1140) 20.

[< *caboclo* + dim. suf. *-inho*. Cf. **caboclo, caboclado.**]
caboclo 'copperish; copper-colored'

1a. person whose skin color indicates mixed ancestry, usually mestizo. *Br* (Hutchinson 1952:27–32; Harris 1964a:58; Sanjek 1971:1129; Aguirre Beltrán 1972:178) cl–20.

1b. descendant of Indians; person with Amerindian phenotype. *Br* (Ramos 1944:30); *Br-n.e.* (Hutchinson 1957:118); *Br-RS* (Coruja et al. 1964:81) 20.

1c. offspring of a white and an Indian; mestizo. *Br-no.* (Kelsey 1940:210) cl ‖ *Br* (Woodbridge 1948:356; Rosenblat 1954:2.107) cl; (Megenney 1978:85) 18; (Ayrosa 1937:71; Malaret 1942:222) mid20; (Wagley 1949:222; Freyre 1964:406; Mörner 1967:70–71) cl–20; (Bailey and Nasatir 1973:766; Burns 1980:547) 20prior; (Ramos 1941:534; Boxer 1962:17; Thompson 1965a:29; Fernandes 1969:461; Alba 1969:34; Azevedo 1970:2.174; Smith 1974:58; Buarque de Holanda 1975:242; Levine 1979:39 and 1980:24) 20.

1d. offspring of an Indian and anyone of some other racial category. *Br* (Harris 1964a:115) 20.

1e. westernized or acculturated mestizo from the interior of the country. *Br* (van den Berghe 1967:62) cl–19.

1f. offspring of a white and an Indian with copperish skin color and straight hair. *Br* (Mattoso 1986:250) prior20.

1g. offspring of a white and an Indian, or mestizo, esp. one from the interior. *Br* (Chamberlain and Harmon 1983:92); *Br-BA* (Amado 1975:557) 20.

1h. offspring of a white man and an Indian woman. *Br* (Cascudo 1962:156–57) 20prior.

1i. river dweller of Indian and white European heritage. *Br-AM* (McCartney 1988:9) late20.

2a. Indian. *Br* (Wagley 1949:222; Freyre 1964:406; Mörner 1967:70–71) cl–20; (Cascudo 1962:156–57) 18; (Baldus and Willems 1939:36) early20prior; (Malaret 1942:222) mid20 ‖ *Br-BA* (Pierson 1942:371) mid20; (Levine 1979:39) 20.

2b. offspring of 2 Indians. *Br* (Diégues 1963:103) 20.

2c. acculturated, civilized, Europeanized, or Brazilianized Indian. *Br* (Johnston 1910:107; Smith 1974:58; Burns 1980:547) 20prior; (Ayrosa 1937:71) mid20 ‖ *Br-BA* (Amado 1975:557) 20.

2d. Indian servant or civilized Indian. *Br* (Baldus and Willems 1939:36) early20prior.

2e. Indian of Br. *Br* (Levine 1980:24) 20; (Bailey and Nasatir 1973:766) 20prior.

3a. offspring of an Indian father and a black mother. *Br* (Woodbridge 1948:356) cl.

3b. offspring of an Indian and a black, usually woman of low social standing. *Br* (Cabral 1982:150) 20.

4a. rustic, backwoods type, of crude manners; hillbilly. *Br* (Freyre 1964:406; Souza 1961:59–60); *Br-BA* (Megenney 1978:85); *Br-sertão* (Almeida Oliveira 1940:53) 20prior ‖ *Br-MG, -RJ, -SP* (Baldus and Willems 1939:36) early20prior ‖ *Br-GO, -MG, -SP* (Ayrosa 1937:81) mid20 ‖ *Br-AM-Manaus* (River tour guide 1987:p.c.); *Br-AM, -n.e.* (Levine 1979:39 and 1980:24) 20.

4b. poor farm laborer who subsists on a small plot of land; sharecropper. *Br* (Fernandes 1969:461); *Br-no.* (Bailey and Nasatir 1973:766) 20.

4c. poor rural person of low social class. *Br Br-AM* (Wagley 1971:71, 101); *Br-AM, -n.e.* (Levine 1980:24) 20.

4d. person from the interior of the country. *Br* (Cascudo 1962:156–57) 20prior ‖ *Br-MG, -RJ, -SP* (Baldus and Willems 1939:36) early20prior.

5. mulatto with copperish skin color and straight hair. *Br-BA* (Amado 1975:557); *Br* (Cascudo 1962:156–57) 20.

[Syn. df. 4a *caipira*. Df. 4b social classification. Df. 4c syns. *tabaréu* in BA, *jeca* in SP, acc. Wagley. Acc. Cascudo, syn. df. 4d *cabouçolo* and *indígena* 18 cent.; df. 5 *mulato acobreado com cabelo corrido*. Acc. Machado (1952:1.431) and Ayrosa, < Tupi *caá* 'forest' + *bóc* 'taken from.' Acc. Baldus and Willems, < Tupi *ka'a'vo* 'person who inhabits the mato;' possibly sim. to Surinam Negro *kabugru*. Acc. Buarque de Holanda, < Tupi *kari'boka* 'rel. to or < white.' Acc. Santamaría (1942:1.248), used in ref. to person's dirty copper skin color. Acc. Alonso (1958:1.820), sim. to *colono* in Co. Other syns. *caatingueiro, caburé, cabo verde, cabra, cafuso, curiboca, cariboca, indígena, jeca, mameluco, roceiro, sertanejo, tabaréu, tapuia, matuto, restingueiro, sertanejo.* Vars. *caboco, cabôucolo, cabôcolo, cabocolo, cobocolor, cabôco, cabouco, cabouculo, cabocro.* Cf. **caboclado, caatingueiro, caipira, curiboca, sertanejo, tapuio.**]

caboclo araçuabo
person whose skin color indicates racial mixture. *Br-BA-Salvador* (Sanjek 1971:1140) 20.

[Cf. **araçuabo, caboclo, caboclo cabelo de flecha.**]

caboclo brabo 'wild *caboclo*'
Indian who is not yet civilized. *Br-no.* (Ayrosa 1937:71–72) 20prior ‖ *Br* (Cabral 1982:150) 20.

[Acc. Ayrosa, *caboclo bravio* [sic]; ant. *caboclo manso*. Possible syn. *íncola*. Cf. **caboclo, caboclo manso.**]

caboclo bravio — See *caboclo brabo*

caboclo cabelo de flecha '*caboclo* with arrow-straight hair'
person whose skin color and hair texture indicate racial mixture, usually between whites and Indians. *Br-BA-Salvador* (Sanjek 1971:1140) 20.
[Cf. **caboclo, caboclo araçuabo, moreno de cabelo bom, moreno de cabelo ruim.**]

caboclo cabo verde 'Cape Verdean *caboclo*'
person whose dark skin color indicates racial mixture, possibly between blacks and Indians. *Br-BA-Salvador* (Sanjek 1971:1140) 20.
[Cf. **cabo verbe, caboclo.**]

caboclo claro 'light *caboclo*'
person whose light skin color indicates racial mixture, possibly between whites and Indians. *Br-BA-Salvador* (Sanjek 1971:1140) 20.
[Cf. **caboclo, caboclo escuro, claro, moreno claro.**]

caboclo de beira
caboclo who resides along a river; riverbank dweller. *Br* (Levine 1980:24) 20.
[Cf. **caboclo.**]

caboclo escuro 'dark *caboclo*'
person whose dark skin color indicates racial mixture, probably with blacks. *Br* (Harris 1964a:58) 20.
[Cf. **caboclo, caboclo claro, caboclo preto, escuro.**]

caboclo manso 'tame *caboclo*'
Indian who is acculturated or civilized. *Br-no.* (Ayrosa 1937:71–72) 20prior.
[Acc. Ayrosa, ant. *caboclo bravio.* Cf. **caboclo, caboclo brabo.**]

caboclo preto 'black *caboclo*'
person, possibly with straight hair, whose black skin color indicates racial mixture, probably with blacks. *Br* (Harris 1970:5) 20.
[Cf. **caboclo, caboclo claro, caboclo escuro, preto.**]

caboco, cabôco — See *caboclo*

caboré
1a. offspring of a black runaway slave who formed part of a *quilombo* and an Indian woman who had been raped by the slave. *Br-interior* (Rosenblat 1954:2.106) cl.
1b. offspring of a black and an Indian. *Br* (Freyre 1964:406; Woodbridge 1948:356) cl; (Ramos 1941:536) mid20; (Ribeiro n.d.:20) n.d.
2a. person whose skin color indicates racial mixture. *Br* (Aguirre Beltrán 1972:178) cl; (Ramos 1947:29) 20.
2b. light-brown-skinned person whose skin color is sim. to that

of the *caboclo. Br-RS* (Coruja et al. 1964:83) 20.

3. light-skinned mestizo. *Br Br-so.* (Cascudo 1962:158) 20.

4a. Indian. *Br-MG* (Diégues 1963:105) 20.

4b. Cariri Indian of RN. *Br-RN* (Cascudo 1962:158) late17.

5. rustic, unacculturated type; hick. *Br-GO, -MG* (Ayrosa 1937:81) mid20prior.

[Syn. df. 5 *caipira.* Acc. Machado (1952–59:1.431–32), Cammarota (1963:19), Granada (1957:1.123), and Cascudo, < Tupi or Tupi-Guarani *caá* 'mato' + *boré* or *poré* 'dweller;' also bird with scientific name *cabure Brasiliensibus.* Acc. Cammarota, in Ar *caburei* 'fierce bird of prey.' Acc. Santamaría (1942:1.249), 'type of owl, gray and rounded with a very sharp beak.' Acc. Cascudo, vars. *caburé, cauré* 'type of hawk' in AM. Other var. *cabaré,* acc. Mellafe. Syns. *caboclo, cafuso.* Cf. **cafuso, caboclo.**]

caboverde — See *cabo verde*

caboverdiano — See *cabo verde*

cabra

1. person whose skin color indicates racial mixture. *Br* (Hutchinson 1952:27–31) 20.

2a. offspring of a black and a mulatto. *Br* (Woodbridge 1948:356) cl; (Souza 1961:61–62; Cascudo 1962:158) 20; (Vergara Martín 1922:231) n.d. ‖ *Br-RS* (Coruja et al. 1964:82) 20 ‖ *Br-n.e., -coast* (Diégues 1963:103, 105) 20 ‖ *Br-BA* (Pierson 1942:371) mid20.

2b. offspring of a black and a mulatto, with very light skin color. *Br* (Mattoso 1986:250) 20.

2c. offspring of a black man and a mulatto woman. *Br* (Vergara Martín 1922:231) n.d.

3. offspring of a white and a black; mulatto. *Br* (Woodbridge 1948:356) cl; (Ramos 1941:537) 20 ‖ *Br-RS* (Coruja et al. 1964:82) 20.

4. person who has lighter skin color, longer and straighter hair, a narrower nose, and fewer black facial features than does a *preto. Br-BA* (Pierson 1942:136) mid20 ‖ *Br-n.e.* (Hutchinson 1957:119; Kottak 1967:43–44) 20.

5a. person who is a mixture of African black, white European, and Indian; dark-skinned mestizo. *Br* (Woodbridge 1948:356; Freyre 1964:406) cl; (Ramos 1941:537) mid20; (Levine 1979:39 and 1980:24) 20.

5b. mestizo of 50% black, 40% Indian, and 10% white, known for being courageous and adventurous and found in folk tales of today. *Br-n.e.* (Kelsey 1940:60) cl.

5c. person who is a descendant of blacks, whites, and Indians and who has light-brown, pallid, or earth-toned skin color. *Br* (Cabral 1982:150–51) 20.

6. offspring of a black and an Indian. *Br* (Baldus and Willems 1939:36–37) mid20.

7a. mestizo with light skin color. *Br-n.e.* (Diégues 1963:105) 20.

7b. mestizo woman with dark skin. *Br* (Woodbridge 1948:356; Freyre 1964:406; Levine 1980:24) 20.

8. brash young person with dark skin, often of low class or social standing. *Br* (Cabral 1982:152) 20.

9. rustic, uncivilized type; hick; hillbilly. *Br-CE* (Ayrosa 1937:81); *Br-CE, -n.e.* (Baldus and Willems 1939:36–37) mid20.

10. bodyguard to a *coronel,* or wealthy landowner. *Br* (Levine 1979:39) 20.

11. person of low social class or standing. *Br* (Cabral 1982:150–51) 20.

[M., f. Alternate m. or f. form *cabrocha.* Df. 2c sim. to Sp. *zambo.* Syn. df. 6 *cariboca.* Syns. df. 8 *caipira* and in so. Br *caboclo.* Other syns. *mestiço, mulato, zambo, cabrocha, cabriola, caboclo escuro, mulato escuro, fulo, bode, cabrito.* Acc. Machado (1952:1.433), att. as 'goat' around 990; *cabrocha* att. from late 19-cent.; meaning 'kid goat' > 'kid, small child' > 'child of dark coloration' > 'anyone old or young from mixed parentage.' Var. *cabre.* Acc. Cabral, dim. derivs. in c.w. and so. Br *cabrochinho, cabrochinha < cabrocha.* Other derivs. *cabrito, cabriola, cabrocha, cabroeira* 'group of *cabras.*' Acc. Cascudo, *cabra-cabriola* 'boogeyman' in Br. Acc. Pierson, popular slang var. *caibra.* Cf. **caboclo, caboré, mulato escuro, cabra de engenho.**]

cabra de engenho

person who works on the *engenho,* or sugar plantation. *Br* (Aguirre Beltrán 1972:178) cl.

[Cf. **cabra, cabre.**]

cabra-seco

black person who is overly aggressive. *Br* (Levine 1979:39) 20.

[M., f. Cf. **cabra.**]

cabre — See *cabra*

cabriola — See *cabra*

cabritinho — See *cabrito*

cabrito

mulatto; dark-skinned person. *Br-sertão* (Almeida Oliveira 1940:54) mid20.

[< *cabra* + dim. suf. *-ito.* Deriv. and syn. *cabritinho.* Other syns. *moreno, mulato, pardo.* Cf. **cabra, caboré, mulato, pardo, moreno.**]

cabrocha — See *cabra*
cabrochinho — See *cabra*
cabrochinha — See *cabra*
caburé — See *caboré*
caburete
offspring of an Indian and a black. *Br* (Johnston 1910:56)
early20prior.
[Sim. to Sp. *zambo* in SA. Cf. **cabra, caboré.**]
café-com-leite 'café-au-lait; coffee-colored'
1. mulatto woman with coffee-brown skin. *Br* (Levine 1980:25)
20.
2. offspring of a white and a black; mulatto; white and black
couple. *Br* (Buarque de Holanda 1975:249) 20.
[M., f. Acc. Levine, sexual connotations; syn. *morena*. Df. 2 sim. to
No. Amer. Engl. *salt-and-pepper.*]
cafre 'infidel'
black slave of the Bantu tribes in southeastern Africa. *Br*
(Péreda Valdés 1937:74) cl.
[Acc. Machado (1952:1.451), Ptg. slavers brought these slaves to the
rest of Europe. Acc. Alonso (1958:1.838), meaning 'inhabitant of ea.
Africa' prevalent since 17 cent. Cf. Sp. **cafre.**]
cafus — See *cafuso*
cafuso
1. offspring of a black and a mulatto. *Br* (Woodbridge 1948:356)
cl.
2a. offspring of a black and an Indian. *Br-no., -n.e.* (Cascudo
1962:165) late19 ‖ *Br* (Woodbridge 1948:356–57; Freyre
1964:407; Poppino 1968:58; Santamaría 1942:1.264; Aguirre
Beltrán 1972:178) cl; (Megenney 1978:85) 18; (Ramos 1947:29)
late19; (Pierson 1942:119, 371; Ramos 1941:536–37, 1944:30, 205,
and 1947:29) mid20; (Zimmerman 1952:95; Souza 1961:66;
Diégues 1963:103, 105; Harris 1964a:87; Thompson 1965a:29;
Bailey and Nasatir 1973:766; Levine 1979:40; Chamberlain and
Harmon 1983:97) 20; (Ribeiro n.d.:20; Vergara Martín 1922:231)
n.d.; (Levine 1980:25) 20prior.
2b. offspring of a black and an Indian with dark, straight hair;
zambo. Br (Mendonça 1935:247) cl–mid20; (Mattoso 1986:250;
Chamberlain and Harmon 1983:97) 20.
3. offspring of a *mameluco* and a black, of a mulatto and an
Indian, of a *curiboca* and an Indian, of a *curiboca* and a black, of a
curiboca and a white, or of a *curiboca* and a mulatto. *Br-PA* (Santa
Rosa 1922:2.131) 19–early20.

[Acc. Souza and Ramos (1947:29), in modern parlance represents physical type of a black person, with very dark skin and high, curly afros. Acc. Levine (1980:25), given name after Ptg. and black slaves penetrated the c.w. and we. interiors of Br from SP. Acc. Zimmerman, intermediate step between a black and an Indian. Acc. Ramos, *linda raça mestiça*. Vars. *cafus, cafuz, cafuzo, cafúzio, carafúzio, carafuso, carafuz, carafuzo*. Syns. *caboré, curiboca, taioca, cabaré, cariboca, caboré, curiboca, cabra, zambo*. Cf. **caboclo, cabra, curiboca, taioca.**]

cafuz — See *cafuso*

cafúzio — See *cafuso*

cafuzo — See *cafuso*

caibra — See *cabra*

caiçara

1. rustic type from the beach area; beach bum. *Br-SP-Santos* (Ayrosa 1937:81) mid20 ‖ *Br-SP* (Buarque de Holanda 1975:250) 20.

2. rustic type; hick. *Br-SP, -RJ* (Buarque de Holanda 1975:250) 20.

[Acc. Buarque de Holanda, < Tupi *kai'sara*; syn. df. 1 *praiano*; syn. df. 2 *caipira*. Acc. Souto Maior (1980:23), also in slang 'vagina.' Cf. **caipira, mameluco, restingueiro,** Sp. **playero.**]

caído 'fallen'

person with dark skin who uses cosmetics to lighten skin and thus pass to a lighter skin color classification. *Br* (Levine 1980:25) 20.

[Past partic. of *cair* 'to fall.' Acc. Levine, *caido* [*sic*].]

caipira 'rustic type; peasant'

1a. inhabitant of the country; hick; rustic type; hillbilly. *Br* (Freyre 1964:407; Souza 1961:68–69; Chamberlain and Harmon 1983:98); *Br-sertão* (Almeida Oliveira 1940:55) 20.

1b. hillbilly from MG. *Br-MG* (Kelsey 1940:150) mid20.

2. uneducated, rural person of crude manners, who is unaware of customary dress habits in urban areas. *Br* (Cascudo 1962:166) 20.

3. inhabitant of the interior of the country. *Br* (Cascudo 1962:166) 20.

[M., f. Acc. Chamberlain and Harmon, colloq. Acc. Ayrosa (1937:79–80), < Tupi *caípora* 'timid, ashamed.' Acc. Souza, < Tupi *caapora* < *cai* or *caai* 'toasted or sunburnt' + *pora* 'skin.' Acc. Buarque de Holanda (1975:251), < Tupi *kai'pira*. Acc. Machado (1952:1.452), origin uncertain but linked with *caipora*, 19-cent. term used in ref. to the constitutionalists during the Brz. liberation struggles of 1828 to 1834. For long list of syns., see Buarque de Holanda and Souza. Cf. **cafuso, caiçara, caipira blanco, caipira caboclo, caipira preto, caipira mulato, caatingueiro, caboclo, mameluco.**]

caipira branco 'white *caipira*'
offspring of white foreigners. *Br* (Souza 1961:68–69) 20.
[M., f. Cf. **branco, caipira.**]

caipira caboclo
offspring of Indians christianized by the first settlers of the interior *sertão. Br* (Souza 1961:68–69) 20.
[M., f. Cf. **caboclo, caboclado, caipira, sertanejo.**]

caipira mulato 'mulatto *caipira*'
offspring of a black, either African or Brazilian, and a white, either Portuguese or Brazilian, or sometimes a *caboclo. Br* (Souza 1961:68–69) 20.
[M., f. Cf. **caipira, mulato.**]

caipira preto 'black *caipira*'
offspring of black Africans no longer found in Br. *Br* (Souza 1961:68–69) 20.
[M., f. Cf. **caipira, preto.**]

caivoca — See *curiboca*

calça curta 'short pants'
rustic type; hick. *Br-SP* (Ayrosa 1937:81) mid20.
[M., f. Syn. *caipira.* Cf. **caipira, cama de vara.**]

cama de vara 'bed of sticks'
rustic type; hick. *Br-SP* (Ayrosa 1937:81) mid20.
[M., f. Syn. *caipira.* Acc. Buarque de Holanda (1975:259), *cama-de-varas* 'rural worker, poor rural dweller.' Cf. **caipira, calça curta.**]

cama-de-vara — See *cama de vara*

camelô
street vendor, usually a *caboclo* or a Portuguese immigrant. *Br* (Levine 1980:26) 20.
[Acc. Levine, *camelo* [*sic*]. Acc. Buarque de Holanda (1975:262), < Fr. *camelot* 'street hawker.' Cf. **caboclo.**]

campeiro 'hick; hillbilly'
rustic type; hick; peasant; country dweller. *Br-RS* (Souza 1961:75) 20.
[< *campo* 'country, field.' Cf. **caipira,** Sp. **campero, campirano, campesino.**]

canarim
native of Goa; Asian. *Br-MG* (Russell-Wood 1982:24) 18.
[Cf. **chinês.**]

canário
black slave. *Br* (Leite de Vasconcellos 1928:363, 368) 16–17.
[Acc. Leite de Vasconcellos, used only after Ptg. overseas discoveries. Also used in ref. to 'canary,' bird introduced from the middle-Atlantic islands, and 'inhabitant of the Canary Islands in the Atlantic Ocean,' through which many African slaves passed on their way to America, acc. Corominas (1973:124). Cf. **guineu, cativo, escravo cativo, preto.**]

candango
1. Portuguese colonist, acc. black Africans native to Br. *Br* (Wagley 1971:90) cl.
2. laborer from northeastern Br coming to Brasília for work. *Br-DF* (Wagley 1971:90) 20.
3. inhabitant of Brasília. *Br* (Wagley 1971:90) 20.
[Acc. Wagley, < Bantu lg.; dfs. 2 and 3 used post-1960. Acc. Buarque de Holanda (1975:267), < Kimbundu *kangundu* 'ordinary, bad.' Cf. **galego.**]

caneludo 'cinnamon-like'
1. person whose skin color is sim. to the color of cinnamon, or reddish-brown. *Br* (Mott 1974:158) early19.
2. person who has long or big legs. *Br-RS* (Coruja et al. 1964:94) 20.
3. Portuguese person. *Br* (Souza 1961:156) 20.
[Acc. Coruja et al., also used in ref. to animals. Syn. df. 3 *galego*. < *canela* 'cinnamon; shank of the leg' + suf. *-udo*. Cf. **candango, galego,** Sp. **canelo, candelo, cano, negro pasudo.**]

cangaceiro — See *mameluco*

capiau — See *mameluco*

cara queimada 'burnt face'
black person, member of the Ewe people of the west African coast. *Br* (Mendonça 1935:79) cl.
[Acc. Mendonça, vulgar, colloq., pejor. Cf. **negro, preto.**]

carafus — See *cafuso*

carafuso — See *cafuso*

carafuz — See *cafuso*

carafúzio — See *cafuso*

carafuzo — See *cafuso*

caraíba
white European, acc. Brazilian Indians; Indian of Carib lg. *Br* (Freyre 1964:408) cl.
[M., f. Acc. Machado (1952:1.502), < Amerindian lg. *caribe* or *caníbal* 'cannibal.' Acc. Buarque de Holanda (1975:278), < Tupi

kara'ib 'astute, intelligent.' Iron. use in ref. to Europeans, since Indians may have thought that the newly arrived Europeans were anthropophagous. Cf. Sp. **caribe.**]

caramutanje
black slave recently arrived from Africa. *Br* (Souza 1961:88) cl.
[Syn. *boçal, negro novo.* Cf. **boçal, canário, crioulo, escravo, negro.**]

carcamano
1. Italian. *Br-RJ* (Chamberlain 1981:420; Buarque de Holanda 1975:281) 20.
2. Arab. *Br-MA* (Buarque de Holanda 1975:281) 20.
[Acc. Chamberlain, found in *gíria* slang of RJ. Acc. Buarque de Holanda, nickname. Cf. **bachicha, galego,** Sp. **carcamán.**]

cariba
foreigner, acc. Indians. *Br* (Souza 1961:89) 20.
[M., f. Cf. **caraíba,** Sp. **caribe.**]

cariboca — See *curiboca*

carijo — See *carijó*

carijó
person whose skin color indicates Indian ancestry. *Br* (Harris 1964a:87; Vianna 1937:84) 20.
[Acc. Santamaría (1942:1.323), 'Indians who lived between Cananea or Cananeia and the Los Patos River or Lagoon in SC, so. Br;' 'pre-Columbian Indian tribe of SoA;' 'tribe of Amazonian Indians;' 'Brz. Carib Indians who live in the upper Yapurá with the Uitotes and Macuches.' Acc. Machado (1952:1.510), < Tupi *caray-yó* 'descendant or deriving from the *caraíbas*,' sim. in meaning to *curiboca,* i.e., 'mixture or spotted with black and white.' Acc. Santamaría, var. *carijo.* Syn. *caboclo.* Cf. **caraíba, carió,** Sp. **caribe.**]

carimboca — See *curiboca*

carió
offspring of an Indian and a black. *Br-PE* (Diégues 1963:106) 18.
[Syns. *cariboca, carijó, curiboca.* Cf. **carijó, curiboca.**]

carioca
native of the city of RJ. *Br* (Cascudo 1962:184) 20prior.
[M., f. Acc. Ayrosa (1937:121–38), < Tupi *carí* 'white, Christian' or *acará* 'flowing river' + *óca* 'house; taken from.' Cf. **candango, paulista.**]

carnijó
person of the Carnijó Indian tribe found in PE. *Br* (Buarque de Holanda 1975:285) 20.
[Syns. *fulniô, formió.* Cf. **bororo, tapanhuna.**]

casaca
rustic type; hick. *Br-PI* (Ayrosa 1937:81) mid20.
[M., f. Syn. *caipira*. Cf. **caipira.**]

casta de Angola 'caste from Angola'
slave from the Angola area of Africa. *Br* (Levine 1980:30) prior20.
[Acc. Levine, includes *benguelas, congos,* and *manicongos.* Cf. **benguela, congo.**]

castelhano 'Castilian'
native of Ur or Ar. *Br-RS* (Coruja et al. 1964:109); *Br* (Buarque de Holanda 1975:293) 20.
[Syn. *oriental,* acc. Coruja et al. Cf. Sp. **brasilero, negro, oriental, paulista.**]

castiço
offspring of a mestizo and an Indian. *Br* (Woodbridge 1948:357) cl; (Santamaría 1942:1.334) mid20prior; (Vergara Martín 1922: 232) n.d.
[Acc. Vergara Martín, Santamaría, and Woodbridge, *castizo* [*sic*]. Acc. Corominas (1954–57:1.723 and 1973:138) and Alonso (1958:1.984), < *casta* 'caste.' Cf. **albino, mestiço,** Sp. **castizo.**]

catarinense — See *barriga verde*

cativo 'captive'
slave. *Br* (Mott 1974:171) early19; (Levine 1980:31) prior20.
[Acc. Cobarruvias (1611:321), used in ref. to 'infidels, or non-Christians.' Also found in 16–17-cent. Portugal, acc. Leite de Vasconcellos (1928:363). Cf. **escravo.**]

cauré — See *caboré*

ceará-bravo
person recently arrived from CE to work in the rubber plantations. *Br-PA* (Buarque de Holanda 1975:302) early20prior.
[M., f. Cf. **cearense, nordestino.**]

cearense 'of Ceará'
1. type of mestizo generally with the traits and habits of an Indian. *Br-AM* (Rosenblat 1954:2.104) cl–20.
2. person from CE; person from northeastern Br. *Br* (Souza 1961:102) 20.
[Acc. Santamaría (1942:1.341), used in SA as df. 1. < *Ceará* 'state in n.e. Br.' Acc. Machado (1952:1.541), ext. in meaning to all persons of n.e. Br. Cf. **baiano, mameluco.**]

cedrino
black person. *Br* (Silva 1987:66–67) late20.
[Acc. Silva, sociological term used in a book by Mari de Wasaré

Baiocchi; < *Cedro* 'ghetto where these black people live;' syns. *do cedro, negro do cedro.* Cf. **negro, preto.**]

charuto 'cigar'
person of color; black person. *Br-sertão* (Almeida Oliveira 1940:66) mid20 ‖ *Br* (Cascudo 1962:203) 20.
[Pejor. Acc. Machado (1952:1.574), < Engl. *cheroot* or *sheroot* < Tamil *churuttu* 'to roll up;' att. 1802. Cf. **negro, preto.**]

china — See *chino*

chineiro
man who procures or prefers *chinas* or prostitutes sexually. *Br-RS, -so.* (Souto Maior 1980:30) 20.
[Cf. **chino.**]

chinês 'Chinese'
person whose skin color is yellowish like that of an Asian. *Br-BA-Salvador* (Sanjek 1971:1141) 20.
[Cf. **chino,** Sp. **asiático.**]

chinita — See *chino*

chino
1. offspring of a mestizo and a black. *Br* (Johnston 1910:56) early20prior.
2. mestizo. *Br-RS* (Coruja et al. 1964:125); *Br* (Tenório d'Albuquerque 1954:92) 20.
3a. wife of a gaucho or an Indian. *Br-RS* (Coruja et al. 1964:125); *Br-so., -ea.* (Cascudo 1962:206) 20.
3b. woman with dark brown skin color. *Br-RS* (Coruja et al. 1964:125); *Br-so., -ea.* (Cascudo 1962:206) 20.
3c. prostitute. *Br* (Tenório d'Albuquerque 1954:92; Souto Maior 1980:30); *Br-so., -ea.* (Cascudo 1962:206) 20.
3d. civilized Indian woman. *Br* (Vergara Martín 1922:234) n.d.
3e. young woman or girl from the interior. *Br* (Cascudo 1962:206) 20.
[F. form *china* for dfs. 3a–3e. Df. 3c ext. from use as 'woman of a soldier,' acc. Tenório d'Albuquerque. Dim. f. form *chinita* for df. 3e, often poetic. Acc. Corominas (1954–57:2.53 and 1973:195), < Quechua *china.* Term of affect. when used with poss. pron. as in *meu chino, minha china,* acc. Tenório d'Albuquerque. Deriv. *chineiro.* Cf. **castiço, chinês, mameluco,** Sp. **asiático, mulato, oriental, pardo.**]

chocolate 'chocolate; chocolate-brown'
black person, esp. male, who does household chores. *Br-n.e.* (Gomes de Matos 1988:p.c.) late20.
[Acc. Gomes de Matos, nickname. Probably derog. Cf. Sp. **negro achocolatado.**]

chulo

1. person whose hair is kinky and skin color is dark brown. *Br-Minas Velhas* (Harris 1956:119) 20.

2. crude person. *Br* (Buarque de Holanda 1975:321) 20.

[Acc. Corominas (1973:199), < Golden Age Sp. slang *chulo* 'boy' < Italian *ciullo* 'kid' < *fanciullo*. Acc. Corominas (1954–57:2.92), first att. 1609. Acc. Corominas (1973:199), att. as 'low class person' in 1666. Possibly rel. to Sp. *cholo*. Cf. **negro, preto,** Sp. **cholo.**]

chumbinho — See *galego*

cidadão de segunda classe — See *mau cidadão*

cigano 'gypsy'

1. person from any background or country who goes from town to town in the interior selling wares, trying to turn a deal, or otherwise causing a nuisance for the locals. *Br* (Souza 1961:110) 20.

2. person from the Far or Middle East. *Br-MG* (Souza 1961:110) 20.

[Syn. df. 2 *judeu*. Cf. Sp. **zíngaro.**]

claro 'light; clear'

1. person with light skin color. *Br* (Harris 1964a:58; Soares and Silva 1987:166); *Br-BA* (Sanjek 1971:1141) 20.

2. mestizo who is 3 parts white. *Br* (Santamaría 1942:1.358) mid20; (Vergara Martín 1922:232–33) n.d.

[Acc. Soares and Silva, df. 1 used in 1976 national domestic survey. Syn. df. 2 *branco*. Cf. **branco, claro branco, mulato claro, negro claro,** Sp. **claro.**]

claro branco 'light white'

person whose skin color is very white. *Br* (Harris 1970:5) 20.

[Cf. **branco, claro.**]

cocada 'cute girl'

brown-skinned woman. *Br* (Souto Maior 1980:32) 20.

[F. Acc. Souto Maior, *mulher morena* [*sic*]. Acc. Buarque de Holanda (1975:339), also 'go-between or message-carrier for lovers.' Cf. **morena, moreno.**]

colono 'colonist'

European immigrant who settled in SP to cultivate coffee plants. *Br-SP* (Bailey and Nasatir 1973:767) 20.

[Cf. Sp. **colono.**]

colored

person of color; black person. *Br* (Chamberlain and Harmon 1983:147) 20.

[M., f. Acc. Chamberlain and Harmon, slang < Engl. *colored*. Cf. **gente de cor, negro, pessoa de cor, preto.**]

comadre 'godmother'
female gossip or busybody. *Br* (Buarque de Holanda 1975:348; Chamberlain and Harmon 1983:147; Gomes de Matos 1988:p.c.) 20.
[F. Acc. Chamberlain and Harmon, colloq. Cf. **cocada.**]

cor de café com leite 'café-au-lait-colored'
person whose skin color is light brown like café au lait. *Br-BA-Salvador* (Sanjek 1971:1141) 20.
[Cf. **café-com-leite,** Sp. **colorado, color achocolatado.**]

cor de canela 'cinnamon-colored'
person whose skin color is reddish-brown like cinnamon. *Br Br-BA-Salvador* (Sanjek 1971:1141); *Br* (Harris 1964a:58) 20.
[Usually in phr. *pessoa de cor de canela.* Cf. **cor de café com leite, canela.**]

cor de cinza 'ashen-colored'
1. person whose skin color is ashen or grayish. *Br Br-BA-Salvador* (Sanjek 1971:1141); *Br* (Harris 1964a:58) 20.
2. *caboclo* or mulatto of medium or brownish skin color. *Br* (Levine 1980:40) 20.
[Cf. **cor de cinza clara,** Sp. **cenizo.**]

cor de cinza clara 'light ashen-colored'
person whose skin color is light gray like ashes. *Br-Arembepe* (Harris and Kottak 1963:203); *Br* (Harris 1964a:58) 20.
[Cf. **claro, cor de cinza.**]

cor de formiga 'ant-colored'
person whose skin color is reddish like an ant's. *Br-BA-Salvador* (Sanjek 1971:1141) 20.
[Acc. Sanjek, *fomiga* [*sic*]. Cf. **cor de cinza.**]

corado bastantemente 'fairly ruddy or bleached'
person with relatively ruddy skin color. *Br* (Russell-Wood 1982:25) cl.
[*Corado* past partic. of *corar* 'to take on color;' 'to redden.' Cf. **avermelhado, roxo, ruivo, vermelho,** Sp. **colorado.**]

coriboca — See *curiboca*

coronel 'colonel'
1. politically important landowner, generally white. *Br-interior* (Buarque de Holanda 1975:387) 20prior; *Br-n.e.* (Gomes de Matos 1988:p.c.) early20–20.
2. rich man who affords expensive lovers. *Br-n.e, -so.* (Souto Maior 1980:35) 20.
[M. Cf. **cangaceiro.**]

cotruco — See *galego*

creolo 'creole'

person who probably has dark skin color. *Br* (Harris 1964a:58); *Br-Arembepe* (Harris and Kottak 1963:203) 20.

[Var. of *crioulo*. Cf. **creoulo, crioulo,** Sp. **criollo.**]

creoulo 'creole'

person who probably has dark skin color. *Br* (Aguirre Beltrán 1972:178) 20.

[Cf. **crioulo.**]

creulo 'creole'

person who has wavy hair and whose skin is the same dark shade of the *chulo* but is smoother. *Br-Minas Velhas* (Harris 1956:119) 20.

[Cf. **chulo, creolo, crioulo.**]

cria

1a. young black reared in the master's house. *Br* (Freyre 1964:410) cl.

1b. child of color born in the master's house. *Br-sertão* (Almeida Oliveira 1940:75) mid20 ‖ *Br-BA* (Pierson 1942:160) prior20.

2. creole; native to a specific place. *Br-RS* (Coruja et al. 1964:150) 20.

3. person of mixed race and low social standing. *Br-RS* (Coruja et al. 1964:150) 20.

[Dfs. 1b and 2 syn. *crioulo*. Also used in ref. to animals. < *criar* 'to rear, engender, raise.' Acc. Pierson, other persons born in the master's house include *irmão de creação, malungo, muleque de estimação, creação.* Cf. **crioulo, muleque, muleque de estimação, piquinini.**]

criolinho africano — See *crioulinho africano*

criolo 'creole'

person who probably has dark skin color. *Br-BA-Salvador* (Sanjek 1971:1141) 20.

[Var. of *crioulo*. Cf. **crioulinho africano, crioulo.**]

crioulinho africano 'little African creole'

young or small person who has dark skin color. *Br-BA-Salvador* (Sanjek 1971:1141) 20.

[Acc. Sanjek, *criolinho* [*sic*]. *Crioulinho* < *crioulo* 'creole' + dim. suf. *-inho.* Cf. **africano, crioulo,** Sp. **criollo.**]

crioulo 'creole'

1. European born in America, considered pure white. *Br* (Esteva Fabregat 1964:281; Barón Castro 1946:793) cl.

2a. person of color; black person. *Br* (Marcgrave 1648:268; Mott 1974:155) cl–17; (Alvarez Nazario 1974:335; Cascudo 1962:251; Chamberlain and Harmon 1983:162) 20 ‖ *Br-sertão* (Mott 1976:14) 20.

2b. black slave born in the master's house. *Br* (Bluteau 1712:2-C.613) early18; (Moraes e Silva 1789:1.349) 18.

2c. black slave born in Br. *Br* (Mattoso 1986:251) prior20.

2d. black person born in Africa; African native; tribal African. *Br* (Paiva 1986:70–71) 20.

2e. offspring of 2 blacks. *Br* (Diégues 1963:103; Mott 1974:155 and 1976:14) 20.

3. slave. *Br* (Bluteau 1712:2-C.613) early18.

4. mulatto with medium-light skin color. *Br* (Levine 1980:42) 20.

5a. person native to the country or region. *Br* (Cowles 1952:206); *Br-RS* (Coruja et al. 1964:151) 20.

5b. native descendant of blacks or whites born in America. *Br* (Cascudo 1962:251) 20prior.

[Acc. Corominas (1954–57:1.943–44 and 1973:178), probably < *cria* + dim. suf. *-oulo* or *-elo*. Var. *criolo*. Derivs. *crioulada* 'group of creoles,' *crioulinho*. Cf. **escravo, mulato, negro,** Sp. **criollo.**]

cristão 'Christian'

any person. *Br-RS* (Coruja et al. 1964:151) 20.

[Ext. from 'Christian.' Sim. to Brz. Ptg. *cara* 'guy.']

cruza 'cross; mixture'

person who is the result of racial mixture. *Br-RS* (Coruja et al. 1964:152) 20.

[Usually f. Cf. Sp. **mezcla.**]

cufuzo — See *cafuso*

cuiabano 'from Cuiabá'

type of mestizo with Indian-like traits or habits. *Br-AM* (Rosenblat 1954:2.104) cl.

[Acc. Rosenblat, *cuyabano* [*sic*]. < *Cuiabá* 'capital of MT' + suf. *-ano*. Cf. **ladino, mameluco,** Sp. **aindiado.**]

culumi — See *culumim*

culumim

Indian boy; small boy; servant; offspring of whites, mestizos, or Indians. *Br* (Freyre 1964:146, 410) cl–20.

[Usually m. Vars. *culumi, curumi, curumim, curubim*. Acc. Machado (1952:1.716), < Tupi *cunumi* 'black boy or child, *moleque*.' Acc. Rodrigues (1986:22), < Old Tupi *cunumí* or *curumí* 'boy.']

Acc. Buarque de Holanda (1975:413), < Tupi *kuru'mi* 'boy.' Cf. **cunhataim, muleque.**]

cunhão-de-ferro — See *gavião*

cunhatã — See *cunhataim*

cunhataim

young girl; offspring of whites, mestizos, or Indians. *Br* (Freyre 1964:146,411) cl–20.

[Usually f. Acc. Machado (1952:1.717), < Tupi *cunhã* 'woman, female animal', < *cû-nha* 'gossip.' Acc. Rodrigues (1986:22), < Old Tupi *cunhã*. Acc. Freyre, < Tupi-Guarani 'young girl'; ant. *culumim*. Acc. Buarque de Holanda (1975:410), < Tupi *kunha'tain* 'adolescent woman'; var. *cunhatã*. Cf. **culumim.**]

cupé — See *galego*

curador 'curer'

witch doctor or any person who prays for the healing of others who have been bitten by poisonous animals. *Br* (Buarque de Holanda 1975:411) 20.

[Cf. **benzedor.**]

curau

rustic type; hick. *Br-SE* (Ayrosa 1937:81) mid20.

[Syn. *caipira*. Cf. **caipira.**]

curiboca

1. offspring of a white and an Indian; mestizo. *Br-AM* (Woodbridge 1948:357) cl; (Rosenblat 1954:2.104; Santamaría 1942: 1.323) mid20; (Diégues 1963:105; Alba 1969:34) 20 ‖ *Br-no.* (Ayrosa 1937:73; Woodbridge 1948:357) mid20 ‖ *Br* (Alba 1969:34) 20; (Vergara Martín 1922:232) n.d.

2. offspring of an Indian and a black. *Br* (Mott 1974:155; Marcgrave 1648:268) cl; (Mott 1974:155 and 1976:14) 18; (Baldus and Willems 1939:36–37) early–mid20; (Ramos 1941:537) mid20; (Diégues 1963:103) 20 ‖ *Br-PA* (Santa Rosa 1922:2.131) late19–early20 ‖ *Br-BA* (Pierson 1942:140) mid20.

3. offspring of a black and a mulatto or *mameluco*. *Br-coast* (Diégues 1963:106) 20.

4. offspring of a white and a *tapuio*. *Br* (Baldus and Willems 1939:36–37) early–mid20.

5. rustic, uncultured type; hick. *Br-no.* (Ayrosa 1937:73) mid20.

[M., f. Df. 1 syn. *mameluco*. Df. 2 syn. *cafuso*, acc. Diégues. Df. 4 syn. *cabra*. Df. 5 syn. *caipira*. Acc. Alba, syns. *caboclo, mameluco*. Acc. Santamaría, < Tupi *cari-boc* 'son or child of the white man.' Acc. Ayrosa, < Tupi *cari-* + *óc* (= *bóc, uoc, voc*) 'taken from.' Acc.

Baldus and Willems, vars. *carimboca, caivoca, carioca.* Other vars. *cariboca, coriboca.* Cf. **cabo verde, caboclo, cabra, cafuso, caipira, carioca, mameluco,** Sp. **mestizo.**]

curumi — See *culumim*

curumim — See *culumim*

cutruco — See *galego*

D

da raça — See *ter pinta*

de cor branca — See *branco*

de cor equívoca 'of dubious color'
person whose skin color, and therefore race, are questionable. *Br* (Russell-Wood 1982:25) cl.
[Desc. phr. Acc. Russell-Wood, vaguely euph. Cf. **de cor fechada, de cor fula.**]

de cor escura — See *escuro*

de cor fechada 'of closed color'
person whose skin color is probably dark. *Br* (Russell-Wood 1982:25) cl.
[Desc. phr. Acc. Russell-Wood, vaguely euph. Cf. **de cor equívoca.**]

de cor fula 'of the color of the Fula people'
person whose skin color is dark like that of an African; black person. *Br* (Russell-Wood 1982:25) cl.
[Desc. phr. Acc. Russell-Wood, vaguely euph. Cf. **de cor equívoca, de cor fechada, fulo,** Sp. **fulo.**]

de cor morena — See *moreno*

de cor parda — See *pardo*

de cor preta — See *preto*

de nação 'of the nation; of the country'
person of nonwhite race or of low class. *Br* (Cabral 1982:541) 20.
[Var. *nação.* Often in phr. *de nação pior* 'of the worst class.' Cf. **ter pinta.**]

do cedro — See *cedrino*

dona de casa 'house lady'
black mistress of the white master. *Br-n.e.* (Kelsey 1940:55) 18–19.
[Cf. **ama, babá,** Sp. **doña.**]

E

emboaba
1. Portuguese settler newly arrived in Br, esp. in the mining areas. *Br* (Bailey and Nasatir 1973:769) cl.
2. Portuguese or coastal-dwelling adventurer who comes in search of gold. *Br-MG* (Burns 1980:548) 18.
3. outsider. *Br-MG* (Burns 1980:548) 20
4. person from the Northeast; northeasterner. *Br-so.* (Silva 1987:171) 20.
[M., f. Df. 3 pejor. Df. 4 derog. Acc. Buarque de Holanda (1975:509), < Tupi. Var. *emboava*. Cf. **galego**.]

emboava — See *emboaba, galego*

escravinho menino mulatinho 'little mulatto slave child'
young child, acc. a priest. *Br* (Leite de Vasconcellos 1928:363) 16–17.
[Also used in Portugal. *Escravinho* < *escravo* 'slave' + dim. suf. *-inho; mulatinho* < *mulato* + dim. suf. *-inho*. Cf. **escravo, mulatinho, mulato, pretinho**.]

escravo 'slave'
slave. *Br* (Bluteau 1713:3-E.224–25) early18.
[Also used in Portugal. Cf. **escravo cativo, preto**.]

escravo cativo 'captive slave'
captured slave. *Br* (Leite de Vasconcellos 1928:363) 16–17.
[Also used in Portugal. Cf. **escravo preto cativo**.]

escravo de aluguel 'rented slave'
slave, generally black, who possessed a skilled trade, whose services were rented out by the master, and who could thus buy personal or family freedom. *Br* (Russell-Wood 1982:34) early18.
[Sim. to *escravo de ganho*. Cf. **escravo, escravo de ganho**.]

escravo de ganho 'earning slave'
slave, usually black, who could hire out as a skilled tradesman and pay the master a set amount in return for personal or family freedom. *Br* (Russell-Wood 1982:34–35) early18.
[Sim. to *escravo de aluguel*. Cf. **escravo, escravo de aluguel, escravo de serviço, negro de ganho**, Sp. **negro de gaño**.]

escravo de serviço 'service slave'
slave, usually a skilled tradesman, whose skills were rented or contracted out by the owner as a sourse of income. *Br* (Levine 1979:85) 19prior.
[Cf. **escravo, escravo de aluguel, escravo de ganho**.]

escravo dos santos
black slave of a missionary. *Br* (Silva 1987:147) cl–prior20.
[Acc. Silva, this slave known for being as badly treated as any other black slave. Cf. **escravo, escravo de serviço, escravo ladino.**]

escravo forro 'freed slave'
slave who is freed by the master. *Br* (Bluteau 1713:4-F.182) early18.
[Also used in Portugal. Cf. **escravo, forro.**]

escravo ladino
slave, usually black, who knows at least rudimentary Portuguese. *Br* (Moraes e Silva 1789:2.3) late18prior.
[Also used in Portugal. Acc. Moraes e Silva, ant. *boçal.* Cf. **bocál, ladino, negro ladino,** Sp. **ladino.**]

escravo ladino da terra
Indian. *Br* (Cascudo 1962:414) cl.
[Acc. Cascudo, *escravo ladino [sic]*, dos da terra. Cf. **escravo ladino.**]

escravo preto 'black slave'
black slave. *Br* (Bluteau 1720:6-P.727) early18.
[Also used in Portugal. Cf. **escravo, preto.**]

escravo preto cativo 'captive black slave'
black captive slave. *Br* (Leite de Vasconcellos 1928:363) 16–17.
[Also used in Portugal. Cf. **escravo cativo, preto.**]

escurinho 'little dark one'
1. person whose skin color is dark. *Br* (Harris 1970:3); *Br-BA* (Sanjek 1971:1141) 20.
2. black person. *Br* (Chamberlain and Harmon 1983:214) 20.
[< *escuro* 'dark' + dim. suf. *-inho.* Acc. Chamberlain and Harmon, colloq., euph. Cf. **escuro.**]

escuro 'dark'
1a. person with dark skin color. *Br* (Harris 1964a:58; Hutchinson 1952:27–31); *Br-BA-Salvador* (Sanjek 1971:1141) cl–20.
1b. person with dark skin color and some Caucasian features; person who is not a *cabo verde, cabra,* or *preto. Br-BA* (Pierson 1942:140) mid20 ‖ *Br-Vila Recôncavo* (Hutchinson 1957:119–20); *Br-n.e.* (Kottak 1967:44) 20.
1c. dark-skinned person, esp. an outsider. *Br-n.e.* (Hutchinson 1957:119) 20.
2a. black person. *Br-Arembepe* (Harris and Kottak 1963:204–5) 20.
2b. person of color; middle-class black person. *Br* (Chamberlain and Harmon 1983:214) 20.
3. mulatto or *caboclo. Br* (Levine 1980:49) 20.

[Dfs. 1b and 1c euph. Acc. Chamberlain and Harmon, df. 2b euph., colloq. Cf. **escurinho, escuro alvo,** Sp. **oscuro.**]

escuro alvo 'white dark one'

person whose skin color is darker than that of the *escuro. Br-BA* (Sanjek 1971:1141) 20.

[Cf. **alvo, escuro, escuro claro.**]

escuro claro 'light dark one'

person whose skin color is lighter than that of the *escuro. Br-BA* (Sanjek 1971:1141) 20.

[Cf. **claro, escravo, escravo alvo.**]

európido

white person. *Br* (Esteva Fabregat 1964:280) 20.

[Acc. Esteva Fabregat, anthro.; syn. *branco.* Also used in SA. Cf. **branco,** Sp. **blanco, európido.**]

F

faiodermo

offspring of a white man and a black woman. *Br* (Cascudo 1962:116) 20.

[Cf. **bode.**]

farofeiro

person, usually poor or of low social class, who brings lunch to eat at the beach. *Br* (Gomes de Matos 1988:p.c.) late20.

[< *farofa* 'manioc flour' + suf. *-eiro.* Acc. Chamberlain and Harmon (1983:228), also 'braggart.' Cf. **bóia-fria.**]

farrapo

person of the lower classes. *Br* (Segovia 1911:141) early20.

[Sim. to Chilean Sp. *roto.* Cf. Sp. **roto.**]

favelado 'ghetto-dweller'

person who lives in a *favela,* or slum. *Br* (Buarque de Holanda 1975:615; Gomes de Matos 1988:p.c.) 20.

[< *favela* + suf. *-ado.* Cf. **bóia-fria, farofeiro.**]

feirante — See *ambulante*

filho das paisagens adustas 'child of burnt lands'

black person. *Br* (Silva 1987:73) early20.

[Acc. Silva, pseudo-scientific term used by Euclides da Cunha. Cf. **besta de carga, filho das paisagens bárbaras.**]

filho das paisagens bárbaras 'child of barbarous lands'

black person. *Br* (Silva 1987:73) early20.

[Acc. Silva, pseudo-scientific term used by Euclides da Cunha. Cf.

besta de carga, filho das paisagens adustas.]
filho de criação 'step-child'
illegitimate offspring of a mulatto or black mother and a white
father. *Br* (Levine 1980:52) cl–20.
[Cf. **cria, crioulo, irmão de criação, mulato.**]
filho de santo 'child of the saint'
1. black person; mulatto. *Br-n.e.* (Boring 1976:414) 20.
2. initiate in the *candomblé* rite. *Br* (Megenney 1988:p.c.)
late20.
[Cf. **filho do reino, mazombo, mulato, negro,** Sp. **santero.**]
filho do reino 'child of the kingdom'
Portuguese citizen living in Br. *Br* (Rosenblat 1954:2.99) cl.
[Sim. to *reinol*; ant. *mazombo,* acc. Rosenblat. Cf. **crioulo, filho de
santo, reinol, mazombo,** Sp. **godo, perulero.**]
forasteiro 'foreigner; outsider'
person from the Northeast; northeasterner. *Br* (Silva 1987:171)
20.
[Acc. Silva, derog. Cf. **gente de fora, intruso, nordestino.**]
formió — See *carnijó*
forro 'freed'
freed slave. *Br* (Levine 1979:95) 19prior.
[Acc. Levine, syn. *liberto.* Cf. **escravo forro.**]
francês 'French'
person whose skin color is probably light. *Br-BA-Salvador*
(Sanjek 1971:1141) 20.
[Acc. Sanjek, f. *francesa.* Cf. Sp. **francés de agua dulce.**]
fugido 'fled; fugitive'
fugitive or runaway slave. *Br* (Pescatello 1975:247) prior20.
[Also used in SA. Cf. **forro,** Sp. **cimarrón.**]
fula — See *fulo*
fulniô — See *carnijó*
fulo
1. black person who generally has light skin color. *Br-BA*
(Megenney 1978:159) 20.
2. offspring of a black and a mulatto. *Br-AL, -BA, -MG* (Souza
1961:152–53; Diégues 1963:105) 20.
3. black person; mulatto. *Br* (Alonso 1958:2.2072–73) 20.
4. neighbor; fisherman. *Br-BA* (Blanco 1978:100–101) 20.
[Acc. Souza, *fula* [*sic*]; syns. df. 2 *cabra, pardo, negro fulo.* Acc.
Blanco, df. 4 has color ref. Acc. Souza and Megenney (1978:159),
< *Fula* 'Fulanese people, native tribe from Guinea in we. Africa,'
thought to be the same as African Fubah tribe 'Islamized blacks

who had mixed with lighter Semitic peoples and who were introduced into Br as slaves.' Var. *fula.* Cf. **cabra, negro angola, negro de Guiné, negro fulo, pardo,** Sp. **fulo.**]

G

galego 'Galician'

1a. Portuguese person during the republican era of 1835 and thereafter. *Br* (Souza 1961:156) 19–20.

1b. Portuguese person. *Br* (Buarque de Holanda 1975:669) 20.

2. foreigner of any nationality. *Br-n.e.* (Buarque de Holanda 1975:669) 20.

3. person with blond hair; blond. *Br-n.e.* (Buarque de Holanda 1975:669) 20.

4. businessman of Jewish origin. *Br-n.e.* (Gomes de Matos 1988:p.c.) late20.

[Derog. Acc. Souza and Buarque de Holanda, syns., generally obs., *abacaxi, bicudo, boaba, boava, candango, caneludo, chumbinho, cotruco, cupé, cutruco, emboaba, emboava, jaleco, japona, labrego, marabuto, marinheiro, maroto, marreta, mascate, mondrongo, novato, parrudo, pé-de-chumbo, portuga, puça, sapatão. talaveira, zelis.* Cf. **emboaba, judeu, polaco,** Sp. **gallego.**]

ganhadeira 'earner'

slave woman, usually black, who bought fish at the market, re-sold it at a higher price, and used the profits to purchase her freedom. *Br* (Russell-Wood 1982:37) cl.

[F. Cf. **escravo de aluguel, escravo de ganho.**]

gato negro 'black cat'

person of mixed race. *Br* (Silva 1987:158) 20.

[Acc. Silva, color designation. Cf. **acastanhado, agalegado, alvo, amarelado, avermelhado, bem branco, negro, negro do gato, preto, vermelho.**]

gauchaço

person who typifies the gaucho par excellence. *Br-RS* (Coruja et al. 1964:220). 20.

[F. *gauchona.* Syns. *gaúcho completo, gaúcho perfeito.* Cf. **gaúcho.**]

gauchão

person who pretends to be a gaucho. *Br-RS* (Coruja et al. 1964:221) 20.

[< *gaúcho* + aug. suf. *-ão.* Cf. **gaúcho.**]

gauchito — See *gaúcho*

gaúcho 'gaucho; cowboy'

1. Argentine peasant or cowboy. *Br* (Morínigo 1966:279) 20.

2a. southern Brazilian cowboy or backwoodsman. *Br-RS* (Lax-

alt 1980:493) 20.
  2b. rustic type; hick. *Br-RS* (Ayrosa 1937:81) mid20.
  3. person from RS. *Br-so.* (Callage 1928:67–68) early–mid20
‖ *Br* (Souza 1961:159–60) 20.
  4. mestizo. *Br* (Laxalt 1980:482) prior20.
  5a. Indian warrior or horseman who lived a nomadic existence
in Ar. *Br-so.* (Callage 1928:67–68) early20prior.
  5b. vagrant Indian. *Br-RS* (Coruja et al. 1964:222–27) 20.
  [Syn. df. 2b *caipira*. Syns. df. 3 *rio-grandense-do-sul, sul-rio-grandense*. Acc. Machado (1952:1.1081–82) and Coruja et al., possibly < Arawak *cauchu* 'vagabond' or *cachu* 'friend.' Acc. Corominas (1973:294), < Amerindian term but generally of uncertain origin. Acc. Coruja et al., derivs. *gauchito* 'small gaucho,' *gauchaço* 'gaucho-like,' *gauchona* 'female gaucho.' Cf. **gauchaço, gauchão, gaudério.**]

gaúcho completo — See *gauchaço*
gaúcho perfeito — See *gauchaço*
gauchona — See *gauchaço, gaúcho*
gaudério
  person from the interior, or frontiersman, known for cattle rustling and thievery. *Br-RS* (Cascudo 1962:345) mid18.
  [Acc. Cascudo, obs. since 19 cent.; replaced by *gaúcho* or *vaqueiro*; vars. *godério, godero*. Acc. Buarque de Holanda (1975:679), < Sp. *gauderio*. Cf. **gaúcho, vaqueiro.**]

gavião 'type of hawk'
  1. person of the Gavião Indian tribe. *Br* (Gomes de Matos 1988:p.c.) 20.
  2. man who has many lovers; great lover. *Br-n.e., -no., -so.* (Souto Maior 1980:63) 20.
  [Syn. df. 2 *cunhão-de-ferro*. Cf. **bororo.**]

gazo 'albino'
  1. person with very light skin color. *Br-BA-Salvador* (Sanjek 1971:1141; Blanco 1978:100) 20.
  2. person with overly white skin and light blue eyes. *Br-sertão* (Zimmerman 1963:94); *Br* (Levine 1980:56) 20.
  3a. white person whose ancestry may not be all white. *Br* (Levine 1980:56) 20.
  3b. person of supposed racial mixture. *Br* (Silva 1987:158) mid20.
  [Acc. Levine, df. 3a iron. Acc. Silva, df. 3b color designation. < *gázeo* 'light bluish-green.' Cf. **gazula, mulato gazo.**]

gazula
  person whose skin color is probably light. *Br* (Harris 1964a:58)

20.

[M., f. Acc. Machado (1952:1.1084), of uncertain origin. Cf. **gazo.**]
genipapo 'genipap fruit'
person whose skin is spotted, thus indicating some black
ancestry. *Br-BA* (Pierson 1942:139) mid20.
[Acc. Pierson, usually in phr. *ter genipapo.* < *genipapapo* 'type of
tropical fruit of which the dark juice is used in ceremonies to paint
the faces of some Brz. Indians.']
gentalha 'riff-raff'
person of the lower classes. *Br-sertão* (Almeida Oliveira
1940:103) mid20 ‖ *Br-RS* (Coruja et al. 1964:228) 20.
[F. Acc. Corominas (1954–57:2.723), sim. to Sp. *gentalla,* < Catalan
gentalla or Italian *gentaglia.* Cf. **gente.**]
gente 'person; people'
person of high social class or distinction, usually of the upper
classes. *Br-Vila Recôncavo* (Hutchinson 1957:113) cl–20.
[Cf. **gentalha, gente sinhá,** Sp. **gente, gente de razón, gente
decente.**]
gente da roça 'country folk'
peasant or person from the countryside; hick. *Br-Minas Velhas*
(Harris 1956:141) 20.
[F. Cf. **caipira, gentalha, gente, gente sinhá.**]
gente de baixo 'lower people'
Portuguese person. *Br-MT-Cuiabá* (Souza 1961:160) 20.
[Acc. Souza, generally obs. Cf. **galego, gentalha, gente, gente
sinhá.**]
gente de cor 'person of color'
person of color; nonwhite person. *Br* (Alvarez Nazario 1974:349;
Mott 1974:182) cl–20.
[Sim. to Engl. *colored people,* Fr. *gens de couleur,* or Mauritian
Creole *dimun kulér,* acc. Chaudenson (1974:79). Also sim. to Sp.
gente de color, persona de color, or *pardo.* Cf. **gente,** Sp. **gente de
color.**]
gente de fora 'outsider'
person from the Northeast; northeasterner. *Br-so.* (Silva
1987:171) 20.
[Derog. Cf. **forasteiro, intruso, nordestino.**]
gente de nação
Jew; descendant of Jews. *Br* (Buarque de Holanda 1975:683)
20.
[Cf. Sp. **jacoibo, ruso.**]
gente fina — See *boa gente, gente sinhá*
gente que tem destaque 'person of distinction'
person of the elite. *Br-MG-Minas Velhas* (Harris 1956:100–

151) 20.

[Sim. to Sp. *gente decente* or *gente de razón.* Cf. **gente.**]

gente sinhá
well-educated person from a good family. *Br* (Cascudo 1962:701) 20prior.

[*Sinhá* 'term of endearment given by slaves to the master's wife or any white woman.' Var. *gente fina.* Cf. **gente.**]

gigolô do índio 'gigolo of the Indian'
researcher, scientist, or other intellectual who has investigated or studied Brazilian Indians, seemingly for personal gain but in the guise of aiding the Indian. *Br* (Silva 1987:70–71) 20.

[Derog. Cf. **gigolô do negro.**]

gigolô do negro 'gigolo of the black'
researcher, scientist, or other intellectual who has investigated or studied, and apparently exploited, Brazilian blacks. *Br* (Silva 1987:70) 20.

[Derog. Acc. Silva, originally 'person who makes money off blacks.' Cf. **gigolô do índio.**]

godeme
any Englishman. *Br* (Souza 1961:161) 19–20.

[Acc. Souza, derog.; perhaps < Engl. *good man,* coined in early 19 cent. Acc. Buarque de Holanda (1975:691), perhaps < Engl. *God damn.* Cf. Sp. **inglés.**]

godério — See *gaudério*

godero — See *gaudério*

grauçá — See *sarará*

grinfo
black person; mulatto. *Br* (Chamberlain and Harmon 1983:274) 20.

[Acc. Chamberlain and Harmon, slang, ext. to 'man, guy, woman, dame.' Acc. Buarque de Holanda (1975:702), syns. *crioulo, moreno.* Perhaps sim. to Sp. *grifo.* Cf. **gringo,** Sp. **grifo, gringo.**]

gringo
1a. foreigner not from the Iberian Peninsula. *Br-RS* (Coruja et al. 1964:232) 20.

1b. foreigner, esp. Italian. *Br-RS* (Coruja et al. 1964:232) 20.

1c. any foreigner. *Br* (Souza 1961:164; Cabral 1982:429) 20.

1d. any foreigner, esp. one with light or blond hair. *Br* (Cabral 1982:429; Chamberlain and Harmon 1983:274) 20.

2. Spanish-speaking person from Spain or RP. *Br* (Souza 1961:164) 20.

[Acc. Chamberlain and Harmon, df. 1d colloq., pejor. Acc. Souza, df. 2 generalized to df. 1c. Acc. Buarque de Holanda (1975:702), < Sp.

of RP *gringo*. Cf. **crioulo,** Sp. **gringo.**]

guajiru

mulatto who has dark reddish or ruddy skin color. *Br* (Diégues 1963:106) mid20prior.

[< Tupi *guajeru* 'type of fruit-bearing plant,' acc. Buarque de Holanda (1975:705). Cf. **mameluco, mulato,** Sp. **guajiro.**]

guarani — See *tupi*

guasca

1. rustic type; hick. *Br-RS* (Ayrosa 1937:81) mid20.

2. person from RS. *Br* (Buarque de Holanda 1975:708) 20.

[M., f. Acc. Ayrosa, syn. *caipira*. Acc. Buarque de Holanda, < Quechua *kuask'a* 'cord'; syn. df. 2 *rio-grandense-do-sul, gaúcho*. Cf. **caipira, gaúcho.**]

guató

person of the Guató Brazilian Indian tribe found in the Upper Paraguay River area. *Br* (Buarque de Holanda 1975:708; Gomes de Matos 1988:p.c.) 20.

[Cf. **bororo, gavião, tapanhuna.**]

guinéu 'Guinean'

slave from the Guinea coast of west Africa. *Br* (D'Azevedo 1903:290) 15–cl.

[Acc. D'Azevedo, syns. *mouro, negro de Guinea, negro de Guiné*.]

gungunhana

black person. *Br* (Schneider 1985:230) 20.

[M., f. Acc. Schneider, < Kimbundu lg. *Gungunhana* 'last king (1884–95) of Gaza or Shanagana in Mozambique.' Cf. **negro, preto.**]

H

henrique 'Henry'

black man who was a member of the black regiments who fought against the Dutch. *Br-n.e.* (Kelsey 1940:56) 19.

[M. < *Henrique (Dias)* 'valorous soldier of this conflict,' acc. Kelsey.]

hispânico — See Sp. **hispano**

homem bom 'good man'

white man of high social standing, usually a plantation owner, who voted and had all the other privileges of his class. *Br* (Nuñez 1980:232) cl.

[M. Opp. to *homem do povo*. Cf. **homem do povo.**]

homem branco 'white man'

white man; person from an upper-class family who owns slaves.

Br (Bluteau 1712:2-B.183) early18.
[M. Also used in Portugal. Cf. **branco.**]

homem de cor 'man of color; colored man'
black person; man of color. *Br* (Hutchinson 1957:109; Degler 1971:179) 20.
[M. Euph. in Ptg., Sp., Engl., and Fr., acc. Hutchinson and Degler. Acc. Degler, phr. apparently proposed by Negro rights groups in the 1920s to replace disrespectful *negro*. Sim. to Fr. *homme de couleur,* Engl. *colored man,* Sp. *hombre de color.* Acc. Buarque de Holanda (1975:731), syns. *mulato, preto.* Cf. **gente de cor,** Sp. **gente de color, hombre de color.**]

homem do povo 'man of the people'
white Portuguese-Brazilian, either poor or of humble origins, who was excluded from receiving land grants. *Br* (Nuñez 1980:232) early cl.
[M. Opp. to *homem bom.* Cf. **homem bom.**]

homem ladino
man who is an expert at some skill; trained person. *Br* (Moraes e Silva 1789:2.3) late18.
[M. Also used in Portugal. Cf. **ladino.**]

homem mestiço 'mestizo'
offspring of parents from different countries. *Br* (Bluteau 1716:5-M.455) early18.
[M. Also used in Portugal. Cf. **mestiço.**]

homem pardo 'brown man'
mulatto. *Br* (Bluteau 1720:6-P.265) early18; (Segovia 1911:134) early20.
[M. Also used in Portugal. Acc. Segovia, syn. *pardo.* Cf. **pardo.**]

homem preto da terra de Benim 'black man from Benin'
black slave. *Br* (Leite de Vasconcellos 1928:369) 15–16.
[M. Also used in Portugal. Acc. Leite de Vasconcellos, *Benym* [*sic*] 'area of we. Africa.' Cf. **homem de cor.**]

homem roto 'broken man'
poorly dressed man; ragamuffin; bum. *Br* (Bluteau 1720:7-R.384) early18.
[M. Also used in Portugal. Cf. Sp. **roto.**]

I

íncola — See *caboclo brabo*

indiano 'person from India; Indian; Asian-Indian'
person from India or the Asian subcontinent. *Br* (Bluteau

1713:4-I.106) early18; (Baldus and Willems 1939:22, 135) early20. [Also used in Portugal. Acc. Bluteau, syn. *indiático*. Acc. Buarque de Holanda (1975:755), syns. *índio, índico, indiático*. Acc. Baldus and Willems, used to distinguish Amerindians (*índios* or *ameríndios*) from Asian Indians.]

indiático — See *indiano*

índico — See *indiano*

índio 'Indian, Amerindian'

1a. Indian; Amerindian; native of the Americas. *Br* (Bluteau 1713:4-I.110) early18; (Esteva Fabregat 1964:280); *Br-n.e.* (Hutchinson 1957:118) 20.

1b. Amazonian Indian; Indian from interior MT. *Br-n.e.* (Hutchinson 1957:118) 20.

2. native of India; Asian Indian. *Br* (Bluteau 1713:4-I.110) early18; Buarque de Holanda 1975:759) 20.

3. non-Amerindian, gaucho worker or employee on a plantation or cattle farm. *Br-so.* (Callage 1928:73) early20 ‖ *Br-RS* (Coruja et al. 1964:246); *Br* (Souza 1961:170) 20.

[Dfs. 1 and 2 also used in Portugal. Acc. Callage, syn. df. 3 *gaúcho*. Cf. **aborígena, indiano, indígena.**]

índio bárbaro 'untamed Indian'

Indian of the Brazilian outback or *sertão*, either an *índio manso* or an *índio bravo*. *Br* (Bluteau 1713:4-I.110) early18.

[Cf. **índio, índio bravo, índio manso.**]

índio bravo 'wild Indian'

uncivilized, unacculturated, or unruly Indian. *Br* (Bluteau 1713:4-I.110) early18; (Johnston 1910:108) early20prior.

[Acc. Johnston, often naked. Cf. **índio bárbaro, índio manso.**]

índio cafuso

free or freed Indian slave. *Br* (Souza 1961:66) 18.

[Acc. Souza, *cafuz* [sic]. Cf. **índio, cafuso.**]

índio da Guiana 'Guyana Indian'

Caribe Indian from the Brazilian-Guyana border area. *Br* (Vergara Martín 1922:238) early20.

[Acc. Vergara Martín, *indio de la Guayana* [sic]. Cf. **índio.**]

índio de corda

Indian slave who continued to be enslaved even after laws forbidding Indian slavery were enacted. *Br* (Levine 1980:66) mid18–19.

[Cf. **índio.**]

índio do Amazonas 'Amazon Indian'

person with Indian-like features, esp. slanted eyes, from the

Manaus area. *Br-AM-Manaus* (hotel bellboy 1987:p.c.) late20.
[Hotel bellboy's own self-description. Cf. **índio.**]

índio ladino — See *ladino*

índio mais escuro 'darker Indian'
Indian with dark skin color. *Br-BA-Salvador* (Sanjek 1971:
1141) 20.
[Possibly indicates racial mixture. Cf. **escuro, índio.**]

índio manso 'tame Indian'
Indian of Br who is easier taught and acculturated than the
índio bravo. Br (Bluteau 1713:4-I.110) early18.
[Cf. **índio, índio bárbaro, índio bravo.**]

índio meio amulatado — See *acaboclado, pardavasco*

índio moreno 'brown Indian'
Indian with brown or dark skin color and possibly brunet hair.
Br (Harris 1970:5) 20.
[Cf. **índio, moreno.**]

índio preto 'black Indian'
Indian whose skin color is very dark, perhaps implying racial
mixture. *Br* (Harris 1970:5) 20.
[Perhaps sim. to Sp. *indio oscuro.* Cf. **índio, preto, índio mais
escuro,** Sp. **indio oscuro.**]

ingênuo 'innocent; simple; naive'
1. dark-skinned child born to a freed slave father. *Br* (Mott
1974:171) early19.
2. free child of a slave mother, who was born after the passage
of the 1871 Rio Branco Law but who remained enslaved until the
age of 21. *Br* (Levine 1979:113) 19.
[Cf. **pardo.**]

intruso 'intruder'
person from the Northeast; northeasterner. *Br-so.* (Silva
1987:171) 20.
[Derog. Cf. **forasteiro, gente de fora, nordestino.**]

irmão de criação 'half-brother; step-brother; house brother'
slave, usually the illegitimate child of the master, reared in the
master's house. *Br* (Levine 1980:68–69) cl.
[Indicates that the person was reared in the same house as other
children but was not legitimate. Cf. **cria, crioulo, filho de
criação.**]

israelense — See *judeu*

israelita — See *judeu*

italiano 'Italian'
Italian. *Br* (Buarque de Holanda 1975:789) 20prior.

[Std. for 'Italian.' Cf. Sp. **nápoles, tano.**]

J

jaboticaba
 descendant of blacks. *Br* (Silva 1987:200) 20.
 [M., f. Cf. **negro, preto.**]
jagunço
 1. person whose racial ancestry is a mixture of Indian, white, and a small part black. *Br* (Reis 1961:324) 20.
 2. *caboclo* who is part black. *Br-n.e.* (Woodbridge 1948:358) cl.
 3. outlaw or other ruffian, usually a *caboclo*. *Br-sertão* (Levine 1980:69) 20.
 [Acc. Buarque de Holanda (1975:795), < *zaguncho* 'type of slingshot.' Acc. Machado (1952:2.1253), att. 19 cent., of uncertain origin. Cf. **caboclo, mameluco, mulato,** Sp. **jíbaro.**]
jaleco
 person from Portugal. *Br* (Souza 1961:178) 20.
 [Nickname. Acc. Machado (1952:2.1254), < Sp. *jaleco* < Algerian Arabic *jalikâ* < Turkish *ielék* 'short jacket.' Cf. **galego, parrudo, portuga.**]
jangadeiro — See *mameluco*
japão — See *japonês*
japona — See *galego*
japonês 'Japanese'
 person from Japan; Japanese. *Br* (Buarque de Holanda 1975:797) 20prior.
 [Acc. Buarque de Holanda, syns. *japão, japônico, nipônico.* Cf. **italiano.**]
japônico — See *japonês*
jeca
 rustic type; hick; low-class rural person. *Br-interior, -SP* (Wagley 1971:101, 262) 20prior.
 [M., f. Acc. Buarque de Holanda (1975:800), < *jeca-tatu* < *Jeca Tatu* 'character in a literary work symbolizing the *caboclo* of the interior.' Acc. Wagley, sim. to *tabaréu* of BA and *caboclo* of AM. Cf. **caboclo, caipira, guasca, tabaréu,** Sp. **jíbaro.**]
jeca-tatu — See *jeca*
judaico — See *judeu*
judeu 'Jewish;
 1. Jewish person; Israeli. *Br* (Buarque de Holanda 1975:805) 20.

2. person from the Far or Middle East. *Br-MG* (Souza 1961:110) 20.

[F. form *judia*. Śyns. df. 1 *israelense, israelita, judaico*. Syn. df. 2 *cigano*. Cf. **cigano, polaco, turco,** Sp. **judío, turco.**]

judia — See *judeu*

L

labrego — See *galego*

ladino 'astute; clever'

1a. black slave brought from the Iberian Peninsula who had learned Portuguese, assimilated some of the culture, and usually worked as a house servant. *Br* (Alvarez Nazario 1974:332; Souza 1961:184; Mörner 1967:16; Freyre 1964:416) cl.

1b. black slave brought from Portugal who had learned Portuguese, assimilated some of the culture, and worked as a field hand or house servant. *Br* (Levine 1979:122–23) 19prior.

1c. slave who could speak Portuguese, knew Christian religion, and had a rudimentary skill as an artisan or craftsman. *Br* (Mattoso 1986:251) 19prior.

2. black or Indian slave who spoke Portuguese and had a skill. *Br* (Cascudo 1962:414) cl.

3. foreigner, esp. black, who had learned to speak Portuguese better than expected. *Br* (Bluteau 1716:5-L.16) early18.

[Df. 3 also used in Portugal. Syns. *indio ladino, negro ladino*. Acc. Alvarez Nazario, Souza, Mörner, and Freyre, as slaves in America, *ladinos* brought higher prices than *boçales* and often worked in domestic service rather than in the fields. Acc. Cobarruvias (1611:747), used in ref. to 'Moor or foreigner who had learned Spanish' in 17 cent. Acc. Corominas (1954–57:3.9–10), Old Ptg. *ladinho*; modern form perhaps < Sp. *ladino*. Cf. Sp. **ladino.**]

lamão — See *alamão*

lançado 'launched, tossed'

white or mulatto who lived among the African native chiefs. *Br* (Mattoso 1986:251) prior20.

[Cf. **mulato.**]

libanês 'Lebanese'

Lebanese; person from Lebanon. *Br* (Buarque de Holanda 1975:835) 20.

[Cf. **turco.**]

liberto 'freed; freed slave'

black or mulatto slave who was given or acquired freedom. *Br*

(Mott 1974:17) early19.
[Syn. *forro.*]
loiro — See *louro*
lourinho 'little blond'
person whose hair and skin color are light. *Br-BA-Salvador* (Sanjek 1971:1141) 20.
[< *louro* 'blond' + dim. suf. -*inho.* Cf. **louro.**]
louro 'blond'
1a. person with blond hair. *Br* (Bluteau 1716:5-L.188–89) early18.
1b. white person with blond hair. *Br-n.e.* (Hutchinson 1957:118) 20.
2a. person who probably has light skin color. *Br* (Harris 1964a:58); *Br-BA* (Sanjek 1971:1141) 20.
2b. person with light skin or hair color, acc. 1980 census. *Br* (Silva 1987:159) 20.
[Df. 1a also used in Portugal. Acc. Hutchinson, df. 1b ant. *moreno* 'brunet.' Df. 2a used in surveys. Acc. Silva, color classification. Acc. Machado (1952:2.1360), att. from 16 cent. as 'light chestnut color.' Var. *loiro.* Cf. **acastanhado, agalegado, alvo, amarelado, avermelhado, bem branco, lourinho, moreno, vermelho,** Sp. **chele, pelicandelo, rubio.**]

M

macaco 'type of monkey; ugly'
black person. *Br* (Chamberlain and Harmon 1983:308) 20.
[Cf. **negro, preto,** Sp. **macaco.**]
macaco de cartola — See *negro pó de arroz*
mãe preta 'black mother'
female slave of color who cared for the master's children. *Br-BA* (Pierson 1942:374) prior20.
[F. only. Var. *mãe-preta.* Cf. **ama, ama de criar, ama de leite, babá, preto,** Sp. **ama.**]
mãe-de-santo — See Sp. **santero**
mãe-preta — See *mãe preta*
malê
1. black Muslim slave. *Br* (Nuñez 1980:293) cl.
2. Brazilian Muslim of African origin now found in small communities in BA and RJ. *Br* (Buarque de Holanda 1975:870) 20.
[Acc. Nuñez, < African word, possibly Arabic. Acc. Buarque de

Holanda, < African origin. Cf. **malê de Salvador, malungo, mandinga, marabu,** Sp. **marabú.**]

malê de Salvador

black person. *Br Br-BA-Salvador* (Silva 1987:71) 20. [Cf. **negro, malê, preto.**]

maleiro — See *baiano*

malinke — See *mandinga*

malungo

1. black slave, acc. fellow slaves on an African slave boat. *Br* (Souza 1961:197; Cascudo 1962:448–49; Freyre 1964:418) cl.

2. young black slave playmate of the master's children. *Br* (Freyre 1964:418) cl; (Levine 1979:134) 19prior.

[Acc. Cascudo, usually in phr. *meu malungo*; < Congolese lg. *m'alungu* < *mualungu* 'on the ship.' Acc. Buarque de Holanda (1975:873), < Kimbundu *ma'lūga* 'companion.' Acc. Freyre, < African word for 'comrade'; also used by mates in the Brz. *quilombos,* or runaway slave camps. Acc. Machado (1952:2.1404), < Kimbundu lg. Sim. to cl. Sp. *carabela* and to modern Amer. Black Engl. *bro* or *blood*. Cf. Sp. **carabela.**]

mamaluco — See *mameluco*

mambebe

person whose skin color perhaps indicates racial mixture. *Br-Arembepe* (Harris and Kottak 1963:203) 20. [Cf. **membebe.**]

mameluco

1. person whose skin color indicates racial mixture. *Br* (Aguirre Beltrán 1972:178) cl–20 ‖ *Br-BA* (Sanjek 1971:1141) 20.

2. person of mixed race. *Br* (Woodbridge 1948:358; Freyre 1964:418) cl; (Levine 1979:135) 20prior.

3. Brazilian half-breed, usually of black and Indian, who hunted savage Indians and put them in their service or sold them as slaves in MG. *Br* (Bayo 1910:133) cl.

4. offspring of a white and a mestizo, whose skin color was cinnamon-brown. *Br* (Segovia 1911:239) early20; (Santamaría 1942:2.224) 20; (Vergara Martín 1922:239–40) n.d.

5a. offspring of a white, usually Portuguese, and an Indian; mestizo. *Br* (Freyre 1964:418; Woodbridge 1948:358; Rosenblat 1954:2.102; Santamaría 1942:2.224; Mott 1974:155; Marcgrave 1648:268; Wagley 1949:216; Poppino 1968:58; Souza 1961:198; Ramos 1944:25; Harris 1964a:116; Mörner 1967:70; Boxer 1962:17) cl; (Russell-Wood 1982:30) cl–18; (Ramos 1947:29) late19; (Ayrosa 1937:163–67) 16–mid20; (Levine 1979:135) 20prior; (Cascudo 1962:451; Reis 1961:324; Diégues 1963:103; Alba

1969:34; Bailey and Nasatir 1973:772) 20; (Ribeiro n.d.:19; Vergara Martín 1922:239–40) n.d. ‖ *Br-n.e.* (Kelsey 1940:60) cl ‖ *Br-BA* (Megenney 1978:85) late18 ‖ *Br-SE* (Mott 1976:14); *Br-BA* (Harris 1964a:87) 20.

5b. offspring of a white European and an Indian, whose skin color is cinnamon-brown. *Br* (Segovia 1911:239) early20.

5c. offspring of a white man and an Indian woman. *Br Br-PA-Belém* (Cascudo 1962:450–51) 20.

6a. offspring of a black and a white, generally European. *Br* (Souza 1961:198) cl; (Moraes e Silva 1789:2.48) 18.

6b. offspring of a white European father and a black mother. *Br* (Bluteau 1716:5-M.276–77) early18.

7. offspring of a white and a *curiboca;* quadroon; person who is 1/4 white. *Br* (Santamaría 1942:2.224; Souza 1961:198); *Br-AM* (Diégues 1963:105) 20.

8. offspring of a white mestizo and a *curiboca. Br* (Vergara Martín 1922:239–40) n.d.

9. offspring of a white, probably European, and a creole, perhaps a black native to Br. *Br* (Vergara Martín 1922:239–40) n.d.

10. offspring of an Indian and a mulatto. *Br* (Moraes e Silva 1789:2.48) 18.

11. *paulista,* or person from SP. *Br* (Alonso 1958:2.2675; Santamaría 1942:2.224) 20.

12. *mineiro,* or person from MG. *Br* (Vergara Martín 1922: 239–40) n.d.

[Df. 2 generic term. Acc. Alba, syns. df. 5a *caboclo, curiboca.* Acc. Kelsey, df. 5a indicates vain or evil person. Syn. df. 7 *quarteirão,* acc. Souza and Santamaría. Possibly < Arabic *mamluk* 'one who is enslaved,' partic. of *malaka* 'to own or govern,' acc. Souza, Corominas (1954–57:3.213–14 and 1973:376), Alonso (1958:2.2675), and Machado (1952:2.1406). Acc. Vergara Martín, perhaps connected to the *mamelucos* of Egypt, since those of America were known for their cruelty against the Indians. Acc. Moraes e Silva, 'Turk raised in the art of warfare;' var. *mamuloco.* Acc. Machado, first att. 1513. Acc. Corominas and Alonso, first att. 1585. Acc. Souza, Cascudo, and Santamaría (1942:2.224), < Tupi *mamaruca* or *mamairuúca* 'mixed, mestizo,' < *mamã* 'to mix' + *ruca* or *yruuca* 'to throw,' thus having no conncection with the *mameluco oriental.* Acc. Buarque de Holanda (1975:874), < Arabic *mamluk* 'slave, servant.' Perhaps the Arabic and Tupi words combined in Br with one reinforcing the other. Syns. with meaning 'mestizo' *tapuio, paroara, vaqueiro* on Marajó Island, no. Br, *cuibano* in MT, *cearense, cangaceiro, jangadeiro, praieiro* in São Francisco area, *capiau* in BA and MG, *caiçara, caipira* in SP; var. *mamaluco,* acc. Reis. Sim. to Fr.

mamelouque or *meamelouc.* Cf. **caipira, cearense, cuiabano, curiboca, mestiço, paroara, tapuio, vaqueiro,** Sp. **mestizo.**]

mamuloco — See *mameluco*

mandinga
African black. *Br* (Cascudo 1962:452) cl.
[M., f. Acc. Cascudo, syn. *malinke.* Acc. Buarque de Holanda (1975:876), these Africans were racially mixed with Berbers or Ethiopians and were of Islamic religion. Cf. **africano, guinéu, negro, preto.**]

mandioqueiro
rustic type; hick. *Br-RN* (Ayrosa 1937:81) mid20 ‖ *Br-MG* (Buarque de Holanda (1975:877) 20.
[< *mandioca* 'manioc root' + suf. *-eiro.* Acc. Ayrosa, syn. *caipira.* Cf. **caipira.**]

marabu
Moslem hermit. *Br* (Pescatello 1975:248) 20.
[Acc. Buarque de Holanda (1975:885), < Fr. *marabout* 'Moslem hermit or saint.' Cf. **malê,** Sp. **marabú.**]

marabuto — See *galego*

mareno
person who is a mixture of Indian, black, and white, whose hair is straight, and whose nose is somewhat broad like that of a black. *Br* (Thompson 1965b:34) 20.
[Possibly var. of *moreno* 'brown.' Cf. **moreno, pardo.**]

marinheiro 'sailor'
1. continental Portuguese. *Br-no.* (Souza 1961:205) 20.
2. any foreigner. *Br-CE* (Buarque de Holanda (1975:891) 20.
[Ext. to all Ptg. as a result of their fame as great sailors. Possibly pejor. Cf. **galego.**]

marosca
mestizo, mulatto, *caboclo,* or other mixed-race woman. *Br-RS* (Coruja et al. 1964:312) 20.
[F. Acc. Machado (1952:2.1438), of unknown origin; att. 1890. Acc. Coruja et al., possibly < *morocha,* < Sp. *moro.* Cf. **caboclo, mestiço, misturado, morocho, mulato.**]

maroto — See *galego*

marreta — See *galego*

marrom 'chestnut-brown'
person whose skin color is chestnut-brown. *Br-BA-Salvador* (Sanjek 1971:1141) 20.
[F. form *marrona.* Acc. Machado (1952:2.1439), < Fr. *marron.* Cf. **acastanhado, moreno, pardo.**]

marrona — See *marrom*

masambo — See *mazombo*

mascate — See *galego*

matuto

rustic type; hick. *Br-AL, -MG, -PB, -PE, -RN, -SP* (Ayrosa 1937:81) mid20.

[Acc. Buarque de Holanda (1975:900), < *mato* 'shrubland' + suf. *-uto.* Cf. **caipira.**]

mau cidadão 'bad citizen'

person of color; black person. *Br* (Silva 1987:200) 20.

[Derog. Syn. **cidadão de segunda classe.** Cf. **bom cidadão, boa gente, gente de cor, gente sinhá.**]

maxacali

person of the Maxacali Brazilian Indian tribe found in northeastern MG near BA. *Br* (Buarque de Holanda 1975:901; Gomes de Matos 1988:p.c.) 20.

[Acc. Gomes de Matos, *maxakalí* [*sic*]. Vars. *maxacari, maxakali, maxakalí.* Cf. **bororo, gavião, tapanhuna.**]

maxacari — See *maxacali*

maxakali — See *maxacali*

maxakalí — See *maxacali*

mazombo

1a. person of foreign parents, usually peninsular Portuguese or European, born in Br. *Br* (Freyre 1964:419; Marcgrave 1648:268; Mott 1974:155) cl; (Bailey and Nasatir 1973:773) n.d. ‖ *Br Br-PE* (Souza 1961:211) prior20 ‖ *Br-SE* (Mott 1976:14) 20.

1b. Brazilian Portuguese person. *Br* (Rosenblat 1954:2.99; Burns 1980:549) cl; (Levine 1979:139) 20prior.

1c. offspring of whites born in Br. *Br* (Diégues 1963:106) cl.

2. black from Africa. *Br* (Alvarez Nazario 1974:356) cl.

[Df. 1a derog. Acc. Bailey and Nasatir, *masambo* [*sic*]. Acc. Souza, originally 'European parentage,' opp. by. *crioulo, filho do reino, reinol.* Acc. Machado (1952:2.1450–51), < African lg. Acc. Alvarez Nazario (1974:356), < *Moçambique* 's.e. African country from which many black slaves were extracted.' Vars. *masambo, moçambo, mosombo, mozombo.* Cf. **crioulo, filho do reino.**]

mbembo

1. white boy or guy, acc. blacks. *Br-MG* (Machado Filho 1964:122) 20prior.

2. superintendent; manager. *Br-MG* (Machado Filho 1964:122) 20prior.

[Acc. Machado Filho, < African lg.; used in diamond mines by black workers in creolized Ptg. Cf. Sp. **bembo.**]

médio 'medium; middle'

moreno whose skin color is medium. *Br-BA-Salvador* (Sanjek 1971:1135) 20.

[Used in ref. to 'medium color,' i.e., brownish, between black and white. Cf. **moreno.**]

meio claro 'medium-light'

moreno whose skin color is medium-light. *Br-BA-Salvador* (Sanjek 1971:1135) 20.

[Cf. **médio, pardavasco,** Sp. **mediopelo.**]

meio pardo — See *pardavasco*

melado 'honey-colored, honey-brown'

person with honey-brown skin color, acc. 1980 census. *Br* (Silva 1987:159) 20.

[Acc. Silva, color classification. Cf. **acastanhado, agalegado, alvo, amarelado, avermelhado, bem branco, branco melado, mestiço, miscigenação, misto, morenado, moreno acanelado, mulato alvacento, vermelho.**]

membebe

person whose skin color probably indicates racial mixture. *Br* (Harris 1964a:58) 20.

[Cf. **mambebe.**]

menelique

person of color, or black person, acc. persons of Italian descent. *Br-SP* (Fernandes 1969:146, 452); *Br* (Levine 1980:85) 20.

[Acc. Levine, perhaps < *moleque.* Acc. Fernandes, derog. var. *minelite.* Cf. **negro, preto.**]

mestiço 'mestizo'

1a. person whose skin color indicates racial mixture; mestizo. *Br-BA* (Sanjek 1971:1141); *Br* (Silva 1987:159) 20.

1b. person of color, usually with brown skin, of middle social standing. *Br-n.e.* (Kelsey 1940:60) mid20.

2. offspring of a white and an Indian; 50% white, 50% Indian; mestizo. *Br* (Mörner 1967:70) cl; (Esteva Fabregat 1964:281) 20.

3. any person of mixed race. *Br-n.e.* (Hutchinson 1957:126); *Br* (Azevedo 1970:2.172) 20 ‖ *Br-BA* (Pierson 1942:139–40) mid20.

4. offspring of a white and a black; mulatto. *Br* (Mörner 1967:70) cl; (Wagley 1949:222) late19; (Nuñez 1980:315) 20.

5. offspring of a mulatto and a *caboclo. Br* (Wagley 1949:223) 20prior.

6. offspring of parents from different nations. *Br* (Bluteau 1716:5-M.455) early18.

[Acc. Silva, df. 1a 1980 census color classification. Acc. Azevedo, syns. df. 3 *pardo, caboclo, mulato, cafuso.* Df. 6 also used in Portugal. Acc. Moraes e Silva (1789:2.76, 78), var. *mistiço.* Sim. to Old Occitan *mestitz* 'bad, low,' Fr. *métis,* Italian *mestrizzo, mestizio.* < Late Latin *misticius* 'mixed,' acc. Alonso (1958:2.2807) and Corominas (1954–57:3.316). Acc. Zaccaria (1927:271–72), Italian *mestizo,* < Ibero-Romance, att. 1585. Derivs. in other lgs. such as *mestiezen* in Curaçao, acc. Hoetink (1973:26), *métif* in the Fr. An, acc. Aguirre Beltrán (1972:178), and *mustifino* or *mustifee* in Jamaica, acc. Reuter (1918:13) and Cassidy (1961:162). Cf. **acastanhado, agalegado, alvo, amarelado, avermelhado, bem branco, moreno acanelado, caboclo, cafuso, mameluco, melado, mestiço claro, misto, moreno, miscigenação, misto, morenado, mulato, mulato alvacento, pardo, vermelho,** Sp. **mestizo.**]

mestiço claro 'light mestizo'

1. offspring of a white and a Caribe Indian. *Br* (Woodbridge 1948:358) cl.

2. offspring of a white and a mestizo. *Br* (Woodbridge 1948:358; Santamaría 1942:2.275) cl.

3. offspring of a *curiboca* and a white. *Br* (Vergara Martín 1922:240) n.d.

[Acc. Vergara Martín, *mestizo claro* [*sic*]. Cf. **claro, mestiço.**]

mina

1. person whose skin color and other nonwhite physical features indicate nonwhite race. *Br* (van den Berghe 1967:71) 20.

2a. black, highly respected, Bahian woman. *Br* (Freyre 1964:420) cl.

2b. black slave woman with light skin color who was used sexually by the Portuguese master. *Br* (Levine 1980:87) prior20.

[M., f. Acc. Freyre, < *Forte de El Mina* on the we. African coast.' Acc. Mattoso (1986:251), < Ashanti, used in ref. to 'black peoples of we. Africa living in present-day Togo.']

mineiro 'miner; person from MG'

offspring of a Guarani Indian and a white Portuguese. *Br-MG* (Vergara Martín 1922:240) n.d.

[Acc. Vergara Martín, syn. *mameluco.* Cf. **mameluco.**]

minelite — See *menelique*

minuano

Indian who dwelled on the north bank of the Paraná River near the mouth of the Salado at the time of America's discovery. *Br* (Santamaría 1942:2.282); *Br-RS* (Buarque de Holanda 1975:927) cl.

[Acc. Santamaría, *minuán* [*sic*]. Acc. Alonso (1958:2.2841), same in SA. Cf. **indígena, índio.**]

miscigenação 'miscegenation'
person of mixed race, acc. 1980 census. *Br* (Silva 1987:159) 20.
[F. Acc. Silva, color classification. Cf. **acastanhado, agalegado, amarelado, avermelhado, bem branco, mestiço, misto, morenado, moreno, vermelho.**]
mistiço — See *mestiço*
misto 'mixed'
person of mixed race, acc. 1980 census. *Br* (Silva 1987:159) 20.
[Acc. Silva, color classification. Syn. *misturado.* Cf. **acastanhado, agalegado, amarelado, avermelhado, bem branco, mestiço, miscigenação, mistura danada, morenado, vermelho.**]
mistura danada 'damned mixture'
offspring of persons from different racial or ethnic backgrounds. *Br* (Levine 1980:88) 20.
[Cf. **misturada, misturo.**]
misturado 'mixed'
1. young mestizo, mulatto, or *caboclo* woman with brown skin color. *Br-RS* (Coruja et al. 1964:308) 20.
2. person of mixed race. *Br* (Buarque de Holanda 1975:931) 20.
[Acc. Coruja et al., df. 1 f. *misturada* [sic]. Syn. df. 2 *mixto.* < *mistura* 'mixture.' Syns. df. 1 *cabocla, mestiça, mulata.* Cf. **caboclo, mestiço, miscigenação, misto, misturo, mulato.**]
misturo
person whose skin color indicates racial mixture. *Br-BA-Salvador* (Sanjek 1971:1141) 20.
[< *mistura* 'mixture.' Cf. **mistura danada, misturada.**]
mixuango — See *muxuango*
mocambeiro
slave who took refuge in a *mocambo,* or runaway slave camp. *Br-PA* (Santa Rosa 1922:2.131) late19–early20.
[< *mocambo* 'runaway slave camp' + suf. *-eiro.* Cf. **quilombola,** Sp. **cimarrón.**]
moçambique 'Mozambique'
1. black person, usually a slave, from Mozambique on the east African coast. *Br* (Mendonça 1935:219) cl.
2. black slave from Mozambique brought to Br via India. *Br* (Nuñez 1980:318) prior20.
[M., f. Cf. **angola, guineu, negro de Angola,** Sp. **mozambique.**]
moçambo — See *mazombo*
mocorongo
1. offspring of a white and a black. *Br-interior* (Woodbridge 1948:358) cl.

2. offspring of a black and an Indian. *Br-interior* (Woodbridge 1948:358) cl.

3a. person of white, black, and Indian ancestry, with skin color ranging from dark to white, black, often curly, hair, and oblique eyes, who lives in the mountains. *Br* (Ramos 1941:537) mid20.

3b. hillbilly; hick. *Br-ea., -so.* (Chamberlain and Harmon 1983:338) 20.

4. black person who is the direct descendant of coffee-plantation slaves. *Br* (Ramos 1944:297) mid20.

[Df. 3b colloq. Acc. Machado (1952:2.1519), < Tupi. Cf. **caboclo, caipira, mameluco.**]

moleca 'young female child'

1. dark-skinned mestizo girl. *Br* (Cabral 1982:526) 20.

2. young girl of the lower classes. *Br* (Cabral 1982:526) 20.

[F. of *moleque.* Var. *molecota.* Cf. **cabra, cabrocha, plebe.**]

molecão

young black child. *Br* (Mattoso 1986:251) prior20.

[Syn. *molecote.* Acc. Mattoso, f. *molecona.* Acc. Alvarez Nazario (1974:338), f. *molecõa.* < *moleque* + aug. suf. *-ão.* Cf. **moleca, moleque,** Sp. **mulecón.**]

molecõa — See *molecão*

molecona — See *molecão*

molecota — See *moleca*

molecote

any boy, either white or of color. *Br* (Cabral 1982:526–27) 20.

[< *moleque* + suf. *-ote.* Acc. Freyre (1964:421), var. *mulecote.* Syn. *molecão.* Cf. **molecota, moleque, mulecote.**]

moleque 'child, kid'

1. small or young black slave. *Br* (Bluteau 1716:5-M.541) early18; (Segovia 1911:131) 19prior.

2a. small black child. *Br* (Moraes e Silva 1789:2.91) late18; (Mattoso 1986:251) prior20; (Cascudo 1962:486) 20.

2b. small black boy, acc. blacks. *Br* (Mendonça 1935:220–21) cl; (Cascudo 1962:486) 20.

2c. small black boy. *Br* (Cascudo 1962:486; Buarque de Holanda 1975:937) 20.

3. street urchin, regardless of color. *Br* (Pierson 1942:139–40) mid20.

4. person who has no dignity or who does not keep appointments. *Br* (Cascudo 1962:486) 20.

[Acc. Bluteau, term taken to Portugal. Acc. Moraes e Silva, syns. df. 2a *pretinho, negro pequeno.* Syn. df. 2c *negrinho.* Acc. Mattoso, other syns. and derivs. *moleca, molequinho* (< *moleque* + dim. suf.

-inho). Acc. Gomes de Matos (1988:p.c.), non-std. var. *muleque.* Acc.
Pierson, < African lg. Acc. Mendonça, < Abundu *muleque* 'boy.' Acc.
Buarque de Holanda (1975:937), < Kimbundu *mu'leke* 'child.' Cf.
moleca, molecote, muleque, Sp. **muleque.**]

molequinho — See *moleque, mulequinho*

mondrongo — See *galego*

morena 'brunet or dark woman'
ideal female type, having dark brown eyes, dark wavy or curly
hair, and white features. *Br-BA* (Nuñez 1980:323) 20.
[Desc. of a sexually attractive or desirable woman, considered more
passionate than other women. Cf. **moreno, mulata quente.**]

morenado 'browned'
person with browned or darkened skin color, acc. 1980 census.
Br (Silva 1987:159) 20.
[Acc. Silva, color classification. Var. *amorenado.* Cf. **acastanhado,
agalegado, alvo, amarelado, amorenado, avermelhado, bem
branco, morenão, vermelho.**]

morenão 'large brown one'
person, perhaps large, with dark brown skin color, acc. 1980
census. *Br* (Silva 1987:159) 20.
[Acc. Silva, color classification. Cf. **acastanhado, agalegado, alvo,
amarelado, avermelhado, bem branco, morenado, moreno,
moreno bronzeado, moreno castanho, moreno claro, moreno
cor de canela, moreno fechado, moreno escuro, moreno
prata, moreno roxo, moreno ruivo, moreno trigueiro, mulato,
vermelho.**]

moreninho 'small brown one'
person whose skin color is brown or brownish. *Br-BA-Salvador*
(Sanjek 1971:1140); *Br* (Silva 1987:159) 20.
[Acc. Silva, 1980 census color classification. < *moreno* + dim. suf.
-inho. Desc. rather than derog. Cf. **acastanhado, agalegado,
alvo, amarelado, avermelhado, bem branco, morenão,
moreninho de cabelo bom, moreninho escuro, moreno,** Sp.
morenito.]

moreninho cabelo bom — See *moreninho de cabelo bom*

moreninho de cabelo bom 'small brown person with good hair'
brown-skinned person with straight (i.e., not kinky) hair
texture. *Br-BA-Salvador* (Sanjek 1971:1140) 20.
[Var. *moreninho cabelo bom.* Desc. rather than derog. Cf.
moreninho, moreninho escuro, moreno, Sp. **morenito
acrespado.**]

moreninho escuro 'small, dark-brown one'
person with dark brown skin color. *Br-BA-Salvador* (Sanjek

319

1971:1140) 20.

[Cf. **escuro, moreninho, moreninho de cabelo bom, moreno, moreno claro.**]

moreno 'brown; brown-skinned one; brunet'

1a. person whose skin color is brown, acc. parish records, literature, surveys, and other documents. *Br* (Vianna 1937:84; Harris 1964a:58; Silva 1987:159); *Br-BA* (Sanjek 1971:1129) 20.

1b. person with brown skin color, acc. national home survey. *Br* (Soares and Silva 1987:166) 20.

2. person of color, generally light-skinned, but often without regard to true skin color. *Br* (Degler 1971:201) 20.

3a. racially mixed person who is considered white socially; social white. *Br* (Thompson 1965a:29) 20.

3b. racially mixed person with dark brown eyes, café-au-lait hair which is wavy or curly, and generally white features. *Br-BA* (Pierson 1942:136–37) mid20.

4a. white person with brunet hair. *Br-n.e.* (Hutchinson 1957:118) 20.

4b. person of mixed race or parentage who generally has brunet hair. *Br-AM-Itá* (Wagley 1953:130 and 1963:121) 20.

4c. person whose skin color looks like that of a white person with a heavy sunburn and who generally has brunet hair. *Br-Minas Velhas* (Harris 1956:119) 20.

4d. person who is not all white, but whose skin color is fair, whose hair is brunet, long, and not curly, and whose features are less black than white. *Br-n.e.* (Hutchinson 1957:120); *Br* (Kottak 1967:44) 20.

4e. dark-skinned person who generally has brunet hair, generally describing the average Brazilian in a non-racial way. *Br* (Shoumatoff 1980:137) 20.

5a. black person. *Br* (Levine 1979:143) 20.

5b. black person; person of color. *Br* (Chamberlain and Harmon 1983:342) 20.

6. mulatto. *Br* (Nuñez 1980:323) 20.

7. gaucho woman; woman of the countryside; young girl. *Br-RS* (Coruja et al. 1964:312) 20.

[Acc. Silva, df. 1a 1980 census color classification. Df. 2 vague euph. used in direct address, acc. Degler. Acc. Pierson, df. 3b represents new ideal in Brz. physical types, perhaps sim. to the idea of the *mulata quente.* Acc. Levine, df. 5a polite; sim. in 1960s and 1970s to *pardo.* Acc. Chamberlain and Harmon, df. 5b colloq., euph.; syn. *escuro.* Df. 7 f. only. Cf. **acastanhado, agalegado, alvo, amarelado, avermelhado, bem branco, escuro, gaúcho,** mameluco, mestiço, morena, moreno alvo, moreno bem chegado, moreno bem suspeito, moreno claro, mouro, mulato, mulata quente, pardo, vermelho, Sp. moreno.]

moreno alvo 'white brown or brunet'
person with brunet hair and/or light brown skin color. *Br-BA-Salvador* (Sanjek 1971:1140) 20.
[Cf. **alvo, moreno, moreno bem claro.**]

moreno bem chegado 'very brown-skinned one'
person with very brown or dark brown skin color, acc. 1980 census. *Br* (Silva 1987:159) 20.
[Acc. Silva, color classification. Cf. **acastanhado, agalegado, alvo, amarelado, avermelhado, bem branco, morenado, moreno, moreno bem claro, moreno bem escuro, moreno bronzeado, moreno castanho, moreno claro, moreno cor de canela, moreno fechado, moreno escuro, moreno prata, moreno roxo, moreno ruivo, moreno trigueiro, mulato, vermelho.**]

moreno bem claro 'very light brown or brunet'
person with light brown skin color. *Br-BA-Salvador* (Sanjek 1971:1140) 20.
[Cf. **claro, moreno, moreno alvo, moreno bem escuro.**]

moreno bem escuro 'very dark brown or brunet'
person with dark brown skin color. *Br-BA-Salvador* (Sanjek 1971:1140) 20.
[Cf. **escuro, moreno, moreno alvo, moreno bem claro,** Sp. **moreno oscuro.**]

moreno bem suspeito 'very suspicious brown or brunet'
person of the upper class, considered white, but often with some black ancestry. *Br-no.* (Wagley 1971:254) late19.
[Cf. **moreno, moreno bem claro, moreno bem escuro.**]

moreno bronzeado 'suntan-brown or brunet'
person with bronzed, suntanned, or dark brown skin color. *Br-BA-Salvador* (Sanjek 1971:1140); *Br* (Silva 1987:159) 20.
[Acc. Silva, 1980 census color classification. Cf. **acastanhado, agalegado, alvo, amarelado, avermelhado, bem branco, morenado, moreno, moreno bem claro, moreno bem escuro, moreno bronzeado, moreno castanho, moreno claro, moreno cor de canela, moreno fechado, moreno escuro, moreno prata, moreno roxo, moreno ruivo, moreno trigueiro, mulato, vermelho.**]

moreno cabelo sarará 'brown or brunet with *sarará*-like hair'
person with dark skin and probably kinky hair. *Br-BA-Salvador* (Sanjek 1971:1140) 20.
[Cf. **cabelo bom, moreno, sarará.**]

moreno cabo verde 'Cape Verdean-like brown or brunet'
person whose skin color is very dark brown. *Br* (Harris 1970:5);
Br-BA (Sanjek 1971:1140) 20.
[Acc. Harris, used in a survey. Cf. **cabo verde, moreno.**]

moreno caboclo *'caboclo*-like brown or brunet'
person whose hair and skin color are brown. *Br* (Harris 1970:5)
20.
[Cf. **caboclo, moreno.**]

moreno canelado 'cinnamon-colored brown or brunet'
person with reddish or cinnamon-colored brown skin color, acc.
1980 census. *Br* (Silva 1987:159) 20.
[Acc. Silva, color classification. Cf. **acastanhado, agalegado, alvo,
amarelado, avermelhado, bem branco, morenado, moreno,
moreno bem claro, moreno bem escuro, moreno bronzeado,
moreno castanho, moreno claro, moreno cor de canela,
moreno fechado, moreno escuro, moreno prata, moreno roxo,
moreno ruivo, moreno trigueiro, mulato, vermelho.**]

moreno castanho 'chestnut brown'
person with chestnut-brown skin color, acc. 1980 census. *Br*
(Silva 1987:159) 20.
[Acc. Silva, color classification. Cf. **acastanhado, agalegado, alvo,
amarelado, avermelhado, bem branco, morenado, moreno,
moreno bem claro, moreno bem escuro, moreno bronzeado,
moreno canelado, moreno cor de canela, moreno fechado,
moreno escuro, moreno prata, moreno roxo, moreno ruivo,
moreno trigueiro, mulato, vermelho.**]

moreno claro 'light brown or brunet'
person whose skin color and/or hair are light brown. *Br-BA*
(Sanjek 1971:1129); *Br* (Hutchinson 1952:27–31; Harris 1964a:58;
Soares and Silva 1987:166–67; Silva 1987:159) 20.
[Acc. Soares and Silva, used in a national home survey. Acc. Silva,
1980 census color classification. Cf. **acastanhado, agalegado,
alvo, amarelado, avermelhado, bem branco, claro, morenado,
moreno, moreno bem claro, moreno bem escuro, moreno
bronzeado, moreno canelado, moreno cor de canela, moreno fechado, moreno escuro, moreno prata, moreno roxo,
moreno ruivo, moreno trigueiro, mulato, vermelho,** Sp.
moreno claro.]

moreno claro caboclado *'caboclo*-like light brown or brunet'
person whose skin color is light brownish. *Br* (Harris 1964a:58);
Br-Arembepe (Harris and Kottak 1963:203) 20.
[Cf. **caboclado, claro, moreno, moreno bem claro, moreno
claro.**]

moreno cor de canela 'cinnamon-colored brown'
person whose skin color is cinnamon-brown. *Br-BA-Salvador* (Sanjek 1971:1140); *Br-sertão* (Zimmerman 1963:94); *Br* (Silva 1987:159) 20.
[Acc. Silva, 1980 census color classification. Cf. **acastanhado, agalegado, alvo, amarelado, avermelhado, bem branco, cor de canela, morenado, moreno, moreno bem claro, moreno bem escuro, moreno bronzeado, moreno canelado, moreno castanho, moreno claro, moreno fechado, moreno escuro, moreno prata, moreno roxo, moreno ruivo, moreno trigueiro, mulato, vermelho.**]

moreno de cabelo bom 'brown or brunet with good hair'
brown-skinned person with straight, not kinky, and probably brown hair. *Br-BA* (Sanjek 1971:1140) 20.
[Cf. **cabelo bom, mestiço de cabelo bom, moreninho de cabelo bom, moreno, moreno cabelo sarará.**]

moreno de cabelo cacheado 'brown with curly or wavy hair'
brown-skinned person with curly or wavy hair. *Br-BA-Salvador* (Sanjek 1971:1140) 20.
[Acc. Sanjek, *cachiado* [*sic*]. Cf. **moreno, moreno de cabelo bom.**]

moreno de cabelo escuhido
person whose skin color is brown and whose hair is probably curly or kinky. *Br-BA-Salvador* (Sanjek 1971:1140) 20.
[*Escuhido* possibly deformation of *esculpido* 'sculpted.' Cf. **moreno, moreno de cabelo bom.**]

moreno de cabelo liso 'brown or brunet with straight hair'
brown-skinned person with straight hair. *Br-BA-Salvador* (Sanjek 1971:1140) 20.
[Cf. **moreno, moreno de cabelo bom.**]

moreno de cabelo ruim 'brown or brunet with bad hair'
brown-skinned person with kinky hair. *Br-BA-Salvador* (Sanjek 1971:1140) 20.
[Used in ref. to person with hair texture like that of a black person, therefore bad or undesirable hair. Cf. **cabelo ruim, moreno, moreno de cabelo bom.**]

moreno de olhos verdes 'brown or brunet with green eyes'
brown-skinned person with green eyes. *Br-n.e., -sertão* (Zimmerman 1963:96) 20.
[Acc. Zimmerman, most preferred type of skin color and features in parts of n.e. Br. Cf. **moreno, moreno de cabelo bom, moreno de cabelo ruim, muxuango.**]

moreno escurinho 'darkish brunet or brown'
person with darkish brown skin color and perhaps brunet hair. *Br-BA-Salvador* (Sanjek 1971:1140) 20.

[Cf. **escuro, moreno, moreno escuro.**]

moreno escuro 'dark brown or brunet'
person with dark skin color and perhaps brunet hair. *Br-BA* (Sanjek 1971:1140); *Br* (Hutchinson 1952:27–31; Harris 1964a:58; Silva 1987:159) 20.

[Acc. Silva, 1980 census color classification. Cf. **acastanhado, agalegado, alvo, amarelado, avermelhado, bem branco, escuro, moreninho escuro, moreno, moreno claro, moreno escurinho, moreno fechado,** Sp. **indio oscuro, moreno oscuro.**]

moreno escuro claro 'light-dark brown or brunet'
person with medium brown skin color, acc. survey. *Br* (Harris 1970:5) 20.

[Phr. is combination of ants. *claro* 'light' and *escuro* 'dark.' Cf. **escuro, moreno, moreno claro, moreno escuro.**]

moreno fechado 'taciturn or dead brown'
person with washed-out brown skin color, acc. 1980 census. *Br* (Silva 1987:159) 20.

[Acc. Silva, color classification. Cf. **acastanhado, agalegado, alvo, amarelado, avermelhado, bem branco, morenado, moreno, moreno bem claro, moreno bem escuro, moreno bronzeado, moreno canelado, moreno claro, moreno cor de canela, moreno escuro, moreno prata, moreno roxo, moreno ruivo, moreno trigueiro, mulato, vermelho.**]

moreno fino 'fine brown or brunet'
dark-skinned person with features considered good, generally those of a white. *Br-n.e.* (Hutchinson 1957:120) 20.

[Syn. *bem moreninho.* Cf. **bem moreninho, moreno.**]

moreno laranjado 'orangish-brown or brunet'
person with orangish-brown skin color. *Br-BA-Salvador* (Sanjek 1971:1140) 20.

[*Laranjado* < *laranja* 'orange' + adj. suf. *-ado.* Cf. **moreno.**]

moreno mestiço 'mestizo-like brown or brunet'
person with mestizo-brown skin color, acc. survey. *Br* (Harris 1970:5) 20.

[Cf. **mestiço, moreno, moreno mulato,** Sp. **moreno o mestizo.**]

moreno mulato 'mulatto-like brown or brunet'
person whose skin color is of one who is not a pure mulatto. *Br-n.e.* (Hutchinson 1957:122–23) 20.

[Acc. Hutchinson, *morena mulata* [sic]. Cf. **moreno, moreno mestiço, mulato.**]

moreno prata 'silver brown'
person with silverish-brown or shiny brown skin color, acc.
1980 census. *Br* (Silva 1987:159) 20.
[Acc. Silva, color classification; f. *morena prata.* Cf. **acastanhado,
agalegado, alvo, amarelado, avermelhado, bem branco,
moreno, moreno castanho, moreno claro, moreno escuro,
moreno fechado, moreno roxo, moreno ruivo, vermelho.**]

moreno preto 'black-brown; dark brown or brunet'
person with dark brown skin color, acc. survey. *Br* (Harris
1970:5) 20.
[Cf. **moreno, moreno mestiço, moreno mulato, preto.**]

moreno roxo 'purple brown or brunet'
person whose skin color is deep brown or purplish-brown. *Br-
BA-Salvador* (Sanjek 1971:1140); *Br* (Silva 1987:159) 20.
[Acc. Silva, 1980 census color classification. Cf. **acastanhado, agalegado, alvo, amarelado, avermelhado, bem branco, moreno,
moreno castanho, moreno claro, moreno escuro, moreno
fechado, moreno mestiço, moreno mulato, moreno preto,
moreno prata, moreno ruivo, roxo, vermelho.**]

moreno ruivo 'reddish-brown'
person whose skin color is reddish-brown, acc. 1980 census. *Br*
(Silva 1987:159) 20.
[Acc. Silva, color classification. Cf. **acastanhado, agalegado, alvo,
amarelado, avermelhado, bem branco, moreno, moreno
castanho, moreno claro, moreno escuro, moreno fechado,
moreno mestiço, moreno mulato, moreno preto, moreno
prata, moreno roxo, roxo, ruivo, vermelho.**]

moreno sarará
person whose skin color is dark brown. *Br* (Harris 1970:5); *Br-
BA* (Sanjek 1971:1140) 20.
[Cf. **moreno, moreno cabelo sarará, sarará.**]

moreno trigueiro 'wheat-colored or light brown'
person whose skin color is light brown, acc. 1980 census. *Br*
(Silva 1987:159) 20.
[Acc. Silva, color classification. Cf. **acastanhado, agalegado, alvo,
amarelado, avermelhado, bem branco, moreno, moreno
castanho, moreno claro, moreno escuro, moreno fechado,
moreno mestiço, moreno mulato, moreno preto, moreno
prata, moreno roxo, roxo, ruivo, trigueiro, vermelho.**]

morocha — See *morocho*

morocho 'brown; brunet'
1. person with brown skin color. *Br-RS* (Coruja et al. 1964:312)
20.

2. young, brown-skinned girl; country girl. *Br-RS* (Coruja et al. 1964:312) 20.

[Df. 2 f. *morocha* < *muruchu* or *muruch'u* 'hard, strong, brown, dark, chestnut-colored,' acc. Alonso (1958:2.2897), Santamaría (1942:2.300), Corominas (1954–57:3.444 and 1973:404), and Cowles (1952:529). Cf. **moreno,** Sp. **morocho.**]

mosca no leite 'fly in the milk'

black person, usually a man, standing alone among a crowd of whites or dressed up in white clothes. *Br* (Chamberlain and Harmon 1983:344) 20.

[M., f. Also acc. Degler (1971:187), 'mixed marriage, marriage between persons of different races or colors.' Cf. **negro, negro pó de arroz, preto.**]

mosombo — See *mazombo*

mouro 'Moor, Moorish'

1. black slave. *Br* (Verlinden 1943:20) 15.

2. slave. *Br* (D'Azevedo 1903:290) 15–cl.

[Acc. Verlinden, syns. *negro, guineu, servo, escravo*; also used in Portugal. Acc. D'Azevedo, df. 2 used in ref. to the quality of the slave rather than the nationality or physical type. Acc. Leite de Vasconcellos (1928:37), *mourisco* 'Moorish Moslem who converted to Christianity after the Reconquest' found in use in Portugal in 16 and 17 cents. and *mouro forro* 'freed Moor' through the 15 cent. Cf. **casta, escravo, guineu, moreno, negro,** Sp. **morisco.**]

mozambo — See *mazombo*

mozombo — See *mazombo*

mucama

1a. black slave woman, generally a young family favorite, used in domestic service as a housemaid, personal maid, or nursemaid. *Br* (Souza 1961:222; Freyre 1964:421) cl.

1b. young, trusted, black slave woman who served the master's wife as a maidservant. *Br* (Segovia 1911:131) 19prior.

1c. trusted black slave woman who generally served the master's wife. *Br* (Mendonça 1935:222–23) 19prior.

2. slave woman of a polygamous black man. *Br* (Ribeiro n.d.:119) n.d.

[F. Acc. Mendonça, Buarque de Holanda (1975:950), Pereda Valdés (1937:77), and Machado (1952:2.1547), < Kimbundu *mukama* 'slave woman, concubine.' Acc. Megenney, term used as a personal name in Gullah, Engl.-based creole lg. of s.e. US coast. Var. *mucamba*. Cf. **ama, babá, dona de casa, mucama de estimação,** Sp. **mucama.**]

mucama de estimação 'favored maid servant'
trusted, black maidservant, often used as a wetnurse for the white child of the master. *Br* (Freyre 1964:421) cl.
[F. Cf. **mucama, muleque de estimação.**]

mucamba — See *mucama*

mulata boa 'good mulatto woman'
sexually attractive mulatto woman. *Br-AM-Itá* (Wagley 1963:121) 20.
[Cf. **mulatinha bonita, mulato.**]

mulata quente 'hot mulatto woman'
sexually ideal, Brazilian woman, usually with light brown skin, dark eyes, and long, straight, dark-brunet hair. *Br* 20.
[F. Quite often the woman so described is simply very attractive and not at all mulatto. Phr. has lost racial meaning. In Br, *cho das mulatas* is normally what Amer. Engl. speakers would call a 'girly show,' rather in Las Vegas or Atlantic City style. Cf. **moreno, mulata boa, mulatinha bonita, mulato.**]

mulataço — See *mulato*

mulatete — See *mulatinho, mulato*

mulatinha bonita 'pretty little mulatto girl'
pretty girl, no matter what race. *Br-AM-Itá* (Wagley 1963:121) 20.
[Cf. **mulatinho, mulato.**]

mulatinho 'little mulatto'
person with the dark skin color sim. to that of a mulatto. *Br-BA-Salvador* (Sanjek 1971:1140); *Br* (Silva 1987:159) 20.
[< *mulato* + dim. suf. *-inho*. Acc. Silva, 1980 census color classification. Irregular syn. *mulatete,* acc. Buarque de Holanda (1975:952). Cf. **acastanhado, agalegado, alvo, amarelado, avermelhado, bem branco, moreninho, moreno, moreno castanho, moreno claro, moreno escuro, moreno fechado, moreno mestiço, moreno mulato, moreno preto, moreno prata, moreno roxo, mulato, roxo, ruivo, trigueiro, vermelho.**]

mulato 'mulatto'
1. person who has dark skin color like that of the mulatto. *Br* (Harris 1964a:58; Silva 1987:159); *Br-BA* (Sanjek 1971:1129) 20.
2a. offspring of a black and a white; mulatto; 50% white, 50% black. *Br* (Woodbridge 1948:359; Marcgrave 1648:268; Mott 1974:155; Alvarez Nazario 1974:351) cl; (Bluteau 1716:5-M.628) early18; (Moraes e Silva 1789:2.103) late18; (Ramos 1947:28–29) late19; (Esteva Fabregat 1964:281) 20prior; (Ramos 1944:23) mid20; (Alonso 1958:2.2919; Diégues 1963:103) 20 ‖ *Br-SE* (Mott 1976:14) 20.

2b. offspring of a black and a white, with pretty features and clear complexion, but of indolent character. *Br* (Ramos 1947:28–29) late19.

2c. person of mixed black and white ancestry. *Br* (Bailey and Nasatir 1973:773) 20.

2d. offspring of a mixture of black African and white Portuguese. *Br* (Thompson 1965a:29) 20.

3. offspring of a mulatto and a white. *Br* (Moraes e Silva 1789:2.103) late18.

4. person whose skin color is yellowish, light, or dark, whose hair is kinky or curly, and who has thin or thick lips and a narrow to wide nose.' *Br-n.e.* (Hutchinson 1957:120; Kottak 1967:44) 20.

5. person whose skin color is darker than that of the *moreno* and who has kinky hair. *Br-Minas Velhas* (Harris 1956:119) 20.

[Acc. Silva, df. 1 1980 census color classification. Acc. Bluteau, df. 2a also used in Portugal. Acc. Sanjek, 1 of 10 most salient racial terms used in Salvador. Acc. Pierson (1942:138), pejor. in mid-20 cent. BA. Syn. *pardo,* acc. Mott (1974:172). Acc. Buarque de Holanda (1975:952), aug. deriv. *mulataço*; dim. deriv. *mulatete.* First applied to 'offspring of European white and Moor' in Europe. Sim. to Engl. *mulatto* and Fr. *mulâtre.* Cf. **branco, escuro, mestiço, moreninho, moreno, mulatinho, negro, pardo, preto, trigueiro,** Sp. **mulato.**]

mulato acobreado 'copper-colored mulatto'
mulatto with kinky hair. *Br* (Cascudo 1962:156) 20.
[Cf. **mulato,** Sp. **cobrizo.**]

mulato alvacento — See *aça, sarará*

mulato bem claro 'very light mulatto'
mulatto whose skin color is very light. *Br* (Harris 1964a:58) 20.
[Cf. **moreno bem claro, mulato, mulato acobreado, mulato bem limpo.**]

mulato bem limpo 'very clean mulatto'
mulatto whose skin color is probably light. *Br-BA-Salvador* (Sanjek 1971:1140) 20.
[Cf. **mulato, mulato bem claro.**]

mulato branco 'white mulatto'
mulatto with white or light skin color, acc. survey. *Br* (Harris 1970:5) 20.
[Cf. **branco, mulato, mulato bem limpo, mulato claro,** Sp. **mulato blanco.**]

mulato caboclo '*caboclo*-like mulatto'
mulatto whose skin color is sim. to that of a *caboclo,* acc. survey. *Br* (Harris 1970:5) 20.

[Cf. **caboclo, mestiço caboclado, mulato, mulato branco, mulato claro.**]

mulato claro 'light mulatto'

1a. mulatto with light skin color. *Br* (Harris 1964a:58; Hutchinson 1952:27–31); *Br-BA-Salvador* (Sanjek 1971:1140) 20.

1b. light mulatto, esp. in certain social circles. *Br Br-Arembepe* (Kottak 1967:40) 20.

1c. light mulatto with straight hair, thin lips, and the narrow nose of a white. *Br-n.e.* (Hutchinson 1957:119) 20.

2. offspring of a black with Semitic or Hamitic ancestry and a white. *Br* (Woodbridge 1948:359) cl.

[Df. 1c sim. to *branco da terra*,' acc. Hutchinson. Var. *mulato-claro*. Cf. **branco da terra, claro, mulato, mulato branco,** Sp. **mulato claro.**]

mulato escuro 'dark mulatto'

1. mulatto whose skin color is dark. *Br-BA-Salvador* (Sanjek 1971:1140); *Br* (Harris 1964a:58; Hutchinson 1952:27–31) 20.

2. dark mulatto, esp. in certain social circles. *Br-n.e.* (Hutchinson 1957:119); *Br Br-Arembepe* (Kottak 1967:40) 20.

[Cf. **escuro, mulato, mulato bem claro, mulato claro,** Sp. **mulato oscuro.**]

mulato gazo 'light-eyed mulatto'

mulatto who probably has light skin color and light green eyes. *Br-BA-Salvador* (Sanjek 1971:1140) 20.

[Cf. **gazula, mulato.**]

mulato índio 'Indian-like mulatto'

mulatto with Indian-like features, acc. survey. *Br* (Harris 1970:5) 20.

[Cf. **índio, mulato, mulato caboclo.**]

mulato mestiço 'mestizo-like mulatto'

mulatto with mestizo-like features, acc. survey. *Br* (Harris 1970:5) 20.

[Phr. could imply mixture of black, white, and Indian races. Cf. **mulato, mulato índio,** Sp. **mulato amestizado.**]

mulato pachola — See *negro pó de arroz*

mulato preto 'black mulatto'

mulatto with black skin color. *Br-BA* (Sanjek 1971:1140) 20.

[Acc. Mellafe (1964:89), in cl. SA, generally 'offspring of a black and a *mulato pardo*' with skin color dark enough to pass for a black person. Cf. **mulato, mulato escuro, mulato pardo, preto,** Sp. **mulato prieto.**]

mulato sarará

mulatto with very dark skin color. *Br* (Harris 1964a:58 and

1970:5) 20.
[Cf. **moreno cabelo sarará, mulato, mulato preto, sarará.**]
mulato triguenho 'wheat-colored mulatto'
light-skinned mulatto. *Br* (Nuñez 1980:329) 20.
[*Triguenho* var. of *trigueiro*. Cf. **mulato, mulato claro, mulato preto, trigueiro.**]
muleca — See *muleque*
mulecote 'large *muleque*'
1. black child, usually a boy, with a sturdily built body. *Br* (Freyre 1964:421) cl.
2. person whose physical type and dark skin generally indicate black ancestry. *Br* (van den Berghe 1967:71) 20.
[Acc. Alvarez Nazario (1974:338), < *muleque* + aug. suf. *-ote,* implying that the boy is now near or beyond puberty. Cf. **moleque, muleque,** Sp. **mulecón, muleque.**]
muleque
young black, usually a slave. *Br* (Santamaría 1942:2.291; Freyre 1964:421) cl.
[F. form *muleca* 'maid in the master's house,' acc. Freyre. Acc. Mieres et al. (1966:94), Machado (1952:2.1524), and Alonso (1958:2.2919), < African lg. Acc. Machado, < Abundu 'child' about 1778. Acc. Alvarez Nazario (1974:338), < Caribbean lgs. *moulékê, muleki,* or *mureko,* 'little boy; boy.' Also possible that these Caribbean lgs. took word from slavers. Acc. Gomes de Matos (1988:p.c.), non-std. var. of *moleque.* In RP area of SA, syn. *negrito* 'little black boy,' acc. Pereda Valdés (1937:77). Vars. *moleque, moleca.* Cf. **moleque, mucama, mulato, negrinho,** Sp. **mulecón, muleque, negrito.**]
muleque companheiro de brinquedo 'little black playmate'
black slave child who played with the master's white child up to adolescence. *Br* (Levine 1980:91) 19.
[Cf. **mucama de estimação, muleque, muleque de estimação.**]
muleque de estimação 'slave child of distinction'
favorite black slave child who had the run of the master's house. *Br* (Freyre 1964:421) cl.
[This child often played with the children of the white master, or perhaps was also a child of the master by a slave woman. Cf. **mucama de estimação, muleque, muleque companheiro de brinquedo.**]
muleque pardo
muleque with dark skin color. *Br* (Aguirre Beltrán 1972:178) cl.
[Cf. **muleque, pardo.**]

mulequinho 'little *muleque*'
1. black child from birth to the age of 6 years. *Br* (Alvarez Nazario 1974:337–38) cl.
2. small black child, usually a boy; *Br* (Freyre 1964:421) cl.
[Acc. Alvarez Nazario (1974:338), < *muleque* + dim. suf. *-inho*. Var. *molequinho*. Sim. to Amer. Engl. *pickaninny*. Cf. **moleque, muleque, negrinho, pretinho**, Sp. **mulequillo, mulequín**.]

mulher de cama 'woman of the bed'
black slave woman kept by white men for sexual relations; black concubine. *Br* (Nuñez 1980:331) prior20.
[F. Cf. **morena, mulata quente**.]

mulher de cor 'woman of color'
any nonwhite woman or woman of color whom a white man marries. *Br* (Levine 1980:91) 19.
[F. Cf. **homem de cor, pessoa de cor**.]

mumbanda
favored black woman slave. *Br* (Levine 1979:145) 19prior.
[F. Acc. Buarque de Holanda (1975:954), < Kimbundu *mi-nbamda* 'woman.' Perhaps sexual connotations. Cf. **mucama de estimação**.]

mushuango — See *muxuango*

musulmí
Brazilian black who practices Islam; black Muslim. *Br* (Levine 1980:92) 20.
[Cf. **marabu, malê, negro, preto**, Sp. **marabú**.]

muxuango
1. offspring of a black and an Indian, often also with a white ancestor, who generally has light or white skin color, blond hair, greenish or blue eyes, thin lips, and an aqualine or white-type narrow nose, and who lives in the lowlands. *Br* (Ramos 1941:537) mid20.
2. offspring of whites and Indians who live in the river lowlands. *Br* (Ramos 1944:206–7) mid20.
3. offspring of a white and a Tupi or Tapuyas Indian, often also with a black ancestor. *Br-coast* (Woodbridge 1948:359) mid20.
4a. rustic type; hick. *Br-RJ* (Ayrosa 1937:81) mid20 ‖ *Br-SP* (Buarque de Holanda 1975:959) 20.
4b. rustic type, often a black, acc. rural dwellers. *Br-RJ* (Nuñez 1980:334) 20
[Acc. Nuñez, < Bantu. Vars. *mixuango, mushuango*.]

N

nação — See *de nação*

nagô

1a. black African of a Sudanic Yoruba tribe. *Br* (Mattoso 1986:251) prior20.

1b. black African of a Yoruba tribe. *Br* (Cascudo 1962:503) cl.

2. black from western Africa. *Br* (Cascudo 1962:503) cl.

[Acc. Cascudo, f. *nagoa*; < Ewe *anagó* 'Yoruba.' Cf. **negro,** Sp. **nagó.**]

nagoa — See *nagô*

nambikwara — See *nhambiquara*

nambiquara — See *nhambiquara*

não-branco 'nonwhite'

any person who is not white; nonwhite; person of color. *Br* (Silva 1987:159) late20.

[Acc. Silva, color designation. Cf. **acastanhado, agalegado, alvo, amarelado, avermelhado, bem branco, branco, gente de cor, pessoa de cor, vermelho,** Sp. **no blanco del todo.**]

nega — See *nego*

negão 'large black'

black friend, acc. a white. *Br* (Silva 1987:159) 20.

[Acc. Silva, color designation. Cf. **acastanhado, agalegado, alvo, amarelado, avermelhado, bem branco, negro, negrinho, vermelho.**]

nego

1. person with dark skin color. *Br-BA-Salvador* (Sanjek 1971:1141) 20.

2a. black person. *Br-BA-Salvador* (Sanjek 1971:1132); *Br* (Chamberlain and Harmon 1983:352) 20.

2b. black person, acc. other blacks. *Br* (Freyre 1964:370) cl.

[< *negro,* acc. Cabral (1982:543) and Freyre. Acc. Sanjek, df. 2a insult., esp. in form *nega,* not used in polite conversation; can be used with affection to refer to children. Acc. Chamberlain and Harmon, df. 2a colloq., affect., vocative; syn. *crioulo.* Acc. Freyre, df. 2b term of endearment among blacks. Acc. Alvarez Nazario (1974:347), derog. among blacks in ref. to a fellow's slave condition in cl. Cabo Verde. Often used as term of endearment in n.e. *Br,* acc. Hutchinson (1957:118), and as endearment between spouses, acc. Wagley (1949:260). Usually in phrs. such as *minha nega, meu nego, nego velho, neguinho* as affect. Extremely pejor. var. **nega.** Other vars. *nêgo, nêgu.* Deriv. *neguinho.* Cf. **negro, negrinho, preto,** Sp. **negrito.**]

negraço — See *negralhão,* Sp. **negrazo**

negrada
1. group of blacks. *Br* (Buarque de Holanda 1975:968) 20.
2. people; group of people. *Br* (Buarque de Holanda 1975:968) 20.
[< *negro.* Acc. Buarque de Holanda, syns. *negraria, negralhada.* Cf. **negro.**]

negralhada — See *negrada*

negralhão 'large black'
large black person. *Br* (Buarque de Holanda 1975:968) 20.
[F. form *negralhona.* Syns. *negraço, negrão.* Sim. to Sp. *negrazo.* Cf. **negro,** Sp. **negrazo.**]

negralhona — See *negralhão, negro*

negrão — See *negralhão, negro*

negreiro
1. trafficker of black slaves; black slave trader. *Br* (Buarque de Holanda 1975:968) prior20.
2. person who prefers blacks sexually. *Br* (Buarque de Holanda 1975:968) 20.
[M., f. Acc. Buarque de Holanda, < *negro* 'black' + suf. *-eiro.* Sim. to Sp. *negrero.* Cf. **negro,** Sp. **mulatero, negrero.**]

negrilho 'small black one'
very young black person. *Br* (Buarque de Holanda 1975:968) 20.
[Acc. Buarque de Holanda, < *negro* + dim. suf. *-ilho.* Cf. **negralhão, negrinho, negro,** Sp. **negrito.**]

negrinho 'little black one'
1. person with dark skin color. *Br-BA-Salvador* (Sanjek 1971:1141) 20.
2. child, acc. parents. *Br-RS* (Coruja et al. 1964:318) 20.
3. small black slave. *Br* (Bluteau 1716:5-N.702) early18.
[Df. 2 term of endearment in 20-cent. RS, acc. Coruja et al. (1964:318). Df. 3 also used in Portugal. Usually in phrs. *meu negrinho, minha negrinha.* < *negro* or *nego* 'black' + dim. suf. *-inho.* Acc. Cabral (1982:544), var. *neguinho.* Cf. **nego, negrilho, negro, pretinho, preto,** Sp. **negrecito, negrín, negrito, negro.**]

negro 'black'
1. person with dark or black skin color. *Br* (Harris 1964a:58; Silva 1987:159); *Br-BA* (Sanjek 1971:1129) 20.
2a. black slave. *Br* (Verlinden 1955:630) 15–early16.
2b. person of black or African race; black African. *Br* (Souza 1961:229) cl; (Bluteau 1716:5-N.702–3) early18.

2c. offspring of two blacks. *Br* (Bluteau 1716:5-N.702–3) early18.

2d. black person. *Br* (Baldus and Willems 1939:164) mid16 ‖ *Br-BA* (Pierson 1942:138) mid20 ‖ *Br Br-Minas Velhas* (Harris 1956:117); *Br* (Degler 1971:201) 20.

2e. person with black features such as dark skin, kinky hair, thick lips, and a flat nose. *Br* (Esteva Fabregat 1964:280–81) 20.

3. Indian. *Br* (Baldus and Willems 1939:164) mid16; (Cascudo 1962:158) early cl.

4. person of nonwhite or non-European race, acc. early Portuguese colonizers. *Br* (Souza 1961:229) cl.

[Acc. Silva, df. 1 1980 census color classification. Dfs. 2a, 2b, 2c also used in Portugal. Acc. Harris and Degler, df. 2d insult., often with weight of No. Amer. Engl. *nigger.* Acc. Sanjek, 1 of 10 most used terms in Salvador. Acc. Buarque de Holanda (1975:968), derivs. *negrão, negrona, negralhão, negralhona, negrote.* Other derivs. *negrada, negraria, negroto.* Cf. **africano, bem branco, crioulo, gente de cor, moreno, moreninho, mulato, não-branco, nego, negralhão, negrilho, negrinho, negrote, negroto, pessoa de cor, pretinho, preto,** Sp. **negro.**]

negro aça, negro-aça, negro-aço — See *preto-aça*

negro alforrado — See *negro forro*

negro angola 'Angolan black'

black person with very dark skin color. *Br* (Cabral 1982:544) 20.

[Acc. Cabral, syns. *negro preto, negro retinto.* Cf. **negro,** Sp. **negro angolo.**]

negro bichado 'wormy black'

sick black slave, esp. one with dysentery, worms, or another such disease. *Br* (Nuñez 1980:343) cl.

[*Bichado < bicha* 'worm.' Cf. **negro calico.**]

negro boçal

black person, usually considered useful only for manual labor, of the lowest social rank. *Br* (Levine 1979:148–49) 20prior.

[Cf. **boçal, negro,** Sp. **negro bozal.**]

negro branco 'white black one'

black person whose skin color is not as dark as is typical for a *negro,* acc. survey. *Br* (Harris 1970:5) 20.

[Cf. **branco, negro,** Sp. **mestizo blanco, mulato blanco.**]

negro calico 'calico black'

poor, illiterate, oppressed, urban black employed in menial labor and characterized by a dirty or shabby appearance. *Br* (Nuñez 1980:344) early20.

[Acc. Nuñez, *calico* 'poor-quality cloth used to make clothing.' Cf. **negro, negro bichado.**]

negro crioulo 'creole black'
black person native to the New World. *Br* (Alvarez Nazario 1974:335) prior20.
[Ants. *negro ladino, negro da terra.* Sim. to Engl. *creole Negro,* LA Fr. *nègre créole.* Cf. **crioulo, ladino, negro, negro ladino,** Sp. **negro criollo.**]

negro da África 'African black'
person whose dark or black skin color indicates African origin. *Br-BA-Salvador* (Sanjek 1971:1141) 20.
[Cf. **africano, branco da terra, negro, negro angola, negro crioulo, negro de Guiné, negro da terra, peça da costa, peça de África.**]

negro da costa 'black from the coast'
person with dark or black skin color. *Br-BA-Salvador* (Sanjek 1971:1141) 20.
[Often anyone from coastal areas in SA or Br is considered to have darker skin color as a result of contact with black slaves. Cf. **negro, negro da África, peça da costa.**]

negro da terra 'black from the land'
1. black slave born in America. *Br* (Azevedo 1964:519) cl.
2. black, Indian; nonwhite. *Br* (Levine 1979:148) cl.
[Cf. **negro, negro crioulo, negro da África, negro de Guiné,** Sp. **negro criollo.**]

negro de cabelo bom 'black with good hair'
person with dark skin color but whose hair texture is not kinky like that of a black. *Br-BA-Salvador* (Sanjek 1971:1141) 20.
[Cf. **moreno de cabelo bom, moreno de cabelo ruim, negro.**]

negro de ganho
black slave artisan or tradesman whom the master hired out to anyone needing special services, who worked for the master's gain, or who worked semi-independently to buy freedom while paying the master a set stipend. *Br* (Levine 1979:148) 19prior; (Levine 1980:95) cl; (Russell-Wood 1982:35) 18 ‖ *Br-BA-Salvador* (Pierson 1942:375, 435) prior20.
[Syn. *escravo de ganho,* acc. Russell-Wood. Var. *negro-de-ganho.* Cf. **negro, preto de aluguel,** Sp. **negro de gaño.**]

negro-de-ganho — See *negro de ganho*

negro de Guiné 'Guinean black'
black slave born in Africa. *Br* (Azevedo 1964:519) cl.
[Cf. **negro, negro angola, negro da África, negro da terra.**]

negro de recado 'message black'
black person, usually a slave, charged with dispatching the master's messages and letters. *Br* (Nuñez 1980:345) cl.
[Cf. **negro, negro de ganho.**]

negro do cedro — See *cedrino*

negro do gato 'black as a cat'
Brazilian Indian. *Br* (Sturm 1985:74, 85) late16.
[Acc. Sturm, derog.; used in ref. to Maracajá Indians. Cf. **negro.**]

negro do gentio da terra 'black from the land'
black person born in Br. *Br* (Souza 1961:229) 20.
[Syn. *crioulo.* Ant. *negro do gentio de Guiné.* Cf. **negro, negro da África, negro crioulo, negro do gentio de Guiné.**]

negro do gentio de Guiné
black person born in Africa. *Br* (Souza 1961:229) 20.
[Syn. *boçal.* Ant. *negro do gentio da terra.* Cf. **negro, negro crioulo, negro da África, negro ladino,** Sp. **negro de Guinea.**]

negro ébano 'ebony black'
black person with very dark skin color. *Br* (Cascudo 1962:508) 16–20.
[Syn. *negro preto,* acc. Cascudo. Cf. **negro, negro preto.**]

negro forro 'free black'
free or freed black slave. *Br* (Mott 1974:157) 18.
[Syn. *negro alforrado.* Acc. Domínguez Ortiz (1952:386), many slave owners sent slaves out to sell wares on the street, either to earn a living on their own or to enhance the owner's coffers. If the slaves did earn their keep, then the master expected a percentage of the earnings. This practice made it possible for some slaves to buy their freedom through saving their money. In this way, slaves could buy their freedom or that of their family, a practice customary throughout cl. SA and Br. Cf. **forro, negro, negro de ganho,** Sp. **negro horro.**]

negro fulo
black person with light skin color and fewer black features, perhaps indicating racial mixture with non-black North Africans before the arrival of the Portuguese and other Europeans in Africa. *Br* (Souza 1961:229; Ramos 1941:537) 20prior.
[Acc. Ramos, < *Fullah* 'African people who were converted to Islam.' Cf. **fulo, negro, negro angola.**]

negro ladino — See *ladino*

negro legítimo 'legitimate black'
black person with dark skin color. *Br-BA-Salvador* (Sanjek 1971:1141) 20.
[Probably indicates pure black with no racial mixture. Cf. **negro.**]

negro metido a besta — See ***negro pó de arroz***

negro mulato escuro 'dark mulatto black'
person whose dark skin color probably indicates racial mixture with black, acc. survey. *Br* (Harris 1970:5) 20.
[Cf. **escuro, mulato, mulato escuro, negro.**]

negro novo 'new black'
1. black slave recently arrived from Africa. *Br-BA* (Pierson 1942:375); *Br* (Cascudo 1962:414) cl; (Souza 1961:42) late17.
2. black slave who had recently arrived from Africa knowing neither the Portuguese lg. nor a skill. *Br* (Cascudo 1962:508) cl.
[Acc. Cascudo, syn. *boçal*; ants. *escravo ladino, ladino.* Acc. Pierson, var. *negro-novo.* Cf. **boçal, ladino, negro, negro da África,** Sp. **negro bozal.**]

negro-novo — See *negro novo*

negro pequeno — See *moleque*

negro pó de arroz 'white-faced or face-powdered black'
any person, esp. black or dark-skinned, trying to pass from the lower classes to the elite, acc. whites and nonwhites. *Br-RJ* (Pinto 1953:221) mid20.
[Acc. Pinto, syns. *branco em comissão* 'delegated white,' *mulato pachola* 'farsical or pedantic mulatto,' *negro metido a besta* 'black putting on airs,' *macaco de cartola* 'monkey or black in a top hat,' *mosca no leite* 'fly in the milk'; all rather pejor.; popular in 1950s. Cf. **mosca no leite.**]

negro preto 'extra black one; black Negro'
black person with very dark skin. *Br* (Harris 1970:5; Cabral 1982:544) 20; (Cascudo 1962:508–9) 16–20.
[Acc. Harris, used in a survey. Acc. Cascudo, syn. *negro ébano.* Acc. Cabral, syns. *negro angola, negro retinto.* Cf. **negro, negro angola, negro ébano, negro retinto, preto,** Sp. **negro prieto.**]

negro retinto 'redyed black'
1. black person with coal-black skin color. *Br* (Souza 1961:229) cl–20.
2. black person with very dark skin color. *Br* (Ramos 1941:537) mid20; (Alvarez Nazario 1974:359; Cabral 1982:544) 20.
[Acc. Ramos, intensifying, generally pejor., used in ref. to former slave status of blacks. Sim. to Sp. *negro atezado* and *negro retinto.* Acc. Cabral, syns. *negro angola, negro preto.* Cf. **negro, negro angola, negro preto, retinto,** Sp. **negro atezado, negro retinto.**]

negro ruim 'bad black'
black person. *Br-AM-Itá* (Wagley 1949:130) mid20; *Br-AM* (Wagley 1963:121) 20.

[Powerful or extreme insult, acc. Wagley. Used to indicate undesirable state or condition of being black. Cf. **moreno cabelo ruim, negro.**]

negro sujo 'dirty black'
black person considered ignorant or uncouth. *Br* (Levine 1980:96) 20prior.
[Acc. Levine, very derog. Cf. **negro, negro pó de arroz, negro ruim,** Sp. **negro sucio.**]

negro velho 'old black'
any person; friend, comrade. *Br* (Cabral 1982:544) 20.
[Acc. Cabral, term of affect. sim. to *o cara, o sujeito, o camarada*; syns. *negrinho, negro, meu negro.* Cf. **negrinho, negro.**]

negróide
person who has traits sim. to those of a black. *Br* (Buarque de Holanda 1975:968) 20.
[Cf. **negro, negrote,** Sp. **negroide.**]

negrona — See *negralhão, negro*

negrota — See *negrote*

negrote 'young black'
1. young black child. *Br* (Buarque de Holanda 1975:968; Cabral 1982:544) 20.
2. any child with black skin. *Br* (Cabral 1982:544) 20.
[Acc. Buarque de Holanda (1975:968), f. *negrota.* Acc. Cabral, syn. *negrinho.* Other syns. *negro pequeno, molecote.* Cf. **mulatinho, negrinho, negro, pretinho.**]

negroto
person with black skin color, acc. 1980 census. *Br* (Silva 1987:159) 20.
[Acc. Silva, color classification. Possibly var. of *negrote.* Cf. **acastanhado, agalegado, alvo, amarelado, avermelhado, bem branco, mulato, negrão, negrilho, negrinho, negro, negrote, nêgu, vermelho.**]

nêgu — See *nego*

neguinho — See *negrinho*

nhambiquara
person of the Nambiquara Brazilian Indian tribe found in northern MT. *Br* (Buarque de Holanda 1975:972; Gomes de Matos 1988:p.c.) 20.
[M., f. Vars. *nambiquara, nambikwara.* Cf. **bororo, gavião, tapanhuna.**]

nhonhô
small child, acc. Brazilian slaves. *Br* (Levine 1980:96) early20prior.

[Acc. Levine, *nhonho* [*sic*]; < *menino* 'child.' Acc. Buarque de Holanda (1975:972), reduplicative apheresis of *sinhô*. Cf. **negrote, sinhô.**]

nipônico — See *japonês*

nordestino 'northeastern; northeasterner'
person from northeastern Br. *Br* (Degler 1971:131) 20.
[Used in ref. to anyone from the *Nordeste* 'region stretching from MA to BA.' Cf. **carioca, gaúcho, paulista, potiguar.**]

norte-rio-grandense — See *potiguar*

novato — See *galego*

novo cristão 'new Christian'
Jew who converted to Christianity. *Br* (Ludwig 1985:38) 16.
[Acc. Ludwig, used in specific ref. to Fernando de Noronha.]

O

oitavão 'octoroon'
1. person whose skin color indicates racial mixture with black. *Br* (Aguirre Beltrán 1972:178) cl.
2. person with 1/8 black ancestry. *Br* (Buarque de Holanda 1975:994) 20prior.
[F. *oitavona*. Cf. **quarteirão,** Sp. **ochavón, octavón.**]

oitavona — See *oitavão*

olho-de-fogo 'eye-of-fire;' type of fish
albino. *Br-RS* (Diégues 1963:106) prior20 ‖ *Br* (Buarque de Holanda 1975:996) 20.
[Acc. Diégues, syn. *preto-aça*; obs. Cf. **negro-aça, preto-aça.**]

oriental 'oriental; easterner'
person from Ur; Uruguayan. *Br-RS* (Coruja et al. 1964:326) 20.
[< *oriente* 'east.' Official name of Ur is *República Oriental del Uruguay.* Cf. **castelhano,** Sp. **oriental.**]

otuque — See *bororo*

P

pai-de-santo
leader, often black, of an Afro-Brazilian religious cult. *Br* (Buarque de Holanda 1975:1017) 20.
[F. form *mãe-de-santo*. Syns. *babá, babalorixá, babaloxá, pai-de-terreiro,* Sp. *santero.* Cf. **babá,** Sp. **santero.**]

pai-de-terreiro — See *pai-de-santo*

pálido 'pallid; pale'
person with pale skin color, acc. 1980 census. *Br* (Silva 1987:159) 20.

[Acc. Silva, color classification. Cf. **acastanhado, agalegado, alvo, amarelado, avermelhado, bem branco, claro, moreno, moreno claro, mulato, negro, verde, vermelho,** Sp. **anémico, pálido.**]

pantera 'panther'
person of mixed race with the skin color of a panther, either dark or black, acc. 1980 census. *Br* (Silva 1987:158) 20.

[M., f. Acc. Silva, color classification. Cf. **acastanhado, agalegado, alvo, amarelado, avermelhado, bem branco, mestiço, moreno, mulato, negro, preto, vermelho,** Sp. **mestizo.**]

papa-mamão 'papaya-gruel; papaya-eater'
person native to the city of Olinda, PE. *Br* (Cascudo 1962:564); *Br-PE-Recife* (Buarque de Holanda 1975:1028) 20.

[< *papar* 'to eat' + *mamão* 'papaya.' Acc. Buarque de Holanda, obs.]

paraense — See *paroara*

paraíba 'Paraíba'
person with the skin color, probably dark, of one from PB, acc. 1980 census. *Br* (Silva 1987:159) 20.

[M., f. Acc. Silva, color classification. Cf. **acastanhado, agalegado, alvo, amarelado, avermelhado, bem branco, moreno, mulato, negro, paroara, preto, queimado de sol, vermelho.**]

pardavasco 'brownish; mulatto-like'
1. person whose skin color indicates racial mixture. *Br* (Aguirre Beltrán 1972:178) cl.

2. offspring of a black and an Indian. *Br* (Woodbridge 1948:359) cl; (Vergara Martín 1922:242) n.d. ‖ *Br-RS* (Coruja et al. 1964:339) 20.

3. offspring of a black and a mulatto who has very dark skin. *Br* (Woodbridge 1948:359; Freyre 1964:423) cl ‖ *Br-BA, -GO, -PE, -so.* (Souza 1961:240); *Br-BA, -GO, -so.* (Diégues 1963:105) 20.

4. offspring of a white and a black; mulatto. *Br* (Woodbridge 1948:359) cl; (Ramos 1941:537) mid20 ‖ *Br-RS* (Coruja et al. 1964:339) 20.

5. dark-skinned person sim. to a mulatto. *Br* (Freyre 1964:423) cl.

[Syns. df. 2 *meio pardo, acaboclado, índio meio amulatado, pardo escuro,* or *pardo carregado.* Acc. Coruja et al., other syn. *pardo* in RS. Acc. Vergara Martín, df. 2 sim. to Sp. *medio pardo.* Acc. Mellafe (1975:115), sim. to Sp. *mulato prieto* 'offspring of a black and a *pardo.*' Acc. Diégues, more pejor. mid-20 cent. Br; indicates

superiority of speaker. Acc. Coruja et al., used to replace *pardusco*.
Acc. Malkiel (1969:198), *pardusco* 'dark gray, grizzly.' Var. *pardovasco*. Cf. **caboré, cafuso, curiboca, mulato, pardo,** Sp.
pardejón.]

pardo 'gray; brown'

1a. person whose dark or brown skin color indicates racial
mixture. *Br* (Wagley 1949:222) late19; (Hutchinson 1952:27–31;
Wagley 1953:130) mid20; (Harris 1964a:58; Fernandes 1969:461;
Soares and Silva 1987:166) 20 ‖ *Br-BA-Salvador* (Sanjek
1971:1141); *Br Br-n.e.* (Kottak 1967:44) 20.

1b. person with brown or tan skin color, acc. 1980 census. *Br*
(Silva 1987:159) 20.

2a. offspring of a white and a black; mulatto. *Br* (Russell-Wood
1982:25) cl; (Moraes e Silva 1789:2.159) late18; (Woodbridge
1948:359; Freyre 1964:423) 19; (Wagley 1949:222) late19; (Souza
1961:240) 20prior; (Ramos 1941:537) mid20; (Bailey and Nasatir
1973:774; Levine 1979:159) 20; (Soares and Silva 1987:171) late20.

2b. mulatto with light skin color. *Br* (Hutchinson 1957:118) 20.

3. offspring of a mulatto and an Indian. *Br* (Woodbridge
1948:359; Santamaría 1942:2.411) cl; (Vergara Martín 1922:242)
n.d.

4. offspring of a white and an Indian; mestizo. *Br* (Woodbridge
1948:359) cl.

5. offspring of a white and a mulatto. *Br* (Souza 1961:240); *Br-
BA* (Diégues 1963:105) 20.

6. offspring of a black and an Indian. *Br* (Mellafe 1964:89) 20.

7a. person of color; nonwhite; racially mixed person. *Br*
(Azevedo 1953:123; Rosenblat 1954:2.108; Mörner 1967:71) cl;
(Diégues 1963:105) 18; (Ramos 1941:535) mid20; (Thompson
1965a:29) 20.

7b. black person. *Br* (Bailey and Nasatir 1973:774; Levine
1979:159) 20.

8a. person who is the result of the fusion of all ethnic types and
with all the possible gradations of skin color. *Br* (Ramos 1944:30)
mid20.

8b. person who is a mixture of black, Indian, and white. *Br*
(Alba 1969:34) 20.

8c. offspring of 2 mulattoes, of 2 blacks, or of a mulatto and a
mameluco. *Br* (Diégues 1963:103) n.d.

[Acc. Silva, color classification. Acc. Russell-Wood, df. 2a euph. for
mulato, to which *pardo* is thought to be morally superior. Acc.
Moraes e Silva, syn. df. 2a *homem pardo*; also used in Portugal. Df.
2b used in census. Syn. df. 6 *zambo*. Df. 7a euph., vague. Df. 7b

polite in 1960s, acc. Levine. Cf. **amulatado, avermalhado, caboclo, cafuso, curiboca, mameluco, mestiço, moreno, mulato, negro, pardavasco, pardo claro, vermelho,** Sp. **pardo.**]

pardo carregado — See *pardavasco*

pardo claro 'light-brown-skinned person'
person with light brown skin color, acc. 1980 census. *Br* (Silva 1987:159) 20.
[Acc. Silva, color classification. Cf. **acastanhado, agalegado, alvo, amarelado, avermelhado, bem branco, claro, moreno claro, mulato claro, vermelho.**]

pardo de matiz claro 'light-brown-skinned person'
person with very light brown skin color. *Br* (Harris 1964b:21) 20.
[Sim. to *branco moreno,* acc. Harris. Cf. **branco moreno, pardo, pardo de matiz escuro.**]

pardo de matiz escuro 'dark-brown-skinned person'
person with very dark brown skin color. *Br* (Harris 1964b:21) 20.
[Sim. to *preto,* acc. Harris. Cf. **pardo, pardo de matiz claro, preto.**]

pardo disfarçado 'disguised brown-skinned person'
person whose skin color indicates racial mixture with black. *Br-SE* (Mott 1976:13) late18–early19.
[*Disfarçado < disfarçar* 'to disguise.' Cf. **pardo.**]

pardo escuro — See *pardavasco*

pardo mais trigueiro
person whose brown skin color is lighter than that of the typical *pardo. Br-SE* (Mott 1976:14) late18–early19.
[Cf. **pardo, pardo disfarçado, pardo trigueiro,** Sp. **trigueño.**]

pardo trigueiro
person with light or wheat-colored skin. *Br-SE* (Mott 1976:14) late18–early19.
[Cf. **pardo, pardo mais trigueiro,** Sp. **trigueño.**]

pardovasco — See *pardavasco*

pardusco — See *pardavasco*

paroara 'type of bird; native of PA'
1. offspring of a white and an Indian. *Br* (Woodbridge 1948:359) cl.
2. mestizo who was acculturated to an Indian life-style; Indianized mestizo. *Br-AM* (Rosenblat 1954:2.104) cl.
3. native of the state of PA in northeastern Br. *Br* (Cascudo

1962:568) 20.

4a. person native of CE or northeastern Br who emigrates to the Amazon region only to return the Northeast. *Br* (Souza 1961:240–41) 20.

4b. northerner who lives in the Amazon region. *Br-no.* (Buarque de Holanda 1975:1038) 20.

[M., f. Syn. df. 3 *paraense*. Var. *paróara*. Df. 4 ext. of df. 3. Acc. Buarque de Holanda (1975:1038), < Tupi *para'wara* 'type of bird.' Cf. **caboclo, cearense, mameluco, mestiço.**]

paróara — See *paroara*

parrudo
native of Portugal; peninsular Portuguese. *Br* (Souza 1961:241) 19–20.

[Derog. nickname. Cf. **galego.**]

patanao
Indian of the upper Amazon River area. *Br* (Vergara Martín 1922:242) n.d.

[Cf. **índio.**]

pau-de-arara — See *bóia-fria*

pau-de-fumo 'firearm'
1. black person. *Br-so.* (Chamberlain and Harmon 1983:385) 20.

2. black man. *Br* (Buarque de Holanda 1975:1049) 20.

[Acc. Chamberlain and Harmon, df. 1 colloq., pejor.; syn. *baiano*. Acc. Buarque de Holanda, df. 2 derog.; syn. *baiano*. Cf. **baiano, negro, preto.**]

paulista 'person from SP'
1. native to or resident of the state of SP in southeastern Br. *Br* (Fernandes 1969:461) 20.

2. offspring of early Portuguese colonizers and Indians of the *meseta* near the city of SP. *Br* (Vergara Martín 1922:242) cl.

3. mestizo who often led expeditions into the interior of Br. *Br* (van den Berghe 1967:60) mid16.

4. mestizo; *mameluco*. *Br* (Vergara Martín 1922:240) n.d.

[Acc. Vergara Martín, person known for cruelty. Acc. van den Berghe, sim. to *bandeirante* or *mameluco*. Cf. **bandeirante, mameluco, mestiço, paulistano.**]

paulistano
resident of or native to the city of SP in the state of SP. *Br* (Fernandes 1969:462) 20.

[Cf. **paulista.**]

pé-de-chumbo 'lead-foot'
native of Portugal; peninsular Portuguese. *Br-RS* (Coruja et al.

1964:350–51) 20.

[Derog. Cf. **galego, parrudo.**]

peça da África — See *peça da costa, peça de África*

peça da costa 'piece from the coast'

black African slave imported to Br. *Br* (Levine 1980:103) cl.

[Acc. Levine, considered crude; syn. *peça da África* 'piece from Africa.' Cf. **escravo, peça das Índias, peça de escravo, peça de Guiné,** Sp. **pieza, pieza de Indias.**]

peça das Índias — See *peça de escravo*

peça de África 'piece from Africa'

black African slave first taken to Portugal for taxation purposes before being sent to America. *Br* (Nuñez 1980:377) 16.

[Cf. **africano, boçal, peça da costa.**]

peça de escravo 'piece of slave'

black African slave. *Br* (Mattoso 1986:252) 17.

[Acc. Mattoso, often used to decide monetary value of the 'head of slave'; syn. *peça das Índias* 'piece from the Indies.' Acc. Megenney (1988:p.c.), could be 1, 1 1/2, 2, or more slaves, depending on the value of each. Cf. **peça da costa,** Sp. **pieza de esclavos, pieza de Índias.**]

peça de Guiné 'piece from Guinea'

black slave at the market, acc. slavers. *Br* (Alvarez Nazario 1974:337) cl.

[Sim. to cl. Sp. *pieza de Indias.* Cf. **peça da costa, peça de África, peça de escravo,** Sp. **pieza, pieza de Indias.**]

peça de Índias 'piece from the Indies'

black slave graded for price in the market acc. age and relative health or physical condition. *Br* (Nuñez 1980:377) 17.

[The younger and healthier the slave, the higher the price. Cf. **peça da costa, peça de Guiné,** Sp. **pieza de Indias.**]

pelé

1. person whose dark skin color is sim. to that of Pelé. *Br* (Harris 1964a:58) 20.

2. any black man or boy. *Br* (Chamberlain and Harmon 1983:394) 20.

[Acc. Chamberlain and Harmon, vocative, slang, pejor. < *Pelé* 'Brz. soccer great,' a very dark skinned man from Santos, SP. Cf. **negro.**]

pele-vermelha 'redskin'

North American Indian. *Br* (Baldus and Willems 1939:175) early20.

[Usually m. Acc. Baldus and Willems, imitation of Engl. *redskin* in ref. to use of cosmetics and paints to decorate skin. Cf. **índio.**]

344

peludo 'hairy; half-breed animal'
rustic type; hick. *Br-MG* (Ayrosa 1937:81) mid20.
[Cf. **caipira.**]

peninsular 'peninsular'
person, generally white, born in the Iberian Peninsula rather
than in America. *Br* (Bailey and Nasatir 1973:775) n.d.
[Cf. Sp. **peninsular.**]

pessoa de cor 'person of color'
mulatto. *Br* (Nuñez 1980:379) 20.
[Sim. to Engl. *person of color* or *colored person,* Fr. *personne de
couleur,* Sp. *persona de color.* Cf. Sp. **persona de color.**]

pessoa de ínfama 'person of the basest class'
person of color or Jew newly converted to Christianity, acc.
church officials. *Br* (Degler 1971:214) 18.
[Sim. to Sp. designation of one who lacks *limpieza de sangre* 'pure
blood.' Cf. **pessoa de sangue infecto.**]

pessoa de sangue infecto 'person with infected blood'
person of color or Jew recently converted to Catholicism. *Br*
(Degler 1971:214) 18.
[Cf. **pessoa de ínfama.**]

pessoal de casa 'house personnel'
black domestic slave who enjoyed a relatively higher status
than the fieldhand slave. *Br* (Nuñez 1980:379) cl.
[Cf. **ama de criar, ama de leite.**]

petiguar — See *potiguar*

piá
1. young Indian or *caboclo. Br* (Freyre 1964:424) cl.
2. young mestizo, or offspring of a white and an Indian; *caboclo.*
Br (Buarque de Holanda 1975:1080) 20.
3. any nonwhite worker on a farm. *Br-RS, -SC* (Buarque de
Holanda 1975:1080) 20.
[Acc. Freyre, term of affect. Acc. Machado (1952:2.1730), < Tupi.
Acc. Buarque de Holanda, < Tupi *pi'á* 'heart, stomach, liver,
innards.']

pinto calçudo 'baggy-pants; shabbily clothed'
person from northeastern Br; northeasterner. *Br-so.* (Silva
1987:171) late20.
[Cf. **gente de fora, nordestino, restingueiro, retirante.**]

pitaquar — See *potiguar*

pitiguar — See *potiguar*

pobre 'poor'
rural or semi-urbanized black person. *Br* (Levine 1980:108) 20.

[Cf. **negro, preto.**]

polaca 'Polish woman'
prostitute who will do any sexual act. *Br-n.e., -PE* (Souto Maior 1980:105–6) 20.
[F. of *polaco*. Cf. **polaco, polonês,** Sp. **polaca.**]

polaco 'Polish; Pole'
1. Polish person; Pole. *Br* (Buarque de Holanda 1975:1110) 20prior.
2. person whose skin color is like that of a Pole, acc. 1980 census. *Br* (Silva 1987:159) 20.
[M., f. Df. 1 derog.; sim. in force or connotation to Eng. *Polack.* Acc. Silva, df. 2 color classification; probably indicates light skin color. Cf. **alemão, avermelhado, boche, moreno claro, paraíba, polaca, polonês,** Sp. **polaca, polaco.**]

polonês 'Polish; Pole'
Polish person; person from Poland. *Br* (Buarque de Holanda 1975:1110) 20prior.
[Var. and syn. *polônio*; derog. syn. *polaco.* Cf. **polaca, polaco,** Sp. **polaca, polaco.**]

polônio — See *polonês*

portuga — See *galego*

português 'Portuguese'
person whose skin color is generally light like that of a person from Portugal. *Br-BA-Salvador* (Sanjek 1971:1141) 20.
[Cf. **galego, parrudo.**]

potiguar
1. Indian of the Potiguar (Tupi) tribe found near the Paraíba do Norte River. *Br* (Buarque de Holanda 1975:1123) prior20.
2. native of RN. *Br* (Buarque de Holanda 1975:1123) 20.
[< Tupi *potï'war* 'shrimp-eater.' Vars. df. 1 *petiguar, pitaguar, pitiguar, potiguara.* Syns. df. 2 *rio-grandense-do-norte, norte-rio-grandense.* Cf. **carioca, gaúcho, paulista.**]

potiguara — See *potiguar*

pouco brancado 'a little whitened'
person who relatively light skin color. *Br-BA-Salvador* (Sanjek 1971:1140) 20.
[Acc. Sanjek, *pouca brancada* [*sic*]. Cf. **branco.**]

pouco claro 'a little light-colored'
person with lightish skin color, acc. 1980 census. *Br* (Silva 1987:159) 20.
[Acc. Silva, color classification; *pouco clara* [*sic*]. Cf. **acastanhado, agalegado, alvo, amarelado, avermelhado, bem branco, claro, moreno claro, mulato claro, pouco brancado, pouco moreno,**

ruivo, vermelho.]
pouco moreno 'a little brownish'
person with brown or brownish skin color, acc. 1980 census. *Br*
(Silva 1987:159) 20.
[Acc. Silva, color classification; *pouco morena* [*sic*]. Cf.
**acastanhado, agalegado, alvo, amarelado, avermelhado, bem
branco, claro, moreno claro, mulato claro, pouco brancado,
pouco claro, ruivo, vermelho.**]
praciano 'plaza-dweller'
person from the city, city dweller, or family person, acc.
sertanejos. Br-sertão (Almeida Oliveira 1940:145) mid20.
[< *praça* 'plaza, town square.' Cf. **sertanejo.**]
praiano — See *caiçara*
praieiro — See *mameluco*
prego 'nail'
1. young black boy with very dark skin color. *Br-BA* (Pierson
1942:139) mid20; (Levine 1980:110) 20.
2. any black person. *Br* (Buarque de Holanda 1975:1129) 20.
[Cf. **negro, negro retinto, preto.**]
pretalhão 'big black'
black person. *Br* (Buarque de Holanda 1975:1136) 20.
[Aug. m. F. *pretalhona.* Syns. *negralhão, negrão.* Cf. **negro,
preto.**]
pretalhona — See *pretalhão*
pretão 'big black one'
man, often large, with dark or black skin color. *Br-BA-Salvador*
(Sanjek 1971:1141) 20.
[Aug. m. < *preto* 'black' + aug. suf. *-ão.* Cf. **brancão, negralhão,
pretalhão, pretinho, preto.**]
pretinho 'small black one'
1. small black slave. *Br* (Bluteau 1720:6-P.727) early18.
2. small black man. *Br* (Moraes e Silva 1789:2.242) late18.
3. person, often small, with dark or black skin color. *Br* (Silva
1987:159); *Br-BA-Salvador* (Sanjek 1971:1141) 20.
[Df. 1 also used in Portugal. Acc. Silva, df. 3 1980 census color classification. < *preto* 'black' + dim. suf. *-inho.* Often affect. Cf.
negrinho, pretão, preto, Sp. **negrito.**]
preto 'black'
1a. person with black skin color. *Br* (Harris 1964a:58; Hutchinson 1952:27–31; Soares and Silva 1987:166; Silva 1987:159); *Br-
BA* (Sanjek 1971:1129) 20.
1b. black person. *Br* (Roback 1944:136) mid20 ‖ *Br* (Mörner
1967:73; Thompson 1965a:29; Harris 1964a:59; Kottak 1967:43;

(Degler 1971:201); *Br-n.e.* (Hutchinson 1957:120) *Br Br-Minas Velhas* (Harris 1956:117) 20.

2. person who has all the features of a black African includir·g shiny black skin, kinky hair, a broad or flat nose, and thick or lar·,e lips. *Br-n.e.* (Hutchinson 1957:118); *Br* (Levine 1979:175) 20.

3. black slave. *Br* (Leite de Vasconcellos 1928:363) 16–17; (Bluteau 1720:6-P.727) early18.

[Df. 1a used in a 1976 household survey, acc. Soares and Silva; acc. Silva, 1980 census color classification. Df. 1b slur, derog., polite, or euph. used instead of *negro*. Syn. df. 2 *preto retinto,* acc. Hutchinson. Acc. Levine, df. 2 lowest rung in racial ladder. Df. 3 also used in Portugal. Acc. Sanjek, 1 of 10 most used terms in Salvador. Cf. **negro, pretão, pretinho, preto-aça, preto retinto,** Sp. **prieto.**]

preto aça — See *preto-aça*

preto-aça 'albino-black'
albino. *Br* (Souza 1961:263) 20.
[< *preto* 'black' + *aça* 'albino animal or person.' Syns. *negro-aça, olho-de-fogo.* Vars. *preto aça, preto-aço.* Cf. **negro-aça, olho-de-fogo.**]

preto-aço — See *preto-aça*

preto amarelo 'yellow black'
person whose dark skin color has a yellowish tinge, acc. survey. *Br* (Harris 1970:5) 20.
[Cf. **amarelo, preto.**]

preto cativo 'captive black'
captured black slave. *Br* (Leite de Vasconcellos 1928:363) 16–17.
[Also used in Portugal. Cf. **cativo, preto.**]

preto claro 'light black'
person with light black skin color. *Br* (Harris 1964a:58 and 1970:5) 20.
[Cf. **claro, moreno claro, preto, preto amarelo, preto retinto.**]

preto como carvão 'black as coal; coal-black'
black person with very dark skin. *Br* (Nuñez 1980:391) 20.
[Cf. **preto, preto escuro, preto negro,** Sp. **negro como un tizón.**]

preto da costa 'black from the coast'
black slave at market. *Br* (Alvarez Nazario 1974:337) cl.
[Syns. *negro da costa, peça de Guiné.* Slave probably captured on the African coast. Sim. to Sp. *pieza de Indias.* Cf. **negro da costa, peça das Índias, peça de Guiné, preto,** Sp. **pieza de Indias.**]

preto de aluguel 'black for rent'
black slave hired out to do labor for the master's own profit. *Br*

(Pescatello 1975:248) prior20.

[Cf. **preto de ganho,** Sp. **negro de gaño.**]

preto de cabelo bom 'black with good hair'

black person with straight or non-kinky hair. *Br-BA-Salvador* (Sanjek 1971:1141) 20.

[Cf. **moreno de cabelo bom, preto.**]

preto de ganho 'black for profit'

black slave who had the master's permission to hire out services for a profit, giving the master a fixed rate. *Br* (Pescatello 1975:248) prior20.

[Sim. to Sp. *negro de gaño.* Cf. **preto de aluguel.**]

preto de qualidade 'black of quality'

good-looking black person. *Br-n.e.* (Hutchinson 1957:121) 20.

[Cf. **preto, preto da costa, preto de raça branca.**]

preto de raça branca 'black of white race'

person of mixed race, usually black African with Berber or Arabic, usually tall, with yellowish or reddish skin color, a round face, and less kinky hair texture and less Negroid features than a pure black person. *Br* (Alvarez Nazario 1974:46) cl.

[Sim. to *moreno branco.* Cf. **moreno branco, mulato, pardo, preto.**]

preto escuro 'dark black'

person with very dark black skin color. *Br* (Harris 1964a:58) 20.

[Cf. **escuro, negro escuro, preto, preto de raça branca.**]

preto forro 'freed black'

freed black slave. *Br* (Leite de Vasconcellos 1928:363) 16–17.

[Also used in Portugal. Ant. *preto cativo.* Cf. **forro, preto, preto cativo.**]

preto legítimo 'legitimate black'

pure black person. *Br* (Shoumatoff 1980:137) 20.

[Cf. **negro legítimo, preto.**]

preto louro 'blond black'

black person with blond hair, acc. survey. *Br* (Harris 1970:5) 20.

[Cf. **louro, preto, preto escuro, preto mestiço.**]

preto mestiço 'mestizo black'

person of mixed race, usually with black, acc. survey. *Br* (Harris 1970:5) 20.

[Cf. **preto, preto louro, preto moreno.**]

preto moreno 'brown or brunet black'

black person with generally brunet hair color. *Br-BA-Salvador* (Sanjek 1971:1141); *Br* (Harris 1970:5) 20.

[Cf. **moreno, preto, preto mestiço, preto negro.**]

preto negro 'black or dark black'

black person with very dark skin color, acc. survey. *Br* (Harris 1970:5) 20.

[Cf. **negro, preto, preto mestiço, preto retinto.**]

preto retinto 'redyed black'

black person with very dark or coal-black skin color. *Br-BA* (Pierson 1942:139) mid20 ‖ *Br* (Degler 1971:103; Levine 1979: 175); *Br-n.e.* (Hutchinson 1957:118) 20.

[Cf. **negro retinto, preto, retinto.**]

preto rico 'rich black'

rich black person, esp. one with a small country estate. *Br* (Nuñez 1980:391) 20prior.

[Cf. **branco rico, preto, preto de qualidade,** Sp. **negro de conuco.**]

preto sarará 'reddish-haired black'

black person with reddish or blondish hair color, acc. survey. *Br* (Harris 1970:5) 20.

[Cf. **preto, preto louro, sarará.**]

puça — See *galego*

puxar para branco 'heading for white'

person whose skin color is not quite white, acc. 1980 census. *Br* (Silva 1987:159) 20.

[Verb phr. Acc. Silva, color classification; *puxa para branca* [*sic*]. Cf. **acastanhado, agalegado, alvo, amarelado, avermelhado, bem branco, branco, moreno, mulato, pardo, ter pinta, trigueiro, vermelho.**]

Q

quadrarão

person of 1/4 black ancestry. *Br* (Aguirre Beltrán 1972:178) cl; (Buarque de Holanda 1975:1163) 20.

[F. *quadrarona.* Acc. Buarque de Holanda, syns. *quadrum, quarterão.* Sim. to Engl. *quadroon* and Fr. *quarteron.* Cf. **terceirão,** Sp. **cuarterón.**]

quadrarona — See *quadrarão*

quadrum — See *quadrarão*

quarterão — See *quadrarão*

quase negro 'almost black'
person whose skin color tends toward dark or black, acc. 1980 census. *Br* (Silva 1987:159) 20.
[Acc. Silva, color classification. Cf. **acastanhado, agalegado, alvo, amarelado, avermelhado, bem branco, moreno claro, mulato claro, pardo, pouco claro, pouco moreno, preto, trigueiro, vermelho.**]

queimadinho de sol 'little suntanned one'
person of color. *Br* (Silva 1987:200) 20.
[Euph. Cf. **gente de cor, negro, preto, queimado de sol, pessoa de cor.**]

queimado de praia 'beach-tanned one'
person with dark or sunburnt skin color, acc. 1980 census. *Br* (Silva 1987:159) 20.
[Euph. Acc. Silva, color classification. Cf. **acastanhado, agalegado, alvo, amarelado, avermelhado, bem branco, queimadinho de sol, queimado de sol, trigueiro, vermelho.**]

queimado de sol 'suntanned one'
person with dark or sunburnt skin color, acc. 1980 census. *Br* (Silva 1987:159) 20.
[Acc. Silva, color classification. Cf. **acastanhado, agalegado, alvo, amarelado, avermelhado, bem branco, moreno, mulato, pardo, queimadinho de sol, queimado de praia, trigueiro, vermelho.**]

quilombola
1. runaway slave, generally black, who went to a *quilombo,* or settlement set up for and by other escaped slaves. *Br* (Mendonça 1935:236) cl–19; (Ramos 1944:190; Freyre 1964:426; Alvarez Nazario 1974:342) cl.
2. escaped slave. *Br* (Ramos 1939:25) cl–prior20.
[M., f. Acc. Machado (1952:2.1835), < African lg. *quilombo,* att. 16 cent. Acc. Alvarez Nazario, < Bantu lg. *quilombo.* Acc. Pereda Valdés (1937:77), < Kimbundu; in RP 'noisy bordello.' Acc. Ribeiro (n.d.:117), < Angolese lg. *quilombo* 'stop where travelers rest from a trip to the African interior' + Tupi verbal suf. *-ora* (> *-ola*). Acc. Alvarez Nazario, *quilómbola* [*sic*]. Cf. **mocambeiro,** Sp. **apalencado, cimarrón, palenquero.**]

quilómbola — See *quilombola*

quimbundo
black person, often small. *Br-MG* (Machado Filho 1964:124) 20.
[Acc. Machado Filho, < *Kimbundu* 'African lg.,' < dim. pref. *ki-* + *mbundo* 'black.' Cf. **angola, quilombola.**]

R

raça brava 'unruly race'
immigrant, known for being feisty or pugnacious, from the Calabria region of Italy. *Br-SP* (Levine 1980:114) 20.
[F. Cf. **galego, parrudo.**]

rapaz negro 'black boy'
small black boy, usually a slave. *Br* (Bluteau 1716:5-N.702) early18.
[M. Also used in Portugal. Cf. **negro.**]

reclame de pixe — See *reclame do pixe*

reclame do pixe 'protest of the tar; bit of the tarbrush'
black person with very dark or pitch-black skin color. *Br-BA* (Pierson 1942:139) mid20; (Levine 1980:117) 20.
[Acc. Levine, *reclame de pixe* [*sic*]; slang. Cf. **negro retinto, preto retinto,** Sp. **negro azabache.**]

regular 'regular'
person with medium skin color, neither black nor white, acc. 1980 census. *Br* (Silva 1987:159) 20.
[Acc. Silva, color classification. Cf. **acastanhado, agalegado, alvo, amarelado, avermelhado, bem branco, claro, médio, moreno, pardavasco, pardo, pouco claro, trigueiro, vermelho,** Sp. **regular.**]

reinol
1a. peninsular Portuguese *Br* (Rosenblat 1954:2.99) cl.
1b. Portuguese born in the Old World who lived permanently or temporarily in Br. *Br* (Burns 1980:550) cl.
2. person born in the Kingdom of Portugal. *Br* (Bluteau 1720:7-R.213) early18.
[Syn. *filho do reino*. Df. 2 also used in Portugal. < *reino* 'kingdom.' Ant. *mazombo* 'person born in Africa.' Pl. *reinóes*. Pl. var. *reinóis*. Cf. **filho do reino, mazombo, parrudo, peninsular,** Sp. **peninsular.**]

restingueiro
1. rustic type; hick; beachcomber. *Br-RN* (Ayrosa 1937:81) mid20 ‖ *Br-so.* (Silva 1987:171) late20.
2. northeasterner. *Br-so.* (Silva 1987:171) late20.
[Acc. Silva, syn. df. 1 *caipira*; syn. df. 2 *nordestino*. Acc. Buarque de Holanda (1975:1227), < *restinga* 'sand dune' + suf. *-eiro*. Other syn. df. 1 *caboclo*. Cf. **caboclo, caiçara, caipira, gente de fora, nordestino,** Sp. **playero.**]

retinho 'redyed'
person with very dark or redyed skin color, acc. 1980 census. *Br*

(Silva 1987:159) 20.

[Acc. Silva, color classification; *retinha* [*sic*]. Probably < var. of *retinto* 'redyed' (< *retingir* 'to dye again, redye'). Cf. **acastanhado, agalegado, alvo, amarelado, avermelhado, bem branco, moreno, mulato, negro, pardo, preto, retinto, trigueiro, vermelho.**]

retinto 'redyed; dark-colored'
very dark-skinned black person. *Br* (Zenón Cruz 1975:1.255) cl–20; (Alvarez Nazario 1974:349) 20.

[Acc. Alvarez Nazario, often pejor.; syn. *negro retinto*. Cf. **negro retinto, preto retinto, retinho,** Sp. **negro retinto, retinto.**]

retirante
1. *sertanejo* or northeastern migrant who flees the *sertão* as a result of prolonged droughts and/or famine. *Br-no.* (Cascudo 1962:657) late19–20 ‖ *Br* (Chamberlain and Harmon 1983:444) 20.

2. person from northeastern Br; northeasterner. *Br* (Silva 1987:171) late20prior.

[Acc. Chamberlain and Harmon, df. 1 colloq. Acc. Silva, df. 2 derog. Cf. **caboclo, gente de fora, noredestino, restingueiro, sertanejo.**]

rio-grandense-do-norte — See *potiguar*

rio-grandense-do-sul — See *gaúcho, guasca*

roceiro
rustic type; hick. *Br-MG, -PA, -RJ* (Ayrosa 1937:81) mid20.

[< *roça* 'countryside' + suf. *-eiro*. Cf. **caipira, gente da roça.**]

rosa 'pink'
person with pinkish skin color, acc. 1980 census. *Br* (Silva 1987:159) 20.

[Acc. Silva, color classification. Cf. **acastanhado, agalegado, alvo, amarelado, avermelhado, bem branco, branco, claro, moreno, queimadinho de sol, rosa queimada, rosado, roxo, ruivo, vermelho.**]

rosa queimada 'burnt or dark pink'
person with dark pink skin color, acc. 1980 census. *Br* (Silva 1987:159) 20.

[Acc. Silva, color classification. Cf. **acastanhado, agalegado, alvo, amarelado, avermelhado, bem branco, branco, claro, moreno, queimadinho de sol, queimado de praia, queimado de sol, rosa, rosado, ruivo, vermelho.**]

rosado 'pinkish color'
person with pinkish skin color, acc. 1980 census. *Br* (Silva 1987:159) 20.

[Acc. Silva, color classification. Cf. **acastanhado, agalegado, alvo, amarelado, avermelhado, bem branco, branco, claro, moreno, queimadinho de sol, queimado de praia, queimado de sol, rosa, rosa queimada, roxo, ruivo, vermelho.**]

roto 'broken'

person from the lower classes. *Br* (Segovia 1911:141) early20.

[Acc. Segovia, syn. *farrapo.* Cf. **farrapo,** Sp. **roto.**]

roxinha — See *roxinho*

roxinho 'little purple one'

1. black person, acc. himself or herself. *Br-Minas Velhas* (Harris 1956:123) 20.

2. young mulatto woman with light skin color. *Br* (Chamberlain and Harmon 1983:448) 20.

[Df. 2 f. only. Acc. Chamberlain and Harmon, *roxinha* [*sic*]. Cf. **pretinho, roxo.**]

roxinho de cabelo bom 'little purplish one with good hair'

black person with straight or otherwise non-kinky hair. *Br-BA-Salvador* (Sanjek 1971:1141) 20.

[Cf. **negro de cabelo bom, roxinho, roxo.**]

roxo 'purple'

1. person with dark skin color. *Br-BA-Salvador* (Sanjek 1971:1141); *Br* (Harris 1964a:58; Silva 1987:159) 20.

2. black person whose skin appears purplish under the sun's rays. *Br-BA* (Pierson 1942:140) mid20.

[Acc. Silva, df. 1 1980 census color classification. Acc. Bluteau (1720:7-R.389), also 'blond, yellow, reddish, golden' in early 18-cent. Portugal and Br. Cf. **acastanhado, agalegado, alvo, amarelado, avermelhado, bem branco, branco, claro, moreno, queimadinho de sol, queimado de praia, queimado de sol, rosa, rosa queimada, roxinho, ruivo, vermelho.**]

roxo claro 'light purple'

person whose skin color appears to be reddish or purplish. *Br-BA-Salvador* (Sanjek 1971:1141); *Br* (Harris 1964a:58) 20.

[Cf. **claro, roxinho, roxo.**]

roxo de cabelo bom 'purple with good hair'

dark-skinned person with straight or non-kinky hair. *Br-BA-Salvador* (Sanjek 1971:1141); *Br* (Harris 1964a:58; Levine 1980:120–21) 20.

[Acc. Levine, rural; pejor. Cf. **moreno de cabelo bom, roxinho de cabelo bom, roxo, roxo claro,** Sp. **pelo bueno.**]

roxo de nação

person native to Russia. *Br* (Bluteau 1720:7-R.390) early18.

[Also used in Portugal. Cf. **gente de nação,** Sp. **ruso.**]

ruim de cabelo — See *ser ruim de cabelo*
ruivo 'reddish'
person with ruddy or reddish skin color and/or red hair. *Br-BA-Salvador* (Sanjek 1971:1141); *Br* (Silva 1987:159) 20.
[Acc. Silva, 1980 census skin color classification. Sim. to Sp. *rubio.* Cf. **acastanhado, agalegado, alvo, amarelado, avermelhado, bem branco, cor de canela, rosa, rosado, roxinho, roxo, vermelho.**]
russiano — See *russo*
russo 'Russian'
1. Russian; person from Russia. *Br* (Buarque de Holanda 1975:1253) 20.
2. Soviet; person from the Soviet Union. *Br* (Buarque de Holanda 1975:1253) 20.
3. person who has skin color, probably white or light, like that of a Russian, acc. 1980 census. *Br* (Silva 1987:159) 20.
[Acc. Buarque de Holanda, syn. df. 2 *soviético*; var. *russiano.* Acc. Silva, df. 3 color classification. Cf. **acastanhado, agalegado, alemão, alvo, amarelado, avermelhado, bem branco, moreno, mulato, pardo, polonês, vermelho,** Sp. **ruso.**]
rústico — See *caipira*

S

sacalagua
offspring of a mulatto and a *somboloro,* the latter of which is an Indian and a black. *Br* (Souza 1961:66) 19prior.
[Acc. Paz Soldán (1938:349), < Sp. refrain '*saca el agua* del bautismo y se verá que no eres sino mezclado.' Acc. Souza, var. *saccalagua;* < Sp. Cf. **somboloro,** Sp. **sacalagua.**]
saccalagua — See *sacalagua*
salta-atrás 'jump-back'
1. offspring of a *mameluco* and a black. *Br-PE-sertão* (Souza 1961:286) 18 ‖ *Br-sertão* (Diégues 1963:106) cl ‖ *Br* (Cascudo 1962:474–75) 18.
2. offspring of a mulatto and a black. *Br-sertão* (Diégues 1963:106) cl.
3. black African slave. *Br-PE* (Cascudo 1962:674–75) late19–20.
[Acc. Diégues, syn. on the coast *curiboca.* Cf. **curiboca, mameluco, sertanejo,** Sp. **saltatrás.**]

sapatão — See *galego*

sapecado 'singed; scorched; toasted-reddish'
person with reddish-brown skin color, acc. 1980 census. *Br*
(Silva 1987:159) 20.
[Acc. Silva, color classification. Cf. **acastanhado, agalegado, alvo,
amarelado, avermelhado, bem branco, morenado, moreno,
mulato, queimadinho de sol, queimado de praia, queimado
de sol, vermelho.**]

saraça 'awkward, clumsy'
mulatto with light skin color. *Br* (Ramos 1941:537; Woodbridge
1948:360) cl–mid20.
[Acc. Corominas (1954–57:4.847), possibly < Sp. *saraga* or Andalusian *sarasa* 'woman of low life; man of feminine gestures, ways,
and tastes.' Acc. Buarque de Holanda (1975:1272), < Malay *sarásah*
'fine cotton cloth.' Cf. **aça, mulato claro, sarará.**]

sarara — See *sarará*

sarará
1. person with reddish, sandy, or blondish hair color and not-so-
dark skin color. *Br* (Hutchinson 1952:27–31; Harris 1964a:58;
Aguirre Beltrán 1972:178); *Br-BA* (Pierson 1942:136) mid20;
(Sanjek 1971:1129) 20.
2a. light-skinned mulatto, usually with kinky hair. *Br* (Woodbridge 1948:360) cl; (Ramos 1941:537) mid20.
2b. light-skinned mulatto with red or reddish hair color. *Br-PE*
(Cascudo 1962:684) 20prior ‖ *Br* (Chamberlain and Harmon
1983:459) 20.
2c. light-skinned mulatto with blondish or reddish, more or less
kinky hair. *Br* (Diégues 1963:106) prior20.
3a. person of mixed race, or mestizo, with reddish or blondish
hair color. *Br* (Buarque de Holanda 1975:1273) 20.
3b. person of mixed race. *Br* (Silva 1987:158) mid20.
3c. person of mixed race, acc. 1980 census. *Br* (Silva 1987:159)
20.
4. black person with light skin color, generally reddish or
blondish kinky hair, Negroid physical traits, and often with blue or
green eyes and freckles. *Br* (Freyre 1964:428) cl; (Kottak 1967:44;
Souza 1961:290) 20 ‖ *Br-n.e.* (Hutchinson 1957:119–20) 20.
5. albino. *Br-GO, -MA* (Buarque de Holanda 1975:1273); *Br*
(Chamberlain and Harmon 1983:459) 20.
6. person from CE, acc. *caboclos* of the Amazon region; *cearense.*
Br-AM (Buarque de Holanda 1975:1273) 20.
[M., f. Df. 2c obs. Acc. Silva, df. 3b skin color designation; df. 3c
skin color classification. Syn. df. 5 *sarassará.* Df. 6 nickname. Acc.

Buarque de Holanda (1975:1273), < Tupi *sara-rá* 'red-haired.' Acc. Souza, < *sarará* 'reddish ant' < *yca-rará*. Acc. Machado (1952: 2.1950), < Tupi *ycá* 'ant' + *ará* 'day' + *ra* 'to be born.' Acc. Buarque de Holanda, < Tupi *sara-rá* 'one with blond or red hair.' Acc. Sanjek, 1 of 10 most used terms in Salvador. Syns. *grauça, mulato alvacento, mulato claro, mulato sarará*. Vars. *sarassará* in MA and GO, *sarara, sarué, saruê*. Cf. **aça, araçuabo, saraça, sarará escuro, sarará legítimo**.]

sarará escuro
dark-skinned *sarará*. *Br* (Harris 1964a:58) 20.
[Cf. **escuro, sarará**.]

sarará legítimo
real or pure *sarará*. *Br-BA-Salvador* (Sanjek 1971:1140) 20.
[Cf. **negro legítimo, sarará**.]

sarará miolo
prototypical *sarará*. *Br-BA-Salvador* (Sanjek 1971:1140) 20.
[*Miolo* 'bone marrow; prototype.' Cf. **sarará, sarará legítimo**.]

sarará preto
sarará with black skin color. *Br-BA-Salvador* (Sanjek 1971:1140) 20.
[Cf. **preto, sarará, sarará legítimo, sarará miolo**.]

sararazado 'like a *sarará*'
person whose skin and hair color are like those of the *sarará*. *Br-BA-Salvador* (Sanjek 1971:1140) 20.
[< *sarará* + adj. suf. *-ado*. Cf. **sarará, sararazão, sararazinho**.]

sararazão
large *sarará*. *Br-BA-Salvador* (Sanjek 1971:1140) 20.
[< *sarará* + aug. suf. *-ão*. Cf. **sarará, sararazado, sararazinho**.]

sararazinho
small *sarará*. *Br-BA-Salvador* (Sanjek 1971:1140) 20.
[< *sarará* + dim. suf. *-inho*. Cf. **sarará, sararazado, sararazão**.]

sarassará — See *sarará*

saraúba
skin color classification, possibly indicating person of mixed race, acc. 1980 census. *Br* (Silva 1987:159) 20.
[Cf. **acastanhado, amarelado, avermelhado, araçuabo, bem branco, morenado, moreno, mulato, preto, sarará, vermelho**.]

sarraceno 'Saracen'
1. slave, possibly Moslem. *Br* (Leite de Vasconcellos 1928:367) 16–17.
2. Arab; Moor. *Br* (Buarque de Holanda 1975:1275) 20.
[Also used in Portugal. Acc. Alonso (1958:3.3718), < Arabic for 'oriental, eastern.' Cf. **escravo, cigano, negro**.]

saruabo — See *araçuabo*

sarué — See *sarará*

saruê — See *sarará*

senhor de engenho 'master of the sugar mill'
landowner, usually white, who enjoyed great wealth and very high social status. *Br* (Levine 1980:37–38) late19.
[Cf. **branco.**]

ser cheio de arte 'to be full of art or airs'
black person who tries to pass for white, perhaps by acting cultured. *Br* (Nuñez 1980:172) 20.
[Verb phr. usually as *é cheio de arte* 'he is just acting white.' Cf. **ser da raça, ter pinta,** Sp. **negro catedrático.**]

ser da raça 'to be of the race'
black person who tries to pass for white. *Br* (Nuñez 1980:173) 20.
[Verb phr. usually as *é da raça* 'he/she is of the (black) race.' Cf. **ser cheio de arte, ser ruim de cabelo, ter pinta.**]

ser ruim de cabelo 'to be of bad hair'
person with some black ancestry. *Br* 20.
[Pejor., joc. *Ruim de cabelo* 'badness of hair' indicates some kinkiness to the hair texture and thus black traits. Cf. **negro, negro cabelo bom, preto, ser da raça,** Sp. **pelo malo.**]

serrano 'highlander'
1. anyone from Cima da Serra or Santa Maria. *Br-RS* (Coruja et al. 1964:443) 20.
2. rustic type; hick. *Br* (Buarque de Holanda 1975:1293) 20.
[Cf. **caipira,** Sp. **serrano.**]

sertanejo
1. person with Amerindian features. *Br-n.e.* (Hutchinson 1957:118) 20.
2. inhabitant of the *sertão* of eastern Br. *Br* (Vergara Martín 1922:244) n.d.; (Santamaría 1942:3.82) mid20.
3. rustic type; hick. *Br* (Buarque de Holanda 1975:1293) 20.
4. person from northeastern Br; northeasterner. *Br-so.* (Silva 1987:171) 20.
[Acc. Silva, syn. df. 3 *caipira*; syns. df. 4 *nordestino, restingueiro, retirante.* < *sertão* 'desert-like area of ea. Br' + suf. *-ejo.* Acc. Vergara Martín and Santamaría, sim. to *llanero* in Ve. Other syns. *caatingueiro, caboclo.* Cf. **caatingueiro, caboclo, caipira, nordestino, restingueiro, retirante.** Sp. **llanero.**]

servo — See *mouro*

siá — See *sinhá*

sinha — See *sinhá*

sinhá

1. white lady of the master's house, acc. slaves. *Br* (Freyre 1964:428) cl.

2a. white wife of the master's house, acc. black slave women. *Br* (Levine 1979:199) cl–19.

2b. wife of the white landlord. *Br-PE* (Cascudo 1962:701) 20prior.

[F. < phonetic corruption of *senhora* 'lady, woman, mistress.' Syns. *sinhá-dona, sinhá moça, sinhá-moça, sinharinha* 'young white lady,' *sinhazinha* 'young white lady.' Acc. Buarque de Holanda (1975: 1305), syns. *siá, sinha.* Cf. **gente sinhá, senhor de engenho, sinhama, sinhô.**]

sinhá-dona — See *sinhá*

sinhá moça, sinhá-moça — See *sinhá*

sinhama

black nursemaid. *Br* (Freyre 1964:429) cl.

[F. < *senhora* 'woman, lady' + *ama* 'nursemaid.' Sim. to Engl. *mammy.* Cf. **ama, ama de criar, babá, sinhá, sinhô.**]

sinharinha — See *sinhá*

sinhazinha — See *sinhá*

sinhô

male child, usually white. *Br-PE* (Cascudo 1962:701) 20prior.

[M. < phonetic corruption of *senhor* 'master, lord, gentleman.' Syn. *sinhozinho.* Cf. **senhor de engenho, sinhá, sinhô-moço.**]

sinhô-moço

young white master or son of the white master, acc. slaves. *Br* (Freyre 1964:429) cl.

[M. Acc. Freyre, familiar, affect. < *sinhô* + *moço* 'boy, lad.' Cf. **senhor de engenho, sinhá.**]

sinhozinho — See *sinhô*

somboloro

offspring of a black and an Indian. *Br* (Souza 1961:66) 19prior.

[Possibly < *sambo* + *louro.* Cf. **louro, sambo, sacalagua, zambo,** Sp. **sambaigo.**]

soviético — See *russo*

sul-rio-grandense — See *gaúcho, guasca*

suleiro — See *sulista*

sulino — See *sulista*

sulista 'southern; southerner'

person from southern Br; southerner. *Br* (Souza 1961:302) 20.

[Syns. *suleiro, sulino.* Cf. **cabeça-chata,** Sp. **sureño.**]

T

tabaréu
1. rustic type; hick; inhabitant of the countryside; low-class rural type. *Br-BA, -PA, -RJ, -SE, -SP* (Ayrosa 1937:81); *Br-sertão* (Almeida Oliveira 1940:160) mid20 ‖ *Br-BA* (Wagley 1971:101); *Br-PE* (Cascudo 1962:714); *Br* (Silva 1987:171) 20.
2. person who works the fields; fieldhand. *Br-Minas Velhas* (Harris 1956:141) 20.
3. person from northeastern Br; northeasterner. *Br* (Silva 1987:171) 20.
[Acc. Buarque de Holanda (1975:1344), < Tupi *taba'ré* 'inclined toward the village'; f. form *tabaroa*. Acc. Wagley, syns. *caboclo* in AM, *jeca* in SP. Acc. Silva, syn. df. 1 *caipira*; syns. df. 2 *nordestino, restingueiro, retirante, sertanejo*. Other syns. *matuto, roceiro*. Acc. Harris, *tabareu* [*sic*]. Cf. **caboclo, caipira, jeca, matuto, roceiro, sertanejo,** Sp. **campirano, campesino, jíbaro.**]

tabaroa — See *tabaréu*

taioca
offspring of a black and an Indian. *Br-no.* (Souza 1961:66) 20.
[Acc. Machado (1952:2.2039), < Tupi. Acc. Buarque de Holanda (1975:1347), < Tupi *ta'yoka* 'reddish-brown ant.' Syns. *cafuso, caboré, curiboca, mestiço.* Cf. **caboré, cafuso, curiboca, mulato,** Sp. **sambo, zambo.**]

talaveira
person from or native to Portugal or its islands. *Br-RS* (Coruja et al. 1964:444) 20.
[M., f. Acc. Coruja et al. and Buarque de Holanda (1975:1348), < *Talavera* 'Spanish city.' Syn. *galego.* Cf. **galego, parrudo, peninsular,** Sp. **gallego.**]

tapa huno — See *tapanhuna*

tapaiúna — See *tapanhuna*

tapaiúno — See *tapanhuna*

tapanhaúna — See *tapanhuna*

tapanhuna
1. offspring of a *cafuso* and a black. *Br* (Woodbridge 1948:360) cl; (Vergara Martín 1922:245) n.d.
2. black African living in Br. *Br* (Buarque de Holanda 1975:1353) 20.
3. Indian of the Tapanhuna tribe of MT. *Br* (Buarque de Holanda 1975:1353) 20.

[M., f. Acc. Buarque de Holanda, probably < Tupi. Vars. *tapanuna,
tapa huno, tapanhaúna, tapanhuno, tapaiúna, tapaiúno.* Cf. **índio,
negro, preto.**]

tapanhuno — See *tapanhuna*

tapanuna — See *tapanhuna*

tapiocano

rustic type; hick. *Br-RJ* (Ayrosa 1937:81) mid20 ‖ *Br*
(Buarque de Holanda 1975:1354) 20.

[Acc. Buarque de Holanda, < *tapioca* + suf. *-ano.* Syn. *caipira.* Cf.
caboclo, caipira, tabaréu.]

tapuia — See *tapuio*

tapuio

1. offspring of a civilized Indian and a black. *Br* (Woodbridge
1948:360) cl.

2a. any Brazilian Indian. *Br* (Freyre 1964:429) cl.

2b. any Indian, acc. whites. *Br-AM* (Baldus and Willems
1939:215–17) early20.

2c. independent or uncivilized Indian, acc. civilized Indians.
Br-AM (Baldus and Willems 1939:215–17) early20.

2d. wild or savage Indian from the interior or *sertão. Br-AM,
-PA* (Cascudo 1962:728) 20prior.

2e. Indian from the northeastern interior. *Br-n.e.* (Diégues
1963:105) 20.

2f. Indian dwelling along the banks of the Amazon River. *Br-
AM* (Santa Rosa 1922:2.39) early20.

3a. person of mixed race. *Br-PA* (Santa Rosa 1922:2.130–31)
early20.

3b. any brown-skinned person of mixed race with straight,
black hair. *Br-RS* (Coruja et al. 1964:447) 20.

3c. any brown-skinned mestizo with straight hair. *Br-BA*
(Buarque de Holanda (1975:1354) 20.

4. rustic type; hick. *Br-AM, -PA* (Ayrosa 1937:81) mid20.

5. offspring of a white and an Indian. *Br-n.e.* (Diégues
1963:105) 20.

6. person with the physical traits of an Amerindian. *Br-AM-Itá*
(Wagley 1963:121) 20.

7. enemy or foreigner, acc. Tupi Indians. *Br* (Vergara Martín
1922:245) prior20.

[Acc. Cascudo, ant. df. 2d *tupi* 'Indian from the coast'; syn. *caboclo.* Acc. Santa Rosa, syn. df. 3a *caboclo.* Acc. Ayrosa, syn. df. 4
caipira. Acc. Diégues, syn. df. 5 *mameluco.* Acc. Wagley, syn. df. 6
caboclo. Acc. Machado (1952:2.2051) and Baldus and Willems,
< Tupi *tapuia.* Acc. Vergara Martín, < Tupi *tapuya* 'anyone not

Tupi, not speaking Tupi, or engaging in war against the Tupi.' Vars.
tapúia, tapoui, tapuya, tapuyja, tapuyia. Cf. **caipira, caboclo,
mameluco, tupi.**]

tapuyana

black person, acc. Indians. *Br* (Ramos 1939:152) 16.
[M., f. Possibly < *tapuia.* Cf. **tapanhuna, tapuia, tupi.**]

ter genipapo — See *genipapo*

ter pimenta do reino 'to have black pepper'

black person with tight, kinky hair texture. *Br-AM* (Wagley
1963:122; Levine 1980:107) 20.
[Verb. phr. Cf. **negro, preto, ter pixaim,** Sp. **pelo malo.**]

ter pinta 'to be tinted; to have a bit of the tarbrush'

social climber of black or mixed race, acc. both whites and
blacks. *Br-n.e.* (Hutchinson 1957:122) 20.
[Verb phr. Syns. *ser da raça, ter sangue.* Sim. to Engl. phr. *to have
a touch of the tarbrush.* Cf. **negro, preto.**]

ter pixaim

black person with kinky hair; person with the kinky hair
texture of a black. *Br-AM* (Wagley 1963:122; Levine 1980:107) 20.
[Verb phr. Acc. Cabral (1982:610), *pixaim* or *pixauim* 'kinky hair.'
Acc. Buarque de Holanda (1975:1096), *pixaim* < Tupi *apixa'ĩ* 'kinky
hair.' Syn. *ter pimenta de reino.* Cf. **negro cabelo ruim, ser ruim
de cabelo, ter pimenta de reino,** Sp. **pelo malo.**]

ter raça 'to have (some of the) race'

Moor; Jew. *Br* (Bluteau 1720:7-R.86) early18.
[Acc. Bluteau, also used in Portugal; pejor.; usually in phrs. *ter raça
de mouro, ter raça de judeu.* Cf. **mouro.**]

ter sangue — See *ter pinta*

ter um pouco da raça 'to have a little of the race'

socially mobile mulatto who enhances his social standing by
marrying a woman with skin color lighter than his own. *Br* (Levine
1980:140) mid20.
[Verb phr. generally used in ref. to man, common in 1940s, acc.
Levine. Cf. **ter pimenta de reino, ter raça, ter sangue.**]

terceirão 'terceroon'

offspring of a white and a mulatto. *Br* (Vergara Martín
1922:245; Santamaría 1942:3.161; Woodbridge 1948:360; Diégues
1963:106) cl.
[< by anal. to *quarteirão.* Sim. to Sp. *cuarterón.* Acc. Cassidy
(1961:162), in Jamaica *terceroon* is next closest to black after the
quadroon. Acc. Mellafe (1975:115), 3rd generation removed from
black, like Engl. octoroon. Cf. Sp. **tercerón.**]

tetudo 'breasted'

offspring of an Indian and a white Portuguese *Br* (Vergara Martín 1922:245) n.d.

[< *teta* 'breast' + suf. *-udo*. Syn. *mestiço*. Cf. **mestiço.**]

tia 'aunt'

black woman, often a servant or slave, who was held in high esteem in the master's house. *Br-n.e.* (Kelsey 1940:56) 18–19.

[F. only. Cf. **mucama,** Sp. **tío.**]

tira-teima

1. person of mixed race. *Br-RJ* (Pinto 1953:217) mid20.

2. person with obvious black physical traits who is rejected by other family members who wish to continue to be considered white. *Br* (Levine 1980:135) 20.

[M., f. Acc. Levine, *tira-teime* [*sic*]; sim. to Engl. *black sheep.*]

tira-teime — See *tira-teima*

tostado 'toasted'

person with toasted or reddish-brown skin color, acc. 1980 census. *Br* (Silva 1987:159) 20.

[Acc. Silva, color classification. Cf. **acastanhado, amarelado, avermelhado, bem branco, claro, morenado, moreno, mulato, queimado de praia, queimado de sol, sapecado, vermelho,** Sp. **tostado.**]

tresalbo 'three white-footed'

offspring of an Indian and a mestizo. *Br* (Santamaría 1942:3.216) cl; (Vergara Martín 1922:245) n.d.

[Acc. Alonso (1958:3.4033), < *tres* 'three' + *albo* 'white,' i.e. 'horse with 3 white feet.' Var. *tresavo.* Sim. to Sp. *castizo, coyote.* Cf. **terceirão,** Sp. **tresalbo.**]

tresavo — See *tresalbo*

trigo 'wheat'

person with wheat-colored or light brown skin, acc. 1980 census. *Br* (Silva 1987:159) 20.

[Acc. Silva, color classification. Cf. **acastanhado, alvo, amarelado, avermelhado, bem branco, moreno, pardo, preto, trigueiro, vermelho,** Sp. **trigueño.**]

trigueiro 'wheat-colored'

person with light-brown or wheat-colored skin. *Br-SE* (Mott 1976:14) late18–20 ‖ *Br* (Silva 1987:159) 20.

[Acc. Buarque de Holanda (1975:1409), var. *triguenho.* Acc. Silva, 1980 census color classification. Cf. **acastanhado, amorenado, avermelhado, branco, morenado, moreno, pardo, preto, tapuio, trigo,** Sp. **trigueño.**]

triguenho — See *trigueiro*

trombadinha 'little hit; little bump'

orphaned or abandoned child or teenager who pickpockets or steals from others on street corners by using a method of bumping. *Br* (Buarque de Holanda 1975:1413; Gomes de Matos 1988:p.c.) 20.

[M., f. Generally poor street urchin, probably of any race.]

tupi 'Tupi'

1. Brazilian Indian. *Br* (Cascudo 1962:751–52) cl–20.

2. Indian from the coast. *Br* (Cascudo 1962:728) prior20.

[Ant. df. 2 *tapuio.* Acc. Buarque de Holanda (1975:1419), < Tupi; general syns. *guarani, tupi-guarani.* Cf. **índio, nhambiquara, tapanhuna, tapuio.**]

tupi-guarani — See *tupi*

turco 'Turk; Turkish'

1. Turk; Turkish; Ottoman. *Br* (Buarque de Holanda 1975: 1420) 20.

2a. Middle Easterner, usually owner of a small business, who speaks Arabic and emigrated to America at the turn of the 20 cent. *Br* (Souza 1961:326) 20.

2b. any Arab or Syrian. *Br* (Buarque de Holanda 1975:1420) 20.

[Often used in ref. to Turk, Syrian, Lebanese, Palestinian, Saudi, or other Arabs. Acc. Buarque de Holanda, df. 2b slang. < Turkish *turc* 'Turk,' acc. Alonso (1958:3.4072). Cf. **árabe, judeu,** Sp. **turco.**]

turututu

person of color, usually a neighbor or a fisherman. *Br-BA* (Blanco 1978:101) 20.

[M., f. Cf. **pessoa de cor.**]

turvo 'dark; opaque'

person with dark skin color, acc. 1980 census. *Br* (Silva 1987:159) 20.

[Acc. Silva, color classification. Cf. **acastanhado, alvo, amarelado, avermelhado, bem branco, morenado, moreno, mulato, pardo, tostado, vermelho.**]

U

urubá

1. black person from BA with a short, roundish face. *Br* (Mendonça 1935:244) cl.

2. black slave with a tattooed face. *Br* (Nuñez 1980:467) cl.

[M., f. Ant. *cara queimada.* Cf. **urubu.**]

urubu 'type of buzzard'
1. black person; person of color. *Br* (Chamberlain and Harmon 1983:505) 20.
2. Indian of the Urubu tribe found in MA. *Br* (Buarque de Holanda 1975:1433) 20.
[Slang, joc.; syn. *baiano,* acc. Chamberlain and Harmon. Cf. **baiano, urubá.**]

V

vaqueano — See *baqueano*
vaqueiro — See *mameluco*
vaquiano — See *baqueano*
verde 'green; delicate; very pallid'
person with very pallid or delicate skin color, acc. 1980 census. *Br* (Silva 1987:159) 20.
[Acc. Silva, color classification. Cf. **acastanhado, alvo, amarelado, avermelhado, bem branco, branco, moreno, mulato, pálido, pardo, rosado, rosa, rosa queimada, tostado, vermelho,** Sp. **anémico, pálido.**]
vermelhaça — See *vermelhaço*
vermelhaço
person with reddish or dark red skin color. *Br-BA-Salvador* (Sanjek 1971:1141; Blanco 1978:100) 20.
[Acc. Sanjek, *vermelhaça* [*sic*]. Acc. Blanco, *vermelhazo* [*sic*]. < *vermelho* 'red, dark red' + suf. *-aço.* Cf. **vermelho.**]
vermelho 'red'
1. person with red skin color, acc. surveys and censuses. *Br* (Harris 1964a:58; Silva 1987:159); *Br-BA* (Sanjek 1971:1141) 20.
2. Indian. *Br* (Ribeiro n.d.:19) 20prior.
[Also used in ref. to 'blond, redhead,' acc. Machado (1952:2.2161). Acc. Silva, df. 1 1980 census color classification. Df. 2 sim. to Engl. *redskin* 'Indian.' Cf. **acastanhado, avermelhado, bem branco, branco, índio, moreno, mulato, pardo, queimado de praia, queimado de sol, rosa, roxo, tostado, verde.**]

X

xavante
person of the Xavante Brazilian Indian tribe found in MT. *Br* (Buarque de Holanda 1975:1477; Gomes de Matos 1988:p.c.) 20.
[Acc. Buarque de Holanda, member of larger *Acuém* tribe. Cf. **bororo, gavião, tapanhuna, tupi, yanomámi.**]

xiano
  Portuguese invader, acc. Indians. *Br* (Freyre 1964:432) cl.
  [Probably of Amerindian origin.]

xibaro — See *xíbaro*

xíbaro
  1. offspring of a *cafuso* and a black. *Br* (Woodbridge 1948:360)
  cl ‖ *Br-PR* (Souza 1961:343) 20.
  2. offspring of a *caboré* and a black. *Br* (Woodbridge 1948:360)
  cl ‖ *Br-PR* (Souza 1961:343) 20.
  3. offspring of a *curiboca* and a black. *Br* (Woodbridge
  1948:360) cl.
  4. offspring of a black and an Indian. *Br* (Ramos 1941:537)
  mid20.
  5. offspring of a *caboclo* and a black. *Br-PR* (Buarque de
  Holanda 1975:1478) 20.
  [Vars. *xibaro, xívaro.* Acc. Buarque de Holanda, < Sp. *jíbaro.* Cf.
  caboré, cafuso, negro, zambo.]

xívaro — See *xíbaro*

Y

yanoáma — See *yanomámi*
yanomám — See *yanomámi*
yanomámá — See *yanomámi*
yanomáme — See *yanomámi*

yanomámi
  person of the Yanomama Brazilian Indian tribe. *Br* (Rodrigues
  1986:89, 134; Gomes de Matos 1988:p.c.) 20.
  [Acc. Rodrigues, vars. *yanoáma, yanomám, yanomámá, yanomáme.*

Z

zambo
  1a. offspring of a black and an Indian; 50% black, 50% Indian.
  Br (Woodbridge 1948:361) cl; (Ramos 1941:537) mid20; (Tenório
  d'Albuquerque 1954:44) 20.
  1b. offspring of a black and an Indian with dark, straight hair.
  Br (Mendonça 1935:247) cl–mid20.

2. offspring of a mulatto and a black. *Br* (Vergara Martín 1922:231) n.d.

[Syn. *cabra,* acc. Woodbridge and Vergara Martín. Syn. *cafuso,* acc. Chamberlain and Harmon (1983:97) and Mendonça. Acc. Tenório d'Albuquerque (1954:44), probably < Sp. via RP. Cf. **cabra, cafuso, zambo cabra.**]

zambo cabra
offspring of a black and a mulatto. *Br* (Woodbridge 1948:361) cl.

[Syns. *zambo grifo, zambo retorno.* Cf. **cabra, zambo, zambo claro, zambo preto.**]

zambo claro 'light *zambo*'
offspring of a *cabra* and an Indian. *Br* (Woodbridge 1948:361) cl; (Vergara Martín 1922:246) n.d.

[Var. *zambo-claro.* Cf. **claro, zambo, zambo cabra, zambo preto.**]

zambo-claro — See *zambo claro*

zambo grifo
offspring of a black and a mulatto. *Br* (Santamaría 1942:3.309; Woodbridge 1948:361) cl.

[Syns. *zambo cabra, zambo retorno.* Cf. **grifo, zambo, zambo cabra, zambo retorno.**]

zambo preto 'black *zambo*'
1. offspring of a *cabra* and a black. *Br* (Woodbridge 1948:361) cl.

2. offspring of a *zambo* and a black; 75% black, 25% Indian. *Br* (León 1924:27; Woodbridge 1948:361; Santamaría 1942:3.309) cl; (Vergara Martín 1922:246) n.d.

3. offspring either of a *caburete* or a *zambo* and a black. *Br* (Johnston 1910:56) early20prior.

[Syn. df. 3 *cafuso.* Cf. **preto, zambo, zambo retorno,** Sp. **zambo prieto.**]

zambo retorno
offspring of a black and a mulatto. *Br* (Woodbridge 1948:361; Santamaría 1942:3.309) cl.

[Syns. *zambo cabra, zambo grifo.* Probably indicates person is of darker skin color than the *zambo.* Cf. **zambo, zambo cabra, zambo grifo.**]

zelis — See *galego*

zumbi
black chieftain of a runaway slave camp. *Br* (Nuñez 1980:503) cl.

[Cf. **marabu, quilombola,** Sp. **palenquero.**]

References

Abalos, David T. 1986. Latinos in the United States: The sacred and the political. Notre Dame, IN: University of Notre Dame Press.

Acuña, Luis Alberto. 1951. Diccionario de bogotanismos. Bogotá: Minerva.

Aguilera Patiño, Luisa. 1951. Diccionario de panameñismos. Boletín de la Academia Argentina de Letras 20:405–506.

Aguirre Beltrán, Gonzalo. 1944. The slave trade in Mexico. Hispanic American Historical Review 24:412–31.

———. 1945. Races in seventeenth-century Mexico. Phylon 6(3): 212–18.

———. 1972 (1st ed., 1946). La población negra de México: Estudio etnohistórico. 2d ed. Mexico: Fondo de Cultura Económica.

Alario di Filippo, Mario. 1964. Léxicon de colombianismos. Cartagena, Co: Editora Bolívar.

Alba, Victor. 1969. The Latin Americans. New York: Frederick A. Praeger.

Alcedo, Antonio de. 1786–89 (trans., 1815; repr., 1970). The geographical and historical dictionary of America and the West Indies. 5 vols. Trans. by G. A. Thompson. New York: Burt Franklin. Repr. by Lenox Hill, New York.

Allen, Irving Lewis. 1983. The language of ethnic conflict: Social organization and lexical culture. New York: Columbia University Press.

Alleyne, Mervyn C. 1963. Review of Alvarez Nazario 1961. Caribbean Studies 3(1):96–98.

Almeida Oliveira, Sebastião. 1940. Expressões do populário sertanejo: Vocabulário e superstições. São Paulo: Civilização Brasileira.

Alonso, Amado. 1967. Estudios lingüísticos: Temas hispanoamericanos. 3d ed. Madrid: Gredos.

Alonso, Martín. 1958. Enciclopedia del idioma: Diccionario histórico y moderno de la lengua española (Siglos XII al XX) etimológico, tecnológico regional e hispanoamericano. 3 vols. Madrid: Aguiar.

Alvar, Manuel. 1987. Léxico del mestizaje hispanoamericano. Madrid: Ediciones Cultura Hispánica, Instituto de Cooperación Iberoamericana.

REFERENCES

Alvarez Nazario, Manuel. 1974 (1st ed., 1961). El elemento afrone-groide en el español de Puerto Rico: Contribución al estudio del negro en América. 2d ed. San Juan, PR: Instituto de Cultura Puertorriqueña.

———. 1982. Orígenes y desarrollo del español en Puerto Rico (siglos XVI y XVII). Río Piedras, PR: Editorial de la Universidad de Puerto Rico.

Amado, Jorge. 1975. Tereza Batista: Home from the wars. Trans. by Barbara Shelby. New York: Avon.

American Heritage Dictionary of the English Language. 1976. Ed. by William Morris. Boston: Houghton Mifflin.

Anderson, James M. 1973. Structural aspects of language change. London: Longman Group Ltd.

André, Jacques. 1949. Étude sur les termes de couleur dans la langue latine. Paris: Klincksieck.

Andrews, George Reid. 1979. Race vs. class association: The Afro-Argentines of Buenos Aires, 1850–1900. Journal of Latin American Studies 11:19–39.

Anshen, Frank. 1982. Creoles studied as a key to language's origin. The speech of slaves now takes scholarly forefront in linguistics. New York Times (August 22, 1982), p. 20E.

Armengol Valenzuela, Pedro. 1914–17. Glosario etimológico de nombres de personas, animales, plantas, ríos y lugares aborígenas de Chile y de algunas otras partes de América. Revista Chilena de Historia y Geografía 10:144–206, 11:218–62, 12:249–96, 13:122–56, 16:281–310, 17:273–304, 18:273–304, 19:273–304, 20:273–304, 21:273–304, 22:273–304, 23:273–304, 24:337–82.

Arnold, Thomas Walker. 1935 (repr., 1961). The preaching of Islam: A history of the propagation of the Muslim faith. Lahore: Sh. Muhammed Ashraf.

Arriola, Jorge Luis. 1941. Pequeño diccionario de voces guatemaltecas. Guatemala: Tipografía Nacional.

Arrom, José Juan. 1951. Criollo: Definición y matices de un concepto. Hispania 34:172–76.

Ayrosa, Plinio. 1937. Têrmos tupís no português do Brasil. São Paulo: Emprêsa Gráfica da 'Revista dos Tribunais.'

Azevedo, Aroldo de. 1970. Brasil: A terra e o homem. Vol. 2: A vida humana. São Paulo: Companhia Editora Nacional.

Azevedo, Thales de. 1951. Um questionário sobre estereótipos raciais. Sociologia 13(1):58–63.

———. 1953. Índios, brancos e pretos no Brasil colonial: As relações inter-raciais na cidade da Bahia. América Indígena 13:119–32.

———. 1964. Mestiçagem e status no Brasil. Sociologia 26(4):519–40.

Bailey, Helen Miller, and Abraham P. Nasatir. 1973. Latin America: The development of its civilization. 3d ed. Englewood Cliffs, NJ: Prentice-Hall.

Baldus, Herbert, and Emilio Willems. 1939. Dicionário de etnologia e sociologia. São Paulo: Companhia Editora Nacional.

Barker, George Carpenter. 1950. Pachuco: An American-Spanish argot and its social functions in Tucson, Arizona. Tucson: University of Arizona Press.

Barnet, Miguel. 1971. Biografía de un cimarrón. 2d ed. Mexico: Siglo veintiuno.

Barón Castro, Rodoldo. 1946. Política racial de España en Indias. Revista de Indias 7:781–802.

Barras de Aragón, F. 1929. Noticias de varios cuadros pintados en el siglo XVIII representando mestizajes y tipos de razas indígenas de América y algunos casos anormales. Memorias de la Real Sociedad de Historia Natural (Madrid) 15:155–68.

Bastide, Roger. 1970. Stereotypes, norms, and interracial behavior in São Paulo, Brazil. In: Race and ethnicity, ed. by Pierre L. van den Berghe. New York: Basic Books Inc.

Bastide, Roger, and Pierre van den Berghe. 1957. Stereotypes, norms and interracial behavior in São Paulo, Brazil. American Sociological Review 22:689–94.

Batres Jáuregui, Antonio. 1892. Vicios del lenguaje y provincialismos de Guatemala: Estudio filológico. Guatemala: Encuadernación y Tipografía Nacional.

Bayo, Ciro. 1910. Vocabulario criollo-español sud-americano. Madrid: Librería de los sucesores de Hernando.

_____. 1931. Manual del lenguaje criollo de Centro y Sudamérica. Madrid: R. Caro Raggio.

Beals, Ralph L. 1969. Indian-mestizo-white relations in Spanish America. In: Tumin 1969, pp. 239–57.

Bentivoglio, Paola. 1977. Observaciones sobre el léxico del cuerpo humano en el habla culta de Caracas. In: Estudios sobre el español hablado en las principales ciudades de América, ed. by Juan M. Lope Blanch, pp. 293–98. Mexico: UNAM.

Blanchard, Raphaël. 1908. Les tableaux de métissage au Méxique. Journal de la Société des Americanistes de Paris, New Series 5:59–66.

_____. 1910. Encore sur les tableaux de métissage du Musée de Méxique. Journal de la Société des Americanistes de Paris, New Series 7:37–60.

Blanco, Antonio. 1971. La lengua española en la historia de California: Contribución a su estudio. Madrid: Ediciones Cultura Hispánica.

REFERENCES

Blanco, Merida Holderness. 1978. Race and face among the poor: The language of color in a Brazilian bairro. Unpublished Ph.D dissertation, Stanford University, Palo Alto, CA.

Blassingame, John W. 1972. The slave community: Plantation life in the antebellum South. New York: Oxford University Press.

Bloch, Oscar. 1932. Dictionnaire étymologique de la langue française. 2 vols. With the collaboration of Walther von Wartburg. Paris: Presses Universitaires de France.

Bluteau, Raphael. 1712–21. Vocabulario portuguez, e latino. 8 vols. Coimbra: Collegio das Artes da Companhia de Jesu, and Lisbon: Officina de Pascoal da Sylva.

———. 1727–28. Supplemento ao Vocabulario portuguez, e latino. 2 vols. Lisbon: Officina de Joseph Antonio da Sylva.

Boggs, Ralph S., et al., comps. 1946. A tentative dictionary of Medieval Spanish. Chapel Hill, NC.

Borah, Woodrow, and Sherburne F. Cook. 1961. Sobre las posibilidades de hacer el estudio histórico del mestizaje sobre una base demográfica. In: Mörner 1961, pp. 64–73.

Boring, Phyllis Z. 1976. Amado and Barroso: Two novelists view race relations in Brazil. CLA Journal 19(3):412–17.

Bourricaud, François. 1975. Indian, mestizo and cholo as symbols in the Peruvian system of stratification. In: Glazer and Moynihan 1975, pp. 350–87.

Boxer, Charles Ralph. 1962. The colour question in the Portuguese empire, 1415–1825. Proceedings of the British Academy 47: 113–38.

Boyd-Bowman, Peter M. 1969. Negro slaves in early colonial Mexico. The Americas 26:134–51.

Boyd-Bowman, Peter M., ed. 1971. Léxico hispanoamericano del siglo XVI. London: Tamesis.

———. 1982. Léxico hispanoamericano del siglo XVIII. Madison, WI: Hispanic Seminary of Medieval Studies.

———. 1983. Léxico hispanoamericano del siglo XVII. Madison, WI: Hispanic Seminary of Medieval Studies.

———. 1984. Léxico hispanoamericano del siglo XIX. Madison, WI: Hispanic Seminary of Medieval Studies.

Brito P., Rafael. 1930. Diccionario de criollismos. San Francisco de Macorís, DR: Imprenta 'ABC' de Carlos F. de Moya.

Brown, Francis J., and Joseph Slabey Roucek, eds. 1939. Our racial and national minorities: Their history, contributions, and present problems. New York: Prentice-Hall.

Brown, Leon Carl. 1967. Color in northern Africa. Daedalus 96:464–82.

Buarque de Holanda Ferreira, Aurélio, ed. 1975. Novo diciónario da língua portuguesa. Rio de Janeiro: Editora Nova Fronteira.

Burma, John H. 1949. Negro population of Latin America. Sociology and Social Research 33:271–74.

Burns, Alan. 1971. Color prejudice. Westport, CT: Negro Universities Press.

Burns, E. Bradford. 1980. A history of Brazil. 2d ed. New York: Columbia University Press.

Bynon, Theodora. 1977. Historical linguistics. Cambridge: Cambridge University Press.

Cabral, Tomé. 1982. Novo dicionário de termos e expressões populares. Fortaleza, CE: Edições da Universidade Federal do Ceará.

Cahnman, Werner J. 1943. The Mediterranean and Caribbean regions—a comparison in race and culture contacts. Social Forces 22(2):209–14.

Callage, Roque. 1928. Vocabulario gaúcho. 2d ed. Porto Alegre: Edição da Livraria do Globo.

Cámara Barbachano, Fernando. 1964. El mestizaje en México: Planteamiento sobre problemáticas socio-culturales. Revista de Indias 24:27–85.

Cammarota, Federico. 1963. Vocabulario familiar y del lunfardo, con notas sobre su origen. Buenos Aires: Gráfico Standard.

Cara-Walker, Ana. 1987. Cocoliche: The art of assimilation and dissimulation among Italians and Argentines. Latin American Research Review 22(3):37–67.

Cartwright, Frederick F. 1972. Disease and history. In collaboration with Michael D. Biddiss. New York: Crowell.

Carvalho-Neto, Paulo de. 1964. Diccionario del folklore ecuatoriano. Quito: Editorial Casa de la Cultura Ecuatoriana.

Cascudo, Luis da Câmara. 1962 (1st ed., 1954). Dicionário do folclore brasileiro. Rio de Janeiro: Ministério da Educação e Cultura, Instituto Nacional do Livro.

Caso, Alfonso. 1948. Definición del indio y de lo indio. América Indígena 8:239–47.

Cassidy, Frederic G. 1961. Jamaica talk: Three hundred years of the English language in Jamaica. London: Macmillan.

Cassidy, Frederic G., and David DeCamp. 1966. Names for albino among Jamaican Negroes. Names 14:129–33.

Castellón, Hildebrando A. 1939. Diccionario de nicaraguanismos. Managua: Talleres Nacionales.

Castillo, Rodolfo. 1974. Los colores y algunos de sus aspectos semánticos. Fremdsprachen 18:145–46.

Castro, Américo. 1948. España en su historia: Cristianos, moros y judíos. Buenos Aires: Losada.

_____. 1973 (1st ed., 1954). La realidad histórica de España. 5th ed. Mexico: Porrúa.

Chamberlain, Bobby J. 1981. Lexical similarities of *lunfardo* and *gíria*. Hispania 64:417–25.

Chamberlain, Bobby J., and Ronald M. Harmon. 1983. A dictionary of informal Brazilian Portuguese, with English index. Washington, DC: Georgetown University Press.

Chance, John K. 1979. On the Mexican mestizo. Latin American Research Review 14(3):153–68.

Chance, John K., and William B. Taylor. 1977. Estate and class in a colonial city: Oaxaca in 1792. Comparative Studies in Society and History 19:454–87.

Chaudenson, Robert. 1974. Le noir et le blanc: La classification raciale dans les parlers créoles de l'océan Indien. Revue de Linguistique Romane 38:75–94.

Chávez González, Rodrigo A. 1937. El mestizaje y su influencia social en América. Guayaquil: Imprenta y Talleres Municipales.

Chiappelli, Fredi, ed. 1976. First images of America: The impact of the New World on the Old. 2 vols. Co-editors: Michael J. B. Allen and Robert L. Benson. Berkeley: University of California Press.

Cobarruvias Orozco, Sebastián de. 1611 (facsimile ed., 1977). Tesoro de la lengua castellana o española. Reproduction of 1611 edition, with the emendations of the 1943 edition. Madrid: Turner.

Cobb, Martha. 1972. Afro-Arabs, blackamoors, and blacks: An inquiry into race concepts through Spanish literature. Black World 21(5):32–40.

Cobos, Rubén. 1983. A dictionary of New Mexico and southern Colorado Spanish. Santa Fe: Museum of New Mexico Press.

Coll y Toste, Cayetano. 1924. Origen etnológico del campesino de Puerto Rico y mestizaje de las razas blanca, india y negra. Boletín Histórico de Puerto Rico (San Juan) 11:127–59, 255–62.

Colón, Germán. 1976. El léxico catalán en la Romania. Madrid: Gredos.

The colours of Brazil. 1986. The Economist 299 (May 10, 1986):42.

Comas, Juan. 1945. La discriminación racial en América. América Indígena 5:73–89, 161–70.

_____. 1966. Manual de antropología física. 2d ed. Mexico: UNAM, Instituto de Investigaciones Históricas, Sección de Antropología.

Conklin, Harold C. 1962. Lexicographical treatment of folk taxonomies. In: Householder and Saporta 1962, pp. 119–41.

Corominas, Juan. 1944. Indianorománica: Estudios de lexicografía hispanoamericana. Revista de Filología Hispánica 6:1–35.

_____. 1954–57. Diccionario crítico etimológico de la lengua castellana. 4 vols. Bern: Francke.

_____. 1973. Breve diccionario etimológico de la lengua castellana. 3d ed. Madrid: Gredos.

Corominas, Juan, and José A. Pascual. 1980–81. Diccionario crítico etimológico castellano e hispánico. 4 (of 6) vols. Madrid: Gredos.

Cortina Gomez, Rodolfo. 1978. Race and identity in Puerto Rican literature. In: Minority literature and the urban experience: Selected proceedings of the 4th annual conference on minority studies, ed. by George E. Carter, James R. Parker, and Sara Bentley. La Crosse, WI: Institute for Minority Studies, University of Wisconsin-La Crosse.

Coruja, Antônio Álvares Pereira, Romaguera Corrêa, Luiz Carlos de Maraes, and Roque Callage. 1964. Vocabulário sul-rio-grandense. Rio de Janeiro: Editora Globo.

Cowles, Ella Nancy. 1952. A vocabulary of American Spanish based on glossaries appended to literary works. Unpublished Ph.D. dissertation, University of Michigan, Ann Arbor.

Crépeau, Pierre. 1973. Classifications raciales populaires et métissage: Essai d'anthropologie cognitive. Montreal: Centre de Recherches Caraïbes, Université de Montreal.

Cumberland, Charles C. 1960. The Sonora Chinese and the Mexican revolution. Hispanic American Historical Review 40:191–211.

Dauzat, Albert, Jean Dubois, and Henri Mitterand. 1964. Nouveau dictionnaire étymologique et historique. 3d ed. Paris: Larousse.

Davenport, Charles B., and Morris Steggerda. 1970. Race crossing in Jamaica. Westport, CT: Negro Universities Press.

Davidson, Basil. 1961. The African slave trade: Precolonial history 1450–1850. Boston: Little, Brown.

D'Azevedo, Pedro A. 1903. Os escravos. Archivo Historico Portuguez 1:289–307.

De Vos, George, and Lola Romanucci-Ross, eds. 1975. Ethnic identity: Cultural communities and change. Palo Alto, CA: Mayfield Publishing.

Deagan, Kathleen A. 1973. Mestizaje in colonial St. Augustine. Ethnohistory 20:55–65.

Degler, Carl N. 1971. Neither black nor white: Slavery and race relations in Brazil and the United States. New York: Macmillan.

Diccionario de la lengua española. 1970 (1st ed., 1726–39). 19th ed. Madrid: Real Academia Española.

Diccionario histórico de la lengua española. 1960–74. 11 fascicles. General directors, Julio Casares and Rafael Lapesa. Madrid: Real Academia Española.

375

REFERENCES

Diégues, Manuel, Jr. 1963. Etnias e culturas no Brasil. 3d ed. Rio de Janeiro: Editora Letras e Artes.

Diggs, Irene. 1953. Color in colonial Spanish America. Journal of Negro History 38:403–27.

Dihigo y López-Trigo, Ernesto. 1966. Los cubanismos en el Diccionario de la Real Academia Española. Madrid: Comisión Permanente de la Associación de Academias de la Lengua Española.

Diretória Geral da Estatística (Brasil). 1873–76. Recenseamento da população do Império do Brasil a que se procedeu no dia 1 de Agosto de 1872. 23 vols. Rio de Janeiro: Leuzinger e Filhos.

Dollard, John. 1957. Caste and class in a southern town. Garden City, NY: Doubleday Anchor Books.

Domínguez, Virginia R. 1973. The middle race. Unpublished Scholar of the House thesis, Yale University, New Haven, CT.

———. 1986. White by definition: Social classification in Creole Louisiana. New Brunswick, NJ: Rutgers University Press.

Domínguez Ortiz, Antonio. 1952. La esclavitud en Castilla durante la edad moderna. In: Instituto 'Balmés' de Sociología 1952, vol. 2, pp. 367–428.

Dunbar-Nelson, Alice. 1916. People of color in Louisiana. Journal of Negro History 1:361–76.

Dunlap, A. R., and C. A. Weslager. 1947. Trends in the naming of tri-racial mixed-blood groups in the eastern United States. American Speech 22:81–87.

Echaiz, René León. 1955. Interpretación histórica del huaso chileno. Santiago de Chile: Editorial Universitaria.

Escalante, Aquiles. 1964. El negro en Colombia. Bogotá: Universidad Nacional de Colombia, Facultad de Sociología.

Espina Pérez, Darío. 1972. Diccionario de cubanismos. Barcelona: M. Pareja.

Esteva Fabregat, Claudio. 1964. El mestizaje en Iberoamérica. Revista de Indias 24:277–354.

Exquemelin, Alexandre Olivier. 1684. The buccaneers of America. Verbatim reprint of the 2d edition of the English translation. London: George Routledge and Sons, Ltd., and New York: E. P. Dutton and Co.

Ferguson, J. Halcro. 1963. El equilibrio racial en América Latina. Trans. by Horacio Martínez. Buenos Aires: Editorial Universitaria de Buenos Aires.

Fernandes, Florestan. 1968. The weight of the past. In: Franklin 1968, pp. 282–301.

———. 1969. The Negro in Brazilian society. Trans. by Jacqueline D. Skiles, A. Brunel, and Arthur Rothwell. Ed. by Phyllis B. Eveleth. New York and London: Columbia University Press.

REFERENCES

Fernández Gómez, Carlos. 1962. Vocabulario de Cervantes. Madrid: Real Academia Española.

_____. 1971. Vocabulario completo de Lope de Vega. 3 vols. Madrid: Real Academia Española.

Fernández Naranjo, Nicolás, and Dora Gómez de Fernández. 1967. Diccionario de bolivianismos. 2d ed. La Paz-Cochabamba: 'Los Amigos del Libro.'

Flórez, Luis. 1969. Léxico del cuerpo humano en Colombia. (Publicaciones del Instituto Caro y Cuervo, 27.) Bogotá: Instituto Caro y Cuervo.

Fontaine, Pierre-Michel, ed. 1985. Race, class and power in Brazil. Los Angeles: UCLA Center for Afro-American Studies.

Fontanella de Weinberg, María Beatriz. 1982. Aspectos del español hablado en el Río de la Plata durante los siglos XVI y XVII. Bahía Blanca, Ar: Departamento de Humanidades, Universidad Nacional del Sur.

Fortune, Armando. 1960. Los orígenes africanos del negro panameño y su composición étnica a comienzos del siglo XVII. Lotería Nacional de Beneficia (Panamá) 56:113–28.

Fox, Geoffrey. 1988. Hispanic communities in the United States. Latin American Research Review 23(3):227–37.

Franklin, John Hope. 1968. Introduction: Color and race in the modern world. In: Franklin 1968, pp. vii–xvi.

Franklin, John Hope, ed. 1968. Color and race. Boston: Houghton Mifflin.

Frazier, E. Franklin. 1957. Race and culture contacts in the modern world. Boston: Beacon.

Frenk Alatorre, Margit. 1953. Designaciones de rasgos físicos personales en el habla de la Ciudad de México. Nueva Revista de Filología Española 7:134–56.

Freyre, Gilberto. 1956. Brazilian melting pot: The meeting of races in Portuguese America. The Atlantic Monthly 197(2):104–8.

_____. 1964. The masters and the slaves (Casa grande & senzala): A study in the development of Brazilian civilization. Trans. by Samuel Putnam. New York: Knopf.

Fried, Jacob. 1961. The Indian and mestizaje in Peru. Human Organization 20:23–26.

Fromkin, Victoria, and Robert Rodman. 1988. An introduction to language. 4th ed. New York: Holt, Rinehart and Winston.

Fuente, Julio de la. 1947. Definición, pase y desaparición del indio en México. América Indígena 7:63–69.

Gagini, Carlos. 1918. Diccionario de barbarismos y provincialismos de Costa Rica. 2d ed. San José, CR: Tipografía Nacional.

Gallo, Cristino. 1980. Language of the Puerto Rican street: A slang dictionary with English cross-reference. Hato Rey, PR: Ramallo Bros., Inc.

Galván, Roberto A., and Richard V. Teschner, comps. 1985 (1st ed., 1975). El diccionario del español chicano / The dictionary of Chicano Spanish. Lincolnwood, IL: Voluntad Publishers of the National Textbook Company.

Gann, Lewis H., and Peter J. Duignan. 1986. The Hispanics in the United States: A history. Stanford, CA: Hoover Institution on War, Revolution and Peace.

Garza Cuarón, Beatriz. 1987. El español hablado en la ciudad de Oaxaca, México: Caracterización fonética y léxica. (Serie Estudios de dialectología mexicana, 2.) Mexico: El Colegio de México.

Garzón, Tobías. 1910. Diccionario argentino ilustrado con numerosos textos. Buenos Aires: Sopena.

Genovese, Eugene D. 1969. The world the slaveholders made: Two essays in interpretation. New York: Pantheon.

Gibson, Charles. 1966. Spain in America. New York: Harper and Row.

Gili y Gaya, Samuel. 1960. Tesoro lexicográfico (1492–1726). vol. 1. Madrid: Consejo Superior de Investigaciones Científicas.

Gillin, John. 1949. Mestizo America. In: Linton 1949, pp. 156–211.

_____. 1961. The social transformation of the mestizo. In: Mörner 1961, pp. 73–78.

Glazer, Nathan, and Daniel P. Moynihan, eds. 1975. Ethnicity: Theory and experience. Cambridge, MA: Harvard University Press.

Gobello, José, and Luciano Payet. 1959. Breve diccionario lunfardo. Buenos Aires: A. Peña Lillo.

Gonzalez de Mireles, Jovita. 1939. Latin Americans. In: Brown and Roucek 1939, pp. 497–509.

González Olle, Fernando. 1962. Los sufijos diminutivos en castellano medieval. (Revista de Filología Española, añejo 75.) Madrid: Consejo Superior de Investigaciones Científicas.

Gooch, Anthony. 1970. Diminutive, augmentative and pejorative suffixes in Modern Spanish: A guide to their use and meaning. 2d ed. Oxford, England: Pergamon.

Goodman, Morris F. 1964. A comparative study of Creole French dialects. The Hague: Mouton.

Grace, Lee Ann. 1976. Los mestizos y los indigenismos: México, 1550–1600. Paper presented at the Colloquium on Hispanic and Luso-Brazilian Linguistics, Oswego, NY, July 24–55, 1976.

Granada, Daniel. 1957 (reproduction of 2d ed. of 1890). Vocabulario rioplatense razonado. 2 vols. Montevideo: Impresora Uruguaya for the Ministerio de Instrucción Pública.

Grenón, Pedro, S.J., comp. 1929–30. Diccionario documentado de nuestra terminología. Córdoba, Ar: Talleres Gráficos de la Penitenciaria.

Grimes, Barbara, ed. 1988. Ethnologue: Languages of the World. 11th ed. Dallas: Summer Institute of Linguistics.

Guarnieri, Juan Carlos. 1957. Nuevo diccionario campesino rioplatense, con las locuciones más usadas en el Uruguay. Montevideo: Florensa y Tafón.

———. 1967. El habla del boliche: Diccionario del lenguaje popular rioplatense. Montevideo: Florensa y Lafón.

———. 1968. Diccionario del lenguaje campesino rioplatense. Montevideo: Florensa y Lafón.

———. 1979. Diccionario del lenguaje rioplatense. Montevideo: Ediciones de la Banda Oriental.

Gutiérrez Saco, M. Yolanda. 1965. Mestizaje peruano-chino. Revista Histórica (Lima) 28:261–67.

Haberly, David T. 1983. Three sad races: Racial identity and national consciousness in Brazilian literature. Cambridge: University Press.

Harris, Marvin. 1952. Race relations in Minas Velhas, a community in the mountain region of central Brazil. In: Wagley 1952.

———. 1956. Town and country in Brazil. New York: Columbia University Press.

———. 1964a. Patterns of race in the Americas. New York: Walker and Co.

———. 1964b. Racial identity in Brazil. Luso-Brazilian Review 1(2):21–28.

———. 1970. Referential ambiguity in the calculus of Brazilian racial identity. Southwestern Journal of Anthropology 26:1–14.

Harris, Marvin, and Conrad Kottak. 1963. The structural significance of Brazilian racial categories. Sociologia 25:203–8.

Harth-Terré, Emilio. 1965. El mestizaje y la miscegenación en los primeros años de la fundación de Lima. Revista Histórica (Lima) 28:132–44.

Heath, Dwight B., and Richard N. Adams, eds. 1965. Contemporary cultures and societies of Latin America: A reader in the social anthropology of Middle and South America and the Caribbean. New York: Random House.

Hernández Aquino, Luis. 1969. Diccionario de voces indígenas de Puerto Rico. Bilbao, Spain: Editorial Vasco Americana, S.A.

Herrera, Alfonso L., and Ricardo E. Cícero. 1895. Catálogo de la colección de antropología del Museo Nacional. Mexico: Imprenta del Museo Nacional.

Hildebrandt, Martha. 1969. Peruanismos. Lima: Moncloa.

Hoetink, Harry. 1973. Slavery and race relations in the Americas: Comparative notes on their nature and nexus. New York: Harper Torchbooks.

Hole, Edwyn. 1958. Andalus: Spain under the Muslims. London: R. Hale Ltd.

Hollanda, Güy de. 1956. Los españoles y las castas. Historia Paraguaya (Anuario del Instituto Paraguayo de Investigaciones Históricas), pp. 69–76.

Hope, T. E. 1971. Lexical borrowing in the Romance languages: A critical study of Italianisms in French and Gallicisms in Italian from 1100 to 1900. 2 vols. New York: New York University Press.

Householder, Fred W., and Sol Saporta, eds. 1962. Problems in lexicography. (Indiana University Publications in Anthropology and Linguistics, 21.) Bloomington: Indiana University Press.

Humboldt, Alexander von. 1941 (1st ed., 1882). Ensayo político sobre el reino de la Nueva España. 6th ed. Paris: Rosa.

Hutchinson, Harry W. 1952. Race relations in a rural community of the Bahian Recôncavo. In: Wagley 1952, pp. 16–46.

_____. 1957. Village and plantation life in northeastern Brazil. Seattle: University of Washington Press.

Ianni, Octávio. 1975. Escravismo e racismo. Anais de História (São Paulo) 7:66–94.

Imbs, Paul, dir. 1978. Trésor de la langue française. Vol. 6. Paris: Éditions du Centre National de la Recherche Scientifique.

Instituto 'Balmés' de Sociología. 1952. Estudios de historia social de España. 2 vols. Madrid: Consejo Superior de Investigaciones Científicas.

Ivory, Annette. 1979. Juan Latino: The struggle of Blacks, Jews, and Moors in Golden Age Spain. Hispania 62:613–18.

Johnson, Lemuel. 1971. The devil, the gargoyle, and the buffoon: The Negro as metaphor in western literature. Port Washington, NY: Kennikat Press.

Johnson, Leroy. 1981. Congolese-Portuguese relationships, 1482–1506. The initial phase. Paper presented for the Center for Afro-American Studies Colloquium, University of Michigan, Ann Arbor, April 15, 1981.

Johnston, Harry Hamilton. 1910. The Negroes in the New World. New York: Macmillan.

Kahane, Henry and Renée. 1962. Notes on the linguistic history of *sclavus*. In: Studi in onore di Lo Gatto and Maver 1962, pp. 345–60.

Kammer, Edward J. 1941. A socio-economic survey of the marsh-dwellers of four southeast Louisiana parishes. Washington, DC: Catholic University of America Press.

Kany, Charles E. 1960a. American-Spanish euphemisms. Berkeley: University of California Press.

_____. 1960b. American-Spanish semantics. Berkeley: University of California Press.

Kelsey, Vera. 1940. Seven keys to Brazil. New York and London: Funk and Wagnalls.

Kiddle, Lawrence B. 1952a. The Spanish language as a medium of cultural diffusion in the age of discovery. American Speech 27:241–56.

_____. 1952b. Spanish loanwords in American Indian languages. Hispania 35:179–84.

Klein, Herbert S. 1968. The slave economies of Cuba and Virginia: A comparison. In: Weinstein and Gatell 1968, pp. 112–31.

Klumpp, Kathleen. 1970. Black traders of north highland Ecuador. In: Whitten and Szwed 1970, pp. 245–62.

Konetzke, Richard. 1946. El mestizaje y su importancia en el desarrollo de la población hispanoamericana durante la época colonial. Revista de Indias 7:7–44, 215–37.

_____. 1961. La legislación española y el mestizaje en América. In: Mörner 1961, pp. 59–64.

König, Karl. 1939. Überseeische Wörter im Französischen (16.–18. Jahrhundert). (Beihefte zur Zeitschrift für romanische Philologie, 91.). Halle: Max Niemeyer.

Kottak, Conrad P. 1967. Race relations in a Bahian fishing village. Luso-Brazilian Review 4(2):35–52.

_____. 1978. Anthropology: The exploration of human diversity. 2d ed. New York: Random House.

Lane-Poole, Stanley. 1893. The Moors in Spain. 5th ed. London: T. Fisher Urwin; New York: G. P. Putnam's Sons.

Laxalt, Robert. 1980. Last of a breed: The Gauchos. National Geographic 158:478–501.

Leite de Vasconcellos Pereira de Mello, José. 1928. Antroponímia portuguesa. Lisbon: Imprensa Nacional.

León, Aurelio de. 1936–37. Barbarismos comunes en México: Solecismos, anglicismos, provincialismos del norte, voces forenses impropias. Mexico: Imprenta Mundial and Porrúa.

León, Nicolás. 1924. Las castas del México colonial o Nueva España: Noticias etno-antropológicas. Mexico: Talleres gráficos del

Museo Nacional de Arqueología, Historia y Etnografía.

Lévi-Provençal, Evariste. 1932. L'Espagne musulmane au Xème siècle: Institutions et vie sociale. Paris: Larose.

———. 1957. España musulmana hasta la caída del Califato de Córdoba (711–1032 de J.C.): Instituciones y vida social e intelectual. Ed. by Ramón Menéndez-Pidal. Trans. by Emilio García Gómez. Madrid: Espasa-Calpe.

Levine, Robert M. 1979. Historical dictionary of Brazil. (Latin American Historical Dictionaries, 19.) Metuchen, NJ: Scarecrow Press.

———. 1980. Race and ethnic relations in Latin America and the Caribbean. Metuchen, NJ: Scarecrow Press.

Lexis: Dictionnaire de la langue française. 1975. Jean Dubois, dir. Paris: Larousse.

Lind, Andrew, ed. 1955. Race relations in world perspective. Papers read at the Conference on Race Relations in World Perspective, Honolulu, 1954. Honolulu: University of Hawaii Press.

Linton, Ralph, ed. 1949. Most of the world: The peoples of Africa, Latin America, and the East today. New York: Columbia University Press.

Lipschütz, Alejandro. 1944. El indoamericanismo y el problema racial en las Américas. 2d ed. Santiago de Chile: Editorial Nascimiento.

Lipski, John M. 1985. The speech of the negros congos of Panama: An Afro-Hispanic dialect. Hispanic Linguistics 2(1):23–47.

———. 1987. Language contact phenomena in Louisiana isleño Spanish. American Speech 62(4):320–31.

Love, Edgar F. 1971. Marriage patterns of persons of African descent in a colonial Mexico City parish. Hispanic American Historical Review 51:79–91.

Lowenthal, David. 1969. Race and color in the West Indies. In: Tumin 1969, pp. 293–312.

Lowenthal, David, and Lambros Comitas, eds. 1973. Consequences of class and color: West Indian perspectives. Garden City, NY: Anchor Books.

Ludwig, Armin K. 1985. Brazil: A handbook of historical statistics. Boston: G. K. Hall.

Lynch, Benito. 1964. El inglés de los güesos. 9th ed. Buenos Aires: Troquel.

MacCurdy, Raymond R. 1950. The Spanish dialect of St. Bernard Parish, Louisiana. Albuquerque: University of New Mexico Press.

Machado, José Pedro. 1952–59. Dicionário etimológico da língua portuguesa. 2 vols. 2d ed. Rio de Janeiro: Editorial Confluência.

Machado, Propício da Silveira. 1966. O gaúcho na história e na lingüística: A formação étnica e social do Rio Grande do Sul e a origem do têrmo 'gaúcho' (subsídios histórico-filológicos). Porto Alegre.

Machado Filho, Aires da Mata. 1964 (1st ed., 1943). O negro e o garimpo em Minas Gerais. Rio de Janeiro: Editora Civilização Brasileira.

Macías, José Miguel. 1885. Diccionario cubano, etimológico, crítico, razonado y comprensivo. Veracruz: Imprenta de C. Trowbridge.

Magnusson, Paul. 1980. There's one. Let's get him. Detroit Free Press, Sunday, February 24, 1980, pp. 1B, 4B.

Malaret, Augusto. 1931 (1st ed., 1925). Diccionario de americanismos. San Juan, PR: Imprenta Venezuela.

_____. 1937. Vocabulario de Puerto Rico. San Juan, PR: Imprenta Venezuela.

_____. 1942, 1944. Diccionario de americanismos (suplemento). Vol. 1: A–E. Vol. 2: F–Z. Buenos Aires: Academia Argentina de Letras.

_____. 1946 (1st ed., 1925). Diccionario de americanismos. 3d ed. Buenos Aires: Emecé Editores.

_____. 1947. Los americanismos en la copla popular y en el lenguaje culto. New York: Vanni.

_____. 1967 (1st ed., 1955). Vocabulario de Puerto Rico. 2d ed. New York: Las Américas.

Maldonado de Guevara y Andrés, Francisco. 1924. El primer contacto de blancos y gentes de color en América: Estudio sobre el diario del primer viaje de Cristóbal Colón. Valladolid: Talleres Tipográficas 'Cuesta'; Berkeley: University of California Press.

Malkiel, Yakov. 1953. 'Apretar', 'pr(i)eto', 'perto': Historia de un cruce hispanolatino. Thesaurus 9:1–135.

_____. 1958. Old Spanish judezno, morezno, pecadezno. Philological Quarterly 37:95–99.

_____. 1969. The case of Old Spanish /sk/ changing to /θk/. Romance Philology 23:188–200.

_____. 1976. Changes in the European languages under a new set of sociolinguistic circumstances. In: Chiappelli 1976, vol. 2, pp. 581–93.

Marcgrave, Jorge. 1648 (repr. 1942). História natural do Brasil. São Paulo: Imprensa Oficial do Estado de São Paulo.

Marcílio, Maria Luiza. 1974. Evolução da população brasileira através dos censos até 1872. Anais de História 6:115–37.

Marden, Charles F., and Gladys Meyer. 1978. Minorities in American society. 5th ed. New York: D. Van Nostrand.

Martínez, Fernando Antonio. 1968. Lexicography. In: Ibero-American and Caribbean linguistics, Current trends in linguistics, vol. 4, ed. by Thomas A. Sebeok, pp. 84–105. The Hague: Mouton.

Martinez-Alier, Verena. 1974. Marriage, class and colour in nineteenth-century Cuba: A study of racial attitudes and sexual values in a slave society. Cambridge: Cambridge University Press.

Mattoso, Katia M. de Queiros. 1986. To be a slave in Brazil, 1550–1888. Trans. by Arthur Goldhammer, with a foreword by Stuart Schwartz. New Brunswick, NJ: Rutgers University Press.

McAlister, Lyle. 1963. Social structure and social change in New Spain. Hispanic American Historical Review 43:349–79.

McCartney, Michael. 1988. Under a roof of thatch in the jungle: A remote base for Amazon excursions. New York Times (Sunday, September 11, 1988), Section 5: Travel, pp. 8–9.

McDavid, Raven I., Jr., and Sarah Ann Witham. 1974. Poor whites and rustics. Names 22:93–103.

McGrath, Eileen E. 1980. Germanía gelfe 'black slave': An alternative hypothesis. Journal of Hispanic Philology 4:257–58.

Megenney, William W. 1978. A Bahian heritage: An ethnolinguistic study of African influences on Bahian Portuguese. (North Carolina Studies in the Romance Languages and Literatures, 198.) Chapel Hill: University of North Carolina Press.

_____. 1983. Common words of African origin used in Latin America. Hispania 66:1–10.

Mellafe, Rolando. 1964. La esclavitud en Hispanoamérica. Buenos Aires: Editorial Universitaria de Buenos Aires.

_____. 1975. Negro slavery in Latin America. Trans. by J. W. S. Judge. Berkeley: University of California Press.

Membreño, Alberto. 1897 (1st ed., 1895). Hondureñismos: Vocabulario de los provincialismos de Honduras. 2d ed. Tegucigalpa: Tipografía Nacional.

Mendonça, Renato. 1935. A influência africana no português do Brasil. 2d ed. São Paulo: Companhia Editora Nacional.

Métraux, Alfred. 1960. The racial landscape of Latin America. UNESCO Courier (October 1960) 13(10):21–22.

Mieres, Celia, Elida Miranda, Eugenia B. de Alberti, and Mercedes R. de Berro. 1966. Diccionario uruguayo documentado. Montevideo: Biblioteca de la Academia Nacional de Letras.

Miller, Michael I. 1987. Multicultural discourse. American Speech 62(2):165–69.

Millones Santagadea, Luis. 1973. Minorías étnicas en el Perú. Lima: Pontificia Universidad Católica.

Montagu, Ashley. 1974. Man's most dangerous myth: The fallacy of race. 5th ed. New York: Oxford University Press.

Monteforte Toledo, Mario. 1959. El mestizaje en Guatemala. Cuadernos Americanos 18(102):169–82.

Moraes e Silva, António de, ed. 1789. Diccionario da lingua portugueza, composto pelo padre Rafael Bluteau. 2 vols. Lisbon: Officina de Simão Thaddeo Ferreira.

_____. 1948. Grande dicionário da língua portuguesa. 10th ed. Ed. by Augusto Moreno, Casdoso Júnior, and José Pedro Machado. Rio de Janeiro: Confluência.

Moreno Navarro, Isidoro. 1973. Los cuadros del mestizaje americano: Estudio antropológico del mestizaje. Madrid: J. Porrúa Turanzas.

Morínigo, Marcos A. 1966. Diccionario de americanismos. Buenos Aires: Muchnik Editores.

Mörner, Magnus. 1960. El mestizaje en la historia de Ibero-América: Informe sobre el estado actual de la investigación. Stockholm: Biblioteca e Instituto de Estudios Ibero-americanos de la Escuela de Ciencias Económicas.

_____. 1961. Teoría y práctica de la segregación en la América colonial española. Boletín de la Academia Nacional de la Historia (Caracas) 44:278–85.

_____. 1967. Race mixture in the history of Latin America. Boston: Little, Brown.

_____. 1973. Legal equality—social equality: A post-abolition theme. Revista/Review Interamericana (Hato Rey, PR) 3(1):24–41.

_____. 1978. Recent research on Negro slavery and abolition in Latin America. Latin American Research Review 13(2):265–89.

Mörner, Magnus, ed. 1961. El mestizaje en la historia de Ibero-América. Mexico: Instituto Panamericano de Geografía e Historia, Comisión de Historia.

Mosél, James N. 1945. Embarrassing moments in Spanish, and how to avoid them: A practical handbook on Spanish usage. New York: Frederick Unger.

Mott, Luiz R. B. 1974. Brancos, pardos, prêtos e índios em Sergipe. Anais de História 6:139–84.

_____. 1976. Pardos e pretos em Sergipe, 1774–1851. Revista do Instituto de Estudos Brasileiros 18:7–37.

Nack, William. 1980. From hard punches, a life of ease. Sports Illustrated 52(25):30–42.

Naranjo Martínez, Enrique. 1934. White Indians. Hispanic American Historical Review 14:95–98.

Naro, Anthony J. 1978. A study on the origins of pidginization. Language 54:314–47.

The New Michaelis Illustrated Dictionary (Michaelis). 1973. 2 vols. 11th ed. São Paulo: Edições Melhoramentos.

Nogueira, Oracy. 1959. Skin color and social class. In: Plantation systems of the New World: Papers and discussion summaries of the seminar held in San Juan, Puerto Rico, pp. 164–79. Washington, DC: Pan American Union.

Nuñez, Benjamin. 1980. Dictionary of Afro-Latin American civilization. Westport, CT: Greenwood Press.

O'Crouley, Pedro Alonso. 1972. A description of the Kingdom of New Spain (1774). Trans. and ed. by Seán Galvin. San Francisco: John Howell-Books.

Olaechea Labayen, Juan B. 1985. El vocabulario racial de la América y en especial la voz 'mestizo.' Boletín de la Real Academia Española 65(234):121–32.

Oliver, Roland, and John D. Fage. 1975. A short history of Africa. 5th ed. Baltimore: Penguin.

Omi, Michael, and Howard Winant. 1986. Racial formation in the United States from the 1960s to the 1980s. New York and London: Routledge and Kegan Paul.

Ortiz Fernández, Fernando. 1924. Glosario de afronegrismos. Havana: Imprenta 'El Siglo XX.'

Otte, Enrique, and Conchita Ruiz-Burruecos. 1963. Los portugueses en la trata de esclavos negros en las postrimerías del siglo XVI. Moneda y Crédito 85:3–40.

Oviedo y Valdés, Gonzalo Fernández de. 1944–45. Historia general y natural de las Indias, islas y tierra-firme del mar Océano. Ed. by José Amador de los Ríos. Vol. 14 (1945). Asunción del Paraguay: Editorial Guaranía; Washington, DC: Catholic University of America Press.

———. 1478–1557 (repr. 1969). De la natural historia de las Indias. (Facsimile ed., University of North Carolina Studies in Romance Languages and Literatures, 85). Chapel Hill: University of North Carolina Press.

Oxford English Dictionary, compact edition. 1971. 2 vols. Oxford: Oxford University Press.

Paiva, Marcelo Rubens. 1986. Blecaute, a novel. São Paulo: Editora Brasiliense.

Pariente, Angel. 1981. La etimología de 'cachopo.' Revista de Filología Española 61:199–224.

Parrish, Charles H. 1946. Color names and color notions. Journal of Negro Education 15:13–20.

Patín Maceo, Manuel A. 1940. Dominicanismos. Ciudad Trujillo: Montalvo.

Patterson, Horace Orlando. 1972. Toward a future that has no past —reflections on the fate of Blacks in the Americas. Public Interest 27:25–62.

_____. 1975. Context and choice in ethnic allegiance: A theoretical framework and Caribbean case study. In: Glazer and Moynihan 1975, pp. 305–49.

Payne, Stanley G. 1973. A history of Spain and Portugal. 2 vols. Madison: University of Wisconsin Press.

Paz Soldán y Unanue, Pedro (pseudonym, Juan de Arona). 1938 (1st ed., 1883–84). Diccionario de peruanismos. Paris: Desclée.

Pereda Valdés, Ildefonso. 1937. El negro rioplatense y otros ensayos. Montevideo: C. García.

_____. 1970. Lo negro y lo mulato en la poesía cubana. Montevideo: Ediciones Ciudadela.

Pérez de Barradas, José. 1948. Los mestizos de América. Madrid: Cultura Clásica y Moderna.

Pescatello, Ann M., ed. 1975. The African in Latin America. New York: Alfred Knopf.

Pichardo y Tapia, Esteban. 1953 (1st ed., 1875). Pichardo novísimo, o diccionario provincial casi razonado de voces y frases cubanas. 9th ed. Ed. by Esteban Rodríguez Herrera. Havana: Selecta.

Pierson, Donald. 1942. Negroes in Brazil: A study of race contact at Bahia. Chicago: University of Chicago Press.

_____. 1955. Race relations in Portuguese America. In: Lind 1955, pp. 433–62.

_____. 1967. Negroes in Brazil: A study of race contact at Bahia. Carbondale and Edwardsville: Southern Illinois University Press.

Pike, Ruth. 1967. Sevillian society in the sixteenth century: Slaves and freedmen. Hispanic American Historical Review 47: 344–59.

Pinkerton, Anne. 1986. Observations on the tú / vos option in Guatemalan Ladino Spanish. Hispania 69(3):690–98.

Pinto, Luis de Aguiar Costa. 1953. O negro em Rio de Janeiro. São Paulo: Brasiliana, Civilização Brasileira.

Pitt-Rivers, Julian. 1967. Race, color, and class in Central America and the Andes. Daedalus 96:542–59.

_____. 1968. Race, color, and class in Central America and the Andes. In: Franklin 1968, pp. 264–81.

Poppino, Rollie E. 1968. Brazil: The land and people. New York: Oxford University Press.

Posner, Rebecca. 1975. Semantic change or lexical change? In: Saltarelli and Wanner 1975, pp. 177–82.

Pottier, Bernard. 1970. Domaine de l'ethnolinguistique. Langages 18:3–11.

———. 1974. Ethnolinguistique et grammaire. Revue de Linguistique Romane 38:418–19.

Price, Richard, ed. 1979. Maroon societies: Rebel slave communities in the Americas. 2d ed. Baltimore and London: Johns Hopkins.

Pulgram, Ernst. 1958. The tongues of Italy: Prehistory and history. New York: Greenwood.

Querol y Roso, Luis. 1931–32. Negros y mulatos de Nueva España: Historia de su alzamiento en Méjico en 1612. Anales de la Universidad de Valencia 12:121–65.

Ramos, Arthur. 1939. The Negro in Brazil. Trans. by Richard Partee. Washington, DC: Associated Publishers, Inc.

———. 1941. Contact of races in Brazil. Social Forces 19:533–38.

———. 1944. Las poblaciones del Brasil. Mexico: Fondo de Cultura Económica.

———. 1947. A mestiçagem no Brasil: Opiniões e estereotípias. Província de São Pedro 8:26–34.

Raveau, F. H. M. 1975. Role of color in identification processes. In: De Vos and Romanucci-Ross 1975, pp. 353–59.

Read, Jan. 1974. The Moors in Spain and Portugal. London: Faber and Faber.

Redfield, Robert. 1942. El indio en México. Revista Mexicana de Sociología 4(3):103–20.

Reis, P. Pereira do. 1961. A miscigenacão e a étnia brasileira. Revista de História 23:323–37.

Reuter, Edward Byron. 1918. The mulatto in the United States, including a study of the rôle of mixed-blood races throughout the world. Boston: R. G. Badger.

Revollo, Pedro María. 1942. Costeñismos colombianos; o apuntamientos sobre lenguaje costeño de Colombia. Barranquilla: Colombia S.A.

Ribeiro, João. n.d. O elemento negro. Introduction and notes by Joaquim Ribeiro. Rio de Janeiro: Record.

Ricardo, Cassiano. 1942. Marcha para Oeste: A influência da bandeira na formação social e política do Brasil. 2d ed. 2 vols. Rio de Janeiro.

Rieff, David (pseudonym of David Sontag). 1987. Going to Miami: Exiles, tourists, and refugees in the New America. Boston: Little, Brown and Co.

Roback, Abraham Aaron. 1944 (repr. 1979). A dictionary of international slurs. Reprint of 1944 edition. Cambridge, MA: Sci-Art Publishers, and Waukesha, WI: Maledicta Press.

Rodrigues, Aryon Dall'Igna. 1986. Línguas brasileiras: Para o conhecimento das línguas indígenas. São Paulo: Edições Loyola.

Rodriguez, Richard. 1982. Hunger of memory: The education of Richard Rodriguez; an autobiography. New York: Bantam.

Rodríguez, Zorobábel. 1875 (repr. 1979). Diccionario de chilenismo. Facsimile edition of 1875 edition. Valparaíso, Chile: Ediciones Universitarias de Valparaíso.

Rodríguez Molas, Ricardo. 1961. Negros libres rioplatenses. Revista de Humanidades (Buenos Aires) 1(1):99–126.

Rogers, Captain Woodes. 1712. A cruising voyage round the world: first to the South-Seas, thence to the East-Indies, and homewards by the Cape of Good Hope. London: Printed for A. Bell at the Cross-Keys and Bible in Cornhil, and B. Lintot at the Cross-Keys between the two Temple-Gates, Fleetstreet.

Román, Manuel Antonio. 1901–18. Diccionario de chilenismos y de otras voces y locuciones viciosas. Santiago de Chile: Imprenta de 'La Revista Católica.'

Romero, Fernando. 1944. The slave trade and the Negro in South America. Hispanic American Historical Review 24:368–86.

———. 1965. El mestizaje negroide en la demografía del Perú. Revista Histórica (Lima) 28:231–48.

Roncal, Joaquín. 1944. The Negro race in Mexico. Hispanic American Historical Review 24:530–40.

Rosenblat, Angel. 1954. La población indígena y el mestizaje en América. 2 vols. Buenos Aires: Nova.

Rout, Leslie B., Jr. 1976. The African experience in Spanish America: 1502 to the present day. London: Cambridge University Press.

Rubin, Vera, ed. 1960. Caribbean studies: A symposium. Seattle: University of Washington Press.

Rubio, Darío. 1919. Nahuatlismos y barbarismos. Mexico: Imprenta Nacional.

Russell-Wood, A. J. R. 1982. The black man in slavery and freedom in colonial Brazil. New York: St. Martin's Press.

Saint-Méry, Médéric Louis Élie Moreau de. 1958 (1st ed., 1796–98, 2 vols.). Description topographique, physique, civile, politique et historique de la partie française de l'isle Saint-Domingue. Edited by B. Maurel and E. Taillemite. 3 vols. Paris: Larose.

Sala, Marius, coord. 1982. El español de América. 2 vols. (Publicaciones del Instituto Caro y Cuervo, 60.) Bogotá: Instituto Caro y Cuervo.

Salazar García, Salomón. 1910. Diccionario de provincialismos y barbarismos centroamericanos. 2d ed. San Salvador: 'La Unión.'

Salesiano. 1938. Vocabulario de palabras—modismos y refranes ticos. Cartago, Costa Rica: Escuela Tipografía Salesiana.

Saltarelli, Mario, and Dieter Wanner, eds. 1975. Diachronic studies in Romance linguistics. The Hague: Mouton.

Sánchez-Albornoz, Nicolás. 1974. The population of Latin America. Trans. by W. A. R. Richardson. Berkeley: University of California Press.

Sanjek, Roger. 1971. Brazilian racial terms: Some aspects of meaning and learning. American Anthropologist 73:1126–43.

Santa Rosa, Henrique de, ed. 1922. Diccionario histórico geográphico e etnográphico do Brasil. Rio de Janeiro: Imprensa Nacional for the Instituto Histórico e Geográphico Brasileiro.

Santamaría, Francisco J. 1942. Diccionario general de americanismos. 3 vols. Mexico: Pedro Robredo.

———. 1974. Diccionario de mejicanismos. 2d ed. Mexico: Porrúa.

Saubidet Gache, Tito. 1943. Vocabulario y refranero criollo con textos y dibujos originales. Buenos Aires: Guillermo Kraft Ltda.

Sayres, William C. 1956. Racial mixture and cultural valuation in a rural Colombian community. América Indígena 16:221–30.

Schneider, John T. 1985. Sub-Saharan extensions in Brazil: The relevance of lexical data. Studies in African Linguistics 16(2): 223–34.

Segovia, Lisandro. 1911. Diccionario de argentinismos, neologismos y barbarismos. Buenos Aires: Coni Hermanos.

Seminario, Lee Anne Durham. 1975. The history of the Blacks, the Jews, and the Moors in Spain. Madrid: Playor.

Shoumatoff, Alex. 1980. The capital of hope. The New Yorker (November 3), pp. 59–163.

Silva, Martiniano J. 1987. Racismo à brasileira: Raízes históricas. Brasília, DF: Thesaurus Editora.

Simmons, Ozzie G. 1955. The criollo outlook in the mestizo culture of coastal Peru. American Anthropologist 57:107–17.

Simonet, D. Francisco Javier. 1888. Glosario de voces ibéricas y latinas entre los mozárabes precedido de un estudio sobre el dialecto hispano-mozárabe. Madrid: Fortanet.

Simpson, George Eaton, and J. Milton Yinger. 1985. Racial and cultural minorities: An analysis of prejudice and discrimination. 5th ed. New York: Plenum Books.

Smith, Raymond T. 1963. Culture and social structure in the Caribbean: Some recent work on family and kinship studies. Comparative Studies in Society and History 6(1):24–46.

Smith, T. Lynn. 1974. Brazilian society. Albuquerque: University of New Mexico Press.

Snowden, Frank M., Jr. 1970. Blacks in Antiquity: Ethiopians in the Greco-Roman experience. Cambridge, MA: Belknap Press of Harvard University.

Soares, Glaucio Ary Dillon, and Nelson do Valle Silva. 1987. Urbanization, race, and class in Brazilian politics. Latin American Research Review 22(2):155–76.

Sobarzo, Horacio. 1966. Vocabulario sonorense. Mexico: Porrúa.

Solano y Pérez Lila, Francisco de. 1975. Estudio socioantropológico de la población rural no indígena de Yucatán, 1700. Revista de la Universidad de Yucatán 17(98):73–149.

Solaún, Mauricio, and Sidney Kronus. 1973. Discrimination without violence: Miscegenation and racial conflict in Latin America. New York: John Wiley and Sons.

Solaún, Mauricio, Eduardo Vélez, and Cynthia Smith. 1987. Claro, trigueño, moreno: Testing for race in Cartagena. Caribbean Review 15(3):18–19.

Soletsky, Albert Z. 1977. Germanía *gelfe* 'black slave.' Journal of Hispanic Philology 2:61.

Souto Maior, Mário. 1980. Diciónario do palavrão e termos afins. 1st ed. (4th ed., 1988, Rio de Janeiro: Record.) Recife: Editora Guarapes.

Souza, Bernardino José de. 1961. Dicionário da terra e da gente do Brasil. 5th ed. (Brasiliana, série grande formato, 19.) São Paulo: Companhia Editora Nacional.

Spaulding, Robert K. 1943. How Spanish grew. Berkeley and Los Angeles: University of California Press.

Steiner, Roger J. 1985. Lexicon in the first Spanish-English dictionary. Hispanic Linguistics 2(1):87–98.

Stephens, Thomas M. 1983. Creole, créole, criollo, crioulo: The shadings of a term. The SECOL Review 7(3):28–39.

Studi in onore di Ettore Lo Gatto e Giovanni Maver. 1962. Florence: Sansoni.

Sturm, Fred Gillette. 1985. 'Estes têm alma como nóa?': Manual da Nóbrega's view of the Brazilian Indian. In: Empire in transition: The Portuguese world in the time of Camões, ed. by Alfred Hower and Richard A. Preto-Rodas, pp. 72–82. Gainesville, FL: University Presses of Florida.

Sundheim, Adolfo. 1922. Vocabulario costeño; o lexicografía de la región septentrional de la República de Colombia. Paris: Librería Cervantes.

Tascón, Leonardo. 1961. Diccionario de provincialismos y barbarismos del Valle del Cauca y quechuismos usados en Colombia. Cali: Biblioteca de la Universidad del Valle.

Tenório d'Albuquerque, Acir. 1954. Gauchismos: A linguagem do Rio Grande do Sul (Influência do castelhano, das línguas africanas, do Guarani, do Tupi e do Quíchua). Porto Alegre: Livraria Sulina.

Terrasse, Henri. 1949–50. Histoire du Maroc des origines à l'établissement du Protectorat français. 2 vols. Casablanca: Atlantides.

Thernstron, Stephan, ed. 1980. Harvard Encyclopedia of American Ethnic Groups. Cambridge, MA: Belknap.

Thompson, Era Bell. 1965a. Does amalgamation work in Brazil? Absorbing Negro through interracial marriage is their answer to race problem. Ebony 20(9):27–41.

———. 1965b. Does amalgamation work in Brazil? The formula is not perfect but so far it works the best. Ebony 20(11):33–42.

Tobón Betancourt, P. Julio. 1953. Colombianismos y otras voces de uso general. 2d ed. Bogotá: Imprenta Nacional.

Torre Revello, José. 1927. Esclavas blancas en las Indias Occidentales. Boletín del Instituto de Investigaciones Históricas (Buenos Aires) 6:263–71.

Trudgill, Peter. 1974. Sociolinguistics: An introduction. New York: Penguin.

Tumin, Melvin M., ed. 1969. Comparative perspectives on race relations. Boston: Little, Brown.

Tumin, Melvin M., and Arnold Feldman. 1969. Social class and skin color in Puerto Rico. In: Tumin 1969, pp. 197–214.

Tuttle, Edward F. 1976. Borrowing vs. semantic shift: New World nomenclature in European languages. In: Chiappelli 1976, vol. 2, pp. 595–611.

Uitti, Karl D. 1963. Review of Householder and Saporta 1962. Romance Philology 16:416–28.

Ullmann, Stephen. 1962. Semantics: An introduction to the science of meaning. New York: Barnes and Noble.

———. 1974. Words and their meanings. (University Lectures, 1974.) Canberra: Australian National University Press.

Unanue, José Hipólito. 1806. Observaciones sobre el clima de Lima y sus influencias en los seres organizados. Lima: Imprenta Real de los Huérfanos.

———. 1914/1975. Obras científicas y literarias. 3 vols. Facsimile edition of 1914 edition. Barcelona: Tipografía La Académica de Serra Hermanos y Russell, and Lima: Editorial Universo.

Urbanski, Edmund Stephen. 1978. Hispanic America and its civilizations: Spanish Americans and Anglo-Americans. Trans. by

Frances Kellam Hendricks and Beatrice Berler. Norman: University of Oklahoma Press.

Urdang, Laurence. 1963. Review of Householder and Saporta 1962. Language 39:586–94.

Valle, Alfonso. 1948. Diccionario del habla nicaragüense. Managua: La Nueva Prensa.

Vallenilla Lanz, Laureano. 1921. Las castas coloniales. Cultura Venezolana (Caracas, November 1921), pp. 108–14.

van den Berghe, Pierre L. 1967. Race and racism: A comparative perspective. New York: John Wiley and Sons.

Vandiver, Marylee Mason. 1949. Racial classifications in Latin American censuses. Social Forces 28:138–46.

Vázquez Ruiz, José. 1981. A propósito de la etimología de *chumbera* y *chumbo*. Revista de Filología Española 61:247–52.

Velasco Valdés, Miguel. 1957. Vocabulario popular mexicano. Mexico: Olimpo.

Velásquez, Rogerio. 1962. Gentilicios africanos del occidente de Colombia. Revista de Folklore (Bogotá) 3:107–48.

Vergara Martín, Gabriel María. 1922. Diccionario etnográfico americano. Madrid: Sucesores de Hernando.

Verlinden, Charles. 1943. L'origine de sclavus = esclave. Bulletin du Cange, Archivum latinitatis Medii Aevi 17:97–128.

_____. 1955. L'esclavage dans l'Europe médiévale. Brugge: De Tempel.

_____. 1964. Esclavage médiéval en Europe et esclavage colonial en Amérique. Cahiers de l'Institut des Hautes Études de l'Amérique Latine (Paris) 6:27–45.

Vianna, Francisco José de Oliveira (= Oliveira Vianna). 1933. Evolução do povo brasileiro. 2d ed. São Paulo: Companhia Editora Nacional.

_____. 1934. Raça e assimilação: Os problemas da raça. Os problemas da assimilação. São Paulo: Companhia Editora Nacional.

_____. 1937. Evolución del pueblo brasileño. Buenos Aires.

Villegas, Francisco. 1952. Glosario del argot costarricense. Unpublished Ph.D. dissertation, University of Michigan, Ann Arbor.

Wade, Peter. 1985. Race and class: The case of South American blacks. Ethnic and Racial Studies 8:233–49.

Wagley, Charles. 1949. Brazil. In: Linton 1949, pp. 212–70.

_____. 1953. Amazon town: A study of man in the tropics. New York: Macmillan.

_____. 1960. Plantation-America. In: Rubin 1960, pp. 3–13.

_____. 1963. Race relations in an Amazon community. In: Wagley 1963, pp. 116–41.

_____. 1969. From caste to class in north Brazil. In: Tumin 1969, pp. 47–62.

_____. 1971. An introduction to Brazil. 2d revised ed. New York and London: Columbia University Press.

Wagley, Charles, ed. 1952 (2d ed., 1963). Race and class in rural Brazil. Paris: UNESCO, and New York: UNESCO.

Wallace, James M. 1984. Urban anthropology in Lima: An overview. Latin American Research Review 19(3):57–85.

Wartburg, Walther von. 1951. Problemas y métodos de la lingüística. Trans. by Dámaso Alonso and Emilio Lorenzo. Annotated by Dámaso Alonso. Madrid: C. Bermejo.

Washburn, Sherwood L. 1963. The study of race. American Anthropologist 65:521–31.

Weinstein, Allen, and Frank Otto Gatell, eds. 1968. American Negro slavery: A modern reader. New York: Oxford University Press.

Westlake, Donald E. 1982. Belize: Will it be another Falkland Islands? The New York Times Magazine (September 19, 1982), pp. 44–45, 100–104.

Whitten, Norman E., Jr. 1965. Class, kinship, and power in an Ecuadorian town: The Negroes of San Lorenzo. Stanford, CA: Stanford University Press.

Whitten, Norman E., Jr., and John F. Szwed, eds. 1970. Afro-American anthropology: Comtemporary perspectives. New York: The Free Press.

Wiarda, Howard J. 1969. The Dominican Republic: Nation in transition. New York: Praeger.

Williams, Eric. 1960. Race relations in Caribbean society. In: Rubin 1960, pp. 54–60.

Wilson, William E. 1939. Some notes on slavery during the Golden Age. Hispanic Review 7:171–74.

Woodbridge, Hensley C. 1948. Glossary of names found in colonial Latin America for crosses among Indians, Negroes, and whites. Journal of the Washington Academy of Sciences 38:353–62.

Yrarrázaval Larrain, José Miguel. 1945. Chilenismos. Santiago de Chile: Imprenta Cultura.

Zaccaria, Enrico. 1927. L'elemento iberico nella lingua italiana. Bologna: L. Cappelli.

Zamboni, Alberto. 1976. L'etimologia. Bologna: Zanichelli.

Zenón Cruz, Isabelo. 1975. Narciso descubre su trasero: El negro en la cultura puertorriqueña. 2d ed. Humacao, PR: Editorial Furidi.

Zimmerman, Ben. 1952 (1963). Race relations in the arid sertão. In: Wagley 1952, pp. 89–135, and Wagley 1963, pp. 82–115.

Index of Places